From the Wadsworth Series in Mass Communication and Journalism

General Mass Communication

Kwadwo Anokwa, Carolyn Lin, and Michael Salwen, *International Communication: Issues and Controversies*

Shirley Biagi, *Media/Impact: An Introduction to Mass Media,* 6th Ed.

Erik Bucy, *Living in the Information Age: A New Media Reader*

John Craft, Frederic Leigh, and Donald Godfrey, *Electronic Media*

Louis Day, *Ethics in Media Communications: Cases and Controversies,* 4th Ed.

Everette E. Dennis and John C. Merrill, *Media Debates: Great Issues for the Digital Age,* 4th Ed.

Robert S. Fortner, *International Communications: History, Conflict, and Control of the Global Metropolis*

Donald Gillmor, Jerome Barron, and Todd Simon, *Mass Communication Law: Cases and Comment,* 6th Ed.

Donald Gillmor, Jerome Barron, Todd Simon, and Herbert Terry, *Fundamentals of Mass Communication Law*

Michele Hilmes, *Only Connect: A Cultural History of Broadcasting in the United States*

Michele Hilmes, *Connections: A Broadcast History Reader*

Kathleen Hall Jamieson and Karlyn Kohrs Campbell, *The Interplay of Influence,* 5th Ed.

Yahya K. Kamalipour, *Global Communication*

Paul Lester, *Visual Communication,* 3rd Ed.

Wayne Overbeck, *Major Principles of Media Law,* 2003 Edition

Glenn G. Sparks, *Media Effects Research: A Basic Overview*

Joseph Straubhaar and Robert LaRose, *Media Now: Communications Media in the Information Age,* 3rd Ed.

Edward Jay Whetmore, *Mediamerica, Mediaworld: Form, Content, and Consequence of Mass Communication,* Updated 5th Ed.

John D. Zelezny, *Communications Law: Liberties, Restraints, and the Modern Media,* 3rd Ed.

John D. Zelezny, *Cases in Communications Law,* 3rd Ed.

Journalism

Paul Adams, *Writing Right for Today's Mass Media: A Textbook and Workbook with Language Exercises*

Douglas Anderson, *Contemporary Sports Reporting,* 2nd Ed.

Dorothy Bowles and Diane L. Borden, *Creative Editing,* 3rd Ed.

Jean Chance and William McKeen, *Literary Journalism: A Reader*

Raymond Dorn, *How to Design and Improve Magazine Layouts,* 2nd Ed.

Heintz-Dietrich Fischer, *Sports Journalism at Its Best: Pulitzer Prize-Winning Articles, Cartoons, and Photographs*

Lionel Fisher, *The Craft of Corporate Journalism*

William Gaines, *Investigative Reporting for Print and Broadcast,* 2nd Ed.

Robert L. Hilliard, *Writing for Television, Radio, and New Media,* 7th Ed.

Lauren Kessler and Duncan McDonald, *When Words Collide,* 5th Ed.

Alice M. Klement and Carolyn Burrows Matalene, *Telling Stories/Taking Risks: Journalism Writing at the Century's Edge*

Ray Laakaniemi, *Newswriting in Transition*

Lisa Miller, *Power Journalism: Computer-Assisted Reporting*

Carole Rich, *Writing and Reporting News: A Coaching Method,* 4th Ed.

Rick Wilber and Randy Miller, *Modern Media Writing*

Photojournalism and Photography

Fred S. Parrish, *Photojournalism: An Introduction*

Public Relations and Advertising

Jerry A. Hendrix, *Public Relations Cases,* 5th Ed.

Todd Hunt and James Grunig, *Public Relations Techniques*

Jerome A. Jewler and Bonnie L. Drewniany, *Creative Strategy in Advertising,* 7th Ed.

Doug Newsom, and Bob Carrell, *Public Relations Writing: Form and Style,* 6th Ed.

Doug Newsom, Judy VanSlyke Turk, and Dean Kruckeberg, *This Is PR: The Realities of Public Relations,* 7th Ed.

Juliann Sivulka, *Soap, Sex, and Cigarettes: A Cultural History of American Advertising*

Gail Baker Woods, *Advertising and Marketing to the New Majority: A Case Study Approach*

Research and Theory

Earl Babbie, *The Practice of Social Research,* 9th Ed.

Stanley Baran and Dennis Davis, *Mass Communication Theory: Foundations, Ferment, and Future,* 3rd Ed.

Sondra Rubenstein, *Surveying Public Opinion*

Rebecca B. Rubin, Alan M. Rubin, and Linda J. Piele, *Communication Research: Strategies and Sources,* 5th Ed.

Roger D. Wimmer and Joseph R. Dominick, *Mass Media Research: An Introduction,* 7th Ed.

Seventh Edition

Mass Media Research

An Introduction

Roger D. Wimmer
Wimmer Research

Joseph R. Dominick
University of Georgia

THOMSON
WADSWORTH

Australia • Canada • Mexico • Singapore • Spain • United Kingdom • United States

THOMSON

WADSWORTH

Publisher: *Holly J. Allen*
Assistant Editor: *Nicole George*
Editorial Assistant: *Amber Fawson*
Technology Project Manager: *Jeanette Wiseman*
Marketing Manager: *Kimberly Russell*
Marketing Assistant: *Neena Chandra*
Advertising Project Manager: *Shemika Britt*
Project Managers, Editorial Production: *Cathy Linberg and Katy German*

Printed in the United States of America
3 4 5 6 7 06 05 04

For more information about our products, contact us at:
Thomson Learning Academic Resource Center
1-800-423-0563

For permission to use material from this text, contact us by:
Phone: 1-800-730-2214
Fax: 1-800-730-2215
Web: http://www.thomsonrights.com

Library of Congress Control Number:
2002102411

ISBN 0-534-56274-4

Print/Media Buyer: *Rebecca Cross*
Permissions Editor: *Charles Hodgkins*
Production Service: *Greg Hubit Bookworks*
Text Designer: *John Edeen*
Cover Designer: *Ross Carron*
Cover Image: *Getty Images/Eduardo Garcia*
Compositor: *Carlisle Communications, Ltd.*
Printer: *Phoenix Color Corp., Book Technology Park*

Wadsworth/Thomson Learning
10 Davis Drive
Belmont, CA 94002-3098
USA

Asia
Thomson Learning
5 Shenton Way #01-01
UIC Building
Singapore 068808

Australia
Nelson Thomson Learning
102 Dodds Street
South Melbourne, Victoria 3205
Australia

Canada
Nelson Thomson Learning
1120 Birchmount Road
Toronto, Ontario M1K 5G4
Canada

Europe/Middle East/Africa
Thomson Learning
High Holborn House
50/51 Bedford Row
London WC1R 4LR
United Kingdom

Latin America
Thomson Learning
Seneca, 53
Colonia Polanco
11560 Mexico D.F.
Mexico

Spain
Paraninfo Thomson Learning
Calle/Magallanes, 25
28015 Madrid, Spain

To Shad & Jeremy and
Carole & Meaghan
—We're happy that so many readers
have kept your names in print.

Preface

In the preface to each edition of our book, we have said that the mass media constantly change. This continues to be true today. Keeping up with the changes in the media is a daily task. For example, the effects of radio-ownership rule changes in the Telecommunications Act of 1996 continue into the 21st century. Satellite TV delivery has forever changed television because viewers have so many programming choices. The accessibility to the print media on the Internet has changed the reading habits for millions of people. The Internet itself has changed how mass media researchers conduct their work. And finally, the events on September 11, 2001, in America have changed how mass media managers design and program the content of their medium. These are only some of the events in mass media that invite investigation.

Approach and Organization

Our goal is to provide you with the tools you need to use mass media research in the professional world through simplified explanation of goals, procedures, and uses of information in mass media research. We want you to be comfortable with research and to recognize its unlimited value; so we use extensive practical applications to illustrate its use in the world today.

As with earlier editions, this book is divided into four parts. In Part One we begin with an overview of mass communication research, including elements, ethics, and sampling. Part Two explores each major approach to research, including qualitative research, content analysis, survey research, longitudinal research, and experimental research. In Part Three we continue with a section on data analysis, covering statistics and hypothesis testing. Part Four concludes the book with a forward-looking section on research applications, including those for print media, electronic media, advertising, public relations, media effects, and mass media research and the Internet.

Features

We are gratified by the feedback we've received from hundreds of professors teaching this course. We hope you will find that this edition reflects the best pedagogy based on the continuous improvements we've made to each edition. The text includes many features that provide additional information and enhance learning and understanding of concepts. Features included are:

- Effective mass media pedagogy
- Extensive coverage of the use of technology in media research
- Websites and search suggestions included throughout the book
- End-of-chapter questions and exercises for practice and review
- InfoTrac® College Edition exercises for further investigation of current issues, strategies, and controversies in mass media research
- Extensive discussion on hypothesis testing clarifies this fundamental research component
- Chapter summaries help you pull together the most important concepts within each chapter

Our website suggestions and InfoTrac College Edition exercise suggestions are current as of mid-2002. However, since Internet content changes daily, some of the suggestions and sites may be relocated or even abandoned. If that is the case, take time to search for related sites—the Internet is an information gold mine.

New to This Edition

In this edition, we have made many changes based on comments from teachers, students, and media professionals who have used our book. All chapters have been updated, a few chapters have been rearranged to meet the requests of several users, and new chapters have been added. Specifically, we've added:

- A new chapter titled "Research in Public Relations" (Chapter 16)
- A new chapter titled "Mass Media Research and the Internet" (Chapter 18) featuring techniques and information on using the Internet in mass media research and a "how-to" guide for doing Internet surveys
- New "Using the Internet" exercises at the end of each chapter
- More than 50 new "An Inside Look" shaded text boxes providing practical information and tips for bringing concepts to life
- Updated examples throughout the text, including current issues such as poll results in the Gore vs. Bush election (Chapter 5, Sampling) and stem cell research (Chapter 3, Ethics)
- Key Terms lists at the end of each chapter

Online Resources

Finally, in an effort to keep up to date with changes in mass media research, we have developed a website for this book for readers who want additional information. Please visit the site at *www.wimmerdominick.com.* On the site, you'll find additional reference materials, articles that expand on some of the topics in the book, a Q&A section for students to submit questions to us, a sampling error calculator, and more. We will update the website whenever we find something of interest to mass media researchers, so visit often. If you have any suggestions for additional content on the site, please contact one of us.

Also, please visit the Book Companion Site at *http://communication.wadsworth.com.* There you will find a glossary, flashcards, crossword puzzle, Internet activities, and InfoTrac College Edition questions.

Your Feedback

As we have stated in the previous six editions: If you find a serious problem in the text or the website, please contact one of us. Each of us will steadfastly blame the other for the problem and will be happy to give you his home telephone number (or forward any email).

Have fun with the book and the website. The mass media research field is still a great place to be!

Roger Wimmer
Denver, Colorado
roger@rogerwimmer.com
www.rogerwimmer.com

Joseph Dominick
Athens, Georgia
joedom@arches.uga.edu

Brief Contents

Contents

Chapter 1

Science and Research

The first question many people ask about mass media research is, "What types of things do you research?" That's a good question, and here are some examples:

- What type of format should a radio station adopt?
- Which songs should a radio station play?
- What type of hosts do listeners want on a radio station's morning show?
- How do viewers evaluate a television pilot for a new TV show?
- Why is a current TV program not performing as well as was planned?
- How effective is advertising on TV, radio, and in all types of print?
- Which ads do readers see most often in their local newspaper?
- Why are newspaper subscriptions declining?
- What should a politician include in campaign messages?
- Who should be the spokesperson for a new consumer product?
- Who should be the host of a new TV game show?
- Are there more violent acts on TV now than 5 years ago?
- What are the elements of a successful magazine cover page?
- Why don't employees read their company's internal newspaper?

The types of questions and problems investigated in mass media research could go on almost forever. But even this short list demonstrates why it's necessary to understand mass media research—because literally every area of the mass media uses research, and anyone who works in the media (or plans to) will be exposed to or involved in research.

Our goal in this book is to introduce you to mass media research and dispel many of the negative thoughts people may have about research, especially a fear of having to use math and statistics. You will find that you do not have to be a math or statistics wizard. The only thing you need is an inquiring mind.

Learning mass media research requires learning terms, concepts, and procedures. However, before we can get into various research approaches, you need to understand just what the term "research" means.

What Is Research?

Regardless of how the word *research* is used, it essentially means the same thing: *an attempt to discover something*. We all do this every day. This book discusses many of the different attempts used to discover something in the mass media. It's that simple.

Research can be very informal, with few, if any, specific plans or steps, or it can be formal, with the researcher following highly defined and exacting procedures. Keep in mind, however, that the lack of exacting procedures in informal research does not mean that the approach is incorrect. Also, know that the use of exacting procedures does not automatically make formal research correct. Both procedures can be good or bad, depending on the specific requirements. The important thing for any researcher (formal or informal) to understand is the correct approach to follow to ensure the best results.

Most people who conduct research are not paid for their efforts. Although the research industry is an excellent field to enter, our approach in this book is to assume that most of you who read this material will not become (or are not now) paid professional researchers. We assume that most of you will work, or are already working, for companies and businesses that use research or that you are merely interested in finding out more about the field. With these ideas in mind, our approach is to explain what research is all about, to show you how to use it to discover something, and to make your life just a bit easier when a research report is put on your desk for you to read or when you face a question that needs to be answered.

Now, back to the idea that all of us are researchers and conduct research every day. Remember that we define research as an attempt to discover something. Every day each of us conducts hundreds or thousands of "research projects." We're not being facetious here. Just consider the number of things you must analyze, test, or evaluate in order to perform daily tasks:

1. Set the water temperature in the shower so you do not freeze or burn.
2. Decide which clothes to put on that are appropriate for the day's activities.
3. Select something to eat for breakfast that will stay with you until lunchtime.
4. Decide what time to leave the house to reach your destination on time.
5. Figure out the most direct route to your destination.
6. Decide whether you should pull over to the side of the road if you hear a siren.
7. Determine how loud to talk to someone.
8. Estimate how fast you need to walk to get across the street and beat the traffic.
9. Evaluate the best way to tell a friend about a problem you have.
10. Figure out when it is time to go home.

The list may seem mundane and boring, but the fact is that when we make any of these decisions, we have to conduct a countless number of tests. We all make many attempts to discover things in order to reach a decision about these events.

In essence, we are all researchers already. This begs the question: Then why read this book? The reason is that there are good ways to attempt to discover something and there are not-so-good ways to attempt to discover something. This book discusses both the good and the bad so you will be able to distinguish between the two. Even if you do not plan to become a paid professional researcher, it is important to learn the best way to collect information and analyze it.

However, you don't have to take only our word that understanding research is valuable. Consider what some people in the media say about research. Larry Barnes, President of Media Resources, Ltd., a Canton, Ohio, supplier of print-based promotions and advertising services, says:

> Research arms us with the best sales tool in the world—instant credibility. The customers we visit are busy with their own responsibilities, and oftentimes our sales call is perceived as an intrusion. When these customers see the basic research we have conducted for them and how it will help them make money, we are immediately considered to be experts in our field and are no longer considered to be an intrusion.

In the radio field, Bob Neil, President/CEO of Cox Radio, Inc., in Atlanta, Georgia, says:

> When I first started in radio, the notion of research was a new idea. In the late 70s and early 80s, very few stations took the time or spent the money to find out what the audience really wanted. I quickly became fascinated

> with research because, as a Program Director, there were so many questions I wanted to ask.
>
> Radio is simply a product, not unlike any other product, and if you are going to succeed, you need to understand who your target is. The only way to do that is through research.

David Hall, Program Director for KFI-AM in Los Angeles, California, takes a more basic approach:

> I work in a business in which I am responsible for knowing what 2 million people like and don't like when they listen to the radio, a product they can neither see nor touch. In fact, it's a product they don't even know they think about. Research is invaluable to me because I'm such a geek that if I put on my radio station what I like, our station would have an audience of about 10 people in a city of 10 million.

The underlying theme presented by these three professionals highlights the business philosophy followed by the senior author for the past 20+ years as a paid professional researcher. That is, there are three basic steps to success in business (and for that matter, in every facet of life):

1. Find out what the people want (customers, audience, readers, family).
2. Give it to them.
3. Tell them that you gave it to them.

Failure is virtually impossible if you follow this three-step philosophy. How can you fail when you give people what they ask for? The way to find out what people want is through research, and that is what this book is all about.

▪ Getting Started

Keep in mind that the focus of this book is to discuss attempts to discover something in the mass media. Although it would be valuable to address other fields of endeavor, this chapter contains discussions of the development of mass media research during the past several decades and the methods used to collect and analyze information. It also includes a discussion of the scientific method of research. The purpose of this chapter is to provide a foundation for the topics discussed in detail in later chapters.

Two basic questions a beginning researcher must learn to answer are (1) how to use research methods and statistical procedures and (2) when to use research methods and statistical procedures. Although developing methods and procedures is a valuable task, the focus for most researchers should be on applications. This book supports the tasks and responsibilities of the applied data analyst (researcher), not the statistician; it does not concentrate on the role of the statistician because the "real world" of mass media research does not require an extensive knowledge of statistics. Instead, the "real world" requires an understanding of what the statistics produce and how to use the results in decision making. After conducting thousands of mass media research studies for more than 25 years, we have concluded that those who wish to become mass media researchers should spend time learning *what to do with the research methods, not how they work*. (For more information, search the Internet for "research methods.")

Although both statisticians and researchers are involved in producing research results, their functions are quite different. (Keep in mind that one person sometimes serves in both capacities.) What do statisticians do? Among other complex activities, they generate statistical procedures, or formulas, called **algorithms.** Researchers then use these algorithms to investigate research questions and hypotheses. The results of this cooperative effort are used to advance our understanding of the mass media.

For example, users of radio and television ratings (mainly produced by The Arbitron

Company and A. C. Nielsen) continually complain about the instability of ratings information. The ratings and shares for radio and television stations in a given market often vary dramatically from one survey period to the next without any logical explanation (see Chapter 14). Users of ratings periodically ask statisticians and the ratings companies to help determine why this problem occurs and to offer suggestions for making syndicated media audience information more reliable. As recently as the fall of 2001, media statisticians recommended larger samples and more refined methods of selecting respondents to correct the instability. Although the problems have not been solved, it is clear that statisticians and researchers can work together. (Search the Internet for "statisticians" to find out the variety of tasks these people perform.)

During the early part of the 20th century, there was no interest in the size of an audience or in the types of people who make up the audience. Since then, mass media leaders have come to rely on research results for nearly every major decision they make. The increased demand for information has created a need for more researchers, both public and private. In addition, within the research field are many specializations. Research directors plan and supervise studies and act as liaisons to management; methodological specialists provide statistical support; research analysts design and interpret studies; and computer specialists provide hardware and software support in data analysis.

Research in mass media is used to verify or refute gut feelings or intuition for decision makers. Although common sense is sometimes accurate, media decision makers need additional objective information to evaluate problems, especially when they make decisions that involve large sums of money. The past 50 years have witnessed the evolution of a decision-making approach that combines research and intuition to produce a higher probability of success.

Research is not limited only to decision-making situations. It is also widely used in theoretical areas to attempt to describe the media, to analyze media effects on consumers, to understand audience behavior, and so on. Every day there are references in the media to audience surveys, public opinion polls, growth projections or status reports of one medium or another, or advertising or public relations campaigns. As philosopher Suzanne Langer (1967) says, "Most new discoveries are suddenly-seen things that were always there." Mass media researchers have a great deal to see, and everyone is exposed to this information every day.

Two final points before we get into media research. First, media research and the need for qualified researchers will continue to grow, but it is difficult to find qualified researchers who can work in the public and private sectors. Second, we strongly urge you to search the Internet for additional information on every topic discussed in this book. We have identified some areas for further investigation, but do not limit your searching to only our suggestions.

▪ The Development of Mass Media Research

Mass media research has evolved in definable steps, and similar patterns have been followed in each medium's needs for research (see Figure 1.1). (As you read the following paragraphs about the development of mass media research, consider the Internet as an example. It is now the newest mass medium.) In Phase 1 of the research, there is an interest in the medium itself. What is it? How does it work? What technology does it involve? How is it similar to or different from what we already have? What functions or services does it provide? Who will have access to the new medium? How much will it cost?

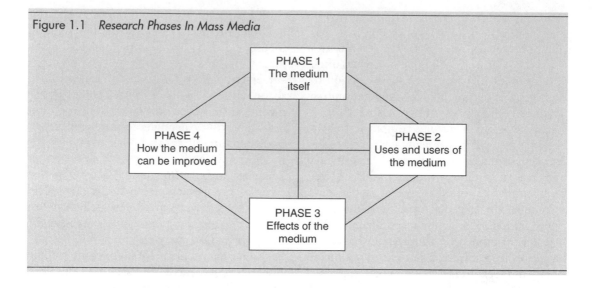

Figure 1.1 *Research Phases In Mass Media*

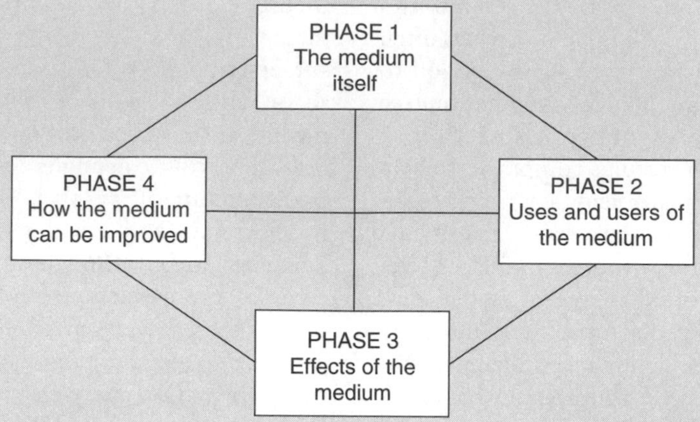

Phase 2 research begins once the medium is developed. In this phase, specific information is accumulated about the uses and the users of the medium. How do people use the medium in real life? Do they use it for information only, to save time, for entertainment, or for some other reason? Do children use it? Do adults use it? Why? What gratifications does the new medium provide? What other types of information and entertainment does the new medium replace? Were original projections about the use of the medium correct? What uses are evident other than those that were predicted from initial research?

Phase 3 includes investigations of the social, psychological, and physical effects of the medium. How much time do people spend with the medium? Does it change people's perspectives about anything? What do the users of the medium want and expect to hear or see? Are there any harmful effects related to using the medium? Does the technology cause any harm? How does the medium help in people's lives? Can the medium be combined with other media or technology to make it even more useful?

In Phase 4 research is conducted to determine how the medium can be improved, either in its use or through technological developments. Can the medium provide information or entertainment to more types of people? How can new technology be used to perfect or enhance the sight or sound of the medium? Is there a way to change the content (programming) to be more valuable or entertaining?

The design of Figure 1.1 is not intended to suggest that the research phases are linear—that when one phase is over, it is never considered again. In reality, once a medium is developed and established, research may be conducted simultaneously in all four phases. For example, although television has been around for more than 50 years, researchers are still investigating the medium itself (satellite-delivered digital audio and video), the uses of TV (pay-per-view programming), effects (violent programming), and improvements (flat-screen TV).

Research is a never-ending process. In most instances a research project designed to answer one series of questions produces a new set of questions no one thought of before. This failure to reach closure may be troublesome to some people, yet it is the essential nature of research.

Figure 1.1 depicts four phases of research. However, in some instances, as in private-sector research, an additional element permeates every phase: How can the medium make money? The largest percentage of research conducted in the private sector relates in some way to money—how to save it, make more of it, or take it away from others. This may not "sit well" with people who view the media as products of artistic endeavor, but this is how the "real world" operates.

At least four major events or social forces have encouraged the growth of mass media research. The first was World War I, which prompted a need to understand the nature of propaganda. Researchers working from a *stimulus-response* point of view attempted to uncover the effects of the media on people (Lasswell, 1927). The media at that time were thought to exert a very powerful influence over their audiences, and several assumptions were made about what the media could and could not do. One theory of mass media, later named the **hypodermic needle** model of communication, suggested that mass communicators need only "shoot" messages at an audience and that those messages would produce preplanned and almost universal effects. The belief then was that all people behave in very similar ways when they encounter media messages. We know now that individual differences among people rule out this rather simplistic view. As DeFleur and Ball-Rokeach (1989) note:

> These assumptions may not have been explicitly formulated at the time, but they were drawn from fairly elaborate theories of human nature, as well as the nature of the social order. . . . It was these theories that guided the thinking of those who saw the media as powerful.

A second contributor to the development of mass media research was the realization by advertisers in the 1950s and 1960s that research data are useful in developing ways to persuade potential customers to buy products and services. Consequently, advertisers encouraged studies of message effectiveness, audience demographics and size, placement of advertising to achieve the highest level of exposure (efficiency), frequency of advertising necessary to persuade potential customers, and selection of the medium that offered the best chance of reaching the target audience.

A third contributing social force was the increasing interest of citizens in the effects of the media on the public, especially on children. The direct result was an interest in research related to violence and sexual content in television programs and in commercials aired during children's programs. Researchers have expanded their focus to include the positive (prosocial) as well as the negative (antisocial) effects of television (see Chapter 17). Investigating violence on television is still an important endeavor, as evidenced by such studies as "The UCLA Television Violence Report" published in January 1998.

Increased competition among the media for advertising dollars was a fourth contributor to the growth of research. Most media managers are now very sophisticated and use long-range plans, management by objectives, and an increasing dependency on data to support the decision-making process. Even program producers seek relevant research data, a task usually assigned to the creative side of program development. In addition, the mass media now focus on audience fragmentation, which means that the masses of people are divided into small groups, or niches (technically referred to as the "demassification" of the mass media). Researchers need information about these groups of people.

The competition among the media for audiences and advertising dollars continues to reach new levels of complexity. The media "survival kit" today includes information about consumers' changing values and tastes, shifts in demographic patterns, and developing trends in lifestyles. Audience fragmentation increases the need for trend studies (fads, new behavior patterns), image studies (people's perceptions of the media and their environment), and segmentation studies (explanations of behavior by types or groups of people). Large research organizations, consultants, and media owners and operators conduct research that was previously considered the sole property of the marketing, psychology, and sociology disciplines. With the advent of increased competition and audience fragmentation, media managers more frequently use marketing strategies in an attempt to discover their position in the marketplace. When this position is identified, the medium is packaged as an "image" rather than a product. (Similarly, the producers of consumer goods such as soap and toothpaste try to sell the "image" of these products because the products themselves are very similar, if not the same, from company to company.)

This packaging strategy involves determining what the members of the audience think, how they use language, how they spend their spare time, and so on. Information on these ideas and behaviors is then woven into the merchandising effort to make the medium seem to be part of the audience. Positioning thus involves taking information from the audience and interpreting the data to use in marketing the medium. (For more information about positioning companies and products in the business and consumer worlds, see Ries & Trout, 1997, 2001.)

Much of the media research before the early 1960s originated in psychology and sociology departments at colleges and universities. Researchers with backgrounds in the media were rare because the mass media were young. But this situation has changed. Media departments in colleges and universities grew rapidly in the 1960s, and media researchers entered the scene. Today mass media researchers dominate the field, and now the trend is to encourage cross-disciplinary studies in which media researchers invite participation from sociologists, psychologists, and political scientists. Because of the pervasiveness of the media, researchers from all areas of science are now actively involved in attempting to answer media-related questions.

Modern mass media research includes a variety of psychological and sociological investigations, such as physiological and emotional responses to television programs, commercials, or music played by radio stations. In addition, computer modeling and other sophisticated computer analyses are now commonplace in media research to determine such things as the potential success of television programs (network or syndicated). Once considered eccentric by some, mass media research is now a legitimate and esteemed field.

Media Research and the Scientific Method

Scientific research is an *organized, objective, controlled, qualitative or quantitative empirical analysis of one or more variables.* The terms that define the scientific research method describe a procedure that has been accepted for centuries. In the 16th century, for example, Tycho Brahe (pronounced TEE-koh BRAH-hee) conducted years of organized and controlled observation to refute many of Aristotle's theories of the universe. (Search the Internet for "Tycho Brahe" to discover more about this fascinating astronomer. Pay particular attention to the role of scientific research in solving Brahe's mysterious death.)

As mentioned earlier, we all conduct research every day. We do this whenever we test a question about anything. Children conduct "research studies" to determine which items are hot and which are cold, how to ride a bicycle or a snowboard, and which persuasive methods work best with parents. Teenagers "test" ideas about driving, dating, and working, and adults "test" ideas about family, finance, and survival.

All research, whether formal or informal, begins with a basic question or proposition about a specific phenomenon. For example, why do viewers select one television program over another? Which sections of the newspaper do people read most often? Which types of magazine covers attract the most readers? Which types of advertising are most effective in selling products and services? These questions can be answered to some degree with well-designed research studies. However, the task is to determine which data collection method can most appropriately provide answers to specific questions.

▪ The Methods of Knowing

There are several possible approaches in answering research questions. Kerlinger (2000), using definitions provided nearly a century ago by C. S. Peirce, discusses four approaches to finding answers, or **methods of knowing:** tenacity, intuition, authority, and science.

A user of the *method of tenacity* follows the logic that something is true because it has always been true. An example is the storeowner who says, "I don't advertise because my parents did not believe in advertising." The idea is that nothing changes—what was good, bad, or successful before will continue to be so in the future.

In the *method of intuition,* or the a priori approach, a person assumes that something is true because it is "self-evident" or "stands to reason." Some creative people in advertising agencies resist efforts to test their advertising methods because they believe they know what will attract customers. To these people, scientific research is a waste of time.

The *method of authority* promotes a belief in something because a trusted source, such as a parent, a news correspondent, or a teacher, says it is true. The emphasis is on the source, not on the methods the source may have used to gain the information. For example, the claim that "consumers will pay hundreds of dollars for a new satellite dish to receive hundreds of television channels because producers of satellite dish companies say so" is based on the method of authority. (During 1994 and 1995, this was shown not to be true. Consumers did not flock to the stores to buy the new delivery system, and research had to be conducted to find out what failed. When changes were made in both product and marketing, sales quickly took off.)

The *scientific method* approaches learning as a series of small steps. That is, one study or one source provides only an indication of what may or may not be true; the "truth" is found through a series of objective analyses. This means that the scientific method is self-correcting in that changes in thought or theory are appropriate when errors in previous research are uncovered. For example, in 1984 Barry Marshall, a medical resident in Perth, Australia, identified a bacterium (*Helicobacter pylori* or *H. pylori*) as the cause of stomach ulcers (not an increase in stomach acid due to stress or anxiety). After several years, hundreds of independent studies proved that Marshall was correct, and in 1996, the Food and Drug Administration (FDA) approved a combination of drugs to fight ulcers—an antacid and an antibiotic. In space exploration, NASA disclosed in early 1998 that water had been found on Earth's moon, changing the centuries-old idea that water could not exist there, and the Hubble telescope provides new information on a daily basis. See *http://hubblesite.org* for more information about Hubble telescope discoveries.

In communications, researchers discovered that the early perceptions of the power of the media (the "hypodermic needle" theory) were incorrect and, after numerous studies, concluded that behavior and ideas are changed by a combination of communication sources and different people's reactions to the same message. Isaac Asimov

AN INSIDE LOOK
The Methods of Knowing

A graduate student from Colorado was interested in how much information he was exposed to each day fell into each of the Methods of Knowing. He designed a class project to count the number of statements or "facts" he heard during one week. In his case, the majority of information he heard over a week's time fell into the categories of tenacity, intuition, and authority. What does this tell you about the information you may be exposed to during a typical day?

(1990, p. 42) states, "One of the glories of scientific endeavor is that any scientific belief, however firmly established, is constantly being tested to see if it is truly universally valid." The scientific method may be inappropriate in many areas of life—for instance, in evaluating works of art, choosing a religion, or forming friendships—but it has been valuable in producing accurate and useful data in mass media research. The next section provides a more detailed look at this method of knowing. See R. K. Tucker (1996) for a discussion of how a person's personality, temperament, or approach to life can affect the way he or she learns things. In addition, for a different perspective of the methods of knowing, go to *http://mrrc.bio.uci.edu/se10/philosophy.html.*

▪ Characteristics of the Scientific Method

Five basic characteristics, or tenets, distinguish the scientific method from other methods of knowing. A research approach that does not follow these tenets is not a scientific approach.

1. *Scientific research is public.* Advances in science require freely available information. Researchers (especially in the academic sector) cannot plead private knowledge, methods, or data in arguing for the accuracy of their findings; scientific research information must be freely communicated from one researcher to another. As Nunnally and Bernstein (1994) note:

> Science is a highly public enterprise in which efficient communication among scientists is essential. Each scientist builds on what has been learned in the past; day by day his or her findings must be compared with those of other scientists working on the same types of problems. . . . The rate of scientific progress in a particular area is limited by the efficiency and fidelity with which scientists can communicate their results to one another.

Researchers therefore must take great care in their published reports to include information on sampling methods, measurements, and data-gathering procedures. Such information allows other researchers to independently verify a given study and support or refute the initial research findings. This process of replication allows for correction and verification of previous research findings. Though not related to media research, the importance of replication in scientific research was underscored in 1992, when physicists were unable to duplicate the fantastic claim made by two University of Utah chemists who said they had produced fusion at room temperature.

Researchers also need to save their descriptions of observations (data) and their research materials so that information not included in a formal report are available to other researchers on request. Nunnally and Bernstein (1994) say, "A key principle of science is that any statement of fact made by one scientist should be independently verifiable by other scientists." Researchers can verify results only if they have access to the original data. It is common practice to keep all raw research materials for at least five years. The material is usually provided free as a courtesy to other researchers, or for a nominal fee if photocopying or additional materials are required.

2. *Science is objective.* Science tries to rule out eccentricities of judgment by researchers. When a study is undertaken, explicit rules and procedures are constructed and the researcher is bound to follow them, letting the chips fall where they may. Rules for classifying behavior are used so that two or more independent observers can classify particular behavior patterns in the same manner. For example, to measure the appeal of a television commercial, researchers might count the number of times a viewer switches channels while the commercial is shown. This is considered an objective measure because any competent observer would report a change in channel. On the other hand, to measure appeal by observing how many viewers make negative facial expressions while the ad is shown would be a subjective approach, since different observers may have different ideas of what constitutes a negative expression. However, an explicit definition of "negative facial expression" might eliminate the coding error.

Objectivity also requires that scientific research deal with facts rather than interpretations of facts. Science rejects its own authorities if their statements conflict with direct observation. As the noted psychologist B. F. Skinner (1953) wrote: "Research projects do not always come out as one expects, but the facts must stand and the expectations fall. The subject matter, not the scientist, knows best." Mass media researchers have often encountered situations in which media decision makers reject the results of a research project because the study did not produce the anticipated results. (In such a case, one might wonder why the research was conducted at all.)

3. *Science is empirical.* Researchers are concerned with a world that is knowable and potentially measurable. (*Empiricism* comes from the Greek word for "experience.") They must be able to perceive and classify what they study and to reject metaphysical and nonsensical explanations of events. For example, a newspaper publisher's claim that declining subscription rates are "God's will" would be rejected by scientists; such an occurrence cannot be perceived, classified, or measured. (Scientists whose areas of research rely on superstition and other nonscientific methods of knowing are said to practice "bad science." For a fascinating discussion on astrology, UFOs, and pseudoscience, see Seeds, 1992, and search the Internet for "empiricism.")

This *does not* mean that scientists avoid abstract ideas and notions; they encounter them every day. However, they recognize that concepts must be strictly defined to allow for observation and measurement. Scientists must link abstract concepts to the empirical world through observations, which may be made either directly or indirectly via various measurement instruments. Typically, this linkage is accomplished by framing an operational definition.

Operational definitions are important in science, and a brief introduction necessitates some backtracking. There are basically two kinds of definitions. A **constitutive definition** defines a *word by substituting other words or concepts for it.* For example, here is a constitutive definition of the concept "artichoke": An artichoke is a green leafy vegetable, a tall composite herb of the *Cynara scolymus* family. In contrast, an **operational definition** *specifies procedures that will allow one to experience or measure a concept*—for example: Go to the grocery store and find the produce

AN INSIDE LOOK
Scientific Research

Although the Internet is a valuable information source, it is also a source for misunderstanding, passing of incorrect information via forwarded email, and perpetuation of urban legends. Look at some of the information passed along on the Internet on *www.urbanlegends.com.* Why do you think these legends are so popular? In which method of knowing do these urban legends belong?

aisle; look for a sign that says "Artichokes"; what's underneath the sign is an artichoke. Although an operational definition assures precision, it does not guarantee validity; a stock clerk may mistakenly stack lettuce under the artichoke sign. This possibility for error underscores the importance of considering both the constitutive definition and the operational definition of a concept to evaluate the trustworthiness of any measurement. Carefully examining the constitutive definition of artichoke indicates that the operational definition might be faulty. (For more information about definitions in general, see Langer, 1967.)

Operational definitions can help dispel some of the strange questions raised in philosophical discussions. For instance, if you have taken a philosophy course, you may have encountered the question, "How many angels can stand on the head of a pin?" The debate ends quickly when the retort is, "Give me an operational definition of an angel, and I'll give you the answer." Any question can be answered as long as there are operational definitions for the independent or dependent variables. For further discussion of operational definitions, see *Psychometric Theory* (Nunnally & Bernstein, 1994) and *The Practice of Social Research* (Babbie, 2001).

4. *Science is systematic and cumulative.* No single research study stands alone, nor does it rise or fall by itself. Astute researchers always use previous studies as building blocks for their own work. One of the first steps in conducting research is to review the available scientific literature on the topic so that the current study will draw on the heritage of past research. This review is valuable for identifying problem areas and important factors that might be relevant to the current study. (Please read Timothy Ferris's preface in *The Whole Shebang,* 1998.)

In addition, scientists attempt to search for order and consistency among their findings. In its ideal form, scientific research begins with a single carefully observed event and progresses ultimately to the formulation of theories and laws. A **theory** is *a set of related propositions that presents a systematic view of phenomena by specifying relationships among concepts.* Researchers develop theories by searching for patterns of uniformity to explain their data. When relationships among variables are invariant (always the same) under given conditions, researchers may formulate a law. A **law** is *a statement of fact meant to explain, in concise terms, an action or set of actions that is generally accepted to be true and universal.* Both theories and laws help researchers search for and explain consistency in behavior, situations, and phenomena.

5. *Science is predictive.* Science is concerned with relating the present to the future. In fact, scientists strive to develop theories because, among other reasons, they are useful in predicting behavior. A theory's ade-

quacy lies in its ability to predict a phenomenon or event successfully. A theory that suggests predictions that are not borne out by data analysis must be carefully reexamined and perhaps discarded. Conversely, a theory that generates predictions that are supported by the data can be used to make predictions in other situations.

Research Procedures

The purpose of the scientific method of research is to provide an objective, unbiased evaluation of data. To investigate research questions and hypotheses systematically, both academic and private-sector researchers follow a basic eight-step procedure. However, merely following the eight research steps does not guarantee that the research is good, valid, reliable, or useful. An almost countless number of intervening variables (influences) can destroy even the best-planned research project. The situation is similar to someone assuming he or she can bake a cake by just following the recipe. The cake may be ruined by an oven that doesn't work properly, spoiled ingredients, altitude, or numerous other problems. The typical research process consists of these eight steps:

1. Select a problem.
2. Review existing research and theory (when relevant).
3. Develop hypotheses or research questions.
4. Determine an appropriate methodology/research design.
5. Collect relevant data.
6. Analyze and interpret the results.
7. Present the results in an appropriate form.
8. Replicate the study (when necessary).

Step 4 includes deciding whether to use **qualitative research** (such as focus groups or one-on-one interviews) with small samples or **quantitative research** (such as telephone interviews), in which large samples are used to allow results to be generalized to the population under study (see Chapter 5 for a discussion of qualitative research).

Steps 2 and 8 are optional in the private sector, where some research is conducted to answer a specific and unique question related to a future decision, such as whether to invest a large sum of money in a developing medium. In this type of project, there generally is no previous research to consult, and there seldom is a reason to replicate the study because a decision is made based on the first analysis. However, if the research produces inconclusive results, the study is revised and replicated.

Each step in the eight-step process depends on all the others to produce a maximally efficient research study. For example, before a literature search is possible, the researcher must have a clearly stated research problem; to design the most efficient method of investigating a problem, the researcher must know what types of studies have been conducted; and so on. In addition, all the steps are interactive—a literature search may refine and even alter the initial research problem, or a study conducted previously by another company or business in the private sector might expedite (or complicate) the current research effort.

▪ Two Sectors of Research: Academic and Private

The practice of research is divided into two major sectors, academic and private, which are sometimes called "basic" and "applied," respectively. We do not use these terms in this text because research in both sectors can be basic or applied. The two sectors are equally important and in many cases work together to solve mass media problems.

Scholars from colleges and universities conduct academic-sector research. Generally, this research has a theoretical or scholarly approach; that is, the results are intended to help explain the mass media and their effects on individuals. Some popular research topics in the theoretical area are the use of media and various media-related items, such as video games and multiple-channel cable systems; differences in consumer lifestyles; effects of media "overload" on consumers; and effects of various types of programming on children.

Nongovernmental companies or their research consultants conduct private-sector research. It is generally applied research; that is, the results are intended to facilitate decision making. Typical research topics in the private sector include media content and consumer preferences, acquisitions of additional businesses or facilities, analysis of on-air talent, advertising and promotional campaigns, public relations approaches to solving specific informational problems, sales forecasting, and image studies of the properties owned by the company.

There are other differences between academic research and private-sector research. For instance, academic research is public. Any other researcher or research organization that wishes to use the information gathered by academic researchers should be able to do so merely by asking the original researcher for the raw data. Most private sector research, on the other hand, generates proprietary data that are considered the sole property of the sponsoring agency and generally cannot be obtained by other researchers. Some private sector research, however, is released to the public soon after it has been conducted (for example, public opinion polls and projections concerning the future of the media). Other studies may be released only after several years, although this practice is the exception rather than the rule.

Another difference between academic research and private-sector research involves the amount of time allowed to conduct the work. Academic researchers generally do not have specific deadlines for their research projects (except when they receive research grants). Academicians usually conduct their research at a pace that accommodates their teaching schedules. Private sector researchers nearly always operate under some type of deadline. The time frame may be imposed by management or by an outside agency or a client that needs to make a decision.

Academic research is generally less expensive to conduct than research in the private sector. This is not to say that academic research is "cheap," because in many cases it is not. But academicians do not need to cover overhead costs for office rent, equipment, facilities, computer analysis, subcontractors, and personnel. Private sector research must consider such expenses, regardless of whether the research is conducted within the company or contracted out to a research supplier. The lower cost of academic researchers sometimes motivates large media companies and groups to use them rather than professional research firms.

Despite these differences, beginning researchers must understand that academic research and private-sector research are not independent of each other. Academicians perform many studies for industry, and private-sector groups conduct research that can be classified as theoretical. (For example, the television networks have departments that conduct social research.) Similarly, many college and university professors act as consultants to (and often conduct private-sector research for) the media industry.

It is important for all researchers to refrain from attaching to academic or private-sector research stereotypical labels such as "unrealistic," "pedantic," and "limited in scope." Research in both sectors, though occasionally differing in cost and scope, uses similar methodologies and statistical analyses. In addition, the two sectors have common research goals: to understand problems and to predict the future. When conducting a study according to the scientific method, researchers must have a clear understanding of what they are investigating, how the phenomenon can be measured or observed, and what procedures are required to test the observations or measurements. Answering a research question or hypothesis requires a conceptualization of the research problem and a logical development of the procedural steps. These steps are discussed in greater detail in the following sections of this chapter.

▪ Research Procedures

The scientific evaluation of any problem must follow a sequence of steps to increase the probability that it will produce relevant data. Researchers who do not follow a prescribed set of steps do not subscribe to the scientific method of inquiry and simply increase the amount of error present in a study. This chapter describes the process of scientific research—from identifying and developing a topic for investigation to replicating the results. The first section briefly introduces the steps in the development of a research topic.

Objective, rigorous observation and analysis characterize the scientific method. To meet this goal, researchers must follow the prescribed steps shown in Figure 1.2. This research model is appropriate to all areas of scientific research.

Selecting a Research Topic

Not all researchers are concerned with selecting a topic to study; some are able to choose and concentrate on a research area that is interesting to them. Many researchers come to be identified with studies of specific types, such as those concerning children and media violence, newspaper readership, advertising, or communications law. These researchers investigate small pieces of a puzzle to obtain a broad picture of their research area. In addition, some researchers become identified with specific *approaches* to research, such as focus groups or historical analysis. In the private sector, researchers generally do not have the flexibility to select topics or questions to investigate. Instead, they conduct studies to answer questions raised by management, or they address the problems and questions for which they are hired, as is the case with full-service research companies.

Although some private-sector researchers are occasionally limited in selecting a topic, they are usually given total control over how the question should be answered (that is, what methodology should be used). The goal of private-sector researchers in every research study is to develop a method that is fast, inexpensive, reliable, and valid. If all these criteria are met, the researcher has performed a valuable task.

Selecting a topic is a concern for many beginning researchers, however, especially those writing term papers, theses, and dissertations. The problem is knowing where to start. Fortunately, many sources are available for research topics; academic journals, periodicals, newsweeklies, and everyday encounters provide a wealth of ideas. This section highlights some primary sources.

Professional Journals

Academic communication journals, such as the *Journal of Broadcasting and Electronic Media*, *Journalism and Mass Communication Quarterly*, and others listed in this section, are excellent sources of information. Although academic journals tend to publish research that is 12 to 24 months old (due to review procedures and the backlog of articles), the articles may provide ideas for research topics. Most authors conclude their research by discussing

Figure 1.2 *Steps in the Development of a Research Project*

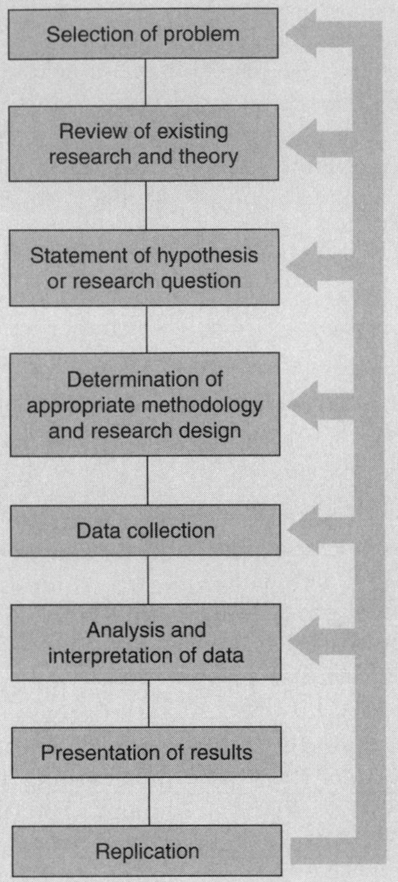

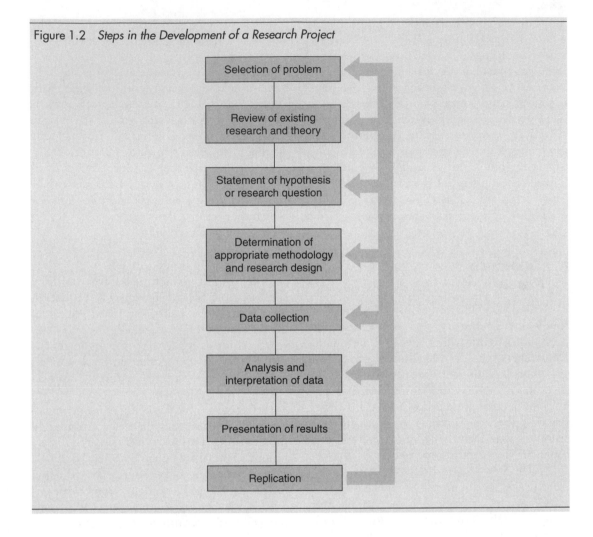

problems they encountered during the study and suggesting topics that need further investigation. In addition, some journal editors build issues around individual research themes, which often can help in formulating research plans. Many high-quality journals cover various aspects of research; some specialize in mass media, and others include media research occasionally. The journals listed below provide a starting point in using academic journals for research ideas.

In addition to academic journals, professional trade publications offer a wealth of information relevant to mass media research. These include *Broadcasting & Cable, Radio & Records, Advertising Age, Electronic Media, Television/Radio Age, Media Decisions, Editor & Publisher, CableVision,* and *Media and Marketing Management.* Other excellent sources for identifying current topics in mass media are the weekly newsletters such as *Media Industry Newsletter, Cable Digest,* and several publications from Paul Kagan and Associates.

Research abstracts, located in most college and university libraries, are also valuable sources for research topics. These volumes contain summaries of research articles published in nearly every academic journal. Of particular

Journals That Specialize in Mass Media Research

- *Critical Studies in Mass Communication*
- *Journalism and Mass Communication Quarterly*
- *Journal of Advertising*
- *Journal of Advertising Research*
- *Journal of Broadcasting and Electronic Media*
- *Journal of Consumer Research*
- *Journal of Radio Studies*
- *Newspaper Research Journal*
- *Public Relations Review*

Journals That Occasionally Publish Mass Media Research

- *American Psychologist*
- *Communication Education*
- *Communication Monographs*
- *Communication Research*
- *Feedback (from the Broadcast Education Association)*
- *Human Communication Research*
- *Journalism Educator*
- *Journal of Communication*
- *Journal of Marketing*
- *Journal of Marketing Research*
- *Multivariate Behavioral Research*
- *Public Opinion Quarterly*
- *Public Relations Quarterly*
- *Quarterly Journal of Speech*

interest to media researchers are *Communication Abstracts, Psychological Abstracts, Sociological Abstracts,* and *Dissertation Abstracts.*

Magazines and Periodicals

Although some educators feel that publications other than professional journals contain only "watered down" articles written for the public, these articles tend to eliminate tedious technical jargon and are often good sources for problems and hypotheses. In addition, more and more articles written by highly trained communications professionals appear in weekly and monthly publications such as *TV Guide, Time,* and *Newsweek.* These sources often provide interesting perspectives on complex problems in communication and many times raise interesting questions that media researchers can pursue.

Research Summaries

Professional research organizations periodically publish summaries that provide a close look at the major research areas in various fields. These summaries are often useful for obtaining information about research topics because they survey a wide variety of studies. Good examples of summary research (also known as "meta-research") in communication are *Television and Human Behavior* by George Comstock and others (1978), The *Effects of Mass Communication on Political Behavior* by Sydney Kraus and Dennis Davis (1967), and *Milestones in Mass Communication Research* by Shearon Lowery and Melvin DeFleur (1995).

The Internet

The Internet brings the world to a researcher's fingertips and must be considered whenever the goal is to find a topic to investigate. Search engines such as *Google, AltaVista,* and *Infoseek* provide a huge number of possible research topics. For example, assume that you have an interest in satellite television. A search for "satellite television" on *www.google.com* produces nearly 650,000 matches. That's a lot of material to consider, but suppose you wonder about the first remote controls for satellite television. That search produces nearly

104,000 items, many of which provide an interesting history about the development of remote controls for television.

A great exercise on the Internet is to search for broad categories. For example, to see the variety of questions that can be answered, search for "How is," "How does," "Why is," or "Why does." In addition, conduct a search for "research topic ideas." You'll find an incredible list of items.

Everyday Situations

Each day people are confronted with various types of communication via radio, television, newspapers, magazines, movies, personal discussions, and so forth. These can be excellent sources of topics for researchers who take an active role in analyzing them. With this in mind, consider the following questions:

- Why do advertisers use specific types of messages in broadcasting or print?
- Why are "Entertainment Tonight," "Jeopardy," and "Wheel of Fortune" so popular?
- Why do so many TV commercials use only video to deliver a message when many people don't always watch TV—they just listen?
- How effective are billboards in communicating information about products?
- What types of people listen to radio talk shows?
- How many commercials in a row can people watch on television or hear on the radio before the commercials lose their effect?
- Why do commercials on radio and television always sound louder than the regular programming?
- What is the appeal of "reality" programs on TV?
- How many people listen to the music channels on cable or satellite TV?
- What types of people buy items from the television shopping channels?
- Does anyone really watch the *Weather Channel*?

These and other questions may become a research idea. Significant studies based on questions arising from everyday encounters with the media and other forms of mass communication have covered investigations of television violence, the layout of newspaper advertisements, advisory warnings on television programs, and approaches to public relations campaigns. Pay attention to things around you and to conversations with others; these contacts can produce a wealth of questions to investigate.

For the sake of experimentation, do a search on the Internet using "everyday situations" and see how many articles and mentions appear; you may be surprised.

Archive Data

Data archives, such as the Inter-University Consortium for Political Research (ICPR) at the University of Michigan, the Simmons Target Group Index (TGI), the Gallup and Roper organizations, and the collections of Arbitron and Nielsen ratings data (see Chapter 15), are valuable sources of ideas for researchers. Historical data may be used to investigate questions different from those that the data were originally intended to address. For example, ratings books provide information about audience size and composition for a particular period in time, but other researchers may use the data for historical tracking, prediction of audiences in the future, changes in the popularity of types of stations and programs, and the relationship between audience ratings and advertising revenue generated by individual stations or an entire market. This process, known as **secondary analysis,** is a marvelous research approach because it saves time and resources.

Secondary analysis provides an opportunity for researchers to evaluate otherwise unavailable data. Becker (1981, p. 240) defines secondary analysis as

> [the] reuse of social science data after they have been put aside by the researcher who gathered them. The reuse of the data can be by the original researcher or someone uninvolved in any way in the initial research project. The research questions examined in the secondary analysis can be related to the original research endeavor or quite distinct from it.

Advantages of Secondary Analysis. Ideally, every researcher should conduct a research project of some magnitude to learn about design, data collection, and analysis. Unfortunately, this ideal situation does not exist. Modern research is simply too expensive. In addition, because survey methodology has become so complex, it is rare to find one researcher or even a small group of researchers who are experts in all phases of large studies.

Secondary analysis is one research alternative that overcomes some of these problems. Using available data is inexpensive. There are no questionnaires or measurement instruments to construct and validate; interviewers and other personnel do not need to be paid; and there are no costs for subjects and special equipment. The only expenses entailed in secondary analysis are those for duplicating materials (some organizations provide their data free of charge) and usually some fee to cover time of handling. Data archives are valuable sources for empirical data. In many cases, archive data provide researchers with information that can be used to address significant media problems and questions.

Although novice researchers can gain some benefit from developing questionnaires and conducting a research project using a small and often unrepresentative sample of subjects, this type of analysis rarely produces results that are externally valid. (External validity is discussed later in this chapter.) Instead of conducting a small study that has limited value to other situations, these people can benefit from using previously collected data. Researchers then have more time to understand and analyze the data (Tukey, 1969). All too often researchers collect data that are quickly analyzed for publication or reported to management and never touched again. It is difficult to completely analyze all data from any research study in just one analysis yet researchers in both the academic and private sectors are guilty of ignoring data gathered earlier.

Many years ago, Tukey (1969, p. 89) argued for data reanalysis, especially for graduate students, but his statement applies to all researchers:

> There is merit in having a Ph.D. thesis encompass all the admitted steps of the research process. Once we recognize that research is a continuing, more or less cyclic process, however, we see that we can segment it in many places. Why should not at least a fair proportion of theses start with a careful analysis of previously collected and presumably already lightly analyzed data, a process usefully spread out over considerable time? Instant data analysis is—and will remain—an illusion.

Arguments for secondary analysis come from a variety of researchers (Glenn, 1972; Hyman, 1972; Tukey, 1969; Hinds, Vogel, & Clarke-Steffen, 1997). It is clear that the research method provides excellent opportunities to produce valuable knowledge. The procedure, however, is not universally accepted—an unfortunate perspective that limits the advancement of knowledge.

Disadvantages of Secondary Analysis. Researchers who use secondary analysis are limited in the types of hypotheses or research questions that can be investigated. The data already exist, and because there is no way to go back for more information, researchers must keep their analyses within the boundaries of the data originally collected.

In addition, there is no guarantee that the data are good. It may be that the data were poorly collected, inaccurate, fabricated, or flawed. Many studies do not include information about research design, sampling procedures, weighting of subjects' responses, or other peculiarities. Although individual researchers in mass media have made their data more readily available (Reid, Soley, & Wimmer, 1981; Wimmer & Reid, 1982), not all follow adequate scientific procedures. This drawback may seriously affect a secondary analysis.

Despite the criticisms of using secondary analysis, the methodology is an acceptable research approach, and detailed justifications for using it should no longer be required. For further information, search the Internet for "secondary analysis."

▪ Determining Topic Relevance

Once a basic research idea has been chosen or assigned, the next step is to ensure that the topic has merit. This is accomplished by answering eight basic questions.

Question 1: Is the Topic Too Broad?

Most research studies concentrate on one small area of a field; researchers do not attempt to analyze an entire field in one study. However, researchers frequently choose topics that are too broad to cover in one study—for example, "the effects of television violence on children" or "the effects of mass media information on voters in a presidential election." To avoid this problem, researchers usually write down their proposed title as a visual starting point and attempt to dissect the topic into a series of questions.

For example, a University of Colorado master's degree student was interested in why viewers like the television shows they watch and how viewers' analyses of programs are similar to or different from the analyses of TV critics. This is a broad topic. First of all, what types of programs will be analyzed? After a great deal of thought about the questions involved, the student settled on the topic of "program element importance" in television soap operas. She asked viewers to identify what is important to them when they watch a soap opera, and she developed a "model" for a successful program.

Question 2: Can the Problem Really Be Investigated?

Aside from being too broad, a topic might prove unsuitable for investigation simply because the question being asked has no answer or at least cannot be answered with the facilities and information available. For example, a researcher who wants to know how people who have no television receiver react to everyday interpersonal communication situations must consider the problem of finding subjects without a TV set in the home. A few such subjects may exist in remote parts of the country, but the question is basically unanswerable due to the current market saturation of television. Thus, the researcher must attempt to reanalyze the original idea to conform with practical considerations. A. S. Tan (1977) solved this particular dilemma by choosing to investigate what people do when their television sets are turned off for a period of time. He persuaded subjects not to watch television for one week and to record their use of other media, their interactions with their family and friends, and so on. (Subjects involved in these types of media-deprivation studies usually cheat and use the medium before the end of the project.)

Another point to consider is whether all the terms of the proposed study can be defined. Remember that all measured variables must have operational definitions. A researcher interested in examining youngsters' use of the media must develop a working definition of the word *youngsters* to avoid confusion. Problems can be eliminated if an operational definition is stated: "Youngsters are children between the ages of 3 and 7 years."

One final consideration is to review available literature to determine if the topic has been previously investigated. Were there any problems in previous studies? What methods were used to answer the research questions? What conclusions were drawn?

Question 3: Can the Data Be Analyzed?

A topic does not lend itself to productive research if it requires collecting data that cannot be measured in a reliable and valid fashion. In other words, a researcher who wants to measure the effects of not watching television should consider whether the information about the subjects' behavior will be adequate and reliable, whether the subjects will answer truthfully, what value the data will have once gathered, and so forth. Researchers also need to have enough data to make the study worthwhile. It would be unacceptable to analyze only 10 subjects in the "television turn-off" example because the results could not be generalized to the entire population. (A sample of 10 may be used for a **pilot study** or test of the research procedures.)

Another consideration is the researcher's previous experience with the statistical method selected to analyze the data; that is, does the researcher really understand the proposed statistical analysis? Researchers need to know how the statistics work and how to interpret the results. All too often researchers design studies that involve advanced statistical procedures they have never used. This tactic almost always creates errors in computation and interpretation. Research methods and statistics should not be selected because they happen to be popular or because a research director suggests a given method, but because they are appropriate for a given study and are understood by the person conducting the analysis. A common error made by beginning researchers—selecting a statistical method without understanding what the method produces—is called the **Law of the Instrument.**

It is much wiser to use simple frequencies and percentages and understand the results than to try to use a high-level statistic and end up confused.

Question 4: Is the Problem Significant?

It is important to determine if a study has merit *before the research is started*; that is, to determine if the study has practical or theoretical value. The first question to ask is: Will the results add knowledge to information already available in the field? The goal of research is to help further the understanding of the problems and questions in a field of study. If a study does not do this, it has little value beyond the experience the researcher acquires from conducting it. Of course, not all research has to be earth shattering. Many researchers waste valuable time trying to develop monumental projects when in fact the smaller problems are more important.

A second question is: What is the real purpose of the study? This question is important because it helps focus ideas. Is the study intended for a class paper, a thesis, a journal article, or a management decision? Each of these projects requires different amounts of background information, levels of explanation, and details about the results generated. For example, applied researchers need to consider whether any useful action based on the data will prove to be feasible, as well as whether the study will answer the question(s) posed by management.

Question 5: Can the Results of the Study Be Generalized?

If a research project is to have practical value beyond the immediate analysis, it must have **external validity**; that is, it must be possible to generalize the results to other situations. For example, a study of the effects of a small-town public relations campaign might be appropriate if plans are made to analyze such effects in several small towns, or if it is a case study not intended for generalization; however, such an analysis has little external validity and cannot be related to other situations.

Question 6: What Costs and Time Are Involved in the Analysis?

In many cases, the cost of a research study is the sole determinant of its feasibility. A researcher may have an excellent idea, but if costs would be prohibitive, the project is abandoned. A cost analysis must be completed very early on. It does not make sense to develop the specific designs and the data-gathering instrument for a project that will be canceled because of lack of funds. Sophisticated research is particularly expensive; the cost of one project can easily exceed $50,000.

A carefully itemized list of all materials, equipment, and other facilities required is necessary before beginning a research project. If the costs seem prohibitive, the researcher must determine whether the same goal can be achieved if costs are shaved in some areas. Another possibility to consider is financial aid from graduate schools, funding agencies, local governments, or other groups that subsidize research projects. In general, private-sector researchers are not severely constrained by expenses; however, they must adhere to budget specifications set by management.

Time is also an important consideration in research planning. Research studies must be designed so that they can be completed in the time available. Many studies fail because the researchers do not allot enough time for each research step, and in many cases, the pressure of deadlines creates problems in producing reliable and valid results (for example, failure to provide alternatives if the correct sample of people cannot be located).

Question 7: Is the Planned Approach Appropriate to the Project?

The best research idea may be needlessly hindered by a poorly planned method of approach. For example, a researcher might wish to measure changes in television viewing habits that may accompany an increase in time spent on the Internet. The researcher could mail questionnaires to a large number of people to determine how their television habits have changed during the past several months. However, the costs of printing and mailing questionnaires, plus follow-up letters and possibly phone calls to increase the response rate, might prove prohibitive.

Could the study be planned differently to eliminate some of the expense? Possibly, depending on its purpose and the types of questions planned. For example, the researcher could collect the data by telephone interviews to eliminate printing and postage costs. Although some questions might need reworking to fit the telephone procedure, the essential information could be collected. A close look at every study is required to plan the best approach. Every procedure in a re-

AN INSIDE LOOK
Occam's Razor

Although Occam's razor is mentioned only briefly here, it is an enormously important concept to remember and it is mentioned several times in the book. It is important not only in research but also in every facet of people's lives. If you are stumped with a sampling problem, a questionnaire design problem, a data analysis problem, or a report problem, always ask yourself, "Is this the easiest way to approach the problem?" In most cases, you'll find the difficulty is that you're making the problem too complex. The same situation often occurs in your everyday life. Always look for the simplest approach to any problem you encounter. It will always be the best approach to follow.

search study should be considered from the standpoint of the **parsimony principle,** or **Occam's razor.** The principle, attributed to 14th-century philosopher William of Occam (also spelled Ockham), states that a person *should not increase, beyond what is necessary, the number of entities required to explain anything, or make more assumptions than the minimum needed.* Applying this principle to media research says that *the simplest research approach is always the best.* (Search the Internet for "Occam" for several interesting articles about the philosopher.)

Question 8: Is There Any Potential Harm to the Subjects?

Researchers must carefully analyze whether their project may cause physical or psychological harm to the subjects under evaluation. Will respondents be frightened in any way? Will they be required to answer embarrassing questions or perform embarrassing acts that may create adverse reactions? Is there a chance that exposure to the research conditions will have lasting effects? Before the start of most public-sector research projects involving humans, subjects are given detailed statements explaining the exact procedures involved in the research to ensure that they will not be injured in any way. These statements protect unsuspecting subjects from exposure to harmful research methods.

Underlying the eight steps in the research topic selection process is the necessity for validity (discussed later in this chapter). In other words, are all the steps (from the initial idea to data analysis and interpretation) the correct ones to follow in trying to answer the question(s)?

Suppose that after you carefully select a research project and convince yourself that it is something you want to do, someone confronts you with this reaction: "It's a good idea, but it can't be done: the topic is too broad, the problem cannot really be investigated, the data cannot be analyzed, the problem is not significant, the results cannot be generalized, it will cost too much, and the approach is wrong." How should you respond? First, consider the criticisms carefully to make sure that you have not overlooked anything. If you are convinced you're on the right track and no harm will come to any subject or respondent, go ahead with the project. It is better to do the study and find nothing than to back off because of someone's criticism. (Almost every major inventor in the past 100 years has been the target of jokes and ridicule.)

Literature Review

Researchers who conduct studies under the guidelines of scientific research never begin a research project without first consulting available literature to learn what has been done, how it was done, and what results were generated. Experienced researchers consider the literature review to be one of the most important steps in the research process. It not only allows them to learn from (and eventually add to) previous research but also saves time, effort, and money. Failing to conduct a literature review is as detrimental to a project as failing to address any of the other steps in the research process.

Before they attempt any project, researchers should ask these questions:

- What type of research has been done in the area?
- What has been found in previous studies?
- What suggestions do other researchers make for further study?
- What has not been investigated?
- How can the proposed study add to our knowledge of the area?
- What research methods were used in previous studies?

Answers to these questions will usually help define a specific hypothesis or research question.

■ Stating a Hypothesis or Research Question

After identifying a general research area and reviewing the existing literature, the researcher must state the problem as a workable hypothesis or research question. A **hypothesis** is *a formal statement regarding the relationship between variables and is tested directly.* The predicted relationship between the variables is either true or false. On the other hand, a **research question** is *a formally stated question intended to provide indications about something; it is not limited to investigating relationships between variables.* Research questions are appropriate when a researcher is unsure about the nature of the problem under investigation. Although the intent is merely to gather preliminary data, testable hypotheses are often developed from information gathered during the research question phase of a study.

Singer and Singer (1981) provide an example of how a topic is narrowed, developed, and stated in simple terms. Interested in whether television material enhances or inhibits a child's capacity for symbolic behavior, Singer and Singer reviewed available literature and then narrowed their study to three basic research questions:

1. Does television content enrich a child's imaginative capacities by offering materials and ideas for make-believe play?
2. Does television lead to distortions of reality for children?
3. Can intervention and mediation by an adult while a child views a program, or immediately afterward, evoke changes in make-believe play or stimulate make-believe play?

The information collected from this type of study could provide data to create testable hypotheses. For example, Singer and Singer might have collected enough valuable information from their preliminary study to test these hypotheses:

1. The amount of time a child spends in make-believe play is directly related to the amount of time spent viewing make-believe play on television.
2. A child's level of distortion of reality is directly related to the amount and

types of television programs the child views.

3. Parental discussions with children about make-believe play before, during, and after a child watches television programs involving make-believe play increase the child's time involved in make-believe play.

The difference between the two sets of statements is that the research questions pose only *general areas* of investigation, whereas the hypotheses are *testable* statements about the relationship(s) between the variables. The only intent in the research question phase is to gather information to help the researchers define and test hypotheses in later projects.

Data Analysis and Interpretation

The time and effort required for data analysis and interpretation depend on the study's purpose and the methodology used. Analysis and interpretation may take from several days to several months. In many private-sector research studies involving only a single question, data analysis and interpretation may be completed in a few minutes. For example, a radio station may be interested in finding out its listeners' perceptions of the morning show team. After a survey is conducted, that question may be answered by summarizing only one or two items on the questionnaire. The summary then may determine the fate of the morning show team.

Every research study must be carefully planned and performed according to specific guidelines. When the analysis is completed, the researcher must step back and consider what has been discovered. The researcher must ask two questions: Are the results internally and externally valid? Are the results accurate? Here, for example, is an excerpt from the conclusion drawn by Singer and Singer (1981, p. 385):

> Television by its very nature is a medium that emphasizes those very elements that are generally found in imagination: visual fluidity, time and space flexibility and make-believe. . . . Very little effort has emerged from producers or educators to develop age-specific programming. . . . It is evident that more research for the development of programming and adult mediation is urgently needed.

Researchers must determine through analysis whether their work is both internally and externally valid. This chapter has touched briefly on the concept of external validity: An externally valid study is one whose results can be generalized to the population. To assess internal validity, on the other hand, one asks: Does the study really investigate the proposed research question?

Internal Validity

Control over research conditions is necessary to enable researchers *to rule out plausible but incorrect explanations of results*. For example, if a researcher is interested in verifying that "y is a function of x," or $y = f(x)$, control over the research conditions is necessary to eliminate the possibility of finding that $y = f(b)$, where b is an extraneous variable. Any such variable that creates a possible but incorrect explanation of results is called an **artifact** (also referred to as an *extraneous variable* or *a confounding variable*). The presence of an artifact indicates a lack of internal validity; that is, the study has failed to investigate its hypothesis.

For example, suppose that researchers discover through a study that children who view television for extended periods have lower grade point averages in school than children who watch only a limited amount of television. Could an artifact have created this finding?

AN INSIDE LOOK

Data Analysis—The Wimmer-Dominick Data Analysis Principle

One thing beginning researchers always find interesting is the ability for seasoned researchers to look at data and say something like, "This looks wrong." The beginners wonder how the veteran knows that. The answer is the Wimmer-Dominick Data Analysis Principle, which states: If something looks wrong in a research study, it probably is.

Here's a real example. In a recent research study using rating scales from 1 to 10, a few responses had mean scores above 10. The data looked wrong and, of course, they were because it's impossible to have a mean greater than 10 on a 1–10 scale. Experience in research will allow you to locate these types of errors. Trust your judgment—if something looks wrong, it probably is wrong.

It may be that children who view fewer hours of television also receive parental help with their school work; parental help (the artifact), not hours of television viewed, may be the reason for the difference in grade point averages between the two groups.

Artifacts in research may arise from several sources. Those most frequently encountered are described next. Researchers should be familiar with these sources to achieve internal validity in the experiments they conduct (Campbell & Stanley, 1963; Cook & Campbell, 1979).

1. *History.* Various events that occur during a study may affect the subjects' attitudes, opinions, and behavior. For example, to analyze an oil company's public relations campaign for a new product, researchers first pretest subjects' attitudes toward the company. The subjects are next exposed to an experimental promotional campaign (the experimental treatment); then a posttest is administered to determine whether changes in attitude occur because of the campaign. Suppose the results indicate that the public relations campaign was a complete failure, that the subjects display a very poor perception of the oil company in the posttest. Before the results are reported, the researchers must determine whether an intervening variable could have caused the poor perception. An investigation discloses that during the period between tests, subjects learned from a television news story that a tanker owned by the oil company spilled millions of gallons of crude oil into the North Atlantic. News of the oil spill—not the public relations campaign—may have acted as an artifact to create the poor perception. The potential to confound a study is compounded as the time increases between a pretest and a posttest.

The effects of history in a study can be devastating, as was shown during the late 1970s and early 1980s, when several broadcast companies and other private businesses perceived a need to develop Subscription Television (STV) in various markets throughout the country where cable television penetration was thought to be very low. An STV service allows a household, using a special antenna, to receive pay television services similar to *Home Box Office* or *Showtime.* Several cities became prime targets for STV because both Arbitron and A. C. Nielsen reported very low cable penetration. Research conducted in these cities supported the Arbitron and Nielsen data. In addition, the research found that people who did not have access to cable television were very receptive to the idea of STV. However, it was discovered later that even as some studies were being conducted, cable companies in the target areas were expanding very rapidly and had wired many previously nonwired neighborhoods. What were once prime targets for STV soon became accessible to cable television. The major problem was that researchers attempting to determine the feasibility of STV failed to consider the historical changes (wiring of the cities) that could affect the results of their research. The result was that many companies lost millions of dollars and STV soon faded away.

2. *Maturation.* Subjects' biological and psychological characteristics change during the course of a study. Growing hungry, tired, or becoming older may influence how subjects respond in a research study. An example of how maturation can affect a research project was seen in the early 1980s, when radio stations around the country began to test their music playlist in auditorium sessions (see Chapter 13). Some unskilled research companies tested as many as 800 songs in one session and wondered why the songs after about 400 tested differently from the others. With only some investigation, researchers discovered that the respondents were physically and emotionally drained once they reached 400 songs (about 70 minutes of testing time), and they merely wrote down any number just to complete the project.

Technology and experience have changed the approach in auditorium music testing. In several studies during 2001, the senior author tested a variety of auditorium music testing methods and found that, among other things, if a professional production company is used to produce consistent hooks (song segments), and sufficient breaks are given for the respondents, it is possible to test as many as 600 songs in one session without compromising the data.

3. *Testing.* Testing itself may be an artifact, particularly when subjects are given similar pretests and posttests. A pretest may sensitize subjects to the material and improve their posttest scores regardless of the type of experimental treatment given to them. This is especially true when the same test is used for both situations. Subjects learn how to answer questions and to anticipate researchers' demands. To guard against the effects of testing, different pretests and posttests are required. Or, instead of being given a pretest, subjects can be tested for similarity (homogeneity) by means of a variable or set of variables that differs from the experimental variable. The pretest is not the only way to establish a **point of prior equivalency** (the point at which the groups were equal before the experiment) between groups—it also can be accomplished through sampling (randomization and matching). For further discussion on controlling confounding variables within the context of an experiment, see Chapter 9.

4. *Instrumentation.* Also known as *instrument decay,* this term refers to the deterioration of research instruments or methods over the course of a study. Equipment may wear out, observers may become more casual in recording their observations, and interviewers who memorize frequently asked questions may fail to present them in the proper order. Some college entrance tests, such as the SAT and ACT, are targets of debate by many researchers and statisticians. The complaints mainly address the concern that the current tests do not adequately measure knowledge of today, but rather what was once considered necessary and important.

5. *Statistical regression.* Subjects who achieve either very high or very low scores on a test tend to regress to the sample or population mean during subsequent testing sessions. Often outliers (subjects whose pretest scores are far from the mean) are selected for further testing or evaluation. Suppose, for example, that researchers develop a series of television programs designed to teach simple mathematical concepts, and they select only subjects who score very low on a mathematical aptitude pretest. An experimental treatment is designed to expose these subjects to

the new television series, and a posttest is given to determine whether the programs increased the subjects' knowledge of simple math concepts. The experimental study may show that indeed, after only one or two exposures to the new programs, math scores increased. But the higher scores on the posttest may not be due to the television programs; they may be a function of **statistical regression.** That is, regardless of whether the subjects viewed the programs, the scores in the sample may have increased merely because of statistical regression to the mean. The programs should be tested with a variety of subjects, not just those who score low on a pretest. (The significance of regression toward the mean is relevant to a variety of areas such as stock market prices and the standings of professional sports teams.)

6. *Experimental mortality.* All research studies face the possibility that subjects will drop out for one reason or another. Especially in long-term studies, subjects may refuse to continue with the project, become ill, move away, drop out of school, or quit work. This **mortality,** or loss of subjects, is sure to have an effect on the results of a study because most research methods and statistical analyses make assumptions about the number of subjects used. It is always better to select more subjects than are actually required—within the budget limits of the study. It is common to lose 50% or more of the subjects from one testing period to another (Wimmer, 1995).

7. *Sample selection.* Most research designs compare two or more groups of subjects to determine whether differences exist on the dependent measurement. These groups must be selected randomly and tested for homogeneity to ensure that results are not due to the type of sample used (see Chapter 4).

8. *Demand characteristics.* The term **demand characteristics** is used to describe subjects' reactions to experimental conditions. Orne (1969) suggests that under some circumstances subjects' awareness of the experimental purpose may be the sole determinant of how they behave; that is, subjects who recognize the purpose of a study may produce only "good" data for researchers.

Novice researchers quickly learn about the many variations of demand characteristics. For example, research studies seeking to find out about respondents' listening and viewing habits always find subjects who report high levels of *NPR* and *PBS* listening and viewing. However, when the same subjects are asked to name their favorite *NPR* or *PBS* programs, many cannot recall even one. (In other words, the respondents are not telling the truth.)

Cross-validating questions are often necessary to verify subjects' responses; by giving subjects the opportunity to answer the same question phrased in different ways, the researcher can spot discrepant, potentially error-producing responses. In addition, researchers can help control demand characteristics by disguising the real purpose of the study; however, researchers should use caution when employing this technique (see Chapter 4).

In addition, most respondents who participate in research projects are eager to provide the information the researcher requests. They are flattered to be asked for their opinions. Unfortunately, this means that they will answer any type of question, even if the question is ambiguous, misleading, vague, or uninterpretable. For example, this book's senior author conducted a telephone study in the early 1990s with respondents in area code 717 of Pennsylvania. An interviewer mistakenly called area code 714 (Orange County, California). For nearly 20 minutes, the respondent in California answered questions about radio stations with W call letters—stations impossible for her to receive on any radio. The problem was discovered during questionnaire validation.

9. *Experimenter bias.* Rosenthal (1969) discusses a variety of ways in which a researcher may influence the results of a study. Bias can enter through mistakes made in observation, data recording, mathematical com-

putations, and interpretation. Whether experimenter errors are intentional or unintentional, they usually support the researcher's hypothesis and are biased (Walizer & Wienir, 1978).

Experimenter bias can also enter into any phase of a research project if the researcher becomes swayed by a client's wishes for a project's end results. Such a situation can cause significant problems for researchers if they do not remain totally objective throughout the entire project, especially when they are hired by individuals or companies to "prove a point" or to provide "supporting information" for a decision (this is usually unknown to the researcher). For example, the news director at a local television station may dislike a particular news anchor and want information to justify the dislike (in order to fire the anchor). A researcher is hired under the guise of finding out whether the audience likes or dislikes the anchor. In this case, it is easy for the news director to intentionally or unintentionally sway the results through conversations with the researcher in the planning stages of the study. It is possible for a researcher, either intentionally or unintentionally, to interpret the results in a way that supports the program director's desire to eliminate the anchor. The researcher may have like/dislike numbers that are very close but may give the "edge" to dislike because of the news director's influence.

Experimenter bias is a potential problem in all phases of research, and those conducting a study must be aware of problems caused by outside influences. Several procedures can help to reduce experimenter bias. For example, individuals who provide instructions to subjects and make observations should not be informed of the purpose of the study. Experimenters and others involved in the research should not know whether subjects belong to the experimental group or the control group (called a *double-blind experiment*), and automated devices such as tape recorders should be used whenever possible to provide uniform instructions to subjects. (See Chapter 10 for more information about control groups.)

Researchers can also ask clients not to discuss the intent of a research project beyond what type of information is desired. In the news anchor example, the program director should say only that information is desired about the like/dislike of the program and should not discuss what decisions will be made following the research. In cases where researchers must be told about the purpose of the project, or where the researcher is conducting the study independently, experimenter bias must be repressed at every phase.

10. *Evaluation apprehension.* Rosenberg's (1965) concept of evaluation apprehension is similar to demand characteristics, but it emphasizes that subjects are essentially afraid of being measured or tested. They are interested in receiving only positive evaluations from the researcher and from the other subjects involved in the study. Most people are hesitant to exhibit behavior that differs from the norm and tend to follow the group even though they may totally disagree with the others. The researcher's task is to try to eliminate this passiveness by letting subjects know that their individual responses are important.

11. *Causal time order.* The organization of an experiment may create problems with data collection and interpretation. It may be that an experiment's results are not due to the stimulus (independent) variable but rather to the effect of the dependent variable. For example, respondents in an experiment that is attempting to determine how magazine advertising layouts influence their purchasing behavior may change their opinions when they read or complete a questionnaire after viewing several ads.

12. *Diffusion or imitation of treatments.* In situations where respondents participate at different times during one day or over several days, or where groups of respondents are studied one after another, respondents may have the opportunity to discuss the project with someone else and contaminate the research project. This is a special problem with focus groups when one group leaves the focus room at the same time a new group enters.

13. *Compensation.* Sometimes individuals who work with a control group (the one that receives no experimental treatment) may unknowingly treat the group differently because the group is "deprived" of something. In this case, the control group is no longer legitimate.

14. *Compensatory rivalry.* In some situations, subjects who know they are in a control group may work harder or perform differently to outperform the experimental group.

15. *Demoralization.* Control group subjects may literally lose interest in a project because they are not experimental subjects. These people may give up or fail to perform normally because they may feel demoralized or angry that they are not in the experimental group.

The sources of internal invalidity are complex and may arise in all phases of research. For this reason, it is easy to see why the results from a single study cannot be used to refute or support a theory or hypothesis. In attempting to control these artifacts, researchers use a variety of experimental designs and try to keep strict control over the research process so that subjects and researchers do not intentionally or unintentionally influence the results. As Hyman (1954) recognized:

> All scientific inquiry is subject to error, and it is far better to be aware of this, to study the sources in an attempt to reduce it, and to estimate the magnitude of such errors in our findings, than to be ignorant of the errors concealed in our data.

▪ External Validity

External validity refers to how well the results of a study can be generalized across populations, settings, and time (Cook & Campbell, 1979). The external validity of a study can be severely affected by the interaction in an analysis of variables such as subject selection, instrumentation, and experimental conditions (Campbell & Stanley, 1963). A study that lacks external validity cannot be projected to other situations; it is valid only for the sample tested.

Most procedures used to guard against external invalidity relate to sample selection. Cook and Campbell (1979) make three suggestions:

1. Use random samples.
2. Use heterogeneous samples and replicate the study several times.
3. Select a sample that is representative of the group to which the results will be generalized.

Using random samples rather than convenience or available samples allows researchers to gather information from a variety of subjects rather than from those who may share similar attitudes, opinions, and lifestyles. As discussed in Chapter 5, a random sample means that everyone (within the guidelines of the project) has an equal chance of being selected for the research study.

Several replicated research projects using samples with a variety of characteristics (heterogeneous) allow researchers to test hypotheses and research questions and not worry that the results will apply to only one type of subject.

Selecting a sample that is representative of the group to which the results will be generalized is basic common sense. For example, the results from a study of a group of high school students cannot be generalized to a group of college students.

A fourth way to increase external validity is to conduct research over a long period of time. Mass media research is often designed as short-term projects that expose subjects to an experimental treatment and then immediately test or measure them. In many cases, however, the immediate effects of a treatment are negligible. In advertising, for example, research studies designed to measure brand awareness are generally based on only one exposure to a commercial or advertisement. It is well known that persuasion and attitude change rarely take place after only one exposure; they require multiple exposures over time. Logically, then, such measurements should be made over weeks or months to take into account the "sleeper" effect—that attitude change may be minimal or nonexistent in the short run and still prove significant in the end.

Presenting Results

The format used to present results depends on the purpose of the study. Research intended for publication in academic journals follows a format prescribed by each journal; research conducted for management in the private sector tends to be reported in simpler terms, often excluding detailed explanations of sampling, methodology, and review of literature. However, all results must be presented in a clear and concise manner appropriate to both the research question and the individuals who will read the report.

Replication

One important point mentioned throughout this book is that the results of any single study are, by themselves, only indications of what might exist. A study provides information that says, in effect, "This is what may be the case." For others to be relatively certain of the results of any study, the research must be replicated. Too often researchers conduct one study and report the results as if they are providing the basis for a theory or a law. The information presented in this chapter, and in other chapters that deal with internal and external validity, argues that this cannot be true.

A research question or hypothesis must be investigated from many different perspectives before any significance can be attributed to the results of one study. Research methods and designs must be altered to eliminate **design-specific results**—that is, results that are based on, and hence specific to, the design used. Similarly, subjects with a variety of characteristics should be studied from many angles to eliminate sample-specific results, and statistical analyses need to be varied to eliminate **method-specific results.** In other words, every effort must be made to ensure that the results of any single study are not created by or dependent on a methodological factor; studies must be replicated.

Researchers overwhelmingly advocate the use of **replication** to establish scientific fact. Lykken (1968) and Kelly, Chase, and Tucker (1979) identify four basic types of replication that can be used to help validate a scientific test:

1. **Literal replication** involves the exact duplication of a previous analysis, including the sampling procedures, experimental conditions, measuring techniques, and methods of data analysis.
2. **Operational replication** attempts to duplicate only the sampling and experimental procedures of a previous analysis, to test whether the procedures will produce similar results.
3. **Instrumental replication** attempts to duplicate the dependent measures used in a previous study and to vary the experimental conditions of the original study.
4. **Constructive replication** tests the validity of methods used previously by deliberately not imitating the earlier study; both the manipulations and the measures differ from those used in the first study. The researcher simply begins with a statement of empirical "fact" uncovered in a previous study and attempts to find the same "fact."

Despite the obvious need to replicate research, mass media researchers generally ignore this important step, probably because many feel that replications are not as glamorous or important as original research. The wise researcher recognizes that even though replications may lack glamour, they most certainly do not lack importance.

▪ *Research Suppliers and Field Services*

Most media researchers do not conduct every phase of every project they supervise. Although they usually design research projects, determine the sample to study, and prepare the measurement instruments, researchers generally do not actually make telephone calls or interview respondents in on-site locations. Instead, the researchers contract with a research supplier or a field service to perform these tasks.

Research suppliers provide a variety of services. A full-service supplier participates in the design of a study, supervises data collection, tabulates the data, and analyzes the results. The company may work in any field (such as mass media, medical and hospital, or banking) or specialize in only one type of research work. In addition, some companies can execute any type of research method—telephone surveys, one-on-one interviews, shopping center interviews (intercepts), or focus groups—whereas others concentrate on only one method.

Field services usually specialize in conducting telephone interviews, mall intercepts, and one-on-one interviews and in recruiting respondents for group administration (*central location testing,* or CLT) projects and focus groups. The latter projects are called **prerecruits** (the company prerecruits respondents to attend a research session). Although some field services offer help in questionnaire design and data tabulation, most concentrate on telephone interviews, mall interviews, and prerecruiting.

Field services usually have focus group rooms available (with one-way mirrors to allow clients to view the session) and test kitchens for projects involving food and cooking. Although some field service facilities are gorgeous and elaborate, others look as though the company just filed for bankruptcy protection. Many field services lease space, or lease the right to conduct research, in shopping malls to conduct intercepts. Some field services are actually based in shopping malls.

Hiring a research supplier or field service is a simple process. The researcher calls the company, explains the project, and is given a price quote. A contract or project confirmation letter is usually signed. In some cases, the price quote is a flat fee for the total project, or a fee plus or minus about 10%, depending on the difficulty of the project. Sometimes costs are based on the cost per interview (CPI), which is discussed shortly.

One term that plays an important role in the research process is **incidence,** which describes how easy it is to find qualified respondents or subjects for a research project. Incidence is expressed as a percentage of 100—the lower the incidence, the more difficult it is to find a qualified respondent or group of respondents. **Gross incidence** is the percentage of qualified respondents reached of all contacts made (such as telephone calls), and **net incidence** is the number of respondents or subjects who actually participate in a project.

For example, assume that a telephone research study requires 100 female respondents between the ages of 18 and 49 who listen to the radio at least 1 hour per day. The estimated gross incidence is 10%. (Radio and television incidence figures can be estimated by using Arbitron and A. C. Nielsen ratings books; in many cases, however, an incidence

AN INSIDE LOOK
Incidence and Phone Calls Required

Although the example just described shows that a total of about 1,818 calls would be required to complete the study, the actual number of dialings is much higher. The term "dialings" includes wrong numbers, busy signals, fax machines, computer modems, disconnected numbers, and so on. In reality, most telephone studies conducted today require about 40 dialings for each completed survey.

is merely a guess on the part of the researcher.) A total of about 1,818 calls will have to be made to recruit the 100 females, not 1,000 calls, as some people may think. The number of calls required is not computed as the target sample size (100 in this example) divided by the incidence (.10), or 1,000. The number of calls computed for gross incidence (1,000) must then be divided by the acceptance rate, or the percentage of the target sample that agrees to participate in the study.

The total calls required is 1,000 divided by .55 (a generally used acceptance rate), or 1,818. Of the 1,818 telephone calls made, 10% (182) will qualify for the interview, but only 55% of those (100) will actually agree to complete the interview (net incidence).

Field services and research suppliers base their charges on net incidence, not gross incidence. Many novice researchers fail to consider this when they plan the financial budget for a project.

There is no "average" incidence rate in research. The actual rate depends on the complexity of the sample desired, the length of the research project, the time of year the study is conducted, and a variety of other factors. The lower the incidence, the higher the cost of a research project. In addition, prices quoted by field services and research suppliers are based on an estimated incidence rate. Costs are adjusted after the project is completed and the actual incidence rate is known. As mentioned earlier, a quote from a field service is usually given with a plus or minus 10% "warning." Some people may think that understanding how a CPI is computed is unnecessary, but the concept is vitally important to any researcher who subcontracts work to a field service or research supplier.

Returning to the CPI discussion, let's assume that a researcher wants to conduct a 400-person telephone study with adults who are between the ages of 18 and 49. A representative of the company first asks for the researcher's estimated incidence and the length of the interview (in minutes). The two figures determine the CPI. Most field services and research suppliers use a chart to compute the CPI, such as the one shown in Table 1.1.

The table is easy to use. To find a CPI, first read across the top of the table for the length of the interview and then scan down the left-hand side for the incidence. For example, the CPI for a 20-minute interview with an incidence of 10% is $30. A researcher conducting a 400-person telephone study with these "specs" will owe the field service or research supplier $12,000 (400 × $30) plus any costs for photocopying the questionnaire, mailing, and tabulating the data (if requested). If the company analyzes the data and writes a final report, the total cost will be between $20,000 and $30,000.

Research projects involving prerecruits, such as focus groups and group administration, involve an additional cost—respondent *co-op* fees, or *incentives*. A telephone study

Table 1.1 *Example CPI Chart (Shows cost-per-completed interview or recruit)*

	Minutes					
Incidence %	5	10	15	20	25	30
5	44.25	45.50	46.50	47.75	49.00	50.00
6	38.00	39.25	40.50	41.75	42.75	44.00
7	34.00	35.00	36.25	37.50	38.50	39.75
8	30.75	32.00	33.00	34.25	35.50	36.50
9	28.50	29.50	30.75	32.00	33.00	34.25
10	26.50	27.75	29.00	30.00	31.25	32.50
20	14.25	15.50	16.75	17.75	19.00	20.25
30	10.25	11.50	12.50	13.75	15.00	16.25
40	8.25	9.50	10.50	11.75	13.00	14.25
50	7.00	8.25	9.50	10.50	11.75	13.00
60	6.50	7.75	9.00	10.00	11.25	12.50
70	6.00	7.25	8.50	9.50	10.75	11.75
80	5.75	7.00	8.00	9.25	10.50	11.50
90	5.50	6.75	8.00	9.00	10.25	11.00
100	5.00	6.50	7.75	9.00	10.00	10.50

respondent generally receives no payment for answering questions. However, when respondents are asked to leave their homes to participate in a project, they are usually paid between $25 and $100.

Costs rise quickly in a prerecruit project. For example, assume that a researcher wants to conduct a group session with 400 respondents instead of using a telephone approach. Rather than paying a field service or a research supplier a CPI to conduct a telephone interview, the payment is for recruiting respondents to attend a session conducted at a specific location. Although most companies have separate rate cards for prerecruiting (they are usually a bit higher than the card used for telephone interviewing), we will assume that the costs are the same. Recruiting costs, then, are $12,000 (400 × $30 CPI), with another $10,000 (minimum) for respondent co-op (400 × $25). Total costs so far are $22,000, about twice as much as those for a telephone study. In addition, other costs must be added to this figure: a rental fee for the room where the study will be conducted, refreshments for respondents, fees for assistants to check in respondents, and travel expenses (another $1,000–$4,000).

Finally, to ensure that 400 people show up (four sessions of 100 each), it is necessary

AN INSIDE LOOK
Research Costs

As with almost everything else in life, fees charged by field services and research suppliers are negotiable, and this process becomes much easier once a researcher has a few years of experience. For example, a researcher may conduct a certain type of study and know that the usual CPI is somewhere around $30.00. If a quote is given for the same type of project that is, say, $50.00 CPI, the researcher already knows the price is too high. What should the researcher do? It's very simple: just tell the field service or supplier that the price is too high. The quote will be reduced.

to overrecruit since not every respondent will show up. In prerecruit projects, field services and research suppliers overrecruit 25% to 100%. In other words, for a 400 "show rate," a company must prerecruit between 500 and 800 people. However, rarely does a prerecruit session hit the target sample size exactly. In many cases, the show rate falls short and a "make-good" session is required (the project is repeated at a later date with another group of respondents to meet the target sample size). In some cases, more respondents than required show for the study, which means that projected research costs may skyrocket over the planned budget.

In most prerecruit projects, field services and research suppliers are paid on a "show basis" only; that is, they receive payment only for respondents who show up, not for the number who are recruited. If the companies were paid on a recruit basis, they could recruit thousands of respondents for each project. The show-basis payment procedure also adds incentive for the companies to ensure that those who are recruited actually show up for the research session.

Although various problems with hiring and working with research suppliers and field services are discussed in Chapter 5, we present two important points here to help novice researchers when they begin to use these support companies.

1. *All suppliers and field services are not equal.* Regardless of qualifications, any person or group can form a research supply company or field service. There are no formal requirements, no tests to take, and no national, state, or regional licenses to acquire. All that's required are a "shingle on the door," advertising in marketing and research trade publications, and (optional) membership in one or more of the voluntary research organizations. It is thus the sole responsibility of researchers to determine which of the hundreds of suppliers available are capable of conducting a professional, scientifically based research project. Over time, experienced researchers develop a list of qualified trustworthy companies. This list comes from experience with a company or from the recommendations of other researchers. In any event, it is important to check the credentials of a research supplier or field service. The senior author has encountered several instances of research supplier and field service fraud during the past 20+ years in the industry.

2. *The researcher must maintain close supervision over the project.* This is true even with the very good companies, not because their professionalism cannot be trusted but rather to be sure that the project is answering the questions that were posed. Because of security considerations, a research supplier may never completely understand why a particular

Table 1.2 *Computing a CPI*

Step		Explanation
1. Gross incidence	1,000	100 ÷ .10
2. Acceptance rate	55%	Standard figure used to determine how many calls are needed.
3. Actual contacts necessary	1,818	1,000 ÷ .55
4. Minutes per contact	4	Number of minutes to find correct respondent (bad numbers, busy lines, etc.)
5. Total contact minutes	7,272	4 × 1,818
6. Productive minutes per hour	40	Average number of minutes interviewers usually work in 1 hour (net of breaks, etc.)
7. Total contact hours	182	7,272 ÷ 40
8. Total interview hours	33	(100 × 20 minutes) ÷ 60
9. Total hours	215	Contact hours + interview hours
10. Hourly rate	$15	Industry standard
11. Total cost	$3,225	215 × $15
12. CPI	$32.25	$3,225 ÷ 100 interviews

project is being conducted, and the researcher needs to be sure that the project will provide the exact information required.

Supplement on Incidence Rates and CPI

Incidence is an important concept in research because it determines both the difficulty and the cost of a research project. Table 1.2 illustrates a standard CPI rate chart. The specific rates shown on the chart are computed through a complicated series of steps. Without exact detail, this supplement explains the general procedure of how each CPI is computed.

As mentioned earlier, CPI is based on the incidence rate and interview length. In prerecruiting, only incidence is considered, but the CPIs are basically the same as those for telephone interviews. To determine a CPI, let us assume we wish to conduct a 100-person telephone study, with an incidence rate of 10% and an interview length of 20 minutes. The computation and an explanation of each step are shown in Table 1.2. As shown in the table, 1,818 contacts must be made. Of these, 10% will qualify for the interview (182) and 55% of these will accept (100). The total number of hours required to conduct the 100-person survey is 215, with a CPI of $32.25.

▪▪▪ Summary

Media research evolved from the fields of psychology and sociology and is now a well-established field in its own right. It is not necessary to be a statistician to be a successful researcher;

it is more important to know how to conduct research and what research procedures can do.

In an effort to understand any phenomenon, researchers can follow one of several methods of inquiry. Of the procedures discussed in this chapter, the scientific approach is most applicable to the mass media because it involves a systematic, objective evaluation of information. Researchers first identify a problem and then investigate it using a prescribed set of procedures known as the scientific method. The scientific method is the only learning approach that allows for self-correction of research findings; one study does not stand alone but must be supported or refuted by others.

The explosion of mass media research is mainly attributable to the rapidly developing technology of the media industry. Because of this growth in research, both applied and theoretical approaches have taken on more significance in the decision-making process of the mass media and in our understanding of the media. At the same time, there continues to be a severe shortage of good researchers in both the academic and private sectors.

This chapter described the processes involved in identifying and developing a topic for research investigation. It was suggested that researchers consider several sources for potential ideas, including a critical analysis of everyday situations. The steps in developing a topic for investigation naturally become easier with experience; the beginning researcher needs to pay particular attention to material already available. He or she should not attempt to tackle broad research questions but should try to isolate a smaller, more practical subtopic for study. The researcher should develop an appropriate method of analysis and then proceed, through data analysis and interpretation, to a clear and concise presentation of results.

The chapter stressed that the results of a single survey or other research approach provide only indications of what may or may not exist. Before the researcher can claim support for a research question or hypothesis, the study must be replicated a number of times to eliminate dependence on extraneous factors.

While conducting research studies, the investigator must be constantly aware of potential sources of error that may create spurious results. Phenomena that affect an experiment in this way are sources of breakdowns in internal validity. Only if differing and rival hypotheses are ruled out can researchers validly say that the treatment was influential in creating differences between the experimental group and the control group. A good explanation of research results rules out intervening variables; every plausible alternative explanation should be considered. However, even when this is accomplished, the results of one study can be considered only as an indication of what may or may not exist. Support for a theory or hypothesis is gained only after several other studies produce similar results.

In addition, if a study is to be helpful in understanding mass media, its results must be generalizable to subjects and groups other than those involved in the experiment. External validity can be best achieved through random sampling (see Chapter 4).

Key Terms

Academic research
Algorithm
Artifact
Causal time order
Central location testing
Confounding variable
Constitutive definition
Constructive replication
CPI
Cross-validating questions
Data archives
Demand characteristics
Design-specific results
Double-blind experiment
Eight steps of research
Empiricism
Evaluation apprehension
Experimenter bias
External validity
Extraneous variable
Field services
Gross incidence
Hypodermic needle theory
Hypothesis
Incidence
Instrument decay
Instrumental replication
Internal validity
Internet search engine
Law
Law of the Instrument
Literal replication
Maturation
Methods of knowing
Method-specific results

Mortality
Net incidence
Occam's razor
Operational definition
Operational replication
Parsimony principle
Pilot study
Point of prior equivalency
Prerecruits
Private sector research
Qualitative research
Quantitative research
Replication
Research question
Research suppliers
Scientific method
Secondary analysis
Statistical regression
Theory
Urban legends

Using the Internet

1. Search engines. Finding information on the Internet is easy with a search engine. Two suggestions are: *www.google.com* and *www.hotbot.com*. See *www.wimmerdominick.com* for other suggestions.
2. Search the Internet for more information about the "hypodermic needle theory" of communication, validity, and reliability.
3. For a list of research suppliers, go to: *www.greenbook.org*.
4. Visit *www.urbanlegends.com* for research topics and to find out what is true and false about information you hear and see.
5. For additional help with research topics and media information, go to: *www.kagan.com*

Questions and Problems for Further Investigation

1. Obtain a recent issue of the *Journal of Broadcasting and Electronic Media, Journalism and Mass Communication Quarterly,* or *Public Opinion Quarterly.* How many articles fit into the research phases depicted in Figure 1.1?
2. How might researchers abuse the scientific research approach?
3. Theories are used as springboards to develop solid bodies of information, yet there are only a few universally recognized theories in mass media research. Why do you think this is true?
4. Some citizens groups have claimed that television has a significant effect on viewers, especially the violence and sexual content of some programs. How might these groups collect data to support their claims? Which method of knowing can such groups use to support their claims?
5. Investigate how research is used to support or refute an argument outside the field of mass media. For example, how do various groups use research to support or refute the idea that motorcycle riders should be required to wear protective helmets? (Refer to publications such as *Motorcycle Consumer News.*)
6. If you are using InfoTrac® College Edition, try using "scientific method" as a key word search term. Note the variety of disciplines that rely on this method.
7. Replication has long been a topic of debate in scientific research, but mass media researchers have not paid much attention to it. Why do you think this is true?
8. An analysis of the effects of television viewing revealed that the fewer hours of television students watched per week, the higher were their scores in school. What alternative explanations or artifacts might explain such differences? How could these variables be controlled?
9. The fact that some respondents will answer any type of question, whether it is a legitimate question or not, may surprise some novice researchers until they encounter it firsthand. Try posing the following question to a friend in another class or at a party: What effects do you think the sinking of Greenland into the Labrador Sea will have on the country's fishing industry?
10. Spend a few hours on the Internet searching for information on topics that interest you. Go to a search engine and type in words such as "viewers," "listeners," or "readers."
11. If you are using InfoTrac College Edition, you can get a good sampling of recent research topics in media research by looking up "mass media research" in the subject guide. Note that popular publications as well as scholarly journals contain articles on this topic.

For additional information on these and related topics, see

http://www.wimmerdominick.com

References and Suggested Readings

Achenback, J. (1991). *Why things are.* New York: Ballantine Books.

Agostino, D. (1980). Cable television's impact on the audience of public television. *Journal of Broadcasting,* 24(3), 347–366.

Anderson, J. A. (1987). *Communication research: Issues and methods.* New York: McGraw-Hill.

Asimov, I. (1990). Exclusion principle survives another stab at its heart. *Rocky Mountain News,* December 9, 1990, p. 42.

Babbie, E. R. (2001). *The practice of social research* (9th ed.). Belmont, CA: Wadsworth.

Barnes, L. Personal correspondence, February 11, 1998.

Beasant, P. (1992). *1000 facts about space.* New Brunswick, Canada: Kingfisher Books.

Becker, L. B. (1981). Secondary analysis. In G. H. Stempel & B. H. Westley (Eds.), *Research methods in mass communications.* Englewood Cliffs, NJ: Prentice-Hall.

Becker, L. B., Beam, R., & Russial, J. (1978). Correlates of daily newspaper performance in New England. *Journalism Quarterly,* 55(1), 100–108.

Berliner, B. (1990). *The book of answers.* New York: Prentice Hall.

Bowers, J. W., & Courtright, J. A. (1984). *Communication research methods.* Glenview, IL: Scott, Foresman.

Brown, J. A. (1980). Selling airtime for controversy: NAB self regulation and Father Coughlin. *Journal of Broadcasting,* 24(2), 199–224.

Burman, T. (1975). *The dictionary of misinformation.* New York: Thomas Crowell.

Campbell, D. T., & Stanley, J. C. (1963). *Experimental and quasi-experimental designs for research.* Skokie, IL: Rand McNally.

Carroll, R. L. (1980). The 1948 Truman campaign: The threshold of the modern era. *Journal of Broadcasting,* 24(2), 173–188.

Cohen, J. (1965). Some statistical issues in psychological research. In B. B. Wolman (Ed.), *Handbook of clinical psychology.* New York: McGraw-Hill.

Cole, J. (1998). *The UCLA Television Violence Report 1997.* Los Angeles: UCLA Center for Communication Policy.

Comstock, G., Chaffee, S., Katzman, N., McCombs, M., & Roberts, D. (1978). *Television and human behavior.* New York: Columbia University Press.

Cook, T. D., & Campbell, D. T. (1979). *Quasi-experimentation: Designs and analysis for field studies.* Skokie, IL: Rand McNally.

Davis, P. J., & Park, D. (1987). *No way: The nature of the impossible.* New York: W. H. Freeman.

DeFleur, M. L., & Ball-Rokeach, S. (1989). *Theories of mass communication* (5th ed.). New York: Longman.

Feldman, D. (1990). *Why do dogs have wet noses?* New York: HarperCollins Publishers.

Ferris, T. (1988). *Coming of age in the Milky Way.* New York: William Morrow.

Ferris, T. (1998). *The whole shebang.* New York: Touchstone.

Glenn, N. (1972). Archival data on political attitudes: Opportunities and pitfalls. In D. Nimmo & C. Bonjean (Eds.), *Political attitudes and public opinion.* New York: David McKay.

Graedon, J., and Graedon, T. (1991). *Graedons' best medicine.* New York: Bantam Books.

Gribben, J., & Rees, M. (1989). *Cosmic coincidences: Dark matter, mankind, and anthropic cosmology.* New York: Bantam Books.

Hall, D. G. Personal correspondence, February 1, 1998.

Haskins, J. B. (1968). *How to evaluate mass communication.* New York: Advertising Research Foundation.

Herzog, H. (1944). What do we really know about daytime serial listeners? In P. Lazarsfeld & F. Stanton (Eds.), *Radio research 1943–44.* New York: Duell, Sloan & Pearce.

Hinds, P. S., Vogel, R. J., Clarke-Steffen, L. (1997) The possibilities and pitfalls of doing a secondary analysis of a qualitative data set. *Qualitative Health Research,* Vol. 7(3): 408–424.

Hirsch, E. D., Kett, J. F., & Trefil, J. (1993). *Dictionary of cultural literacy: What every American needs to know.* New York: Houghton Mifflin.

Hough, D. L. (1995). Are you hanging it out too far? *Motorcycle Consumer News,* 26(9), 38–41.

Hsia, H. J. (1988). *Mass communication research methods: A step-by-step approach.* Hillsdale, NJ: Lawrence Erlbaum.

Hyman, H. H. (1954). *Interviewing in social research.* Chicago: University of Chicago Press.

Hyman, H. H. (1972). *Secondary analysis of sample surveys.* New York: John Wiley.

Katz, E., & Lazarsfeld, P. F. (1955). *Personal influence.* New York: Free Press.

Kelly, C. W., Chase, L. J., & Tucker, R. K. (1979). Replication in experimental communication research: An analysis. *Human Communication Research,* 5, 338–342.

Kerlinger, F. N. (2000). *Foundations of behavioral research* (4th ed.). New York: Holt, Rinehart & Winston.

Klapper, J. (1960). *The effects of mass communication.* New York: Free Press.

Kraus, S., & Davis, D. (1967). *The effects of mass communication on political behavior.* University Park: Pennsylvania State University Press.

Langer, S. K. (1967). *Philosophy in a new key: A study in the symbolism of reason, rite, and art* (3rd ed.). Cambridge, MA: Harvard University Press.

Lasswell, H. D. (1927). *Propaganda technique in the World War.* New York: Alfred A. Knopf.

Lazarsfeld, P., Berelson, B., & Gaudet, H. (1948). *The people's choice.* New York: Columbia University Press.

Lowery, S. A., & DeFleur, M. L. (1995). *Milestones in mass communication research* (3rd ed.). White Plains, NY: Longman.

Lykken, D. T. (1968). Statistical significance in psychological research. *Psychological Bulletin,* 21, 151–159.

Murphy, J. H., & Amundsen, M. S. (1981). The communication effectiveness of comparative advertising for a new brand on users of the dominant brand. *Journal of Advertising,* 10(1), 14–20.

Neil, R. F. Personal correspondence, February 1, 1998.

Nesselroade, J. R., & Cattell, R. B. (Eds.). (1988). *Handbook of multivariate experimental psychology* (2nd ed.). New York: Plenum Press.

Nunnally, J. C., & Bernstein, I. H. (1994). *Psychometric theory* (3rd ed.). New York: McGraw-Hill.

Orne, M. T. (1969). Demand characteristics and the concept of quasi-controls. In R. Rosenthal & R. L. Rosnow (Eds.), *Artifact in behavioral research.* New York: Academic Press.

Poundstone, W. (1986). *Bigger secrets.* New York: Houghton Mifflin.

Reid, L. N., Soley, L. C., & Wimmer, R. D. (1981). Replication in advertising research: 1977, 1978, 1979. *Journal of Advertising,* 10, 3–13.

Rensberger, B. (1986). *How the world works.* New York: Quill.

Ries, A., & Trout, J. (2001). *Positioning: The battle for your mind* (2nd ed). New York: McGraw-Hill.

Ries, A., & Trout, J. (1997). *Marketing warfare.* New York: McGraw-Hill.

Rosenberg, M. J. (1965). When dissonance fails: On eliminating evaluation apprehension from attitude measurement. *Journal of Personality and Social Psychology,* 1, 28–42.

Rosenthal, R. (1969). *Experimenter effects in behavioral research.* New York: Appleton-Century-Crofts.

Rubin, R. B., Rubin, A. M., & Piele, L. J. (1996). *Communication research: Strategies and sources* (4th ed.). Belmont, CA: Wadsworth.

Seeds, M. A. (1992). *Foundations of astronomy.* Belmont, CA: Wadsworth.

Sharp, N. W. (1988). *Communications research: The challenge of the information age.* Syracuse, NY: Syracuse University Press.

Singer, D. G., & Singer, J. L. (1981). Television and the developing imagination of the child. *Journal of Broadcasting,* 25, 373–387.

Skinner, B. F. (1953). *Science and human behavior.* New York: Macmillan.

Sutton, C. (1984). *How did they do that?* New York: Quill.

Sybert, P. J. (1980). MBS and the Dominican Republic. *Journal of Broadcasting,* 24(2), 189–198.

Tan, A. S. (1977). Why TV is missed: A functional analysis. *Journal of Broadcasting,* 21, 371–380.

True, J. A. (1989). *Finding out: Conducting and evaluating social research* (2nd ed.). Belmont, CA: Wadsworth.

Tucker, R. K. (1996). S.O.B.s: *The handbook for handling super difficult people.* Bowling Green, OH: OptimAmerica, Ltd.

Tukey, J. W. (1969). Analyzing data: Sanctification or detective work? *American Psychologist,* 24, 83–91.

Tuleja, T. (1982). *Fabulous fallacies: More than 300 popular beliefs that are not true.* New York: Harmony Books.

Walizer, M. H., & Wienir, P. L. (1978). *Research methods and analysis: Searching for relationships.* New York: Harper & Row.

Weaver, R. M. (1953). *The ethics of rhetoric.* Chicago: Henry Regnery.

Whitcomb, J., & Whitcomb, C. (1987). *Oh say can you see: Unexpected anecdotes about American history.* New York: Quill.

Williams, F. (1988). *Research methods and the new media.* New York: Free Press.

Wimmer, R. D. (1995). *Los Angeles radio listening: A panel study.* Denver: The Eagle Group.

Wimmer, R. D., & Reid, L. N. (1982). Willingness of communication researchers to respond to replication requests. *Journalism Quarterly,* 59, 317–319.

Wimmer Research. (2001). Proprietary research conducted by Roger Wimmer.

Winston, D. (1998). Digital democracy and the new age of reason. Internet post of speech presented at the Democracy and Digital Media conference, May 27, 1998.

Chapter 2

Elements of Research

Chapter 1 presented an overview of the research process. In this chapter, we define and discuss four basic elements of this process: concepts and constructs, measurement, variables, and scales. A clear understanding of these elements is essential to conducting precise and meaningful research.

Concepts and Constructs

A **concept** is a term that expresses an abstract idea formed by generalizing from particulars and summarizing related observations. For example, a researcher might observe that a public speaker becomes restless, starts to perspire, and continually fidgets with a pencil just before giving a speech. The researcher might summarize these observed patterns of behavior and label them "speech anxiety." On a more ordinary level, the word *table* is a concept that represents a wide variety of observable objects, ranging from a plank supported by concrete blocks to a piece of furniture commonly found in dining rooms. Typical concepts in mass media research include terms such as *advertising effectiveness, message length, media usage,* and *readability.*

Concepts are important for at least two reasons. First, they simplify the research process by combining particular characteristics, objects, or people into more general categories. For example, a researcher may study families that own computers, modems, VCRs, CD players, cell phones, and DVD machines. To make it easier to describe these families, the researcher calls them "Taffies" and categorizes them under the concept of "technologically advanced families." Now, instead of describing each of the characteristics that makes these families unique, the researcher has a general term that is more inclusive and convenient to use.

Second, concepts simplify communication among those who have a shared understanding of them. Researchers use concepts to organize their observations into meaningful summaries and to transmit this information to others. Researchers who use the concept of "agenda setting" to describe a complicated set of audience and media activities find that their colleagues understand what is being discussed. Note that people must share an understanding of a concept in order for the concept to be useful. For example, when teenagers use the word *phat* to describe an activity, most of their peers understand perfectly what is meant by the concept, although adults may not.

A **construct** is a concept that has three distinct characteristics. First, it is an abstract idea that is usually broken down into dimensions represented by lower-level concepts. In other words, a construct is a combination of concepts. Second, because of its abstraction, a construct usually cannot be observed directly. Third, a construct is usually designed for some particular research purpose so that its exact meaning relates only to the context in which it is found. For example, the construct "involvement" has been used in many advertising studies (Pokrywczynski, 1986). It is a construct that is difficult to see directly, and it includes the concepts of attention, interest, and arousal. Researchers can observe only its likely or presumed manifestations. In some contexts involvement means a subject's involvement with the product; in others it refers to involvement with the message or even with the medium. Its precise meaning depends on the research context.

AN INSIDE LOOK
Mass Media Variables

Analysis of why people like certain movies, magazines, newspapers, or radio or television shows has historically been very difficult because of the number of variables to consider. Even when researchers develop a relatively stable set of variables to measure, assessing popularity of the media is difficult because respondents say something like, "It depends on my mood." As a media researcher, how would you address this problem?

To take another example, in mass communication research, the term *authoritarianism* represents a construct defined to describe a certain type of personality; it comprises nine different concepts, including conventionalism, submission, superstition, and cynicism. Authoritarianism itself cannot be seen; some type of questionnaire or standardized test must determine its presence. The results of such tests indicate what authoritarianism might be and whether it is present under given conditions, but the tests do not provide exact definitions for the construct itself.

The empirical counterpart of a construct or concept is called a **variable.** Variables are important because they link the empirical world with the theoretical; they are the phenomena and events that can be measured or manipulated in research. Variables can have more than one value along a continuum. For example, the variable "satisfaction with pay-per-view TV programs" can take on different values—a person can be satisfied a lot, a little, or not at all—reflecting in the empirical world what the concept "satisfaction with pay-per-view TV programs" represents in the theoretical world.

Researchers try to test a number of associated variables to develop an underlying meaning or relationship among them. After suitable analysis, the most important variables are retained and the others are discarded. These important variables are labeled **marker variables** because they seem to define or highlight the construct under study. After further analysis, new marker variables may be added to increase understanding of the construct and to permit more reliable predictions.

Concepts and constructs are valuable tools in theoretical research, but, as noted in Chapter 1, researchers also function at the observational, or empirical, level. To understand how this is done, it is necessary to examine variables and to know how they are measured.

▪ Independent and Dependent Variables

Variables are classified in terms of their relationship with one another. It is customary to talk about independent and dependent variables: **Independent variables** are systematically varied by the researcher, and **dependent variables** are observed and their values presumed to depend on the effects of the independent variables. In other words, the *dependent variable is what the researcher wishes to explain.* For example, assume an investigator is interested in determining how the angle of a camera shot affects an audience's perception of the credibility of a television newscaster. Three versions of a newscast are videotaped: one shot from a very low angle, another from a high angle, and a third from eye level. Groups of subjects are randomly assigned to view one of the three versions and complete a questionnaire to measure the newscaster's credibility. In this experiment, the camera angle is the independent variable. The experimenter, who selects only three of the camera angles possible, systematically varies its values. The dependent variable to be measured is the perceived credibility of the newscaster. If the researcher's assumption is correct, the newscaster's credibility will vary according to the camera angle. (The values of the dependent variable are not manipulated; they are simply observed or measured.)

Keep in mind that the distinction between types of variables depends on the purposes of the research. An independent variable in one study may be a dependent variable in another. Also, a research task may involve examining the relationship of more than one independent variable to a single dependent variable. For example, the researcher in the previous example could investigate the effects not only of camera angles but also of the newscaster's manner, or style, in closing the program on his or her credibility (as perceived by the viewers). Moreover, in many instances multiple dependent variables are measured in a single study. This type of study is called a **multivariate analysis.**

Discrete and Continuous Variables

Two forms of variables are used in mass media investigation. A **discrete variable** includes only a finite set of values; it cannot be divided into subparts. For instance, the number of children in a family is a discrete variable because the unit is a person. It does not make much sense to talk about a family size of 2.24 because it is hard to conceptualize 0.24 of a person. Political affiliation, population, and gender are other discrete variables.

A **continuous variable** can take on any value (including fractions) and can be meaningfully broken into smaller subsections. Height is a continuous variable. If the measurement tool is sophisticated enough, it is possible to distinguish between one person 72.113 inches tall and another 72.114 inches tall. Time spent watching television is another example; it is perfectly meaningful to say that Person A spent 3.12115 hours viewing while Person B watched 3.12114 hours. The average number of children in a family is a continuous variable; thus, in this context, it may be perfectly meaningful to refer to 0.24 of a person.

When dealing with continuous variables, researchers should keep in mind the distinction between the variable and the measure of the variable. If a child's attitude toward television violence is measured by counting his or her positive responses to six questions, then there are only seven possible scores: 0, 1, 2, 3, 4, 5, and 6. It is entirely likely, however, that the underlying variable is continuous even though the measure is discrete. In fact, even if a fractionalized scale were developed, it would still be limited to a finite number of scores. As a generalization, most of the measures in mass media research tend to be discrete approximations of continuous variables.

Variables measured at the nominal level are always discrete variables. Variables measured at the ordinal level are generally discrete, although there may be some underlying continuous measurement dimension. (Nominal and ordinal levels are discussed later in the chapter.) Variables measured at the interval or ratio level can be either discrete (number of magazine subscriptions in a household) or continuous (number of minutes per day spent reading magazines). Both the level of measurement and the type of variable under consideration are important in developing useful measurement scales.

Other Types of Variables

In nonexperimental research, where there is no active manipulation of variables, different terms are sometimes substituted for independent and dependent variables. The variable that is used for predictions or is assumed to be causal (analogous to the independent variable) is sometimes called the **predictor,** or **antecedent, variable.** The variable that is predicted or assumed to be affected (analogous to the dependent variable) is sometimes called the **criterion variable.**

Researchers often wish to control certain variables to eliminate unwanted influences. These **control variables** are used to ensure that the results of the study are due to the independent variables, not to another source. However, a control variable need not always be used to eliminate an unwanted influence. On occasion, researchers use a control variable such as age, gender, or socioeconomic status to divide subjects into specific, relevant categories. For example, in studying the relationship between newspaper readership and reading ability, researchers know that IQ will affect the relationship and must be controlled; thus, subjects may be selected based on IQ scores or placed in groups with similar scores.

One of the most difficult steps in any type of research is to identify all the variables that may create spurious or misleading results. Some researchers refer to this problem as **noise.** Noise can occur in even very simple research projects. For example, a researcher might design a telephone survey to ask respondents to name the local radio station they listened to most during the past week. The researcher uses an open-ended question—that is, provides no specific response choices—and the interviewer writes down each respondent's answer. When the completed surveys are tabulated, the researcher notices that several people mentioned radio station WAAA. But if the city has a WAAA-AM and a WAAA-FM, which station gets the credit? The researcher cannot arbitrarily assign credit to the AM station or to the FM station; nor can credit be split because this may distort the description of the actual listening habits.

Interviewers could attempt callbacks to everyone who said "WAAA," but this is not suggested for two reasons: (1) the likelihood of reaching all the people who gave that response is low, and (2) even if the first condition is met, some respondents may not recall which station they originally mentioned. The researcher is therefore unable to provide a reliable analysis of the data because not all possible intervening variables were considered. (The researcher should have predicted this problem and the interviewers should have been instructed to find out in each case whether WAAA meant the AM or the FM station.)

People who unknowingly provide false information create another type of research noise. For example, people who keep diaries for radio and television surveys may err in recording the station or channel they tune in; that is, they may listen to or watch station KAAA but incorrectly record "KBBB." (This problem is partially solved by the use of *people meters;* see Chapter 14.) In addition, people often answer a multiple-choice or yes/no research question at random because they do not wish to appear ignorant or uninformed. To minimize this problem, researchers should construct their measurement instruments with great care. Noise is always present, but a large and representative sample should decrease the effects of some research noise. (In later chapters, noise is referred to as "error.")

With experience, researchers learn to solve many simple problems in their studies. In many situations, however, researchers understand that total control over all aspects of the research is impossible, and they account for the impossibility of achieving perfect control in the interpretation of their results.

Defining Variables Operationally

In Chapter 1, we stated that an operational definition specifies the procedures to be followed in experiencing or measuring a concept. Research depends on observations, and observations cannot be made without a clear

Table 2.1 *Examples of Operational Definitions*

Study	Variable	Operational Definition
Henning and Vorderer (2001)	Need for cognition	Summated scores on a 6-point Likert Scale to eight cognition items
Wu (2000)	Press freedom	Scale of press freedom ranging from 1 to 100 taken from yearly evaluations by the Freedom House organization
Bae (2000)	Unique news story	News story covered by only one network on a given news day
Buijen and Valkenburg (2000)	Children's gift ideas	Children were asked to write down their two most favorite Christmas wishes
Hindman (2000)	Rural vs. urban	If respondent lived in a Metropolitan Area as defined by the Census Bureau

statement of what is to be observed. An operational definition is such a statement.

Operational definitions are indispensable in scientific research because they enable investigators to measure relevant variables. In any study, it is necessary to provide operational definitions for both independent variables and dependent variables. Table 2.1 lists examples of such definitions taken from research studies in mass communication.

Kerlinger (2000) identifies two types of operational definitions, *measured* and *experimental.* A measured operational definition specifies how to measure a variable. For instance, a researcher investigating *dogmatism* and media use might operationally define the term dogmatism as a subject's score on the Twenty-Item Short Form Dogmatism Scale. An experimental operational definition explains how an investigator has manipulated a variable. Obviously, this type of definition is used when the independent variable is defined in a laboratory setting. For example, in a study on the impact of television violence, the researcher might manipulate media violence by constructing two 8-minute films. The first film, labeled "the violent condition," could contain scenes from a boxing match. The second film, labeled "the nonviolent condition," could depict a swimming race. Similarly, source credibility might be manipulated by alternately attributing an article on health to the *New England Journal of Medicine* and to the *National Enquirer.*

Operationally defining a variable forces a researcher to express abstract concepts in concrete terms. Occasionally, after unsuccessfully struggling with the task of making a key variable operational, the researcher may conclude that the variable as originally conceived is too vague or ambiguous and must be redefined. Because operational definitions are expressed so concretely, they can communicate exactly what the terms represent. For instance, a researcher might define "political knowledge" as the number of correct answers on a 20-item true/false test. Although it is possible to argue about the validity of the definition, there is no confusion as to what the statement "Women possess more political knowledge than men" actually means.

Finally, there is no single foolproof method for operationally defining a variable. No operational definition satisfies everybody. The investigator must decide which method is best suited for the research problem at hand.

The numerous articles and examples available from an Internet search of "operational definition" illustrate the various methods.

▪ Qualitative and Quantitative Research

Mass media research, like all research, can be qualitative or quantitative. **Qualitative research** involves several methods of data collection, such as focus groups, field observation, in-depth interviews, and case studies. In all of these methods, the questioning approach is varied. In other words, although the researcher enters the project with a specific set of questions, follow-up questions are developed as needed. The variables in qualitative research may or may not be measured or quantified.

In some cases, qualitative research has certain advantages. The methods allow a researcher to view behavior in a natural setting without the artificiality that sometimes surrounds experimental or survey research. In addition, qualitative techniques can increase a researcher's depth of understanding of the phenomenon under investigation. This is especially true when the phenomenon has not been investigated previously. Finally, qualitative methods are flexible and allow the researcher to pursue new areas of interest. A questionnaire is unlikely to provide data about questions that were not asked, but a person conducting a field observation or focus group might discover facets of a subject that were not considered before the study began.

There are, however, some disadvantages associated with qualitative methods. First, sample sizes are sometimes too small (sometimes as small as one) to allow the researcher to generalize the data beyond the sample selected for the particular study. For this reason, qualitative research is often the preliminary step to further investigation rather than the final phase of a project. The information collected from qualitative methods is often used to prepare a more elaborate quantitative analysis, although the qualitative data may in fact constitute all the information needed for a particular study.

Reliability of the data can also be a problem, since single observers are describing unique events. Because a person doing qualitative research must become closely involved with the respondents, it is possible to lose objectivity when collecting data. A researcher who becomes too close to the study may lose the necessary professional detachment.

Finally, if qualitative research is not properly planned, the project may produce nothing of value. Qualitative research appears to be easy to conduct, but projects must be carefully planned to ensure that they focus on key issues. Although this book is primarily concerned with quantitative research, we discuss several qualitative methods in Chapter 5.

Quantitative research also involves several methods of data collection, such as telephone surveys, mail surveys, and Internet surveys. In these methods, the questioning is static or standardized—all respondents are asked the same questions.

In the past some researchers claimed that the difference between qualitative and quantitative research related to only two things:

1. Qualitative research uses smaller samples of subjects or respondents.
2. Because of the small sample size, results from qualitative research could not be generalized to the population from which the samples were drawn.

While some qualitative research may be affected by these two points, the fact is that sample sizes in both qualitative and quantitative can be the same.

Quantitative research requires that the variables under consideration be measured. This form of research is concerned with how often a variable is present and generally uses numbers to communicate this amount.

AN INSIDE LOOK

Qualitative and Quantitative Research

The only difference between qualitative and quantitative research is the style of questioning. Qualitative research uses flexible questioning; quantitative uses standardized questions. Assuming that sample sizes are large enough and that the samples are adequately selected, the results from both methods can be generalized to the population from which the sample was drawn.

Quantitative research has certain advantages. One is that the use of numbers allows greater precision in reporting results. For example, the Violence Index (Gerbner, Gross, Morgan & Signorielli, 1980), a quantitative measuring device, makes it possible to report the exact increase or decrease in violence from one television season to another, whereas qualitative research could report only whether there was more or less violence.

For the past several years, some friction has existed in the mass media field and in other disciplines between those who favor quantitative methods and those who prefer qualitative methods. Most researchers have now come to realize that both methods are important in understanding any phenomenon. In fact, the term *triangulation,* commonly used by marine navigators, frequently comes up in conversations about communication research. If a ship picks up signals from only one navigational aid, it is impossible to know the vessel's precise location. However, if signals from more than one source are detected, elementary geometry can be used to pinpoint the ship's location. In this book, the term **triangulation** refers to the use of both qualitative methods and quantitative methods to fully understand the nature of a research problem.

Although most of this book is concerned with skills relevant to quantitative research, we do not imply that quantitative research is in any sense better than qualitative research. It is not. Each approach has value and the decision to use one or the other depends on the goals of the research.

The Nature of Measurement

The importance of mathematics to mass media research is difficult to overemphasize. As pointed out by measurement expert J. P. Guilford (1954, p. 1):

> The progress and maturity of a science are often judged by the extent to which it has succeeded in the use of mathematics. . . . Mathematics is a universal language that any science or technology may use with great power and convenience. Its vocabulary of terms is unlimited. . . . Its rules of operation . . . are unexcelled for logical precision.

The idea behind **measurement** is simple: A researcher assigns numerals to objects, events, or properties according to certain rules. Examples of measurement are everywhere: "She or he is a 10" or "Unemployment increased by 1%" or "The earthquake measured 5.5 on the Richter scale." Note that the definition contains three central concepts: numerals, assignment, and rules. A numeral is a symbol, such as V, X, C, or 5, 10, 100. A *numeral* has no implicit quantitative meaning. When it is given quantitative meaning, it becomes a number and can be used in mathematical and statistical computations. *Assignment* is the designation of numerals or numbers to certain objects or events. A simple measurement system might entail assigning the numeral 1 to the people who obtain most of their news from television, the numeral 2 to those who get most of their news from a newspaper, and the numeral 3 to those who receive most of their news from some other source.

Rules specify the way that numerals or numbers are to be assigned. Rules are at the heart of any measurement system; if they are faulty, the system will be flawed. In some situations, the rules are obvious and straightforward. To measure reading speed, a stopwatch and a standardized message may be sufficient. In other instances, the rules are not so apparent. Measuring certain psychological traits, such as "source credibility" or "attitude toward violence," calls for carefully explicated measurement techniques.

Additionally, in mass media research and in much of social science research, investigators usually measure indicators of the properties of individuals or objects rather than the individuals or objects themselves. Concepts such as "authoritarianism" or "motivation for reading the newspaper" cannot be observed directly; they must be inferred from presumed indicators. Thus, if a person endorses statements such as "Orders from a superior should always be followed without question" and "Law and order are the most important things in society," it can be deduced that he or she is more authoritarian than someone who disagrees with the same statements.

Measurement systems strive to be isomorphic to reality. **Isomorphism** means *identity or similarity of form or structure.* In some research areas, such as the physical sciences, isomorphism is not a problem because there is usually a direct relationship between the objects being measured and the numbers assigned to them. For example, if an electric current travels through Substance A with less resistance than it does through Substance B, it can be deduced that A is a better conductor than B. Testing more substances can lead to a ranking of conductors, where the numbers assigned indicate the degrees of conductivity. The measurement system is isomorphic to reality.

Table 2.2 *Illustration of Isomorphism*

Person	Test score	"True" score
A	1	0
B	3	1
C	6	6
D	7	7
E	8	12

In mass media research, the correspondence is seldom that obvious. For example, imagine that a researcher is trying to develop a scale to measure the "persuasibility" of people in connection with a certain type of advertisement. A test is developed and given to five people. The scores are displayed in Table 2.2. Now imagine that an omniscient being is able to disclose the "true" persuasibility of the same five people. These scores are also shown in Table 2.2. For two people, the test scores correspond exactly to the "true" scores. The other three scores miss the "true" scores, but there is a correspondence between the rank orders. Also note that the "true" persuasibility scores range from 0 to 12 and the measurement scale ranges from 1 to 8. To summarize, there is a general correspondence between the test and reality, but the test is far from an exact measure of what actually exists.

Unfortunately, the degree of correspondence between measurement and reality is rarely known in research. In some cases, researchers are not even sure they are actually measuring what they are trying to measure (validity). In any event, researchers must carefully consider the degree of isomorphism between measurement and reality. This topic is discussed in greater detail later in the chapter.

Levels of Measurement

Scientists have distinguished four different ways to measure things, or four different levels of measurement, depending upon the rules that are used to assign numbers to objects or events. The operations that can be performed with a given set of scores depend on the level of measurement achieved. The four levels of measurement are nominal, ordinal, interval, and ratio.

The **nominal level** is the weakest form of measurement. In nominal measurement, numerals or other symbols are used to classify persons, objects, or characteristics. For example, in the physical sciences, rocks can generally be classified into three categories: igneous, sedimentary, and metamorphic. A geologist who assigns a 1 to igneous, a 2 to sedimentary, and a 3 to metamorphic has formed a nominal scale. Note that the numerals are simply labels that stand for the respective categories; they have no mathematical significance. A rock that is placed in Category 3 does not have more "rockness" than those in Categories 2 and 1. Other examples of nominal measurement are the numbers on football jerseys and license plates and Social Security numbers. An example of nominal measurement in mass media is classifying respondents according to the medium they depend on most for news. Those depending most on TV may be in Category 1, those depending most on newspapers in Category 2, those depending on magazines in Category 3, and so on.

The nominal level, like all levels, possesses certain formal properties. Its basic property is equivalence. If an object is placed in Category 1, it is considered equal to all other objects in that category. Suppose a researcher is attempting to classify all the advertisements in a magazine according to primary appeal. If an ad has economic appeal, it is placed in Category 1; if it uses an appeal to fear, it is placed in Category 2; and so on. Note that all ads using "fear appeal" are equal even though they may differ on other dimensions such as product type or size, or use of illustrations.

Another property of nominal measurement is that all categories are *exhaustive* and *mutually exclusive*. This means that each measure accounts for every possible option and that each measurement is appropriate to only one category. For instance, in the example of primary appeals in magazine advertisements, all possible appeals need to be included in the analysis (exhaustive): economic, fear, morality, religion, and so on. Each advertisement is placed in one and only one category (mutually exclusive).

Nominal measurement is frequently used in mass media research. Hinkle and Elliot (1989) divided science coverage by supermarket tabloids and mainstream newspapers into medical coverage and hard technology stories and discovered that tabloids had far more medical stories. Weinberger and Spotts (1989) divided the use of humorous devices in British and American ads into six nominal categories—pun, understatement, joke, ludicrous, satire, and irony—and found that the use of humor was similar in both countries.

Even a variable measured at the nominal level may be used in higher-order statistics if it is converted into another form. The result of this conversion process is known as **dummy variables.** For example, political party affiliation could be coded as follows:

Republican	1
Democrat	2
Independent	3
Other	4

This measurement scheme could be interpreted incorrectly to imply that a person classified as "Other" is three units "better" than a person classified as a "Republican." To measure political party affiliation and use the data in higher-order statistics, a researcher must convert the variable into a more neutral form.

One way to convert the variable to give equivalent value to each option is to recode it as a dummy variable that creates an "either/or" situation for each option; in this example, a person is either a "Republican" or something else. For example, a binary coding scheme could be used:

Republican	001
Democrat	010
Independent	100
Other	000

This scheme treats each affiliation equivalently and allows the variable to be used in higher-order statistical procedures. Note that the final category "Other" is coded using all zeros. A complete explanation for this practice is beyond the scope of this book; basically, however, its purpose is to avoid redundancy, since the number of individuals classified as "Other" can be found from the data on the first three options. If, in a sample of 100 subjects, 25 are found to belong in each of the first three options, then it is obvious that there are 25 in the "Other" option. (For more information on the topic of dummy variable coding, see Kerlinger & Pedhazur, 1997.)

Objects measured at the **ordinal level** are usually ranked along some dimension, such as from smallest to largest. For example, one might measure the variable "socioeconomic status" by categorizing families according to class: lower, lower middle, middle, upper middle, or upper. A rank of 1 is assigned to lower, 2 to lower middle, 3 to middle, and so forth. In this situation, the numbers have some mathematical meaning: Families in Category 3 have a higher socioeconomic status than families in Category 2. Note that nothing is specified with regard to the distance between any two rankings. Ordinal measurement often has been compared to a horse race without a stopwatch. The order in which the horses finish is relatively easy to determine, but it is difficult to calculate the difference in time between the winner and the runner-up.

An ordinal scale possesses the property of *equivalence.* Thus, in the previous example, all families placed in a category are treated equally, even though some might have greater incomes than others. It also possesses the property of order among the categories. Any given category can be defined as being higher or lower than any other category. Common examples of ordinal scales are rankings of football or basketball teams, military ranks, restaurant ratings, and beauty pageant results.

Ordinal scales are frequently used in mass communication research. Schweitzer (1989) ranked 16 factors that were important to the success of mass communication researchers. In a study of electronic text news, Heeter, Brown, Soffin, Stanley, and Salwen (1989) rank-ordered audience evaluations of the importance of 25 different issues in the news and found little support of an effect on content, known as **agenda setting.**

When a scale has all the properties of an ordinal scale and also the intervals between adjacent points on the scale are of equal value, the scale is at the **interval level.** The most obvious example of an interval scale is temperature. The same amount of heat is required to warm an object from 30 to 40 degrees as to warm it from 50 to 60 degrees. Interval scales incorporate the formal *property of equal differences;* that is, numbers are assigned to the positions of objects on an interval scale in such a way that one may carry out arithmetic operations on the differences between them.

One disadvantage of an interval scale is that it lacks a true zero point, or a condition of nothingness. For example, it is difficult to conceive of a person having zero intelligence or zero personality. The absence of a true zero point means that a researcher cannot make statements of a proportional nature;

for example, someone with an IQ of 100 is not twice as smart as someone with an IQ of 50, and a person who scores 30 on a test of aggression is not three times as aggressive as a person who scores 10. Despite this disadvantage, interval scales are frequently used in mass communication research. Zohoori (1988) constructed a "motivations for using TV" scale by presenting respondents with a list of 11 reasons for viewing television. The response options were "not at all like me," coded 1; "a little like me," coded 2; and "a lot like me," coded 3. Baran, Mok, Land, and Kang (1989) developed a five-point agree/disagree interval scale to measure a person's worth as seen by others by eliciting responses to seven statements such as "It's likely that I'd have this woman/man as a friend" and "It's fairly likely that this man/woman is punctual."

Scales at the **ratio level** of measurement have all the properties of interval scales plus one more: the existence of a true zero point. With the introduction of this fixed zero point, ratio judgments can be made. For example, since time and distance are ratio measures, one can say that a car traveling at 50 miles per hour is going twice as fast as a car traveling at 25. Ratio scales are relatively rare in mass media research, although some variables, such as time spent watching television or number of words per story, are ratio measurements. For example, Gantz (1978) measured news recall ability by asking subjects to report whether they had seen or heard 10 stories taken from the evening news. Scores could range from 0 to 10 on this test. Giffard (1984) counted the length of wire service reports related to 101 developed or developing nations. Theoretically, scores could range from zero (no coverage) to hundreds of words.

As discussed in Chapter 9, researchers who use interval or ratio data can use parametric statistics, which are specifically designed for these data. Procedures designed for use with "lower" levels of measurement can also be used with data at a higher level of measurement. Statistical procedures designed for higher-level data, however, are generally more powerful than those designed for use with nominal or ordinal levels of measurement. Thus, if an investigator has achieved the interval level of measurement, parametric statistics should generally be used. Statisticians disagree about the importance of the distinction between ordinal scales and interval scales and about the legitimacy of using interval statistics with data that may in fact be ordinal. Without delving too deeply into these arguments, we suggest that the safest procedure is to assume interval measurement unless there is clear evidence to the contrary, in which case ordinal statistics should be used. For example, ordinal statistics should be used for a research task in which a group of subjects ranks a set of objects. On the other hand, parametric procedures are justified if subjects are given an attitude score constructed by rating responses to various questions.

Most statisticians seem to feel that statistical analysis is performed on the numbers yielded by the measures, not on the measures themselves, and that the properties of interval scales belong to the number system (Nunnally & Bernstein, 1994; Roscoe, 1975). Additionally, there have been several studies in which various types of data have been subjected to different statistical analyses. These studies suggest that the distinction between ordinal data and interval data is not particularly crucial in selecting an analysis method (McNemar, 1969).

▪ Measurement Scales

A scale represents a composite measure of a variable; it is based on more than one item. Scales are generally used with complex variables that do not easily lend themselves to single-item or single-indicator measurements. Some items, such as age, newspaper circulation, or number of radios in the house, can be adequately measured without scaling techniques. Measurement of other variables, such as attitude toward TV news or gratification received from going to a movie theater, generally requires the use of scales. Several scaling techniques have been developed over the years. This section discusses only the better-known methods. Search the Internet for additional information about all types of measurement scales.

Simple Rating Scales

Rating scales are common in mass media research. Researchers frequently ask respondents to rate a list of items such as a list of programming elements that can be included in a radio station's weekday morning show, or to rate how much respondents like radio or TV on-air personalities.

The researcher's decision is to decide which type of scale to use: 1 to 3? 1 to 5? 1 to 7? 1 to 10? 1 to 100? Or even a 0–9 scale, which is commonly used by researchers who don't have computer software to accept double-digit numbers (10). Selecting a type of scale is largely a matter of personal preference, but there are a few things to consider:

1. *A scale with more points rather than fewer points allows for greater differentiation on the item or items being rated.* For example, assume we are rating the importance of programming elements contained in a radio station's weekday morning show. Will a 1–3 scale or 1–10 scale, when the respondents are told that, "The higher the number, the more important the element is to you" provide more information? Obviously, the 1–10 scale provides the broadest differentiation.

Broad differentiation in opinions, perceptions, and feelings is important because it gives the researcher more information. Artificially restricting the range of ratings is known as **factor fusion,** which means that opinions, perceptions, and feelings are squeezed into a smaller space. It's better for the respondents and the researcher to have more rating points than fewer rating points.

2. *Our experience shows that males and females, all age groups, and all races and nationalities most readily like to use a* 1–10 *scale.* This is true because the 1–10 scale is universally used, particularly in sporting events like the Olympics. Virtually everyone understands the 1–10 rating scale. A 10 is best or perfect, a 1 is worst or incorrect. Our experience also shows that researchers should not use a 0–9 or 1–9 rating scale because, quite frankly, respondents do not associate well with a "9" as the highest number.

3. *When using simple rating scales, it is best to tell respondents that, "The higher the number, the more you agree," or "The higher the number, the more you like."* Over thousands of research studies, we have found this approach better than telling respondents, "Use a scale of 1 to 10, where '1' means *Dislike* and '10' means *Like a lot.*"

Transforming Scales

On occasion, a researcher will conduct a study using one scale and then later want to compare those data to other data using a different rating scale. For example, let's say that a researcher uses a 1–7 rating scale and wants to convert the results to a 1–100 scale. What can be done?

The procedure is always the same: divide the smaller rating scale into the larger to produce a multiplier to transform the scale. For the transformation of 1–7 to 1–100, first divide 100 by 7, which is 14.2857, then multiply this number times each of the 1–7 elements to compute the converted 1–100 scale numbers. The new, transformed (rounded) ratings are:

1 = 14
2 = 29
3 = 43
4 = 57
5 = 71

6 = 86
7 = 100

What about transforming a 5-point scale to a 7-point scale? The procedure is the same: Divide 7 by 5, which produces a multiplier of 1.4. This number is multiplied times each of the numbers in the 5-point scale to produce a transformed scale:

1 = 1.4
2 = 2.8
3 = 4.2
4 = 5.6
5 = 7.0

If you transform scores the other way, such as a 10-point scale to a 5-point scale, simply divide each of the numbers in the scale by the multiplier.

Specialized Rating Scales

Thurstone Scales. Thurstone scales are also called *equal-appearing interval scales* because of the technique used to develop them. They are typically used to measure the attitude toward a given concept or construct. To develop a Thurstone scale, a researcher first collects a large number of statements (Thurstone recommends at least 100) that relate to the concept or construct to be measured. Next, judges rate these statements along an 11-category scale in which each category expresses a different degree of favorableness toward the concept. The items are then ranked according to the mean or median ratings assigned by the judges and are used to construct a questionnaire of 20 to 30 items that are chosen more or less evenly from across the range of ratings. The statements are worded so that a person can agree or disagree with them. The scale is then administered to a sample of respondents whose scores are determined by computing the mean or median value of the items agreed with. A person who disagrees with all the items has a score of zero.

One advantage of the Thurstone method is that it is an interval measurement scale. On the downside, this method is time-consuming and labor-intensive. Thurstone scales are not often used in mass media research, but they are common in psychology and education research.

Guttman Scaling. Guttman scaling, also called *scalogram* analysis, is based on the idea that items can be arranged along a continuum in such a way that a person who agrees with an item or finds an item acceptable will also agree with or find acceptable all other items expressing a less extreme position. For example, here is a hypothetical four-item Guttman scale:

1. Indecent programming on TV is harmful to society.
2. Children should not be allowed to watch indecent TV shows.
3. Television station managers should not allow indecent programs on their stations.
4. The government should ban indecent programming from TV.

Presumably, a person who agrees with Statement 4 will also agree with Statements 1–3. Furthermore, if we assume the scale is valid, then a person who agrees with Statement 2 will also agree with Statement 1 but will not necessarily agree with Statements 3 and 4. Because each score represents a unique set of responses, the number of items a person agrees with is the person's total score on a Guttman scale.

A Guttman scale requires a great deal of time and energy to develop. Although they do not appear often in mass media research, Guttman scales are fairly common in political science, sociology, public opinion research, and anthropology.

Likert Scales. Perhaps the most commonly used scale in mass media research is the Likert scale, also called the summated rating approach. A number of statements are developed with respect to a topic, and respondents can strongly agree, agree, be neutral, disagree, or strongly disagree with the statements (see Figure 2.1). Each response option is weighted, and each subject's responses are added to produce a single score on the topic.

This is the basic procedure for developing a Likert scale:

1. Compile a large number of statements that relate to a specific dimension. Some statements are positively worded; some are negatively worded.
2. Administer the scale to a randomly selected sample of respondents.
3. Code the responses consistently so that high scores indicate stronger agreement with the attitude in question.
4. Analyze the responses and select for the final scale those statements that most clearly differentiate the highest from the lowest scorers.

Semantic Differential Scales. Another commonly used scaling procedure is the **semantic differential** technique. As originally conceived by Osgood, Suci, and Tannenbaum (1957), this technique is used to measure the meaning an item has for an individual. Research indicated that three general

Figure 2.1 *Sample of Likert Scale Items*

1. Only U.S. citizens should be allowed to own broadcasting stations.

Response		Score Assigned
________	Strongly agree	5
________	Agree	4
________	Neutral	3
________	Disagree	2
________	Strongly Disagree	1

2. Prohibiting foreign ownership of broadcasting stations is bad for business.

Response		Score Assigned
________	Strongly agree	1
________	Agree	2
________	Neutral	3
________	Disagree	4
________	Strongly Disagree	5

Note: To maintain attitude measurement consistency, the scores are reversed for a negatively worded item. Question 1 is a positive item; Question 2 is a negative item.

Figure 2.2 *Sample Form for Applying the Semantic Differential Technique*

Time Magazine

Biased ______ : _ : ______ : ______ : ______ : ______ : ______ Unbiased
Trustworthy ______ : _ : ______ : ______ : ______ : ______ : ______ Untrustworthy
Valuable ______ : _ : ______ : ______ : ______ : ______ : ______ Worthless
Unfair ______ : _ : ______ : ______ : ______ : ______ : ______ Fair

factors—activity, potency, and evaluation—were measured by the semantic differential. Communication researchers were quick to adapt the evaluative dimension of the semantic differential for use as a measure of attitude.

To use the technique, a name or a concept is placed at the top of a series of seven-point scales anchored by bipolar attitudes. Figure 2.2 shows an example of this technique as used to measure attitudes toward *Time* magazine. The bipolar adjectives that typically "anchor" such evaluative scales are *pleasant/unpleasant, valuable/worthless, honest/dishonest, nice/awful, clean/dirty, fair/unfair,* and *good/bad.* However, we recommend that a unique set of anchoring adjectives be developed for each particular measurement situation. For example, Markham (1968), in his study of the credibility of television newscasters, uses 13 variable sets, including *deep/shallow, ordered/chaotic, annoying/pleasing,* and *clear/hazy.* Robinson and Shaver (1973) present a collection of scales commonly used in social science research. (Search the Internet for "semantic differential" to find several examples of how the technique is used.)

Strictly speaking, the semantic differential technique attempts to place a concept in semantic space through the use of an advanced multivariate statistical procedure called **factor analysis.** When researchers borrow parts of the technique to measure attitudes, or images or perceptions of objects, persons, or concepts, they are not using the technique as originally developed. Consequently, perhaps a more appropriate name for this technique is bipolar rating scales.

▪ Reliability and Validity

Using any scale without prior testing results is poor research. At least one pilot study should be conducted for any newly developed scale to ensure its reliability and validity. To be useful, a measurement must possess these two related qualities. A measure is reliable if it consistently gives the same answer. **Reliability** in measurement is the same as reliability in any other context. For example, a reliable person is one who is dependable, stable, and consistent over time. An unreliable person is unstable and unpredictable and may act one way today and another way tomorrow. Similarly, if measurements are consistent from one session to another, they are reliable and can be believed to some degree.

In understanding measurement reliability, you may think of a measure as containing two components. The first represents an individual's "true" score on the measuring instrument. The second represents random error and does not provide an accurate assessment of what is being measured. Error can slip into the measurement process from several sources. Perhaps a question was worded ambiguously, or a person's pencil slipped as he or she was filling out a measuring instrument.

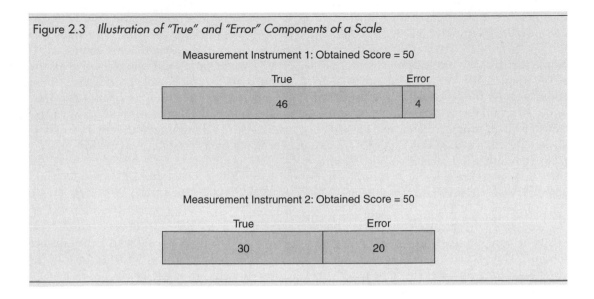

Figure 2.3 *Illustration of "True" and "Error" Components of a Scale*

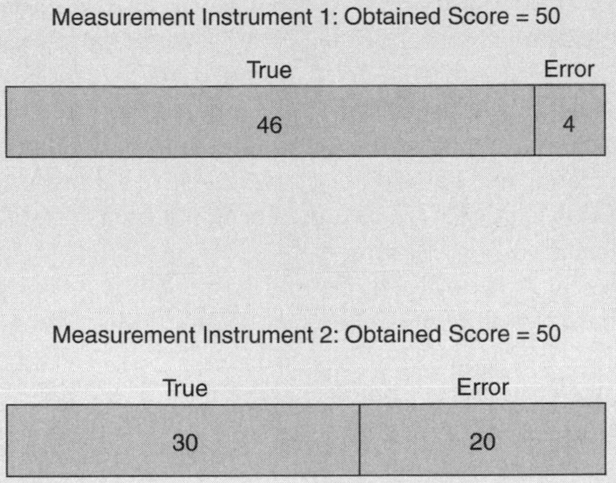

Whatever the cause, all measurement is subject to some degree of random error. Figure 2.3 illustrates this concept. As is evident, Measurement Instrument 1 is highly reliable because the ratio of the true component of the score to the total score is high. Measurement Instrument 2 is unreliable because the ratio of the true component to the total is low.

A completely unreliable measurement measures nothing at all. If a measure is repeatedly given to individuals and each person's responses at a later session are unrelated to his or her earlier responses, the measure is useless. If the responses are identical or nearly identical each time the measure is given, the measure is reliable; it at least measures something, though not necessarily what the researcher intended. (This problem is discussed later in this chapter.)

The importance of reliability should be obvious now. Unreliable measures cannot be used to detect relationships between variables. When the measurement of a variable is unreliable, it is composed mainly of random error, and random error is seldom related to anything else.

Reliability is not a unidimensional concept. It consists of three different components: stability, internal consistency, and equivalency.

Stability refers to *the consistency of a result or of a measure at different points in time.* For example, suppose that a test designed to measure proofreading ability is administered during the first week of an editing class and again during the second week. The test possesses stability if the two results are consistent. Caution should be exercised whenever stability is used as a measure of reliability, since people and things can change over time. In the proofreading example, it is possible for a person to score higher the second time because some people might actually improve their ability from Week 1 to Week 2. In this case, the measure is not really unstable—actual change occurred.

An assessment of reliability is necessary in all mass media research and should be reported along with other facets of the research as an aid in interpretation and evaluation. One commonly used statistic for assessing reliability is the correlation coefficient, denoted as r_{xx}. Chapter 9 provides a more detailed examination of the correlation coefficient. For now let's say only that r_{xx} is a number ranging from −1.00 to + 1.00 and is used to gauge the strength of a relationship between two variables. When r_{xx} is high—that is, approaching +1.00—the relationship is strong. A negative number indicates a negative relationship (high scores on one variable are associated with low scores on the other), and a positive number indicates a positive relationship (a high score goes with another high score). In measuring reliability, a high positive r_{xx} is desired.

One method that uses correlation coefficients to compute reliability is the test-retest method. This procedure measures the stability component of reliability. The same people are measured at two different points in time, and a coefficient between the two scores is computed. An r_{xx} that approaches +1.00 indicates that a person's score at Time A was similar to his or her score at Time B, showing consistency over time. There are two limitations to the test-retest technique. First, the initial administration of the measure might affect scores on the second testing. If the measuring device is a questionnaire, a person might remember responses from session to session, thus falsely inflating reliability. Second, the concept measured may change from Time A to Time B, thus lowering the reliability estimate.

Internal consistency involves examining the consistency of performance among the items that compose a scale. If separate items on a scale assign the same values to the concept being measured, the scale possesses internal consistency. For instance, suppose a researcher designs a 20-item scale to measure attitudes toward newspaper reading. For the scale to be internally consistent, the total score on the first half of the test should correlate highly with the score on the second half of the test. This method of determining reliability is called the *split-half technique.*

Only one administration of the measuring instrument is made, but the test is split into halves and scored separately. For example, if the test is in the form of a questionnaire, the even-numbered items might constitute one half and the odd-numbered items the other half. A correlation coefficient is then computed between the two sets of scores. Since this coefficient is computed from a test that is only half as long as the final form, it is corrected by using the following formula:

$$r_{xx} = \frac{2(r_{oe})}{1 + r_{oe}}$$

where r_{oe} is the correlation between the odd items and the even items. (Search the Internet for "split-half reliability" for additional information and examples.)

Another common reliability coefficient is alpha (sometimes referred to as Cronbach's alpha), which uses the analysis of variance approach to assess the internal consistency of a measure (see Chapter 12).

The **equivalency** component of reliability, sometimes referred to as **cross-test reliability,** assesses the relative correlation between two parallel forms of a test. Two instruments that use different scale items or different measurement techniques are developed to measure the same concept. The two versions are then administered to the same group of people during a single time period, and the correlation between the scores on the two forms of the test is taken as a measure of the reliability. The major problem with this method, of course, is developing two forms of a scale that are perfectly equivalent. The less parallel the two forms, the lower the reliability.

A special case of the equivalency component occurs when two or more observers judge the same phenomenon, as is the case in content analysis (see Chapter 6). This type of reliability is called **intercoder reliability** and is used to assess the degree to which a result can be achieved or reproduced by other observers. Ideally, two individuals who use the same operational measure and the same measuring instrument should reach the same results. For example, if two researchers try to identify acts of violence in television content based on a given operational definition of violence, the degree to which their results are consistent is a measure of intercoder reliability. Disagreements reflect a difference either in perception or in the way the original definition was interpreted. Special formulas for computing intercoder reliability are discussed in Chapter 6.

In addition to being reliable, a measurement must have validity if it is to be of use in studying variables. A valid measuring device measures what it is supposed to measure. Or, to put it another way, determining validity requires an evaluation of the congruence between the operational definition of a variable and its conceptual or constitutive definition. Assessing validity requires some judgment on the part of the researcher. In the following discussion of the major types of measurement validity, note that each one depends at least in part on the judgment of the researcher. Also, validity is almost never an all-or-none proposition; it is usually a matter of degree. A measurement rarely turns out to be totally valid or invalid. Typically it winds up somewhere in the middle.

Concerning measurement, there are four major types of validity, and each has a corresponding technique for evaluating the measurement method—*face validity, predictive validity, concurrent validity,* and *construct validity.*

The simplest and most basic kind of validity, **face validity,** is achieved by examining the measurement device to see whether, on the face of it, it measures what it appears to measure. For example, a test designed to measure proofreading ability could include accounting problems, but this measure would lack face validity. A test that asks people to read and correct certain paragraphs has more face validity as a measure of proofreading skill. Whether a measure possesses face validity depends to some degree on subjective judgment. To minimize subjectivity, the relevance of a given measurement should be judged independently by several experts.

Checking a measurement instrument against some future outcome assesses **predictive validity.** For example, scores on a test to predict whether a person will vote in an upcoming election can be checked against actual voting behavior. If the test scores allow the researcher to predict with a high degree of accuracy which people will actually vote and which will not, then the test has predictive validity. Note that it is possible for a measure to have predictive validity and at the same time lack face validity. The sole factor in determining validity in the predictive method is the measurement's ability to forecast future behavior correctly. The concern is not with what is being measured but with whether the measurement instrument can predict something. Thus, a test to determine whether a person will become a successful mass media researcher could conceivably consist of geometry problems. If it predicts the ultimate success of a researcher reasonably well, the test has predictive validity but little face validity. The biggest problem associated with predictive validity is determining the criteria against which test scores are to be checked. What, for example, constitutes a "successful mass media researcher"? One who obtains an advanced degree? One who publishes research articles? One who writes a book?

Concurrent validity is closely related to predictive validity. In this method, however, the measuring instrument is checked against some present criterion. For example, it is possible to validate a test of proofreading ability by administering the test to a group of professional proofreaders and to a group of nonproofreaders. If the test discriminates well between the two groups, it can be said to have concurrent validity. Similarly, a test of aggression might discriminate between one group of children who are frequently detained after

Figure 2.4 *Types of Validity*

Judgment-based	Criterion-based	Theory-based
Face validity	Predictive validity Concurrent validity	Construct validity

school for fighting and another group who have never been reprimanded for antisocial behavior.

The fourth type of validity, **construct validity,** is the most complex. In simplified form, construct validity involves relating a measuring instrument to some overall theoretic framework to ensure that the measurement is logically related to other concepts in the framework. Ideally, a researcher should be able to suggest various relationships between the property being measured and the other variables. For construct validity to exist, the researcher must show that these relationships are in fact present. For example, an investigator might expect the frequency with which a person views a particular television newscast to be influenced by his or her attitude toward that program. If the measure of attitudes correlates highly with the frequency of viewing, there is some evidence for the validity of the attitude measure. Similarly, construct validity is present if the measurement instrument under consideration does not relate to other variables when there is no theoretic reason to expect such a relationship. Therefore, if an investigator finds a relationship between a measure and other variables that is predicted by a theory and fails to find other relationships that are not predicted by a theory, there is evidence for construct validity. For example, Milavsky, Kessler, Stipp, and Rubens (1982) established the validity of their measure of respondent aggression by noting, as expected, that boys scored higher than girls and that high aggression scores were associated with high levels of parental punishment. In addition, aggression was negatively correlated with scores on a scale measuring prosocial behavior. Figure 2.4 summarizes the four types of validity.

Before closing this discussion, we should point out that reliability and validity are related. Reliability is necessary to establish validity, but it is not a sufficient condition; a reliable measure is not necessarily a valid one. Figure 2.5 shows this relationship. An X represents a test that is both reliable and valid; the scores are consistent from session to session and lie close to the true value. An O represents a measure that is reliable but not valid; the scores are stable from session to session but they are not close to the true score. A + represents a test that is neither valid nor reliable; scores vary widely from session to session and are not close to the true score.

▪▪▪ Summary

Understanding empirical research requires a basic knowledge of concepts, constructs, variables, and measurement. Concepts summarize related observations and express an abstract notion that has been formed by generalizing from particulars. Connections among concepts form propositions that, in turn, are used to build theories. Constructs consist of combinations of concepts and are also useful in building theories.

Figure 2.5 *Relationship of Reliability and Validity*

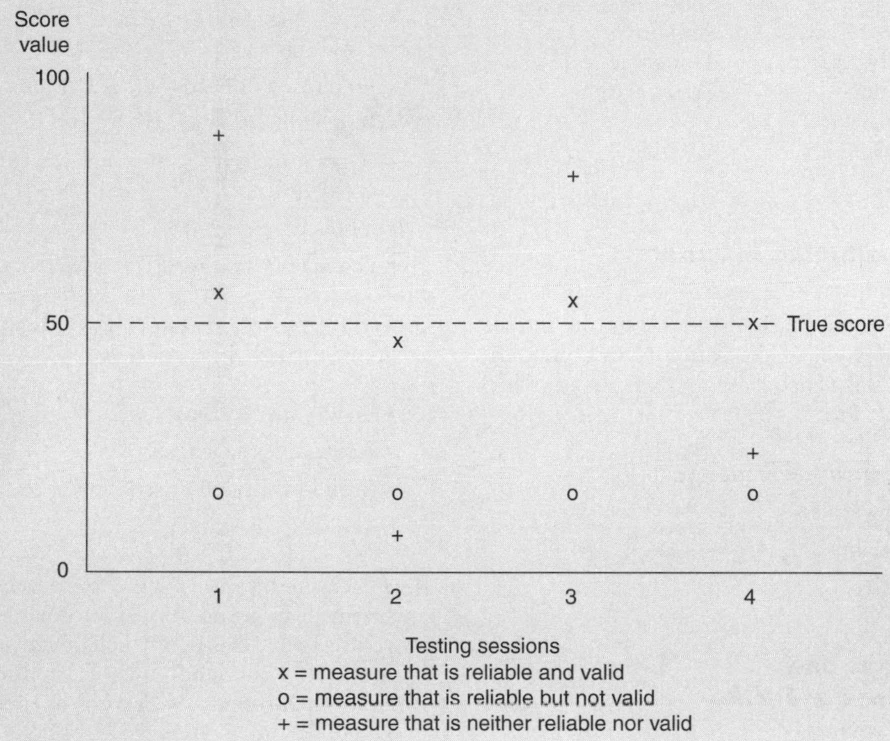

Variables are phenomena or events that take on one or more different values. Independent variables are manipulated by the researcher, whereas dependent variables are what the researcher attempts to explain. All variables are related to the observable world by operational definitions. Researchers frequently use scales to measure complex variables. Thurstone, Guttman, Likert, and semantic differential scales are used in mass media research.

Measurement is the assignment of numerals to objects, events, or properties according to certain rules. The four levels of measurement are nominal, ordinal, interval, and ratio. To be useful, a measurement must be both reliable and valid.

Key Terms

Agenda setting
Antecedent variable
Concept
Concurrent validity
Construct
Construct validity
Continuous variable
Control variable
Criterion variable
Cronbach's alpha
Cross-test reliability
Dependent variable
Discrete variable
Dummy variable
Equivalency
Face validity
Factor analysis
Factor fusion
Guttman scale
Independent variable
Intercoder reliability
Internal consistency
Interval level
Isomorphism
Likert scale
Marker variable
Measurement
Multivariate analysis
Noise
Nominal level

Ordinal level
Predictive validity
Predictor variable
Qualitative research
Quantitative research
Rating scale transformation
Ratio level
Reliability
Semantic differential
Split-half technique
Stability
Thurstone scale
Triangulation
Validity
Variable

Using the Internet

There are many articles available on the Internet about almost all of the concepts and terms discussed in this chapter. As an experiment, search the Internet for:

- Operational definition
- Rating scales
- Reliability
- Validity

Questions and Problems for Further Investigation

1. Provide conceptual and operational definitions for the following items:

   - Artistic quality
   - Objectionable song lyrics
   - Programming appeal
   - Sexual content
   - Violence

   Compare your definitions to those of others in the class. Would there be any difficulty in conducting a study using these definitions? Have you demonstrated why so much controversy surrounds the topics, for example, of sex and violence on television? What can you find on the Internet about these terms?

2. What type of data (nominal, ordinal, interval, or ratio) is associated with each of the following concepts or measurements?

   - Baseball team standings
   - A test of listening comprehension
   - A. C. Nielsen's list of the top 10 television programs
   - Frequency of heads versus tails on coin flips
   - Baseball batting averages
   - A scale measuring intensity of attitudes toward violence
   - VHF channels 2–13
   - A scale for monitoring your weight over time

3. Try to develop a measurement technique to examine each of these concepts:

   - Newspaper reading
   - Aggressive tendencies
   - Brand loyalty (in purchasing products)
   - Television viewing

4. Search the Internet for the four levels of measurement to get additional information. While you're there, check for "reliability" and "validity." In your validity search, find the article entitled "Grounds of Validity of the Laws of Logic: Further Consequences of Four Incapacities" by Charles S. Peirce [*Journal of Speculative Philosophy* 2 (1869), 193–208]. The article is rather "lofty" sounding, but it may provide some interesting research ideas.

5. The semantic differential is a widely used measurement technique in social science. If you are using InfoTrac College Edition, find three recent studies that have used this method. What concepts were measured?

For additional information on these and related topics, see

http://www.wimmerdominick.com

References and Suggested Readings

Anderson, J. A. (1987). *Communication research: Issues and methods.* New York: McGraw-Hill.

Babbie, E. R. (2001). *The practice of social research* (9th ed.). Belmont, CA: Wadsworth.

Bae, H. S. (2000). Product differentiation in national TV newscasts. *Journal of Broadcasting and Electronic Media, 44*(1), 62–77.

Baran, S. B., Mok, J. J., Land, M., & Kang, T. Y. (1989). You are what you buy. *Journal of Communication, 39*(2), 46–55.

Bergen, L. A., & Weaver, D. (1988). Job satisfaction of daily newspaper journalists and organization size. *Newspaper Research Journal, 9*(2), 1–14.

Bloom, M. (1986). *The experience of research.* New York: Macmillan.

Buijen, M. & Valkenburg, P. (2000). The impact of television advertising on children's Christmas wishes. *Journal of Broadcasting and Electronic Media, 44*(3), 456–470.

Carroll, R. (1989). Market size and TV news values. *Journalism Quarterly, 66*(1), 48–56.

Chadwick, B., Bahr, H., & Albrecht, S. (1984). *Social science research methods.* Englewood Cliffs, NJ: Prentice-Hall.

Demers, D. (1994). Effect of organizational size on job satisfaction of top editors at U.S. dailies. *Journalism Quarterly, 71*(4), 914–925.

Emmert, P., & Barker, L. L. (1989). *Measurement of communication behavior.* White Plains, NY: Longman.

Fischer, P. M., Richards, J. V., Berman, E. J., & Krugman, D. M. (1989). Recall and eye-tracking study of adolescents viewing tobacco advertisements. *Journal of the American Medical Association, 261,* 840–889.

Gantz, W. (1978). How uses and gratifications affect recall of television news. *Journalism Quarterly, 55*(4), 664–672.

Gerbner, G., Gross, L., Morgan, M., & Signorielli, N. (1980). The mainstreaming of America: Violence profile no. 11. *Journal of Communication, 30*(3), 10–29.

Giffard, C. (1984). Developed and developing nations' news in U.S. wire service files to Asia. *Journalism Quarterly, 61*(1), 14–19.

Guilford, J. P. (1954). *Psychometric methods.* New York: McGraw-Hill.

Heeter, C., Brown, N., Soffin, S., Stanley, C., & Salwen, M. (1989). Agenda setting by electronic text news. *Journalism Quarterly, 66*(1), 101–106.

Henning, B. & Vorderer, P. (2001). Psychological escapism: Predicting the amount of television viewing by need for cognition. *Journal of Communication, 51*(1), 100–120.

Hindman, D. B. (2000). The rural-urban digital divide. *Journalism and Mass Communication Quarterly, 77*(3), 549–560.

Hinkle, G., & Elliot, W. R. (1989). Science coverage in three newspapers and three supermarket tabloids. *Journalism Quarterly, 66*(2), 353–358.

Hsia, H. J. (1988). *Mass communication research methods: A step-by-step approach.* Hillsdale, NJ: Lawrence Erlbaum.

Jacobs, R. (1995). Exploring the determinants of cable television subscriber satisfaction. *Journal of Broadcasting and Electronic Media, 39*(2), 262–274.

Kaid, L., Chanslor, M., & Hovind, M. (1992). The influence of program and commercial type on political advertising effectiveness. *Journal of Broadcasting and Electronic Media, 36*(3), 303–320.

Kerlinger, F. N. (2000). *Foundations of behavioral research* (4th ed.). New York: Holt, Rinehart & Winston.

Kerlinger, F. N., & Pedhazur, E. (1997). *Multiple regression in behavioral research* (3rd ed.). New York: Holt, Rinehart & Winston.

Krugman, D. M., & Johnson, K. F. (1991). Differences in the consumption of traditional broadcast and VCR movie rentals. *Journal of Broadcasting and Electronic Media, 35*(2), 213–232.

Lin, C. A., & Atkin, D. J. (1989). Parental mediation and rulemaking for adolescent use of television and VCRs. *Journal of Broadcasting and Electronic Media, 33*(1), 53–69.

Lindlof, T. R. (Ed.). (1987). *Natural audiences: Qualitative research of media uses and effects.* Norwood, NJ: Ablex.

Markham, D. (1968). The dimensions of source credibility for television newscasters. *Journal of Communication, 18*(1), 57–64.

Mason, E. J., & Bramble, W. J. (1989). *Understanding and conducting research* (2nd ed.). New York: McGraw Hill.

McNemar, Q. (1969). *Psychological statistics* (4th ed.). New York: John Wiley.

Milavsky, J., Kessler, R., Stipp, H., & Rubens, W. (1982). *Television and aggression.* New York: Academic Press.

Nunnally, J. C., & Bernstein, I. H. (1994). *Psychometric theory* (4th ed.). New York: McGraw-Hill.

Osgood, C., Suci, G., & Tannenbaum, P. (1957). *The measurement of meaning.* Urbana: University of Illinois Press.

Pokrywczynski, J. (1986). *Advertising effects and viewer involvement with televised sports.* Unpublished doctoral dissertation, University of Georgia, Athens.

Robinson, J., & Shaver, P. (1973). *Measures of social psychological attitudes* (2nd ed.). Ann Arbor, MI: Institute for Social Research.

Roscoe, J. (1975). *Fundamental research statistics for the behavioral sciences.* New York: Holt, Rinehart & Winston.

Schweitzer, J. C. (1989). Factors affecting scholarly research among mass communication faculty. *Journalism Quarterly, 66*(2), 410–417.

Shah, H., & Gayatri, G. (1994). Development news in elite and non-elite newspapers in Indonesia. *Journalism Quarterly,* 71(2), 411–420.

Smith, M. J. (1988). *Contemporary communication research methods.* Belmont, CA: Wadsworth.

Wanta, W., & Leggett, D. (1988). Hitting paydirt: Capacity theory and sports announcers' use of clichés. *Journal of Communication,* 38(4), 82–89.

Weinberger, M. G., & Spotts, H. E. (1989). Humor in U.S. versus U.K. TV commercials. *Journal of Advertising,* 18(2), 39–44.

Whitmore, E., & Tiene D. (1994). Viewing Channel One: Awareness of current events by teenagers. *Mass Comm Review,* 21(1/2), 67–75.

Williams, F., Rice, R. E., & Rogers, E. M. (1988). *Research methods and the new media.* New York: Free Press.

Wu, H. D. (2000). Systemic determinants of international news coverage. *Journal of Communication,* 50(2), 110–130.

Zohoori, A. R. (1988). A cross-cultural analysis of children's television use. *Journal of Broadcasting and Electronic Media,* 32(1), 105–113.

Chapter 3

Research Ethics

The ethical problems of doing scientific research made major headlines in 2001. The federal government suspended various medical research projects at Johns Hopkins University after the death of a healthy research volunteer. The case highlighted the need for researchers to inform subjects of all possible risks that might come with research participation. Scientists also debated the pros and cons of research using stem cells taken from human embryos and the ethics of cloning a human being. Accordingly, this chapter focuses on an area that is not part of the research process itself but is nevertheless vital to the execution of any research project: ethics. Although mass media researchers may not face the kind of ethical problems faced by researchers in the biological and medical sciences, they should be no less aware of the ethical implications of their research.

Ethics and the Research Process

Most mass media research involves observations of human beings—asking them questions or examining what they have done. In this probing process, however, the researcher must ensure that the rights of the participants are not violated. This concern for rights requires a consideration of ethics: distinguishing right from wrong and proper from improper. Unfortunately, there are no universal definitions for these terms. Instead, several guidelines, broad generalizations, and suggestions have been endorsed or at least tacitly accepted by most in the research profession. These guidelines do not provide an answer to every ethical question that may arise, but they can help make researchers more sensitive to the issues.

Before discussing these specific guidelines, let's pose some hypothetical research situations involving ethics.

- A researcher at a large university hands questionnaires to the students in an introductory mass media course and tells them that if they do not complete the forms, they will lose points toward their grade in the course.
- A researcher is conducting a mail survey about attendance at X-rated motion pictures. The questionnaire states that the responses will be anonymous. Unknown to the respondents, however, each return envelope is marked with a code that enables the researcher to identify the sender.
- A researcher volunteers for duty at a college newspaper and secretly observes and records the discussions of reporters and editors about what stories should be carried.
- A researcher shows one group of children a violent television show and another group a nonviolent program. Afterward, the children are sent to a public playground, where they are told to play with the children who are already there. The researcher records each instance of violent behavior exhibited by the young subjects.
- Subjects in an experiment are told to submit a sample of their news writing to an executive of a large newspaper. They are led to believe that whoever submits the best work will be offered a job at the paper. In fact, the "executive" is a confederate in the experiment and severely criticizes everyone's work.

These examples of ethically flawed study designs should be kept in mind while you read the following guidelines to ethics in mass media research.

▪ *Why Be Ethical?*

Ethical behavior is the right thing to do. The best reason to behave ethically is the personal knowledge that you have acted in a morally appropriate manner. In addition, there are other cogent reasons that argue for ethical behavior. Unethical behavior may have an adverse effect on research participants. Just one experience with an ethically questionable research project may completely alienate a respondent. A person who was improperly deceived into thinking that he or she was being evaluated for a job at a newspaper when it was all just an experiment might not be so willing to participate in another study. Since mass communication research depends upon the continued goodwill and cooperation of respondents, it is important to shield them from unethical research practices.

Moreover, unethical research practices reflect poorly on the profession and may result in an increase in negative public opinion. Many readers have probably heard about the infamous Tuskegee syphilis study in which impoverished African-American men suffering from syphilis were studied without their consent and left untreated so that researchers could study the progress of the disease (see Jones, 1981, for a complete description). The distrust and suspicion engendered by this experiment in the African-American community have yet to subside and have been cited as a factor in the rise of some conspiracy theories about the spread of AIDS (Thomas & Quinn, 1981). It is fortunate that the mass communication research community has not had an ethical lapse of this magnitude, but the Tuskegee experiment illustrates the harmful fallout that can result from an unethical research project.

Unethical research usually does not result from some sinister motivation. Instead, it generally comes from pressures on researchers to cut corners in an attempt to publish an article or gain prestige or impress other colleagues. Nonetheless, it is behavior that is potentially serious and little tolerated within the community of mass media scholars.

▪ *General Ethical Theories*

The problem of determining what is right and proper has been examined for hundreds of years. At least three general types of theories have evolved to suggest answers: (1) rule-based or **deontological** theories, (2) balancing or **teleological** theories, and (3) **relativistic** theories.

The best-known deontological theory is the one associated with the philosopher Immanuel Kant. Kant posited moral laws that constituted **categorical imperatives**—principles that define appropriate action in any and all situations. Following these categorical imperatives represents a moral duty for all humans. To define a categorical imperative, a person should ask whether or not the behavior in question is something that he or she would like to see universally implemented. In other words, a person should act in a way that he or she wants all others to act. Note that in many ways Kant's thinking parallels what we might call the Golden Rule: Do unto others as you would have them do unto you.

A mass media researcher, for example, might develop a categorical imperative about deception. Deception is not something that a researcher wants to see universally practiced by all; nor does the researcher wish to be deceived. Therefore, deception is something that should not be used in research, no matter what the benefits and no matter what the circumstances.

The teleological or balancing theory is best exemplified by what philosopher John Stuart Mill called **utilitarianism.** In this theory, the good that may come from an action is weighed against or balanced against the possible harm. The individual then acts in a way that maximizes good and minimizes harm. In other words, the ultimate test for determining the rightness of some behavior depends upon the outcomes that result from this behavior. The end may justify the means.

A mass media researcher who follows the utilitarian approach must balance the good that will come from a research project against its possible negative effects. In this situation, a researcher might decide it is appropriate to use deception in an experiment if the positive benefits of the knowledge obtained outweigh the possible harmful effects of deceiving the subjects. Note that a researcher might use a different course of action depending upon which ethical theory is used as a guide.

The relativism approach argues that there is no absolute right or wrong way of behaving. Instead, ethical decisions are determined by the culture within which a researcher is working. Indeed, behavior that is judged to be wrong in one culture may be judged ethical in another. One of the ways that the ethical norms of a culture may be established is through the creation of codes of behavior or of good conduct that spell out what most researchers in the field think are desirable or undesirable behaviors. Thus a researcher confronted with a particular ethical problem might look to these codes for guidance.

These three theories help form the basis for the ethical principles discussed next.

▪ *Ethical Principles*

General ethical principles are difficult to construct in the research area. There are, however, at least four relevant principles. First is the principle of **autonomy,** or self-determination, which has its roots in the categorical imperative. Denying autonomy is not something that a researcher wishes to see universally practiced. Basic to this concept is the demand that the researcher respects the rights, values, and decisions of other people. The reasons for a person's action should be respected and the actions not interfered with. This principle is exemplified by the use of informed consent in the research procedure.

A second ethical principle important to social science research is **nonmaleficence.** In short, it is wrong to intentionally inflict harm on another. A third ethical principle—**beneficence**—is usually considered in tandem with nonmaleficence. Beneficence stipulates a positive obligation to remove existing harms and to confer benefits on others. These two principles operate together, and often the researcher must weigh the harmful risks of research against its possible benefits (for example, an increase in knowledge or a refinement of a theory). Note how the utilitarian theory relates to these principles.

A fourth ethical principle, the principle of **justice,** is related to both deontological and teleological theories of ethics. At its general level, this principle holds that people who are equal in relevant respects should be treated equally. In the research context, this principle should be applied when new programs or policies are being evaluated. The positive results of such research should be shared with all. It would be unethical, for example, to deny the benefit of a new teaching procedure to children because they were originally chosen to be in the control group rather than in the group that received the experimental procedure. Benefits should be shared with all who are qualified.

It is clear that mass media researchers must follow some set of rules to meet their ethical obligations to their subjects and respondents. Cook (1976), discussing the laboratory approach, offers one such code of behavior that represents norms in the field:

- Do not involve people in research without their knowledge or consent.
- Do not coerce people to participate.
- Do not withhold from the participant the true nature of the research.
- Do not actively lie to the participant about the nature of the research.
- Do not lead the participant to commit acts that diminish his or her self-respect.
- Do not violate the right to self-determination.
- Do not expose the participant to physical or mental stress.
- Do not invade the privacy of the participant.
- Do not withhold benefits from participants in control groups.
- Do not fail to treat research participants fairly and to show them consideration and respect.

To this list we add:

- Always treat every respondent or subject with unconditional human regard. (That is, accept and respect a person for what he or she is, and do not criticize the person for what he or she is not.)

Are ethical principles transmitted from one generation of researchers to another? A study by McEuen, Gordon, and Todd-Mancillas (1990) that examined Ph.D. programs in communication found that no program offered a graduate-level course devoted to the study of research ethics. About 70% of the programs, however, did offer one or more courses that were partly devoted to ethics instruction. Their survey also revealed that the four ethical issues that received the most attention were subjects' confidentiality, subjects' right of withdrawal, informed consent, and dealing with institutional review boards.

Specific Ethical Problems

The following subsections discuss some of the common areas where mass media researchers might encounter ethical dilemmas.

Voluntary Participation and Informed Consent

An individual is entitled to decline to participate in any research project or to terminate participation at any time. Participation in an experiment, survey, or focus group is always voluntary, and any form of coercion is unacceptable. Researchers who are in a position of authority over subjects (as when a teacher/researcher hands questionnaires to university students) should be especially sensitive to implied coercion: Even though the researcher might tell the class that failure to participate will not affect grades, many students may not believe this. In such a situation, it is better to keep the questionnaires anonymous and for the person in authority to be absent from the room while the survey is administered.

Voluntary participation is not a pressing ethical issue in mail and telephone surveys because respondents are free to hang up the phone or to throw away the questionnaire. Nonetheless, a researcher should not attempt to induce subjects to participate by misrepresenting the organization sponsoring the research or by exaggerating its purpose or importance. For example, telephone interviewers should not be instructed to identify themselves as representatives of the "Department of Information" to mislead people into thinking the survey is government-sponsored. Likewise, mail questionnaires should not be constructed to mimic census forms, tax returns, Social Security questionnaires, or other official government forms.

Closely related to voluntary participation is the notion of **informed consent.** For people to volunteer for a research project, they need to know enough about the project to make an intelligent choice. Researchers have the responsibility to inform potential subjects or respondents of all features of the project that can reasonably be expected to influence participation. Respondents should understand that an interview may take as long as 45 minutes, that a second interview is required, or that after completing a mail questionnaire they may be singled out for a telephone interview.

In an experiment, informed consent means that potential subjects must be warned of any possible discomfort or unpleasantness that might be involved. Subjects should be told if they are to receive or administer electric shocks, be subjected to unpleasant audio or visual stimuli, or undergo any procedure that might cause concern. Any unusual measurement techniques that may be used must be described. Researchers have an obligation to answer candidly and truthfully, as far as possible, all the participants' questions about the research.

Experiments that involve deception (as described in the next subsection) cause special problems about obtaining informed consent. If deception is absolutely necessary to conduct an experiment, is the experimenter obligated to inform subjects that they may be deceived during the upcoming experiment? Will such a disclosure affect participation in the experiment? Will it also affect the experimental results? Should the researcher compromise by telling all potential subjects that deception will be involved for some participants but not for others?

Another problem is deciding exactly how much information about a project a researcher must disclose in seeking informed consent. Is it enough to explain that the experiment involves rating commercials, or is it necessary to add that the experiment is designed to test whether subjects with high IQs prefer different commercials from those with low IQs? Obviously, in some situations the researcher cannot reveal everything about the project for fear of contaminating the results. For example, if the goal of the research is to examine the influence of peer pressure on commercial evaluations, alerting the subjects to this facet of the investigation might change their behavior in the experiment.

Problems might occur in research that examines the impact of mass media in non-literate communities—for example, the research subjects might not comprehend what they were told regarding the proposed investigation. Even in literate societies, many people fail to understand the implications for confidentiality of the storage of survey data on computer disks. Moreover, an investigator might not have realized in advance that some subjects would find part of an experiment or survey emotionally disturbing.

In 1992 the American Psychological Association (APA) released its statement on "Ethical Principles of Psychologists and Code of Conduct," which addresses a wide range of ethical issues of relevance to that discipline. Since mass communication researchers face many of the same ethical issues faced by psychologists, it seems useful to quote from that document several provisions concerning informed consent:

- Researchers should use language understandable to participants to obtain consent.
- Researchers should tell participants they can withdraw from the research.
- Researchers should inform participants of the important things that might affect their decision (such as discomfort and loss of confidentiality).
- If participation in a research project is a course requirement or an opportunity

for extra credit, students should be given a choice of alternative activities.

- Prior consent must be obtained if participants will be filmed, taped, or recorded in any form unless the research involves natural observation in public places.

Examine the APA's Code of Conduct at *www.apa.org/ethics/code.* As of mid-2001, the APA was working on a revised version of this document.

Research findings provide some indication of what research participants should be told in order to ensure informed consent. Epstein, Suedefeld, and Silverstein (1973) found that subjects wanted a general description of the experiment and what was expected of them; they wanted to know whether danger was involved, how long the experiment would last, and the experiment's purpose. As for informed consent and survey participation, Sobal (1984) found wide variation among researchers about what to tell respondents in the survey introduction. Almost all introductions identified the research organization and the interviewer by name and described the research topic. Less frequently mentioned in introductions were the sponsor of the research and guarantees of confidentiality or anonymity. Few survey introductions mentioned the length of the survey or that participation was voluntary. Greenberg and Garramone (1989) reported the results of a survey of 201 mass media researchers that disclosed that 96% usually provided guaranteed confidentiality of results, 92% usually named the sponsoring organization, 66% usually told respondents that participation is voluntary, and 61% usually disclosed the length of the questionnaire. Brody, Gluck, and Aragon (1997) surveyed subjects in psychological experiments and found that 41% of them had had negative experiences. A major reason for the negative experience was the invasiveness of the experiment, which suggests that the unpleasant aspects of the research were not well explained during the informed consent process.

Finally, one must consider the form of the consent to be obtained. Written consent is a requirement in certain government-sponsored research programs and may also be required by many university research review committees, as discussed later in this section in connection with guidelines promulgated by the federal government. In several generally recognized situations, however, signed forms are regarded as impractical. These include telephone surveys, mail surveys, personal interviews, and cases in which the signed form itself might represent an occasion for breach of confidentiality. For example, a respondent who has been promised anonymity as an inducement to participate in a face-to-face interview might be suspicious if asked to sign a consent form after the interview. In these circumstances, the fact that the respondent agreed to participate is taken as implied consent.

As a general rule, the greater the risk of potential harm to subjects, the greater the need to obtain a consent statement. Figure 3.1 is an example of a typical consent form.

Concealment and Deception

Concealment and deception are encountered most frequently in experimental research. **Concealment** is the withholding of certain information from the subjects; **deception** is deliberately providing false information. Both practices raise ethical problems. The difficulty in obtaining consent has already been mentioned. A second problem derives from the general feeling that it is wrong for experimenters to lie to or otherwise deceive subjects.

Many critics argue that deception transforms a subject from a human being into a manipulated object and is therefore demeaning to the participant. Moreover, once subjects have been deceived, they are likely to

Figure 3.1 *Example of a Typical Consent Form*

The purpose of this research is to explore possible relationships between watching daytime TV talk shows and perceptions of social reality. You will be asked questions about your general TV viewing, your viewing of daytime talk shows and your attitudes about interpersonal relationships. This questionnaire will take about 20 minutes to complete. Please answer every question as accurately as possible. Participation is voluntary. Your grades will not be affected if you choose not to participate. Your participation will be anonymous. No discomfort, stress, or risks are anticipated.

I agree to participate in the research entitled "Talk Show Viewing and Social Reality" conducted by ______________________________, in the Department of Mass Communication at the University of ______________________________, (telephone number ________________). I understand that this participation is entirely voluntary. I can withdraw my consent at any time without penalty and have the results of this participation, to the extent that they can be identified as mine, returned to me, removed from the research record, or destroyed.

______________________________ ______________________________

Signature of Researcher (date) Signature of Participant (date)

Research at the University of ______________________ that involves human participants is overseen by the Institutional Review Board. Questions or problems regarding your rights as a participant should be addressed to ____________________________________, (telephone number ____________. email address __________________________).

expect to be deceived again in other research projects. At least two research studies seem to suggest that this concern is valid. Stricker and Messick (1967) reported finding a high incidence of suspicion among subjects of high school age after they had been deceived. Fillenbaum (1966) found that one-third to one-half of subjects were suspicious at the beginning of an experiment after having experienced deception in a prior research project.

On the other hand, some researchers argue that certain studies could not be conducted at all without the use of deception. They use the utilitarian approach to argue that the harm done to those who are deceived is outweighed by the benefits of the research to scientific knowledge. Indeed, Christensen (1988) suggests that it may be immoral to fail to investigate important areas that cannot be investigated without the use of deception. He also argues that much of the sentiment against deception in research exists because deception has been analyzed only from the viewpoint of abstract moral philosophy. The subjects who were "deceived" in many experiments did not perceive what was done to them as deception but viewed it as a necessary element in the research procedure. Christensen illustrates the relativistic approach when he suggests that any decision regarding the use of deception should take into account the context and aim of the deception. Research suggests that subjects are most disturbed when deception violates their privacy or increases their risk of harm.

Obviously, deception is not a technique that should be used indiscriminately. Kelman (1967) suggests that before the investigator settles on deception as an experimental tactic, three questions should be examined:

1. How significant is the proposed study?
2. Are alternative procedures available that would provide the same information?
3. How severe is the deception? (It is one thing to tell subjects that the experimentally constructed message they are reading was taken from the *New York Times;* it is another to report that the test a subject has just completed was designed to measure latent suicidal tendencies.)

Another set of criteria is put forth by Elms (1982), who suggests five necessary and sufficient conditions under which deception can be considered ethically justified in social science research:

1. When there is no other feasible way to obtain the desired information
2. When the likely benefits substantially outweigh the likely harm
3. When subjects are given the option to withdraw at any time without penalty
4. When any physical or psychological harm to subjects is temporary
5. When subjects are debriefed about all substantial deception and the research procedures are made available for public review

Together the suggestions of Kelman and Elms offer researchers good advice for the planning stages of investigations.

When an experiment is concluded, especially one involving concealment or deception, it is the responsibility of the investigator to debrief subjects. Debriefing should be thorough enough to remove any lasting effects that might have been created by the experimental manipulation or by any other aspect of the experiment. Subjects' questions should be answered and the potential value of the experiment stressed. How common is debriefing among mass media researchers? In the survey cited in Greenberg and Garramone (1989), 71% of the researchers reported they usually debrief subjects, 19% debrief sometimes, and 10% rarely or never debrief subjects. Although it is an ethical requirement of most experiments, the practice of debriefing has yet to be embraced by all investigators.

The APA's 1992 statement of principles contains the following provisions concerning deception:

- Deception should not be used unless it is justified by the study's scientific value and other nondeceptive techniques are not feasible.
- Subjects should never be deceived about factors that might have an impact on their informed consent.
- If deception is used, subjects should be debriefed as promptly as possible.

The American Sociological Association's guidelines for research contain similar language:

- Sociologists do not use deceptive techniques unless (1) they have determined that their use will not be harmful to research participants; is justified by the study's prospective scientific, educational, or applied value; and that equally effective alternative procedures that do not use deception are not feasible, and (2) unless they have obtained the approval of institutional review boards.
- Sociologists never deceive research participants about significant aspects of the research that would affect their willingness to participate, such as physical risks, discomfort, or unpleasant emotional experiences.

No data are available on how often deception is used in mass media research. Some information, however, is available from the psychology field. In a study of 23 years of articles published in a leading psychology journal,

Sieber (1995) found that 66% of all studies published in 1969 used deception, compared to 47% in 1992. Since a good deal of psychological research utilizes the experimental approach (see Chapter 10), a strategy not used nearly as often in mass communication research, the percentages for media research would probably be significantly lower.

Protection of Privacy

The problem of protecting the privacy of participants arises more often in field observation and survey research than in laboratory studies. In field studies, observers may study people in public places without their knowledge (for example, individuals watching TV at an airport lounge). The more public the place, the less a person has an expectation of privacy and the fewer ethical problems are encountered. There are, however, some public situations that present ethical concerns. Is it ethical, for example, for a researcher to pretend to browse in a video rental store when in fact the researcher is observing who rents pornographic videos? What about eavesdropping on people's dinner conversations to determine how often news topics are discussed? To minimize ethical problems, a researcher should violate privacy only to the minimum degree needed to gather the data.

When they take a survey, respondents have a right to know whether their privacy will be maintained and who will have access to the information they provide. There are two ways to guarantee privacy: by assuring anonymity and by assuring confidentiality. A promise of **anonymity** is a guarantee that a given respondent cannot possibly be linked to any particular response. In many research projects, anonymity is an advantage because it encourages respondents to be honest and candid in their answers. Strictly speaking, personal and telephone interviews cannot be anonymous because the researcher can link a given questionnaire to a specific person, household, or telephone number. In such instances, the researcher should promise **confidentiality;** that is, respondents should be assured that even though they can be identified as individuals, their names will never be publicly associated with the information they provide. A researcher should never use "anonymous" in a way that is or seems to be synonymous with "confidential."

Additionally, respondents should be told who *will* have access to the information they provide. The researcher's responsibility for assuring confidentiality does not end once the data have been analyzed and the study concluded. Questionnaires that identify persons by name should not be stored in public places, nor should other researchers be given permission to examine confidential data unless all identifying marks have been obliterated. The APA's statement does not contain much guidance on issues of privacy and confidentiality. It does say that researchers should inform subjects if they are planning to share or use data that are personally identifiable. The American Sociological Association's guidelines are more detailed. In part they include the following provisions:

- Sociologists take reasonable precautions to protect the confidentiality rights of research participants, students, employees, clients, or others.
- Confidential information provided by research participants, students, employees, clients, or others is treated as such by sociologists even if there is no legal protection or privilege to do so. Sociologists have an obligation to protect confidential information, and not allow information gained in confidence from being used in ways that would unfairly compromise research participants, students, employees, clients, or others.
- Sociologists may confront unanticipated circumstances when they become

aware of information that is clearly health- or life-threatening to research participants, students, employees, clients, or others. In these cases, sociologists balance the importance of guarantees of confidentiality with other principles in this Code of Ethics, standards of conduct, and applicable law.

- Confidentiality is not required with respect to observations in public places, activities conducted in public, or other settings where no rules of privacy are provided by law or custom. Similarly, confidentiality is not required in the case of information available from public records.

Federal Regulations Concerning Research

In 1971 the Department of Health, Education, and Welfare (HEW) drafted rules for obtaining informed consent from research participants, which included full documentation of informed consent procedures. In addition, the government set up a system of **institutional review boards** (IRBs) to safeguard the rights of human subjects. In 1995 there were more than 700 IRBs at medical schools, colleges, universities, hospitals, and other institutions. At most universities, IRBs have become part of the permanent bureaucracy. They hold regular meetings and have developed standardized forms that must accompany research proposals that involve human subjects or respondents. For a description of how a typical IRB operates, consult *www.nova.edu/cwis/ogc/intro*.

In 1981 the Department of Health and Human Services (HHS, successor to HEW) softened its regulations concerning social science research. The department's *Policy for the Protection of Human Research Subjects* exempts studies that use existing public data, research in educational settings about new instructional techniques, research involving the use of anonymous education tests, and survey, interview, and observational research in public places, provided the subjects are not identified and sensitive information is not collected. Signed consent forms are deemed unnecessary if the research presents only a minimal risk of harm to subjects and involves no procedures for which written consent is required outside the research context. This means that signed consent forms are no longer necessary in the interview situation because a person does not usually seek written consent before asking a question. Although the new guidelines apparently exempt most nonexperimental social science research from federal regulation, IRBs at some institutions still review all research proposals that involve human subjects, and some IRBs still follow the old HEW standards. In fact, some IRB regulations are even more stringent than the federal guidelines. As a practical matter, a researcher should always build a little more time into the research schedule to accommodate IRB procedures.

You can read the online version of the HHS's Office for Human Research Protections guidelines at *http://ohrp.osophs.dhhs.gov/irb/irb_guidebook*.

Ethics in Data Analysis and Reporting

Researchers are responsible for maintaining professional standards in analyzing and reporting their data. The ethical guidelines in this area are less controversial and more clear-cut. One cardinal rule is that researchers have a moral and ethical obligation to refrain from tampering with data: Questionnaire responses and experimental observations may not be fabricated, altered, or discarded. Similarly, researchers are expected to exercise reasonable care in processing the data to guard against needless errors that might affect the results.

Another universal ethical principle is that authors should not plagiarize. The work of

AN INSIDE LOOK
Ethical Matters

The death of a research subject at Johns Hopkins sparked new interest in the adequacy of the IRBs that examine research projects for compliance with federal and university regulations. An examination of the IRB process discovered that many IRBs were overburdened with stacks of research applications and did not give many proposals the degree of scrutiny that may have been required.

In late 2001, E. Greg Koski, the new director of the U.S. Office of Human Research Protections (OHRP), stated that the U.S. government's system for protecting human subjects needed some significant changes. At the top of the list of possible reforms was a call to universities and institutions to voluntarily improve their protections of research subjects. In addition, the new director recommended that researchers who do not adequately protect volunteers should be barred from doing research. Koski also urged that more uniform national standards be developed to guide IRBs at various institutions and that more nonscientists and members of the general public be added to IRBs.

In a related development, the American Association of University Professors proposed that universities recruit more social scientists to serve on IRBs. Some researchers have complained that many boards are dominated by members from the biological and physical sciences, who have little experience with the kind of research done by social scientists. This concern was noted by the new director of the OHRP, who stated that the concerns of social scientists would be a top priority.

someone else should not be reproduced without giving proper credit to the original author. Somewhat related, only those individuals who contribute significantly to a research project should be given authorship credit. This last statement addresses the problem of piggybacking, when a subordinate is pressured by someone in authority to include the superior's name on a manuscript even though the superior had little input into the finished product. The definition of a "significant contribution" might be fuzzy at times; generally, however, to be listed as an author, a person should play a major role in conceptualizing, analyzing, or writing the final document.

Another problem that sometimes crops up involves the order of authorship of an article or a report. If there are two or more researchers involved, who gets listed as first author ("top billing")? Ideally, all those involved should decide upon the order of authorship at the beginning of a project, subject to later revision if changes in contribution should happen. Usually, the first author is the one who made the biggest contribution to the work.

Finally, special problems are involved when university faculty do research with students. (This topic is discussed later in the chapter.)

Researchers should never conceal information that might influence the interpretation of their findings. For example, if 2 weeks elapsed between the testing of an experimental group and the testing of a control group, this delay should be reported so that other researchers can discount the effects of history and maturation on the results. Every research report should contain a full and complete description of method, particularly any departure from standard procedures.

Since science is a public activity, researchers have an ethical obligation to share their findings and methods with other researchers. All questionnaires, experimental materials, measurement instruments, instructions to subjects, and other relevant items should be made available to those who wish to examine them.

Finally, all investigators are under an ethical obligation to draw conclusions from their data that are consistent with those data. Interpretations should not be stretched or distorted to fit a personal point of view or a favorite theory, or to gain or maintain a client's favor. Nor should researchers attribute greater significance or credibility to their data than the data justify. For example, when analyzing correlation coefficients obtained from a large sample, a researcher could achieve statistical significance with an r of only, for example, .10. It would be perfectly acceptable to report a statistically significant result in this case, but the investigator should also mention that the predictive utility of the correlation is not large and, specifically, that it explains only 1% of the total variation. In short, researchers should report their results with candor and honesty.

Ethics in the Publication Process

Publishing the results of research in scholarly journals is an important part of the process of scientific inquiry. Science is a public activity, and publication is the most efficient way to share research knowledge. In addition, success in the academic profession is often tied to a successful publication record. Consequently, certain ethical guidelines are usually followed with regard to publication procedures. From the perspective of the researcher seeking to submit an article for publication, the first ethical guideline comes into play when the article is ready to be sent off for review. The researcher should submit the proposed article to only one journal at a time because simultaneous submission to several sources is inefficient and wasteful. When an article is submitted for review to an academic journal, it is usually sent to two, three, or more reviewers for evaluation. Simultaneous submission means that several sets of referees spend their time pointing out the same problems and difficulties that could have been reported by a single set. This duplication of effort is unnecessary and might delay consideration of other articles waiting for review.

A related ethical problem concerns attempts to publish nearly identical or highly similar articles based on the same data set. For example, suppose a researcher has data on the communication patterns in a large organization. The investigator writes up one article emphasizing the communication angle for a communication journal and a second article with a management slant for a business journal. Both articles draw upon the same database and contain comparable results. Is this practice ethical? This is not an easy question to answer. Some journal editors apparently do not approve of writing multiple papers from the same data; others suggest that this practice is acceptable, provided submissions are made to journals that do not have overlapping audiences. In addition, there is the sticky question of how different one manuscript has to be from another in order to be considered a separate entity. Campbell (1987) discusses these and other vexing issues.

On the other side of the coin, journal editors and reviewers have ethical obligations to those who submit manuscripts to be evaluated. Editors and reviewers should not let the decision process take an inordinate amount of time; a prompt and timely decision is owed to all contributors. (Most editors of mass communication journals try to notify their contributors of their decision within 3 months.) Reviewers should try to provide positive and helpful reviews; they should not do "hatchet jobs" on articles submitted to them. Moreover, reviewers should not unjustly squelch manuscripts that argue against one of their pet ideas or contradict or challenge some of their own research. Each contributor to a journal should receive an objective and impartial review. Neither should reviewers quibble needlessly over minor points in an article or demand unreasonable changes. Reviewers also owe contributors consistency. Authors find it frustrating to revise their manuscripts according to a reviewer's wishes only to find that, on a second reading, the reviewer has a change of mind and prefers the original version.

Ryan and Martinson (1999) surveyed nearly 100 scholars whose articles had appeared in two mass communication journals during the mid-1990s. They found that the three biggest complaints of these authors were (1) editors who didn't reach a decision about a manuscript in a reasonable amount of time; (2) editors who blamed delays on reviewers; and (3) reviewers who did not have expertise in the area represented by the manuscript.

A Professional Code of Ethics

Formalized codes of ethics have yet to be developed by all professional associations involved in mass media research. One organization that has developed a code is the American Association for Public Opinion Research (shown in the box on page 79).

Ethical Problems of Student-Faculty Research

Schiff and Ryan (1996) list several ethical dilemmas that can occur in a college setting, including using undergraduate classes in research and claiming joint authorship of articles based on student theses and dissertations. With regard to the first problem, they found that about 36% of a sample of 138 faculty members who had recently chaired thesis or dissertation committees reported that using a research class to collect data for a thesis or dissertation was unethical and that 65% thought it was unethical to require undergraduate classes to participate in thesis or dissertation research. (Note that Schiff and Ryan were investigating the ethics involved in using undergraduates for dissertation or thesis research—not research projects conducted by faculty members. Presumably, however, the numbers should be similar.)

Schiff and Ryan found uniform ethical norms concerning authorship of articles stemming from theses and dissertations. About 86% of the respondents stated that requiring students to list a professor as coauthor on any article stemming from the thesis or dissertation as a condition for directing the project was unethical.

The APA's Ethics Committee provides some guidelines with regard to the joint authorship of articles based on a dissertation or thesis:

- The dissertation adviser may receive only second authorship.
- Secondary authorship for the adviser may be considered obligatory if the adviser supplies the database, designates variables, or makes important interpretive contributions.
- If the adviser suggests the general topic, is significantly involved in the design or instrumentation of the project, or substantially contributes to the writing, then the student may offer the adviser second authorship as a courtesy.
- If the adviser offered only financial aid, facilities, and periodic critiques, then secondary authorship is inappropriate.

Some researchers, however, argue that a dissertation should comprise original and independent work and that involvement by the researcher sufficient to merit co-authorship may be too much involvement (Audi, 1990).

American Association for Public Opinion Research Code of Professional Ethics and Practices

I. Principles of Professional Practice in Conduct of Our Work

A. We shall exercise due care in gathering and processing data, taking all reasonable steps to assure the accuracy of results.

B. We shall exercise due care in the development of research designs and in the analysis of data.

1. We shall recommend and employ only research tools and methods of analysis which, in our professional judgment, are well suited to the research problem at hand.
2. We shall not select research tools and methods of analysis because of their capacity to yield a misleading conclusion.
3. We shall not knowingly make interpretations of research results, nor shall we tacitly permit interpretations, which are inconsistent with the data available.
4. We shall not knowingly imply that interpretations should be accorded greater confidence than the data actually warrant.

C. We shall describe our findings and methods accurately and in appropriate detail in all research reports.

II. Principles of Professional Responsibility in Our Dealings with People

A. The Public

1. We shall cooperate with legally authorized representatives of the public by describing the methods used in our studies.
2. When we become aware of the appearance in public of serious distortions of our research we shall publicly disclose what is required to correct the distortions.

B. Clients and Sponsors

1. When undertaking work for a private client we shall hold confidential all proprietary information obtained about the client's business affairs and about the finding of research conducted for the client, except when the dissemination of the information is expressly authorized by the client or becomes necessary under terms of Section II-A-2.
2. We shall be mindful of the limitations of our techniques and facilities and shall accept only those research assignments which can be accomplished within these limitations.

C. The Profession

1. We shall not cite our membership in the Association as evidence of professional competence, since the Association does not so certify any persons or organizations.
2. We recognize our responsibility to contribute to the science of public opinion research and to disseminate as freely as possible the ideas and findings which emerge from our research.

D. The Respondent

1. We shall not lie to survey respondents or use practices and methods which abuse, coerce, or humiliate them.
2. Unless the respondent waives confidentiality for specified uses, we shall hold as privileged and confidential all information that tends to identify a respondent with his or her responses. We shall also not disclose the names of respondents for nonresearch purposes.

AN INSIDE LOOK

Ethics: Broadcast Research

A few years ago, the senior author of this text was contacted by a radio station general manager (GM) who stated, "My morning show host is a pain in the neck and I want to fire him. I'd like you to conduct a telephone study to back up my opinions." What would you say to the GM? Would you take the job?

The Rights of Students As Research Participants

College students provide much of the data in social science research. In psychology, for example, more than 70% of studies use students (Korn, 1988). In fact, it is the rare liberal arts major who has not participated in (or had a request to participate in) social science research. The ethical dimensions of this situation have not been overlooked. Korn (1988) suggests a "bill of rights" for students who agree to be research subjects:

- Participants should know the general purpose of the study and what they will be expected to do. Beyond this, they should be told everything a reasonable person would want to know in order to participate.
- Participants have the right to withdraw from a study at any time after beginning participation in the research.
- Participants should expect to receive benefits that outweigh the costs or risks involved. To achieve the educational benefit, participants have the right to ask questions and to receive clear, honest answers. If they don't receive what was promised, they have the right to remove their data from the study.
- Participants have the right to expect that anything done or said during their participation in a study will remain anonymous or confidential, unless they specifically agree to give up this right.
- Participants have the right to decline to participate in any study and may not be coerced into research. When learning about research is a course requirement, an equivalent alternative to participation should be available.
- Participants have the right to know when they have been deceived in a study and why the deception was used. If the deception seems unreasonable, participants have the right to withhold their data.
- When any of these rights is violated or participants have objections about a study, they have the right and responsibility to inform the appropriate university officials.

▪ ▪ ▪ Summary

Ethical considerations in conducting research should not be overlooked. Nearly every research study could affect subjects in some way, either psychologically or physically. Researchers who deal with human subjects must ensure that all precautions are taken to avoid any potential harm to subjects. This includes carefully planning a study and debriefing subjects upon completion of a project.

Key Terms

Anonymity
Autonomy
Beneficence
Categorical imperative
Concealment
Confidentiality
Deception
Deontological theories
Ethics
Informed consent
Institutional review boards
Justice
Nonmaleficence
Relativism
Relativistic theories
Teleological theories
Utilitarianism
Voluntary participation

Using the Internet

The Internet is full of articles and discussions of research ethics. The importance of ethics in research became an immediate concern in late 2001, when genetics researchers publicized that they had successfully cloned a human cell. In most cases, the condemnation of the research was not based on what was known about the research, but what the research implicated.

While genetics research may involve topics that are more volatile than those that mass media researchers may encounter, it is still necessary to consider the ethical nature of any mass media research study conducted.

Review some of the information about ethics that is available on the Internet. What would you do if your study is condemned as unethical?

Questions and Problems for Further Investigation

1. Using the five examples on page 66, suggest alternative ways of conducting each study that would be ethically acceptable.
2. In your opinion, what types of media research are unfair to respondents? What types of studies encroach on the guidelines discussed in this chapter?
3. In your opinion, is it wrong for researchers to give respondents the impression that they are being recruited for a particular study when the researchers actually have another purpose in mind? What are the limits to this behavior?
4. The World Wide Web has raised new issues concerning research and plagiarism. If you are using InfoTrac College Edition, look for articles that discuss this growing problem.

For additional information on these and related topics, see

http://www.wimmerdominick.com

References and Suggested Readings

Audi, R. (1990). The ethics of graduate teaching. In S. M. Cahn (Ed.), *Morality, responsibility and the university.* Philadelphia: Temple University Press.

Beauchamp, T., Faden, R., Wallace, R. J., & Walters, L. (Eds.). (1982). *Ethical issues in social science research.* Baltimore: Johns Hopkins University Press.

Bower, R., & deGasparis, P. (1978). *Ethics in social research.* New York: Praeger.

Brody, J. L., Gluck, J. P., & Aragon, A. (1997). Participants' understanding of the process of psychological research: Informed consent. *Ethics and Behavior,* 7(4), 285–298.

Campbell, D. J. (1987). Ethical issues in the publication process. In S. L. Payne & B. H. Charnov (Eds.), *Ethical problems for academic professionals.* Springfield, IL: Charles C Thomas.

Christensen, L. (1988). Deception in psychological research. *Personality and Social Psychology Bulletin,* 14(4), 664–675.

Cook, S. (1976). Ethical issues in the conduct of research in social relations. In C. Sellitz, L. Wrightsman, & S. Cook (Eds.), *Research methods in social relations.* New York: Holt, Rinehart & Winston.

Elmes, D. G., Kantowitz, B. H., & Roediger, H. L. (1995). *Research methods in psychology* (5th ed.). New York: West Publishing.

Elms, A. (1982). Keeping deception honest. In T. Beauchamp, R. Faden, R. J. Wallace, & L. Walters (Eds.), *Ethical issues in social science research.* Baltimore: Johns Hopkins University Press.

Epstein, Y., Suedefeld, P., & Silverstein, S. (1973). The experimental contract. *American Psychologist,* 28, 212–221.

Fillenbaum, S. (1966). Prior deception and subsequent experimental performance. *Journal of Personality and Social Psychology,* 4, 532–537.

Greenberg, B. S., & Garramone, G. M. (1989). Ethical issues in mass communication research. In G. H.

Stempel & B. H. Westley (Eds.), *Research methods in mass communication* (2nd ed.). Englewood Cliffs, NJ: Prentice-Hall.

Jones, J. H. (1981). *Bad blood: The Tuskegee syphilis experiment.* New York: Free Press.

Kelman, H. (1967). Human use of human subjects: The problem of deception in social psychological experiments. *Psychological Bulletin,* 67, 111.

Kelman, H. (1982). Ethical issues in different social science methods. In T. Beauchamp, R. Faden, R. J. Wallace, & L. Walters (Eds.), *Ethical issues in social science research.* Baltimore: Johns Hopkins University Press.

Korn, J. H. (1988). Students' roles, rights, and responsibilities as research participants. *Teaching of Psychology,* 15(2), 74–78.

Mann, T. (1994). Informed consent for psychological research. *Psychological Science,* 5(3), 140–143.

McEuen, V., Gordon, R., & Todd-Mancillas, W. (1990). A survey of doctoral education in communication research ethics. *Communication Quarterly,* 38(3), 281–290.

Ryan, M., & Martinson, D. L. (1999). Perceived problems in evaluation of mass communication scholarship. *Journalism and Mass Communication Educator,* 54(1), 69–78.

Saslow, C. (1994). *Basic research methods.* New York: McGraw-Hill.

Schiff, F., & Ryan, M. (1996). Ethical problems in advising theses and dissertations. *Journalism and Mass Communication Educator,* 51(1), 23–35.

Sieber, J. (1992). *Planning ethically responsible research.* Newbury Park, CA: Sage.

Sieber, J. (1995). Deception methods in psychology. *Ethics and Behavior,* 5(1), 67–85.

Sobal, J. (1984). The content of survey introductions and the provision of informed consent. *Public Opinion Quarterly,* 48(4), 788–793.

Stricker, L., & Messick, J. (1967). The true deceiver. *Psychological Bulletin,* 68, 1320.

Thomas, S. B., & Quinn, S. C. (1981). The Tuskegee syphilis study. *American Journal of Public Health,* 81(4), 1498–1505.

Chapter 4

Sampling

- *Population and Sample*
- *Probability and Nonprobability Samples*
- *Sample Size*
- *Sampling Error*

Summary

Key Terms

Using the Internet

Questions and Problems for Further Investigation

References and Suggested Readings

When it comes to research, we live in a world of small sample statistics. This chapter describes the basics of the sampling methods used in mass media research. However, because sampling theory has become a distinct discipline in itself, there are some studies, such as nationwide surveys, that require consultation of more technical discussions of sampling (for example, Cochran, 1977; Kish, 1965).

Population and Sample

One goal of scientific research is to describe the nature of a **population**—*a group or class of subjects, variables, concepts, or phenomena.* In some cases, an entire class or group is investigated, as in a study of prime-time television programs during the week of September 10–16. The process of examining every member of such a population is called a **census.** In many situations, however, an entire population cannot be examined due to time and resource constraints. Studying every member of a population is also generally cost-prohibitive and may, in fact, confound the research because measurements of large numbers of people often affect measurement quality.

The usual procedure in these instances is to take a sample from the population. A **sample** is a *subset of the population that is representative of the entire population.* An important word in this definition is representative. A sample that is not representative of the population, regardless of its size, is inadequate for testing purposes because the results cannot be generalized.

The sample selection process is illustrated using a Venn diagram (see Figure 4.1); the population is represented by the larger of the two circles. A census would test or measure every element in the population (A), whereas a sample would measure or test a segment of the population (A_1). Although in Figure 4.1 it might seem that the sample is drawn from only one portion of the popula-

Figure 4.1 *A Venn Diagram. As Used in the Process of Sample Selection*

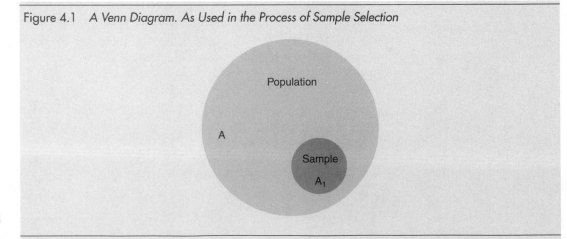

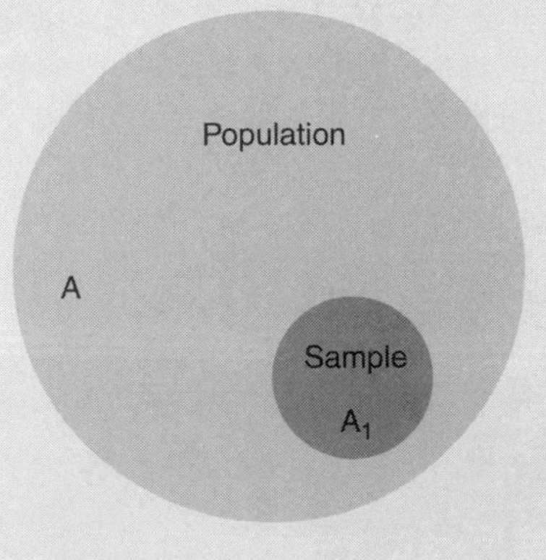

AN INSIDE LOOK

Measurement Error

A recent example of measurement error, and one that will certainly be discussed for decades, is the ballot counting fiasco in Florida for the 2000 presidential race between George W. Bush and Al Gore. As of this writing, several organizations were still involved in attempting to find the real vote count in Florida. Search the Internet for information about this topic to uncover the latest results.

tion, it is actually selected from every portion. If a sample is chosen according to proper guidelines and is representative of the population, then the results from a study using the sample can be generalized to the population. The results must be generalized with some caution, however, because of the error that is inherent in all sample-selection methods. Theoretically, when a population is studied, only **measurement error** (that is, inconsistencies produced by the instrument used) is present. But when a sample is drawn from the population, the procedure introduces the likelihood of **sampling error** (that is, the degree to which measurements of the units or subjects selected differ from those of the population as a whole). Because a sample does not provide the exact data that a population would, the potential error must be taken into account.

A classic example of how sampling error can affect the results of a research study occurred during the 1936 presidential campaign. *Literary Digest* had predicted, based on the results of a sample survey, that Alf Landon would beat Franklin D. Roosevelt. Although the *Literary Digest* sample included more than a million voters, it was composed mainly of affluent Republicans. Consequently, it inaccurately represented the population of eligible voters in the election. The researchers who conducted the study had failed to consider the population **parameters** (characteristics) before selecting their sample. Of course, FDR was reelected in 1936, and it may be no coincidence that the *Literary Digest* went out of business shortly thereafter.

Have the polls improved? The following list shows the final poll results from several national polls conducted for the 2000 presidential contest between George W. Bush (Republican) and Al Gore (Democrat).

Source	Bush%	Gore%
Actual Vote	48	48
ABC	48	45
CBS	44	45
CNN/USA Today/Gallup	48	46
Harris	47	47
NBC/Wall Street Journal	47	44
Newsweek	45	43
Reuters/MSNBC	46	48
Washington Post	48	45

The polling results shows that researchers have become better at predicting the outcome of elections. Considering the margin of error (about $\pm 3.0\%$ to $\pm 4.0\%$), the polls accurately predicted the final election results.

▪ Probability and Nonprobability Samples

A **probability sample** is selected according to mathematical guidelines whereby each unit's

AN INSIDE LOOK
Sampling

Sampling is an important part of all research, but sampling is often misunderstood by beginning researchers. The usual question is, "How can 500 people represent the opinions and attitudes of people in New York (or any other city)?" If you are a beginner, keep this in mind: If sampling is conducted correctly, the sample will usually represent the characteristics of that population.

The most important part of any sampling procedure is to avoid bias of any kind—each respondent should have an equal chance of being selected. The **sampling design** (scheme used to select respondents) *must* be free from bias.

chance for selection is known. A **nonprobability sample** does not follow the guidelines of mathematical probability. However, the most significant characteristic distinguishing the two types of samples is that probability sampling allows researchers to calculate the amount of sampling error present in a research study; nonprobability sampling does not.

There are four issues to consider when deciding whether to use a probability or a nonprobability sample:

- *Purpose of the study.* Some research studies are not designed to be generalized to the population but rather to investigate variable relationships or collect exploratory data for designing questionnaires or measurement instruments. A nonprobability sample is often appropriate in these situations.
- *Cost versus value.* The sample should produce the greatest value for the least investment. If the cost of a probability sample is too high in relation to the type and quality of information collected, then a nonprobability sample is a possible alternative.
- *Time constraints.* In many cases researchers collecting preliminary information operate under time constraints imposed by sponsoring agencies, management directives, or publication guidelines. Since probability sampling is often time-consuming, a nonprobability sample may meet the need temporarily.
- *Amount of acceptable error.* In preliminary or pilot studies, where error control is not a prime concern, a nonprobability sample is usually adequate.

Although nonprobability samples may have merit in some cases, it is always best to use a probability sample when a study is conducted to support or refute a significant research question or a hypothesis and the results will be generalized to the population.

Probability sampling generally incorporates some type of systematic selection procedure, such as a table of random numbers, to ensure that each unit has an equal chance of being selected. However, it does not always guarantee a representative sample from the population, even when systematic selection is followed. It is possible to randomly select 50 members of the student body at a university in order to determine the average number of hours the students spend watching television during a typical week and, by extraordinary coincidence, end up with 50 students who do not own a TV set. Such an event is unlikely, but possible, and this underscores the need to replicate any study.

AN INSIDE LOOK
Volunteer Samples

Some people involved in research claim that the worry about volunteer samples is a waste of time. Their claim is that all research conducted in mass media (as well as all behavioral research) uses volunteer samples all the time—that in fact there are probably few, if any, behavioral research projects conducted with a truly random sample. Why? Because respondents in research projects must agree to participate. We cannot force a person to answer questions. Some critics say that because researchers ask questions of only those people who agree (volunteer) to answer them, the argument about using a random sample is moot.

Types of Nonprobability Samples

Mass media researchers frequently use nonprobability sampling, particularly in the form of available samples, samples using volunteer subjects, and purposive samples. Mall intercepts use nonprobability sampling. An **available sample** (also known as a **convenience sample**) is a collection of readily accessible subjects for study, such as a group of students enrolled in an introductory mass media course or shoppers in a mall. Although available samples can be helpful in collecting exploratory information and may produce useful data in some instances, the samples are problematic because they contain unknown quantities of error. Researchers need to consider the positive and negative qualities of available samples before using them in a research study.

Available samples are the subject of heated debate in many research fields. Critics argue that regardless of what results they generate, available samples do not represent the population and therefore have no external validity. Proponents of using available samples claim that if a phenomenon, characteristic, or trait does in fact exist, then it should exist in any sample. Available samples can be useful in pretesting questionnaires or other preliminary (*pilot study*) work. They often help eliminate potential problems in research procedures, testing, and methodology before the final research study is attempted.

Subjects who constitute a **volunteer sample** also form a nonprobability sample, since the individuals are not selected mathematically. There is concern in all areas of research that persons who willingly participate in research projects differ greatly from nonvolunteers and may consequently produce erroneous research results. Rosenthal and Rosnow (1969) identified the characteristics of volunteer subjects based on several studies and found that such subjects, in comparison with nonvolunteers, tend to exhibit higher educational levels, higher occupational status, greater need for approval, higher intelligence levels, and lower levels of authoritarianism. They seem to be more sociable, more "arousal-seeking," and more unconventional; they are more likely to be first children; and they are generally younger.

These characteristics mean that the use of volunteer subjects may significantly bias the results of a research study and may lead to inaccurate estimates of various population parameters (Rosenthal & Rosnow, 1969). Also, available data seem to indicate that volunteers may, more often than nonvolunteers, provide data that support a researcher's hypothesis. In some cases volunteer subjects are necessary—for example, in comparison tests of products or services. However, volunteers should be used carefully because, as with available samples, the data have an unknown quantity of error.

Although volunteer samples have been shown to be inappropriate in scientific research, the media and Internet websites inappropriately legitimize volunteers through the various polls conducted on radio and television stations, TV networks, the Internet, newspapers, and magazines. The media almost daily report the results of the latest viewer, listener, or reader poll about some local or national concern. Although some media occasionally state that the polls are not scientific studies, the results are presented as such. The media are deceiving unwary listeners and viewers because the results are only indications, not scientific "proof."

A **purposive sample** includes subjects or elements selected for specific characteristics or qualities and eliminates those who fail to meet these criteria. Purposive samples are often used in advertising studies where researchers select subjects who use a particular type of product and ask them to compare it with a new product. A purposive sample is chosen with the knowledge that it is not representative of the general population. In a similar method, the **quota sample,** subjects are selected to meet a predetermined or known percentage. For example, a researcher interested in finding out how VCR owners differ from non-VCR owners in their use of television may know that 40% of a particular population owns a VCR. The sample the researcher selects, therefore, would be composed of 40% VCR owners and 60% non-VCR owners (to reflect the population characteristics).

Another nonprobability sampling method is to select subjects haphazardly based on appearance or convenience, or because they seem to meet certain requirements (for example, the subjects "look" as if they qualify for the study in progress). Haphazard selection involves researcher subjectivity and introduces error—**sampling bias**—because the researcher usually favors selection based on certain characteristics. Some haphazard samples give the illusion of a probability sample; these must be approached carefully. For example, interviewing every tenth person who walks by in a shopping center is haphazard because not everyone in the population has an equal chance of walking by that particular location. Some people live across town; some shop in other centers; and so on.

Some researchers, research suppliers, and field services try to work around the problems associated with convenience samples in mall intercepts by using a procedure based on what is called "The Law of Large Numbers." Essentially, the researchers interview thousands of respondents instead of hundreds. The presumption (and the sales approach used on clients) is that the large number of respondents eliminates the problems of convenience sampling and somehow compensates for the fact that the sample is not random. *It does not.* The large number approach is a *convenience sample.* It is not a random sample, which is described next.

Types of Probability Samples

The most basic type of probability sampling is the simple **random sample** where *each subject or unit in the population has an equal chance of being selected.* If a subject or unit is drawn from the population and removed from subsequent selections, the procedure is known as random sampling *without replacement*—the most widely used random sampling method. Random sampling with replacement involves returning the subject or unit to the population so that it has a chance of being chosen another time. Sampling with replacement is often used in more complicated research studies such as nationwide surveys.

Researchers usually use a table of random numbers to generate a simple random sample. For example, a researcher who wants to analyze 10 prime time television programs out of a population of 100 programs to determine how the medium portrays elderly people can take a random sample from the 100 programs by numbering each show from 00 to 99 and then selecting 10 numbers from a table of random numbers, such as the brief listing in Table 4.1. First, a starting point in the table is selected at random. There is no specific way to choose a starting point; it is an arbitrary decision. The researcher then selects the remaining 9 numbers by going up, down, left, or right on the table—or even randomly throughout the table. For example, if the researcher goes down the table from the starting point of 44 until a sample of 10 has been drawn, the sample would include television programs numbered 44, 85, 46, 71, 17, 50, 66, 56, 3, and 49.

Simple random samples for use in telephone surveys are often obtained by a process called **random digit dialing,** or RDD. One RDD method involves randomly selecting four-digit numbers (usually generated by a computer or through the use of a random numbers table) and adding them to the three-digit exchange prefixes in the city in which the survey is conducted. A single four-digit series may be used once, or it may be added to all the prefixes.

Unfortunately, many of the telephone numbers generated by this method of RDD are invalid because some phones have been disconnected, some numbers have not yet been assigned, and so on. Therefore it is best to produce at least three times the number of telephone numbers needed; if a sample of 100 is required, then at least 300 numbers should be generated to allow for invalid numbers.

A second RDD method that tends to decrease the occurrence of invalid numbers involves adding from one to three random digits to a telephone number selected from a phone directory or a list of phone numbers. One first selects a number from a list of telephone numbers (a directory or list purchased from a supplier). Assume that the number 448–3047 was selected from the list. The researcher then simply adds a predetermined number, say 6, to produce 448–3053; or a predetermined two-digit number, say 21, to get 448–3068; or even a three-digit number, say 112, to produce 448–3159. Each variation of the method helps to eliminate many of the invalid numbers produced in pure random number generation, since telephone companies tend to distribute telephone numbers in series, or blocks. In this example, the block "30" is in use, and there is a good chance that random add-ons to this block will be residential telephone numbers.

Random number generation is possible via a variety of methods. However, two rules are always applicable: (1) each unit or subject in the population must have an equal chance of being selected, and (2) the selection procedure must be free from subjective intervention by the researcher. The purpose of random sampling is to reduce sampling error; violating random sampling rules only increases the chance of introducing such error into a study.

Similar in some ways to simple random sampling is a procedure called **systematic random sampling,** in which every nth subject or unit is selected from a population. For example, to obtain a sample of 20 from a population of 100, or a sampling rate of 1/5, a researcher randomly selects a starting point and a **sampling interval.** Thus, if the number 11 is chosen as the starting point, then the sample will include the 20 subjects or items numbered 11, 16, 21, 26, and so on. To add further randomness to the process, the researcher may randomly select both the starting point and

Table 4.1 *Random Numbers*

38	71	81	39	18	24	33	94	56	48	80	95	52	63	01	93	62
27	29	03	62	76	85	37	00	44	11	07	61	17	26	87	63	79
34	24	23	64	18	79	80	33	98	94	56	23	17	05	96	52	94
32	44	31	87	37	41	18	38	01	71	19	42	52	78	80	21	07
41	88	20	11	60	81	02	15	09	49	96	38	27	07	74	20	12
95	65	36	89	80	51	03	64	87	19	06	09	53	69	37	06	85
77	66	74	33	70	97	79	01	19	44	06	64	39	70	63	46	86
54	55	22	17	35	56	66	38	15	50	77	94	08	46	57	70	61
33	95	06	68	60	97	09	45	44	60	60	07	49	98	78	61	88
83	48	36	10	11	70	07	00	66	50	51	93	19	88	45	33	23
34	35	86	77	88	40	03	63	36	35	73	39	44	06	51	48	84
58	35	66	95	48	56	17	04	41	99	79	87	85	01	73	33	65
98	48	03	63	53	58	03	87	97	57	16	38	46	55	96	66	80
83	12	51	88	33	98	68	72	79	69	88	41	71	55	85	50	31
56	66	06	69	40	70	43	49	35	46	98	61	17	63	14	55	74
68	07	59	51	48	87	64	79	19	76	46	68	50	55	01	10	61
20	11	75	63	05	16	96	95	66	00	18	86	66	67	54	68	06
26	56	75	77	75	69	93	54	47	39	67	49	56	96	94	53	68
26	45	74	77	74	55	92	43	37	80	76	31	03	48	40	25	11
73	39	44	06	59	48	48	99	72	90	88	96	49	09	57	45	07
34	36	64	17	21	39	09	97	33	34	40	99	36	12	12	53	77
26	32	06	40	37	02	11	83	79	28	38	49	32	84	94	47	32
04	52	85	62	24	76	53	83	52	05	14	14	49	19	94	62	51
33	93	35	91	24	92	47	57	23	06	33	56	07	94	98	39	27
16	29	97	86	31	45	96	33	83	77	28	14	40	43	59	04	79

Simple Random Sampling

Advantages
1. Detailed knowledge of the population is not required.
2. External validity may be statistically inferred.
3. A representative group is easily obtainable.
4. The possibility of classification error is eliminated.

Disadvantages
1. A list of the population must be compiled.
2. A representative sample may not result in all cases.
3. The procedure can be more expensive than other methods.

Systematic Sampling

Advantages
1. Selection is easy.
2. Selection can be more accurate than in a simple random sample.
3. The procedure is generally inexpensive.

Disadvantages
1. A complete list of the population must be obtained.
2. Periodicity may bias the process.

the sampling interval. For example, an interval of 11 with a starting point of 29 generates the numbers 40, 51, 62, 73, and so on.

Systematic samples are used frequently in mass media research. They often save time, resources, and effort when compared to simple random samples. In fact, since the procedure so closely resembles a simple random sample, many researchers consider systematic sampling to be as effective as the random procedure. The method is widely used to select subjects from lists such as telephone directories, *Broadcasting/Cablecasting Yearbook,* and *Editor & Publisher.*

The accuracy of systematic sampling depends on the adequacy of the **sampling frame,** or the complete list of members in the population. Telephone directories are inadequate sampling frames in most cases because not all phone numbers are listed and some people do not have telephones at all. However, lists that include all the members of a population have a high degree of precision. Before deciding to use systematic sampling, one should consider the goals and purpose of a study and the availability of a comprehensive list of the population. If such a list is not available, then systematic sampling is probably ill advised.

One major problem associated with systematic sampling is **periodicity;** that is, the arrangement or order of the items in the population list may bias the selection process. For example, consider the problem mentioned

Stratified Sampling

Advantages
1. Representativeness of relevant variables is ensured.
2. Comparisons can be made to other populations.
3. Selection is made from a homogeneous group.
4. Sampling error is reduced.

Disadvantages
1. A knowledge of the population prior to selection is required.
2. The procedure can be costly and time-consuming.
3. It can be difficult to find a sample if incidence is low.
4. Variables that define strata may not be relevant.

earlier of analyzing television programs to determine how the elderly are portrayed. Quite possibly, ABC may have aired every 10th program listed; the result would be a nonrepresentative sampling of the three networks.

Periodicity also causes problems when telephone directories are used to select samples. The alphabetical listing does not allow each person or household an equal chance of being selected. One way to solve the problem is to cut each name from the directory, place them all in a "hat," and draw names randomly. Obviously, this would take days to accomplish and it is not a real alternative. An easier way to use a directory is to tear the pages loose, mix them up, randomly select pages, and then randomly select names. Although this procedure does not totally solve the problem, it is generally accepted when simple random sampling is impossible. If periodicity is eliminated, systematic sampling can be an excellent sampling methodology.

Although a simple random sample is the usual choice in most research projects, some researchers do not wish to rely on randomness. In some projects, researchers want to guarantee that a specific subsample of the population is adequately represented, and no such guarantee is possible using a simple random sample. A **stratified sample** is the approach used to get adequate representation of a subsample. The characteristics of the subsample (strata or segment) may include almost any variable: age, gender, religion, income level, or even individuals who listen to specific radio stations or read certain magazines. The strata may be defined by an almost unlimited number of characteristics; however, each additional variable or characteristic makes the subsample more difficult to find. Therefore incidence drops.

Stratified sampling ensures that a sample is drawn from a homogeneous subset of the population—that is, from a population that has similar characteristics. Homogeneity helps researchers to reduce sampling error. For example, consider a research study on subjects' attitudes toward two-way, interactive cable television. The investigator, knowing that cable subscribers tend to have higher achievement levels, may wish to stratify the population according to education. Before randomly selecting subjects, the researcher divides the population into three education levels: grade school, high school, and college. Then, if it is determined that 10% of the population completed college, a random sample proportional to the population should contain 10% of the population who meet this standard. As Babbie (2001) notes:

Cluster Sampling

Advantages

1. Only part of the population need be enumerated.
2. Costs are reduced if clusters are well defined.
3. Estimates of cluster parameters are made and compared to the population.

Disadvantages

1. Sampling errors are likely.
2. Clusters may not be representative of the population.
3. Each subject or unit must be assigned to a specific cluster.

> Stratified sampling ensures the proper representation of the stratification variables to enhance representation of other variables related to them. Taken as a whole, then, a stratified sample is likely to be more representative on a number of variables than a simple random sample.

Stratified sampling can be applied in two different ways. **Proportionate stratified sampling** includes strata with sizes based on their proportions in the population. If 30% of the population is adults ages 18–24, then 30% of the total sample will be subjects in this age group. This procedure is designed to give each person in the population an equal chance of being selected. Disproportionate stratified sampling is used to oversample or overrepresent a particular stratum. The approach is used basically because that stratum is considered important for marketing, advertising, or other similar reasons. For example, a radio station that targets 25- to 54-year-olds may have ratings problems with the 25- to 34-year-old group. In a telephone study of 500 respondents, the station management may wish to have the sample represented as follows: 70% in the 24–34 group, 20% in the 35–49 group, and 10% in the 50–54 group. This distribution would allow researchers to break the 25–34 group into smaller groups such as males, females, fans of specific stations, and other subcategories and still have reasonable sample sizes.

The usual sampling procedure is to select one unit or subject at a time, but this requires the researcher to have a complete list of the population. In some cases there is no way to obtain such a list. One way to avoid this problem is to select the sample in groups or categories; this procedure is known as **cluster sampling.** For example, analyzing magazine readership habits of people in Wisconsin would be time-consuming and complicated if individual subjects were randomly selected. With cluster sampling, one can divide the state into districts, counties, or zip code areas and select groups of people from these areas.

Cluster sampling creates two types of errors: errors in defining the initial clusters and errors in selecting from the clusters. For example, a zip code area may contain mostly residents of a low socioeconomic status who are unrepresentative of the rest of the state; if selected for analysis, such a group may confound the research results. To help control such error, it is best to use small areas or clusters, both to decrease the number of elements in each cluster and to maximize the number of clusters selected (Babbie, 2001).

In many nationwide studies, researchers use a form of cluster sampling called **multistage sampling,** in which individual households or persons (not groups) are selected.

Figure 4.2 *Census Tracts*

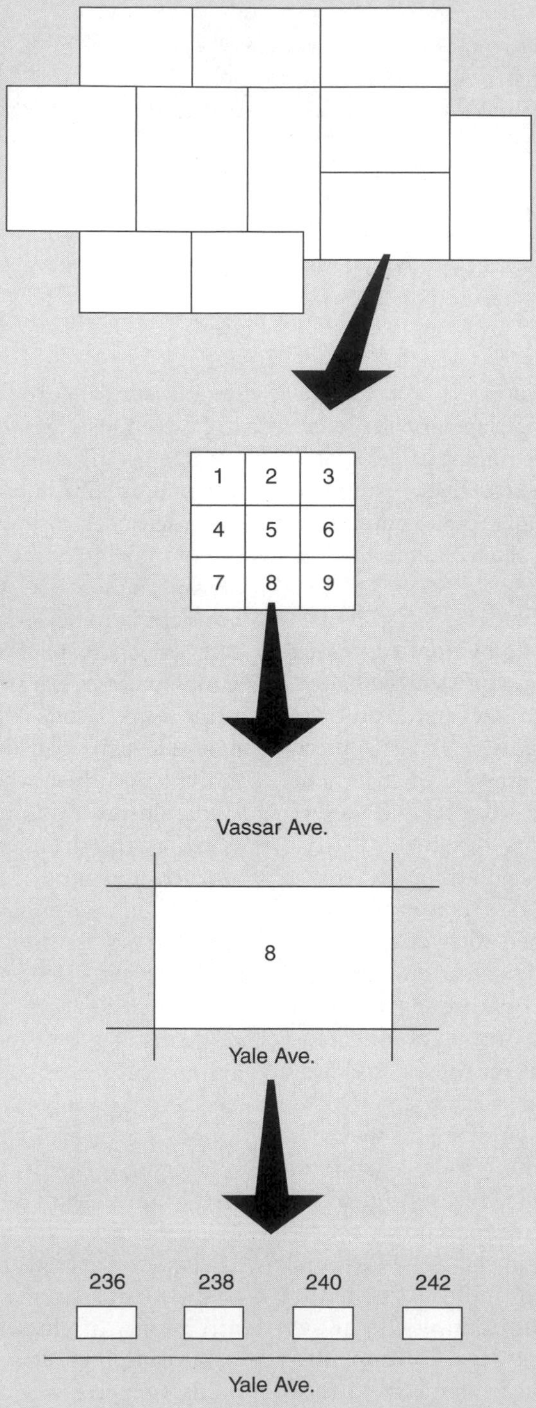

Figure 4.2 illustrates a four-stage sequence for a nationwide survey. First, a cluster of counties (or another specific geographic area) in the United States is selected. Researchers then narrow this cluster by randomly selecting a county, district, or block group within the principal cluster. Next, individual blocks are selected within each area. Finally, a convention such as "the third household from the northeast corner" is established. Applying the selection formula in the stages just described can thus identify the individual households in the sample.

In many cases researchers also need to randomly select an individual in a given household. Researchers usually cannot count on being able to interview the person who happens to answer the telephone. *Demographic quotas* may be established for a research study, which means that a certain percentage of all respondents must be of a certain gender or age. In this type of study, researchers determine which person in the household should answer the questionnaire by using a form of random numbers table, as illustrated in Table 4.2.

To get a random selection of individuals in the selected households, the interviewer simply asks each person who answers the telephone, "How many people are there in your home who are age 12 or older?" If the first respondent answers "Five," the interviewer asks to speak to the fifth-oldest (in this case the youngest) person in the home. Each time a call is completed, the interviewer checks off on the table the number representing the person questioned. If the next household called also has five family members, the interviewer moves to the next number in the 5 column and asks to talk to the third-oldest person in the home.

The same table can be used to select respondents by gender; that is, the interviewer could ask, "How many men who are age 12 or older live in your home?" The interviewer could then ask for the nth-oldest male, or female, according to the requirements of the survey.

Since the media are complex systems, researchers frequently encounter complicated sampling methods. These are known as *hybrid situations*. Consider some researchers attempting to determine the potential for videotext distribution of a local newspaper to cable subscribers. This problem requires investigating readers and nonreaders of the newspaper

Table 4.2 *Example of Matrix for Selecting Respondents at Random*

	Number of people in household						
	1	2	3	4	5	6	7
Person to interview:	1	2	1	3	5	5	7
		1	3	4	3	2	6
			2	2	1	4	1
				1	2	6	4
					4	1	3
						3	2
							5

AN INSIDE LOOK
National Sampling

Most novice researchers believe that conducting a study using a national sample is an impossible task, particularly in reference to obtaining a national sample. On the contrary, national studies are very simple to conduct because there are dozens of survey sampling companies that can provide almost any type of national sample. If you're interested in conducting a national study, search the Internet for survey sampling companies. The only thing you need to do is explain the type of respondent you're interested in interviewing or studying. The company can develop a list for you in a few hours.

in addition to cable subscribers and nonsubscribers. The research therefore requires random sampling from the following four groups:

Group A	Subscribers/Readers
Group B	Subscribers/Nonreaders
Group C	Nonsubscribers/Readers
Group D	Nonsubscribers/Nonreaders

The researcher must identify each subject as belonging to one of these four groups. If three variables are involved, sampling from eight groups is required, and so on. In other words, researchers are often faced with very complicated sampling situations that involve numerous steps.

The term **snowball sampling** is most often used in academic research. In private sector research, this approach is known as "referrals." In either case, the method is the same. A researcher (research company or field service) randomly contacts a few qualified respondents and then asks these people for the names of friends, relatives, or acquaintances they know who may also qualify for the research study. These referrals are then contacted to determine if they qualify for the research. While this sampling procedure sounds legitimate, the authors do not recommend the procedure for *any* legitimate research because the sample may be completely biased. A researcher may find that the sample consists only of respondents from a club, organization, or group.

▪ Sample Size

Determining an adequate sample size is one of the most controversial aspects of sampling. How large must a sample be to provide the desired level of confidence in the results? Unfortunately, there is no simple answer. Certain sample sizes are suggested for various statistical procedures, but no single sample-size formula or method is available for every research method or statistical procedure. For this reason, we advise you to consult sampling texts for information concerning specific techniques (Cochran, 1977; Raj, 1972).

The size of the sample required for a study depends on at least one or more of the following seven factors: (1) project type, (2) project purpose, (3) project complexity, (4) amount of error tolerated, (5) time constraints, (6) financial constraints, and (7) previous research in the area. (An eighth factor in private sector research is how much the client is willing to spend.) Research designed as a preliminary search for general indications generally does not require a large sample. However, projects intended to answer significant questions (those designed to provide information for decisions involving large sums of money or decisions that may affect people's lives) require high levels of precision and therefore large samples.

A few general principles guide researchers in determining an acceptable sample size.

These suggestions are not based on mathematical or statistical theory, but they provide a starting point in most cases.

1. A primary consideration in determining sample size is the research method used. Focus groups (see Chapter 5) use samples of 6–12 people, but the results are not intended to be generalized to the population from which the respondents are selected. Samples with 10–50 subjects are commonly used for pretesting measurement instruments and pilot studies, and for conducting studies that will be used for only heuristic value.

2. Researchers often use samples of 50, 75, or 100 subjects per group (such as adults 18–24 years old). This base figure is used to "back in" to a total sample size. For example, assume a researcher is planning to conduct a telephone study with adults aged 18–54. Using the normal mass media age spans of 18–24, 25–34, 35–44, and 45–54, the researcher would probably consider a total sample of 400 as satisfactory (100 per age group, or "cell"). However, the client may also wish to investigate the differences in opinions and attitudes among men and women, which produces a total of eight age cells. In this case, a sample of 800 would be used—100 for each of the cell possibilities. Realistically, however, not many clients in private sector research are willing to pay for a study with a sample of 800 respondents (approximately $58,000 for a 20-minute telephone interview). More than likely, the client would accept 50 respondents in each of the eight cells, producing a total sample of 400 (8 × 50).

3. Cost and time considerations always control sample size. Although researchers may wish to use a sample of 1,000 for a survey, the economics of such a sample are usually prohibitive. Research with 1,000 respondents can easily cost more than $70,000. Most research is conducted using a sample size that conforms to the project's budget. If a smaller sample is forced on a researcher by someone else (a client or a project manager), the results must be interpreted accordingly—that is, with caution. However, considering that reducing a sample size from 1,000 to 400 (for example) reduces the sampling error by only a small percentage, researchers may be wise to consider using smaller samples for most projects.

4. Multivariate studies always require larger samples than do univariate studies because they involve analyzing multiple response data (several measurements on the same subject). One guideline recommended for multivariate studies is as follows: 50 = very poor; 100 = poor; 200 = fair; 300 = good; 500 = very good; 1,000 = excellent (Comrey & Lee, 1992). Other researchers suggest using a sample of 100 plus 1 subject for each dependent variable in the analysis (Gorsuch, 1983).

5. For panel studies, central location testing, focus groups, and other prerecruit projects, researchers should always select a larger sample than is actually required. The larger sample compensates for those subjects who drop out of research studies for one reason or another, and allowances must be made for this in planning the sample selection. High dropout rates are especially prevalent in panel studies, where the same group of subjects is tested or measured frequently over a long period of time. Usually researchers can expect 10–25% of the sample to drop out of a study before it is completed, and 50% or more is not uncommon.

6. Use information available in published research. Consulting other research provides a starting point. If a survey is planned and similar research indicates that a representative sample of 400 has been used regularly with reliable results, then a sample larger than 400 may be unnecessary.

7. Generally speaking, the larger the sample, the better. However, a large unrepresentative sample ("The Law of Large Numbers") is as meaningless as a small unrepresentative sample, so researchers should not consider numbers alone. Quality is always more important in sample selection than mere size. During our 25 years of research, we have found that a sample size of less than 30 in a given cell (such as females, 18–24) produces unstable results. For more information about sampling, see Tukey, 1986.

▪ Sampling Error

Since researchers deal with samples from a population, there must be some way for them to compare the results of (or make inferences about) what was found in the sample to what exists in the target population. The comparison allows researchers to determine the accuracy of their data and involves the computation of error. All research involves three types of error—**sampling error, measurement error,** and **random error** (also called unknown, or uncontrollable, error). Sampling error is also known as **standard error.** The different sources of error are additive; that is, total error is the sum of the three different sources. This section discusses sampling error in mass media research.

Sampling error occurs when measurements taken from a sample do not correspond to what exists in the population. For example, assume we wish to measure attitudes toward a new television program by 18–24-year-old viewers in Denver, Colorado. Further, assume that all the viewers produce an average score of 6 on a 10-point program appeal measurement scale. Some viewers may dislike the program and rate the show 1, 2, or 3; some may find it mediocre and rate it 4, 5, 6, or 7; and the remaining viewers may like the show a lot and rate it 8, 9, or 10. The differences among the 18–24-year-old viewers provide an example of how sampling error may occur. If we asked each viewer to rate the show in a separate study and each one rated the program a 6, then no error exists. However, an error-free sample is highly unlikely.

Respondent differences do exist; some dislike the program, and others like it. Although the average program rating is 6 in the hypothetical example, it is possible to select a sample from the target population that does not match the average rating. A sample could be selected that includes only viewers who dislike the program. This would misrepresent the population because the average appeal score would be lower than the mean score. Computing the percentage of sampling error allows researchers to assess the risk involved in accepting research findings as "real."

Computing sampling error is appropriate *only with probability samples*. Sampling error cannot be computed with research that uses nonprobability samples because not everyone has an equal chance of being selected. This is one reason nonprobability samples are used only in preliminary research or in studies where error rates are not considered important.

Sampling error computations are essential in research and are based on the concept of the **central limit theorem.** In its simplest form, the theorem states that the sum of a large number of independent and identically distributed random variables (or **sampling distributions**) has an approximate **normal distribution.** A theoretical sampling distribution is the set of all possible samples of a given size. This distribution of values is described by a bell-shaped curve or **normal curve** (also known as a *Gaussian distribution,* after German mathematician and astronomer Karl F. Gauss, who used the concept to analyze observational errors). The normal distribution is important in computing sampling error because sampling errors (a sampling distribution) that are made in repeated measurements tend to be normally distributed.

Computing standard error is a process of determining, with a certain amount of confidence, the difference between a sample and the target population. Error can occur by chance or through some fault of the research procedure. However, when probability sampling is used, the incidence of error can be de-

Figure 4.3 *Areas under the Normal Curve*

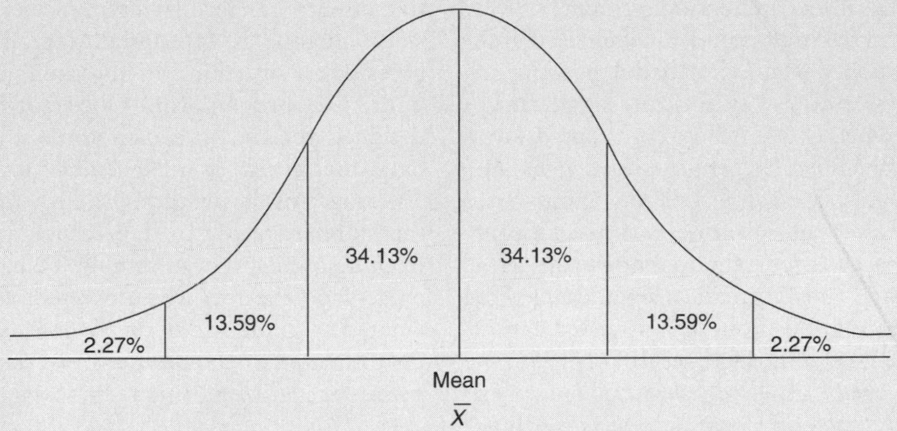

termined because of the relationship between the sample and the normal curve. A normal curve, as shown in Figure 4.3, is symmetrical about the mean or midpoint, which indicates that an equal number of scores lies on either side of the midpoint.

Confidence Level and Confidence Interval

Sampling error involves two concepts: **confidence level** and **confidence interval.** After a research project has been conducted, the researcher estimates the accuracy of the results in terms of a level of confidence that the results lie within a specified interval. For example, a researcher may say he is 95% confident (*confidence level*) that his finding—in which 50% of his study's respondents named "MTV" as their favorite cable channel—is within ±5% (*confidence interval*) of the true population percentage.

In every normal distribution, the standard deviation defines a standard unit of distance from the midpoint of the distribution to the outer limits of the distribution. These standard deviation interval units (values) are used in establishing the confidence interval that is accepted in a research project. In addition, the standard deviation units indicate the amount of standard error. For example, using an interval (confidence interval) of −1 or +1 standard deviation unit—1 standard error—says that the probability is that 68% of the samples selected from the population will produce estimates within that distance from the population value (1 standard deviation unit; see Figure 4.3).

Researchers use a number of different confidence intervals. Greater confidence in results is achieved when the data are tested at higher levels, such as 95%. Research projects that are preliminary in nature or whose results are not intended to be used for significant decision making can and should use more conservative confidence levels, such as 68%. Conducting research that deals with human subjects is difficult enough on its own, without further complicating the work with highly restrictive confidence levels. The researcher must balance necessity with practicality. For instance, a researcher might need to ask whether her investigation concerning tastes and preferences in music needs to be tested at a confidence level of 95% or 99%. The answer is no. In fact, the necessity for confidence levels and confidence intervals in behavioral research is under debate. Research is often judged as good or bad depending on whether a study is "statistically significant," not on whether the study contributed anything to the advancement of knowledge. Statistical significance alone does not anoint a research project as scientific; a nonsignificant finding is as important to knowledge as a study that "finds" statistical significance. For more information about the misguided nature of statistical significance, see Tukey, 1986.

The areas under the normal curve in Table 3 of Appendix 1 are used to determine other confidence intervals. For example, the 68% confidence interval (.34 on either side of the mean) corresponds to 1.00 standard error; the 95% interval corresponds to 1.96 standard errors; and the 99% interval corresponds to 2.576 standard errors. If the statistical data from the sample fall outside the range set by the researcher, the results are considered significant.

Computing Sampling Error

The essence of statistical hypothesis testing is to draw a sample from a target population, compute some type of statistical measurement, and compare the results to the theoretical sampling distribution. The comparison determines the frequency with which sample values of a statistic are expected to occur.

The *expected value* of a statistic is the mean of the sampling distribution. The standard error is the standard deviation of the sampling distribution. There are several ways to compute standard (sampling) error, but no single method is appropriate for all sample types or all situations. In addition, error formulas vary in complexity. One error formula, designed for use with dichotomous (yes/no) data, that estimates audience size for certain TV programs during certain time periods uses the standard error of a percentage derived from a simple random sample. If the sample percentage (the ones who answered yes) is designated as p, the size of the sample as N, and the estimated or standard error of the sample percentage as $SE(p)$, this is the formula:

$$SE(p) = \sqrt{\frac{p(100 - p)}{N}} \times Z \textit{ for associated confidence level}$$

Suppose a sample of 500 households produces a rating (or estimate of the percentage of viewers) of 20 for a particular show. This means that 20% of those households were turned to that channel at that time. At the 95% confidence level, the formula can be used to calculate the standard error of this viewership percentage as follows:

$$SE(p) = \sqrt{\frac{20(80)}{500}} \times 1.96 = \pm 3.5\%$$

At the 99% confidence level, the sampling error percentage is:

$$SE(p) = \sqrt{\frac{20(80)}{500}} \times 2.57 = \pm 4.6\%$$

Confidence Level %	*Associated Z value to use in Sample Error Formula*
68	1.00
95	1.96
99	2.57

Table 4.3 Finding Error Rate Using a Rating of 20 (68% Confidence Level)

Sample size	Error	Lower limit	Upper limit
600	±1.63	18.37	21.63
700	±1.51	18.49	21.51
800	±1.41	18.59	21.41
900	±1.33	18.67	21.33
1,000	±1.26	18.74	21.26
1,500	±1.03	18.97	21.03

This information can be used to calculate confidence intervals at various confidence levels. For example, to calculate the confidence interval at the .68 confidence level, simply add and subtract 1 standard error from the percentage. See Table 4.3 (Note that 68% of the normal curve is encompassed by plus and minus 1 standard error.) Thus we are 68% confident that the true rating lies somewhere between 18.21 (20 − 1.79) and 21.79 (20 + 1.79).

If we want to have greater confidence in our results, we can calculate the confidence interval at the .95 confidence level by multiplying by the associated Z value for 2 standard deviation units, which is $1.96 \times SE(p)$. In our example with 500 respondents and a TV rating of 20%, the sampling error at the 95% confidence level would be ±3.50.

Standard error is directly related to sample size. The error figure improves as the sample size is increased, but in decreasing increments. Thus an increase in sample size does not provide a big gain, as illustrated by Table 4.4. As can be seen, even with a sample of 1,500, the standard error is only .75 better than with the sample of 500 computed above. A researcher needs to determine if the increase in time and expense created by 1,000 additional subjects justifies such a proportionally small increase in precision.

Table 4.4 shows the amount of error at the 95% and 99% confidence level for measurements that contain dichotomous variables (such as yes/no). For example, using a 95% confidence level, with a sample of 1,000 and a 30% "yes" response to a question, the probable error due to sample size alone is ±2.8. This means that we are 95% sure that our values for this particular question fall between 27.2% and 32.8%.

Sampling error is an important concept in all research areas because it provides an indication of the degree of accuracy of the research. Research studies published by large audience measurement firms such as Arbitron and A. C. Nielsen are required by the Electronic Media Ratings Council (EMRC) to include simplified charts to assist in determining sampling error. In addition, each company provides some type of explanation about error, such as the Arbitron statement entitled "Description of Methodology" contained in every ratings book section:

> Arbitron estimates are subject to statistical variances associated with all surveys which use a sample of the universe . . . the accuracy of Arbitron estimates, data and reports and their statistical evaluators cannot be determined to any precise mathematical value or definition.

Table 4.4 *Sampling Error at 95% and 99% Confidence Levels*

Sampling Error at 95% Confidence Level

Result is:	1% or 99%	5% or 95%	10% or 90%	15% or 85%	20% or 80%	25% or 75%	30% or 70%	35% or 65%	40% or 60%	45% or 55%	50%
Sample Size											
10	6.2	13.5	18.6	22.1	24.8	26.8	28.4	29.6	30.4	30.8	31.0
20	4.4	9.6	13.1	15.6	17.5	19.0	20.1	20.9	21.5	21.8	21.9
30	3.6	7.8	10.7	12.8	14.3	15.5	16.4	17.1	17.5	17.8	17.9
40	3.1	6.8	9.3	11.1	12.4	13.4	14.2	14.8	15.2	15.4	15.5
50	2.8	6.0	8.3	9.9	11.1	12.0	12.7	13.2	13.6	13.8	13.9
75	2.3	4.9	6.8	8.1	9.1	9.8	10.4	10.8	11.1	11.3	11.3
100	2.0	4.3	5.9	7.0	7.8	8.5	9.0	9.3	9.6	9.8	9.8
200	1.4	3.0	4.2	4.9	5.5	6.0	6.4	6.6	6.8	6.9	6.9
300	1.1	2.5	3.4	4.0	4.5	4.9	5.2	5.4	5.5	5.6	5.7
400	.98	2.1	2.9	3.5	3.9	4.2	4.5	4.7	4.8	4.9	4.9
500	.87	1.9	2.6	3.1	3.5	3.8	4.0	4.2	4.3	4.4	4.4
600	.80	1.7	2.4	2.9	3.2	3.5	3.7	3.8	3.9	4.0	4.0
700	.74	1.6	2.2	2.6	3.0	3.2	3.4	3.5	3.6	3.7	3.7
800	.69	1.5	2.1	2.5	2.8	3.0	3.2	3.3	3.4	3.4	3.5
900	.65	1.4	2.0	2.3	2.6	2.8	3.0	3.1	3.2	3.3	3.3
1,000	.62	1.4	1.9	2.2	2.5	2.7	2.8	3.0	3.0	3.1	3.1
1,200	.56	1.2	1.7	2.0	2.3	2.5	2.6	2.7	2.8	2.8	2.8
2,000	.44	.96	1.3	1.6	1.8	1.9	2.0	2.1	2.1	2.2	2.2
3,000	.36	.78	1.1	1.3	1.4	1.5	1.6	1.7	1.8	1.8	1.8
4,000	.31	.68	.93	1.1	1.2	1.3	1.4	1.5	1.5	1.5	1.5
5,000	.28	.60	.83	.99	1.1	1.2	1.3	1.3	1.4	1.4	1.4
10,000	.20	.43	.59	.70	.78	.85	.90	.93	.96	.98	.98

Table 4.4 *(continued)*

Sampling Error at 99% Confidence Level											
Result is:	1% or 99%	5% or 95%	10% or 90%	15% or 85%	20% or 80%	25% or 75%	30% or 70%	35% or 65%	40% or 60%	45% or 55%	50%
Sample Size											
10	8.1	17.7	24.4	29.0	32.5	35.2	37.2	38.8	39.8	40.4	40.6
20	5.7	12.5	17.2	20.5	23.0	24.9	26.3	27.4	28.2	28.6	28.7
30	4.7	10.2	14.1	16.8	18.8	20.3	21.5	22.4	23.0	23.3	23.5
40	4.0	8.9	12.2	14.5	16.3	17.6	18.6	19.4	19.9	20.2	20.3
50	3.6	7.9	10.9	13.0	14.5	15.7	16.7	17.3	17.8	18.1	18.2
75	3.0	6.5	8.9	10.6	11.9	12.9	13.6	14.2	14.5	14.8	14.8
100	2.6	5.6	7.7	9.2	10.3	11.1	11.8	12.3	12.6	12.8	12.9
200	1.8	4.0	5.5	6.5	7.3	7.9	8.3	8.7	8.9	9.0	9.1
300	1.5	3.2	4.5	5.3	5.9	6.4	6.8	7.1	7.3	7.4	7.4
400	1.3	2.8	3.9	4.6	5.1	5.6	5.9	6.1	6.3	6.4	6.4
500	1.1	2.5	3.4	4.1	4.6	5.0	5.3	5.5	5.6	5.7	5.7
600	1.0	2.3	3.1	3.7	4.2	4.5	4.8	5.0	5.1	5.2	5.2
700	1.0	2.1	2.9	3.5	3.9	4.2	4.5	4.6	4.8	4.8	4.9
800	.90	2.0	2.7	3.2	3.6	3.9	4.2	4.3	4.5	4.5	4.5
900	.85	1.9	2.6	3.1	3.4	3.7	3.9	4.1	4.2	4.3	4.3
1,000	.81	1.8	2.4	2.9	3.3	3.5	3.7	3.9	4.0	4.0	4.1
2,000	.57	1.3	1.7	2.1	2.3	2.5	2.6	2.7	2.8	2.9	2.9
3,000	.47	1.0	1.4	1.7	1.9	2.0	2.2	2.2	2.3	2.3	2.3
4,000	.40	.89	1.2	1.5	1.6	1.8	1.9	1.9	2.0	2.0	2.0
5,000	.36	.79	1.1	1.3	1.5	1.6	1.7	1.7	1.8	1.8	1.8
10,000	.26	.56	.77	.92	1.0	1.1	1.2	1.2	1.3	1.3	1.3

Statistical error due to sampling is found in all research studies. Researchers must pay specific attention to the potential sources of error in any study. Producing a study riddled with error is tantamount to never having conducted the study at all. If the magnitude of error were subject to accurate assessment, researchers could simply determine the source of error and correct it. Since this is not possible, they must accept error as part of the research process, attempt to reduce its effects to a minimum, and remember always to consider its presence when interpreting their results.

To use these tables, first find the response percentage in a column at the top of the table, then find the sample size in the left-hand column—then go across for the appropriate sampling error estimate. For example, if 50% of the respondents in a sample of 400 agree with a specific statement, the estimated amount of error associated with this answer is ±4.9%. That is, the "actual" response ranges from between 45.1% to 54.9%. At the 99% confidence level, the estimated amount of error associated with the answer is ±6.4%.

Finite Population Correction Factor

Some researchers contend that if sampling is done without replacement for a small population, it is necessary to adjust the computed sampling error by a factor known as the **Finite Population Correction Factor (FPCF).** The usual approach is to use FPCF if the sample is more than 5% of the population. The correction factor supposedly accounts for the fact that a parameter can better be estimated from a small population when a large portion of that population's units are sampled.

FPCF is calculated using this formula:

$$FPCF = \sqrt{\frac{N - n}{N - 1}}$$

Where N = population and n = sample size. This number is then multiplied by the sampling error values using the formula shown on page 100.

The problem with FPCF is the assumption that a smaller population, such as TV or radio station employees, contains less variance than a larger population. This assumption falls into the category of decisions made by, "It seems like." In other words, it seems as if a finite (or small) population has less variance and therefore it must be true. While there are several studies on the Internet discussing the value of FPCF, none of them addresses the assumption that a smaller population possesses less variance than a larger, or infinite sample.

Sample Weighting

In an ideal study, a researcher has enough respondents or subjects with the required demographic, psychographic (why people behave in specific ways), or lifestyle characteristics. The ideal sample, however, is rare due to the time and budget constraints of most research. Instead of canceling a research project because of sampling inadequacies, most researchers utilize a statistical procedure known as **weighting,** or *sample balancing*. That is, when the subject totals in given categories do not reach the necessary population percentages, subjects' responses are multiplied (weighted) to allow for the shortfall. A single subject's responses may be multiplied by 1.3, 1.7, 2.0, or any other figure to reach the predetermined required level.

Subject weighting is a controversial data manipulation technique, especially in broadcast ratings. The major question is just how much one subject's responses can be weighted and still be representative. Weighting is discussed in greater detail in Chapter 13.

▪ ▪ ▪ Summary

To make predictions about events, concepts, or phenomena, researchers must perform detailed, objective analyses. One procedure to use in such analyses is a census, in which every member of the population is studied. Conducting a census for each research project is impractical, however, and researchers must resort to alternative methods. The most widely used alternative is to select a random sample from the population, examine it, and make predictions from it that can be generalized to the population. There are several procedures for identifying the units that make up a random sample.

If the scientific procedure is to provide valid and useful results, researchers must pay close attention to the methods they use in selecting a sample. This chapter described several types of samples commonly used in mass media research. Some are elementary and do not require a great deal of time or resources; others entail great expense and time. Researchers must decide what costs and time are justified in relation to the results generated.

Sampling procedures must not be considered lightly in the process of scientific investigation. It makes no sense to develop a research design for testing a valuable hypothesis or research question and then nullify this effort by neglecting correct sampling procedures. These procedures must be continually scrutinized to ensure that the results of an analysis are not sample-specific—that is, that the results are not based on the type of sample used in the study.

Key Terms

Available sample
Census
Central limit theorem
Cluster sample
Confidence interval
Confidence level
Convenience sample
Finite Population Correction Factor
Gaussian distribution
Law of Large Numbers
Measurement error
Multistage sampling
Nonprobability sample
Normal curve
Normal distribution
Parameters
Periodicity
Population
Probability sample
Proportionate stratified sampling
Purposive sampling
Quota Sampling
Random digit dialing
Random error
Random sample
Sample
Sample balancing
Sample weighting
Sampling bias
Sampling design
Sampling error
Sampling frame
Sampling interval
Snowball sample
Standard error
Stratified sampling
Systematic random sampling
Volunteer sample

Using the Internet

1. Search the Internet for "sampling." One good site to get you started is located at: *http://jan.ucc.nau.edu/,mezza/nur390/Mod3/sampling.*
2. If you need a random number generator, go to: *www.randomizer.org.*
3. A handy sampling error calculator is located at: *www.rogerwimmer.com.*
4. Go to *www.surveysystem.com/sscalc.htm* for a sample size calculator.

Questions and Problems for Further Investigation

1. Using available samples in research has long been a target for heated debate. Some researchers say that available samples are inaccurate representations of the population; others claim that if a concept or phenomenon exists, it should exist in an available sample as well as in a random sample. Which argument do you support? Explain your answer.
2. Many research studies use small samples. What are the advantages and disadvantages of this practice? Can any gain other than cost savings be realized by using a small sample in a research study?

3. What sampling technique might be appropriate for the following research projects?

   - A pilot study to test whether people understand the directions to a telephone questionnaire
   - A study to determine who buys videocassette recorders
   - A study to determine the demographic makeup of the audience for a local television show
   - A content analysis of commercials aired during Saturday morning children's programs
   - A survey examining the differences between newspaper readership in high-income households and low-income households

4. Check the Internet for updates on sampling information.
5. One of the controversies surrounding the census in the year 2000 involved sampling. If you are using Info Trac College Edition, find articles that deal with this topic and explain what the controversy was about. (Hint: Search using "statistical sampling" as a key word.)

For additional information on these and related topics, see

http://www.wimmerdominick.com

References and Suggested Readings

Make sure to check the Internet for additional information about sampling. Search for topics such as "research sampling," "books on sampling," "types of research sample," and "random sample."

Babbie, E. R. (2001). *The practice of social research* (9th ed.). Belmont, CA: Wadsworth.

Blalock, H. M. (1972). *Social statistics*. New York: McGraw-Hill.

Cochran, W. G. (1977). *Sampling techniques* (3rd ed.). New York: John Wiley.

Comrey, A. L., & Lee, H. B. (1992). *A first course in factor analysis* (2nd ed.). Hillsdale, NJ: Lawrence Erlbaum.

Fletcher, J. E. (Ed.). (1981). *Handbook of radio and TV broadcasting*. New York: Van Nostrand Reinhold.

Gorsuch, R. L. (1983). *Factor analysis* (2nd ed.). Philadelphia: W. B. Saunders.

Gy, P., & Royle, A. G. (Translator). (1998). *Sampling for analytical purposes*. New York: John Wiley.

Hanson, M. H., et al. (1993). *Sample survey methods and theory*. New York: John Wiley.

Kish, L. (1965). *Survey sampling*. New York: John Wiley.

Nunnally, J. C., & Bernstein, I. H. (1994). *Psychometric theory* (3rd ed.). New York: McGraw-Hill.

Raj, D. (1972). *The design of sample surveys*. New York: McGraw-Hill.

Rosenthal, R., & Rosnow, R. L. (1969). *Artifact in behavioral research*. New York: Academic Press.

Tukey, J. W. (1986). *The collected works of John W. Tukey, Vols. III and IV*. Belmont, CA: Wadsworth and Brooks/Cole.

Walizer, M. H., & Wienir, P. L. (1978). *Research methods and analysis: Searching for relationships*. New York: Harper & Row.

Chapter 5

Qualitative Research Methods

Part Two proceeds from a general discussion of research to specific research techniques. Chapter 5 discusses qualitative analysis, which relies mainly on the analysis of visual data (observations) and verbal data (words) that reflect everyday experience. Chapter 6 discusses content analysis, which focuses on words and other message characteristics but is conducted in a more systematic and measured way. Chapter 7 discusses survey research, which relies on greater quantification and greater measurement sophistication than either qualitative research or content analysis. However, this sophistication comes with a price: Increasing quantification narrows the types of research questions that can be addressed. That is, research depth is sacrificed to gain research breadth. Chapter 8 discusses longitudinal research, and, finally, Chapter 9 concludes Part Two with a discussion of experimental methods, which are among the most precise, complex, and intricate of methodologies.

■ Aims and Philosophy

Discussing the qualitative approach to research can be confusing because, as Potter (1996) ably demonstrates, there is no commonly accepted definition of the term *qualitative.* In fact, some qualitative researchers resist defining the term at all for fear of limiting the technique. The task is further complicated because of the several levels of reference connected with the term. The word *qualitative* has been used to refer to (1) a broad philosophy and approach to research, (2) a research methodology, and (3) a specific set of research techniques. To better understand this area, it is helpful to step back and examine some general considerations related to social science research.

Neuman (1997) and Blaikie (1993) suggest that there are three distinct approaches to social science research: positivism (or objectivism), interpretive, and critical. Each of these represents a model or a **paradigm** for research—*an accepted set of theories, procedures, and assumptions about how researchers look at the world.* Paradigms are based on axioms, or statements that are universally accepted as true. Paradigms are important because they are related to the selection of research methods.

The *positivist* paradigm is the oldest and still the most widely used in mass media research. Derived from the writings of philosophers such as Comte and Mill, positivism is the paradigm most used in the natural sciences. When the social sciences developed, researchers modified this technique for their own purposes. The positivist paradigm involves such concepts as quantification, hypotheses, and objective measures. The positivist paradigm is the one that underlies the approach of this book.

Interpretive social science traces its roots to Max Weber and Wilhelm Dilthey. The aim of this paradigm is to understand how people in everyday natural settings create meaning and interpret the events of their world. This paradigm became popular in mass media research during the 1970s and 1980s and gained added visibility in the 1990s and the new century.

The *critical* paradigm draws on analysis models used in the humanities. Critical researchers are interested in such concepts as the distribution of power in society and political ideology. Though useful in many cases, a consideration of the critical paradigm is beyond the scope of this book. Interested readers should consult Hall (1982). At the risk of oversimplification, in the rest of this section we compare the positivist and interpretive paradigms.

The positivist paradigm differs from the interpretive paradigm along three main dimensions. First, the two methods have a different philosophy of reality. For the positivist researcher, reality is objective; it exists apart from researchers and can be seen by all. In other words, it is out there. For the interpretive researcher, there is no single reality. Each observer creates reality as part of the research process. It is subjective and exists only in reference to the observer. Perhaps a classic example will help here. If a tree falls in the forest and there is no one there to hear it, does it make any noise? On the one hand, a positivist would answer yes. Reality doesn't depend on an observer; it exists independently. On the other hand, an interpretive researcher would say no noise was made. Reality exists only in the observer. Furthermore, the positivist researcher believes that reality can be divided into component parts, and knowledge of the whole is gained by looking at the parts. In contrast, the interpretive researcher examines the entire process, believing that reality is holistic and cannot be subdivided.

Second, the two methods have different views of the individual. The positivist researcher believes all human beings are basically similar and looks for general categories to summarize their behaviors or feelings. The interpretive investigator believes that human beings are fundamentally different and cannot be pigeonholed.

Third, positivist researchers aim to generate general laws of behavior and explain many things across many settings. In contrast, interpretive scholars attempt to produce a unique explanation about a given situation or individual. Whereas positivist researchers strive for breadth, interpretive researchers strive for depth.

The practical differences between these approaches are perhaps most apparent in the research process. The following five major research areas demonstrate significant differences between the positivist and interpretive approaches:

1. *Role of the researcher.* The positivist researcher strives for objectivity and is separated from the data. The interpretive researcher is an integral part of the data; in fact, without the active participation of the researcher, no data exist.

2. *Design.* For a positivist, the design of a study is determined before it begins. In interpretive research, the design evolves during the research; it can be adjusted or changed as the research progresses.

3. *Setting.* The positivist researcher tries to limit contaminating and confounding variables by conducting investigations in controlled settings. The interpretive researcher conducts studies in the field, in natural surroundings, trying to capture the normal flow of events without controlling extraneous variables.

4. *Measurement instruments.* In positivist research, measurement instruments exist apart from the researcher; another party could use the instruments to collect data in the researcher's absence. In interpretive research, the researcher is the instrument; no other individual can substitute.

5. *Theory building.* Where the positivist researcher uses research to test, support, or reject theory, the interpretive researcher develops theories as part of the research process—theory is "data driven" and emerges as part of the research process, evolving from the data as they are collected.

A researcher's paradigm has a great influence on the specific research methods that he or she uses. As Potter (1996, p. 36) explains: "Two scholars who hold different beliefs [paradigms] . . . may be interested in examining the same phenomenon but their beliefs will lead them to set up their studies very differently because of their differing views of evidence, analysis and the purpose of the research." The positivist approach is most closely associated with quantitative content analysis, surveys, and experiments, techniques discussed in detail in subsequent chapters. The interpretive approach is most closely connected with the specific research methods discussed in this chapter. Research methods, however, are not conscious of the philosophy that influenced their selection. It is not unusual to find a positivist using focus groups or intensive interviewing, two methods commonly categorized as qualitative, in connection with a quantitative study. Nor is it rare to find an interpretive researcher using numbers from a survey or content analysis. Thus the guidelines for focus groups that are discussed in this chapter, or the discussion of survey research in a subsequent chapter, are relevant to both paradigms. Although the methods may be the same, however, the research goal, the research question, and the way the data are interpreted are quite different.

To use a concrete example, assume that a positivist researcher is interested in testing the hypothesis that viewing negative political ads increases political cynicism. The researcher conducts a focus group to help develop a questionnaire that measures cynicism and exposure to what the researchers define as *negative advertising*. A statistical analysis is then conducted to see if these two items are related and if the hypothesis is supported.

An interpretive researcher interested in the same question might also conduct a focus group, but the questions discussed in the group concentrate on how group members interpret a political ad, what meanings they derive from a negative ad, the context of their viewing, and what makes them feel cynical toward politics. The focus groups stand alone as the source of data for the analysis. The interpretive researcher uses induction to try to find commonalities or general themes in participants' remarks. Thus both researchers use focus groups, a method traditionally defined as qualitative, but each uses the method somewhat differently.

Despite their differences, many researchers now use a combination of the quantitative and qualitative approaches in order to understand fully the phenomenon they are studying. As Miles and Huberman (1994, p. 20) state:

> It is getting harder to find any methodologists solidly encamped in one epistemology or the other. More and more "quantitative" methodologists . . . are using naturalistic and phenomenological approaches to complement tests, surveys, and structured interviews. On the other side, an increasing number of ethnographers and qualitative researchers are using predesigned conceptual frameworks and prestructured instrumentation. . . . Most people now see the world with more ecumenical eyes.

Cooper, Potter, and Dupagne (1994) document the importance of qualitative methods in the field. They report that although almost 60% of published mass communication research studies conducted since 1971 have used quantitative methods, qualitative techniques were used either exclusively (33%) or partially in the other 40%.

Although qualitative research can be an excellent way to collect and analyze data, researchers must keep in mind that the results of such studies have interpretational limits. Researchers interested in generalizing results should use large samples or consider other methods. In most cases, qualitative research studies use small samples—respondents or units that are not representative of the population from which they are drawn. Like quantitative research, qualitative research is a useful mass media research tool only when its limitations are recognized. All too often, the results from small-sample qualitative projects are interpreted as though they had been collected with large-sample quantitative techniques. This approach can only cause problems in the end. Decisions are highly likely to be incorrect if they are based on small-sample research.

Qualitative Research Definition—A Final Note

While most qualitative research projects use small samples that eliminate the ability of the researcher to generalize the results to the population, the truth is that it's easy to increase sample size to avoid this problem. This is often done in both private- and public-sector research and, therefore, eliminates the primary argument against using qualitative research. So what's the problem?

Well, if large sample sizes are used, then the difference between qualitative research and quantitative research must relate to something else. It does—it relates to how questions are asked. When all the clouds of controversy are eliminated, the difference between qualitative research and quantitative research boils down to this:

- Qualitative research uses a flexible questioning approach. Although a basic set of questions is designed to start the project, the researcher can change questions or ask follow-up questions at any time.
- Quantitative research uses a static or standardized set of questions. All respondents are asked the same questions. Although follow-up questions (and skips) can be designed into a questionnaire, they must be included in the questionnaire or measurement instrument before the research project begins.

▪ Data Analysis in Qualitative Research

Before examining some specific types of qualitative research, let's discuss qualitative data and methods of analysis in general. Qualitative data come in a variety of forms, such as notes made while observing in the field, interview transcripts, documents, diaries, and journals. In addition, a researcher accumulates a great deal of data during the course of a study. Organizing, analyzing, and making sense of all this information pose special challenges for the researcher using qualitative methods.

Unlike the quantitative approach, which waits until all the numbers are in before analysis begins, data analysis in qualitative studies is done early in the collection process and continues throughout the project. In addition, quantitative researchers generally follow a deductive model in data analysis: Hypotheses are developed prior to the study, and relevant data are then collected and analyzed to determine whether the hypotheses are confirmed or not confirmed. In contrast, qualitative researchers use an inductive method: Data are collected relevant to some topic and are grouped into appropriate and meaningful categories; explanations emerge from the data themselves.

Preparing the Data

To facilitate working with the large amounts of data generated by a qualitative analysis, the researcher generally first organizes the information along a temporal dimension. In other words, the data are arranged in chronological order according to the sequence of events that occurred during the investigation. Furthermore, each piece of information should be coded to identify the source. Multiple photocopies of the notes, transcripts, and other documents should be made.

The data are then organized into a preliminary category system. These categories might arise from the data themselves, or they might be suggested by prior research or theory. Many researchers prefer to do a preliminary run-through of the data and jot possible category assignments in the margins. For example, a qualitative study of teenage radio listening might produce many pages of interview transcripts. The researcher would read the comments and might write "peer group pressure" next to one section and "escape" next to another. When the process is finished, a preliminary category system may have emerged from the data. Other researchers prefer to make multiple copies of the data, cut them into coherent units of analysis, and physically sort them into as many categories as might be relevant. Finally, several software programs are available that help organize qualitative data.

Moreover, many qualitative researchers like to have a particular room or other space that is specially suited for the analysis of qualitative data. Typically, this room has bulletin boards or other arrangements for the visual display of data. Photocopies of notes, observations written on index cards, large flowcharts, and marginal comments can then be conveniently arrayed to simplify the analysis task. This "analytical wallpaper" approach is particularly helpful when there are several members of the research team working on the project because it is an efficient way to display the data to several people at once.

Finally, the researcher is the main instrument in qualitative data collection and analysis and therefore must do some preparation before beginning the task of investigation. Maykut and Morehouse (1994) describe this preparation as **epoche,** the process by which the researcher tries to remove or at least become aware of prejudices, viewpoints, or assumptions that might interfere with the analysis. Epoche helps the researcher put aside personal viewpoints so that the phenomenon under study may be seen for itself.

Analysis Techniques

Qualitative data can be analyzed with many different techniques. This section discusses two of the best known: the constant comparative technique and the analytical induction technique.

The **constant comparative technique** was first articulated by Glaser and Strauss (1967) and has subsequently been refined (Lincoln & Guba 1985). At a general level, the process consists of four steps:

1. Comparative assignment of incidents to categories
2. Elaboration and refinement of categories
3. Searching for relationships and themes among categories
4. Simplifying and integrating data into a coherent theoretical structure

Each of these steps is discussed in turn.

Comparative assignment of incidents to categories. After the data have been prepared for analysis, the researcher puts each unit of analysis into a set of provisional categories. As each new unit is examined, it is compared to the other units previously assigned to that category to see whether its inclusion is appropriate. It is possible that some initial categories may have only one or two incidents assigned to them while others may have a large number. If some units of analysis do not fit any preexisting category, new classifications may have to be created. Units that fit into more than one category should be copied and included where relevant. Throughout the process, the emphasis is on comparing units and finding similarities among the units that fit into the category.

For example, suppose a researcher is doing a qualitative study about why individuals subscribe to online services such as America Online. Interviews are conducted with several people and transcribed. The researcher then defines each individual assertion as the unit of analysis and writes each statement on an index card. The first two cards selected for analysis mention getting news faster from online services. The researcher places both of these into a category tentatively labeled "news." The next statement talks about email; it does not seem to belong to the first category and is set aside. The next card mentions chat lines; the researcher decides this reason is similar to the one that mentioned email and creates a new category called "interpersonal communication." The process is then repeated with every unit of analysis, which can be a long and formidable task. At some point during the process, however, the researcher begins to fine-tune and refine the categories.

Elaboration and refinement of categories. During the category refinement stage, the researcher writes rules or propositions that attempt to describe the underlying meaning that defines the category. Some rules for inclusion might be rewritten and revised throughout the study. These rules not only help to focus the study but also allow the researcher to start to explore the theoretical dimensions of the emerging category system. The ultimate value of these rules, however, is that they reveal what you are learning about your chosen topic and help you determine your research outcome.

After scanning all the data cards in the "interpersonal communication" category, a researcher might write a proposition such as "People subscribe to online services in order to expand their circle of casual friends." Similar statements are written for the other categories.

Searching for relationships and themes among categories. The third phase of the method involves searching for relationships and common patterns across categories. The researcher examines the propositional statements and looks for meaningful connections. Some propositions are probably strong enough to stand alone; others might be related in several important ways. Whatever the situation, the goal of this phase is to generate assertions that can explain and further clarify the phenomenon under study.

In our online example, the researcher might note that several propositions refer to the notion of expansion. People use online services to expand their shopping opportunities, to enlarge their pool of potential chess opponents, or to have a greater number of news sources. The analyst then generalizes that the expansion of one's informational space is an essential reason for subscribing.

Simplifying and integrating data into a coherent theoretical structure. In the final phase of the process, the report summarizing the research is written. All the results of the foregoing analyses are integrated into some coherent explanation of the phenomenon. The researcher attempts to offer a brief explanation but in sufficient detail to convey an idea of the scope of the project. The goal of this phase of the project is to arrive at an understanding of the people and events being studied.

The **analytic induction strategy** blends hypothesis construction and data analysis. It consists of the following steps (adapted from Stainback & Stainback 1988):

1. Define a topic of interest and develop a hypothesis.
2. Study a case to see whether the hypothesis works. If it doesn't work, reformulate it.
3. Study other cases until the hypothesis is in refined form.
4. Look for "negative cases" that might disprove the hypothesis. Reformulate again.
5. Continue until the hypothesis is adequately tested.

Note that in this method, an explanation for the phenomenon, in the form of a hypothesis, is generated at the beginning of the study. This process contrasts with the constant comparative technique, in which an explanation is derived as the result of the research.

Perhaps the best way to demonstrate how the analytic induction approach works is with a simplified example. Let's suppose that a researcher is interested in explaining why people watch home shopping channels. Colleagues tell the researcher that the answer is obvious: People watch because they want to buy the merchandise. The researcher is not convinced of this but decides to use this explanation as an initial hypothesis and finds a person who is known to be a heavy viewer of these channels. During the interview, the person says that although she has ordered a couple of things off the air, her primary reason for watching is to find out about new and unusual products.

Armed with this information, the researcher reformulates the hypothesis: People watch the home shopping channels to buy and find out about new products. Another viewer is interviewed and reports essentially the same reasons but also adds that he uses the prices advertised on the channel to comparison shop. Once again, the hypothesis is refined. The researcher posits that the home shopping channels are viewed for practical consumer-related reasons: finding bargains, learning about products, and comparing prices.

At this point, the researcher tries to find cases that might not fit the new hypothesis. A colleague points out that all the people interviewed so far have been affluent, with substantial disposable income and that perhaps people who are less well-off economically might watch the home shopping channels for other reasons. The researcher interviews a viewer from a different economic background and discovers that this person watches because he finds the people who do the selling entertaining to watch. Once again, the initial hypothesis is modified to take this finding into account.

The researcher then finds other respondents from different economic levels to check the validity of this new hypothesis and continues to gather data until no more cases can be located that do not fit the revised hypothesis.

This process can be exhausting, and it can be difficult for the researcher to determine an exact stopping point. One might always argue that there are still cases in the environment that would not support the hypothesis, but the researcher simply did not find them.

Reliability and Validity in Qualitative Data

Qualitative researchers must pay attention to several different concerns that may call the credibility of their research into question. First, there is the matter of the completeness of the data. If a qualitative researcher does a sloppy job taking notes or otherwise recording what was observed, there is the possibility that incorrect interpretations may be drawn from the data. A second problem concerns selective perception. A qualitative researcher cannot simply dismiss data that do not fit his or her favored interpretation of the data. The researcher must analyze these cases and offer explanations as to why they don't seem to fit. Finally, qualitative research often raises the question of reactivity—the act of observing some situation changes the situation itself. Would the same things have occurred if the researcher was not there? Reactivity is a difficult problem to overcome, but researchers must try to minimize it whenever possible. Taken together, these three factors suggest that qualitative researchers, much like quantitative researchers, must pay attention to the reliability and validity of their data.

The concepts of reliability and validity, however, have different connotations for qualitative data. As we discuss later, quantitative methods use distinct and precise ways to calculate indexes of reliability and several articulated techniques that help establish validity. These concepts, however, do not translate well into the interpretive paradigm. As Lindlof (1995) points out, interpretive research recognizes the changing nature of behavior and perception over time. Nonetheless, though envisioned differently, reliability and validity are no less important in qualitative research. They help readers determine how much confidence can be placed in the outcomes of the study and whether they can believe the researcher's conclusions. Or as Lindlof (1995, p. 238) puts it: "Basically, we want to inspire confidence in readers (and ourselves) that we have achieved right interpretations." Or as Hammersly (1992) expressed it, validity is achieved when the description of the observed phenomenon accurately depicts what was observed.

Rather than emphasizing reliability and validity, Maykut and Morehouse (1994) address the trustworthiness of a qualitative research project. They summarize four factors that help build credibility:

1. *Multiple methods of data collection.* This factor is similar to the notion of triangulation that was discussed in Chapter 2. The use of interviews along with field observations and analysis of existing documents suggests that the topic was examined from several different perspectives, which helps build confidence in the findings.

2. *Audit trail.* This factor is essentially a permanent record of the original data used for analysis and the researcher's comments and analysis methods. The audit trail allows others to examine the thought processes involved in the researcher's work and allows them to assess the accuracy of her or his conclusions.

3. *Member checks.* In this technique, research participants are asked to read your notes and conclusions and tell whether you have accurately described what they told you.

4. *Research team.* This method assumes that team members keep one another honest and on target when describing and interpreting their data. Sometimes an outside person is asked to observe the process and raise questions of possible bias or misinterpretation where appropriate.

Creswell (1998) suggests another method to aid verification—*debriefing*. This consists of having an individual outside the project question the meanings, methods, and interpretations of the researcher.

The balance of this chapter discusses four common qualitative techniques: field observations, focus groups, intensive interviews, and case studies.

▪ Field Observations

Field observation was rarely used in mass media research before 1980. Cooper, Potter, and Dupagne (1994) found that about 2% of all published studies from 1965 to 1989 relied on observation. Recently, however, field observations have become more common in the research literature (Anderson 1987; Lindlof 1987, 1991, 1995).

Field observation is useful for collecting data and for generating hypotheses and theories. Like all qualitative techniques, it is concerned more with description and explanation than with measurement and quantification. Figure 5.1 shows that field observations are classified along two major dimensions: (1) the degree to which the researcher participates in the behavior under observation, and (2) the degree to which the observation is concealed.

Quadrant 1 in Figure 5.1 represents overt observation. In this situation, the researcher is identified when the study begins, and those under observation are aware that they are being studied. Furthermore, the researcher's role is only to observe, refraining from participation in the process under observation. Quadrant 2 represents overt participation. In this arrangement, those being observed also know the researcher, but unlike the situation represented in Quadrant 1, the researcher goes beyond the observer role and becomes a participant

Figure 5.1 *Dimensions of Field Observation*

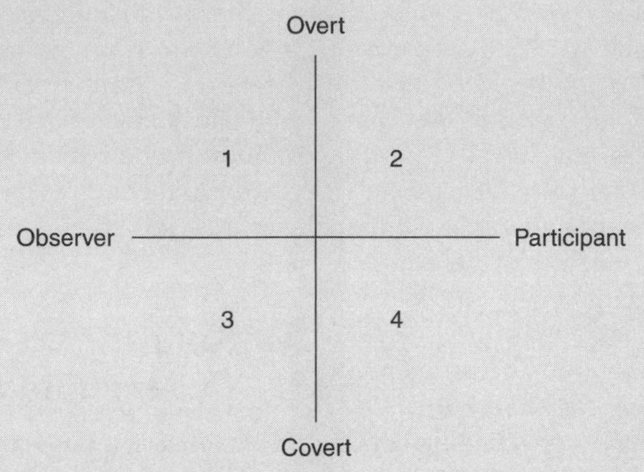

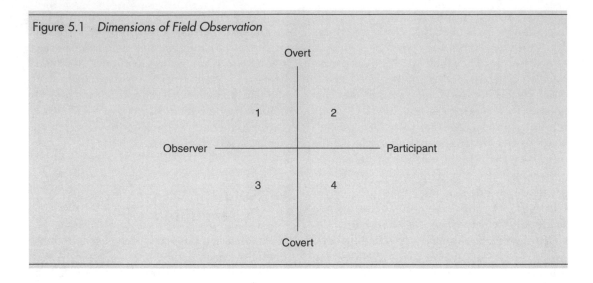

in the situation. Quadrant 3 represents the situation where the researcher's role is limited to that of observer, but those under observation are not aware they are being studied. Quadrant 4 represents a study in which the researcher participates in the process under investigation but is not identified as a researcher.

To illustrate the difference between the various approaches, assume that a researcher wants to observe and analyze the dynamics of writing comedy for television. The researcher could choose the covert observer technique and pretend to be doing something else (such as fixing a computer) while actually observing the TV writing team at work. Or the researcher could be introduced as someone doing a study of comedy writing and watch the team in action. If the research question is best answered by active participation, the researcher might be introduced as a researcher but still participate in the writing process. If the covert participant strategy is used, the researcher might be introduced as a new writer just joining the group (such an arrangement might be made with the head writer, who would be the only person to know the identity of the researcher). The choice of technique depends upon the research problem, the degree of cooperation available from the group or individual observed, and ethical considerations. On the one hand, covert participation may affect subjects' behavior and raise the ethical question of deception. On the other hand, the information gathered may be more valid if subjects are unaware of being scrutinized.

Some examples of field observation studies in mass media research include Gieber's (1956) classic study of gatekeeping (information flow) in the newsroom and Epstein's (1974) description of network news operations. Lemish (1987) used overt observation in her study of television viewing by infants and toddlers. Researchers visited the homes of 16 families and observed the viewing behavior of infants during 1- to 2-hour periods. Similarly, Moriarty and Everett (1994) conducted a study where researchers observed family members watching television and recorded their behaviors on a moment-to-moment basis during several 45-minute viewing episodes. Durham (1999) observed peer group interactions among adolescent girls in order to study the impact of the media on teenage girls' sexuality. Bielby, Harrington and Bielby (1999) observed meetings of soap opera fan clubs in their study of the way fans relate to soap opera characters.

Advantages of Field Observations

Although field observation is not an appropriate technique for every research question, it does have several unique advantages. For one thing, many mass media problems and questions cannot be studied using any other methodology. Field observation often helps the researcher to define basic background information necessary to frame a hypothesis and to isolate independent and dependent variables. For example, a researcher interested in how creative decisions in advertising are made could observe several decision-making sessions to see what happens. Field observations often make excellent pilot studies because they identify important variables and provide useful preliminary information. In addition, since the data are gathered firsthand, observation is not dependent on the subjects' ability or willingness to report their behavior. For example, young children may lack the reading or verbal skills necessary to respond to a questionnaire concerning their TV viewing behavior, but such data are easily gathered by the observational technique.

A field observation is not always used as a preliminary step to other approaches. Sometimes it alone is the only appropriate approach, especially when quantification is difficult. Field observation is particularly suitable for a study of the gatekeeping process in a network television news department because it is difficult to quantify gatekeeping.

Field observation may also provide access to groups that would otherwise be difficult to observe or examine. For example, a questionnaire sent to producers of X-rated movies is not likely to have a high return rate. An observer, however, may be able to establish mutual trust with such a group and persuade them to respond to rigorous questioning.

Field observation is usually inexpensive. In most cases it requires only writing materials or a small tape recorder. Expenses increase if the problem under study requires several observers, extensive travel, or special equipment (such as videorecording machines).

Perhaps the most noteworthy advantage of field observation is that the study takes place in the natural setting of the activity being observed and thus can provide data rich in detail and subtlety. Many mass media situations, such as a family watching television, are complex and constantly subjected to intervening influences. Field observation, because of the opportunity for careful examination, allows observers to identify these otherwise unknown variables.

Disadvantages of Field Observations

On the negative side, field observation is a poor choice if the researcher is concerned with external validity. Validation is difficult partly because the representativeness of the observations made is potentially questionable and partly because of problems in sampling. Observing the TV viewing behavior of a group of children at a day care center can provide valuable insights into the social setting of television viewing, but it probably has little correlation with what preschoolers do in other places and under different circumstances. Besides, since field observation relies heavily on a researcher's perceptions and judgments and on preconceived notions about the material under study, experimenter bias may favor specific preconceptions of results, while observations to the contrary are ignored or distorted. Potential bias is why it is rare to use only one observer in a field observation study—observations should be *cross-validated* by second or third observers.

Finally, field observations suffer from the problem of **reactivity**. The very process of being observed may influence the behavior

AN INSIDE LOOK

Reactivity

The reaction of respondents in any type of research study is an important element to consider. An example that relates to research is how people react when they learn that they are being filmed. This reaction is especially evident in group settings such as protests or other political activities. Experienced mass media researchers learn to anticipate reactivity and account for it in their research designs.

under study. Of course, reactivity can be a problem with other research methods, but it is most often mentioned as a criticism of field observation (Chadwick, Bahr, & Albrecht 1984). Lull (1985) provides perspective on observer effects using data taken from an observational study of families' TV viewing behavior. He found that the presence of an observer in the house did have some impact on behavior. About 20% of parents and 25% of children reported that their overall behavior was affected by the presence of an observer. Most of those who were affected thought that they became nicer or more polite and formal because of the observer's presence. As for differences in the key behavior under study, 87% said that the observer's presence had no effect on their TV viewing activity. Additionally, among those who reported an observer effect, there were no systematic differences in the distribution of changes. About the same number said that they watched more because of the observer as said they watched less. Obviously, additional studies of different groups in different settings are needed before this problem is fully understood, but Lull's data suggest that although reactivity is a problem with observational techniques, its impact may not be as drastic as some suggest.

In any case, at least two strategies are available to diminish the impact of selective perception and reactivity. One is to use several observers to cross-validate the results. A second strategy is triangulation, or supplementing observational data with data gathered by other means (for example, questionnaires or existing records). Accuracy is sought by using multiple data collection methods.

Field Observation Techniques

There are at least six stages in a typical field observation study: choosing the research site, gaining access, sampling, collecting data, analyzing data, and exiting.

Choosing the Research Site. The nature of the research question or area of inquiry usually suggests a behavior or a phenomenon of interest. Once it is identified, the next step is to select a setting where the behavior or phenomenon occurs with sufficient frequency to make observation worthwhile. The settings also should fit the recording forms and instruments the observer plans to use. For example, videotaping requires adequate lighting for the camera to operate.

Possible research venues can be identified from personal experience, from talking with other researchers, from interviews with people who frequent the site, or from newspaper and magazine stories. Anderson (1987) suggests that researchers select two or three research sites and then "hang around" (Anderson's terminology) each one to discover their main advantages and disadvantages. He cautions researchers that the site must be permanent and stable enough to permit observations over a period of time. Lindlof (1995) suggests a similar process that he labels "casing the scene." He suggests that researchers gain an understanding of what is possible from a site and make sure that the site holds the potential for fruitful data collection.

Qualitative researchers should avoid choosing sites where they are well known or have some involvement. Studying one's own workplace, for example, is difficult because the researcher's preconceptions may preclude observations that are more objective. Furthermore, at a site where the researcher is a familiar figure, other individuals may find it difficult to relate to a colleague or friend in the new role of researcher.

Gaining Access. Once the site is selected, the next step is to establish contact. Williamson, Karp, and Dalphin (1992) note that the degree of difficulty faced by researchers in gaining access to settings depends on two factors: (1) how public the setting is and (2) the willingness of the subjects in the setting to be observed. The easiest setting to enter is one that is open to the public and that gives people little reason to keep their behavior secret (for example, a place in which people are watching TV in public—an airport, a bar, a dormitory viewing room). The most difficult setting to enter is one in which entry is restricted because participants have good reason to keep their activities secret (for example, a place in which one could observe the behavior of hostage takers).

Observing a formal group (such as a film production crew) often requires permission from management and perhaps union officials. School systems and other bureaucracies usually have a special unit to handle requests from researchers and to help them obtain necessary permissions.

Gaining permission to conduct field observation research requires persistence and public relations skills. Researchers must decide how much to disclose about the nature of the research. Usually it is not necessary to provide a complete explanation of the hypothesis and procedures unless there are objections to sensitive areas. Researchers interested in observing which family member actually controls the television set might explain that they are studying patterns of family communication. After the contact is made, rapport must be established with the subject(s). Bogdan and Taylor (1998) suggest the following techniques for building rapport: establish common interests with the participants; start relationships slowly; if appropriate, participate in common events and activities; and do not disrupt participants' normal routines.

Lindlof (1995) suggests these ways of gaining access:

- Identify the scene's gatekeeper and attempt to persuade him or her of the project's relevance.
- Find a sponsor who can vouch for the usefulness of the project and can help locate participants.
- Negotiate an agreement with participants.

Neuman (1997) illustrates entry and access as an access ladder. The bottom rung represents the easiest situation in which the researcher is looking for public information. The highest rung on the ladder, which requires the most time spent in the field site, involves gaining access to sensitive events and information.

Sampling. Sampling in field observation is more ambiguous than in most other research approaches. First, there is the problem of how many individuals or groups to observe. If the focus of the study is communication in the newsroom, how many newsrooms should be observed? If the topic is family viewing of television, how many families should be included? Unfortunately, there are no guidelines to help answer these questions. The research problem and the goals of the study are indicators of the appropriate sample size; for example, if the results are intended for generalization to a population, studying one subject or group is inadequate.

Another problem is deciding what behavior episodes or segments to sample. The observer cannot be everywhere and see everything, so what is observed becomes a de facto sample of what is not observed. If an observer views one staff meeting in the newsroom, this meeting represents other unobserved meetings; one conversation at the coffee machine represents all such conversations. Representativeness must be considered even when researchers cannot follow the principles of probability sampling.

Most field observations use purposive sampling, where observers draw on their knowledge of the subject(s) under study and sample only from the relevant behaviors or events. Sometimes previous experience and study of the activity in question suggest what needs to be examined. In a study of newsroom decision making, for example, researchers would want to observe staff meetings because they are an important part of the process. However, restricting the sampling to observations of staff meetings would be a mistake because many decisions are made at the water fountain, at lunch, and in the hallways. Experienced observers tend not to isolate a specific situation but instead to consider even the most insignificant situation for analysis. For most field observations, researchers need to spend some time simply getting the feel of the situation and absorbing the pertinent aspects of the environment before beginning a detailed analysis.

Here are some sampling strategies that might be used (Lindlof, 1995):

- *Maximum variation sampling:* Settings, activities, events, and informants are chosen purposefully to yield as many different and varied situations as possible.
- *Snowball sampling:* A participant refers the researcher to another person who can provide information. This person, in turn, mentions another, and so forth.
- *Typical case sampling:* In contrast to the maximum variation technique, the researcher chooses cases that seem to be most representative of the topic under study.

A more extensive listing of 16 possible sampling strategies is found in Miles and Huberman (1994), including *extreme case sampling,* which looks for highly unusual examples of the phenomenon under study, and *politically important case sampling,* which examines cases that have attracted major attention.

Collecting Data. The traditional data collection tools—notebook and pencil—have been supplemented if not supplanted by other instruments in recent years. As early as 1972, Bechtel, Achelpohl, and Akers installed television cameras in a small sample of households to document families' TV viewing behavior. Two cameras, automatically activated when the television set was turned on, videotaped the scene in front of the set. However, even though a camera can record more information than an observer, Bechtel reported that the project was difficult because of problems in finding consenting families, maintaining the equipment, and interpreting tapes shot at low light levels.

Similarly, Anderson (1987) notes that, even though the advantages offered by audio and video recording are tempting, there are five major drawbacks to their use:

1. Recording devices take time away from the research process because they need regular calibration and adjustment to work properly.
2. The frame of the recording is different from the frame of the observer; a hu-

man observer's field of view is about 180°, whereas a camera's is about 60°.

3. Recordings have to be cataloged, indexed, and transcribed, adding extra work to the project.
4. Recordings take behavior out of context.
5. Recordings tend to fragment behavior and distract attention from the overall process.

Consequently, researchers must weigh the pros and cons carefully before deciding to use recording equipment for observations.

Note taking in the covert participant situation requires special attention. Continually scribbling away on a notepad is certain to draw attention and suspicion to the note taker and might expose the study's real purpose. In this type of situation, researchers should make mental notes and transcribe them at the first opportunity. If a researcher's identity is known initially, the problem of note taking is eliminated. Regardless of the situation, it is not wise for a researcher to spend a lot of time taking notes; subjects are already aware of being observed, and note taking can make them uneasy. Brief notes jotted down during natural breaks in a situation attract a minimum of attention and can be expanded later.

Field notes constitute the basic corpus of data in any field study. In these notes, the observers record not only what happened and what was said, but also personal impressions, feelings, and interpretations of what was observed. A useful procedure is to separate personal opinions from the descriptive narrative by enclosing the former in brackets.

How much should be recorded? It is always better to record too much information than too little. A seemingly irrelevant observation made during the first viewing session might become significant later in the project. If the material is sensitive or if the researcher does not wish it known that research is taking place, notes may be written in abbreviated form or in code. In addition to firsthand observation, three other data collection techniques are available to field researchers: diary keeping, unobtrusive measures, and document analysis. With the first technique, an investigator routinely supplements his or her field notes by keeping a research diary. This diary consists of personal feelings, sentiments, occasional reflections, and other private thoughts about the research process itself; the writings augment and help interpret the raw data contained in the field notes. Moreover, the researcher may ask the individuals under study to keep a diary for a specified length of time. This enables the researcher to learn about behaviors that take place out of his or her sight and extends the horizontal dimension of the observation. Individuals may be instructed to track certain habits—such as the reading of books or magazines during a specific time of day—or to record general feelings and thoughts—such as the way they felt while watching commercials on TV.

One form of diary keeping actually provides researchers with a glimpse of the world as seen through the eyes of the subject(s). The researcher gives the subjects still cameras and asks them to make photographic essays or to keep photographic diaries. Analysis of these photographs might help determine how the subjects perceive reality and what they find important. To illustrate, Ziller and Smith (1977) asked current and former students of the University of Florida to take photographs that described the school. The perceptions of the two groups were different: Current students brought in pictures of buildings, and former students brought in pictures of people.

A second data collection technique available to the field researcher is unobtrusive measurement. This technique helps overcome the problem of reactivity by searching out naturally occurring phenomena relevant to the research task. The people who provide data through unobtrusive measurement are unaware that they are providing information for a research project. Covert observation, as previously mentioned, is obviously a technique of this type, but there are also other very subtle ways to collect data. It might be possible, for example, to determine the popularity of radio stations in a given market by asking auto mechanics to keep track of the dial positions of the radio pushbuttons of cars brought in for repair. Or, in another case, an investigator might use the parking lot at an auto race to discover which brand of tires appears most often on cars owned by people attending the race. Such information might enable tire companies to determine whether their sponsorship of various races has an impact.

Webb, Campbell, Schwartz, and Sechrest (1968) identify two general types of unobtrusive measurements: erosion and accretion. The first type, erosion, estimates wear and tear on a specific object or material. For example, to determine what textbooks are used heavily by students, a researcher might note how many passages in the text are highlighted, how many pages are dogeared, whether the book's spine is creased, and so on. Accretion, on the other hand, quantifies deposits that have built up over time, such as the amount of dust that has built up on the cover of a textbook.

Accretion and erosion measurement methods, however, do have drawbacks. First, they are passive measures and out of the control of the researcher. Second, other factors might influence what is being observed. Compulsively neat students, for example, might dust their books every day, whether or not they open them, thus providing a misleading accretion measurement. For these reasons, unobtrusive measurements are usually used to support or corroborate findings from other observational methods rather than to draw conclusions from.

Finally, existing documents may represent a fertile source of data for the qualitative researcher. In general terms, two varieties of documents are available for analysis: public and private. Public documents include police reports, newspaper stories, transcripts of TV shows, data archives, and so on. Other items may be less recognizable as public documents, however; messages on computer bulletin boards, company newsletters, tombstones, posters, graffiti, and bumper stickers can all fit into this category. Any of these messages may represent a rich source of data for the qualitative researcher. Shamp (1991), for example, analyzed messages that had been left on computer bulletin boards to examine users' perceptions of their communication partners. Priest (1992) used transcripts of the "Donahue" TV program to structure in-depth interviews with people who appeared on the show.

Private documents, on the other hand, include personal letters, diaries, memos, faxes, home movies and videos, telephone logs, appointment books, reports, and so on. For example, a public relations researcher interested in examining the communication flow among executives in an organization might find copies of memos, faxes, appointments, and telephone logs of special interest.

Much like unobtrusive measurements, document analysis also has occasional disadvantages: missing documents, subjects unwilling to make private documents available, ethical problems with the use of private records such as diaries and letters, and so on. To reduce the possibility of error when working with archival data, Berg (1997) urges researchers to use several data collection methods.

Analyzing Data. We have discussed some general considerations of qualitative data analysis. Concerning the specific technique of field observation, data analysis consists of primarily filing the information and analyzing its content. Constructing a filing system is an important step in observation. The purpose of the filing system is to arrange raw field data in an orderly format that is amenable to systematic retrieval later. (The precise filing categories are determined by the data.) From the hypothetical study of decision making in the newsroom, filing categories might include

AN INSIDE LOOK
Ethical Concerns in Qualitative Research

All the ethical principles discussed in Chapter 3 have applications in qualitative research, but the nature of qualitative research raises some additional concerns. With regard to informed consent, it may be necessary for a qualitative researcher to disclose all the details of the project that might make the respondent's life more difficult. A prospective informant for a project using intensive interviewing should be told about the significant time commitment involved if he or she participates in the research. Participation might also mean traveling to the interview site, agreeing to have the interview audiotaped, and possibly being reinterviewed in the future. All these facts should be revealed to the informant in order to fulfill the obligation of informed consent.

Further, what if covert observation reveals evidence of illegal activity, such as spouse abuse? Is the researcher obligated to share that knowledge with the appropriate authorities? What about promises of confidentiality to the participant? Suppose a researcher is examining the way people watch television in a public place, such as a sports bar. As part of the research, the researcher promises confidentiality and conducts intensive interviews with the staff. The interviews reveal a couple of disgruntled employees.

During the project, the sports bar burns down under suspicious circumstances and police suspect arson. The investigators hear about the research project and ask to see the notes and transcripts of the intensive interviews. Should the researcher turn over the notes? Issues such as these must be considered before the project begins.

the headings "Relationships," "Interaction—Horizontal," "Interaction—Vertical," and "Disputes." An observation may be placed in more than one category. It is a good idea to make multiple copies of notes; periodic filing of notes during the observation period will save time and confusion later.

Once all the notes have been assigned to their proper files, a rough content analysis is performed to search for consistent patterns. Perhaps, for example, most decisions in the newsroom are made in informal settings such as hallways rather than in formal settings such as conference rooms. Perhaps most decisions are made with little superior–subordinate consultation. At the same time, deviations from the norm should be investigated. Perhaps all reporters except one are typically asked their opinions on the newsworthiness of events; why the exception?

The overall goal of data analysis in field observation is to arrive at a general understanding of the phenomenon under study. In this regard, the observer has the advantage of flexibility. In laboratory and other research approaches, investigators must at some point commit themselves to a particular design or questionnaire. If it subsequently becomes apparent that a crucial variable was left out, little can be done. In field observation, however, the researcher can analyze data during the course of the study and change the research design accordingly.

Exiting. A participant must have a plan for leaving the setting or the group under study. Of course, if everyone knows the participant, exiting is not a problem. Exiting from a setting that participants regularly enter and leave is also not a problem. Exiting can be difficult, however, when participation is covert. In some instances, the group may have become dependent on the researcher in some way, and the departure may have a negative effect on the group as a whole. In other cases, the sudden revelation that a group has been infiltrated or duped by an outsider might be unpleasant or distressing to some. The researcher has an ethical obligation to do everything possible to prevent psychological, emotional, or physical injury to those being studied. Consequently, leaving the scene must be handled with diplomacy and tact.

▪ Focus Groups

The **focus group**, or group interviewing, is a research strategy for understanding audience attitudes and behavior. From 6 to 12 people are interviewed simultaneously, with a moderator leading the respondents in a relatively unstructured discussion about the focal topic. The identifying characteristic of the focus group is controlled group discussion, which is used to gather preliminary information for a research project, to help develop questionnaire items for survey research, to understand the reasons behind a particular phenomenon, to see how a group of people interpret a certain phenomenon, or to test preliminary ideas or plans. A brief guide for conducting focus groups may be found on our website at http://www.wimmerdominick.com. The following discussion of advantages and disadvantages is generally from a positivist perspective. Lunt and Livingstone (1996) provide a discussion of the focus group method with more of an interpretive perspective.

Advantages of Focus Groups

Focus groups allow researchers to collect preliminary information about a topic or a phenomenon. They may be used in pilot studies to detect ideas that will be investigated further using another research method, such as a telephone survey, or some other qualitative method. A second important advantage is that focus groups can be conducted very quickly. Most of the time is spent recruiting the respondents. A field service that specializes in recruiting focus groups can usually recruit respondents in 7 to 10 days, depending on the type of participant required.

The cost of focus groups also makes the approach an attractive research method. In the private sector, most sessions can be conducted for about $1,000–$4,500 per group, depending on the type of respondent required, the part of the country in which the group is conducted, and the moderator or company used to conduct the group. When respondents are difficult to recruit or when the topic requires a specially trained moderator, a focus group may cost much more. However, the cost is not excessive if the groups provide valuable data for further research studies. Focus groups used in academic research, of course, cost much less.

Researchers also like focus groups because of the flexibility in question design and follow-up. In conventional surveys, interviewers work from a rigid series of questions and are instructed to follow explicit directions in asking the questions. A moderator in a focus group, however, works from a list of broad questions as well as more refined probe questions; hence, it is easy to follow up on important points raised by participants in the group. The ability to clear up confusing responses from subjects makes focus groups valuable in the research process.

Most professional focus group moderators use a procedure known as an **extended focus group,** in which respondents are required to complete a written questionnaire before the group session begins. The pregroup questionnaire, which covers the material that will be discussed during the group session, forces that respondents to "commit" to a particular answer or position before entering the group. This commitment eliminates one potential problem created by group dynamics—namely, the person who does not wish to offer an opinion because he or she is in a minority.

Finally, focus group responses are often more complete and less inhibited than those from individual interviews. One respondent's remarks tend to stimulate others to pursue lines of thinking that might not have been elicited in a situation involving just one individual. With a competent moderator, the discussion can have a beneficial snowball effect, as one respondent comments on the views of another. A skilled moderator also can detect the opinions and attitudes of those who are less articulate by noting facial expressions and other nonverbal behavior while others are speaking.

Disadvantages of Focus Groups

Focus group research is not free of complications; the approach is far from perfect. Some of the problems are discussed here; others are given at our website.

A self-appointed group leader who monopolizes the conversation and attempts to impose his or her opinion on other participants dominates some groups. Such a person usually draws the resentment of the other participants and may have an extremely adverse effect on the performance of the group. The moderator needs to control such situations tactfully before they get out of hand.

A focus group is an inappropriate technique for gathering quantitative data. If quantification is important, it is wise to supplement the focus group with other research tools that permit more specific questions to be addressed to a more representative sample. Many people unfamiliar with focus group research incorrectly assume that the method will answer the question "how many" or "how much." In fact, focus group research is intended to gather qualitative data to answer questions such as "why" or "how." Many times people who hire a person or company to conduct a focus group are disappointed with the results because they expected exact numbers and percentages. Focus groups do not provide such information. As suggested earlier, focus groups depend heavily on the skills of the moderator, who must know when to probe for further information, when to stop respondents from discussing irrelevant topics, and how to involve all respondents in the discussion. All these things must be accomplished with professionalism, since one sarcastic or inappropriate comment to a respondent may have a chilling effect on the group's performance.

Looked at from the positivist perspective, focus groups have other drawbacks as well. The small focus group samples are usually composed of volunteers and do not necessarily represent the population from which they were drawn; the recording equipment or other physical characteristics of the location may inhibit respondents; and if the respondents are allowed to stray too far from the topic under consideration, the data produced may not be useful.

Methodology of Focus Groups

There are seven basic steps in focus group research:

1. *Define the problem.* This step is similar in all types of scientific research: A well-defined problem is established on the basis of previous investigation or out of curiosity. For example, television production companies that produce pilot programs for potential series often conduct 10 to 50 focus groups with target viewers to determine the groups' reactions to each concept.

2. *Select a sample.* Because focus groups are small, researchers must define a narrow audience for the study. The type of sample depends on the purpose of the focus group; the sample might consist of consumers who watch a particular type of television program, men aged 18–34 who listen to a certain type of music, or teenagers who purchase more than 10 record albums a year.

3. *Determine the number of groups necessary.* To help eliminate part of the problem of selecting a representative group, most researchers conduct two or more focus groups on the same topic. They can then compare results to determine whether any similarities or differences exist; or one group may be used as a basis for comparison with the other group. A focus group study using only one group is rare because there is no way to know whether the results are group-specific or characteristic of a wider audience.

4. *Prepare the study mechanics.* We present a more detailed description of the mechanical aspects of focus groups at our website. Suffice it to say here that this step includes arranging for the recruitment of respondents (by telephone or possibly by shopping center intercept), reserving the facilities at which the groups will be conducted, and deciding what type of recording (audio, video, or both) will be used. The moderator must be selected and briefed about the purpose of the group. In addition, the researcher needs to determine the amount of co-op money each respondent will receive for participating. Respondents usually receive between $25 and $50 for attending, although professionals such as doctors and lawyers may require up to $500 or more for co-op.

5. *Prepare the focus group materials.* Each aspect of a focus group must be planned in detail; nothing should be left to chance—in particular, the moderator must not be allowed to "wing it." The screener questionnaire is developed to recruit the desired respondents; recordings and other materials the subjects will hear or see are prepared; any questionnaires the subjects will complete are produced (including the presession questionnaire); and a list of questions is developed for the presession questionnaire and the moderator's guide.

Generally, a focus group session begins with some type of shared experience, so that the individuals have a common base from which to start the discussion. The members may listen to or view a tape or examine a new product, or they may simply be asked how they answered the first question on the presession questionnaire.

The existence of a moderator's guide (see website) does not mean that the moderator cannot ask questions not contained in the guide. Quite the opposite is true. The significant quality of a focus group is that it allows the moderator to probe respondents' comments during the session. A professional moderator is able to develop a line of questioning that no one thought about before the group began, and the questioning usually provides important information. Professional moderators who have this skill receive substantial fees for conducting focus groups.

6. *Conduct the session.* Focus groups may be conducted in a variety of settings, from professional conference rooms equipped with one-way mirrors to hotel rooms rented for the occasion. In most situations, a professional conference room is used. Hotel and motel rooms are used when a focus facility is not available.

7. *Analyze the data and prepare a summary report.* The written summary of focus group interviews depends on the needs of the study and the amount of time and money available. At one extreme, the moderator/researcher may simply write a brief synopsis of what was said and offer an interpretation of the subjects' responses. For a more elaborate content analysis or a more complete description of what happened, the sessions can be transcribed so that the moderator or researcher can scan the comments and develop a category system, coding each comment into the appropriate category. Focus groups conducted in the private sector rarely go beyond a summary of the groups; clients also have access to the audiotapes and videotapes if they desire.

Examples of Focus Groups

Morrison and Krugman (2001) conducted a series of four focus groups with adults who demonstrated different levels of computer-mediated technologies in their homes. Respondents reported that there were different areas of the home and different functions assigned to television and to computers. In their study of MTV videos, McKee and Pardun (1999) conducted seven focus groups composed of college students. Each group watched two music videos that contained religious imagery and was asked to write down and then discuss their perceptions of the visual images. Finally, Steele (1999) conducted eight focus groups among teens that examined media influences on teen sexuality. The eight groups produced more than 30 hours of taped material.

Intensive Interviews

Intensive interviews, or in-depth interviews, are essentially a hybrid of the one-on-one interview approach discussed in Chapter 7. Intensive interviews are unique for these reasons:

- They generally use smaller samples.
- They provide detailed background about the reasons why respondents give specific answers. Elaborate data concerning respondents' opinions, values, motivations, recollections, experiences, and feelings are obtained.
- Intensive interviews allow for lengthy observation of respondents' nonverbal responses.
- They are usually very long. Unlike personal interviews used in survey research that may last only a few minutes, an intensive interview may last several hours and may take more than one session.
- Intensive interviews are customized to individual respondents. In a personal interview, all respondents are usually asked the same questions. Intensive interviews allow interviewers to form questions based on each respondent's answers.
- They can be influenced by the interview climate. To a greater extent than with personal interviews, the success of intensive interviews depends on the rapport established between the interviewer and the respondent.

Advantages and Disadvantages of Intensive Interviews

The most important advantage of the in-depth interview is the wealth of detail that it provides. Furthermore, when compared to more traditional survey methods, intensive interviewing provides more accurate responses on sensitive issues. The rapport between respondent and interviewer makes it easier to approach certain topics that might be taboo in other approaches. In addition, there may be certain groups for which intensive interviewing is the only practical technique. For example, a study of the media habits of U.S. senators would be hard to carry out as an observational study. Also, it would be difficult to get a sample of senators to take the time to respond to a survey questionnaire. In some cases, however, such persons might be willing to talk to an interviewer.

On the negative side, generalizability is sometimes a problem. Intensive interviewing is typically done with a nonrandom sample. Since interviews are usually nonstandardized, each respondent may answer a slightly different version of a question. In fact, it is very likely that a particular respondent may answer questions not asked of any other respondent. Another disadvantage of in-depth interviews is that they are especially sensitive to interviewer bias. In a long interview, it is possible for a respondent to learn a good deal of information about the interviewer. Despite practice and training, some interviewers may inadvertently communicate their attitudes

AN INSIDE LOOK
Locating Respondents

In most cases, identifying and contacting respondents for intensive interviewing is not difficult. In a few cases, however, this can be a downright challenge. Consider the problems faced by Priest (1992) in her study of self-disclosure on television. She wished to recruit subjects who had appeared on TV talk shows and had revealed something intimate and personal about themselves. For obvious reasons, the full names and addresses of such people are rarely given when they appear. In addition, executive producers of "Oprah," "Donahue," and "Sally Jesse Raphael" were unwilling to assist Priest in contacting guests. What to do?

Priest taped several months of "Donahue" for clues about how to reach the show's guests. On several occasions, a guest was identified by name, and a place of residence was mentioned later during the interview. One panel member mentioned the more tolerant atmosphere in San Francisco. The researcher found her name in the San Francisco phone book and called her. Some guests came with their therapists; since the therapists were usually identified, Priest was able to call them and ask that her request for an interview be forwarded to their patients. Potential respondents were given a toll-free number they could call. One guest had mentioned that she worked at a McDonald's restaurant in a certain town. The researcher called the various McDonalds in that area until the person was located. A couple was reached by addressing a letter to them in care of the show. Another man had mentioned frequenting a local bar in New York City. Priest wrote him a letter in care of the bar, and he called the toll-free number. Eventually the researcher was able to locate and interview 24 informants, including a transsexual lesbian, a sex priestess, an incest survivor, and a "swinging" couple. Her experience suggests that qualitative researchers need imagination and perseverance when building their samples.

through loaded questions, nonverbal cues, or tone of voice. The effect of this on the validity of a respondent's answers is difficult to gauge. Finally, intensive interviewing presents problems in data analysis. A researcher given the same body of data taken from an interview may wind up with interpretations significantly different from those of the original investigator.

Procedures

The problem definition, respondent recruiting, and data collection and analysis procedures for intensive interviews are similar to those used in personal interviews. The primary differences with intensive interviews are listed here:

- Co-op payments are usually higher, generally $100 to $1,000.
- The amount of data collected is tremendous. Analysis may take several weeks to several months.
- Interviewees may become extremely tired and bored. Interviews must be scheduled several hours apart, which lengthens the data collection effort.
- Because of the time required, it is very difficult to arrange intensive interviews. This is especially true for respondents who are professionals.
- Small samples do not allow for generalization to the target population.

Berg (1997) provides further details concerning the in-depth interview technique.

Examples of Intensive Interviews

In her study of ethical sensitivity in TV news, Lind (1997) did intensive interviews with 27 television news viewers in Chicago. She found that it was more accurate to describe ethical sensitivity in terms of type rather than level. Albada (2000) conducted intensive interviews with parents and children, focusing on what they thought about how families are portrayed on TV. The interview results suggested that there were several perspectives concerning the degree of realism in the depiction of TV families. Phalen (2000) carried out two-hour interviews with 14 female managers at radio and television stations. The responses to her open-ended questions suggested that her respondents experienced bias against female managers and instances of sexual harassment. Phalen's study illustrates the utility of the intensive interviewing technique when it comes to examining potentially sensitive issues.

▪ Case Studies

The case study method is another common qualitative research technique. Simply put, a **case study** uses as many data sources as possible to systematically investigate individuals, groups, organizations, or events. Case studies are conducted when a researcher needs to understand or explain a phenomenon. They are frequently used in medicine, anthropology, clinical psychology, management science, and history. Sigmund Freud wrote case studies of his patients; economists wrote case studies of the cable TV industry for the FCC; and the list goes on and on.

On a more formal level, Yin (1994) defines a case study as an empirical inquiry that uses multiple sources of evidence to investigate a contemporary phenomenon within its real-life context, in which the boundaries between the phenomenon and its context are not clearly evident. This definition highlights how a case study differs from other research strategies. For example, an experiment separates a phenomenon from its real-life context. The laboratory environment controls the context. The survey technique tries to define the phenomenon under study narrowly enough to limit the number of variables to be examined. Case study research includes both single cases and multiple cases. Comparative case study research, frequently used in political science, is an example of the multiple case study technique.

Merriam (1988) lists four essential characteristics of case study research:

1. *Particularistic.* This means that the case study focuses on a particular situation, event, program, or phenomenon, making it a good method for studying practical, real-life problems.
2. *Descriptive.* The final product of a case study is a detailed description of the topic under study.
3. *Heuristic.* A case study helps people to understand what's being studied. New interpretations, new perspectives, new meaning, and fresh insights are all goals of a case study.
4. *Inductive.* Most case studies depend on inductive reasoning. Principles and generalizations emerge from an examination of the data. Many case studies attempt to discover new relationships rather than verify existing hypotheses.

Advantages of Case Studies

The case study method is most valuable when the researcher wants to obtain a wealth of information about the research topic. Case studies provide tremendous detail. Many times researchers want such detail when they do not know exactly what they are looking for. The case study is particularly advantageous to the researcher who is trying to find clues and ideas for further research (Simon,

1985). This is not to suggest, however, that case studies are to be used only at the exploratory stage of research. The method can also be used to gather descriptive and explanatory data.

The case study technique can suggest why something has occurred. For example, in many cities in the mid-1980s, cable companies asked to be released from certain promises made when negotiating for a franchise. To learn why this occurred, a multiple case study approach, examining several cities, could have been used. Other research techniques, such as the survey, might not be able to reveal all the possible reasons behind this phenomenon. Ideally, case studies should be used in combination with theory to achieve maximum understanding.

The case study method also affords the researcher the ability to deal with a wide spectrum of evidence. Documents, historical artifacts, systematic interviews, direct observations, and even traditional surveys can all be incorporated into a case study. In fact, the more data sources that can be brought to bear in a case, the more likely it is that the study will be valid.

Disadvantages of Case Studies

There are three main criticisms. The first has to do with a general lack of scientific rigor in many case studies. Yin (1994) points out that "too many times, the case study researcher has been sloppy, and has allowed equivocal evidence or biased views to influence the . . . findings and conclusions" (p. 21). It is easy to do a sloppy case study; rigorous case studies require a good deal of time and effort.

The second criticism is that the case study is not amenable to generalization. If the main goal of the researcher is to make statistically based normative statements about the frequency of occurrence of a phenomenon in a defined population, some other method may be more appropriate. This is not to say that the results of all case studies are idiosyncratic and unique. In fact, if generalizing theoretic propositions is the main goal, then the case study method is perfectly suited to the task.

Finally, like participant observation, case studies are often time-consuming and may occasionally produce massive quantities of data that are hard to summarize. Consequently, fellow researchers are forced to wait years for the results of the research, which too often are poorly presented. Some authors, however, are experimenting with nontraditional methods of reporting to overcome this last criticism (see Peters & Waterman, 1982).

Conducting a Case Study

The precise method of conducting a case study has not been as well documented as the more traditional techniques of the survey and the experiment. Nonetheless, there appear to be five distinct stages in carrying out a case study: design, pilot study, data collection, data analysis, and report writing.

Design. The first concern in case study design is what to ask. The case study is most appropriate for questions that begin with "how" or "why." A research question that is clear and precise focuses the remainder of the efforts in a case study. A second design concern is what to analyze. What constitutes a "case"? In many instances, a case is an individual, several individuals, or an event or events. If information is gathered about each relevant individual, the results are reported in the single or multiple case study format; in other instances, however, the precise boundaries of the case are harder to pinpoint. A case might be a specific decision, a particular organization at a certain time, a program, or some other discrete event. One rough guide for determining what to use as the unit of analysis is the available research literature.

AN INSIDE LOOK
Data Collection

Just as with all steps in a research project (and computers) it is necessary to keep duplicates of all information. One mass media researcher, who is a colleague of the authors, lost three years of qualitative data when his office building burned. Unfortunately, he did not make duplicate copies of his data. Don't make the same mistake.

Since researchers want to compare their findings with the results of previous research, it is sometimes a good idea not to stray too far from what was done in past research.

Pilot Study. Before the pilot study is conducted, the case study researcher must construct a study **protocol.** This document describes the procedures to be used in the study and also includes the data-gathering instrument or instruments. A good case study protocol contains the procedures necessary for gaining access to a particular person or organization and the methods for accessing records. It also contains the schedule for data collection and addresses logistical problems. For example, the protocol should note whether a copy machine is available in the field to duplicate records, whether office space is available to the researchers, and what supplies are needed. The protocol should also list the questions central to the inquiry and the possible sources of information to be tapped in answering these questions. If interviews are to be used in the case study, the protocol should specify the questions to be asked.

Once the protocol has been developed, the researcher is ready to begin the pilot study. A **pilot study** is used to refine both the research design and the field procedures. Variables that were not foreseen during the design phase can emerge during the pilot study, and problems with the protocol or with study logistics can also be uncovered. The pilot study also allows the researchers to try different data-gathering approaches and to observe different activities from several trial perspectives. The results of the pilot study are used to revise and polish the study protocol.

Data Collection. At least four sources of data can be used in case studies. Documents, which represent a rich data source, may take the form of letters, memos, minutes, agendas, historical records, brochures, pamphlets, posters, and so on. A second source is the interview. Some case studies make use of survey research methods and ask respondents to fill out questionnaires; others may use intensive interviewing.

Observation/participation is the third data collection technique. The general comments made about this technique earlier in this chapter apply to the case study method as well. The fourth source of evidence used in case studies is the physical artifact—a tool, a piece of furniture, or even a computer printout. Although artifacts are commonly used as a data source in anthropology and history, they are seldom used in mass media case study research. (They are, however, frequently used in legal research concerning the media.)

Most case study researchers recommend using multiple sources of data, thus permitting triangulation of the phenomenon under study (Rubin, 1984). In addition, multiple sources help the case study researcher improve the reliability and validity of the study. Not surprisingly, a study of the case study method found that the ones that used multiple sources of evidence were rated higher than those that relied on a single source (Yin, Bateman, & Moore, 1983).

Data Analysis. Unlike more quantitative research techniques, there are no specific formulas or "cookbook" techniques to guide the researcher in analyzing the data. Consequently, this stage is probably the most difficult in the case study method. Although it is impossible to generalize to all case study situations, Yin (1994) suggests three broad analytic strategies: pattern matching, explanation building, and time series.

In the *pattern-matching strategy,* an empirically based pattern is compared with one or more predicted patterns. For instance, suppose a newspaper is about to initiate a new management tool: regular meetings between top management and reporters, excluding editors. Based on organizational theory, a researcher might predict certain outcomes—namely, more stress between editors and reporters, increased productivity, and weakened supervisory links. If analysis of the case study data indicates that these results do in fact occur, some conclusions about the management change can be made. If the predicted pattern does not match the actual one, the initial study propositions have to be questioned.

In the analytic strategy of *explanation building,* the researcher tries to construct an explanation about the case by making statements about the cause or causes of the phenomenon under study. This method can take several forms. Typically, however, an investigator drafts an initial theoretical statement about some process or outcome, compares the findings of an initial case study against the statement, revises the statement, analyzes a second comparable case, and repeats this process as many times as necessary. Note that this technique is similar to the general approach of analytical induction discussed earlier. For example, to explain why some new communication technologies are failing, a researcher might suggest lack of managerial expertise as an initial proposition. But an investigator who examined the subscription television industry might find that lack of management expertise is only part of the problem, that inadequate market research is also a factor. Armed with the revised version of the explanatory statement, the researcher next examines the direct broadcast satellite industry to see whether this explanation needs to be further refined, and so on, until a full and satisfactory answer is achieved.

In *time series analysis,* the investigator tries to compare a series of data points to some theoretic trend that was predicted before the research, or to some alternative trend. If, for instance, several cities have experienced newspaper strikes, a case study investigator might generate predictions about the changes in information-seeking behaviors of residents in these communities and conduct a case study to see whether these predictions are supported.

Report Writing. The case study report can take several forms. The report can follow the traditional research study format—problem, methods, findings, and discussion—or it can use a nontraditional technique. Some case studies are best suited to a chronological arrangement, whereas comparative case studies can be reported from the comparative perspective. No matter what form is chosen, the researcher must consider the intended audience of the report. A case study report for policy makers is written in a style different from one to be published in a scholarly journal.

Examples of Case Studies

Hindman's (1998) case study examined how an inner-city newspaper dealt with the conflict between its mission as a mainstream paper and community pressure to become an alternative, advocacy publication. In their case study of the introduction of commercial television in India, Crabtree and Malhotra (2000) interviewed business personnel, observed practices at a commercial TV operation, monitored the content of commercial TV, and examined organizational documents. Tovares (2000) examined the development of "Latino USA," a news program about Latino issues. His case study involved personal interviews with the staff, direct observation, and examination of archival materials.

Qualitative Research and Ethnography. This discussion of qualitative research necessitates a brief explanation of terminology in relation to **ethnography.** The term *ethnographic research* is sometimes used as a synonym for *qualitative research* (Lindlof, 1991). Ethnography, however, is in fact a special kind of qualitative research. As first practiced by anthropologists and sociologists, ethnography was the process in which researchers spent long periods of time living with and observing other cultures in a natural setting. This immersion in the other culture helped the researcher understand another way of life as seen from the native perspective. Recently, however, the notion of ethnography has been adapted to other areas: political science, education, social work, and communication. These disciplines were less interested in describing the way of life of an entire culture and more concerned with analyzing smaller units: subgroups, organizations, institutions, professions, audiences, and so on. To reduce confusion, Berg (1997) suggests referring to the traditional study of entire cultures as *macro-ethnography* and to the study of smaller units of analysis as *micro-ethnography.* The latter approach is the one most often used by mass communication researchers.

Regardless of whether it is focusing on an entire culture or on a cultural subunit, ethnography is characterized by four qualities:

1. It puts the researcher in the middle of the topic under study; the researcher goes to the data rather than the other way around.
2. It emphasizes studying an issue or topic from the participants' frame of reference.
3. It involves spending a considerable amount of time in the field.
4. It uses a variety of research techniques including observation, interviewing, diary keeping, analysis of existing documents, photography, videotaping, and so on.

Item 4 seems to distinguish ethnographic research from other forms of qualitative research; indeed, ethnographic research relies upon an assortment of data collection techniques. Although other qualitative research projects can be conducted adequately using only one method, ethnographic research generally uses several of the four common qualitative techniques discussed in this chapter; field observations, intensive interviewing, focus groups, and case studies.

▪ Writing the Qualitative Research Report

As suggested in our website, writing a quantitative research report is fairly straightforward. Writing the qualitative report, however, is more complicated. In the first place, it's difficult to condense qualitative data into numerical tables and charts. Qualitative data come in the form of sentences, extended quotes, paragraphs of description, and even pictures and diagrams. Second, there is less standardization of the methods used by qualitative researchers. Quantitative researchers generally use techniques such as a telephone survey or an experiment whose methods require relatively little description. On the other hand, a qualitative researcher may use a technique that is particular to one given setting or a combination of techniques in varying situations. Indeed, it's possible that the qualitative researcher might even create entirely new ways of gathering data. As a result, the section of a qualitative report that describes the methods used in the study can be lengthy and complex. Third, qualitative researchers may try to give readers a subjective "feel" for the research setting. There may be lengthy descriptions of the research surroundings, the people involved, and the researcher's subjective thoughts about the project. Finally, while quantitative reports are written in an efficient, predictable, albeit unexciting style, qualitative reports can use more free-form and literary styles. Much qualitative research is written in a loose narrative style that employs many devices used in novels and short stories. Keyton (2001), for example, describes three separate styles that can be adopted by the authors of qualitative reports: realist (a dispassionate third-person point of view), confessional (first-person point of view that reveals much about the author), and impressionist (writer uses metaphors and vivid imagery to get point across).

As is probably obvious from the above, qualitative reports are generally much longer than their quantitative counterparts. Indeed, it is not surprising to find that many qualitative studies done in an academic setting are published in book form rather than in journal articles.

With that as a preamble, what follows is a general format for structuring the qualitative report.

1. *The Introduction.* Similar to its quantitative counterpart, the introduction provides an overview of the project, the precise research question or problem statement, the study's justification and why the reader should be interested in it. Unlike the quantitative report, the literature review section may not be extensive. In many qualitative studies, there may not be much literature available. In addition, many qualitative researchers prefer not to do an exhaustive literature review for fear of unduly influencing their perceptions of the research situation.

2. *The Method.* This section includes a number of topics that explain what was done in the study:

a. The method or methods used to collect data and an explanation of why a particular method was chosen. For example, the sensitive nature of the data suggested that intensive interviews might be most appropriate.

b. The research setting. The researcher must provide the reader with a context for judging the suitability of the setting and to try to give a "feel" of the study.

c. Sampling. Participants or respondents can be recruited in a variety of ways, and the researcher must describe the recruitment method(s) used. The discussion should also include the sample size and the criteria used for terminating data gathering.

d. Data collection. This section should explain how the data were collected, such as field notes from observation, focus group transcripts, tapes of intensive interviews, or diaries. The explanation should be detailed so that another researcher could replicate the collection method.

3. *Findings.* This is generally the longest section in the qualitative report. Since qualitative research generates a lot of data, the biggest challenge in presenting the findings is reducing the data to a manageable size. Ideally, the report should not be too thick and ominous; nor should it be too thin and inconsequential. Two guiding principles can help with making the data manageable. First, remember that it's impossible to say everything in a research report. Try to select those vignettes, quotes, or examples that most vividly illuminate the findings. Second, choose data that illustrate the variety of information collected, including situations that were uncommon or atypical.

An overall organizational scheme will make the report more understandable. Some possibilities for arranging the findings section might include (Chenail, 1995):

- Organize the material chronologically.
- Present the most important findings first.
- Use a dramatic presentation and save the most important points till the end.
- Arrange the data according to some theoretical or conceptual scheme.

The findings section should also strike a balance between description and analysis. Detailed quotes or examples should be followed by analysis and generalizations. Qualitative researchers need to guard against the **error of segregation** that occurs when the data are separated so far from the analysis that readers cannot make the connection. One possible arrangement that guards against this problem is:

- Present a summary of the general finding.
- Show an example of this finding.
- Comment on the example.
- Show a second example.
- Comment on the second example.
- When finished with examples, make a transition to next general finding.

4. *Discussion.* This section should include a summary, additional implications of the study that might be explored in future research, and a discussion of the strengths and weaknesses of the study.

▪▪▪ Summary

Mass media research can be influenced by the research paradigm that directs the researcher. This chapter discussed the differences between the positivist approach, which generally favors quantitative methods, and the interpretive approach, which favors qualitative methods. We described four main qualitative techniques: field observations, focus groups, intensive interviews, and case studies.

Field observation is the study of a phenomenon in natural settings. The researcher may be a detached observer or a participant in the process under study. The main advantage of this technique is its flexibility; it can be used to develop hypotheses, to gather preliminary data, or to study groups that would otherwise be inaccessible. Its biggest disadvantage is the difficulty in achieving external validity.

The *focus group,* or group interviewing, is used to gather preliminary information for a research study or to gather qualitative data concerning a research question. The advantages of the focus group method are the ease of data collection and the depth of information that can be gathered. Among the disadvantages: The quality of information gathered during focus groups depends heavily on the group moderator's skill, and focus groups can only complement other research because they provide qualitative, not quantitative, data.

Intensive interviewing is used to gather extremely detailed information from a small sample of respondents. The wealth of data that can be gathered with this method is its primary advantage. Because intensive interviewing is usually done with small, nonrandom samples, however, generalizability is sometimes a disadvantage. Interviewer bias can also be a problem.

The *case study* method draws from as many data sources as possible to investigate an event. Case studies are particularly helpful when a researcher desires to explain or understand some phenomenon. Some problems with case studies are that they can lack scientific rigor, they can be time-consuming to conduct, and the data they provide can be difficult to generalize from and to summarize. The qualitative research report should include an introductory section, a description of methods, findings, examples, and a discussion.

Key Terms

Analytic induction strategy
Audit trail
Case study
Constant comparative technique
Epoche
Error of segregation
Ethnography
Extended focus group
Field observation
Focus group
Intensive interview
Interpretive
Paradigm
Pilot study
Positivist
Protocol
Reactivity

Using the Internet

There are many useful sites on the web for qualitative researchers; a sample follows.

1. *http://nav.webring.com/hub?ring=qualres&id=12&hub* This is the address of the Qualitative Research Web Ring, which focuses on qualitative research and would be of interest to graduate students, faculty, and anyone else interested in all aspects of qualitative research. As of late 2001, there were 19 sites linked in the ring.
2. *http://www.ualberta.ca/,jrnorris/qual.html* The address of QualPage. This site contains general information about books, discussion forums, electronic journals, papers, conferences, and many other items of interest to a qualitative researcher.
3. *www.focusgroups.com* This site contains a listing of focus group facilities in metropolitan areas across the United States. There are, for example, three research organizations in Fort Wayne, Indiana, that can arrange focus group research.
4. *http://www.pewcenter.org/doingcj/pubs/cases/* The Pew Center site contains links to six case studies about civic journalism. Although the studies themselves are more journalistic than academic, they do provide good examples of the different ways case studies can be structured.
5. *http://www.qsrinternational.com/products/nvivo.ht* QSR International manufactures software that is useful for qualitative analysis of transcripts and other texts. This page describes NVivo, one of several programs currently available to aid in qualitative data analysis. The program helps researchers see patterns and themes in textual data.

Questions and Problems for Further Investigation

1. Develop a research topic that is appropriate for a study by each of these methods:
   - Intensive interview
   - Field observation
   - Focus group
2. Suggest three specific research topics that are best studied by the technique of covert participation. Are any ethical problems involved?
3. Select a research topic that is suitable for study using the focus group method; then assemble six or eight of your classmates or friends and conduct a sample interview. Select an appropriate method for analyzing the data.
4. Examine recent journals in the mass media research field and identify instances where the case study method was used. For each example, specify the sources of data used in the study, how the data were analyzed, and how the study was reported.
5. What can a positivist researcher learn from an interpretive researcher? What can the interpretive researcher learn from the positivist researcher?
6. Some researchers claim that, excluding data collection, there are no fundamental differences between qualitative and quantitative research. What is your opinion about this perspective?
7. If you are using InfoTrac College Edition, you can discover the many disciplines that use qualitative research. Perform an advanced search using the title option (ti). Find articles with the word "qualitative" in the title. Count how many different research areas are represented.

For additional information on these and related topics, see

http://www.wimmerdominick.com

References and Suggested Readings

Albada, K. F. (2000). The public and private dialog about the American family on television. *Journal of Communication, 50*(4), 79–110.

Anderson, J. A. (1987). *Communication research: Issues and methods*. New York: McGraw-Hill.

Bechtel, R., Achelpohl, C., & Akers, R. (1972). Correlates between observed behavior and questionnaire responses on television viewing. In E. Rubinstein, G. Comstock, & J. Murray (Eds.), *Television and social behavior* (Vol. IV). Washington, DC: U.S. Government Printing Office.

Berg, B. (1997). *Qualitative research methods* (2nd ed.). Boston: Allyn & Bacon.

Bickman, L., & Hency, T. (1972). *Beyond the laboratory: Field research in social psychology*. New York: McGraw-Hill.

Bielby, D. D., Harrington, C. L., & Bielby, W. T. (1999). Whose stories are they? *Journal of Broadcasting & Electronic Media, 43*(1), 35–51.

Blaikie, N. W. (1993). *Approaches to social enquiry*. Cambridge, MA: Polity Press.

Bogdan, R., & Taylor, S. (1998). *Introduction to qualitative research methods* (3rd ed.). New York: John Wiley.

Brent, E. E., & Anderson, R. E. (1990). *Computer applications in the social sciences*. Philadelphia: Temple University Press.

Brown, J., Dykers, C., Steele, J., & White, A. (1994). Teenage room culture. *Communication Research, 21*(6), 813–827.

Browne, D. (1983). The international newsroom. *Journal of Broadcasting, 27*(3), 205–231.

Calder, B. J. (1977). Focus groups and the nature of qualitative marketing research. *Journal of Marketing Research, 14*, 353–364.

Chadwick, B., Bahr, H., & Albrecht, S. (1984). *Social science research methods*. Englewood Cliffs, NJ: Prentice-Hall.

Chenail, R. J. (1995). Presenting qualitative data. *The Qualitative Report, 2*(3), 1–12.

Cooper, R., Potter, W., & Dupagne, M. (1994). A status report on methods used in mass communication research. *Journalism Educator, 48*(4), 54–61.

Cox, K. D., Higginbotham, J. B., & Burton, J. (1976). Applications of focus group interviewing in marketing. *Journal of Marketing, 40*, 77–80.

Crabtree, R., & Malhotra, S. (2000). The genesis and evolution of commercial television in India. *Journal of Broadcasting and Electronic Media, 44*(3), 364–385.

Creswell, J. W. (1998). *Qualitative inquiry and research design*. Thousand Oaks, CA: Sage.

Dimmick, J., & Wallschlaeger, M. (1986). Measuring corporate diversification. *Journal of Broadcasting and Electronic Media, 30*(1), 1–14.

Durham, M. G. (1999). Girls, media and the negotiation of sexuality. *Journalism and Mass Communication Quarterly, 76*(2), 193–216.

Elliot, S. C. (1980). *Focus group research: A workbook for broadcasters*. Washington, DC: National Association of Broadcasters.

Epstein, E. J. (1974). *News from nowhere*. New York: Vintage.

Erickson, F. (1986). Qualitative methods in research on teaching. In M. C. Wittrock (Ed.), *Handbook of research on teaching*. New York: Macmillan.

Fletcher, A., & Bowers, T. (1991). *Fundamentals of advertising research* (4th ed.). Belmont, CA: Wadsworth.

Gieber, W. (1956). Across the desk: A study of 16 telegraph editors. *Journalism Quarterly, 33*, 423–432.

Glaser, B., & Strauss, A. (1967). *The discovery of grounded theory*. Chicago: Aldine.

Hall, S. (1982). The rediscovery of ideology. In M. Gurevitch, T. Bennett, J. Curran, & J. Woollacott (Eds.), *Culture, society and the media* (pp. 56–90). New York: Methuen.

Hammersly, M. (1992). *What's wrong with ethnography? Methodological explorations*. London: Routledge.

Hindman, E. B. (1998). Spectacles of the poor: Conventions of alternative news. *Journalism and Mass Communication Quarterly, 75*(1), 177–193.

Keyton, J. (2001). *Communication research*. Mountain View, CA: Mayfield.

Lemish, D. (1987). Viewers in diapers: The early development of television viewing. In T. R. Lindlof (Ed.), *Natural audiences*. Norwood, NJ: Ablex.

Lincoln, Y., & Guba, E. (1985). *Naturalistic inquiry*. Beverly Hills, CA: Sage.

Lind, R. A. (1997). Ethical sensitivity in viewer evaluations of a TV news investigative report. *Human Communication Research, 23*(4), 535–561.

Lindlof, T. R. (1987). *Natural audiences: Qualitative research of media uses and effects*. Norwood, NJ: Ablex.

Lindlof, T. R. (1991). The qualitative study of media audiences. *Journal of Broadcasting and Electronic Media, 35*(1), 23–42.

Lindlof, T. R. (1995). *Qualitative communication research methods*. Thousand Oaks, CA: Sage.

Lull, J. (1985). Ethnographic studies of broadcast media audiences. In J. Dominick & J. Fletcher (Eds.), *Broadcasting research methods*. Boston: Allyn & Bacon.

Lunt, P., & Livingstone, S. (1996). Rethinking the focus group in media and communications research. *Journal of Communication, 46*(2), 79–89.

Maykut, P., & Morehouse, R. (1994). *Beginning qualitative research.* Bristol, PA: The Falmer Press.

McKee, K. B., & Pardun, C. J. (1999). Reading the video: A qualitative study of religious images in music videos. *Journal of Broadcasting and Electronic Media,* 43(1), 110–122.

Merriam, S. B. (1988). *Case study research in education.* San Francisco: Jossey-Bass.

Miles, M. B., & Huberman, A. M. (1994). *Qualitative data analysis* (2nd ed.). Beverly Hills, CA: Sage Publications.

Moriarty, S., & Everett, S. (1994). Commercial breaks: A viewing behavior study. *Journalism Quarterly,* 71(2), 346–355.

Morrison, M., & Krugman, D. (2001). A look at mass and computer mediated technologies. *Journal of Broadcasting and Electronic Media,* 45(1), 118–134.

Neuman, W. L. (1997). *Social research methods.* Boston: Allyn & Bacon.

Peters, J. J., & Waterman, R. (1982). *In search of excellence.* New York: Harper & Row.

Phalen, P. F. (2000). An agenda for research on women and the organizational culture of broadcasting. *Journal of Broadcasting and Electronic Media,* 44(2), 230–247.

Potter, W. J. (1996). *An analysis of thinking and research about qualitative methods.* Mahwah, NJ: Lawrence Erlbaum.

Priest, P. J. (1992). *Self disclosure on television.* Unpublished doctoral dissertation, University of Georgia, Athens.

Robertson, L., Kelley, A. B., O'Neill, B., Wixom, C. W., Elswirth, R. S., & Haddon, W. (1974). A controlled study of the effect of television messages of safety belt use. *American Journal of Public Health,* 64, 1074–1084.

Rubin, H. (1984). *Applied social research.* Columbus, OH: Charles E. Merrill.

Shamp, S. A. (1991). Mechanomorphism in perception of computer communication partners. *Computers in Human Behavior,* 17, 147–161.

Simon, J. (1985). *Basic research methods in social science* (3rd ed.). New York: Random House.

Stainback, S., & Stainback, W. (1988). *Understanding and conducting qualitative research.* Dubuque, IA: Kendall/Hunt.

Steele, J. R. (1999). Teenage sexuality and media practice. *Journal of Sex Research,* 36(4), 331–341.

Tovares, R. (2000). Latino USA: Constructing a news and public affairs program. *Journal of Broadcasting and Electronic Media,* 44(3), 471–486.

Tull, D., & Hawkins, D. (1990). *Marketing research* (5th ed.). New York: Macmillan.

Webb, E. J., Campbell, D. T., Schwartz, R. D., & Sechrest, L. (1968). *Unobtrusive measures.* Chicago: Rand McNally.

Westley, B. H. (1989). The controlled experiment. In G. H. Stempel & B. H. Westley (Eds.), *Research methods in mass communication* (2nd ed.). Englewood Cliffs, NJ: Prentice-Hall.

Williamson, J. B., Karp, D. A., & Dalphin, J. R. (1992). *The research craft* (2nd ed.). Boston: Little, Brown.

Wolf, M. (1987). How children negotiate television. In T. R. Lindlof (Ed.), *Natural audiences: Qualitative research of media uses and effects* (pp. 58–94). Norwood, NJ: Ablex.

Woodside, A., & Fleck, R. (1979). The case approach to understanding brand choice. *Journal of Advertising Research,* 19(2), 23–30.

Woodward, B., & Bernstein, C. (1974). *All the president's men.* New York: Simon & Schuster.

Yin, R. (1994). *Case study research* (3rd ed.). Newbury Park, CA: Sage Publications.

Yin, R., Bateman, P., & Moore, G. (1983). *Case studies and organizational innovation.* Washington, DC: Cosmos Corporation.

Ziller, R. C., & Smith, D. C. (1977). A phenomenological utilization of photographs. *Journal of Phenomenological Psychology,* 7, 172–185.

Chapter 6

Content Analysis

This chapter discusses content analysis, a specific research approach used frequently in all areas of the media. The method is popular with mass media researchers because it is an efficient way to investigate the content of the media, such as the number and types of commercials or advertisements in broadcasting or the print media. The beginning researcher will find content analysis a valuable tool in answering many mass media questions.

Modern content analysis can be traced back to World War II, when Allied intelligence units painstakingly monitored the number and types of popular songs played on European radio stations. By comparing the music played on German stations with that on other stations in occupied Europe, the Allies were able to measure with some degree of certainty the changes in troop concentration on the continent. In the Pacific theater, communications between Japan and various island bases were carefully tabulated; an increase in message volume to and from a particular base usually indicated some new operation involving that base.

At about the same time, content analysis was used in attempts to verify the authorship of historical documents. These studies (Yule, 1944) were concerned primarily with counting words in documents of questionable authenticity and comparing their frequencies with the same words in documents whose authors were known. More recently, this technique was used to attribute the authorship of 12 disputed "Federalist Papers" to James Madison (Martindale & McKenzie, 1995). These literary detective cases demonstrated the usefulness of quantification in content analysis.

After the war, researchers used content analysis to study propaganda in newspapers and radio. In 1952 Bernard Berelson published *Content Analysis in Communication Research*, which signaled that the technique had gained recognition as a tool for media scholars.

In 1968, Tannenbaum and Greenberg reported that content analysis of newspapers was the largest single subject of master's theses in mass communication. A later publication (Comstock, 1975) listed more than 225 content analyses of television programming. Concern over the portrayal of violence on television and the treatment of women and minority groups in print and television advertising and in music videos further popularized the content analysis technique among mass media researchers. From 1977 to 1985, 21% of the quantitative studies published in the *Journal of Broadcasting and Electronic Media* were content analyses (Moffett & Dominick, 1987). A study by Cooper, Potter, and Dupagne (1994) found that 25% of all quantitative studies in mass communication from 1965 to 1989 were content analyses. Riffe and Freitag (1997) found that about 25% of the 1,977 full-length research articles published in *Journalism and Mass Communication Quarterly* from 1971 to 1995 were content analyses. This popularity shows no signs of decreasing. *Communication Abstracts* listed more than 90 content analytic studies for 1999 and 2000, indicating that it is still a favored research technique.

Definition of Content Analysis

There are many definitions of *content analysis*. Walizer and Wienir (1978) define it as any systematic procedure devised to examine the content of recorded information; Krippendorf (1980) defines it as a research technique for making replicable and valid references from data to their context. Kerlinger's (2000) definition is fairly typical: Content analysis is a method of studying and analyzing communication in a systematic, objective, and quantitative manner for the purpose of measuring variables.

Kerlinger's definition involves three concepts that require elaboration. First, content analysis is *systematic*. This means that the content to be analyzed is selected according to explicit and consistently applied rules: Sample selection must follow proper procedures, and each item must have an equal chance of being included in the analysis. Moreover, the evaluation process must be systematic: All content under consideration is to be treated in exactly the same manner. There must be uniformity in the coding and analysis procedures and in the length of time coders are exposed to the material. Systematic evaluation simply means that one and only one set of guidelines is used for evaluation throughout the study. Alternating procedures in an analysis is a sure way to confound the results.

Second, content analysis is *objective;* that is, the researcher's personal idiosyncrasies and biases should not enter into the findings. If replicated by another researcher, the analysis should yield the same results. Operational definitions and rules for the classification of variables should be sufficiently explicit and comprehensive that other researchers who repeat the process will arrive at the same decisions. Unless a clear set of criteria and procedures is established that fully explains the sampling and categorization methods, the researcher does not meet the requirement of objectivity and the reliability of the results may be called into question. Perfect objectivity, however, is seldom achieved in a content analysis. The specification of the unit of analysis and the precise makeup and definition of relevant categories are areas in which individual researchers must exercise subjective choice. (Reliability, as it applies to content analysis, is discussed at length later in the chapter.)

Third, content analysis is *quantitative*. The goal of content analysis is the accurate representation of a body of messages. Quantification is important in fulfilling that objective, because it aids researchers in the quest for precision. The statement "Seventy percent of all prime-time programs contain at least one act of violence" is more precise than "Most shows are violent." Additionally, quantification allows researchers to summarize results and to report them succinctly. If measurements are to be made over intervals of time, comparisons of the numerical data from one time period to another can help simplify and standardize the evaluation procedure. Finally, quantification gives researchers additional statistical tools that can aid in interpretation and analysis.

Note, however, that quantification should not blind the researcher to other ways of assessing the potential impact or effects of the content. The fact that some item or behavior was the most frequently occurring element in a body of content does not necessarily make that element the most important. For example, a content analysis of the news coverage of the conflict in Northern Ireland in 2001 might disclose that 90% of the coverage showed nonviolent scenes. The other 10% that contained violence, however, might have been so powerful and so sensational that their impact on the audience was far greater than the nonviolent coverage.

▪ Uses of Content Analysis

Over the past decade, the symbols and messages contained in the mass media have become increasingly popular research topics in both the academic sector and the private sector. The national Parent Teachers Association has offered do-it-yourself training in rough forms of content analysis so that local members can monitor television violence levels in their viewing areas. The Center for Media Education's website contains a content analysis sheet designed to help audience members evaluate how well local TV stations are complying with the Children's Television Act. Public relations firms use content analysis to monitor the subject matter of company publications, and some labor unions now conduct content analyses of the mass media to examine their images. The *Media Monitor* publishes periodic studies of how the media treat social and political issues.

Although it is difficult to classify and categorize studies as varied and diverse as those using content analysis, the studies are generally done for one of five purposes. The following discussion of these aims illustrates some ways in which this technique can be applied.

Describing Communication Content

Several recent studies have cataloged the characteristics of a given body of communication content at one or more points in time. These studies demonstrate content analysis used in the traditional, descriptive manner: to identify what exists. For example, Kim (2000) described how the U.S. press covered the Tiananmen pro-democracy movement. Cann and Mohr (2001) examined the gender of journalists on Australian TV newscasts, and Tuggle and Huffman (2001) described how live reports were used in local TV newscasts. One of the advantages of content analysis is its potential to identify trends over long periods of time. Scharrer (2001), for example, traced the portrayal of sitcom fathers from the 1950s to the 1990s.

These descriptive studies also can be used to study societal change. For example, changing public opinion on various controversial issues could be gauged with a longitudinal study (see Chapter 8) of letters to the editor or newspaper editorials. Statements about what values are judged to be important by a society could be inferred from a study of the nonfiction books on the bestseller list at different points in time. Greenberg and Collette (1997), for example, analyzed changes in the demographic makeup of new characters added to the broadcast networks' new programs from 1966 to 1992.

Testing Hypotheses of Message Characteristics

A number of analyses attempt to relate certain characteristics of the source of a given body of message content to the characteristics of the messages that are produced. As Holsti (1969) points out, this category of content analysis has been used in many studies that test hypotheses of form: "If the source has characteristic *A*, then messages containing elements *x* and *y* will be produced; if the source has characteristic *B*, then messages with elements *w* and *z* will be produced." Hollifield (1997) compared coverage of the proposal for a National Information Infrastructure by the communication industry trade press, the general trade press, and newspapers. She found that the trade press was less likely to cover the social implications of policy proposals. Liebler and Smith (1997) discovered that male and female network news correspondents both used male sources more often than female sources in their reporting. Finally, Furnham and Farragher (2000) found that sex role stereotyping in ads was greater in New Zealand television than in British TV.

Comparing Media Content to the "Real World"

Many content analyses are reality checks in which the portrayal of a certain group, phenomenon, trait, or characteristic is assessed against a standard taken from real life. The congruence of the media presentation and the actual situation is then discussed. Probably the earliest study of this type was by Davis (1951), who found that crime coverage in Colorado newspapers bore no relationship to changes in state crime rates. The National Commission on the Causes and Prevention of Violence used content analysis data collected by Gerbner (1969) to compare the world of television violence with real-life violence. Taylor and Bang (1997) compared the portrayal of three minority groups in magazine ads with their incidence in the general population and found that Latino-Americans were the most underrepresented group in U.S. magazine advertising. Finally, Dixon and Linz (2000) compared the TV depictions of African-Americans and Latinos as lawbreakers to real-life data.

Assessing the Image of Particular Groups in Society

Ever-growing numbers of content analyses have focused on exploring the media image of certain minority or otherwise notable groups. In many instances, these studies are conducted to assess changes in media policy toward these groups, to make inferences about the media's responsiveness to demands for better coverage, or to document social trends. For example, Greenwald (1990) analyzed the coverage of women in the business sections of two metropolitan newspapers. She found that women were the main subjects in only 5 of 180 stories. Taylor and Stern (1997) traced the portrayals of Asian-Americans in television ads during the mid-1990s and reported that only 10% of the ads featured an Asian-American model. Roy and Harwood (1997) found that the elderly were underrepresented but portrayed positively in TV commercials. More recently, Mastro and Greenberg (2000) analyzed the depiction of African-American and Latino characters on television.

Establishing a Starting Point for Studies of Media Effects

The use of content analysis as a starting point for subsequent studies is relatively new. The best known example is **cultivation analysis,** in which the dominant message and themes in media content are documented by systematic procedures and a separate study of the audience is conducted to see whether these messages are fostering similar attitudes among heavy media users. Gerbner, Gross, Signorielli, Morgan, and Jackson-Beeck (1979) discovered that heavy viewers of television tend to be more fearful of the world around them. In other words, television content—in this case, large doses of crime and violence—may cultivate attitudes more consistent with its messages than with reality. Other work that has used a similar framework includes Pfau, Mullen, Deidrich, and Garrow's (1995) study of public perception of attorneys and the viewing of prime-time television programs featuring lawyers and Signorielli and Kahlenberg's (2001) study of the way occupations were portrayed on television. Cultivation analysis is discussed further in Chapter 17.

Content analysis is also used in a study of agenda setting. An analysis of relevant media content is necessary in order to determine the importance of news topics. Subsequent audience research looks at the correspondence between the media's agenda and the audience's agenda. Corbett and Mori (1999), for example, performed a content analysis of news coverage of breast cancer in their examination of agenda setting, and Roessler (1999) content analyzed news coverage on radio, TV, and the newspaper in his examination of political agenda setting.

AN INSIDE LOOK

Content Analysis: Coder Perception Versus Audience Perception

One problem with using content analysis as a starting point for studies of audience effects is the possibility of falsely assuming that what trained coders see in a body of content is the same as what audience members perceive. For example, a study of the cultivation effects of TV content on viewers' attitudes toward sexual practices might start with an analysis of the sexual content of specific television programs. Coders might be trained to count how many provocatively dressed characters appear; how many instances of kissing, embracing, caressing, and other forms of sexual behavior occur; and so on. When the coders are finished with this aspect of the study, they could rank-order a list of TV programs with regard to their sexual content. Audience viewings of these shows could then be correlated with audience attitudes toward sexual matters. The trouble is that the researchers do not know whether the audience defines the term *sexual content* in the same way the coders do. For example, many in the audience might not define all forms of kissing as sexual. Or perhaps programs such as MTV's "Loveline" or "The New Newlywed Game," where sexual activity is only talked about and implied rather than acted out, are also influential in shaping audience attitudes. Since these shows would probably score low on most of the measures used by coders to gauge sexual content, the influence of these shows might be overlooked.

Limitations of Content Analysis

Content analysis alone cannot serve as a basis for making statements about the effects of content on an audience. A study of Saturday morning cartoon programs on television might reveal that 80% of these programs contain commercials for sugared cereal, but this finding alone does not allow researchers to claim that children who watch these programs will want to purchase sugared cereals. To make such an assertion, an additional study of the viewers is necessary (as in cultivation analysis). Content analysis cannot serve as the sole basis for claims about media effects.

Also, the findings of a particular content analysis are limited to the framework of the categories and the definitions used in that analysis. Different researchers may use varying definitions and category systems to measure a single concept. In mass media research, this problem is most evident in studies of televised violence. Some researchers rule out comic or slapstick violence in their studies, whereas others consider it an important dimension. Obviously, great care should be exercised in comparing the results of different content analysis studies. Researchers who use different tools of measurement naturally arrive at different conclusions.

Another potential limitation of content analysis is a lack of messages relevant to the research. Many topics or characters receive little exposure in the mass media. For example, a study of how Asians are portrayed in U.S. television commercials would be difficult because such characters are rarely seen (of course, this fact in itself might be a significant finding). A researcher interested in this topic must be prepared to examine a large body of media content to find sufficient quantities for analysis.

Finally, content analysis is frequently time-consuming and expensive. The task of examining and categorizing large volumes of content is often laborious and tedious. Plowing through 100 copies of the *New York Times* or 50 issues of *Newsweek* takes time and patience. In addition, if television content is selected for analysis, there must be some means of preserving the programs for detailed examination. Typically, researchers videotape programs for analysis, but this requires access to one or more VCRs and large supplies of videotape—materials not all researchers can afford.

▪ Steps in Content Analysis

In general, a content analysis is conducted in several discrete stages. Although the steps are listed here in sequence, they need not be followed in the order given. In fact, the initial stages of analysis can easily be combined. Nonetheless, the following steps may be used as a rough outline:

1. Formulate the research question or hypothesis.
2. Define the population in question.
3. Select an appropriate sample from the population.
4. Select and define a unit of analysis.
5. Construct the categories of content to be analyzed.
6. Establish a quantification system.
7. Train coders and conduct a pilot study.
8. Code the content according to established definitions.
9. Analyze the collected data.
10. Draw conclusions and search for indications.

Formulating a Research Question

One problem to avoid in content analysis is the syndrome of "counting for the sake of counting." The goal of the analysis must be clearly articulated to avoid aimless exercises in data collection that have little utility for mass media research. For example, after counting the punctuation marks used in the *New York Times* and *Esquire,* one might make a statement such as "*Esquire* used 45% more commas, but 23% fewer semicolons than the *New York Times*." The value of such information for mass media theory or policy making is dubious. Content analysis should not be conducted simply because the material exists and can be tabulated.

As with other methods of mass media research, content analyses should be guided by well-formulated research questions or hypotheses. A basic review of the literature is a required step. The sources for hypotheses are the same as for other areas of media research. It is possible to generate a research question based on existing theory, prior research, or practical problems, or as a response to changing social conditions. For example, a research question might ask whether the growing acceptability of motorcycles has produced a change in the way motorcyclists are depicted in TV shows. Or a content analysis might be conducted to determine whether the public affairs programming of group-owned television stations differs from that of other stations. Well-defined research questions or hypotheses lead to the development of accurate and sensitive content categories, which in turn helps to produce data that are more valuable.

Defining the Universe

This stage is not as grandiose as it sounds. To "define the universe" is to specify the boundaries of the body of content to be considered, which requires an appropriate operational definition of the relevant population. If researchers are interested in analyzing the content of popular songs, they must define what is meant by a "popular song": All songs listed in *Billboard's* "Hot 100" chart or on the back page of *Radio & Records?* The top

AN INSIDE LOOK
Content Analysis and Ethics

Most content analyses of Internet content raise few ethical problems, but there may be situations where ethical questions can arise. Examining the content of a web site, for example, seems safe. On the other hand, consider the situation where a researcher wants to examine the content of a chat room that's devoted to some special topic. Is it ethically necessary for the researcher to inform the group that their messages are being monitored? Must the researcher obtain consent from the people who are being monitored? Suppose a person wanted to see how members of a support group reacted to a problem. Is it ethical for that researcher to post a fake message on a listserv and then analyze the responses? In that same connection, suppose a researcher is interested in rumor transmission. Is it ethical to start a rumor online and then monitor how it spreads? These and similar situations deserve close ethical scrutiny.

50 songs? The top 10? They must also ask what time period will be considered: The past 6 months? This month only? A researcher who intends to study the image of minority groups on television must first define what the term *television* means. Does it include broadcast and cable networks? Pay television? Videocassettes? Is it evening programming, or does it also include daytime shows? Will the study examine news content or confine itself to dramatic offerings?

Two dimensions are usually used to determine the appropriate universe for a content analysis—the topic area and the time period. The topic area should be logically consistent with the research question and related to the goals of the study. For example, if a researcher plans a study of U.S. involvement in Bosnia, should the sample period extend back to the time when Bosnia was part of Yugoslavia? Finally, the time period to be examined should be sufficiently long so that the phenomenon under study has enough time to occur.

By clearly specifying the topic area and the time period, the researcher is meeting a basic requirement of content analysis: a concise statement that spells out the parameters of the investigation. For example:

> This study considers TV commercials broadcast in prime time in the New York City area from September 1, 2000, to August 31, 2002

or

> This study considers the news content on the front pages of the *Washington Post* and the *New York Times,* excluding Sundays, from January 1 to December 31 of the past year.

Selecting a Sample

Once the universe is defined, a sample is selected. Although many of the guidelines and procedures discussed in Chapter 4 are applicable here, the sampling of content involves some special considerations. On one hand, some analyses are concerned with a finite amount of data and it may be possible to conduct a census of the content. For example, Skill and Robinson (1994) analyzed a census of all television series that featured families from 1950 to 1989, a total of 497 different series, and Greenberg and Collette (1997) performed a census of all new major characters added to the broadcast networks' program lineup from 1966 to 1992, a total of 1,757 characters. On the other hand, in the more typical situation, the researcher has such a vast amount of content available that a census is not practical. Thus a sample must be selected.

Most content analysis in mass media involves multistage sampling. This process typically consists of two stages (although it may entail three). The first stage is usually to take a sampling of content sources. For example, a researcher interested in the treatment of the environmental movement by American newspapers would first need to sample from among the 1,600 or so newspapers published each day. The researcher may decide to focus primarily on the way big-city dailies covered the story and opt to analyze only the leading circulation newspapers in the 10 largest American cities. To take another example, a researcher interested in the changing portrayal of elderly people in magazine advertisements would first need to sample from among the thousands of publications available. In this instance, the researcher might select only the top 10, 15, or 25 mass-circulation magazines. Of course, it is also possible to sample randomly if the task of analyzing all the titles is too overwhelming. A further possibility is to use the technique of stratified sampling discussed in Chapter 4. A researcher studying the environmental movement might wish to stratify the sample by circulation size and to sample from within the strata composed of big-city newspapers, medium-city newspapers, and small-city newspapers. The magazine researcher might stratify by type of magazine: news, women's interests, men's interests, and so on. A researcher interested in television content might stratify by network or by program type.

Once the sources have been identified, the second step is to select the dates. In many studies, the time period from which the issues are to be selected is determined by the goal of the project. If the goal is to assess the nature of news coverage of the 2000 election campaign, the sampling period is fairly well defined by the actual duration of the story. If the research question is about changes in the media image of President Bill Clinton following allegations of improper use of the presidential pardon, content should be sampled before, at the time of, and after the allegations. But within this period, what editions of newspapers and magazines and which television programs should be selected for analysis? It would be a tremendous amount of work to analyze each issue of *Time, Newsweek,* and *U.S. News & World Report* over a 5-year period. It is possible to sample from within that time period and obtain a representative group of issues. A simple random sample of the calendar dates involved is one possibility: After a random start, every *n*th issue of a publication is selected for the sample. This method cannot be used without planning, however. For instance, if the goal is 50 edition dates and an interval of 7 is used, the sample might include 50 Saturday editions (periodicity). Since news content is not distributed randomly over the days of the week, such a sample will not be representative.

Another technique for sampling edition dates is stratification by week of the month and by day of the week. A sampling rule that no more than two days from one week can be chosen is one way to ensure a balanced distribution across the month. Another procedure is to construct a *composite week* for each month in the sample. For example, a study might use a sample of one Monday (drawn at random from the four or five possible Mondays in the month), one Tuesday (drawn from the available Tuesdays), and so on, until all weekdays have been included. How many edition dates should be selected? Obviously, this depends on the topic under study. If an investigator is trying to describe the portrayal of Mexican-Americans on prime-time television, several dates have to be sampled to ensure a representative analysis. If there is an interest in analyzing the geographic sources of news stories, a smaller number of dates is needed because almost every story is relevant.

The number of dates should be a function of the incidence of the phenomenon in question: The lower the incidence, the more dates must be sampled.

There are some rough guidelines for sampling in the media. Stempel (1952) drew separate samples of 6, 12, 18, 24, and 48 issues of a newspaper and compared the average content of each sample size in a single subject category against the total for the entire year. He found that each of the five sample sizes was adequate and that increasing the sample beyond 12 issues did not significantly improve sampling accuracy. Riffe, Aust, and Lacy (1993) demonstrated that a composite week sampling technique was superior to both a random sample and a consecutive day sample when dealing with newspaper content. Similarly, Riffe, Lacy, and Drager (1996) studied the optimum sample sizes for an analysis of weekly newsmagazines, and Lacy, Robinson, and Riffe (1995) did the same for weekly newspapers. They found that a monthly stratified sample of 12 issues was the most efficient sample for both magazines and newspapers. The next most efficient method was a simple random sample of 14 issues.

In television, Gerbner, Gross, Jackson-Beeck, Jeffries-Fox, and Signorielli (1977) demonstrated that, at least for the purpose of measuring violent behavior, a sample of one week of fall programming and various sample dates drawn throughout the year produced comparable results. Riffe, Lacy, Nagovan, and Burkum (1996) examined sample sizes for content analysis of broadcast news and found that two days per month chosen at random proved to be the most efficient method. As a general rule, however, the larger the sample, the better—within reason, of course. If too few dates are selected for analysis, the possibility of an unrepresentative sample is increased. Larger samples, if chosen randomly, usually run less risk of being atypical.

There may be times, however, when purposive sampling is useful. As Stempel (1989) points out, a researcher might learn more about newspaper coverage of South Africa by examining a small sample of carefully selected papers (for example, those that subscribe to the international/national wire services or have correspondents in South Africa) than by studying a random sample of 100 newspapers. Riffe and Freitag (1997) confirm the importance of purposive sampling in content analysis. They found that 68% of all the content analyses in *Journalism Quarterly* from 1971 to 1995 used a purposive sample.

Another problem that can arise during the sampling phase is systematic bias in the content itself. For example, a study of the amount of sports news in a daily paper might yield inflated results if the sampling was done only in April, when three or more professional sports are simultaneously in season. A study of marriage announcements in the Sunday *New York Times* for the month of June from 1932 to 1942 revealed no announcement of a marriage in a synagogue (Hatch & Hatch, 1947). It was later pointed out that the month of June usually falls within a period during which traditional Jewish marriages are prohibited. Researchers familiar with their topics can generally discover and guard against this type of distortion.

Once the sources and the dates have been determined, there may be a third stage of sampling. A researcher might wish to confine his or her attention to the specific content within an edition. For example, an analysis of the front page of a newspaper is valid for a study of general reporting trends but is probably inadequate for a study of social news coverage. Figure 6.1 provides an example of multistage sampling in content analysis.

Selecting a Unit of Analysis

The next step is to select the **unit of analysis,** which is the smallest element of a content analysis but also one of the most important. In written content, the unit of analysis might be a single word or symbol, a theme (a single

Figure 6.1 *Multistage Sampling in a Hypothetical Analysis Study*

Research Question: Have there been changes in the types of products advertised in men's magazines from 1980 to 2000?

Sampling Stage 1: Selection of Titles
Men's magazines are defined as those magazines whose circulation figures show that 80% or more of their readers are men. These magazines will be divided into two groups: large and medium circulation.
Large circulation: reaches more than 1,000,000 men.
Medium circulation: reaches between 500,000 and 999,999 men.
From all the magazines that fall into these two groups, three will be selected at random from each division, for a total of six titles.

Sampling Stage 2: Selection of Dates
Three issues from each year will be chosen at random from clusters of four months. One magazine will be selected from the January, February, March, and April issues, and so on. This procedure will be followed for each magazine, yielding a final sample of 30 issues per magazine, or a total of 180 issues.

Sampling Stage 3: Selection of Content
Every other display ad will be tabulated, regardless of its size.

assertion about one subject), or an entire article or story. In television and film analyses, units of analysis can be characters, acts, or entire programs. Specific rules and definitions are required for determining these units to ensure closer agreement among coders and fewer judgment calls.

Certain units of analysis are simpler to count than others. It is easier to determine the number of stories on the "CBS Evening News" that deal with international news than the number of acts of violence in a week of network television because a story is a more readily distinguishable unit of analysis. The beginning and ending of a news story are fairly easy to discern, but suppose that a researcher trying to catalog violent content is faced with a long fistfight among three characters? Is the whole sequence one act of violence, or is every blow considered an act? What if a fourth character joins in? Does it then become a different act?

Operational definitions of the unit of analysis should be clear-cut and thorough; the criteria for inclusion should be apparent and easily observed. These goals cannot be met without effort and some trial and error. As a preliminary step, researchers must form a rough draft of a definition and then sample representative content to look for problems. This procedure usually results in further refinement and modification of the operational definition. Table 6.1 presents typical operational definitions of units of analysis taken from mass media research.

Constructing Content Categories

At the heart of any content analysis is the category system used to classify media content. The precise makeup of this system, of course, varies with the topic under study. As Berelson (1952, p. 147) points out, "Particular studies have been productive to the extent that the categories were clearly formulated and well-adapted to the problem and the content."

Table 6.1 *Samples and Operational Definitions of Units of Analysis*

Researcher(s)	Topic	Universe	Sample	Unit of Analysis
Bramlett-Solomon and Subramanian (1999)	Depiction of elderly in magazine ads	All ads in *Life* and *Ebony,* 1990–1997	All ads in all issues except classifieds	Character's over 65, or with gray hair or extensive wrinkling or using walking aid
Kim (2000)	Coverage of pro-democracy movement in China	All prodemocracy stories in *N.Y. Times* and *Washington Post,* May–June, 1980, and June–July, 1989	All prodemocracy stories in 1980; systematic sample of 64 from 1989	Each paragraph in the news story
Mastro and Greenberg (2000)	Racial minorities on TV	Fall, 1996, prime time broadcast TV programs	Randomly constructed composite week for each broadcast network	Programs containing a minority character; minority characters in a prominent role
Signorielli and Kahlenberg (2001)	Occupations in prime time TV	Prime time broadcast TV, 1990–1998	One week of programs per year in either Fall or Spring	Occupations of characters in major, minor, or supporting roles
Lauzen and Dozier (1999)	Women behind the scenes in 1994–1995 TV season	Top 65 sitcoms and dramas in the 1995–1996 season	One episode of each program	Gender of behind-the-scenes workers as inferred from program credits

To be serviceable, all category systems should be mutually exclusive, exhaustive, and reliable. A category system is **mutually exclusive** if a unit of analysis can be placed in one and only one category. If the researcher discovers that certain units fall simultaneously into two categories, then the definitions of those categories must be revised. For example, suppose researchers attempt to describe the ethnic makeup of prime-time television characters using the following category system: (1) African-American, (2) Jewish, (3) white, (4) Native American, and (5) other. Obviously, a Jewish person falls into two categories at once, thus violating the exclusivity rule. Or, to take another example, a researcher might start with these categories in an attempt to describe the types of programming on network television: (1) situation comedies, (2) children's shows, (3) movies, (4) documentaries, (5) action/adventure programs, (6) quiz and talk shows, and (7) general drama. This list might look acceptable at first glance, but a program such as "NYPD Blue" raises questions. Does it belong in the action/adventure category or in the general drama category? Definitions must be highly specific to ensure accurate categorization.

In addition to exclusivity, content analysis categories must have the property of **exhaustivity:** There must be an existing slot into which every unit of analysis can be placed. If investigators suddenly find a unit of analysis that does not logically fit into a predefined category, they have a problem with their category system. Taken as a whole, the category system should account for every unit of analysis. Achieving exhaustivity is usually not difficult in mass media content analysis. If one or two unusual instances are detected, they can be put into a category labeled "other" or "miscellaneous." (If too many items fall into this category, however, a reexamination of the original category definitions is called for; a study with 10% or more of its content in the "other" category is probably overlooking some relevant content characteristic.) An additional way to assure exhaustivity is to dichotomize or trichotomize the content: Attempts at problem solving might be defined as aggressive and nonaggressive, or statements might be placed in positive, neutral, and negative categories. The most practical way to determine whether a proposed categorization system is exhaustive is to pretest it on a sample of content. If unanticipated items appear, the original scheme requires changes before the primary analysis can begin.

The categorization system should also be **reliable;** that is, different coders should agree in the great majority of instances about the proper category for each unit of analysis. This agreement is usually quantified in content analysis and is called **intercoder reliability.** Precise category definitions generally increase reliability, whereas sloppily defined categories tend to lower it. Pretesting the category system for reliability is highly recommended before researchers begin to process the main body of content. Reliability is crucial in content analysis, as discussed in more detail later in this chapter.

Researchers may face the question of how many categories to include in constructing category systems. Common sense, pretesting, and practice with the coding system are valuable guides to aid the researcher in steering between the two extremes of developing a system with too few categories (so that essential differences are obscured) and defining too many categories (so that only a small percentage falls into each, thus limiting generalizations). As a general rule, many researchers suggest that too many initial categories are preferable to too few, since it is usually easier to combine several categories than it is to subdivide a large one after the units have been coded.

Establishing a Quantification System

Quantification in content analysis can involve all four of the levels of data measurement discussed in Chapter 3, although usually only nominal, interval, and ratio data are used. At the nominal level, researchers simply count the frequency of occurrence of the units in each category. Thus Signorielli, McLeod, and Healy (1994) analyzed commercials on MTV and found that 6.5% of the male characters were coded as wearing somewhat sexy clothing and none were coded as being dressed in very sexy outfits; among the female characters, however, the corresponding percentages were 24% and 29%. The topics of conversation on daytime television, the themes of newspaper editorials, and the occupation of prime-time television characters can all be quantified by means of nominal measurement.

At the interval level, it is possible to develop scales for coders to use to rate certain attributes of characters or situations. For example, in a study dealing with the images of women in commercials, each character might be rated by coders on several scales like these:

Independent __:__:__:__:__ Dependent
Dominant __:__:__:__:__ Submissive

Scales such as these add depth and texture to a content analysis and are perhaps more interesting than the surface data obtained through nominal measurement. However, rating scales inject subjectivity into the analysis and may jeopardize intercoder reliability unless careful training is undertaken.

At the ratio level, measurements in mass media research are generally applied to space and time. In the print media, column-inch measurements are used to analyze editorials, advertisements, and stories about particular events or phenomena. In television and radio, ratio-level measurements are made concerning time: the number of commercial minutes, the types of programs on the air, the amount of the program day devoted to programs of various types, and so on. Interval and ratio data permit the researcher to use some powerful statistical techniques. For example, Cho and Lacy (2000) used a regression equation (see Chapter 13) to explain variations in coverage of international news that were due to organizational variables.

Training Coders and Doing a Pilot Study

Placing a unit of analysis into a content category is called **coding.** It is the most time-consuming and least glamorous part of a content analysis. Individuals who do the coding are called coders. The number of coders involved in a content analysis is typically small; a brief examination of a sampling of recent content analyses indicated that typically two to six coders are used.

Careful training of coders is an integral step in any content analysis and usually results in a more reliable analysis. Although the investigator may have a firm grasp of the operational definitions and the category schemes, coders may not share this close knowledge. Consequently, they must become thoroughly familiar with the study's mechanics and peculiarities. To this end, researchers should plan several lengthy training sessions in which sample content is examined and coded. These sessions are used to revise definitions, clarify category boundaries, and revamp coding sheets until the coders are comfortable with the materials and procedure. Detailed instruction sheets should also be provided to coders.

Next, a pilot study is done to check intercoder reliability. The pilot study should be conducted with a fresh set of coders who are given some initial training to impart familiarity with the instructions and the methods of the study. Some argue that fresh coders are preferred for this task because intercoder reliability (among coders who have worked for long periods of time developing the coding scheme) might be artificially high. As Lorr and McNair (1966, p. 133) suggest, "Interrater agreement for a new set of judges given a reasonable but practical amount of training . . . would represent a more realistic index of reliability."

Ahuvia (2001) tries to address this issue by suggesting a type of content analysis called "reception based" analysis. In this technique, a number of coders who are similar to the consumers of the content report their own subjective interpretations of the content. The researcher can then examine the degree of agreement and disagreement and make interpretations as to how the content is likely to be interpreted by the audience. To continue the above example, if a researcher is interested in the effects of sexual content on adolescents, a reception analysis would use adolescent coders. These coders would not be given any predetermined rules about cod-

Figure 6.2 *Standardized Coding Sheet for Studying TV Cartoons*

Character Description Code Sheet

Program name ______________________

A. Character number ______________

B. Character name or description ______________________

C. Role	1-Major	3-Other (individual)
	2-Minor	4-Other (group)
D. Species		
1-Human	4-Robot	7-Other (specify):
2-Animal	5-Animated object	
3-Monster/Ghost	6-Indeterminate	______________
E. Sex		
1-Male 2-Female	3-Indeterminate	4-Mixed (group)
F. Race		
1-White	4-Robot	7-Other (specify):
2-African-American	5-Native American	
3-Animal	6-Indeterminate	______________
G. Age		
1-Child	3-Adult	5-Indeterminate
2-Teenager	4-Mature adult	6-Mixed (group)

ing but would simple use their own intuitive meaning for "sexual content."

They would then code a selected body of content. The degree of agreement among coders is then used as a finding. For example, if half the coders think that talking about sex does not count as "sexual content" and the other half disagrees, that suggests that there is a good deal of variance in the way that content is interpreted which might have implications for its possible effects. Ahuvia argues that there is no reason why different coders have to agree on the meaning of content. Creating consensus where none actually exists may distort the findings.

Coding the Content

Standardized sheets are usually used to ease coding. These sheets allow coders to classify the data by placing check marks or slashes in predetermined spaces. Figure 6.2 is an example of a standardized coding sheet, and Figure 6.3 is the coder instruction sheet that accompanies it. If data are to be tabulated by hand, the coding sheets should be constructed to

Figure 6.3 *Coder Instruction Sheet That Accompanies Form Shown in Figure 6.2*

Character Description Code Sheet Instructions

Code all characters that appear on the screen for at least 90 seconds and/or speak more than 15 words (include cartoon narrator when applicable). Complete one sheet for each character to be coded.

A. Character number, code two-digit program number first (listed on page 12 of this instruction book), followed by two-digit character number randomly assigned to each character (starting with 01).

B. Character name: list all formal names, nicknames, or dual identity names (code dual identity behavior as one character's actions). List description of character if name is not identifiable.

C. Role
   1-*Major*: major characters share the majority of dialogue during the program, play the largest role in the dramatic action, and appear on the screen for the longest period of time during the program.
   2-*Minor*: all codeable characters that are not identified as major characters.
   3-*Other* (*individual*): one character that does not meet coding requirements but is involved in a behavioral act that is coded.
   4-*Other* (*group*): two or more characters that are simultaneously involved in a behavioral act but do not meet coding requirements.

D. Species
   1-*Human*: any character resembling man, even ghost or apparition if it appears in human form (e.g., the Ghostbusters)
   2-*Animal*: any character resembling bird, fish, beast, or insect; may or may not be capable of human speech (e.g., muppets, smurfs, Teddy Ruxpin)
   3-*Monster/Ghost*: any supernatural creature (e.g., my pet monster, ghosts)
   4-*Robot*: mechanical creature (e.g., transformers)
   5-*Animated object*: any inanimate object (e.g., car, telephone) that acts like a sentient being (speaks, thinks, etc.). Do not include objects that "speak" through programmed mechanical means (e.g., recorded voice playback through computer).
   6-*Indeterminate*
   7-*Other*: if species is mixed within group, code as mixed here and specify which of the species are represented.

E. 1-Male 2-Female 3-Indeterminate: use this category sparingly (if animal has low masculine voice, code as male) 4-Mixed (group only)

Note: The remainder of the instructions continue in this format.

allow for rapid tabulation. Some studies code data on 4-by-6-inch index cards, with information recorded across the top of the card. This enables researchers to quickly sort the information into categories. Templates are available to speed the measurement of newspaper space. Researchers who work with television generally videotape the programs and allow coders to stop and start the tape at their own pace while coding data.

When a computer is used in tabulating data, the data are usually transferred directly to a spreadsheet or data file or perhaps to mark-sense forms or optical scan sheets (answer sheets scored by computer). These forms save time and reduce data errors.

Computers are useful not only in the data-tabulation phase of a content analysis but also in the actual coding process. Computers perform with unerring accuracy any coding task in which the classification rules are unambiguous. There are many software programs available that can aid in the content analysis of text documents. Some of the more common are TextSmart, VBPro, and ProfilerPlus. Programs such as Executive Producer and Camera can assist in the analysis of visual content

Many documents and publications in online databases such as Nexis can be searched for key topics and phrases in a matter of seconds. This ease of searching comes with a price, however. As Kaufman, Dykers, and Caldwell (1993) discovered, an online content analysis conducted with Nexis and Vu/Text produced different results from a conventional hand-count content analysis of the same sources.

Analyzing the Data

The descriptive statistics discussed in Chapters 11–13, such as percentages, means, modes, and medians, are appropriate for content analysis. If hypothesis tests are planned, then common inferential statistics (whereby results are generalized to the population) are acceptable. The chi-square test is the most commonly used because content analysis data tend to be nominal in form; however, if the data meet the requirements of interval or ratio levels, then a *t*-test, ANOVA, or Pearson's *r* may be appropriate. Krippendorf (1980) discusses other statistical analyses, such as discriminant analysis, cluster analysis, and contextual analysis.

Interpreting the Results

If an investigator is testing specific hypotheses concerning the relationships between variables, the interpretation will be evident. If the study is descriptive, however, questions may arise about the meaning or importance of the results. Researchers are often faced with a "fully/only" dilemma. Suppose, for example, that a content analysis of children's television programs reveals that 30% of the commercials are for snacks and candy. What is the researcher to conclude? Is this a high amount or a low amount? Should the researcher report, "*Fully* 30% of the commercials fell into this category," or should the same percentage be presented as "*Only* 30% of the commercials fell into this category"? Clearly, the investigator needs some benchmark for comparison; 30% may indeed be a high figure when compared to commercials for other products or for those shown during adult programs.

In a study done by one of the authors, the amount of network news time devoted to the various states was tabulated. It was determined that California and New York receive 19% and 18%, respectively, of non-Washington, DC, national news coverage. By themselves, these numbers are interesting, but their significance is somewhat unclear. In an attempt to aid interpretation, each state's relative news time was compared to its population, and an "attention index" was created by subtracting the ratio of each state's population to the national population from its percentage of news coverage. This provided a listing of states that were either "over-covered" or "under-covered" (Dominick, 1977). To aid in their interpretation, Whitney, Fritzler, Jones, Mazzarella, and Rakow (1989) created a sophisticated "attention ratio" in their replication of this study.

▪ Reliability

The concept of reliability is crucial to content analysis. If a content analysis is to be objective, its measures and procedures must be reliable. A study is reliable when repeated measurement of the same material results in similar decisions or conclusions. Intercoder reliability refers to levels of agreement among independent coders who code the same content using the same coding instrument. If the results fail to achieve reliability, something is amiss with the coders, the coding instructions, the category definitions, the unit of analysis, or some combination of these. To achieve acceptable levels of reliability, the following steps are recommended:

1. *Define category boundaries with maximum detail.* A group of vague or ambiguously defined categories makes reliability extremely difficult to achieve. Coders should receive examples of units of analysis and a brief explanation of each to fully understand the procedure.
2. *Train the coders.* Before the data are collected, training sessions in using the coding instrument and the category system must be conducted. These sessions help eliminate methodological problems. During the sessions, the group as a whole should code sample material; afterward, they should discuss the results and the purpose of the study. Disagreements should be analyzed as they occur. The end result of the training sessions is a "bible" of detailed instructions and coding examples, and each coder should receive a copy.
3. *Conduct a pilot study.* Researchers should select a subsample of the content universe under consideration and let independent coders categorize it. These data are useful for two reasons: Poorly defined categories can be detected, and chronically dissenting coders can be identified. To illustrate these problems, consider Tables 6.2 and 6.3.

In Table 6.2, the definitions for Categories I and IV appear to be satisfactory. All

Table 6.2 *Detecting Poorly Defined Categories from Pilot Study Data**

	Categories			
Coders	I	II	III	IV
A	1,3,7,11	2,5,6,8,12,13	10	4,9,14
B	1,3,7,11	5,8,10,12	2,6,13	4,9,14
C	1,3,7,11	2,8,12,13	5,6,10	4,9,14
D	1,3,7,11	5,6	2,8,10,12,13,14	4,9

*Arabic numerals refer to items.

Table 6.3 *Identifying a Chronic Dissenter from Pilot Study Data**

	Coders		
Items	A	B	C
1	I	I	II
2	III	III	I
3	II	II	II
4	IV	IV	III
5	I	II	II
6	IV	IV	I
7	I	I	III
8	II	II	I

*Roman numerals refer to categories.

four coders placed Units 1, 3, 7, and 11 in the first category; in Category IV, Item 14 is classified consistently by three of the four coders and Items 4 and 9 by all four coders. The confusion apparently lies in the boundaries between Categories II and III. Three coders put Items 2, 6, and/or 13 in Category II, and three placed some or all of these numbers in Category III. The definitions of these two categories require reexamination and perhaps revision because of this ambiguity.

Table 6.3 illustrates the problem of the chronic dissenter. Although Coders A and B agree 7 of 8 times, Coders B and C agree only 2 of 8 times and Coders A and C agree only once. Obviously, Coder C is going to be a problem. As a rule, the investigator would carefully reexplain to this coder the rules used in categorization and examine the reasons for his or her consistent deviation. If the problem persists, it may be necessary to dismiss the coder from the analysis.

When the initial test of reliability yields satisfactory results, the main body of data is coded. After the coding is complete, it is recommended that a subsample of the data, probably between 10% and 25%, be reanalyzed by independent coders to calculate an overall intercoder reliability coefficient. Lacy and Riffe (1996) note that a reliability check based on a probability sample may contain sampling error. They present a formula for calculating the size of the intercoder reliability sample that takes this error into account.

Intercoder reliability can be calculated by several methods. Holsti (1969) reports this formula for determining the reliability of nominal data in terms of percentage of agreement:

$$\text{Reliability} = \frac{2M}{N_1 + N_2}$$

where M is the number of coding decisions on which two coders agree, and N_1 and N_2 are the total number of coding decisions by the first and second coder, respectively. Thus, if two coders judge a subsample of 50 units and agree on 35 of them, the calculation is

$$\text{Reliability} = \frac{2(35)}{50 + 50} = .70$$

This method is straightforward and easy to apply, but it is criticized because it does not take into account some coder agreement that occurs strictly by chance, an amount that is a function of the number of categories in the analysis. For example, a two-category system has 50% reliability simply by chance, a five-category system generates a 20% agreement by chance, and so on. To take this into account, Scott (1955) developed the *pi* index, which corrects for the number of categories used and also for the probable frequency of use:

$$\text{Reliability} = \frac{\begin{matrix}\text{\% observed} \\ \text{agreement}\end{matrix} - \begin{matrix}\text{\% expected} \\ \text{agreement}\end{matrix}}{1 - \text{\% expected agreement}}$$

A hypothetical example demonstrates the use of this index. Suppose that two coders are assigning magazine advertisements to the five categories shown below and obtain the following matrix of agreement:

		Coder A					
	Categories	1	2	3	4	5	Marginal Totals
	1	42	2	1	3	0	48
	2	1	12	2	0	0	15
Coder B	3	0	0	10	0	2	12
	4	0	2	1	8	1	12
	5	2	0	1	2	8	13
Marginal Totals		45	16	15	13	11	100

The percentage of observed agreement is found by adding the numbers in the diagonals (42 + 12 + 10 + 8 + 8 = 80) and dividing by N (80/100 = .80). The percentage of agreement expected by chance is a little more complicated. It is found by multiplying the marginal totals for each cell of the diagonal, dividing by the total N, summing across the cells, and converting the result to a percentage. For example, for the cell in row 1 and column 1: $45 \times 48/100 = 21.6$, or .216. For the cell in row 2 and column 2: $16 \times 15/100 = 2.4$, or .024, and so on for all the five cells along the diagonal of the matrix. This calculation yields an expected proportion of .288. Now we can calculate Scott's *pi*:

$$\text{Reliability} = \frac{.80 - .288}{1 - .288} = .719$$

This same technique can be used to calculate reliability when there are more than two coders. In this instance, the statistic is called Cohen's kappa (Cohen, 1960; Fleiss, 1971), and the formula is slightly modified:

$$\text{Kappa} = \frac{\%\ \text{observed} - \%\ \text{expected}}{N \times M - \%\ \text{expected}}$$

where N is the total number of objects coded and M is the number of coders.

Estimating reliability with interval data requires care. Several studies have used the correlation method called the Pearson r, a method that investigates the relationship between two items. The Pearson r can range from -1.00 to $+1.00$. In estimates of reliability in content analysis, however, if this measure has a high value, it may indicate either that the coders were in agreement or that their ratings were associated in some systematic manner.

For example, suppose an interval scale ranging from 1 to 10 is used to score the degree of favorableness of a news item to some person or topic. (A score of 1 represents very positive; 10 represents very negative.) Assume that two coders are independently scoring the same 10 items. Table 6.4 shows two possible outcomes. In Situation I, the coders agree on every item, and r equals 1.00. In Situation II, the coders disagree on every item by three scale positions, yet r still equals 1.00. Clearly, the uses of this estimate are not equally reliable in the two situations.

Krippendorf (1980) circumvents this dilemma by presenting what might be termed an "all-purpose reliability measure," *alpha*, which can be used for nominal, ordinal, interval, and ratio scales and for more than one coder. Though somewhat difficult to calculate, alpha is the equivalent of Scott's *pi* at the nominal level with two coders and represents an improvement over r in the interval situation.

What is an acceptable level of intercoder reliability? The answer depends on the research context and the type of information coded. In some instances, little coder judgment is needed to place units into categories (for example, counting the number of words per sentence in a newspaper story or tabulating the number of times a network correspondent contributes a story to the evening news), and coding becomes a mechanical or clerical task. In this case, one expects a fairly

Table 6.4 *False Equivalence As a Reliability Measure When r Is Used*

	Situation I			Situation II	
Items	Coder 1	Coder 2	Items	Coder 1	Coder 2
1	1	1	1	1	4
2	2	2	2	2	5
3	3	3	3	3	6
4	3	3	4	3	6
5	4	4	5	4	7
6	5	5	6	5	8
7	6	6	7	6	9
8	6	6	8	6	9
9	7	7	9	7	10
10	7	7	10	7	10
	$r = 1.00$			$r = 1.00$	

high degree of reliability, perhaps approaching 100%, since coder disagreements probably result from only carelessness or fatigue. If a certain amount of interpretation is involved, however, reliability estimates are typically lower. In general, the greater the amount of judgmental leeway given to coders, the lower the reliability coefficients are. As a rule of thumb, most published content analyses typically report a minimum reliability coefficient of about 90% or above when using Holsti's formula, and about .75 or above when using *pi* or *alpha.*

Note that the previous discussion assumed that at least two independent coders categorized the same content. In some situations, however, *intracoder* reliability also might be assessed. These circumstances occur most frequently when only a few coders are used because extensive training must be given to ensure the detection of subtle message elements. To test intracoder reliability, the same individual codes a set of data twice, at different times, and the reliability statistics are computed using the two sets of results.

▪ Validity

In addition to being reliable, a content analysis must yield valid results. As indicated in Chapter 3, *validity* is usually defined as the degree to which an instrument actually measures what it sets out to measure. This raises special concerns in content analysis. In the first place, validity is intimately connected with the procedures used in the analysis. If the sampling design is faulty, if categories overlap, or if reliability is low, the results of the study probably possess little validity. Additionally, the adequacy of the definitions used in a content analysis bears directly on the question of validity. For example, a great deal of content analysis has focused on the depiction of televised violence; different investigators have offered different definitions of what constitutes a violent act. The question of validity emerges when one tries to decide whether each of the various definitions actually encompasses what one might logically refer to as violence. The debate between Gerbner and the television networks vividly illustrates this problem. The definition of violence propounded by Gerbner and his associates in 1977 included accidents, acts of nature, or violence that might occur in a fantasy or a humorous setting. However, network analysts do not consider these phenomena to be acts of violence (Blank, 1977). Both Gerbner and the networks offered arguments in support of their decisions. Which analysis is more valid? The answer depends in part on the plausibility of the rationale that underlies the definitions.

This discussion relates closely to a technique traditionally called *face validity.* This validation technique assumes that an instrument adequately measures what it purports to measure if the categories are rigidly and satisfactorily defined and if the procedures of the analysis have been adequately conducted. Most descriptive content analyses rely on face validity, but other techniques are available.

The use of *concurrent validity* in content analysis is exemplified in a study by Clarke and Blankenburg (1972). These investigators attempted a longitudinal study of violence in TV shows dating back to 1952. Unfortunately, few copies of the early programs were available, and the authors were forced to use program summaries in *TV Guide*. To establish that such summaries would indeed disclose the presence of violence, the authors compared the results of a subsample of current programs coded from these synopses to the results obtained from a direct viewing of the same programs. The results were sufficiently related to convince the authors that their measurement technique was valid. However, this method of checking validity is only as good as the criterion measurement: If the direct-viewing technique is itself invalid, then there is little value in showing that synopsis coding is related to it.

Only a few studies have attempted to document *construct validity.* One instance involves the use of sensationalism in news stories. This construct has been measured by semantic differentials and factor analysis in an attempt to isolate its underlying dimensions, and it is related to relevant message characteristics (Tannenbaum, 1962; Tannenbaum & Lynch, 1960). Another technique that investigators occasionally use is *predictive validity.* For example, certain content attributes from wire stories might allow a researcher to predict which items a newspaper will carry.

In summary, several different methods are used in content analysis to assess validity. The most common is face validity, which is appropriate for some studies. It is recommended, however, that the content analyst also examine other methods to establish the validity of a given study.

▪ Examples of Content Analysis

Table 6.5, which summarizes four content analyses, lists the purpose of the analysis, the sample, the unit of analysis, illustrative categories, and the type of statistic used for each study.

▪ Content Analysis and the Internet

As Stempel and Stewart (2000) put it, the Internet provides both opportunities and challenges for content researchers. On the opportunity side of the ledger, the Internet opens up huge new areas of content that can be studied. Some of the possibilities include the con-

Table 6.5 *Summaries of Content Analytic Studies*

Researcher(s)	Purpose of Study	Sample	Units of Analysis	Representative Categories	Statistics
Dixon and Linz (2000)	To assess representations of blacks, Latinos, and whites and law breakers and law defenders	Random sample of local news programs in Orange and Los Angeles counties	Characters in a crime story	blacks, whites, Latinos, other	Chi square
Kaye and Sapolsky (2001)	To gauge changes in offensive language on TV after adoption of ratings system	All broadcast network prime time programs on three randomly selected weeks	Instances of verbal, implied, gestural, or visual offensive language	Dirty words, sexual words, excretory words, other	Chi square
Cho and Lacy (2000)	To examine international news coverage in local newspapers in Japan	Randomly selected issues of 48 randomly selected local newspapers	Space (in square centimeters) devoted to international news	International conflict and wire-service news	Multiple regression
Chan-Olmstead and Park (2000)	To assess how TV stations are using their websites	Sample of stations stratified by market size	Station's complete website	News, advertising, programming, and promotional content	Cramer's V correlation coefficient

tent of banner or pop-up ads, chat room discussions, personal web pages, email, homepages of commercial media, political campaign websites, online news coverage, and message boards. Second, content can be searched quickly and efficiently by using search engines and electronic archives. If a newspaper, for example, has an online archive of past editions, a search for a research term such as "elections" can be done in a matter of seconds. Third, the content exists in cyberspace and not on paper or some other medium. Researchers don't have to physically obtain, store, and maintain hard copies of the material.

On the challenge side, sampling can be an issue. Sample frames may not exist for many topics. For example, suppose a researcher wanted to do a content analysis of medical web sites. What sites should be sampled? There is probably no comprehensive list of web sites. (A *Google* search using the exact phrase "medical web sites" turned up more than 7,000 hits, and many of these were links to other sites for various medical specialties.) Trying to find an adequate sampling frame for such a study would be a daunting task. On the other hand, a researcher may be lucky enough to find an acceptable listing. Dominick (1999), for example, conducted a study of the content of personal pages on the web. Fortunately, Yahoo had a listing of 40,000 personal pages that served as a sample frame.

A second challenge concerns the fluid nature of the Internet. New sites are added all the time; other sites cease to exist. The content of existing sites is constantly changing. A content analysis done in April might not find the same results as one done in May. Researchers should make sure that all coders are viewing the same material. Some sites may offer both a text only and a graphic version of the site. These versions will probably have different content features. This changeability also has implications for calculating intercoder reliability. Reliability should be checked as quickly as possible to minimize the problem of changing content. Finally, in many situations there are challenges in determining the unit of analysis. Is it the home page or the whole web site? Some sites have more web pages than other sites. Does this introduce a bias? Are links to other sites included? What about audio and video material? McMillan (2000) discusses these and other problems in doing web content analysis.

Additional examples of content analysis applied to the Internet include Ha and Lincoln's (1998) study of the interactivity of business web sites, Evans' (2001) analysis of Internet discussion groups devoted to herbal medicine, and the study of broadcast TV stations' web sites done by Chan-Olmstead and Park (2000).

▪ ▪ ▪ Summary

Content analysis is a popular technique in mass media research. Many of the steps followed in laboratory and survey studies are also involved in content analysis; in particular, sampling procedures need to be objective and detailed, and operational definitions are mandatory.

Coders must be carefully trained to gather accurate data. Interpreting a content analysis, however, requires more caution: No claims about the impact of the content can be drawn from an analysis of the message in the absence of a study that examines the audience. A content analysis should demonstrate acceptable intercoder reliability and validity.

Key Terms

Coding
Composite week
Cultivation analysis
Exhaustivity
Intercoder reliability
Mutually exclusive
Scott's *pi*
Unit of analysis
Universe

Using the Internet

There are several useful Internet sites for a content analysis researcher.

1. Content: The Internet Mailing List features discussion of the theoretical, methodological, and technological aspects of quantitative text and image analysis. Appropriate topics for discussion have included: software and hardware for content analysis; research design in content analysis (e.g., sampling issues, coding instruments, and protocols); statistics for content analysis; teaching content analysis; and the role of content analysis in an era of online information flows and interactive media. You can subscribe to Content by going to *www.gsu.edu/~wwwcom/*
2. Another site that is helpful is *www.content-analysis.de*. A few of the features on this site include descriptions of content analysis software, bibliographies, and examples of content analysis research.
3. A general discussion of content analysis that contains information about content analytic methods and a glossary of important terms can be found at *http://writing.colostate.edu/references/research/content/contents.htm*.

Questions and Problems for Further Investigation

1. Define a unit of analysis that could be used in each of these content analyses:
   a. Problem solving on television
   b. News emphasis in a daily newspaper and a weekly newspaper
   c. Changes in the values expressed by popular songs
   d. The role of women in editorial cartoons
   e. Content of personal web pages on the Internet
2. Using the topics in Question 1, define a sample selection procedure appropriate for each.
3. Generate two content analyses that could be used as preliminary tests for an audience study.
4. Conduct a brief content analysis of one of the topics listed next. (Train a second individual in the use of the category system that you develop, and have this person independently code a subsample of the content.)
   - Similarities and differences between local newscasts on two television stations
   - Changes in the subject matter of movies from 1992 to 2002
   - The treatment of the elderly on network television
5. Using the topic you selected in Question 4, compute a reliability coefficient for the items that were scored by both coders.

For additional information on these and related topics, see

http://www.wimmerdominick.com

References and Suggested Readings

Ahuvia, A. (2001). Traditional, interpretive and reception-based content analysis. *Social Indicators Research,* 54(2), 139–172.

Berelson, B. (1952). *Content analysis in communication research.* New York: Free Press.

Blank, D. (1977). The Gerbner violence profile. *Journal of Broadcasting,* 21, 273–279.

Bramlett-Solomon, S., & Subramanian, G. (1999). Nowhere near picture perfect: Images of the elderly in Life and Ebony magazines, 1990–1997. *Journalism and Mass Communication Quarterly,* 76(3), 565–572.

Brown, S. (1998, April 20). Television violence stays constant. *Broadcasting & Cable,* p. 20.

Cann, D. J., & Mohr, P. B. (2001). Journalist and source gender in Australian television news. *Journal of Broadcasting and Electronic Media,* 45(1), 162–174.

Chan-Olmstead, S. M., & Park, J. S. (2000). From on-air to online world: Examining the content and structures of broadcast TV stations' web sites. *Journalism and Mass Communication Quarterly,* 77(2), 321–339.

Chang, W. (1975). A typology study of movie critics. *Journalism Quarterly,* 52(4), 721–725.

Cho, H., & Lacy, S. (2000). International conflict coverage in Japanese local daily newspapers. *Journalism and Mass Communication Quarterly,* 77(4), 830–845.

Clarke, D., & Blankenburg, W. (1972). Trends in violent content in selected mass media. In G. Comstock & E. Rubinstein (Eds.), *Television and social behavior: Media content and control.* Washington, DC: U.S. Government Printing Office.

Cohen, J. (1960). A coefficient of agreement for nominal scales. *Educational and Psychological Measurement,* 20(1), 37–46.

Comstock, G. (1975). *Television and human behavior: The key studies.* Santa Monica, CA: Rand Corporation.

Cooper, R., Potter, W. J., & Dupagne, M. (1994). A status report on methods used in mass communication research. *Journalism Educator,* 48(4), 54–61.

Corbett, J. B., & Mori, M. (1999). Medicine, media and celebrities: News coverage of breast cancer, 1960–1995. *Journalism and Mass Communication Quarterly,* 76(2), 229–249.

Davis, F. (1951). Crime news in Colorado newspapers. *American Journal of Sociology,* 57, 325–330.

Dixon, T. L., & Linz, D. (2000). Overrepresentation and underrepresentation of African-Americans and Latinos as lawbreakers on television news. *Journal of Communication,* 50(2), 131–154.

Dominick, J. (1977). Geographic bias in national TV news. *Journal of Communication,* 27, 94–99.

Dominick, J. (1999). Who do you think you are? Personal pages and self-presentation on the world wide web. *Journalism and Mass Communication Quarterly,* 76(4), 646–658.

Evans, W. (2001). Mapping mainstream and fringe medicine on the Internet. *Science Communication,* 22(3), 292–300.

Fleiss, J. L. (1971). Measuring nominal scale agreement among many raters. *Psychological Bulletin,* 76, 378–382.

Furnham, A., & Farragher, E. (2000). A cross-cultural content analysis of sex-role stereotyping in television advertisements. *Journal of Broadcasting and Electronic Media,* 44(3), 415–437.

Gerbner, G. (1969). The television world of violence. In D. Lange, R. Baker, & S. Ball (Eds.), *Mass media and violence.* Washington, DC: U.S. Government Printing Office.

Gerbner, G., Gross, L., Jackson-Beeck, M., Jeffries-Fox, S., & Signorielli, N. (1977). One more time: An analysis of the CBS "Final Comments on the Violence Profile." *Journal of Broadcasting,* 21, 297–304.

Gerbner, G., Gross, L., Signorielli, N., Morgan, M., & Jackson-Beeck, M. (1979). The demonstration of power: Violence profile no. 10. *Journal of Communication,* 29(3), 177–196.

Gerbner, G., Holsti, O., Krippendorf, K., Paisley, W., & Stone, P. (1969). *The analysis of communication content.* New York: John Wiley.

Greenberg, B. (1989). On other perceptions toward message analysis. *American Behavioral Scientist,* 33(2), 183–186.

Greenberg, B. S., & Collette, L. (1997). The changing faces on TV. *Journal of Broadcasting and Electronic Media,* 41(1), 1–13.

Greenwald, M. S. (1990). Gender representations in newspaper business sections. *Newspaper Research Journal,* 11(1), 68–79.

Ha, L., & Lincoln, J. E. (1998). Interactivity reexamined: A baseline analysis of early business web sites. *Journal of Broadcasting and Electronic Media,* 42(4), 456–474.

Hatch, D., & Hatch, M. (1947). Criteria of social status as derived from marriage announcements in the New York Times. *American Sociological Review,* 12, 396–403.

Hennessee, J., & Nicholson, J. (1972, May 28). NOW says: TV commercials insult women. *New York Times Magazine,* pp. 12–14.

Hinkle, G., & Elliott, W. R. (1989). Science coverage in three newspapers and three supermarket tabloids. *Journalism Quarterly,* 66(2), 353–358.

Hollifield, C. A. (1997). The specialized press and industry-related political communication. *Journalism and Mass Communication Quarterly,* 74(4), 757–772.

Holsti, O. (1969). *Content analysis for the social sciences and humanities.* Reading, MA: Addison-Wesley.

Kaufman, P., Dykers, C., & Caldwell, C. (1993). Why going online can reduce reliability. *Journalism Quarterly,* 70(4), 824–832.

Kaye, B. K., & Sapolsky, B. S. (2001). Offensive language in prime time television: Before and after content ratings. *Journal of Broadcasting and Electronic Media,* 45(2), 303–319.

Kepplinger, H. M. (1989). Content analysis and reception analysis. *American Behavioral Scientist,* 33(2), 175–182.

Kerlinger, F. N. (2000). *Foundations of behavioral research* (4th ed.). New York: Holt, Rinehart & Winston.

Kim, S. T. (2000). Making a difference: U.S. press coverage of the Kwangju and Tiananmen pro-democracy movements. *Journalism and Mass Communication Quarterly,* 77 (1), 22–36.

Krippendorf, K. (1980). *Content analysis: An introduction to its methodology.* Beverly Hills, CA: Sage Publications.

Lacy, S., & Riffe, D. (1996). Sampling error and selecting intercoder reliability samples for nominal content categories. *Journalism and Mass Communication Quarterly,* 73(4), 963–973.

Lacy, S., Robinson, K., & Riffe, D. (1995). Sample size in content analysis of weekly newspapers. *Journalism and Mass Communication Quarterly,* 72(2), 336–345.

Lauzen, M. M., & Dozier, D. D. (1999). Making a difference in prime time: Women on screen and behind the screen in the 1994–1995 television season. *Journal of Broadcasting and Electronic Media,* 43(1), 1–19.

Liebler, C. M., & Smith, S. J. (1997). Tracking gender differences. *Journal of Broadcasting and Electronic Media,* 41(1), 58–68.

Littleton, C. (1995, Sept. 25). Violence study finds promising signs. *Broadcasting and Cable,* p. 20.

Lorr, M., & McNair, D. (1966). Methods relating to evaluation of therapeutic outcome. In L. Gottschalk & A. Auerbach (Eds.), *Methods of research in psychotherapy.* Englewood Cliffs, NJ: Prentice-Hall.

Martindale, C., & McKenzie, D. (1995). On the utility of content analysis in author attribution. *Computers and the Humanities,* 29(4), 259–270.

Mastro, D. E., & Greenberg, B. (2000). The portrayal of racial minorities on prime time television. *Journal of Broadcasting and Electronic Media,* 44(4), 690–703.

McMillan, S. J. (2000). The microscope and the moving target. The challenge of applying content analysis to the world wide web. *Journalism and Mass Communication Quarterly,* 77(1), 80–98.

Moffett, E. A., & Dominick, J. R. (1987). Statistical analysis in the *Journal of Broadcasting,* 1970–1985. *Feedback,* 28(2), 13–20.

Morris, R. (1994). Computerized content analysis in management research. *Journal of Management,* 20(4), 903–931.

Pfau, M., Mullen, L., Deidrich, T., & Garrow, K. (1995). Television viewing and public perceptions of attorneys. *Human Communication Research,* 21(3), 307–330.

Riffe, D., Aust, C., & Lacy, S. (1993). The effectiveness of random, consecutive day and constructed week sampling in newspaper content analysis. *Journalism Quarterly,* 70(1), 133–139.

Riffe, D., & Freitag, A. (1997). A content analysis of content analyses. *Journalism and Mass Communication Quarterly,* 74(4), 873–882.

Riffe, D., Lacy, S., & Drager, M. W. (1996). Sample size in content analysis of weekly news magazines. *Journalism and Mass Communication Quarterly,* 73(3), 635–644.

Riffe, D., Lacy, S., & Fico, F. G. (1998). *Analyzing media messages.* Mahwah, NJ: Lawrence Erlbaum.

Riffe, D., Lacy, S., Nagovan, J., & Burkum, L. (1996). The effectiveness of simple and stratified random sampling in broadcast news content analysis. *Journalism and Mass Communication Quarterly,* 73(1), 159–168.

Roessler, P. (1999). The individual agenda designing process. *Communication Research,* 26(6), 666–700.

Roy, A., & Harwood, J. (1997). Under-represented, positively portrayed: Older adults in television commercials. *Journal of Applied Communication Research,* 25(1), 39–56.

Scharrer, E. (2001). From wise to foolish: The portrayal of the sitcom father, 1950s–1990s. *Journal of Broadcasting and Electronic Media,* 45(1), 23–40.

Scott, W. (1955). Reliability of content analysis: The case of nominal scale coding. *Public Opinion Quarterly,* 17, 321–325.

Signorielli, N., McLeod, D., & Healy, E. (1994). Gender stereotypes in MTV commercials. *Journal of Broadcasting and Electronic Media,* 38(1), 91–101.

Signorielli, N., & Kahlenberg, S. (2001). Television's word of work in the nineties. *Journal of Broadcasting and Electronic Media,* 45(1), 4–22.

Skill, T., & Robinson, J. (1994). Four decades of families on television. *Journal of Broadcasting and Electronic Media,* 38(4), 449–464.

Stempel, G. H. (1952). Sample size for classifying subject matter in dailies. *Journalism Quarterly,* 29, 333–334.

Stempel, G. H. (1989). Content analysis. In G. H. Stempel & B. H. Westley, *Research methods in mass communications.* Englewood Cliffs, NJ: Prentice-Hall.

Stempel, G. H., & Stewart, R. K. (2000). The internet provides both opportunities and challenges for mass communication researchers. *Journalism and Mass Communication Quarterly,* 77(3), 549–560.

Tannenbaum, P. (1962). Sensationalism: Some objective message correlates. *Journalism Quarterly,* 39, 317–323.

Tannenbaum, P., & Greenberg, B. (1968). Mass communication. *Annual Review of Psychology,* 19, 351–386.

Tannenbaum, P., & Lynch, M. (1960). Sensationalism: The concept and its measurement. *Journalism Quarterly,* 37, 381–392.

Taylor, C. R., & Bang, H. K. (1997). Portrayals of Latinos in magazine advertising. *Journalism and Mass Communication Quarterly,* 74(2), 285–303.

Taylor, C. R., & Stern, B. B. (1997). Asian-Americans: Television advertising and the model minority stereotype. *Journal of Advertising,* 26(2), 47–61.

Tuggle, C. A., & Huffman, S. (2001). Live reporting in television news: Breaking news or black holes? *Journal of Broadcasting and Electronic Media,* 45(2), 335–344.

Walizer, M. H., & Wienir, P. L. (1978). *Research methods and analysis: Searching for relationships.* New York: Harper & Row.

Whitney, D. C., Fritzler, M., Jones, S., Mazzarella, S., & Rakow, L. (1989). Source and geographic bias in network television news: 1982–1984. *Journal of Broadcasting and Electronic Media,* 33(2), 159–174.

Wilhoit, G., & Sherrill, K. (1968). Wire service visibility of U.S. senators. *Journalism Quarterly,* 45, 42–48.

Yule, G. (1944). *The statistical study of literary vocabulary.* Cambridge, England: Cambridge University Press.

Chapter 7

Survey Research

Audience and consumer surveys are commonplace in all areas of life. This is immediately evident by searching the Internet for "audience surveys" or "consumer surveys." Decision makers in businesses, consumer and activist groups, politics, and the media use survey results as part of their daily routine. Fortunately, the increased use of surveys has created changes in the way many of the studies are conducted and reported. More attention is given to sample selection, questionnaire design, and error rates.

Survey research requires careful planning and execution, and the research must take into account a wide variety of decisions and problems. The purpose of this chapter is to introduce the basics of survey research, and we strongly urge you to search the Internet for more information on every topic discussed here.

Descriptive and Analytical Surveys

There are two major types of surveys: descriptive and analytical. A **descriptive survey** attempts to describe or document current conditions or attitudes—that is, to explain what exists at the moment. For example, the Department of Labor regularly conducts surveys on the rate of unemployment in the United States. Professional pollsters survey the electorate to learn its opinions of candidates or issues. Broadcast stations and networks continually survey their audiences to determine programming tastes, changing values, and lifestyle variations that might affect programming. In descriptive surveys, the interest is in discovering the current situation in the area under study.

An **analytical survey** attempts to describe and explain *why* situations exist. In this approach, two or more variables are usually examined to investigate research questions or test research hypotheses. The results allow researchers to examine the interrelationships among variables and to develop explanatory inferences. For example, television station owners survey the market to determine how lifestyles affect viewing habits or to determine whether viewers' lifestyles can be used to predict the success of syndicated programming. On a broader scale, television networks conduct yearly surveys to determine how the public's tastes and desires are changing and how these attitudes relate to viewers' perceptions of the three major commercial networks.

Advantages and Disadvantages of Survey Research

Surveys have several advantages:

1. They can be used to investigate problems in realistic settings. Newspaper reading, television viewing, radio listening, and consumer behavior patterns can be examined where they happen rather than in a laboratory or screening room under artificial conditions.

2. The cost of surveys is reasonable when one considers the amount of information gathered. Researchers also can control expenses by selecting from four major types of surveys: mail, telephone, personal interview, and group administration.

3. A large amount of data can be collected with relative ease from a variety of people. Surveys allow researchers to examine many variables (demographic and lifestyle information, attitudes, motives, intentions, and so on) and to use a variety of statistics to analyze the data.

4. Surveys are not constrained by geographic boundaries; they can be conducted almost anywhere.

5. Data helpful to survey research already exist. Data archives, government documents, census materials, radio and television rating books, and voter registration lists can be used as *primary sources* (main sources of data) or as *secondary sources* (supportive data) of information. With archive data, it is possible to conduct an entire survey study without ever developing a questionnaire or contacting a single respondent.

While survey research has many advantages over other research approaches, it is not a perfect research methodology:

1. The most important disadvantage is that independent variables cannot be manipulated the way they are in laboratory experiments. Without control over independent variables, the researcher cannot be certain whether the relationships between independent variables and dependent variables are causal or noncausal. That is, a survey may establish that A and B are related, but it is impossible to determine solely from the survey results that A causes B. Causality is difficult to establish because many intervening and extraneous variables are involved. Time series studies can sometimes help correct this problem.

2. Inappropriate wording or placement of questions within a questionnaire can bias results. The questions must be worded and organized unambiguously to collect the desired information. This problem is discussed in detail later in the chapter.

3. The wrong respondents may be included in survey research. For example, in telephone interviews, a respondent may claim to be 18 to 24 years old but may in fact be well over 30 years old; a mail survey may be completed by a teenager when the target respondent is a parent in the household.

4. Some survey research is becoming difficult to conduct. This is especially true with telephone surveys, where answering machines, call blocking, caller IDs, various state and local regulations against calling people at home, and respondents unwilling to participate lower the incidence rates (the percentage of people who agree to participate in the survey). Telemarketers (telephone salespeople) are continually affecting mass media research (and all other legitimate research) because more and more people refuse to participate in legitimate studies for fear of attempts by the interviewer to try to sell something.

Despite these problems, however, surveys can produce reliable and useful information. They are especially useful for collecting information on audiences and readership.

▪ Constructing Questions

Although most people think that survey design is simple—just list a series of questions—the fact is that survey design takes a lot of practice. Part of this practice is to understand five basic rules of questionnaire design:

1. Understand the goals of the project so that only relevant questions are included.
2. Questions should be clear and unambiguous.
3. Questions must accurately communicate what is required from the respondents.

AN INSIDE LOOK

Questionnaire Design

There can be significant differences when designing questionnaires for academic use and those used for the private sector. Academic research usually requires additional explanations, procedures, and anonymity guarantees. Because of the differences, it is extremely important to contact the appropriate academic committee that oversees research to ensure that all rules are followed *before* designing any type of academic research project.

4. Don't assume respondents understand the questions they are asked.
5. Follow Occam's Razor in question development and order.

Questionnaire design depends on the choice of data collection technique. Questions written for a **mail survey** must be easy to read and understand because respondents are unable to obtain explanations. **Telephone surveys** cannot use questions with long lists of response options; the respondent may forget the first few responses by the time the last ones are read. Questions written for **group administration** must be concise and easy for the respondents to answer. In a **personal interview,** an interviewer must tread lightly with sensitive and personal questions because his or her physical presence might make the respondent less willing to answer. (These procedures are discussed in detail later in this chapter.)

The design of a questionnaire must always reflect the basic purpose of the research. A complex research topic such as media use during a political campaign requires more detailed questions than does a survey to determine a favorite radio station or magazine. Nonetheless, there are several general guidelines to follow regarding wording of questions and question order and length. In addition, search the Internet for "constructing questions" for numerous examples and software programs about the topic.

Types of Questions

Surveys can consist of two basic types of questions: open-ended and closed-ended. An **open-ended question** requires respondents to generate their own answers, such as:

> What could your favorite radio station change so that you would listen more often?
>
> ______________________________
>
> ______________________________
>
> What type of television program do you prefer to watch?
>
> ______________________________
>
> ______________________________
>
> Why do you subscribe to the *Daily Record?*
>
> ______________________________
>
> ______________________________

Open-ended questions give respondents freedom in answering questions and an opportunity to provide in-depth responses. Furthermore, they give researchers the opportunity to ask, "Why did you say that?" or "Could you explain your answer in more detail?" The flexibility to follow up on, or probe, certain questions enables the interviewers to gather information about the respondents' feelings and the motives behind their answers.

Also, open-ended questions allow for answers that researchers did not foresee in

> AN INSIDE LOOK
> ### Open-Ended Questions
>
> Open-ended questions always include an opportunity for interviewers to ask for additional information. From experience, we have learned that interviewers should ask the respondent "What else?" instead of "Anything more," or "Is that all." The "what else" does not give the respondent the same opportunity to say, "Nothing."

designing the questionnaire—answers that may suggest possible relationships with other answers or variables. For example, in response to the question, "Which radio stations do you have programmed on the buttons in the vehicle you drive most often?" the manager of a local radio station might expect to receive a list of the local radio stations. However, a subject may give an unexpected response, such as, "I have no idea. I thought the stations were programmed by the car dealer." This forces the manager to reconsider his or her perceptions of radio listeners.

Finally, open-ended questions are particularly useful in a pilot test of a study. Researchers may not know what types of responses to expect from subjects, so open-ended questions are used to allow subjects to answer in any way they wish. From the list of responses provided by the subjects, the researcher may select the items most often mentioned and include them in multiple-choice or forced-choice questions. Using open-ended questions in a pilot study generally saves time and resources, since all possible responses are more likely to be included on the final measurement instrument, avoiding the need to reconduct the analysis.

The major disadvantage associated with open-ended questions is the amount of time needed to collect and analyze the responses. Open-ended responses require interviewers to record long answers. In addition, because there are so many types of responses, a content analysis of each open-ended question must be completed to produce data that can be tabulated (see Chapter 6). A content analysis groups common responses into categories, essentially making the question closed-ended. The content analysis results are then used to produce a codebook to code the open-ended responses. A **codebook** is a menu or list of quantified responses. For example, "I hate television" may be coded as a 5 for input into the computer.

In the case of **closed-ended questions,** respondents select an answer from a list provided by the researcher. These questions are popular because they provide greater uniformity of response and the answers are easily quantified. The major disadvantage is that researchers often fail to include some important responses. Respondents may have an answer different from those that are supplied. One way to solve the problem is to include an "Other" response followed by a blank space to give respondents an opportunity to supply their own answer. The "Other" responses are then handled just like an open-ended question; a content analysis of the responses is completed to develop a codebook. A pilot study or pretest of a questionnaire usually solves most problems with closed-ended questions.

Problems in Interpreting Open-ended Questions. Open-ended questions often cause a great deal of frustration. In many cases, respondents' answers are bizarre. Sometimes respondents do not understand a question and provide answers that are not relevant to anything. Sometimes interviewers have difficulty understanding respondents, or they may have problems spelling what the respondents say. In these cases, researchers must interpret the answers and determine which code is appropriate.

The following examples are actual comments (called **verbatims**) from telephone surveys and self-administered surveys conducted by the senior author. They show that even the best-planned survey questionnaire can produce a wide range of responses. The survey question asked, "How do you describe the programming on your favorite radio station?"

- The station is OK, but it's geared to Jerry Atrics.
- I only listen to the station because my poodle likes it.
- It sounds like it is run by people who don't know what they're doing.
- I don't listen to that station because I live on Chinese time.
- It's great. It has the best floormat in the city.
- The station is good, but sometimes it makes me want to vomit.
- It's my favorite, but I really don't like it since my mother does.
- My parrot is just learning to talk, and the station teaches him a lot of words.
- My kids hate it, so I turn it up real loud.
- It sounds great with my car trunk open.
- There is no way for me to answer that question before I eat dinner.

And then there was a woman who, when asked what her spouse does for a living, wrote "Arrow Space Engeneer." Research is not always easy to conduct, especially when trying to decipher comments made by respondents.

General Guidelines

Before we examine specific types of questions appropriate in survey research, here are some general dos and don'ts about writing questions:

1. *Make questions clear.* This is logical, but many researchers become so closely associated with a problem that they can no longer put themselves in the respondents' position. What might be perfectly clear to researchers might not be nearly as clear to the respondent. For example, after finding out which radio stations a respondent has been listening to more lately, the researcher might ask, "Why have you been listening to WXXX more lately?" and expect to receive an answer such as "I like the music a lot more." But the respondent might say, "It's the only station my radio can pick up." The question would be much clearer to a respondent if asked in this form: "Which radio station, or stations, if any, do you enjoy listening to more lately as compared to a few months ago?" Questionnaire items must be phrased precisely so that respondents know what is being asked.

Making questions clear also requires avoiding difficult or specialized words, acronyms, and stilted language. In general, the level of vocabulary commonly found in newspapers or popular magazines is appropriate for a survey. Questions should be phrased in everyday speech, and social science jargon and technical words should be eliminated. For example, "If you didn't have a premium channel, would you consider PPV?" might be better phrased, "If you didn't have a pay channel like Home Box Office or Showtime, would you consider a service where you pay a small amount for individual movies or specials you watch?"

The item "Should the city council approve the construction of an interactive cable TV system?" assumes that respondents know what "interactive cable TV systems" are. A better approach is, "An interactive cable television system is one in which viewers can send messages back to the cable company as well as receive normal television. Do you think the city council should approve such a system for this community?"

The clarity of a question can be affected by double or hidden meanings in the words that are not apparent to researchers. For example, the question "How many television shows do you think are a little too violent—most, some, few, or none?" contains such a problem. Some respondents who feel that all TV shows are extremely violent will answer "none" based on the question's wording. These subjects reason that all shows are more than "a little too violent"; therefore the most appropriate answer to the question is "none." (Deleting the phrase "a little" from the question helps avoid this problem.) In addition, the question inadvertently establishes the idea that at least some shows are violent. The question should read, "How many television shows, if any, do you think are too violent—most, some, few, or none?" Questions should be written so they are fair to all types of respondents.

2. *Keep questions short.* To be precise and unambiguous, researchers sometimes write long and complicated questions. Yet, respondents who are in a hurry to complete a questionnaire are unlikely to take the time to figure out the precise intent of the person who drafted the items. Short, concise items that will not be misunderstood are best. A good question should not contain more than two short sentences.

3. *Remember the purposes of the research.* It is important to include in a questionnaire only items that relate directly to what is being studied. For example, if the occupational level of the respondents is not relevant to the purpose of the survey, the questionnaire should not ask about it. Beginning researchers often add questions for the sake of developing a longer questionnaire, or because the information "will be interesting to find out." Any question that is included only because it would "be interesting to find out the answer" should be deleted from the questionnaire.

4. *Do not ask double-barreled questions.* A **double-barreled question** is one that asks two or more questions in the same sentence. Whenever the word "and" appears in a question, the sentence structure should be examined to see whether more than one question is being asked. Consider "The ABC network has programs that are funny and sexually explicit. Do you agree or disagree?" Since a program may be funny but not necessarily sexually explicit, a respondent could agree with the second part of the question even though he or she disagrees with the first part. This question should be split into two items.

5. *Avoid biased words or terms.* Consider the following item: "In your free time, would you rather read a book or just watch television?" The word "just" in this example injects a pro-book bias into the question because it implies that there is something less desirable about watching television. Similarly, "Where did you hear the news about the president's new economic program?" is mildly biased against newspapers; the word "hear" suggests that "radio," "television," or "other people" is a more appropriate answer. Items that start with "Do you agree or disagree with so-and-so's proposal to . . ." usually bias a question. If the name "Adolf Hitler" is inserted for "so-and-so," the item becomes overwhelmingly negative. Inserting "the president" creates a potential for both positive bias and negative bias. Any time a specific person or source is mentioned in a question, the possibility of bias arises.

6. *Avoid leading questions.* A **leading question** is one that suggests a certain response (either literally or by implication) or contains a

hidden premise. For example, "Like most Americans, do you read a newspaper every day?" suggests that the respondent should answer in the affirmative or run the risk of being unlike most Americans. The question "Do you still use marijuana?" contains a hidden premise. This type of question is called a **double bind**; regardless of how the respondent answers, an affirmative response to the hidden premise is implied—in this case, that the respondent has used marijuana at some point.

7. *Do not use questions that ask for highly detailed information.* The question "In the past 30 days, how many hours of television have you viewed with your family?" is unrealistic. Few respondents could answer it. A more realistic approach is to ask, "How many hours did you spend watching television with your family yesterday?" A researcher interested in a 30-day period should ask respondents to keep a log or diary of family viewing habits.

8. *Avoid potentially embarrassing questions unless they are absolutely necessary.* Most surveys need to collect data of a confidential or personal nature, but an overly personal question may cause embarrassment and inhibit respondents from answering honestly—asking the respondent's income, for example. Many people are reluctant to tell their income to strangers conducting a survey. A straightforward "What is your annual income?" often prompts the reply "None of your business." It is better to preface a reading of the following list with the question, "Which of these categories includes your household's total annual income?"

_____ Under $25,000
_____ $25,000–$29,999
_____ $30,000–$39,999
_____ $40,000–$49,999
_____ $50,000–$59,999
_____ $60,000 or more

The categories are broad enough to allow respondents some privacy, but narrow enough for statistical analysis. In 2000, the average household income in the United States was $55,253. The income classifications depend on the purpose of the questionnaire and the geographic and demographic distribution of the subjects. The $60,000 upper level in the example is too low in several parts of the country.

Other potentially sensitive areas are people's sex lives, drug use, religion, business practices, and trustworthiness. In all these areas, care should be taken to ensure respondents' confidentiality and anonymity, when possible.

The simplest type of closed-ended question is one that provides a dichotomous response, usually "agree/disagree" or "yes/no." For example:

Local television stations should have longer weather reports in the late evening news.

_____ Agree
_____ Disagree
_____ No opinion

Although such questions provide little sensitivity to different degrees of conviction, they are the easiest to tabulate of all question forms. Whether they provide enough sensitivity or information about the purpose of the research project are questions the researcher must seriously consider.

The **multiple-choice question** allows respondents to choose an answer from several options. Here is an example:

In general, television commercials tell the truth . . .

_____ All of the time
_____ Most of the time

_____ Some of the time

_____ Rarely

_____ Never

Multiple-choice questions should include all possible responses. A question that excludes any significant response usually creates problems. For example:

What is your favorite television network?

_____ ABC

_____ CBS

_____ NBC

Subjects who prefer PBS, Turner, UPN, WB, Fox, or any other network cannot answer the question as presented.

Additionally, multiple-choice responses must be **mutually exclusive:** There should be only one response option per question for each respondent. For instance:

How many years have you been working in the newspaper industry?

_____ Less than 1 year

_____ 1–5 years

_____ 5–10 years

Which blank would a person with exactly 5 years of experience check? One way to correct this problem is to reword the responses, such as in the following item:

How many years have you been working in the newspaper industry?

_____ Less than 1 year

_____ Between 1 and 5 years

_____ More than 5 years

Rating scales are also used widely in mass media research (see Chapter 2). They can be arranged horizontally or vertically:

There are too many commercials on TV.

_____ Strongly agree	(coded as 5 for analysis)
_____ Agree	(coded as 4)
_____ Neutral	(coded as 3)
_____ Disagree	(coded as 2)
_____ Strongly disagree	(coded as 1)

What is your opinion of the local news on Channel 9?

Fair	____	____	____	____	____	Unfair
	(5)	(4)	(3)	(2)	(1)	

Semantic differential scales are another form of rating scale frequently used to rate persons, concepts, or objects (see Chapter 2). These scales use bipolar adjectives with seven scale points:

How do you perceive the term *public television?*

Uninteresting	_____	_____	_____	_____	_____	_____	_____	Interesting
Good	_____	_____	_____	_____	_____	_____	_____	Bad
Dull	_____	_____	_____	_____	_____	_____	_____	Exciting
Happy	_____	_____	_____	_____	_____	_____	_____	Sad

Researchers are often interested in the relative perception of several concepts or items. In such cases, the *rank-ordering* technique is appropriate:

Here is an alphabetical list of several common occupations. Please rank them in terms of their prestige. Put a 1 next to the profession that has the most prestige, a 2 next to the one with the second most, and so on. (The list is alphabetical to avoid presentation bias.)

_____ Banker
_____ Lawyer
_____ Newspaper reporter
_____ Police officer
_____ Politician
_____ Teacher
_____ Television news reporter

Asking respondents to rank more than a dozen objects is not recommended because the process can become tedious and the discriminations exceedingly fine. Furthermore, ranking data imposes limitations on the statistical analysis that can be performed.

The **checklist question** is often used in pilot studies to refine questions for the final project. For example:

What things do you look for in a new television set? (Check as many as apply.)

_____ Automatic fine-tuning
_____ Cable ready
_____ Picture within a picture (the ability to view more than one channel at a time)
_____ Portable
_____ Remote control
_____ Stereo sound
_____ Other

In this case, the most frequently checked answers may be used to develop a multiple-choice question; the unchecked responses are dropped.

Forced-choice questions are frequently used in media studies designed to gather information about lifestyles, and they are always listed in pairs. Forced-choice questionnaires are usually very long—sometimes containing dozens of questions—and repeat questions (in a different form) on the same topic. The answers for each topic are analyzed for patterns, and a respondent's interest in that topic is scored. A typical forced-choice questionnaire might contain the following pairs:

Select one statement from each of the following pairs of statements:

_____ Advertising of any kind is a waste of time and money.
_____ I learn a lot from all types of advertising.
_____ The government should regulate television program content.
_____ The government should not regulate television program content.
_____ I listen to the radio every day.
_____ I only listen to the radio when I'm alone.

Respondents generally complain that neither of the responses to a forced-choice question is satisfactory, but they have to select one or the other. From a series of questions on the same topic (violence, lifestyles, career goals), a pattern of behavior or attitude usually develops.

Fill-in-the-blank questions are used infrequently by survey researchers; however, some studies are particularly suited for them. In advertising copy testing, for example, they are often used to test subjects' recall

Figure 7.1 *A "Feeling Thermometer" for Recording a Subject's Degree of Like or Dislike*

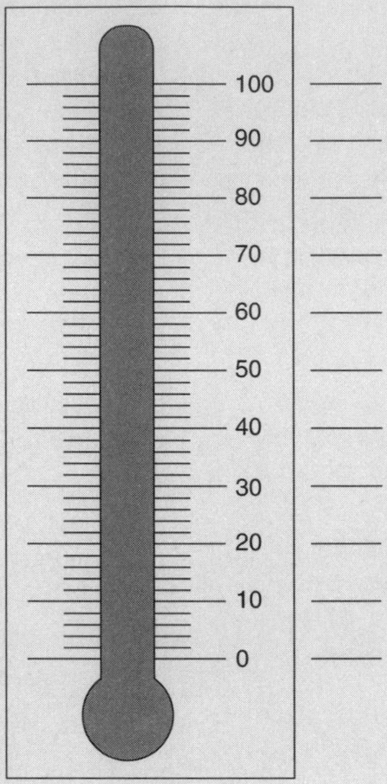

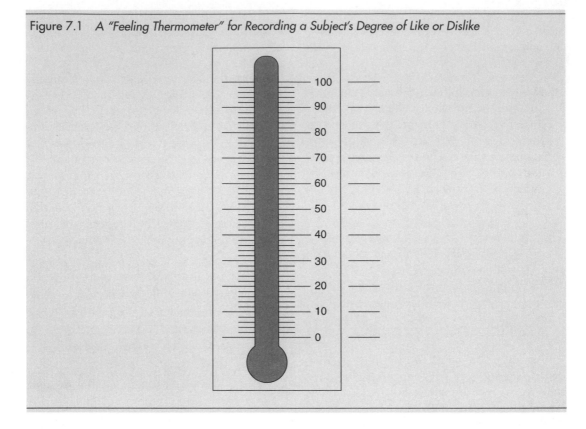

of a commercial. After seeing, hearing, or reading a commercial, subjects receive a script of the commercial in which a number of words have been randomly omitted (often every fifth or seventh word). Subjects are required to fill in the missing words to complete the commercial. Fill-in-the-blank questions also can be used in information tests—for example,

> "The local news anchors on Channel 4 are _____" or "The headline story on the front page was about _____."

Tables, graphs, and figures are also used in survey research. Some ingenious questioning devices have been developed to help respondents more accuratcly describe how they think and feel. For example, the University of Michigan Survey Research Center developed the **feeling thermometer,** with which subjects can rate an idea or object. The thermometer, which is patterned after a normal mercury thermometer, offers an easy way for respondents to rate their degree of like or dislike in terms of "hot" or "cold" (see Figure 7.1). For example:

> How would you rate the coverage your local newspaper provided on the recent school board campaign? (Place an X near the number on the thermometer that most accurately reflects your feelings; 100 indicates strong approval, and 0 reflects strong disapproval.)

A search on the Internet for "feeling thermometer" shows the diverse use of the scale.

Some questionnaires designed for children use other methods to collect information.

Figure 7.2 *A Simple Picture Scale for Use with Young Children*

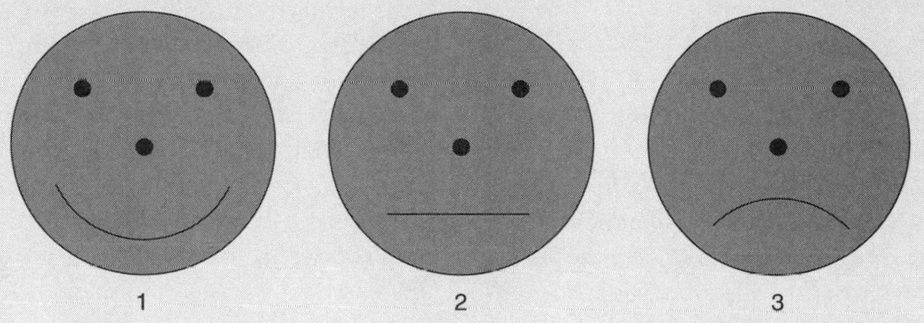

Since young children have difficulty assigning numbers to values, one logical alternative is to use pictures. For example, the interviewer might read the question "How do you feel about Saturday morning cartoons on television?" and present the faces in Figure 7.2 to elicit a response from a 5-year-old. Zillmann and Bryant (1975) present a similar approach with their "Yucky" scale.

▪ Questionnaire Design

The approach used in asking questions as well as the physical appearance (in a self-administered questionnaire) can affect the **response rate** (the percentage of respondents who complete the questionnaire among those who are contacted). The time and effort invested in developing a good questionnaire always pay off with more usable data. This section offers some useful suggestions. [Note: Many of the suggestions about questionnaire design and layout discussed here are intended for paper questionnaires, not **CATI (computer-aided telephone interviewing)**, which precludes problems such as skip patterns and rotation of questions. However, all researchers must understand all of the idiosyncrasies of questionnaire design in order to work with paper questionnaires or review a CATI-designed questionnaire.]

Introduction

One way to increase the response rate in any survey is to prepare a persuasive introduction to the survey. Backstrom and Hursh-Cesar (1986) suggest six characteristics of a successful introduction to a questionnaire; namely, the introduction should be short, realistically worded, nonthreatening, serious, neutral, and pleasant but firm.

Although some academic research requires that the purpose of the survey be explained in detail to respondents, this is usually not the case in private-sector research. In private-sector research, there is no need to explain the purpose or value of a survey to respondents, or to tell them how long the survey will take to complete. For example, in a telephone survey, telling the respondents that "the survey will take only a few minutes" gives them the opportunity to say they do not have time to talk. The introduction should be short so that the respondent can begin writing answers or the interviewer can start asking questions.

Here is an example of an effective introduction for a telephone survey conducted by a field service to show how the interviewer immediately gets into the questionnaire:

> Hi, my name is ________________________ with [INSERT COMPANY NAME]. We're conducting an *opinion* survey about radio in the Chicago area and I'd like to ask you a few questions. We're not trying to sell anything, and this is not a contest or promotion. We're interested only in your opinions. Please tell me which of these age groups you belong to—under 18, 18 to 24, 25 to 34, 35 to 44, 45 to 54, or over 54? [TERMINATE IF UNDER 18 OR OVER 54.]

With some modifications, the same introduction is appropriate for a self-administered questionnaire. The introduction would include the second, third, and fourth sentences along with a final sentence that says, "Please answer the questions as completely and honestly as possible."

The goal of the introduction in telephone surveys is to get into the interview as quickly as possible so the respondent does not have a chance to say "no" and hang up. This may sound overly aggressive, but it works. (Note, however, that many academic research review boards would not approve such an approach and would require that a statement such as "May I continue?" be included before going on with the interview.) The introduction in self-administered questionnaires should be as simple as possible.

Regardless of the survey approach used, a well-constructed introduction usually generates higher response rates than a simple "Please answer the following questions. . . ."

Instructions

All instructions necessary to complete the questionnaire should be clearly stated for respondents or interviewers. These instructions vary depending on the type of survey conducted (search the Internet for "questionnaire instructions" for a variety of suggestions). Mail surveys and self-administered questionnaires usually require the most specific instructions because respondents are not able to ask questions about the survey. Respondents and interviewers should understand whether the correct response consists of circling or checking an item, placing items in a specific order, or skipping an item.

Procedural instructions for respondents are often highlighted with a different typeface, capital letters, or some graphic device, perhaps arrows or lines. The following is an example from a mail survey:

> Do you have a favorite radio station that you listen to most of the time?
>
> _____Yes   _____No
>
> | If yes, please briefly explain why on the lines below. |
> |---|
>
> ____
>
> ____
>
> ____

Some questionnaires require respondents to rank a list of items. In this case, the instructions must clearly describe which response represents the highest value:

> Please rate the following magazines in order of importance to you. Place a 1 next to the magazine you prefer most, a 2 next to the magazine in second place, and so on up to 5.
>
> _____ *American Iron Magazine*
>
> _____ *Better Homes and Gardens*
>
> _____ *Consumer Reports*
>
> _____ *Popular Science*
>
> _____ *Time*

Fowler (1993) offers these suggestions for designing a self-administered questionnaire:

AN INSIDE LOOK
Questionnaire Design

The best way to start designing a questionnaire is to write down a "laundry list" of questions that need to be answered. In this stage, don't worry about how the questions will be asked or what form the questions will take. This list will also help you design the flow of the questionnaire: what should be asked first, second, third, and so on.

- Make the questionnaire self-explanatory.
- Limit the questions to closed-ended items. Checking a box or circling an answer should be the only task required.
- Use only a limited number of question forms.
- Lay out and type the questionnaire in a clear and uncluttered way.
- Limit the amount of instructions. Respondents can be confused easily.

Fowler's second suggestion is too strict. Respondents of most ages are usually able to answer open-ended questions with the same ease (or complication) as closed-ended questions. Whether open-ended or closed-ended, all questions should be pretested to determine if the directions for answering are clear.

Instructions for interviewers are usually typed in capital letters and enclosed in parentheses, brackets, or boxes. For example, instructions for a telephone survey might look like this:

> We'd like to start by asking you some things about television. First, what are your favorite TV shows? [RECORD]
>
> 1. ________ 2. ________
>
> 3. ________ 4. ________

RECORD ALL NAMES OF TV SHOWS. PROBE WITH "ARE THERE ANY MORE?" TO GET AT LEAST THREE SHOWS.

Screener questions, or **filter questions,** are used to eliminate unwanted respondents or to include only respondents who have specific characteristics or who answer questions in a specific manner. These questions often require respondents or interviewers to skip one or more questions. Skips must be clearly specified (recall that a CATI-designed questionnaire will automatically skip to the next question). Here is an example:

> In a typical week, do you listen to radio stations on the AM dial?
>
> ____ Yes [ASK Q.16]
>
> ____ No [SKIP TO Q.17]

A survey using this question might be designed to question only respondents who listen to AM radio. The screener question immediately determines whether the subject falls into this group. If the respondent says "no," the interviewer (or respondent if the survey is self-administered) may skip a certain number of questions or terminate the survey immediately.

When interviewers are used, as is the case in telephone and one-on-one interviews, the questionnaires must have easy-to-follow instructions, including how many responses to take for open-ended questions, simple skip patterns, and enough space to record answers if survey responses are recorded. Telephone questionnaires must include everything an interviewer will say, including introductions, explanations, definitions, transitions, and pronunciations. The last point is particularly important because interviewers should sound as if they know the topic. For example, the name of the rock singer Sade should have a phonetic spelling in parentheses ("Sha-Day") following its first appearance in the questionnaire. Otherwise an interviewer is sure to say something like, "Do you think music by the singer 'Say-dee' should be played on your favorite radio station?"

All instructions should be clear and simple. A confusing questionnaire impairs the effectiveness of the interviewer, lowers the number of respondents who complete the test, and increases costs.

Question Order

All surveys flow better when the early questions are simple and easy to answer. Researchers often include one or two "warm-up" questions about the topic under investigation so respondents become accustomed to answering questions and begin thinking about the survey topic. Preliminary questions can also serve as motivation to create interest in the questionnaire. Demographic data, personal questions, and other sensitive items should be placed at the end of the questionnaire to allow the interviewer to establish a rapport with each respondent or, for a self-administered questionnaire, to relieve any suspicions. Although some respondents may still refuse to answer personal items or may hang up the telephone, at least the main body of data is already collected. Age and gender information are usually included in the first part of a questionnaire, so at least some respondent identification is possible.

The questionnaire should be organized in a logical sequence, proceeding from the general to the specific. Questions on similar topics should be grouped together, and the transitions between question sections should be clear and logical.

Poor question order may bias a respondent's answers. For example, suppose that, after several questions about the presence of violence in society, the respondent is asked to rank the major problems facing the country today from the following list:

_____ Communism
_____ Corrupt government
_____ High prices
_____ Violence on TV
_____ War

Violence on TV might receive a higher ranking than it would if the ranking question had been asked before the series of questions on violence. Or, to take another example, suppose a public relations researcher is attempting to discover the public's attitudes toward a large oil company. If the questionnaire that begins with attitudinal questions concerning oil spills and inflated profits asks respondents to rate certain oil companies, it is likely that the ratings of all the companies will be lower because of general impressions created by the earlier questions.

There is no easy solution to the problem of question "contamination." Obviously, some questions have to be asked before others. Perhaps the best approach for researchers is to be sensitive to the problem and check for it in a pretest. If they think question order A, B, C may have biasing effects, then they should test another version using the order C, B, A. Completely neutral positioning is not always possible, however, and when bias may enter because of how responses are ordered, the list of items should be rotated. The command [ROTATE] after a question indicates that the interviewer must change the order of responses for each subject (performed automatically by a CATI-designed questionnaire). In self-administered questionnaires, different question orders can be printed, but make sure that the data are input and analyzed correctly. If several versions of a questionnaire are used, it's easy to get them confused.

Layout

The physical design of the questionnaire is another important factor in survey research. A badly typed, poorly reproduced questionnaire is not likely to attract many responses in a mail survey. Nor does a cramped questionnaire with 40 questions to a page create a positive attitude in respondents. Response categories should be adequately spaced and presented in a nonconfusing manner. For example, the following format might lead to problems:

> There are too many commercials on television.
>
> Do you Strongly agree _____ Agree _____ Have no opinion _____ Disagree _____ Strongly disagree? _____

A more effective and less confusing method is to provide a vertical ordering of the response choices:

> There are too many commercials on television.
>
> _____ Strongly agree
>
> _____ Agree
>
> _____ No opinion
>
> _____ Disagree
>
> _____ Strongly disagree

Some researchers recommend avoiding blanks altogether because respondents and interviewers tend to make large check marks or Xs that cover more than one blank, making interpretation difficult. If blanks are perceived as a problem, boxes to check or numbers to circle are satisfactory. In any case, the response form should be consistent throughout the questionnaire. Format changes generally create confusion for both respondents and interviewers. Finally, each question must have enough space for answers. This is especially true for open-ended questions. Nothing is more discouraging to respondents and interviewers than to be confronted with a presentation like this:

> What would you change on your favorite radio station? ____________________
>
> ________________________________
>
> Why do you go to the movies? __________
>
> ________________________________
>
> Who are your favorite movie stars? ______
>
> ________________________________
>
> What are your favorite television shows?
>
> ________________________________
>
> ________________________________

If a research budget limits the amount of paper for questionnaires, subjects can be asked to add further comments on the back of the survey.

Questionnaire Length

Questionnaire length is an important concern in any survey because it directly relates to the completion rate. Long questionnaires cause fatigue, respondent mortality, and low completion rates. Shorter questionnaires guarantee higher completion rates.

Unfortunately, there are no strict guidelines to help in deciding how long a questionnaire should be. The length depends on a variety of factors:

- Amount of money in the research budget
- Purpose of the survey
- Type of problems or questions to be investigated
- Age of respondents involved in the survey
- Type and complexity of questions in the questionnaire
- Location in the country where the study is conducted

AN INSIDE LOOK
Questionnaire Design

Two hints can make the questionnaire development process go much more smoothly: (1) read the questionnaire out loud or call up a friend and conduct the interview—errors are easier to detect; and (2) if possible, put the questionnaire aside for a day or two and come back to it—sometimes it's easy to become too involved in questionnaire development and overlook a simple problem.

- Specific setting of the testing situation
- Time of year
- Time of day
- Type of interviewer (professional or amateur)

In most cases, questionnaire length is determined by trial-and-error. A survey that has more than 10% incompletes or breakoffs (the respondent hangs up during a telephone survey) is probably too long. The length of the survey may not be the only problem, however, so it's important to take a close look at the questionnaire for other problems.

Our experience during the past 25 years has shown the following time limits as maximum:

Type of Survey	Maximum Time Limit
Self-administered mail	60 min.
Self-administered in a group situation supervised by a researcher	60 min.
One-on-one interview	60 min.
Telephone	20 min.
Shopping center intercept	10 min.

Telephone interviewing can be a difficult approach to use because it takes talent to keep respondents answering questions on the telephone. Professional interviewers can usually hold respondents' attention for about 20 minutes. After 20 minutes, there is a severe dropoff in incidence due to breakoffs.

▪ Pretesting

Without a doubt, the best way to discover whether a research instrument is adequately designed is to pretest it—that is, conduct a ministudy with a small sample to determine whether the study approach is correct and to help refine the questions. Areas of misunderstanding or confusion can be easily corrected without wasting time or money.

There are several ways to pretest a questionnaire. When an acceptable draft of the questionnaire is completed, a focus group can be used to discuss the questionnaire with potential respondents. However, this is usually too expensive. The best pretest in telephone surveys is for interviewers to call 10 to 20 people and do a run-through. Any problems quickly emerge. Self-administered questionnaires should be pretested with the type of respondent who will participate in the actual study. Once again, any problems should be noted immediately.

In any type of pretesting situation, it is appropriate to discuss the project with respondents after they complete the questionnaire. They can be asked whether they understood the questions, whether the questions were simple to answer, and so on. Respondents are almost always willing to help researchers.

▪ Gathering Survey Data

Once a questionnaire is developed and one or more pretests or pilot studies have been conducted, the next step is to gather data from an appropriate group of respondents. The four basic methods for doing this are mail survey, telephone survey, personal interview, and group administration. Researchers can also use variations and combinations of these four methods, such as disk-by-mail surveys and mall interviews. Each procedure has definite advantages and disadvantages that must be considered before a choice is made. The remainder of this chapter highlights the characteristics of each method.

Mail Surveys

Mail surveys involve sending self-administered questionnaires to a sample of respondents. Stamped reply envelopes are enclosed to encourage respondents to send their completed questionnaires back to the researcher. Mail surveys are popular in some types of businesses because they can secure a lot of information without spending a lot of time and money. However, novice researchers must understand that mail surveys are usually difficult to conduct because most respondents simply throw the questionnaire in the trash can. In research terms, the response rate for mail surveys is very low—usually under 40%.

The general stages of a mail survey are discussed next. Although the steps are listed in numerical sequence, many of them are often done in a different order or even simultaneously.

1. *Select a sample.* Sampling is usually accomplished from a prepared frame that contains the names and addresses of potential respondents (see Chapter 4). The most common sampling frame is the **mailing list,** a collection of names and addresses of respondents who belong to a narrowly defined group, which commercial sampling companies prepare.
2. *Construct the questionnaire.* As discussed earlier, mail questionnaires must be concise and specific because no interviewer is present with the respondent to correct misunderstandings, answer questions, or give directions.
3. *Write a cover letter.* A brief note explaining the purpose and importance of the questionnaire usually increases the response rate.
4. *Assemble the package.* The questionnaire, cover letter, and return envelope are stuffed into mailing envelopes. Researchers sometimes choose to use bulk mail with first-class return envelopes. Another method is to send questionnaires via first-class mail and use business reply envelopes for responses. This allows researchers to pay postage *only for* the questionnaires actually returned. Postal options always depend on the research budget.
5. *Mail the surveys.* Bulk mail regulations require sorting envelopes into zip code areas.
6. *Monitor return rates.*
7. *Send follow-up mailings.* The first follow-up should be sent two weeks after the initial mailing, and a second (if necessary) two weeks after the first. The follow-up letter can be sent to the entire sample or only to the subjects who fail to answer.
8. *Tabulate and analyze data.*

Advantages. Mail surveys cover a wide geographic area for a reasonable cost. They are often the only way to gather information from people who live in hard-to-reach areas of the country (or in other countries). Mail surveys also allow for selective sampling through the use of specialized mailing lists. In addition to those mentioned, lists are available that include only people with annual incomes exceeding $50,000, consumers who have bought a car within the past year, subscribers to a particular magazine, or residents of a specific zip code area. If researchers need to collect information from a highly specialized audience, mail surveys are often better than other approaches.

Another advantage of the mail survey is that it provides anonymity; some respondents are more likely to answer sensitive questions candidly. Questionnaires can be completed at home or in the office, which affords respondents a sense of privacy. People can answer questions at their own pace, and they have an opportunity to look up facts or check past information. Mail surveys also eliminate interviewer bias because there is no personal contact.

Probably the biggest advantage of this method is its low cost. Mail surveys do not require a large staff of trained interviewers. The only costs are for printing, mailing lists, envelopes, and postage. When compared to other data collection procedures, the mail survey has the lowest cost per completed questionnaire.

Disadvantages. First, mail questionnaires must be self-explanatory. No interviewer is present to answer questions or to clear up misunderstandings. Mail surveys are also the slowest form of data collection. Returns start to trickle in a week or so after the initial mailing and continue to arrive for several weeks thereafter. It may even be months before some responses are returned. Many researchers set a cutoff date, after which returns are not included in the analysis.

Another problem with mail surveys is that researchers never know exactly who answers the questions. For example, assistants may complete a survey sent to corporate executives. A survey sent to the "male head-of-household" may be completed by a child in the home. Furthermore, replies are often received only from people who are interested in the survey, and this injects bias into the results. The biggest disadvantage of the mail survey is the low return rate. A typical survey (depending on area and type of survey) will achieve a response rate of 5%–40%. This low return casts doubt on the reliability of the findings.

Increasing Response Rates. Survey researchers have investigated a number of ways to improve return rates, but there are no surefire guarantees. In a meta-analysis (the findings of several studies are treated as independent observations and combined to calculate an overall or average effect) of numerous studies concerning mail surveys, Fox, Crask, and Kim (1989) found that, on the average, response rates can be increased in a variety of ways. In descending order of importance, the following procedures tend to increase mail survey response rates: university sponsorship, stamped return postage as opposed to business reply, written prenotification of the survey sent to the respondent, postcard follow-up, first-class outgoing postage, questionnaire color (green paper as opposed to white), notification of cutoff date, and stamped outgoing postage rather than metered stamping.

In addition, The Eagle Group in 1995 found these ideas to be very successful in increasing response rates in mail surveys (as much as 50%):

- A drawing of some type that offers a prize of a color TV, stereo, or CD player.
- Telephone calling cards with 30 minutes of time (activated when the questionnaire is returned).
- A $10 bill.

Telephone Surveys

Telephone surveys and personal interviews use trained interviewers who ask questions orally and record the responses, usually on a computer terminal. The respondents generally do not see the actual questionnaire. Since telephone and personal interviewing techniques have certain similarities, much of what follows applies to both.

Telephone surveys fill a middle ground between mail surveys and personal interviews. They offer more control and higher response rates than most mail surveys, but they are limited in the types of questions that can be asked. Telephone interviews are generally more expensive than mail surveys but less expensive than face-to-face interviews. Because of these factors, telephone surveys seem to represent a compromise between the other two techniques, and this may account for their enormous popularity in mass media research.

Interviewers are extremely important to both telephone surveys and personal surveys. An interviewer ideally should function as a neutral medium through which the respondents' answers are communicated to the researcher. The interviewer's presence and manner of speaking should not influence respondents' answers in any way. Adequate training and instruction can minimize the bias that the interviewer might inject into the data. For example, if an interviewer shows disdain or shock over an answer, it is unlikely that the respondent will continue to answer questions in a totally honest manner. Showing agreement with certain responses might prompt similar answers to other questions. Skipping questions, carelessly asking questions, and being impatient with the respondent also cause problems.

As an aid to minimizing interviewer bias, the National Association of Broadcasters has published the following recommendations for interviewers:*

- Read the questions exactly as worded. Ask them in the exact order listed. Skip questions only when the instructions on the questionnaire tell you to. There are no exceptions.
- Never suggest an answer, try to explain a question, or imply what kind of reply is wanted. Don't prompt in any way.
- If a question is not understood, say "Let me read it again," and repeat it slowly and clearly. If it is still not understood, report a "no answer."
- Report answers and comments exactly as given, writing them out fully. If an answer seems vague or incomplete, probe with neutral questions, such as "Will you explain that?" or "How do you mean that?" Sometimes just waiting a bit will tell the respondent you want more information.
- Act interested, alert, and appreciative of the respondent's cooperation, but never comment on his or her replies. Never express approval, disapproval, or surprise. Even an "Oh" can cause a respondent to hesitate or refuse to answer further questions. Never talk up or down to a respondent.
- Follow all instructions carefully, whether you agree with them or not.
- Thank each respondent. Leave a good impression for the next interviewer.
- Discuss any communication problems immediately with the researcher in charge.

A general procedure for conducting a telephone survey follows. Again, the steps are presented in numerical order, but it is possible to address many tasks simultaneously.

1. *Select a sample.* Telephone surveys require researchers to specify clearly the geographic area to be covered and to identify the type of respondent to be interviewed in each household contacted. Many surveys are restricted to people over 18, heads of households, and so forth. The sampling procedure used depends on the purpose of the study (see Chapter 4).

2. *Construct the questionnaire.* Telephone surveys require straightforward and uncomplicated response options. For example, ranking a long list of items is especially

*From *A Broadcast Research Primer,* 1976, pp. 37–38. Reprinted with permission (edited).

AN INSIDE LOOK

International Telephone Surveys

Several mass media research companies in the United States also conduct media research in several countries around the world. However, the procedures are not always the same. For example, in several countries it's virtually impossible to conduct telephone surveys since too few households own telephones. In these situations, door-to-door surveys are used. Research companies based in the United States must make several adjustments when conducting research in other parts of the world.

difficult over the telephone, and this should be avoided. The survey should not exceed 10 minutes for nonprofessional interviewers; interviews up to 20 minutes long require professionals who are trained to keep respondents on the telephone.

3. *Prepare an interviewer instruction manual.* This document should cover the basic mechanics of the survey (what numbers to call, when to call, how to record times, and so on). It should also specify which household member to interview and provide general guidelines on how to ask the questions and how to record the responses.

4. *Train the interviewers.* Interviewers need to practice going through the questionnaire to become familiar with all the items, response options, and instructions. It is best to train interviewers in a group using interview simulations that allow each person to practice asking questions. It is good practice to pretest interviewers as well as the questionnaire.

5. *Collect the data.* Data collection is most efficient when conducted from one central location (assuming enough telephone lines are available). Problems that develop are easier to remedy, and important questions raised by one interviewer can easily be communicated to the rest of the group. A central location also makes it easier for researchers to check (validate) the interviewers' work. The completion rate should be monitored daily.

6. *Make necessary callbacks.* Additional calls (usually no more than two) should be made to respondents whose lines were busy or who did not answer during the first session. Callbacks on a different day or evening tend to have a greater chance of reaching someone willing to be interviewed.

Backstrom and Hursh-Cesar (1986, p. 134) offer the following advice about callbacks:

> About 95% of all telephone interviews are successfully completed within three calls. However, we have rules for the number of callbacks to make if the first call results in a busy signal or a no answer. . . . We generally permit only three calls—one original and two callbacks—but if any of these calls produce busy signals or [future interview] appointments, we allow up to five calls total. . . .

Backstrom and Hursh-Cesar's comment that about 95% of the interviews are successfully completed with three calls is a bit optimistic. Generally speaking, three callbacks produce a contact about 75% of the time. In some cases, to achieve 95%, six or more callbacks are required.

When the first call produces a busy signal, the rule is to wait one-half hour before calling again. If the first call produced a "no answer," wait 2 to 3 hours before calling again, assuming it is still a reasonable hour to call. If evening calls produce no answer, call the following day.

Figure 7.3 *Sample Telephone Interview Disposition Sheet*

Phone number ______________________________

Call	#1	_____	#2	_____	#3	_____	#4	_____	#5	_____
	Date	_____	Date	_____	Date	_____	Date	_____	Date	_____
	Time	_____	Time	_____	Time	_____	Time	_____	Time	_____

Code

1 Completed interview

2 Answering machine

3 Busy

4 No answer

5 Refusal

6 Appointment to call again
(when ____________________________________)

7 Nonworking number (out of order, disconnected, nonexistent)

8 Nonresidential number

9 Reached but respondent not available (out of town, hospital, etc.)

10 Reached but not interviewed (ineligible household, speech/physical problem, age disqualification)

In addition, interviewers should keep track of the disposition or status of their sample numbers. Figure 7.3 shows a sample disposition sheet.

7. *Verify the results.* When all questionnaires are complete, a small subsample of each interviewer's respondents should be called to check that the information they provided was accurately recorded. Respondents should be told during the initial survey that they may receive an additional call at a later date. This alerting tends to eliminate any confusion when subjects receive a second call. A typical procedure is to ask the subject's first name in the interview so that it can be used later. The interviewer should ask, "Were you called a few days ago and asked questions about television viewing?" The verification can begin from there—two or three of the original questions are asked again (preferably open-ended and sensitive questions, since interviewers are most likely to omit these).

8. *Tabulate the data.* Along with the normal data analysis, telephone researchers generally compute response rates for the following items: completed interviews, initial refusals, unqualified respondents, busy signals, language barriers, no answers, terminates, breakoffs, and disconnects.

Advantages. The cost of telephone surveys tends to be reasonable. The sampling involves minimal expense, and there are no significant transportation costs. Callbacks are

> *AN INSIDE LOOK*
>
> **Telephone Surveys**
>
> Researchers who plan to conduct a telephone survey should expect to make about 40 dialings per completed interview, although this will vary depending on the type of survey conducted. In other words, a survey of 100 respondents with an incidence of about 15% will require about 4,000 phone calls.

simple and economical. The variety of telephone plans from AT&T, MCI, Sprint, and others enable researchers to conduct telephone surveys from any location.

Compared to mail surveys, telephone surveys can include more detailed questions, and, as stated earlier, interviewers can clarify misunderstandings that might arise during the administration of the questionnaire.

The response rates of telephone surveys for mass media research (once a qualified respondent is contacted) are generally high, especially when multiple callbacks are used. This is because most people enjoy answering questions about what they see, hear, or read. In addition, phone surveys are much faster than mail. A large staff of interviewers can collect the data from the designated sample in a very short time—400 surveys can be completed in less than 7 days.

Disadvantages. First, much of what is called survey "research" by telephone is not research at all but an attempt to sell people something. Unfortunately, many companies disguise their sales pitch as a "survey." This falsified approach has made many respondents suspicious about telephone calls to their home and prompts many potential respondents to terminate an interview before it has started.

Additionally, it is impossible to include questions that involve visual demonstrations. A researcher cannot hold up a picture of a product and ask whether the respondent remembers seeing it advertised. Another potentially severe problem is that not everyone in a community is listed in the telephone directory, the most often used sampling frame. Not everyone has a telephone, and many people have unlisted phone numbers; also, some numbers are listed incorrectly, and others are too new to be listed. These problems would not be serious if the people with no telephones or with unlisted numbers were just like those listed in the phone book. Unfortunately, researchers generally have no way of checking for such similarities or differences, so it is possible that a sample obtained from a telephone directory may be significantly different from the population. (See Chapter 4 concerning random digit dialing.)

Finally, telephone surveys require a large number of "dialings" to successfully interview the number of respondents required for a study. To demonstrate this, Table 7.1 shows a summary of the telephone call disposition sheets from 50 randomly selected telephone studies conducted by Wimmer Research in 2000–2001. The studies include respondents between the ages of 18 and 54 and investigated topics such as radio listening, television viewing, automotive purchases, and other nonmedia topics.

The data in Table 7.1 show what a professional interviewer faces during a typical workday. Of more than three-quarters of a million dialings, only 2.5% were completed interviews; thus, of every 100 dialings made, only 2.5 will result in a completed interview. There aren't many other jobs with a success rate this low.

Table 7.1 *50-Study Call Disposition Summary*

Call Result	Number	Percent of Total
No answer/machine*	443,200	56.3
Initial Refusal	99,350	12.6
Busy	74,600	9.5
Did not qualify	34,550	4.4
Call back	30,550	3.9
Disconnect	28,400	3.6
Wrong age	26,000	3.3
Business	9,400	1.2
Computer/modem	6,750	0.9
Over age/sex quota	5,250	0.7
Language barrier	3,750	0.5
Security	3,000	0.4
Breakoff	2,800	0.4
Complete	20,000	2.5
TOTAL CALLS	787,600	

*Probably includes a significant number of caller ID rejections.

Personal Interviews

Personal interviews usually involve inviting a respondent to a field service location or a research office (called a **one-on-one interview**). Sometimes interviews are conducted at a person's place of work or at home. There are two basic types of interviews—structured and unstructured. In a **structured interview,** standardized questions are asked in a predetermined order; relatively little freedom is given to interviewers. In an **unstructured interview,** broad questions are asked that allow interviewers freedom to determine what further questions to ask to obtain the required information. Structured interviews are easy to tabulate and analyze, but they do not achieve the depth or expanse of unstructured interviews. Conversely, the unstructured type elicits more detail but takes a great deal of time to score and analyze.

The steps in constructing a personal interview survey are similar to those for a telephone survey. The following list discusses instances in which the personal interview differs substantially from the telephone method:

1. *Select a sample.* Drawing a sample for a personal interview is essentially the same as selecting a sample in any other research method. In one-on-one interviews, respondents are selected based on a predetermined set of screening requirements. In door-to-door interviews, a multistage sample is used to select first a general area, then a block or a neighborhood, and finally a random household from which a person will be chosen (see Figure 4.2 on page 94).

2. *Construct the questionnaire.* Personal interviews are flexible: Detailed questions are easy to ask, and the time taken to complete the survey can be greatly extended—many personal interviews take up to one hour. Researchers can also use visual exhibits, lists, and photographs to ask questions, and respondents can be asked to sort photos or materials into categories, or to point to their answers on printed cards. Respondents can have privacy and anonymity by marking ballots, which can then be slipped into envelopes and sealed.

3. *Prepare an interviewer instruction guide.* The detail needed in an instruction guide depends on the type of interview. One-on-one interviewer guides are not very detailed because there is only one location, respondents are prerecruited by a field service, and interviewing times are prearranged. Door-to-door interviewer guides contain information about the household to select, the respondent to select, and an alternative action to take in the event the target respondent is not at home. Interviewer guides often have instructions on how to conduct the interview, how to dress, how to record data, and how to ask questions. (Keep in mind that although door-to-door interviews are mentioned in this chapter, they are rarely used in the United States because of cost and hesitancy of respondents to participate.)

4. *Train the interviewers.* Training is important because the questionnaires in a personal interview are longer and more detailed. Interviewers should receive instructions on establishing a rapport with subjects, on administrative details (for example, time and length of interviews and interviewer salaries), and on asking follow-up questions. Several practice sessions are necessary to ensure that the project's goals are met and that interviewers follow the established guidelines.

5. *Collect the data.* Personal interviews are both labor- and cost-intensive. These problems are why most researchers prefer to use telephone or mail surveys. A personal interview project can take several days to several weeks to complete because turnaround is slow. One interviewer can complete only a handful of surveys each day. In addition, costs for salaries and expenses escalate quickly. It is common for research companies to charge as much as $1,000 per respondent in a one-on-one situation.

Interviewers gather data either by writing down answers or by audiotaping or videotaping the respondents' answers. Both methods are slow, and detailed transcriptions and editing are often necessary.

6. *Make necessary callbacks.* Each callback requires an interviewer to return to a household originally selected or to the location used for the original interview. Additional salary, expenses, and time are required.

7. *Verify the results.* As with telephone surveys, a subsample of each interviewer's completed questionnaires is selected for verification. Respondents can be called on the phone or reinterviewed in person.

8. *Tabulate the data.* Data tabulation procedures for personal interviews are essentially the same as with any other research method. A codebook must be designed, questionnaires coded, and data input into a computer.

Advantages. Many advantages of the personal interview technique have already been mentioned. It is the most flexible means of obtaining information because the face-to-face situation lends itself easily to questioning in greater depth and detail. Also, some information can be observed by the interviewer during the interview without adding to the length of the questionnaire. Additionally, the interviewer can develop a rapport with the respondents and may be able to elicit replies to sensitive questions that would remain unanswered in a mail or telephone survey. The identity of the respondent is known or can be controlled in the personal interview survey. Whereas in a mail survey all members of a family might confer on an answer, this can usually be avoided in a face-to-face interview. Finally, once an interview has begun, it is harder for respondents to terminate the interview before all the questions have been asked. In a telephone survey, the respondent can simply hang up the telephone.

Disadvantages. As mentioned, time and costs are the major drawbacks to the personal interview technique. Another major disadvantage is the problem of interviewer bias. The physical appearance, age, race, gender, dress, nonverbal behavior, and comments of the interviewer may prompt respondents to answer questions untruthfully. Moreover, the organization necessary for recruiting, training, and administering a field staff of interviewers is much greater than that required for other data collection procedures. If a large number of interviewers are needed, it is necessary to hire field supervisors to coordinate their work, which makes the survey even more expensive. Finally, if personal interviews are conducted during the day, most of the respondents will not be employed outside the home. If it is desirable to interview respondents who have jobs outside the home, interviews must be scheduled on the weekends or during the evening.

One alternative now used in personal interviews is a self-administered interview that respondents answer on a personal computer. Respondents are usually invited to the research company or field service to participate in the project by answering questions presented to them on the computer.

A hybrid of personal interviewing is intensive, or in-depth, interviewing, which is discussed in Chapter 5.

Computer-Assisted Personal Interviewing (CAPI)

A recent methodology developed by a small number of research companies is Computer-Assisted Personal Interviewing (CAPI), where portable laptop computers are used for in-person interview surveys.

The respondent or a professional interviewer enters the data directly into the computer and the results are later uploaded to a master computer for analysis.

Advantages. The main advantage of this approach is that the research questionnaire is taken to the respondent rather than the respondent answering the phone or attending a research location. Complicated questions and visual aids may be used in this approach.

Disadvantages. If CAPI involves respondent data entry, it requires that the respondent is able to use a computer and can accurately input his or her responses. In addition, while CAPI may open the geographic area where respondents are contacted, data collection remains slow because only one questionnaire is completed at a time. Finally, while CAPI may be valuable for certain applications, this use of a computer may actually be a technological step backwards. The goal of research in most cases is speed, and CAPI does not reduce the time required to collect data.

Mall Interviews

Although mall interviews are essentially a form of the personal interviews just discussed, their recent popularity and widespread use warrant individual consideration.

During the late 1980s, mall intercepts became one of the most popular research approaches among marketing and consumer researchers. Schleifer (1986) found that of all the people who participated in a survey in 1984, 33% were mall intercepts. In addition, *Marketing News* (1983) stated that 90% of the market researchers it surveyed in the United States use mall intercepts. Both figures have risen since those studies were conducted.

Although mall intercepts use convenience samples so sampling error cannot be determined, the method has become the standard for many researchers. It is rare to enter a shopping mall without seeing an interviewer with a clipboard trying to stop a shopper. The method has become commonplace, but some shoppers resent the intrusion. In fact, shoppers often take paths to avoid the interviewers they can so easily detect.

The procedures involved in conducting mall intercepts are the same as those for personal interviews. The only major difference is that it is necessary to locate the field service that conducts research in the particular mall of interest. Field services pay license fees to mall owners to allow them to conduct research on the premises. Not just any field service can conduct research in any mall.

One recent trend in mall intercept research is the use of a personal computer for data collection. As with one-on-one interviews conducted in a field service, the respondents simply answer questions posed to them on the computer monitor.

Advantages. Mall intercepts are a quick and inexpensive way to collect personal data.

Disadvantages. Most of the disadvantages of mall intercepts have been discussed in other sections of this book. The three major problems are that convenience sampling restricts the generalizability of the results (not all people in a given area shop at the same mall); the interviews must be short (no more than about 10 minutes); and there is no control over data collection (researchers are at the mercy of the field service to conduct a proper interview).

Disk-By-Mail Surveys

During the late 1980s, a high-tech form of mail surveys appeared that offered great promise. The procedure is called **disk-by-mail surveys,** or **DBM.** The name of the survey approach essentially explains the procedure: Respondents are sent computer disks that contain a self-administered questionnaire, and they are asked to complete it by using a personal computer.

The interest in DBM survey died quickly, primarily because of the Internet, which is discussed in the next section.

Internet Surveys

During the late 1990s, researchers naturally capitalized on the popularity of the Internet, and collecting questionnaire data via the Internet is now commonplace. The process is very simple: A respondent is recruited by telephone, letter, or email and is sent, via email, a questionnaire to complete. When finished, the respondent simply transmits the questionnaire back to the research company or the business that is conducting the study.

Advantages. Internet research is generally inexpensive and is very easy to conduct because researchers never have to leave their office. Respondents can be shown almost any type of visual aid or played almost any type of audio material. The data can be collected very quickly.

Disadvantages. The primary disadvantage of Internet research is that there is no way yet to ensure that the person recruited for the study is actually the person who completes the questionnaire. For example, an adult may be recruited for a study, but the adult may ask a child in the house to answer the questions. Internet research, like any electronic gathering procedure, has no control over data-gathering procedures. This lack of control may have a profound negative effect on the results gathered and the decisions made. Internet research is discussed in detail in Chapter 18.

Group Administration

Group administration combines some of the features of mail surveys and personal interviews. In the group-administered survey, a group of respondents is gathered together (prerecruited by a field service) and given individual copies of a questionnaire or asked to participate in a group interview (a large focus group). The session can take place in a natural setting, but it is usually held at a field service location or a hotel ballroom. For example, respondents may be recruited to complete questionnaires about radio or television stations; students in a classroom may complete questionnaires about their newspaper reading habits; or an audience may be asked to answer questions after viewing a sneak preview of a new film.

The interviewer in charge of the session may or may not read questions to respondents. Reading questions aloud may help respondents who have reading problems, but this is not always necessary. (It is possible to screen respondents for reading or language skills.) The best approach is for several interviewers to be present in the room so that individual problems can be resolved without disturbing the other respondents.

Some group-administered sessions include audio and video materials for respondents to analyze. The session allows respondents to proceed at their own pace, and in most cases interviewers allow respondents to ask questions, although this is not a requirement.

Advantages. The group administration technique has certain advantages. For example, a group-administered questionnaire can be longer than the typical questionnaire used in a mail survey. Since the respondents are usually assembled for the sole purpose of completing the questionnaire, the response rates are usually quite high. The opportunity for researchers to answer questions and handle problems that might arise generally means that fewer items are left blank or answered incorrectly.

Disadvantages. On the negative side, if a group-administered survey leads to the perception that some authority sanctions the study, respondents may become suspicious or uneasy. For example, if a group of teachers is brought together to fill out a questionnaire, some might think that the survey has the approval of the local school administration and that the results will be made available to their superiors. Also, the group environment makes interaction possible among the respondents; this can make the situation more difficult for the researcher to control. In addition, not all surveys can use samples that can be tested together in a group. Surveys often require responses from a wide variety of people, and mixing respondents together may bias the results.

Finally, group administration can be expensive. Costs usually include recruiting fees, co-op payments, hotel rental, refreshments, and salaries for interviewers. These are the typical costs for group sessions:

CPI	\$25–\$1,000 per person
Co-op	\$25–\$150 per person
Hotel	\$200–\$1,000 per night
Refreshments	\$0–\$50 per person
Audio/video rental	\$0–thousands of dollars
Hosts	\$0–\$100 per host
Parking fees	\$0–\$25 per person
Interviewers/ assistants	\$0–hundreds of dollars
Travel expenses	\$0–thousands of dollars

▪ Achieving a Reasonable Response Rate

No matter which type of survey is conducted, it is virtually impossible to obtain a 100% response rate. Researchers have more control with some types of surveys (personal interview) and less with others (mail survey). However, regardless of the situation, not all respondents will be available for interviews and not all will cooperate. Consequently, the researcher must try to achieve the highest response rate possible under the circumstances.

What constitutes an acceptable response rate? Obviously, the higher the response rate, the better: As more respondents are sampled, response bias is less likely. But is there a minimum rate that should be achieved? Not everyone agrees on an answer to this question, and it is difficult to develop a standard because of the variety of research studies conducted, the method of recruiting used, the research topic, time of year when the study is conducted, and where the study is conducted. However, the authors' experience in more than 20 years of research provides these response rate ranges:

- Mail surveys: 1%–4%
- Telephone surveys: 10%–75%
- Internet survey *click-through rate* (CTR), where Internet users click on a link to participate in a survey: 1%–30%
- Shopping-center intercept: 5%
- Personal (face-to-face) interviews: 40% (depends on recruiting method)

As far as academic journals are concerned, a survey of research articles published in the

1999–2001 issues of *Journalism and Mass Communication Quarterly, Journal of Broadcasting and Electronic Media,* and the *Journal of Communication* disclosed that the completion rates for telephone surveys ranged from 31% to 71%, with an average rate of about 54%. The completion rates for a mail survey ranged from 21% to 70%, with an average rate of about 45%. The mail survey completion rates that were the highest were surveys mailed to a specific occupational group (such as reporters or public relations practitioners) that used two or three follow-up mailings.

Regardless of the response rate, the researcher is responsible for examining any possible biases in response patterns. Were females more likely to respond than males? Older people more likely to respond than younger ones? Whites more likely than minorities? A significant lack of response from a particular group might weaken the strength of any inferences from the data to the population under study. To be on the safe side, the researcher should attempt to gather information from other sources about the people who did not respond; by comparing such additional data with those from respondents, the researcher may be able to determine whether underrepresentation introduced any bias into the results.

Using common sense will help increase the response rate. In telephone surveys, respondents should be called when they are likely to be at home and receptive to interviewing. Do not call when people are likely to be eating or sleeping. In a one-on-one situation, the interviewer should be appropriately attired. In addition, the researcher should spend time tracking down some of the nonrespondents and asking them why they refused to be interviewed or why they did not fill out the questionnaire. Responses such as "The interviewer was insensitive and pushy," "The questionnaire was delivered with postage due," and "The survey sounded like a ploy to sell something" can be illuminating.

Along with common sense, certain elements of the research design can have a significant impact on response rates. Yu and Cooper (1983), in their survey of 93 published studies, made these discoveries that continue to be important today:

- Monetary incentives increased the response rate, with larger incentives being the most effective.
- Preliminary notification, personalization of the questionnaire, a follow-up letter, and assertive "foot in the door" personal interview techniques all significantly increased the response rate.
- A cover letter, the assurance of anonymity, and a statement of a deadline did not significantly increase the response rate.
- Stressing the social utility of the study and appealing to the respondent to help out the researcher did not affect response rates.

While there are numerous suggestions about how to increase response rates, our experience over the past 25 years shows that the best incentive is money. How much money? That depends on the area of the country, but in broad terms, researchers can expect to pay a minimum of $50.00 per respondent in most research studies not using telephones. (Telephone research remains the only research method that does not require a co-op payment to the respondent. This will probably change in the near future.)

▪ General Problems in Survey Research

Although surveys are valuable tools in mass media research, several obstacles are frequently encountered. Experience in survey research confirms the following points:

1. Subjects or respondents are often unable to recall information about themselves

or their activities. This inability may be caused by memory failure, nervousness related to being involved in a research study, confusion about the questions asked, or some other intervening factor. Questions that are glaringly simple to researchers may cause significant problems for respondents.

For example, radio station managers often want to ask respondents which radio stations they have set on their vehicle's radio pushbuttons. The managers are surprised to discover the number of people who not only do not know which stations are programmed on their radio buttons, but do not know how many buttons are on their radio.

2. Due to a respondent's feelings of inadequacy or lack of knowledge about a particular topic, the respondent may often provide "prestigious" answers rather than admit to not knowing something. This is called **prestige bias.** For example, as mentioned earlier in the book, some respondents claim to watch public TV and listen to public radio when, in fact, they do not.

3. Subjects may purposely deceive researchers by giving incorrect answers to questions. Almost nothing can be done about respondents who lie. A large sample may discount this type of response. However, there is no acceptable and valid method to determine whether a respondent's answers are truthful; the answers must be accepted as they are given, although one way to discover deception is to ask the same question two or three times throughout the survey (using different question approaches).

4. Respondents often give elaborate answers to simple questions because they try to "figure out" what the purpose of a study is and what the researcher is doing. People are naturally curious, but they become even more curious when they are the focus of a scientific research project. In addition, some respondents use a research study as a soapbox for their opinions. These people want to have all of their opinions known and use the research study to attempt to deliver the messages.

5. Surveys are often complicated by the inability of respondents to explain their true feelings, perceptions, and beliefs—not because they do not have any, but because they cannot put them into words. The question "Why do you like to watch soap operas?" may be particularly difficult for some people. They may watch them every day, but respond by saying only "Because I like them." Probing respondents for further information may help, but not in every case.

Conducting survey research is an exciting process. It is fun to find out why people think in certain ways or what they do in certain situations. But researchers must continually remain aware of obstacles that may hinder data collection, and they must deal with these problems. The United States is the most surveyed country in the world, and many citizens now refuse to take part in any type of research project. Researchers must convince respondents and subjects that their help is important in making decisions and solving problems.

The face of survey research is continually changing. One-on-one and door-to-door interviews are now very difficult to conduct. This means there is a greater emphasis on mail surveys, mall intercepts, and electronic data-gathering procedures. In telephone surveys, for example, computer-assisted telephone interviewing (CATI) is now common.

CATI uses video display terminals operated by interviewers to present questions and accept respondent answers, thus eliminating the need for the traditional pencil-and-paper questionnaires. The computer displays the proper questions in the proper order, so there is no possibility of the interviewer making an error by asking the wrong questions or skipping the right ones. The process makes data coding easier because the interviewer enters the respondent's answers through the keyboard. Groves and Mathiowetz (1984) and Wimmer (1995) found that there is little difference in results with CATI and non-CATI techniques. The response rates, reactions of the interviewers and respondents, and quality of data were virtually equivalent. CATI interviews tended to take slightly more time, but this was balanced by the presence of fewer interviewer errors due to skipping questions. As new software is developed in this area, it seems likely that a greater proportion of surveys will use the CATI technique.

Other new techniques include computer-generated, voice-synthesized surveys in which respondents answer by pushing Touch-Tone telephone buttons; 800 telephone numbers for recruited respondents to call to answer questions asked by an interviewer or computer; pop-up surveys on the Internet; and various types of touch-sensitive TV screens that present questionnaires to respondents. Survey research approaches change almost every day.

▪ ▪ ▪ Summary

Survey research is an important and useful method of data collection. The survey is also one of the most widely used methods of media research, primarily because of its flexibility. Surveys, however, involve a number of steps. Researchers must decide whether to use a descriptive or analytical approach; define the purpose of the study; review the available literature in the area; select the survey approach, questionnaire design, and sample; analyze and interpret the data; and finally decide whether to publish or disseminate the results. These steps are not necessarily taken in that order, but all must be considered in conducting a survey.

To ensure that all the steps in the survey process are in harmony, researchers should conduct one or more pilot studies to detect any errors in the approach. Pilot studies save time, money, and frustration because an error that could void an entire analysis sometimes surfaces at this stage.

Questionnaire design is also a major step in any survey. This chapter included examples to show how a question or an interviewing approach may elicit a specific response. The goal in questionnaire design is to avoid bias in answers. Question wording, length, style, and order may affect a respondent's answers. Extreme care must be taken when developing questions to ensure that they are neutral. To achieve a reasonable response rate, researchers should consider including an incentive, notifying survey subjects beforehand, and personalizing the questionnaire. Also, researchers should mention the response rate when they report the results of the survey.

Finally, researchers must select the most appropriate survey approach from among four basic types: mail, telephone, personal interview, and group administration. Each approach has advantages and disadvantages that must be weighed. The type of survey used will depend on the purpose of the study, the amount of time available to the researcher, and the funds available for the study. In the future, survey researchers may depend less on the face-to-face survey and more on computer-assisted telephone interviewing.

Key Terms

Analytical surveys
Breakoffs
Call disposition sheet
CATI
Checklist question
Closed-ended question
Codebook
Descriptive surveys
Disk-by-mail survey
Door-to-door survey
Double-barreled question
Double bind
Feeling thermometer
Filter question
Forced-choice question
Group administered survey
Leading question
Mail survey
Mailing list
Mall intercept
Multiple-choice question
Mutually exclusive
One-on-one interview
Open-ended question
Personal interview
Pop-up Internet survey
Prestige bias
Response rate
Screener question
Structured interview
Telephone survey
Unstructured interview
Verbatims

Using the Internet

1. As with nearly every topic discussed in this text, the Internet offers a variety of information about survey research. To start your journey, first conduct searches for "survey research," "surveys," "questionnaire design," and "Internet research."
2. Use your imagination when searching the Internet. For example, in addition to searching for "questionnaire design," search for "problems with questionnaire design," or "developing questionnaires," or "best use of questionnaires."
3. Ask your instructor for a copy of the sample questionnaire located on the website for this text: *www.wimmerdominick.com.*

Questions and Problems for Further Investigation

1. Develop five research questions or hypotheses that can be tested by survey research. What approaches can be used to collect data on these topics?
2. Nonresponse is a problem in all survey research. In addition, many people refuse to participate in surveys at all. Write a cover letter for a survey on television viewing habits.
3. Define a target group and design questions to collect information on the following topics:
   a. Political party affiliation
   b. Attitudes toward television soap operas
   c. Attitudes toward newspaper editorials
   d. Attitudes toward the number of television commercials
   e. Public television viewing habits
4. Locate one or more survey studies in journals on mass media research. Answer the following questions in relation to the article(s):
   a. What was the purpose of the survey?
   b. How were the data collected?
   c. What type of information was produced?
   d. Did the data answer a particular research question or hypothesis?
   e. Were any problems evident with the survey and its approach?
5. Design a survey to collect data on a topic of your choice. Be sure to address these points:
   a. What is the purpose of the survey? What is its goal?
   b. What research questions or hypotheses are tested?
   c. Are any operational definitions required?
   d. Develop at least 10 questions relevant to the problem.
   e. Describe the approach to be used to collect data.
   f. Design a cover letter or an interview schedule for the study.
   g. Conduct a pretest to test the questionnaire.
6. Although it originated in England, the survey technique is most often used in the United States. What about survey research in other nations and other cultures? If you are using InfoTrac College Edition, you can find online articles from the October 1998 issue of the *American Behavioral Scientist* that describe some of the challenges of doing survey research in other countries.

For additional information on these and related topics, see

http://www.wimmerdominick.com

References and Suggested Readings

Babbie, E. R. (1990). *Survey research methods* (2nd ed.). Belmont, CA: Wadsworth.

Backstrom, C., & Hursh-Cesar, G. (1986). *Survey research* (2nd ed.). New York: John Wiley.

Beville, H. Jr. (1988). *Audience ratings* (Rev. ed.). Hillsdale, NJ: Lawrence Erlbaum.

Brighton, M. (1981). Data capture in the 1980s. Communicare: *Journal of Communication Science,* 2(1), 12–19.

Chaffee, S. H., & Choe, S. Y. (1980). Time of decision and media use during the Ford–Carter campaign. *Public Opinion Quarterly,* 44, 53–70.

Dillman, D. (1978). *Mail and telephone surveys.* New York: John Wiley.

The Eagle Group. (1995). Proprietary research conducted by the senior author.

Erdos, P. L. (1974). Data collection methods: Mail surveys. In R. Ferber (Ed.), *Handbook of marketing research.* New York: McGraw-Hill.

Fletcher, J. E., & Wimmer, R. D. (1981). *Focus group interviews in radio research.* Washington, DC: National Association of Broadcasters.

Fowler, F. (1993). *Survey research methods* (2nd ed.). Newbury Park, CA: Sage Publications.

Fox, R. J., Crask, M. R., & Kim, J. (1989). Mail survey response rate. *Public Opinion Quarterly,* 52(4), 467–491.

Groves, R., & Mathiowetz, N. (1984). Computer-assisted telephone interviewing: Effects on interviewers and respondents. *Public Opinion Quarterly,* 48(1), 356–369.

Hornik, J., & Ellis, S. (1989). Strategies to secure compliance for a mall intercept interview. *Public Opinion Quarterly,* 52(4), 539–551.

Hsia, H. J. (1988). *Mass communication research methods: A step-by-step approach.* Hillsdale, NJ: Lawrence Erlbaum.

Kerlinger, F. N. (1986). *Foundations of behavioral research* (3rd ed.). New York: Holt, Rinehart & Winston.

Lavrakas, P. J. (1993). *Telephone survey methods: Sampling, selection, and supervision* (2nd ed.). Newbury Park, CA: Sage Publications.

Marketing News. (1983). Inflation adjusted spending is on rise for consumer research. *Marketing News,* 17(1), 13.

Miller, D. C. (1991). *Handbook of research design and social measurement* (5th ed.). New York: Longman.

National Association of Broadcasters. (1976). *A broadcast research primer.* Washington, DC: NAB.

Oppenheim, A. N. (1992). *Questionnaire design and attitude measurement.* New York: Pinter.

Poindexter, P. M. (1979). Daily newspaper nonreaders: Why they don't read. *Journalism Quarterly,* 56, 764–770.

Rea, L. M., Parker, R. A., & Shrader, A. (1997). *Designing and conducting survey research: A comprehensive guide.* New York: Jossey-Bass.

Rosenberg, M. (1968). *The logic of survey analysis.* New York: Basic Books.

Schleifer, S. (1986). Trends in attitudes toward and participation in survey research. *Public Opinion Quarterly,* 50(1), 17–26.

Sewell, W., & Shaw, M. (1968). Increasing returns in mail surveys. *American Sociological Review,* 33, 193.

Sharp, L., & Frankel, J. (1983). Respondent burden: A test of some common assumptions. *Public Opinion Quarterly,* 47(1), 36–53.

Singer, E., & Presser, S. (Eds.) (1989). *Survey research methods: A reader.* Chicago: University of Chicago Press.

Wakshlag, J. J., & Greenberg, B. S. (1979). Programming strategies and the popularity of television programs for children. *Journal of Communication,* 6, 58–68.

Walizer, M. H., & Wienir, P. L. (1978). *Research methods and analysis: Searching for relationships.* New York: Harper & Row.

Weisberg, H. F., & Bowen, B. D. (1996). *An introduction to survey research and data analysis* (3rd ed.). Glenview, IL: Scott, Foresman.

Williams, F., Rice, R. E., & Rogers, E. M. (1988). *Research methods and the new media.* New York: Free Press.

Wimmer, R. D. (1976). *A multivariate analysis of the uses and effects of the mass media in the 1968 presidential campaign.* Unpublished doctoral dissertation, Bowling Green University, Ohio.

Wimmer, R. D. (1995). *Comparison of CATI and non-CATI interviewing.* Unpublished company paper. Denver: The Eagle Group.

Winkler, R. L., & Hays, W. L. (1975). *Statistics: Probability, inference and decision* (2nd ed.). New York: Holt, Rinehart & Winston.

Yu, J., & Cooper, H. (1983). A quantitative review of research design effects on response rates to questionnaires. *Journal of Marketing Research,* 20(1), 36–44.

Zillmann, D., & Bryant, J. (1975). Viewers' moral sanctions of retribution in the appreciation of dramatic presentations. *Journal of Experimental Social Psychology,* 11, 572–582.

Chapter 8

Longitudinal Research

- *Development*
- *Types of Longitudinal Studies*
- *Special Panel Designs*
- *Analyzing Causation in Panel Data*
- *Combining Qualitative and Quantitative Data in Longitudinal Research*
- *Longitudinal Research on the Internet*
- *Longitudinal Design in Experiments*

Summary

Key Terms

Using the Internet

Questions and Problems for Further Investigation

References and Suggested Readings

Most of the research discussed to this point has been cross-sectional. In cross-sectional research, data are collected from a representative sample at only one point in time. Longitudinal research, in contrast, involves the collection of data at different points in time. Although longitudinal investigations are relatively rare in mass communication research, several longitudinal studies have been among the most influential and provocative in the field.

Of the 14 studies Lowery and DeFleur (1995) consider to be milestones in the evolution of mass media research, four involve the longitudinal approach: Lazarsfeld, Berelson, and Gaudet's *The People's Choice* (1944), which introduced the two-step flow model; Katz and Lazarsfeld's *Personal Influence* (1955), which examined the role of opinion leaders; the *Surgeon General's Report on Television and Social Behavior,* particularly as used in the study by Lefkowitz, Eron, Walder, and Huesmann (1972), which found evidence that viewing violence on television caused subsequent aggressive behavior; and the 10-year update of the Lefkowitz et al. report (Pearl, Bouthilet, & Lazar, 1982), which cited the longitudinal studies that affirmed the link between TV violence and aggression. Other longitudinal studies also figure prominently in the field, including the elaborate panel study done for NBC by Milavsky, Kessler, Stipp, and Rubens (1982), the cross-national comparisons cited in Huesmann and Eron (1986), and the studies of mass media in elections as summarized by Peterson (1980). Thus, although it is not widely used, the longitudinal method can produce theoretically and socially important results.

■ Development

Longitudinal studies have a long history in the behavioral sciences. In psychology, in particular, they have been used to trace the development of children and the clinical progress of patients. In medicine, longitudinal studies have been used widely to study the impact of disease and treatment methods. Sociologists studying the 1924 election campaign did the pioneering work in political science. Somewhat later, Newcomb (1943) conducted repeated interviews of Bennington College students from 1935 to 1939 to examine the impact of a liberal college environment on respondents who came from conservative families.

In the mass communication area, the first major longitudinal study was done by Lazarsfeld, Berelson, and Gaudet (1944) during the 1940 presidential election. Lazarsfeld pioneered the use of the panel technique in which the same individuals are interviewed several times. Lazarsfeld also developed the 16-fold table, one of the earliest statistical techniques to attempt to derive causation from longitudinal survey data. Another form of longitudinal research, **trend studies** (in which different people are asked the same question at different points in time) began showing up in mass media research in the 1960s. One of the most publicized trend studies was the continuing survey of media credibility done by the Roper organization. Trend studies by Gallup and Harris, among others, also gained notoriety during this time.

More recently, the notion of cohort analysis, a method of research developed by demographers, has become popular. Cohort analysis involves the study of specific populations, usually all those born during a given period, as they change over time. Other significant developments in longitudinal research have taken place as more sophisticated techniques for analyzing longitudinal data were developed. More technical information about advanced computational strategies for longitudinal data is contained in Magnusson, Bergman, Rudinger, and Torestad (1991) and in Toon (2000).

Cross-lagged correlation was widely discussed during the 1960s and 1970s. Cross-lagged correlations are done when information about two variables is gathered from the same sample at two different times. The correlations between variables at the same point in time are compared with the correlations at different points in time. Three other forms of analysis using advanced statistical techniques have had relevance in longitudinal studies: path analysis, log-linear models, and structural equations. Path analysis is used to chart directions in panel data. Log-linear models are used with categorical panel data and involve the analysis of multivariate contingency tables. LISREL (LInear Structural RELations), a model developed by Joreskog (1973), is another statistical technique that has broad application in longitudinal analysis.

▪ Types of Longitudinal Studies

The three main types of longitudinal studies are trend study, cohort analysis, and panel study. Each is discussed in this section.

Trend Studies

The trend study is probably the most common type of longitudinal study in mass media research. Recall that a trend study samples different groups of people at different times from the same population. Trend studies are common around presidential election time. Suppose that 3 months before an election a sample of adults is drawn; 57% report that they intend to vote for Candidate A and 43% for Candidate B. A month later a different sample drawn from the same population shows a change: 55% report that they are going to vote for A and 45% for B. This is a simple example of a trend study. Trend studies provide information about net changes at an aggregate level. In the example, we know that in the period under consideration, Candidate A lost 2% of his support. We do not know how many people changed from B to A or from A to B, nor do we know how many stayed with their original choice. We know only that the net result was a 2-point loss for A. To determine both the gross change and the net change, a panel study is necessary.

Advantages. Trend studies are valuable in describing long-term changes in a population. They can establish a pattern over time to detect shifts and changes in some event. Broadcast researchers, for example, compile trend studies that chart fluctuations in viewing levels for the major networks. Another advantage of trend studies is that they can be based on a comparison of survey data originally constructed for other purposes. Of course, in utilizing such data, the researcher needs to recognize any differences in question wording, context, sampling, or analysis techniques from one survey to the next. Hyman (1987) provides extensive guidance on the secondary analysis of survey data. The growing movement to preserve data archives and the ability of the Internet to make retrieval and sharing much easier will help this technique gain in popularity. *The Gale Guide to Internet Databases* lists online databases that might be useful for mass media researchers. Also, see Using the Internet section at the end of this chapter.

Secondary analysis saves time, money, and personnel; it also makes it possible for researchers to understand long-term change. In fact, mass media researchers might want to consider what socially significant data concerning media behaviors should be collected and archived at regular intervals. Economists have developed regular trend indicators to gauge the health of the economy, but mass communication scholars have developed almost no analogous social indicators of the media or audiences.

Disadvantages. Trend analysis is only as good as the underlying data. If data are unreliable, false trends will show up in the results. Moreover, to be most valuable, trend analysis must be based on consistent measures. Changes in the way indexes are constructed or the way questions are asked produce results that are not comparable over time.

Examples of Trend Studies. Both university and commercial research firms have asked some of the same questions for many national and statewide trend studies. For example, in the United States, a question about satisfaction with the president's performance has been asked hundreds of times, dating back to the administration of Harry Truman. *Public Opinion Quarterly* has a regular section entitled "The Polls" that allows researchers to construct trend data on selected topics. In recent issues the following trend data have appeared: (1) a 10-year sampling of public opinion about terrorism in the United States, (2) a 33-year sampling of attitudes toward China, and (3) a 29-year compilation of public attitudes about the women's movement. Of specific interest in the field of mass media research are the trend data on changing patterns of media credibility, compiled for more than three decades by the Roper organization (summarized in Mayer, 1993). Among other trend studies are the Violence Index constructed by Gerbner and his associates (Gerbner, Gross, Signorielli, Morgan, & Jackson-Beeck, 1979) and the trend study by Xiaoming (1994) that documents demographic trends in the television viewing habits of adults from the 1960s to the 1990s. Robinson and Levy (1996) studied the use of news media and general knowledge and Lubbers, Scheepers, and Vergeer (2000) conducted a trend study about newspaper reading and attitudes toward ethnic minorities that spanned 5 years. Kincaid's (2000) trend study estimated the impact of a mass media campaign about contraceptives done in the Philippines. In the professional area, the local market diary surveys in radio and television done by the Arbitron Company and A. C. Nielsen are examples of trend studies.

Cohort Analysis

To the Romans, a "cohort" was 1 of the 10 divisions of a military legion. For research purposes, a *cohort* is any group of individuals who are linked in some way or who have experienced the same significant life event within a given period. Usually the "significant life event" is birth, in which case the group is termed a *birth cohort.* There are, however, many other kinds of cohorts, including marriage (for example, all those married between 1980 and 1985), divorce (for example, all those divorced between 1985 and 1990), education (the class of 1990), and others (all those who attended college during the Vietnam era).

Any study in which some characteristic of one or more cohorts is measured at two or more points in time is a **cohort analysis.** Cohort analysis attempts to identify a *cohort effect:* Are changes in the dependent variable due to aging, or are they present because the sample members belong to the same cohort? To illustrate, suppose that 50% of college seniors report that they regularly read news magazines, whereas only 10% of college freshmen in the same survey give this answer.

How might the difference be accounted for? One explanation is that freshmen change their reading habits as they progress through college. Another is that this year's freshman class is composed of people with reading habits different from those who were enrolled 3 years earlier.

There are two ways to distinguish between these explanations. One way involves questioning the same students during their freshman year and again during their senior year and comparing their second set of responses to those of a group of current freshmen. (This is the familiar panel design, which is discussed in detail later.) Or a researcher can take two samples of the student population, at Time 1 and Time 2. Each survey has different participants—the same people are not questioned again, as in a panel study—but each sample represents the same group of people at different points in their college career. Although we have no direct information about which individuals changed their habits over time, we do have information on how the cohort of people who entered college at Time 1 had changed by the time they became seniors. If 15% of the freshmen at Time 1 read news magazines and if 40% of the seniors at Time 2 read them, we can deduce that students change their reading habits as they progress through college.

Typically, a cohort analysis involves data in more than one cohort, and a standard table for presenting the data from multiple cohorts was proposed by Glenn (1977). Table 8.1 is such a table. It displays news magazine readership for a number of birth cohorts. Note that the column variable (read down) is age, and the row variable (read across) is the year of data collection. Because the interval between any two periods of measurement (that is, surveys) corresponds to the age class intervals, cohorts can be followed over time. When the intervals are not equal, the progress of cohorts cannot be followed with precision.

Table 8.1 *Percentage Who Regularly Read News Magazines*

	Year		
Age	1992	1996	2000
18–21	15	12	10
22–25	34	32	28
26–29	48	44	35

This type of table allows a researcher to make three types of comparisons. First, reading down a single column is analogous to a cross-sectional study and presents comparisons among different age cohorts at one point in time (*intercohort differences*). Second, reading across the rows shows trends at each age level that occur when cohorts replace one another. Third, reading diagonally toward the right reveals changes in a single cohort from one time to another (an *intracohort study*). Thus, Table 8.1 suggests that news magazine reading increases with age (reading down each column). In each successive time period, the percentage of younger readers has diminished (reading across the rows), and the increase in reading percentage as each cohort ages is about the same (reading diagonally to the right).

The variations in the percentages in the table can be categorized into three kinds of effects. (For the moment, we assume that there is no variation due to sampling error or to changing composition in each cohort as it ages.) First, influences produced by the sheer fact of maturation, or growing older, are called **age effects.** Second, influences associated with members in a certain birth cohort are called **cohort effects.** Finally, influences associated with each particular time period are called **period effects.**

To recognize these various influences at work, examine the hypothetical data in

Table 8.2 *Cohort Table Showing Pure Age Effect*

	Year		
Age	1992	1996	2000
18–21	15	15	15
22–25	20	20	20
26–29	25	25	25
Average	20	20	20

Table 8.3 *Cohort Table Showing Pure Period Effect*

	Year		
Age	1992	1996	2000
18–21	15	20	25
22–25	15	20	25
26–29	15	20	25
Average	15	20	25

Table 8.4 *Cohort Table Showing Pure Cohort Effect*

	Year		
Age	1992	1996	2000
18–21	15	10	5
22–25	20	15	10
26–29	25	20	15
Average	20	15	10

Tables 8.2, 8.3, and 8.4. Again, we assume that the dependent variable is the percentage of the sample who regularly read a news magazine. Table 8.2 demonstrates a "pure" age effect. Note that the rows are identical and the columns show the same pattern of variation. Apparently it does not matter when a person was born or in which period he or she lived. As the individual becomes older, news magazine readership increases. For ease of illustration, Table 8.2 shows a linear effect, but this is not necessarily the only effect possible. For example, readership might increase from the first age interval to the next but not increase from the second to the third.

Table 8.3 shows a "pure" period effect. There is no variation by age at any period; the columns are identical, and the variations from one period to the next are identical. Furthermore, the change in each cohort (read diagonally to the right) is the same as the average change in the total population. The data in this table suggest that year of birth and maturation have little to do with news magazine reading. In this hypothetical case, the time period seems to be most important. Knowing when the survey was done enables the researcher to predict the variation in news magazine reading.

Table 8.4 shows a "pure" cohort effect. Here the cohort diagonals are constant, and the variation from younger to older respondents is in the opposite direction from the variation from earlier to later survey periods. In this table, the key variable seems to be date of birth. Among those who were born between 1971 and 1974, news magazine readership was 15% regardless of their age or when they were surveyed.

Of course, these pure patterns rarely occur in actual data. Nonetheless, an examination of Tables 8.2, 8.3, and 8.4 can help develop sensitivity to the patterns one can detect in analyzing cohort data. In addition, the tables illustrate the logic behind the analysis. Glenn (1977) and Mason, Mason,

Table 8.5 *Cohort Analysis of Daily Newspaper Reading (percent reading paper everyday)**

	Year		
Age	1972	1982	1991
18–22	47	28	20
28–32	66	55	39
38–42	78	51	60

*Data excerpted from Peiser (2000b). Readers are urged to consult the article for the full cohort table and Peiser's interpretation.

Winsborough, and Poole (1973) also present tables showing pure effects.

An example using actual data might also be helpful. Table 8.5 contains excerpts from a cohort analysis done by Peiser (2000a) that examined the cohort effect on newspaper readership. Although these data represent only part of the cohort data analyzed by Peiser, they do represent his general findings.

As can be seen from Table 8.5, there is an apparent age effect (read down the columns). With minor exception, older people are more likely to be newspaper readers. In addition, reading across the rows suggests that younger people are reading less than older people. Finally, a possible cohort effect can be detected by looking at the diagonals.

Advantages. Cohort analysis is an appealing and useful technique because it is highly flexible. It provides insight into the effects of maturation and social, cultural, and political change. In addition, it can be used with either original data or secondary data. In many instances, a cohort analysis can be less expensive than experiments or surveys.

Disadvantages. The major disadvantage of cohort analysis is that the specific effects of age, cohort, and period are difficult to untangle through purely statistical analysis of a standard cohort table. In survey data, much of the variation in percentages among cells is due to sampling variability. There are no uniformly accepted tests of significance appropriate to a cohort table that allow researchers to estimate the probability that the observed differences are due to chance. Moreover, as a cohort grows older, many of its members die. If the remaining cohort members differ in regard to the variable under study, the variation in the cohort table may simply reflect this change. Finally, as Glenn (1977) points out, no matter how a cohort table is examined, three of the basic effects—namely, age, cohort, and period—are confounded. Age and cohort effects are confounded in the columns; age and period effects in the diagonals; and cohort and period effects in each row. Even the patterns of variations in the "pure" cohort Tables 8.2, 8.3, and 8.4 could be explained by a combination of influences.

Several authors have developed techniques to try to sort out these effects. Three of the most useful are Palmore's (1978) triad method, the constrained multiple regression model (Rentz, Reynolds, & Stout, 1983), and the goodness-of-fit technique (Feinberg & Mason, 1980). If the researcher is willing to make certain assumptions, these methods can provide some tentative evidence about the probable influences of age, period, and cohort. Moreover, in many cases there is only one likely or plausible explanation for the variation. Nonetheless, a researcher should exercise caution in attributing causation to any variable in a cohort analysis. Theory and evidence from outside sources should be utilized in any interpretation. For example, in his study of the influences of television watching and newspaper reading on cohort differences in verbal ability, Glenn (1994) assumed that there were no period effects on changes in adult vocabulary during the duration of his study. As a result, he was able to demonstrate a cohort effect suggesting that decreases in verbal ability were associated with a decline in newspaper reading and an increase in TV viewing.

A second disadvantage of the technique is sample mortality. If a long period is involved or if the specific sample group is difficult to reach, the researcher may have some empty cells in the cohort table or some that contain too few members for meaningful analysis.

Examples of Cohort Analysis. Cohort analysis is widely used in advertising and marketing research. For example, Rentz, Reynolds, and Stout (1983) conducted a cohort analysis of consumers born in four time periods: 1931–1940, 1941–1950, 1951–1960, and 1961–1970. Soft drink consumption was the dependent variable. Multiple regression analysis was used to help separate the three possible sources of variation. The results indicated a large cohort effect, suggesting that soft drink consumption does not decrease as successive cohorts age. Cohort analysis is also useful in the study of public opinion. Wilson (1996) conducted a cohort study that examined patterns of prejudice and found that the most recent cohorts of Americans showed no tendency to be less prejudiced than their predecessors. Jennings (1996) analyzed cohort data on political knowledge gathered from a sample of twelfth-graders and their parents and found both period and cohort effects. More recently, Peiser (2000b) looked at cohort trends in media use.

Panel Studies

Panel studies measure the same sample of respondents at different points in time. Unlike trend studies, panel studies can reveal information about both net change and gross change in the dependent variable. For example, a study of voting intentions might reveal that between Time 1 and Time 2, 20% of the panel switched from Candidate A to Candidate B and 20% switched from Candidate B to Candidate A. Where a trend study would show a net change of zero because the gross changes simply canceled each other out, the panel study would show a high degree of volatility in voting intention.

Similar to trend and cohort studies, panel studies can make use of mail questionnaires, telephone interviews, personal interviews, or the Internet via web panels. Television networks, advertising agencies, and marketing research firms use panel studies to track changes in consumer behavior. Panel studies can reveal shifting attitudes and patterns of behavior that might go unnoticed with other research approaches; thus trends, new ideas, fads, and buying habits are among the variables investigated. For a panel study on the effectiveness of political commercials, for example, all members of the panel would be interviewed periodically during a campaign to determine whether and when each respondent makes a voting decision.

Depending on the purpose of the study, researchers can use either a continuous panel, consisting of members who report specific attitudes or behavior patterns on a regular basis, or an interval panel, whose members agree to complete a certain number of measurement instruments (usually questionnaires) only when the information is needed. Panel studies produce data suitable for sophisticated statistical analysis and enable researchers to predict cause-and-effect relationships.

Advantages. Panel data are particularly useful in answering questions about the dynamics of change. For example, under what conditions do voters change political party affiliation? What are the respective roles of mass media and friends in changing political attitudes? Moreover, repeated contacts with the respondents may help reduce their suspicions, so that later interviews yield more information than the initial encounters. Of course, the other side to this benefit is the sensitization effect, discussed under "Disadvantages." Finally, panel studies help solve the

AN INSIDE LOOK
Panel Studies

Panel studies are rarely used in research because of their enormous expense. An "easy" national study with 1,000 respondents over 5 years may cost at least $100,000 per year. One of the most significant problems in this type of research is getting respondents to commit for anything more than one interview.

problems normally encountered when defining a theory on the basis of a one-shot case study. Since the research progresses over a period of time, the researcher can allow for the influences of competing stimuli on the subject.

Disadvantages. On the negative side, panel members are often difficult to recruit because of an unwillingness to fill out questionnaires or submit to interviews several times. The number of initial refusals in a panel study fluctuates, depending on the amount of time required, the prestige of the organization directing the study, and the presence or absence of some type of compensation. One analysis of the refusal rates in 12 marketing panel studies found a range of 15%–80%, with a median of about 40% (Carman, 1974). Wimmer (2001) found that even a cash incentive may not increase a respondent's willingness to participate in a panel study.

Once the sample has been secured, the problem of mortality emerges—panel members drop out for one reason or another. Because the strength of panel studies is that they interview the same people at different times, this advantage diminishes as the sample size decreases. Sullivan, Rumptz, Campbell, Eby, and Davidson (1996) present several helpful techniques that have been shown to minimize sample mortality:

- Offer a stipend or payment to panel members.
- Establish the credibility and value of the research project.
- Gather detailed information about panel member's friends, coworkers, and family who might know the whereabouts of the respondent.
- Contact the panel member between data collection waves.
- Give panel members a card with a phone number to call if they change addresses.

Another serious problem is that respondents often become sensitized to measurement instruments after repeated interviewing, thus making the sample atypical. For example, panelists who know in advance that they will be interviewed about public TV watching might alter their viewing patterns to include more PBS programs (or fewer). Menard (1991) suggests that a revolving panel design might overcome the sensitization problem. In this design, after the first measurement period, new members replace some of the original members of the panel. (This is the procedure A.C. Nielsen uses with its metered national sample.) For example, a researcher concerned that increased PBS viewing is the result of sensitization, could interview 100 viewers during Week 1 and then replace 25 of the original sample with new panel members in Week 2. The viewing data from those who had been interviewed twice could then be compared with the data from those who participated in a single interview. (Researchers who use replacement should not replace more than 25% of the original sample in replications of the first measurement.)

AN INSIDE LOOK
Panel Studies: Minimizing Attrition

One of the most common causes of attrition in panel research is the inability to locate the original respondents for a follow-up study. The longer the time lag between the two waves of data collection, the more severe this problem becomes. A variety of tracking strategies are available, however, for persistent researchers who wish to overcome this problem. Call, Otto, and Spenner (1982) offer the following suggestions for finding those missing respondents:

- Use the U.S. Postal Service to find forwarding addresses.
- Check with the phone company for new phone numbers.
- Question family and relatives for current location.
- Ask neighbors for current information.
- Interview former classmates.
- Enlist the aid of a high school class reunion committee.
- Check with former employers.
- Examine records of college alumni associations.
- Inquire at churches in the area.
- Examine driver's license registration records.
- Utilize military locator services.
- Hire a professional tracking company (such as Equifax or Tracers Company of America).

Finally, respondent error is always a problem in situations that depend on self-administered measurement instruments. For example, panelists asked to keep a diary over a certain period may not fill it out until immediately before it is due. And, of course, panel studies require much more time and can be quite expensive.

Examples of Panel Studies. Perhaps the most famous example of the panel technique in mass media research is the collection of national television audience data by the A. C. Nielsen Company. Nielsen's sample consists of approximately 5,000 households located across the United States. These homes are equipped with people meters—devices that record when the television set is turned on, which channel is tuned in, and who is watching. (See Chapter 14 for more information about people meters.) Other panels are maintained by such commercial research organizations as Market Facts, Inc., National Family Opinion, Inc., and the Home Testing Institute.

A study by Bolton and Drew (1991) illustrated the advantage in using a panel study to understand the process of change in a specific area. In their longitudinal study of the impact of changes in telephone service, they found that changes in the evaluation of individual components of telephone service (for example, absence of static, quality of voice) were influenced quickly by a service change but that changes in the general evaluations of telephone service were noticeable only after 6 months. Outside the marketing area, a well-publicized panel study was carried out with the support of the National Broadcasting Company (Milavsky et al., 1982). The overall purpose of this study was to isolate any possible causal influence on aggression among young people from viewing violence on television. Three panel studies were conducted, with the most ambitious involving boys aged 7–12. In brief, the methodology in the study involved collecting data on aggression, TV viewing, and a host of sociological variables from children in Minneapolis, Minnesota, and Fort Worth, Texas, on six occasions. About 1,200 boys participated in the study. The time lags between each wave of data collection were deliberately varied so that the effects of TV viewing could be analyzed over different durations. Thus, there was a 5-month lag between Waves 1 and 2, a 4-month lag between Waves 2 and 3, and a 3-month lag between Waves 3 and 4. The lag between Waves 1 and 6 constituted the longest elapsed time (3 years). As is the case in all panel studies, the NBC study suffered from attrition. The particular design, however, magnified the effects of attrition. When respondents left the sixth grade, they frequently left the panel. Consequently, only a small number of children (58 of the 1,200 who participated) were available for observing and analyzing the long-term effects of viewing violence on TV.

The participant losses reported by the NBC team illustrate the impact of year-to-year attrition on a sample of this age group. About 7% of the sample was lost in the first year, approximately 37% in the first 2 years, and 63% over all 3 years.

The study also illustrates how a panel design influences the statistical analysis. The most powerful statistical test would have incorporated data from all six waves and simultaneously examined all the possible causal relationships. This was impossible, however, because due to the initial study design and subsequent attrition, the sample size fell below minimum standards. Instead, the investigators worked with each of the 15 possible wave pairs in the sample. The main statistical tests used the analytical technique of partial regression coefficients to remove the impact of earlier aggression levels. In effect, the researchers sought to determine whether TV viewing at an earlier time added to the predictability of aggression at a later time, once the aggression levels present before the test began had been statistically discounted. After looking at all the resulting coefficients for all the possible wave pairs, the investigators concluded that there was no consistent statistically significant relationship between watching violent TV programs and later acts of aggression. Nonetheless, they did find a large number of small but consistently positive coefficients that suggested the possibility of a weak relationship that might not have been detected by conventional statistical methods. Upon further analysis, however, the researchers concluded that these associations were due to chance. This study has value for anyone interested in longitudinal research. Many of the problems encountered in panel studies and the compromises involved in doing a 3-year study are discussed in great detail.

The panel technique continues to be popular for studying the impact of TV violence. Singer, Singer, Desmond, Hirsch, and Nicol (1988) used this technique to examine the effects of family communication patterns, parental mediation, and TV viewing on children's perceptions of the world and their aggressive behavior. Ninety-one first- and second-graders were interviewed during the first phase of the study. One year later, 66 of the original sample were reinterviewed. Concerned about the effects of attrition, the researchers compared their final sample with the original on a wide range of demographic variables and found that attrition did not cause any significant differences between the two groups. Singer and colleagues found that family communication patterns during the first phase were strong predictors of children's cognitive scores but were only weakly related to emotional and behavioral variables. The influence of TV viewing on aggression was greatest among heavy viewers who were least exposed to parental mediation.

Potter (1992) used a three-wave panel study across 5 years to examine how adolescents' perceptions of television's reality changed over time. The design was such that no respondent was present in all three waves. Of the 287 original respondents in Wave 1, 196 were tested again in Wave 2. Of the 443 original respondents in Wave 2, 115 were also measured in Wave 3. Valkenburg and Van Der Voort (1995) conducted a 1-year panel study of Dutch children to investigate the influence of television on children's daydreaming. They found that children's daydreaming styles in Year 1 did not influence TV viewing behavior in Year 2 but that TV viewing in Year 1 did influence daydreaming in Year 2. Koolstra and Van Der Voort (1996) collected panel data from elementary school children at three successive 1-year intervals to assess the impact of TV on children's leisure-time reading. About 20% of the sample was lost to attrition.

▪ Special Panel Designs

Panel data can be expensive to obtain. Moreover, analysis cannot begin until at least two waves of data are available. For many panel studies, this may take years. Researchers who have limited time and resources might consider one of the alternatives discussed next.

Schulsinger, Mednick, and Knop (1981) outlined a research design called a **retrospective panel.** In this method, the respondent is asked to recall facts or attitudes about education, occupations, events, situations, and so on, from the past. These recalled factors are then compared with a later measure of the same variable, thus producing an instant longitudinal design. Belson (1978) used a variation of this design in his study of the effects of exposure to violent TV shows on the aggressive behavior of teenage boys when he asked his respondents to recall when they first started watching violent TV programs.

There are several problems with this technique. Many people have faulty memories; some deliberately misrepresent the past; and others try to give a socially desirable response. Only a few research studies have examined the extent to which retrospective panel data might be misleading. Powers, Goudy, and Keith (1978) reanalyzed data from a 1964 study of adult men. In 1974 all the original respondents who could be located were reinterviewed and asked about their answers to the 1964 survey. In most instances, the recall responses presented respondents in a more favorable light than did their original answers. Interestingly, using the 1974 recall data produced almost the same pattern of correlations as using the 1964 data, suggesting that recall data might be used, albeit with caution, in correlational studies. In 1974 Norlen (1977) reinterviewed about 4,700 persons originally questioned in 1968. Of those reinterviewed, 464 had originally reported that they had written a letter to the editor of a newspaper or magazine, but in 1974 about a third of this group denied ever having written to a newspaper or magazine. Auriat (1993) found that respondents were more likely to recall correctly the month of a major life event (in this case, a family move) than they were the year. In addition, women were slightly better than men at remembering exact dates. Clearly, the savings in time and money accrued by using retrospective data must be weighed against possible losses in accuracy.

A **follow-back panel** selects a cross-sectional sample in the present and uses archival data from an earlier point in time to create the longitudinal dimension of the study. The advantages of such a technique are clear: Changes that occurred over a great many years can be analyzed in a short time period. This design is also useful in studying dwindling populations, because the researcher can assemble a sample from baseline investigations conducted earlier, probably at great expense. The disadvantages are also obvious. The follow-back panel depends on archival data, and archives do not contain many variables that interest mass media researchers. In addition, the resulting sample in a follow-back design may not represent all possible entities. For example, a follow-back study of the managerial practices of small radio stations will not represent stations that went out of business and no longer exist.

A **catch-up panel** involves selecting a cross-sectional study done in the past and locating all possible units of analysis for observation in the present. The catch-up design is particularly attractive if the researcher has a rich source of baseline data in the archive. Of course, this is usually not the case because most data sources lack enough identifying information to allow the investigator to track down the respondents. When the appropriate data exist, however, the catch-up study can be highly useful. In effect, Lefkowitz and colleagues (1972) used a catch-up technique in their study of TV watching and child aggression. After a lapse of 10 years, the investigators tracked down 735 of 875 youths who had participated in a survey of mental health factors when they were in the third grade. These individuals were recontacted and asked questions similar to those they had answered as young children. Huesmann and his colleagues (Huesmann, 1986) caught up with this panel one more time when the panel members were 30 years old. After reinterviewing 409 subjects from the original pool of 875, the authors concluded that this 22-year panel study demonstrated that viewing TV violence can have harmful lifelong consequences.

Another problem associated with the catch-up panel involves the comparability of measures. If the earlier study was not constructed to be part of a longitudinal design, the original measurement instruments have to be modified. For example, a study of 10-year-olds might have used teacher ratings to measure aggressiveness; however, such a measure is not appropriate with 20-year-olds.

Finally, the researcher in the catch-up situation is confined to the variables measured in the original study. In the intervening time, new variables might have been identified as important, but if those variables were not measured during the original survey, they are unavailable to the researcher. Figure 8.1 shows the similarities and differences among retrospective, follow-back, and catch-up panel designs.

▪ Analyzing Causation in Panel Data

The panel design provides an opportunity for the researcher to make statements about the causal ordering among different variables. Three conditions are necessary for determining cause and effect. The first is time order. Causation is present if and only if the cause precedes the effect. Second, causation can occur only if some tendency for change in A results in change in B. In other words, there is an association between the two variables. Third, before effects are attributed to causes, all other alternative causes must be ruled out. Cross-sectional surveys, for which the data are collected at a single point in time, can meet only two of these three criteria. A cross-sectional survey allows the researcher to say that Variables A and B are associated. A skillfully constructed questionnaire and statistical controls such as partial correlation can help the researcher rule out alternative explanations. Nonetheless, only if the time order between A and B is evident can statements of cause be inferred. For example, a person's education is typically acquired before his or her occupational status. Thus, the statement that education is a cause of occupational status (all other things being equal) can be inferred. If there is no distinguishable temporal sequence in the data (as is the case with viewing violence on TV and aggressive behavior), causal statements are conjectural. In a panel study, the variables are measured across time, which makes causal inferences more defensible.

Figure 8.1 *Comparison of Retrospective, Follow-back, and Catch-up Designs*

Retrospective panel

Step 1: Select current sample.
Step 2: Interview sample about past recollections concerning topic of interest.
Step 3: Collect current data on topic of interest.
Step 4: Compare data.

Follow-back panel

Step 1: Select current sample.
Step 2: Collect current data on topic of interest.
Step 3: Locate archival data on sample regarding topic of interest.
Step 4: Compare data.

Catch-up panel

Step 1: Locate archival data on topic of interest.
Step 2: Select current sample by locating as many respondents as possible for whom data exist in the archive.
Step 3: Collect current data on topic of interest.
Step 4: Compare data.

However, there are two important points: On the one hand, the interval between measurement periods must be long enough to allow the cause to produce an effect. For example, if it takes a full year for exposure to TV violence to have an effect on viewers' aggressive behavior, then a panel study with only 6 months between measurement periods will not discover any effect. On the other hand, if a cause produces an effect that does not remain stable over the long run, an overly long interval between measurement waves will fail to discover an effect. Continuing the example, let us suppose that exposure to TV violence produces an effect that appears 3 months after exposure but quickly disappears. A panel survey with 6 months between waves will totally miss observing this effect. The hard part, of course, is determining the proper time intervals. Most researchers rely on past research and appropriate theories for some guidelines.

Many statistical techniques are available for determining a causal sequence in panel data. A detailed listing and explanation of the computations involved are beyond the scope of this book. Nonetheless, some of the following references will be helpful to readers who desire more detailed information. Menard (1991) discusses common methods for analyzing panel data measured at the interval level. Similarly, Toon (2000) gives computational methods for analyzing panel data, including the increasingly popular log-linear technique. Asher (1983) provides a detailed discussion of path analysis. Trumbo (1995) describes statistical methods for analyzing panel data including time series analysis and Granger verification and illustrates their use in a longitudinal study of agenda setting.

Finally, the most mathematically sophisticated technique, linear structural equations, or LISREL, is discussed in Joreskog (1973), Long (1976), and Hayduk (1996). Since it appears that the LISREL method has much to recommend it (it was used in the NBC panel study discussed previously), researchers who intend to do panel studies should be familiar with its assumptions and techniques.

Combining Qualitative and Quantitative Data in Longitudinal Research

Although the discussion up until now has examined longitudinal research from the traditional quantitative survey perspective, it is possible to combine quantitative and qualitative data in a study that extends over time. One possible technique involves selecting a smaller sample of people at each measurement interval for more intensive study. These people might participate in focus groups or in-depth interviews.

Using both qualitative and quantitative techniques provides certain advantages. First, the qualitative data can aid in the interpretation of the quantitative data and provide insights that might have been missed. For example, qualitative data used in conjunction with a panel survey looking at media exposure and vote choice might reveal why certain changes occurred among sample respondents. Additionally, qualitative data might suggest new hypotheses that could be examined in subsequent waves of data collection. To continue with the above example, focus group data could suggest that exposure to negative advertising might play a key role in determining vote choice. This relationship could be examined quantitatively the next time the panel survey is conducted. Using both approaches, however, requires more effort on the part of the researcher and increases the time spent in analyzing and interpreting the data.

McMillan (2001) combined qualitative and quantitative data in her longitudinal study of health-related websites. Data from an email survey found that sites with more financial backing were more likely to survey and that the technological sophistication of the site had no relation to its long-term viability. Qualitative data revealed that site managers considered promotion and marketing as keys to their survival. Wenger (1999) provides another example, showing the advantages of combining these two techniques.

Longitudinal Research on the Internet

The Internet has made it possible to collect longitudinal data online. An Internet survey panel is made up of individuals who have been prerecruited to participate in a number of surveys over time. There are obvious advantages to this arrangement. A large number of individuals can be recruited to serve as potential panel members. This makes it easier for researchers to target and collect data from low-incidence groups (e.g., HDTV owners). Data collection over the Internet is rapid, and researchers can access previously collected demographic information from their respondents.

Internet panels also have disadvantages. As with other online data-gathering techniques, Internet panels may not be representative of the entire population. Not every household has Internet access and not everyone is skilled at completing online surveys. Second, Internet panels may suffer from the "churn" problem, a situation in which respondents sign up for the panel and then get bored or lose interest and drop out. As a result, the potential mortality rates for longitudinal samples become a concern. Third, it's possible that web panel members become "professional respondents" whose answers

> **AN INSIDE LOOK**
> **Professional Respondents**
>
> Most researchers will eventually hear a complaint about the use of professional respondents, or people who are involved in many research projects and are therefore considered "atypical." While this phenomenon may exist, it is not as significant as many critics believe. For example, respondents involved in many auditorium music tests do not differ significantly in their song ratings from respondents who have participated only once.

are influenced by their participation in panel studies (Dennis, 2001). For example, a panel member who fills out several online questionnaires over a period of months about his or her online shopping habits might be encouraged to do even more online shopping.

Many private research companies offer Internet panel research to their clients. *Esearch.com,* for example, has a pool of more than 200,000 respondents that increases by about 5,000 members a month. Knowledge Networks Inc. equipped 40,000 randomly selected U.S. households with Microsoft WebTVs for answering ongoing questions via the Internet. Harris Interactive has the largest pool of potential online panelists. As of 2001, the company reported that their world-wide online research panel had more than 7 million members.

▪ Longitudinal Design in Experiments

Although the preceding discussion was concerned with survey research, experimental research has a longitudinal dimension that should not be overlooked. Many research designs are based on a single exposure to a message, with the dependent variable measured almost immediately afterward. This procedure might be appropriate in many circumstances, but a longitudinal treatment design may be necessary to measure subtle, cumulative media effects. Furthermore, delayed assessment is essential to determine the duration of the impact of certain media effects. (For example, how long does it take a persuasive effect to disappear?)

Bryant, Carveth, and Brown (1981) illustrated the importance of the longitudinal design to the experimental approach. In investigating TV viewing and anxiety, they divided their subjects into groups and assigned to each a menu of TV shows they could watch. Over a 6-week period, one group was assigned a light viewing schedule, and a second was directed to watch a large number of shows that depicted a clear triumph of justice. A third group was assigned to view several shows in which justice did not triumph. One of the dependent variables was also measured over time. The investigators obtained voluntary viewing data by having students fill out diaries for another 3 weeks. The results of this study indicated that the cumulative exposure to TV shows in which justice does not prevail seems to make some viewers more anxious, thus offering some support to Gerbner's cultivation hypothesis.

A study by Wicks (1992) exposed 46 subjects to a TV newscast or newspaper account of several stories. Subjects were then told to think about the stories for 2 days. Upon retesting, the subjects had higher recall scores than they had immediately after viewing or reading, thus demonstrating the "hypernesia" effect. More recently, Rossler and Brosius (2001) in their study of the cultivation phenomenon exposed their experimental subjects to screenings of TV talk shows for 5 consecutive days and measured the impact of this exposure a week later. Their data showed that a limited cultivation effect did occur. Clearly, the longitudinal design can be of great value in experimental research.

▪▪▪ Summary

Longitudinal research involves the collection of data at different points in time. The three types of longitudinal study are trend, cohort, and panel. A trend study asks the same questions of different groups of people at different points in time. A cohort study measures some characteristic of a sample whose members share some significant life event (usually the same age range) at two or more points in time. In a panel study, the same respondents are measured at least twice. One advantage of the panel design is that it allows the researcher to make statements about the causal ordering of the study variables, and several different statistical methods are available for this task.

Key Terms

Age effect	Follow-back panel
Catch-up panel	Longitudinal research
Cohort analysis	Panel study
Cohort effect	Period effect
Cross-sectional research	Retrospective panel
Cross-lagged correlation	Trend studies

Using the Internet

There are many archives that are valuable resources for media researchers interested in longitudinal data. Here are a few examples:

1. National Opinion Research Center—General Social Survey. Among other things, this database contains data on newspaper readership, radio listening and TV viewing from 1972 to the late 1990s. *www.icpsr.umich.edu/GSS/index*
2. The Odum Institute for Research in the Social Sciences. This database at the University of North Carolina requires a subscription for access to all of its contents but some data are open to all. It contains a searchable database of public opinion poll data from 1970 to the present. *www.irss.unc.edu*
3. The Gallup Organization. The web site for this well-known polling organization contains data covering the period 1985–2000 on mass media use, media credibility, bias, and source of most news. *www.gallup.com*
4. The Roper Center. This web site requires a membership fee (but many universities are members) to access data on public opinion polls that date back to the 1930s. *www.ropercenter.uconn.edu*
5. The Pew Center. The Pew Center specializes in studies that look at the public's attitudes toward the news media. A data archive contains polling results from 1997 to the present. *www.people-press.org*

For additional information on these and related topics, see

http://www.wimmerdominick.com

Questions and Problems for Further Investigation

1. Search recent issues of scholarly journals for examples of longitudinal studies. Which of the three designs discussed in this chapter is used? Try to find additional longitudinal studies done by commercial research firms. What design is used most often?
2. What mass media variables are best studied using the cohort method?
3. What are some possible measures of media or audience characteristics that might be regularly made and stored in a data archive for secondary trend analysis?
4. How might a panel study make use of laboratory techniques?

References and Suggested Readings

Asher, H. (1983). *Causal modeling* (2nd ed.). Beverly Hills, CA: Sage Publications.

Auriat, N. (1993). A comparison of event dating accuracy between the wife, the husband, and the couple, and the Belgian population register. *Public Opinion Quarterly,* 57(2), 165–190.

Belson, W. (1978). *Television violence and the adolescent boy.* Hampshire, England: Saxon House.

Bolton, R. N., & Drew, J. H. (1991, January). A longitudinal analysis of the impact of service changes on customer attitudes. *Journal of Marketing,* 55, 1–9.

Bryant, J., Carveth, R., & Brown, D. (1981). Television viewing and anxiety. *Journal of Communication,* 31(1), 106–119.

Call, V., Otto, L., & Spenner, K. (1982). *Tracking respondents.* Lexington, MA: Lexington Books.

Carman, J. (1974). Consumer panels. In R. Ferber (Ed.), *Handbook of marketing* research. New York: McGraw-Hill.

Dennis, J. M. (2001). Are internet panels creating professional respondents? *Marketing Research,* 13 (2), 34–38.

Feinberg, S. E., & Mason, W. M. (1980). Identification and estimation of age-period-cohort models in the analysis of archival data. In K. F. Schuessler (Ed.), *Sociological methodology.* San Francisco: Jossey-Bass.

Gerbner, G., Gross, L., Signorielli, N., Morgan, M., & Jackson-Beeck, M. (1979). The demonstration of power: Violence profile no. 10. *Journal of Communication,* 29(3), 177–196.

Glenn, N. (1977). *Cohort analysis.* Beverly Hills, CA: Sage Publications.

Glenn, N. (1994). Television watching, newspaper reading and cohort differences in verbal ability. *Sociology of Education,* 67(2), 216–230.

Hayduk, L. A. (1996). *LISREL: Issues, debates, strategies.* Baltimore: Johns Hopkins University Press.

Huesmann, L. R. (1986). Psychological processes promoting the relation between exposure to media violence and aggressive behavior by the viewer. *Journal of Social Issues,* 42(3), 125–139.

Huesmann, L. R., & Eron, L. D. (1986). *Television and the aggressive child.* Hillsdale, NJ: Lawrence Erlbaum.

Hyman, H. H. (1987). *Secondary analysis of sample.* Middletown, NY: Wesleyan University Press.

Jennings, M. K. (1996). Political knowledge over time and across generations. *Public Opinion Quarterly,* 60(2), 228–252.

Joreskog, K. (1973). A general method for estimating a linear structural equation system. In A. Goldberger & O. Duncan (Eds.), *Structural equations models in the social sciences.* New York: Seminar Press.

Katz, E., & Lazarsfeld, P. F. (1955). *Personal influence.* New York: Free Press.

Kincaid, D. L. (2000). Mass media, ideation and behavior. *Communication Research,* 27(6), 723–764.

Koolstra, C. M., & Van Der Voort, T. H. (1996). Longitudinal effects of television on children's leisure-time reading. *Human Communication Research,* 23(1), 4–35.

Lazarsfeld, P., Berelson, B., & Gaudet, H. (1944). *The people's choice.* New York: Columbia University Press.

Lefkowitz, M., Eron, L. D., Walder, L. O., & Huesmann, L. R. (1972). Television violence and child aggression. In E. Rubinstein, G. Comstock & J. Murray (Eds.), *Television and adolescent aggressiveness.* Washington, DC: U.S. Government Printing Office.

Lindstrom, P. B. (1997). The Internet: Nielsen's longitudinal research on behavior changes in use of this counterintuitive medium. *Journal of Media Economics,* 10(2), 35–40.

Long, J. (1976). Estimation and hypothesis testing in linear models containing measurement error. *Sociological Methods and Research,* 5, 157–206.

Lowery, S., & DeFleur, M. (1995). *Milestones in mass communication research* (3rd ed.). White Plains, NY: Longman.

Lubbers, M., Scheepers, P., & Vergeer, M. (2000). Exposure to newspapers and attitudes toward ethnic minorities. *Howard Journal of Communication,* 11(2), 127–144.

Magnusson, D., Bergman, L., Rudinger, G., & Torestad, B. (1991). *Problems and methods in longitudinal research.* Cambridge: Cambridge University Press.

Markus, G. (1979). *Analyzing panel data.* Beverly Hills, CA: Sage Publications.

Mason, K., Mason, W., Winsborough, H., & Poole, W. K. (1973, April). Some methodological issues in cohort analysis of archival data. *American Sociological Review,* pp. 242–258.

Mayer, W. (1993). Trends in media usage. *Public Opinion Quarterly,* 57(4), 593–610.

McMillan, S. J. (2001). Survival of the fittest online: A longitudinal study of health-related websites. *Journal of Computer Mediated Communication,* 6(3), *www.ascusc.org/jcmc/vol6/issue3/mcmillan.html*

Menard, S. (1991). *Longitudinal research.* Newbury Park, CA: Sage Publications.

Milavsky, J., Kessler, R. C., Stipp, H. H., & Rubens, W. S. (1982). *Television and aggression.* New York: Academic Press.

Newcomb, T. (1943). *Personality and social change.* New York: Dryden.

Norlen, V. (1977). Response errors in the answers to retrospective questions. *Statistik Tidskrift,* 4, 331–341.

Palmore, E. (1978). When can age, period and cohort effects be separated? *Social Forces,* 57, 282–295.

Pearl, D., Bouthilet, L., & Lazar, J. (1982). *Television and behavior: Ten years of scientific progress and implications for the eighties*. Washington, DC: U.S. Government Printing Office.

Peiser, W. (2000a). Cohort replacement and the downward trend in newspaper readership. *Newspaper Research Journal,* 21(2), 11–23.

Peiser, W. (2000b). Cohort trends in media use in the United States. *Mass Communication & Society,* 3(2/3), 185–203.

Peterson, T. (1980). *The mass media election*. New York: Praeger.

Potter, W. J. (1992). How do adolescents' perceptions of television reality change over time? *Journalism Quarterly,* 69(2), 392–405.

Powers, E., Goudy, W., & Keith, P. (1978). Congruence between panel and recall data in longitudinal research. *Public Opinion Quarterly,* 42(3), 380–389.

Rentz, J., Reynolds, F., & Stout, R. (1983, February). Analyzing changing consumption patterns with cohort analysis. *Journal of Marketing Research,* 20, 12–20.

Robinson, J. P., & Levy, M. R. (1996). News media use and an informed public. *Journal of Communication,* 46(2), 129–135.

Rossler, P., & Brosius, H. B. (2001). Do talk shows cultivate adolescents' views of the world? A prolonged-exposure experiment. *Journal of Communication,* 51(1), 143–163.

Schulsinger, F., Mednick, S., & Knop, J. (1981). *Longitudinal research*. Boston: Nijhoff Publishing.

Singer, J. L., Singer, D. G., Desmond, R., Hirsch, B., & Nicol, A. (1988). Family mediation and children's cognition, aggression and comprehension of television. *Journal of Applied Developmental Psychology,* 9(3), 329–347.

Sullivan, C. M., Rumptz, M. H., Campbell, R., Eby, K. K., & Davidson, W. S. (1996). Retaining participants in longitudinal community research. *Journal of Applied Behavioral Science,* 32(3), 262–276.

Toon, T. W. (2000). *A primer in longitudinal data analysis*. London: Sage Publications.

Trumbo, C. (1995). Longitudinal modeling of public issues. *Journalism and Mass Communication Monographs,* 152 (August 1995), 1–53.

Valkenburg, P., & Van Der Voort, T. (1995). The influence of television on children's daydreaming styles. *Communication Research,* 22(3), 267–287.

Wenger, G. C. (1999). Advantages gained by combining qualitative and quantitative data in a longitudinal study. *Journal of Aging Studies,* 13(4), 369–377.

Wicks, R. (1992). Improvement over time in recall of media information. *Journal of Broadcasting and Electronic Media,* 36(3), 287–302.

Wilson, T. (1996). Cohort and prejudice. *Public Opinion Quarterly,* 60(2), 253–274.

Wimmer, R. D. (2001). *An analysis of panel study participation methods: Replication of 1995 results*. Denver: Wimmer Research.

Xiaoming, H. (1994). Television viewing among American adults in the 1990s. *Journal of Broadcasting and Electronic Media,* 38(3), 353–360.

Chapter 9

Experimental Research

Although the experimental method is the oldest approach in mass media research and continues to provide a wealth of information for researchers and critics of the media, experimental research is used infrequently in the mass media. A 1994 survey by Cooper, Potter, and Dupagne (1994) found that from 1965 to 1989 only 15% of published quantitative studies used the experimental method. In contrast, nearly 50% relied on surveys.

Due to their infrequent use, we examine only the more basic techniques in this chapter, with discussions of the controlled laboratory experiment, quasi-experimental designs, and field experiments. For more information about advanced experimental procedures, you should consult Montgomery (1997), Christensen (1997), and the Internet.

▪ Advantages and Disadvantages of Laboratory Experiments

There are several reasons to use the experimental method:

1. *Evidence of causality.* Experiments help establish cause and effect. Although some researchers argue whether we can ever really *prove* a cause-and-effect link between two variables, the experiment is undoubtedly the best social science research method for establishing causality. The researcher controls the time order of the presentation of two variables and thus makes sure that the cause actually precedes the effect. In addition, the experimental method allows the researcher to control other possible causes of the variable under investigation.

2. *Control.* As suggested, control is an advantage of the experimental method. Researchers have control over the environment, the variables, and the subjects. Laboratory research allows researchers to isolate a testing situation from the competing influences of normal activity. Researchers are free to structure the experimental environment in almost any way. Lighting and temperature levels, proximity of subjects to measuring instruments, soundproofing, and nearly every other aspect of the experimental situation can be arranged and altered. Environmental control, however, has its drawbacks, and the artificially created environment of the laboratory is one of the main disadvantages of the technique.

Laboratory studies also allow researchers to control the numbers and types of independent and dependent variables selected and the way these variables are manipulated. Variable control strengthens internal validity and helps eliminate confounding influences. Gilbert and Schleuder (1990), for example, were able to control almost every detail of their laboratory analysis of the effects of color and complexity in still photographs.

The experimental approach also allows researchers to control subjects, including control over the selection process, assignment to the control or the experimental group, and exposure to experimental treatment. Limits can be placed on the number of subjects who participate in a study, and specific types of subjects can be selected for exposure in varying degrees to the independent variable. For example, researchers may select subjects according to which medium they use for news information and vary each subject's exposure to commercials of different types to determine which is the most effective.

AN INSIDE LOOK

Causality

One fallacy of research is that all research proves something. Research rarely proves anything; rather, it provides an indication of something, such as an indication of a relationship between watching TV and performance in school. Review the characteristics of the scientific method in Chapter 1 to support the idea that scientific research rarely proves anything 100%.

3. *Cost.* In relative terms, the cost of an experiment can be low when compared to other research methods. For example, an advertising researcher can examine the impact of two different ad designs using an experimental design with as few as 40 to 50 subjects. A comparable test done in the field would be far more costly.

4. *Replication.* Finally, the experimental method permits replication. Typically the conditions of the study are clearly spelled out in the description of an experiment, which makes it easier for others to replicate. In fact, classic experiments are often repeated, sometimes under slightly different conditions, to ensure that the original results were not unique in some way.

The experimental technique, however, is not perfect. It has three major disadvantages.

1. *Artificiality.* Perhaps the biggest problem with using this technique is the artificial nature of the experimental environment. The behavior under investigation must be placed in circumstances that afford proper control. Unfortunately, much behavior of interest to mass media researchers is altered when studied out of its natural environment. Critics claim that the sterile and unnatural conditions created in the laboratory produce results that have little direct application to real-world settings, where subjects are continually exposed to competing stimuli. Miller (1991) notes that critics of the laboratory method often resort to ambiguous and disjunctive arguments about the artificiality of the procedure; he suggests that contrasting the "real" world with the "unreal" world may, in fact, be merely a problem in semantics. The main point, he claims, is that both the laboratory method and the field method investigate communication behavior, and if viewed in this way, it is meaningless to speak of behavior as "real" or "unreal": All behavior is real.

Miller also notes that it is unsatisfactory and unscientific to dodge the problem of artificiality in laboratory procedures by including a disclaimer in a study indicating that the findings are applicable only to a particular audience, to the environmental conditions of the analysis, and to the period during which the study was conducted. Since external validity is a major goal of scientific research, a disclaimer of this nature is counterproductive. If researchers are not willing to expand their interests beyond the scope of a single analysis, such studies have only heuristic value; they make little or no contribution to the advancement of knowledge in mass media.

Many researchers have conducted field experiments in an attempt to overcome the artificiality of the laboratory. Although field experiments take place in natural surroundings, they are subject to problems with control.

2. *Researcher (experimenter) bias.* Experiments can be influenced by experimenter bias (see Chapter 1). Rosenthal and Jacobson (1966) discovered that researchers who were told what findings to expect had results more

in line with the research hypothesis than researchers who were not told what to expect. To counteract this problem, some researchers use the **double-blind technique,** in which neither subjects nor researchers know whether a given subject belongs to the control group or to the experimental group.

3. *Limited scope.* Finally, some research questions simply don't lend themselves to the experimental approach. Many of the more interesting research topics in mass communication are concerned with the collective behavior of perhaps millions of people. Experiments on this scale are much too massive to conduct. Consider, for example, the **cultivation effect** (discussed in more detail in Chapter 17), which involves the long-term impact of television on society. Any experimental design that would "test" the cultivation effect would be too time-consuming, expensive, and ethically questionable to take place. Although it is possible to conduct some smaller-scale experiments on this topic with small groups of subjects, it is unclear how these experiments relate to the larger-scale phenomenon.

▪ Conducting Experimental Research

The experimental method involves both manipulation and observation. In the simplest form of an experiment, researchers manipulate the independent variable and then observe the responses of subjects on the dependent variable. Although every experiment is different, most researchers agree that the following eight steps should be followed when conducting an experiment:

1. *Select the setting.* Many experiments are best conducted in a laboratory or in another environment under the direct control of the researcher. Others are best conducted in more natural surroundings where the researcher has little, if any, control over the experimental situation. This latter type of experiment is discussed in more detail later in this chapter.

2. *Select the experimental design.* The appropriate design depends upon the nature of the hypothesis or the research question, types of variables to be manipulated or measured, availability of subjects, and amount of resources available.

3. *Operationalize the variables.* In the experimental approach, independent variable(s) are usually operationalized in terms of the manipulation done to create them. Dependent variables are operationalized by constructing scales or rules for categorizing observations of behavior.

4. *Decide how to manipulate the independent variable.* To manipulate the independent variable (or variables), a set of specific instructions, events, or stimuli are developed for presentation to the experimental subjects. There are two types of manipulations: straightforward and staged.

In **straightforward manipulation,** written materials, verbal instructions, or other stimuli are presented to the subjects. For example, Baran, Mok, Land, and Kang (1989) used a straightforward manipulation of their independent variable—product positioning. One group of subjects was presented with a "generic" shopping list that contained items such as ice cream, frozen dinner, mustard, and coffee. Another group saw the "practical" list with items such as *Borden's* ice cream, *Swanson's* frozen dinner, *French's* mustard, and *Maxwell House* coffee. A third group was presented with the "upscale" list consisting of *Lean Cuisine* frozen dinner, *Grey Poupon* mustard, *General Foods International Coffees,* and similar items. Each group was then asked to make judgments about the character of the person to whom the list belonged. As predicted by the researchers, the shopping lists had an impact on the way subjects evaluated the general goodness and responsibility of the lists' authors. Leshner, Reeves, and

Nass (1998) manipulated the source of a television news story by attributing it to either a general news source (one of the four broadcast TV networks) or a specialized channel (CNN or a regional news network). News that appeared on the specialized channels was evaluated more positively than the same news on a general channel.

In a **staged manipulation,** researchers construct events and circumstances that enable them to manipulate the independent variable. Staged manipulations can be relatively simple or rather elaborate. They frequently involve the use of a confederate, a person who pretends to be a subject but who is actually part of the manipulation.

For example, staged manipulations and confederates have been used in experiments that examine the impact of media portrayals of antisocial behavior. In their study of rock music videos, Hansen and Hansen (1990) showed half of their sample three music videos that depicted antisocial behavior; the other half of the sample viewed three rock videos depicting a more "neutral" type of behavior. The subjects then watched a videotaped job interview of a person applying for a position with the campus TV station's rock video program. One version of this tape showed the applicant (who was actually a confederate of the researchers) making an obscene gesture while the interviewer's back was turned. Subjects who had previously viewed the rock videos depicting "neutral" behaviors evaluated the applicant's behavior more negatively than did the subjects who saw the videos depicting antisocial behaviors.

Hoyt (1977) investigated the effects of television coverage on courtroom behavior. In a staged manipulation of three groups of subjects, he separately questioned the groups about a film they had just viewed. One group answered questions in the presence of a TV camera at the front of the room; a second group answered questions with the camera concealed behind a full-length mirror; and a third group answered questions without being filmed. Hoyt found no differences in subjects' verbal behaviors across the three conditions.

No matter what manipulation technique is used, a general principle for the researcher to follow is to construct or choose a manipulation that is as strong as possible to maximize potential differences between the experimental groups. If, for example, a researcher is trying to assess the effects of different degrees of newspaper credibility on audience perceptions of the accuracy of a story, one condition might attribute the story to the *New York Times* and another might attribute it to the *National Enquirer* or the *National Star.* A strong manipulation maximizes the chances that the independent variable has an effect.

5. *Select and assign subjects to experimental conditions.* Recall from Chapter 1 that, to ensure external validity, experimental subjects should be selected randomly from the population under investigation. The various random sampling techniques discussed in Chapter 4 are also appropriate for selecting subjects for experimental studies.

6. *Conduct a pilot study.* A pilot study with a small number of subjects will reveal problems and allow the researcher to make a manipulation check—a test to see whether the manipulation of the independent variable actually has the intended effect. For example, suppose a researcher wants to assess the effect of the viewer's involvement in a TV show on how well the viewer remembers the ads in the show. The researcher constructs TV shows labeled "high involvement" (a cliff-hanger with lots of suspense), "medium involvement" (a family drama), and "low involvement" (a Senate committee hearing taped from *C-SPAN*). To check whether these programs actually differ in involvement, the researcher must measure the degree to which subjects were actually involved with the programs under each of the conditions. Such a check might include a self-report, an observational report (such as counting the number of

AN INSIDE LOOK
Confounding Variables

Whenever you conduct a research study and are ready to interpret the results, go through every step of the research to determine what could have produced the results. Don't immediately accept that your data are correct.

times a subject looked away from the screen), or even a physiological measure. If the check shows that the manipulation was not effective, the researcher can change the manipulation before the main experiment is conducted. (It is also a good idea to include a manipulation check in the main experiment itself.)

7. *Administer the experiment.* After the bugs are out and the manipulation is checked, the main phase of data collection begins. Experimental manipulations can be carried out on either individuals or groups. The dependent variable is measured, and the subjects are debriefed. During debriefing, the researcher explains the purpose and the implications of the research. If the manipulation required deception, the researcher must explain why and how the deception was used. (See Chapter 3 for more about deception and other ethical problems of research.)

8. *Analyze and interpret the results.* The subjects' scores on the dependent variable(s) are tabulated, and the data are subjected to statistical analysis. Many statistics discussed in Chapters 10 and 12 are used to analyze the results of experiments. Finally, the researcher must decide what the results mean—the most difficult task in many experiments.

▪ Control of Confounding Variables

As discussed in previous chapters, researchers must ensure the internal validity of their research by controlling for the effects of **confounding variables** (*extraneous variables*) that might contaminate their findings. These variables can be controlled through the environment, experimental manipulations, experimental design, or assignment of subjects; all of these items are under the researcher's direct supervision. This section concentrates on techniques used to ensure that the various groups in an experiment are comparable before the experimental treatment is administered. This is an important consideration because it helps to rule out all of the possible alternative explanations based on the natural differences among people.

Perhaps an example will illustrate this point. Suppose a researcher wants to determine whether different versions of a TV commercial's musical soundtrack have different impacts on what is remembered from that ad. The researcher uses a media research class as the sample and assigns an ad with a rap soundtrack to the students in the first three rows. Students in the last three rows view the same ad but hear a heavy metal soundtrack. Both groups are then given a recall test, and the results show that the group that heard the rap soundtrack remembered more information from the ad. How confident should the researcher be of this conclusion? Not too confident: It is entirely possible that the people who sat in the first three rows of the class are different from those who sat in the back. The "fronters" might have chosen the front seats because they are more intelligent, more attentive, and more alert than the "backers," who might have sat in the rear of the room so they could sleep, talk, or otherwise amuse themselves. Consequently, the superior performance of the "fronters" might be due to these factors rather than to the effectiveness of the soundtrack.

How can researchers assure that their groups are equivalent? There are three main techniques: randomizing, matching, and including the confounding variable in the design.

Randomization

A powerful technique for eliminating the influence of extraneous variables is **randomization:** randomly assigning subjects to various treatment groups. Random assignment means that each subject has an equal chance of being assigned to each treatment group. This method works because the variables to be controlled are distributed in approximately the same way in all groups. In the preceding example, suppose that the researcher had randomly assigned students to one group or the other instead of assigning them according to where they sat. It is highly probable that the average level of intelligence in the two groups would have been the same, as would have been their levels of attentiveness and alertness, thus ruling out those variables as alternative explanations. In addition, randomization would equalize some other confounding factors that the researcher might have overlooked. Random assignment would avoid the presence of a disproportionate number of men or women in one or the other group, which skews the results. The same might be said for geographic background: Randomization would provide for proportionate numbers of urban versus rural residents in each group.

There are several ways randomization can be achieved. If there are only two groups in the experiment, the researcher might simply flip a coin. If heads comes up, the subject goes to Group 1; if tails, Group 2. Experimental designs with more than two groups might use a table of random numbers to assign subjects. In a four-group design, a two-digit random number might be assigned to each subject. Those assigned 00–24 are placed in Group 1; 25–49 in Group 2; 50–74 in Group 3; and 75–99 in Group 4.

Randomization, however, is not perfect. The smaller the sample size in the experiment, the greater the risk that randomization will produce nonequivalent groups. This is another reason that researchers must use an adequate sample size in an experiment.

Matching

Another way to control for the impact of confounding variables is to match subjects on characteristics that may relate to the dependent variable. There are two primary methods of **matching.** The first, *matching by constancy,* makes a variable uniform for all of the experimental groups. For example, let's say a researcher is interested in assessing the impact of playing two types of video games on aggressiveness in children. Past research strongly suggests that gender is related to the levels and types of aggressive acts performed. To match the sample by constancy and control for gender effects, the researcher may decide to perform the experiment using only boys or only girls in the sample.

The second type of matching involves *matching by pairing.* In this method, subjects are paired on a similar value of a relevant variable before being assigned to different groups. Using the video game example, suppose the researcher suspects that a subject's prior level of aggressive tendencies has an impact on how that subject is affected by violent video games. The researcher would administer a test of aggressiveness to all subjects and calculate their scores. For simplicity's sake, let us say that there are only three possible scores on this test: low, medium, and high. The researcher would find two people who scored high on this test, pair them up, and then as-

Importance of Pretesting

The following scenario illustrates the importance of pretesting in an experiment. A researcher was planning to conduct a study with high school students. After completing the laborious process of securing approval from the appropriate authorities, the researcher scheduled a date and showed up bright and early to collect the data. About 70 students were assembled in the auditorium, and the school's principal had given the researcher 45 minutes to collect the data. No problem, thought the researcher. The subjects merely had to listen to a few musical selections and fill out rating scales. The researcher passed out the sheets containing the rating scales and told students to get their pencils or pens ready. At this point the students looked perplexed, and many protested that they did not have pencils or pens with them. Unlike the college students that the researcher was used to, high school students do not routinely carry pens or pencils.

With the allotted time quickly running out, the researcher ran to the principal's office and asked to borrow pencils. Luckily, there were several boxes in the supply cabinet. The researcher hurried back into the auditorium and started to pass out the pencils when he suddenly discovered that they were not sharpened. A frenzied search of the auditorium revealed exactly one pencil sharpener that probably dated from the 1930s. Needless to say, the experiment had to be rescheduled. Since that experience the researcher has never failed to run a pretest before doing an experiment, and always brings along plenty of pencils!

sign one at random to one treatment group and the other to the second. A similar procedure would be followed for those scoring low and medium. When finished, the researcher would be confident that equal numbers of high-, medium-, and low-aggression subjects were placed in each treatment group. This process, of course, is not necessarily restricted to pairs. If an experiment had three groups, subjects could be matched as triplets and then randomly assigned to groups.

In addition to gaining control over confounding variables, matching subjects increases the sensitivity of the experimental design. Since the treatment groups become more homogeneous, smaller differences that might have been obscured by individual variations can be detected.

On the other hand, this method does have some disadvantages. Matching by constancy limits the generalizability of the study and restricts the size of the population available for sampling. Both forms of matching also require at least some prior knowledge about the subjects and may require the extra effort of a pretest.

Including the Confounding Variable in the Design

Another way to control the impact of confounding variables in an experiment and to increase the sensitivity of the experiment is to incorporate the confounding variable(s) into the design. For instance, let's return to the video game example. Instead of controlling for the effects of gender by restricting the study to only boys or to only girls, the researcher might include gender as an independent variable. After the sample is divided by gender, each male or female would be randomly assigned to a condition. The resulting design would have four groups: males who play video game A, males who play video game B, females who play video game A, and females who play video game B. (Note that this is an example of the factorial design described later in this chapter.) An added benefit of this design is that it can provide information about the interaction—the combined effects of the confounding variable and independent variable of interest. Again, there are disadvantages to this method. Including another factor in the design increases the number of subjects needed for the experiment and also increases the time and energy necessary to complete it.

For several additional discussions and articles, search the Internet for "confounding variables."

Experimental Design

When used in the context of experimental research, the word *design* can have two different meanings. On the one hand, it can refer to the statistical procedures used to analyze the data, and it is common to hear about an analysis of variance design or a repeated-measures *t*-test design. On the other hand, *design* can refer to the total experimental plan or structure of the research. Used in this sense, it means selecting and planning the entire experimental approach to a research problem. This chapter uses the latter meaning. The appropriate statistical techniques for the various experimental designs in this chapter are discussed in Part Three.

An **experimental design** does not have to be a complicated series of statements, diagrams, and figures; it may be as simple as

Pretest > Experimental treatment > Posttest

Although other factors, such as variable and sample selection, control, and construction of a measurement instrument, enter into this design, the diagram does provide a legitimate starting point for research.

To facilitate the discussion of experimental design, the following notations are used to represent specific parts of a design (Campbell & Stanley, 1963):

- R represents a random sample or random assignment.
- X represents a treatment or manipulation of the independent variables so that the effects of these variables on the dependent variables can be measured.
- O refers to a process of observation or measurement; it is usually followed by a numerical subscript indicating the number of the observation (O_1 = Observation 1).

A left-to-right listing of symbols, such as R O_1 X O_2, indicates the order of the experiment. In this case, subjects are randomly selected or assigned to groups (R) and then observed or measured (O_1). Next, some type of treatment or manipulation of the independent variable is performed (X), followed by a second observation or measurement (O_2). Each line in experimental notation refers to the experience of a single group. Consider the following design:

R	O_1	X	O_2
R	O_1		O_2

This design indicates that the operations in the experiment are conducted simultaneously on two different groups. Notice that the second group, the control group, does not receive the experimental treatment.

Basic Experimental Designs

Each experimental design makes assumptions about the type of data the researcher wants to collect because different data require different research methods. Several questions need to be answered by the researcher before any type of design is constructed:

1. What is the purpose of the study?
2. What is to be measured or tested?
3. How many factors (independent variables) are involved?
4. How many levels of the factors (degrees of the independent variables) are involved?
5. What type of data is desired?
6. What is the easiest and most efficient way to collect the data?
7. What type of statistical analysis is appropriate for the data?
8. How much will the study cost?
9. How can these costs be trimmed?
10. What facilities are available for conducting the study?
11. What types of studies have been conducted in the area?
12. What benefits will be received from the results of the study?

The answer to each question has a bearing on the sequence of steps a study should follow. For example, if a limited budget is available for the study, a complicated, four-group research design cannot be conducted. Or if previous studies have shown the "posttest only" design to be useful, another design may be unjustified.

Not all experimental designs are covered in this section; only the most widely used are considered. The sources listed at the end of the chapter provide more information about these and other designs.

Pretest–Posttest Control Group. The pretest–posttest control group design is a fundamental and widely used procedure in all research areas. The design controls many of the rival hypotheses generated by artifacts; the effects of maturation, testing, history, and other sources are controlled because each group faces the same circumstances in the study. As shown in Figure 9.1, subjects are randomly selected or assigned, and each group is given a pretest. Only the first group, however, receives the experimental treatment. The difference between O_1 and O_2 for Group 1 is compared to the difference between O_1 and O_2 for Group 2. If a significant statistical difference is found, it is assumed that the experimental treatment was the primary cause.

Posttest-Only Control Group. When researchers are hesitant to use a pretest because of the possibility of subject sensitization to the posttest, the design in Figure 9.1 can be altered to describe a posttest-only control group (see Figure 9.2). Neither group has a pretest, but Group 1 is exposed to the treatment variable, followed by a posttest. The two groups are compared to determine whether a statistical significance is present.

The posttest-only control group design is also widely used to control rival explanations. Both groups are equally affected by maturation, history, and so on. Also, both normally call for a *t*-test, a test to compare the significance between two groups, to determine whether a significant statistical difference is present (see Chapter 12).

Figure 9.1 *Pretest–Posttest Control Group Design*

R	O_1	X	O_2
R	O_1		O_2

Figure 9.2 *Posttest-Only Control Group Design*

R	X	O_1
R		O_2

Figure 9.3 *Solomon Four-Group Design*

R	O_1	X	O_2
R	O_3		O_4
R		X	O_5
R			O_6

Figure 9.4 *Hypothetical Data for Solomon Four-Group Design*

Group				
1	R	20 (O_1)	X	40 (O_2)
2	R	20 (O_3)		20 (O_4)
3	R		X	40 (O_5)
4	R			20 (O_6)

Solomon Four-Group Design. The Solomon four-group design combines the first two designs and is useful if pretesting is considered to be a negative factor (see Figure 9.3). Each alternative for pretesting and posttesting is accounted for in the design, which makes it attractive to researchers.

For example, consider the hypothetical data presented in Figure 9.4. The numbers represent college students' scores on a test of current events knowledge. The X represents a program of regular newspaper reading. If the newspaper reading had an effect, O_2 should be significantly different from O_1 and also significantly different from O_4. In addition, O_2 should be significantly different from O_6 and also from O_3. If we assume that the 20-point difference shown in Figure 9.4 is significant, it appears that the independent variable in our example is indeed having an effect on current events knowledge. Note that other informative comparisons are also possible in this design. To assess the possible effects of pretesting, O_4 can be compared with O_6. Comparing O_1 and O_3 allows the researcher to check on the efficacy of randomization, and any possible pretest manipulation interaction can be detected by comparing O_2 and O_5.

The biggest drawback of the Solomon four-group design is a practical one—the design requires four separate groups, which means more subjects, more time, and more money. Further, some results produced from this design can be difficult to interpret. For example, what does it mean if O_2 is significantly greater than O_4 even though O_5 is significantly less than O_6?

Factorial Studies

Research studies involving the simultaneous analysis of two or more independent variables are called **factorial designs,** and each independent variable is called a **factor.** The approach saves time, money, and resources and allows researchers to investigate the interaction between the independent variables. That is, in many instances it is possible that two or more variables are *interdependent* (dependant on each other) in the effects they produce on the dependent variable, a relationship that could not be detected if two simple randomized designs were used.

The term *two-factor design* indicates that two independent variables are manipulated; a *three-factor design* includes three independent variables; and so on. (A *one-factor design* is a simple random design because only one independent variable is involved.) A factorial design for a study must have at least two factors or independent variables.

Factors may also have two or more levels. Therefore, the 2 × 2 factorial design has two independent variables, each with two levels. A 3 × 3 factorial design has three levels for

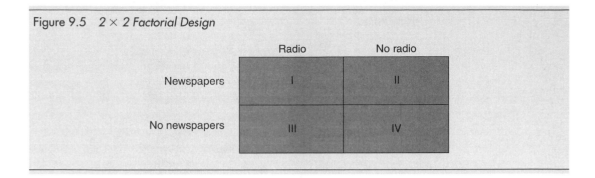

Figure 9.5 *2 × 2 Factorial Design*

	Radio	No radio
Newspapers	I	II
No newspapers	III	IV

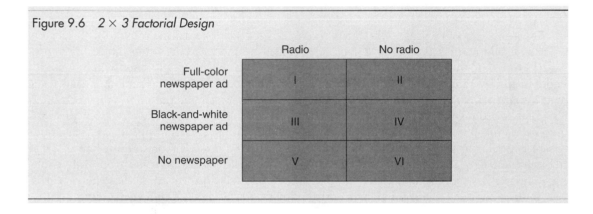

Figure 9.6 *2 × 3 Factorial Design*

	Radio	No radio
Full-color newspaper ad	I	II
Black-and-white newspaper ad	III	IV
No newspaper	V	VI

each of the two independent variables. A 2 × 3 × 3 factorial design has three independent variables: The first has two levels, and the second and third have three levels each.

To demonstrate the concept of levels, imagine that a TV station program director (PD) wants to study the success of a promotional campaign for a new movie-of-the-week series. The PD plans to advertise the new series on radio and in newspapers. Subjects selected randomly are placed into one of the cells of the 2 × 2 factorial design in Figure 9.5. This allows for the testing of two levels of two independent variables—exposure to radio and exposure to newspapers.

Four groups are involved in the study: Group I is exposed to both newspaper material and radio material; Group II is exposed to only newspaper; Group III is exposed to only radio; and Group IV serves as a control group and receives no exposure to either radio or newspaper. After the groups have undergone the experimental treatment, the PD can administer a short questionnaire to determine which medium, or combination of media, worked most effectively.

A 2 × 3 factorial design, which adds a third level to the second independent variable, is illustrated in Figure 9.6. This design demonstrates how the PD might investigate the relative effectiveness of full-color versus black-and-white newspaper advertisements while also measuring the impact of the exposure to radio material.

Assume the PD wants to include promotional advertisements on television as well as use radio and newspaper. The third factor produces a 2 × 2 × 2 factorial design. This

Figure 9.7 *2 × 2 × 2 Factorial Design*

	Radio		No radio	
	TV	No TV	TV	No TV
Newspaper	I	II	III	IV
No newspaper	V	VI	VII	VIII

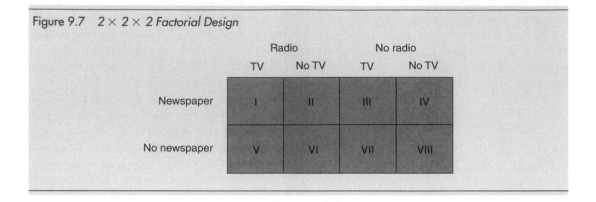

three-factor design in Figure 9.7 shows the eight possibilities of a 2 × 2 × 2 factorial study. Note that the subjects in Group I are exposed to newspaper, radio, and television announcements, whereas those in Group VIII are not exposed to any of the announcements.

The testing procedure in the three-factor design is similar to that of previous methods. Subjects in all eight cells are given some type of measurement instrument, and differences between the groups are tested for statistical significance. For example, Perry and colleagues (1997) used a 2 × 2 × 2 factorial design to study the impact of humorous commercials on the enjoyment of an entertainment program. Factor 1 was gender (male or female), factor 2 was the degree of humor in a program (low or high), and factor 3 was the degree of humor in commercials during the program (low or high). The results showed that the humor level of the commercials in the program influenced program enjoyment. No other main effects or interaction effects were found.

Other Experimental Designs

Research designs are as unique and varied as the questions and hypotheses they help to study. Designs of different types yield different types of information. If information about the effects of multiple manipulations is desired, a **repeated-measures design** (several measurements of the same subject) is appropriate. In this design, instead of assigning different people to different manipulations, the researcher exposes the same subjects to multiple manipulations. The effects of the various manipulations appear as variations within the same person's performance rather than as differences *between* groups of people.

One obvious advantage of the repeated-measures design is that fewer subjects are necessary because each subject participates in all conditions. Furthermore, since each subject acts as his or her own control, the design is quite sensitive to detecting treatment differences. On the other hand, repeated-measures designs are subject to *carryover effects:* The effects of one manipulation may still be present when the next manipulation is presented. Another possible disadvantage is that the subjects experience all of the various experimental conditions and they may figure out the purpose behind the experiment. As a result, they may behave differently than they would have if they were unaware of the study's goal.

If the researcher thinks that the order of presentation of the independent variables in a repeated-measures design will be a problem, a **Latin square design** is appropriate. Figure 9.8 shows an example of a Latin square design for a repeated-measures experiment with four subjects. Notice that each

AN INSIDE LOOK
Repeated-Measures Designs

In many research studies, it doesn't matter if the respondents or subjects "figure out" the purpose of the research. In many cases, there is nothing to figure out. For example, a commonly used repeated-measures design in radio research is the auditorium music test, where respondents rate several hundred song segments. There is nothing hidden in the research and the respondents' rating of one song have no effect on the ratings of other songs. In other words, the respondents don't learn anything from one song to the next.

Figure 9.8 *Latin Square Design*

Subjects	Experimental conditions			
A	1	2	3	4
B	2	3	4	1
C	3	4	1	2
D	4	1	2	3

subject is exposed to all conditions and that each of the four conditions appears only once per row and once per column. The Latin square arrangement also can be used when repeated measures are made on independent groups rather than on individual subjects.

Quasi-Experimental Designs

Sometimes the researcher does not have the luxury of randomly assigning subjects to experimental conditions. Suppose, for example, a researcher knows that a local radio station is about to be sold and is interested in determining the effects of this change of ownership on employee morale. The researcher measures the morale of a sample of employees at the station before and after the sale. At the same time, the researcher collects data on morale from a sample of employees at a comparable station in the same community. This design is similar to the pretest–posttest control group design discussed on page 227, but it does not involve the random assignment of subjects to experimental groups. Using Campbell and Stanley's (1963) terminology, we call it a **quasi-experiment.** Quasi-experiments are a valuable source of information, but there are design faults that must be considered in the interpretation of the data.

Figure 9.9 *Pretest–Posttest Nonequivalent Control Group Design*

O_1	X	O_2
O_3		O_4

Note: The line dividing the two groups indicates that no random assignment occurred.

This chapter discusses only two types of quasi-experimental designs: the pretest–posttest nonequivalent control group design and the interrupted time series design. For more information, consult Campbell and Stanley (1963) and Cook and Campbell (1979).

Pretest–Posttest Nonequivalent Control Group Design. This approach, illustrated in Figure 9.9, is the one used by the hypothetical researcher studying employee morale

Figure 9.10 *Interrupted Time Series Design*

O_1 O_2 O_3 O_4 O_5 X O_6 O_7 O_8 O_9 O_{10}

at radio stations. One group is exposed to the experimental manipulation and is compared to a similar group that is not exposed. The pre- and posttest differences are compared to determine whether the experimental condition had an effect.

In the radio station example, assume the pretest of employee morale showed that the workers at both radio stations had the same morale level before the sale. The posttest, however, showed that the morale of the employees at the sold station decreased significantly after the sale, but the morale level at the other (control) station remained constant. This result indicates that the station sale had an impact on morale. However, this may not be true. The two groups might have been different on other variables at the time of the pretest. For example, suppose the two groups of employees were of different ages. It is possible that the effect of the station sale on older employees produced the difference. The quasi-experimental design does not rule out this alternative selection-treatment interaction explanation.

Interrupted Time Series Design. In this arrangement, illustrated in Figure 9.10, a series of periodic measurements is made of a group. The series of measurements is interrupted by the experimental treatment, and then measurements are continued.

This design can rule out threats to internal validity. If there is a significant difference between O_5 and O_6, maturation can be ruled out by examining the scores for all the intervals before the manipulation. If maturation did occur, it would probably produce differences between O_1 and O_2, O_2 and O_3, and so on. If the only difference is between O_5 and O_6, then maturation is not a plausible explanation. The same logic can be applied to rule out the sensitizing effects of testing. The biggest threat to the internal validity in this design is history. It is possible that any apparent changes occurring after the experimental manipulation might be due to some other event that occurred at the same time as the experimental treatment. Donohew, Lorch, and Palmgreen (1998) describe an example of an interrupted time series design. Monthly samples of 100 teenagers were interviewed about their exposure to anti-marijuana public service announcements and their attitudes toward marijuana use in two matched cities over a 32-month period. A 4-month public service announcement campaign featuring the anti-marijuana public service announcements took place in both cities at different times. Comparison of the month-to-month data revealed changes in attitudes and behaviors.

▪ Field Experiments

Experiments conducted in a laboratory can be disadvantageous for many research studies because of certain problems they present: They are performed in controlled conditions that are unlike natural settings; they are generally considered to lack external validity; and they usually necessitate subject awareness of the testing situation. Because of these shortcomings, many researchers prefer to use field experiments (Haskins, 1968).

The exact difference between laboratory experiments and field experiments has been a subject of debate for years, especially with regard to the "realism" of the situations involved. Many researchers consider field and laboratory experiments to be on opposite ends of the "realism" continuum. However, the main difference between the two approaches is the setting. As Westley (1989, p. 129) points out:

> The laboratory experiment is carried out on the researcher's own turf; the subjects come into the laboratory. In the field experiment, the researcher goes to the subject's turf. In general, the physical controls available in the laboratory are greater than those found in the field. For that reason, statistical controls are often substituted for physical controls in the field.

The presence or absence of rules and procedures to control the conditions and the subjects' awareness or unawareness of being subjects can also distinguish the two approaches. If the researcher maintains tight control over the subjects' behavior and the subjects are placed in an environment they perceive to be radically different from their everyday life, the situation is probably better described as a laboratory experiment. On the other hand, if the subjects function primarily in their everyday social roles with little investigator interference or environmental restructuring, the case is probably closer to a field experiment. Basically, the difference between laboratory experiments and field experiments is one of degree.

Advantages of Field Experiments

The major advantage of field experiments is their external validity: Since study conditions closely resemble natural settings, subjects usually provide a truer picture of their normal behavior and are not influenced by the experimental situation. For example, consider a laboratory study designed to test the effectiveness of two versions of a television commercial. One group views Version A, and the other group views Version B. Both groups are then given a questionnaire to measure their willingness to purchase the advertised product. Based on these results, it may be concluded that Version B is more effective in selling the product. Although this may actually be the case, the validity of the experiment is questionable because the subjects knew they were being studied. (See the discussion of demand characteristics in Chapter 1.) Another problem is that answering a questionnaire cannot be equated to buying a product. Furthermore, viewing commercials in a laboratory setting is different from the normal viewing situation, in which competing stimuli (crying children, ringing telephones, and so on) are often present.

In a field experiment, these commercials might be tested by showing Version A in one market and Version B in a similar, but different, market. Actual sales of the product in both markets might then be monitored to determine which commercial was the more successful in persuading viewers to buy the product. As can be seen, the results of the field experiment have more relevance to reality, but the degree of control involved is markedly less than in the laboratory experiment.

Some field studies have the advantage of being nonreactive. **Reactivity** is the influence that a subject's awareness of being measured or observed has on his or her behavior. Laboratory subjects are almost always aware of being measured. Although this is also true of some field experiments, many can be conducted without the subjects' knowledge of their participation.

Field experiments are useful for studying complex social processes and situations. In their study of the effects of the arrival of television in an English community, Himmelweit, Oppenheim, and Vince (1958) recognized the advantages of the field experiment. Since television has an impact on several lifestyle variables, the researchers used a range of analysis techniques, including diaries, personal interviews, direct observation, questionnaires, and teachers' ratings of students, to document this impact. Such a broad topic area does not easily lend itself to laboratory research.

Field experiments can be inexpensive. Most studies require no special equipment or facilities; however, expenses increase rapidly with the size and scope of the study (Babbie, 1997). Finally, the field experiment may be the only research option to use. For example, suppose a researcher is interested in examining patterns of communication at a television station before and after a change in management—a problem difficult, if not impossible, to simulate in a laboratory. The only practical option is to conduct the study in the field—that is, at the station.

Disadvantages of Field Experiments

The disadvantages of the field experiment are mostly practical ones. However, some research is impossible to conduct because of ethical considerations. The difficult question of the effects of television violence on young viewers provides a good example of this problem. Probably the most informative study that could be performed in this area would be a field experiment in which one group of children is required to watch violent television programs and another similar group to watch only nonviolent programs. The subjects could be carefully observed over a number of years to check for any significant difference in the number of aggressive acts committed by the members of each group. However, the ethics involved in controlling the television viewing behavior of children and in possibly encouraging aggressive acts are extremely questionable. Therefore, scientists have resorted to laboratory and survey techniques to study this problem.

On a more practical level, field experiments often encounter external hindrances that cannot be anticipated. For example, a researcher may spend weeks planning a study to manipulate the media use of students in a summer camp, only to have camp counselors or a group of parents cancel the project because they do not want the children to be used as "guinea pigs." Also, it takes time for researchers to establish contacts, secure cooperation, and gain necessary permissions before beginning a field experiment. In many cases this phase of the process may take weeks or months to complete.

Finally, and perhaps most importantly, researchers cannot control all the intervening variables in a field experiment. The presence of extraneous variables affects the precision of the experiment and the confidence of the researchers in its outcome.

Types of Field Experiments

There are two basic categories of field experiments: those in which the researcher manipulates the independent variable(s) and those in which independent variable manipulation occurs naturally as a result of other circumstances. To illustrate the first type, suppose that a researcher is interested in investigating the effects of not being able to read a newspaper. A possible approach would be to select two comparable samples and not allow one of the samples to read any newspapers for a period of time; the second sample (the control group) would continue to read the newspaper as usual. A comparison could then be made to determine whether abstinence from newspapers has any effect in other areas of life, such as interpersonal communication. In this example, reading the newspaper is the independent variable that has been manipulated.

The second type of field experiment involves passive manipulation of independent variables. Suppose a community with no satellite television system is scheduled for installation in the future. In an attempt to gauge the effects of satellite service on television viewing and other media use, a researcher might begin studying a large sample of television set owners in the community long before the satellite service is available. A few months after it is introduced, the researcher could return to the original sample, sort out the households that subscribed to satellite and those that did not, and then determine the effects of the satellite service. In this case, there is no control over the independent variable (satellite service); the researcher is merely taking advantage of existing conditions.

Note that in some field experiments, the researcher is not able to assign subjects randomly to treatment groups. As a result, many field experiments are classified as quasi-experiments. As Cook and Campbell (1979) point out, the extent to which causal statements can be made from the results of these studies depends upon the ability to rule out alternative explanations. Consequently, researchers who use field experiments must pay close attention to threats to internal validity.

Examples of Field Experiments

Tan (1977) was interested in what people would do during a week without television. He recruited a sample of 51 adults and paid them each $4 a day not to watch television for an entire week. Before depriving these subjects of television, Tan requested that they watch television normally for a 1-week period and keep a detailed diary of all their activities. At the start of the experimental week, Tan's assistants visited the subjects' homes and taped up the electrical plugs on their television sets to lessen temptation. Again, the subjects were requested to record their activities for the week. To maintain some control over the experiment, the assistants visited the subjects' homes periodically during the week to ensure that the television was not being viewed.

One week later, the diaries completed during the week of deprivation were collected, and the data were compared to the week of normal television viewing. Tan discovered that when deprived of television, subjects turned more to radio and newspapers for entertainment and information. They also tended to engage in more social activities with their friends and family.

This study illustrates some of the strengths and weaknesses of field experiments. In the first place, they are probably the only viable technique available to investigate this particular topic. A survey (see Chapter 7) does not permit the researcher to control whether the subjects watch television, and it would be impossible in the United States to select a representative sample composed of people who do not own a television set. Nor would it be feasible to bring people into the laboratory for an entire week of television deprivation.

On the other hand, the ability of the field researcher to control independent variables is not conclusively demonstrated here: Tan had no way to be sure that his sample subjects actually avoided television for the entire week. Subjects could have watched at friends' homes or at local bars, or even at home by untaping the plugs. Moreover, Tan mentioned that several individuals who fell into the initial sample refused to go without television for only $4 per day. As a result, the nonprobability sample did not accurately reflect the general makeup of the community.

Smith and Hand (1987) took advantage of a natural occurrence in their field experiment on the effects of viewing pornography. One XXX rated film was shown every year at the small college that served as the site of the research. About one-third of all the male students on campus typically attend this film at its annual showing. One week before the film was shown, the investigators surveyed 230 female students of the college about their contact with aggression. The same measurement was taken on the Monday following the film and then again a week later. The researchers then analyzed the amount of violence experienced by females whose male companions had seen the film as compared to females whose male companions had not seen the film. The results showed no differences in the amount of violence experienced by the two groups of females.

This study represents one of the few times that the effects of exposure to pornographic films have been studied experimentally outside of the laboratory. Nonetheless, the study suffers from some common limitations of field experiments. First, the researchers were unable to make random assignments of sample subjects. As a consequence, this study is more accurately described as a quasi-experiment. The males who went to the film may have been different from those who stayed away. Second, the researchers had no control over the content of the film that was shown. The actual film may have been too mild to elicit much aggression. Third, the researchers could not control how many females or which particular females had contact with males who attended the movie. They were able to find only 38 of 230 whose companions saw the film. These 38 might not be typical of the rest of the population.

Williams (1986) and her colleagues conducted an elaborate field experiment on the impact of television on a community. In 1973 she was able to identify a Canadian town that, because of its peculiar geographic location, was unable to receive television. This particular town, however, was scheduled to acquire television service within a year. Given this lead time, the researchers could match the town with two others that were similar in population, area, income, transportation systems, education, and other variables. Residents of the three towns completed questionnaires that measured a large number of variables, including aggressive behavior, personality traits, reading ability, creativity, sex-role perceptions, intelligence, and vocabulary. Two years later the research team went back to the three communities, and residents completed a posttest with questions that measured the same variables as before. The design of this field experiment is illustrated in Figure 9.11. Note that it is a variation of the quasi-experimental pretest–posttest nonequivalent control group design discussed earlier.

Figure 9.11 *Design of Canadian Field Experiment*

Town	Time one	Time two
A	No TV reception	One TV channel
B	One TV channel	Two TV channels
C	Four TV channels	Four TV channels

This field experiment provided a wealth of data. Among other things, the researchers found that the arrival of TV apparently slowed down the acquisition of reading skills, lowered attendance at outside social events, fostered more stereotypical attitudes toward sex roles, and increased children's verbal and physical aggression.

Two rather ambitious field experiments were conducted by Milgram and Shotland (1973) with the cooperation of the *CBS* television network. The researchers arranged to have three versions of the then popular television series "Medical Center" constructed. One version depicted antisocial behavior that was punished by a jail sentence; another portrayed antisocial behavior that went unpunished; and a third contained prosocial (favorable) behavior. The antisocial behavior consisted of scenes of a distraught young man smashing a plastic charity collection box and pocketing the money.

In the first experiment, the researchers used two methods to recruit subjects: Ads placed in New York City newspapers promised a free transistor radio to anyone willing to view a 1-hour television show, and business reply cards containing the same message were passed out to pedestrians near several subway stops. Subjects were asked to report to a special television theater to view the program. Upon arrival, each person was randomly assigned to one of four groups, and each group was shown a different program (the three programs described earlier plus a different nonviolent show used as a control). After viewing the program (with no commercial interruptions) and completing a short questionnaire about it, the subjects were instructed to go to an office in a downtown building to receive their free radio.

The downtown office, monitored by hidden cameras, was part of the experiment. The office contained a plastic charity collection box with about $5 in it, and a notice informed the subjects that no more transistor radios were available. Their behavior on reading the notice was the dependent variable: How many would emulate the antisocial act seen in the program and take the money from the charity box? Milgram and Shotland found no differences in antisocial behavior among the groups of viewers; no one broke into the charity box.

The second study tried to gauge the immediate effects of televised antisocial acts on viewers. Subjects were recruited from the streets of New York City's Times Square area and ushered into a room with a color television set and a plastic charity collection box containing $4.45. A hidden camera monitored the subjects' behavior, even though they were told that they would not be observed. Although this time some subjects broke into the box, once again no differences emerged between the groups.

These two studies demonstrate several positive and negative aspects of field experiments. In the first place, Milgram and Shotland had to secure the cooperation of *CBS* to conduct their expensive experiments. Second, volunteer subjects were used, and it is reasonable to assume that the sample was unrepresentative of the general population. Third, in the first experiment the researchers did not control for the amount of time that passed between viewing the program and arriving at the testing center. Some participants arrived 24 hours after watching "Medical Center," whereas others came several days later. Clearly, the subjects' experiences during this interval may have influenced their responses. Finally, Milgram and Shotland reported that the second experiment had to be terminated early because some of the subjects started resorting to behavior that the researchers could not control. On the positive side, the first experiment clearly shows the potential of the field experiment to simulate natural conditions and to provide a nonreactive setting. Upon leaving the theater after seeing the program, subjects had no reason to believe that they would be participating in another phase of the research. Consequently, their behavior at the supposed gift center was probably genuine and not a reaction to the experimental situation.

The Milgram and Shotland studies also raise the important question of ethics in field experiments. Subjects were observed without their knowledge and apparently were never told about the real purpose of the study, or even that they were involved in a research study. Does the use of a hidden camera constitute an invasion of privacy? Does the experimental situation constitute entrapment? How about the subjects who stole the money from the charity box? Have they committed a crime? Field experiments can sometimes pose difficult ethical considerations, and these points *must be dealt with before the experiment is conducted,* not afterward, when harm may already have been inflicted on the subjects.

Two field experiments concerned the impact of media on politics. Donsbach, Brosius, and Mattenklott (1993) compared the perceptions of people who attended a political event in person with those of people who saw different versions of the same event on television. They concluded that participants in the event and those who saw the television coverage did not differ significantly in their perceptions of the event and the people involved. Those who watched the TV versions, however, were more likely to hold polarized opinions than those who had seen the event in person. Cappella and Jamieson (1994) conducted a field experiment that evaluated the effects of *adwatches*—analyses by some TV networks of misleading political ads during the 1992 presidential election. The researchers recruited subjects from 12 cities across the country and paid respondents $10 per day for participating in the study—165 individuals provided useful data. Six groups of respondents were given videotapes that contained several news items and different versions of an adwatch report. The number of exposures per group was also manipulated. One group received a tape that contained only the news reports. All respondents were instructed to view the tapes at home. After exposure, each participant was asked questions about the tapes including information about the particular adwatch he or she had viewed. Results showed that exposure to the adwatches had an impact on the perceived fairness and importance of the ad.

This study is another illustration of the complexity that can be involved in a field experiment. The experimental tapes were constructed with the cooperation of *CNN;* each research location had to have a research coordinator on site; participants had to be paid for their efforts; and so forth. In addition, it points out some of the difficulties in control and generalization. Respondents were volunteers; they might not be a representative sample of the total population. The researchers could not control exposure to other sources of political information. Some sensitization to the study's purpose might have occurred. Field experiments can go a long way toward providing more external validity, but substantial efforts can be involved in carrying out the study.

▪ ▪ ▪ Summary

Mass media researchers have a number of research designs from which to choose when analyzing a given topic. The laboratory experiment has been a staple in mass media research for several decades. Though criticized by many researchers as being artificial, the method offers a number of advantages that make it particularly useful to some researchers. Of specific importance is the researcher's ability to control the experimental situation and to manipulate experimental treatments.

This chapter also described the process of experimental design—the researcher's blueprint for conducting an experiment. The experimental design provides the steps the researcher will follow to accept or reject a hypothesis or research question. Some experimental designs are simple and take very little time to perform; others involve many different groups and numerous treatments.

Quasi-experimental designs are used when random selection and random assignment of subjects are not possible. Field experiments take place in natural settings, which aids the generalizability of the results but introduces problems of control.

Key Terms

Confounding variables
Cultivation effect
Double-blind technique
Experimental design
Factor
Factorial designs
Field experiment
Interrupted Time Series
Laboratory experiment
Latin square design
Manipulation check
Matching
Posttest-only control group
Pretesting
Pretest–posttest control group
Pretest–Posttest nonequivalent control group
Quasi-experimental design
Randomization
Reactivity
Repeated-measures design
Solomon four-group
Staged manipulation
Straightforward manipulation

Using the Internet

1. The Internet is literally packed with information about experimental research. To get an idea of what is available, conduct a search for "experimental research procedures."
2. See *http://commfaculty.fullerton.edu/jreinard/internet.htm* for a great list of links to various mass media research sources.

Questions and Problems for Further Investigation

1. Develop four research questions or hypotheses for any mass media area. Which of the designs described in this chapter is best suited to investigate the problems?
2. What are the advantages and disadvantages of each of the following four experimental designs?

a.	X	O_1		
		O_2		
b.	R		X	O_1
c.	R	O_1	X	O_2
	R		X	O_3
d.	R	O_1	X	O_2

3. A good example of the experimental technique as it relates to mass communication research is Ward's (1992) study of the effectiveness of sidebar graphics on reader comprehension, which appears in the Summer 1992 issue of *Journalism Quarterly*. Read this study and note how the independent variable was manipulated.
4. What research questions are best answered by field experiments?
5. Search the Internet for examples of experimental research. Do not limit yourself to only media research.
6. If you are using InfoTrac College Edition, conduct a search to find recent examples of field experiments. (Hint: Search for articles that have "field experiment" in the title.) What methods did the researchers use to control extraneous influences?

For additional information on these and related topics, see

http://www.wimmerdominick.com

References and Suggested Readings

Babbie, E. R. (1997). *The practice of social research* (7th ed.). Belmont, CA: Wadsworth.

Baran, S. B., Mok, J. J., Land, M., & Kang, T. Y. (1989). You are what you buy. *Journal of Communication,* 39(2), 46–55.

Bruning, J. L., & Kintz, B. L. (1997). *Computational handbook of statistics* (4th ed.). Chicago: Scott, Foresman.

Campbell, D. T., & Stanley, J. C. (1963). *Experimental and quasi-experimental designs and research.* Skokie, IL: Rand McNally.

Cappella, J., & Jamieson, K. (1994). Broadcast adwatch effects. *Communication Research,* 21(3), 342–365.

Christensen, L. B. (1997). *Experimental methodology.* Boston: Allyn & Bacon.

Cook, T. D., & Campbell, D. T. (1979). *Quasiexperimentation: Designs and analysis for field studies.* Skokie, IL: Rand McNally.

Cooper, R., Potter, W., & Dupagne, M. (1994). A status report on methods used in mass communication research. *Journalism Educator,* 48(4), 54–61.

Donohew, L., Lorch, E. P., & Palmgreen, P. (1998). Applications of a theoretic model of information exposure to health interventions. *Human Communication Research,* 24(3), 454–468.

Donsbach, W., Brosius, H., & Mattenklott, A. (1993). How unique is the perspective of television? A field experiment. *Political Communication,* 10(1), 37–53.

Gilbert, K., & Schleuder, J. (1990). Effects of color and complexity in still photographs on mental effort and memory. *Journalism Quarterly,* 67(4), 749–756.

Hansen, C., & Hansen, R. (1990, December). Rock music videos and antisocial behavior. *Basic and Applied Social Psychology,* 11, 357–369.

Haskins, J. B. (1968). *How to evaluate mass communication.* New York: Advertising Research Foundation.

Haskins, J. B. (1981). A precise notational system for planning and analysis. *Evaluation Review,* 5(1), 33–50.

Himmelweit, H., Oppenheim, A. W., & Vince, P. (1958). *Television and the child.* London: Oxford University Press.

Hoyt, J. L. (1977). Courtroom coverage: The effects of being televised. *Journal of Broadcasting,* 21(41), 487–496.

Keppel, G. (1991). *Design and analysis: A researcher's handbook* (3rd ed.). Englewood Cliffs, NJ: Prentice-Hall.

Leshner, G., Reeves, B., & Nass, C. (1998). Switching channels: The effects of TV channels on the mental representation of television news. *Journal of Broadcasting and Electronic Media,* 42(1), 21–33.

McBurney, D. H. (1990). *Experimental psychology.* Belmont, CA: Wadsworth.

Milgram, S., & Shotland, R. (1973). Television and antisocial behavior. New York: Academic Press.

Miller, D. C. (1991). *Handbook of research design and social measurement* (5th ed.). White Plains, NY: Longman.

Montgomery, D. C. (1997). *Design and analysis of experiments.* New York: John Wiley.

Nunnally, J. C. (1994). *Psychometric theory* (3rd ed.). New York: McGraw-Hill.

Perry, S. D., Jenzowsky, S. A., Hester, J. B., King, C. M., & Yi, H. (1997). The influence of commercial humor on program enjoyment and evaluation. *Journalism and Mass Communication Quarterly,* 74(2), 388–399.

Roscoe, J. T. (1975). *Fundamental research statistics for the behavioral sciences.* New York: Holt, Rinehart & Winston.

Rosenberg, M. J. (1965). When dissonance fails: On eliminating evaluation apprehension from attitude measurement. *Journal of Personality and Social Psychology,* 1, 28–42.

Rosenthal, R. (1976). *Experimenter effects in behavioral research* (2nd ed.). New York: Irvington.

Rosenthal, R., & Jacobson, L. (1966). Teacher's expectancies: Determinants of pupils' IQ gains. *Psychological Reports,* 19, 115–118.

Rosenthal, R., & Rosnow, R. L. (1969). *Artifact in behavioral research.* New York: Academic Press.

Smith, M. D., & Hand, C. (1987). The pornography/aggression linkage: Results from a field study. *Deviant Behavior,* 8(4), 389–400.

Tan, A. S. (1977). Why TV is missed: A functional analysis. *Journal of Broadcasting,* 21, 371–380.

Walizer, M. H., & Wienir, P. L. (1978). *Research methods and analysis: Searching for relationships.* New York: Harper & Row.

Ward, D. (1992). The effectiveness of sidebar graphics. *Journalism Quarterly,* 69(2), 318–328.

Westley, B. H. (1989). The controlled experiment. In G. H. Stempel & B. H. Westley (Eds.), *Research methods in mass communication.* Englewood Cliffs, NJ: Prentice-Hall.

Williams, T. B. (1986). *The impact of television.* New York: Academic Press.

Chapter 10

Introduction to Statistics

Statistics are mathematical *methods to collect, organize, summarize, and analyze data.* Statistics cannot perform miracles. Statistics alone will not "correct" a misdirected, poorly phrased, or ambiguous research question or hypothesis, or a study that uses sloppy measurement and design and contains numerous errors. Statistics provide valid and reliable results only when the data collection and research methods follow established scientific procedures.

The science of statistics and the ease with which they can be used have changed dramatically since the development of mini- and microcomputers. Only a few decades ago, researchers spent weeks or months performing hand-calculated statistical procedures—calculations that now take only minutes or seconds on a hand-held calculator or PC. In addition, there are now dozens of excellent computer software programs to calculate nearly any type of statistical test, and these software packages have made statistical analysis very simple.

Much of the groundwork for statistics was established in 1835 by Lambert Adolphe Quetelet ('kay-tuh-lay), a Belgian mathematician and astronomer, with his paper entitled *On Man and the Development of His Faculties*. In addition to other techniques, Quetelet developed the ideas behind the normal distribution and formed the basics of probability theory from preliminary work by French mathematician and physicist Pierre-Simon Laplace (la-'plas) and others.

Quetelet's background is similar to that of others who were instrumental in the development of statistics. Almost all were Renaissance men involved in such disciplines as astronomy, mathematics, physics, and philosophy.

This chapter introduces descriptive statistics and some of the methods used in mass media research. We encourage you to consult statistics books and the Internet for more information.

Descriptive Statistics

Descriptive statistics reduce data sets to allow for easier interpretation. If you asked a random sample of 100 people how long they listened to the radio yesterday and recorded all 100 answers on a sheet of paper, it would be difficult to draw conclusions by simply looking at that list. Analysis of this information is much easier if the data are organized in some meaningful way—and this is the function of descriptive statistics. These statistical methods allow researchers to take random data and organize them into some type of order.

During a research study, investigators typically collect data that are measurements or observations of the people or items in a sample. These data usually have little meaning or usefulness until they are displayed or summarized using one of the techniques of descriptive statistics. Mass media researchers use two primary methods to make their data more manageable: data distributions and summary statistics.

Data Distributions

A **distribution** is simply a collection of numbers. Table 10.1 shows a hypothetical distribution of 20 respondents' answers to the question, "How many hours did you spend in the past two days listening to the radio and watching TV?" The distribution may look nice, but it is difficult to draw any conclusions or to generalize from this collection of unordered scores.

Table 10.1 *Distribution of Responses to "How many hours did you spend in the past two days listening to the radio and watching TV?"*

Respondent	Hours	Respondent	Hours
A	12	K	14
B	9	L	16
C	18	M	23
D	8	N	25
E	19	O	11
F	21	P	14
G	15	Q	12
H	8	R	19
I	11	S	21
J	6	T	11

As a preliminary step toward making these numbers more manageable, the data may be arranged in a **frequency distribution**—a table of the scores ordered according to magnitude and their frequency of occurrence. Table 10.2 presents the data from the hypothetical radio/TV survey in a frequency distribution.

Now the data begin to show a pattern. Note that the typical frequency distribution table includes two columns. The column on the left contains all the values of the variable under study; the column on the right shows the number of occurrences of each value. The sum of the frequency column is the number (N) of persons or items in the distribution.

A frequency distribution can also be constructed using grouped intervals, each of which contains several score levels. Table 10.3 shows the data from the hypothetical survey with the scores grouped together in intervals. This table is a more compact frequency distribution than Table 10.2, but the scores have lost their individual identity.

Table 10.2 *Frequency Distribution of Responses to "How many hours did you spend in the last two days listening to the radio and watching TV?"*

Hours	Frequency (N = 20)
6	1
8	2
9	1
11	3
12	2
14	2
15	1
16	1
18	1
19	2
21	2
23	1
25	1

Table 10.3 *Frequency Distribution of Radio and TV Listening and Viewing Hours Grouped in Intervals*

Hours	Frequency
0–10	4
11–15	8
16–20	4
21–25	4

Table 10.4 *Frequency Distribution with Columns for Percentage, Cumulative Frequency, and Cumulative Frequency as a Percentage of N*

Hours	Frequency	Percentage	*cf*	*cf* percentage of N
6	1	5	1	5
8	2	10	3	15
9	1	5	4	20
11	3	15	7	35
12	2	10	9	45
14	2	10	11	55
15	1	5	12	60
16	1	5	13	65
18	1	5	14	70
19	2	10	16	80
21	2	10	18	90
23	1	5	19	95
25	1	5	20	100
	N = 20	100%		

Other columns can be included in frequency distribution tables such as proportions or percentages. To obtain the percentage of a response, simply divide the frequency of the individual responses by *N*, the total number of responses in the distribution. Percentages allow comparisons to be made between different frequency distributions that are based on different values of *N*.

Some frequency distributions include the **cumulative frequency** (*cf*), constructed by adding the number of scores in one interval to the number of scores in the intervals above it. Table 10.4 displays the frequency distribution from Table 10.2 with the addition of a percentage column, a cumulative frequency column, and a column showing cumulative frequency as a percentage of *N*.

Sometimes it is best to present data in graph form. The graphs shown in this section contain the same information as frequency distributions. Graphs usually consist of two perpendicular lines, the *x-axis,* or **abscissa** (horizontal), and the *y-axis,* or **ordinate** (vertical). Over the years, statisticians have developed certain standards regarding graphic format. One common standard is to list the scores along the *x*-axis and the frequency or relative frequency along the *y*-axis. Thus, the height of a line or bar indicates the frequency of a score. One common form of graph is the **histogram,** or **bar chart,** where frequencies are represented by vertical bars. Figure 10.1 is a histogram constructed from the data in Table 10.1. Note that the scores on the *x*-axis are actually the scores (hours) listed from the

AN INSIDE LOOK
Tables and Graphs

Don't worry about constructing data tables and graphs because they are easy to produce with spreadsheets. For example, *Excel* includes a graphing macro to produce almost any type of graph.

lowest value to the highest; the *y*-axis shows the frequency of scores.

If a line is drawn from the midpoint of each interval at its peak along the *y*-axis to each adjacent midpoint/peak, the resulting graph is called a **frequency polygon.** Figure 10.2 shows a frequency polygon superimposed on the histogram from Figure 10.1. As can be seen, the two figures display the same information.

A **frequency curve** is similar to a frequency polygon except that the points are connected by a continuous, unbroken curve instead of by lines. The curve assumes that any irregularities shown in a frequency polygon are simply due to chance and that the variable being studied is distributed continuously over the population. Figure 10.3 superimposes a frequency curve onto the frequency polygon shown in Figure 10.2.

Frequency curves are described in relation to the **normal curve,** a symmetrical bell-shaped curve whose properties are discussed more fully later in this chapter. Figure 10.4 illustrates the normal curve and shows the ways in which a frequency curve can deviate from it. These patterns of deviation are called skewness.

Skewness refers to the concentration of scores around a particular point on the *x*-axis. If this concentration lies toward the low end of the scale, with the tail of the curve trailing off to the right, the curve is called a *right skew.*

Figure 10.1 *Histogram of Radio Listening/TV Viewing*

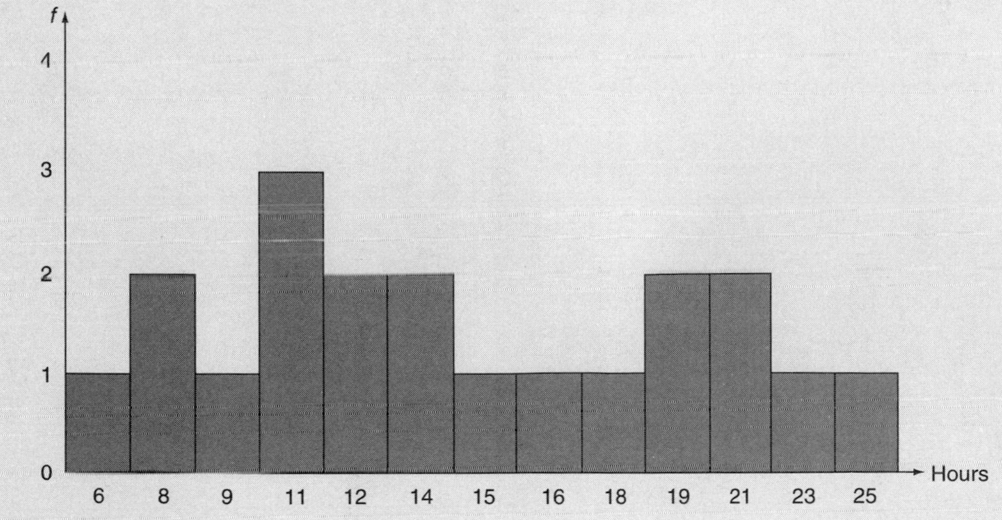

Figure 10.2 *Frequency Polygon of Radio Listening/TV Viewing Hours Superimposed on a Histogram of the Same Data*

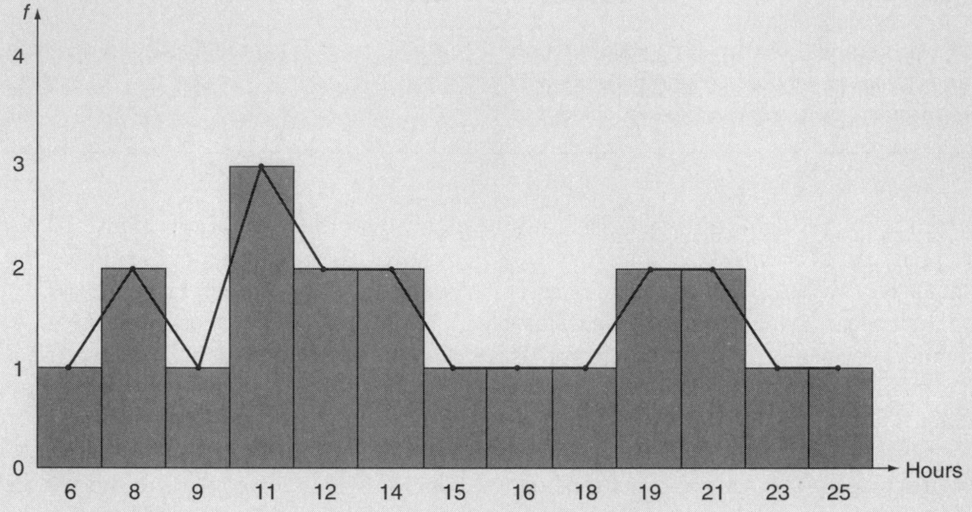

Figure 10.3 *Frequency Curve (Shaded) of Radio Listening/TV Viewing Hours Superimposed on a Frequency Polygon of the Same Data*

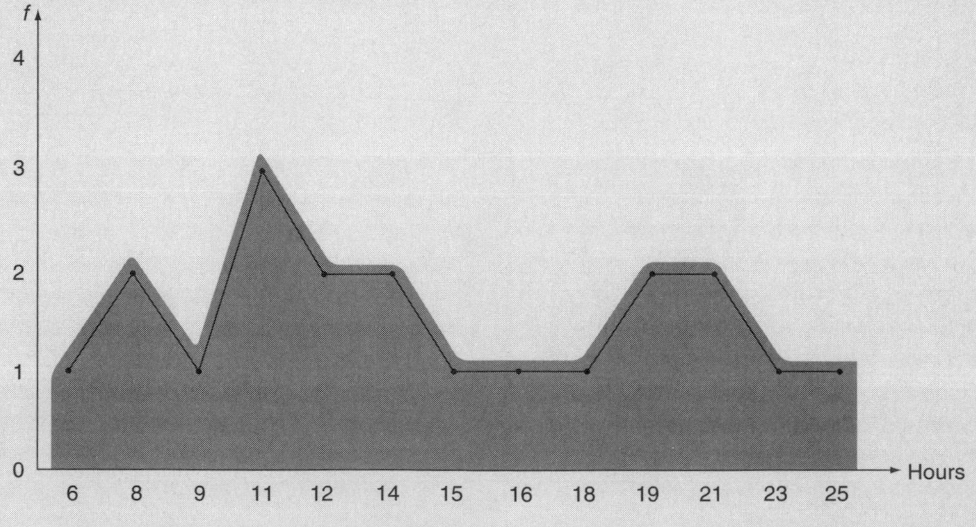

AN INSIDE LOOK
Skewness

Although the word skewness is still a valid statistical term, the fact is that it's not used much in research. Instead, variations of the word "lean" are used. In other words, researchers may say that the data *lean* one way or another, such as, "The data lean to the younger demographic groups." (In other words, there are more younger respondents or subjects in the data distribution.)

Conversely, if the tail of the curve trails off to the left, it is a *left skew.* If the halves of the curve are identical, it is *symmetrical,* or normal.

A normal distribution of data is not skewed in either direction. If data produce a curve that deviates substantially from the normal curve, then the data may have to be transformed in some way (discussed later in this chapter) to achieve a more normal distribution.

Summary Statistics

The data in Table 10.1 can be condensed still further through the use of **summary statistics** that help make data more manageable by measuring two basic tendencies of distributions: central tendency and dispersion, or variability.

Central Tendency. Central tendency statistics answer the question, What is a typical score? The statistics provide information about the grouping of the numbers in a distribution by giving a single number that characterizes the entire distribution. Exactly what constitutes a "typical" score depends on the level of measurement and the purpose for which the data will be used.

For every distribution, three characteristic numbers can be identified. One is the **mode** (Mo), or the score or scores that occur most frequently. Calculation is not necessary to determine the mode; it is found by inspecting the distribution. For the data in Table 10.1, the mode is 11.

Though easy to determine, the mode has some serious drawbacks as a descriptive statistic. It focuses attention on only one possible score and can hide important facts about the data when considered by itself. This is illustrated by the data in Table 10.5. The mode is 70, but the most striking feature about the numbers is the way they cluster around 30. Another serious drawback is that a distribution of

Figure 10.4 *Skewness and the Normal Curve*

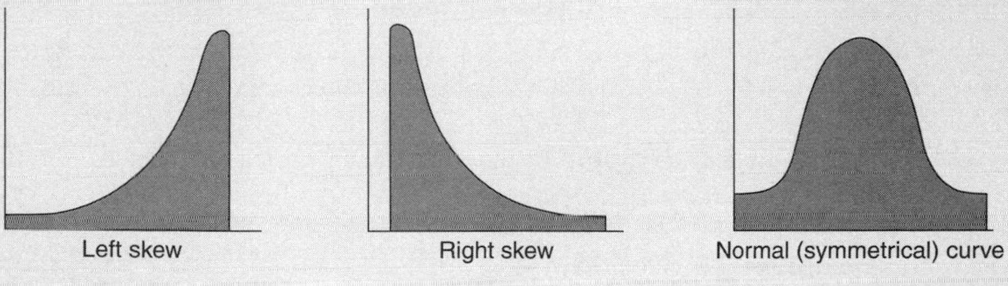

Table 10.5 *The Mode As a Potentially Misleading Statistic*

Score	f
70	2
35–69	0
34	1
33	1
32	1
31	1
30	1
29	1
28	1
27	1
26	1

scores can have more than one mode. When this happens, the mode does not provide an effective way of analyzing data.

A second summary statistic is the **median** (Mdn), which is the midpoint of a distribution—half of the scores lie above it and half lie below it. If the distribution has an odd number of scores, the median is the middle score; if there is an even number, the median is a hypothetical score halfway between the two middle scores. To determine the median, the scores are ordered from smallest to largest, then the midpoint is identified by inspection. (The median is 14 in the sample data in Table 10.1.)

Consider another example for the median with nine scores:

0 2 2 5 (6) 17 18 19 67

The median score is 6 because there are four scores above this number and four below it. Now consider these 10 scores:

0 2 2 5 6 17 18 19 67 75
↑
11.5

In this example, no score neatly bisects this distribution. To determine the median, the two middle scores must be added and divided by 2:

$$\text{Mdn} = \frac{6 + 17}{2} = 11.5$$

When several scores in the distribution are the same, computing the median becomes more complicated. See *Comprehending Behavioral Statistics* by Hurlburt (1998, p. 52) for a detailed description of how to compute the median when there are duplications of middle scores.

The third type of central tendency statistic is the **mean.** The mean represents the average of a set of scores and is probably the most familiar summary statistic. Mathematically speaking, we define the mean as the *sum of all scores divided by N,* the total number of scores. Since the mean is used widely in both descriptive statistics and inferential statistics, it is described here in detail.

As a first step, some basic statistical notation is required:

X = any score in a series of scores
$\overline{X}$ = the mean (read "X bar"; M is also commonly used to denote the mean)
Σ = summation (symbol is Greek capital letter **sigma**)
N = the total number of scores in a distribution

Using these symbols, we can write the formula for the calculation of the mean as

$$\overline{X} = \frac{\Sigma X}{N}$$

This equation indicates that the mean is the sum of all scores (ΣX) divided by the total number of scores (N). From the data in Table 10.1, the mean is

$$\overline{X} = \frac{293}{20} = 14.65$$

If the data are contained in a frequency distribution, a slightly different formula is used to calculate the mean:

$$\overline{X} = \frac{\Sigma fX}{N}$$

In this case X represents the midpoint of any given interval, and f is the frequency of that interval. Table 10.6 uses this formula to calculate the mean of the frequency distribution in Table 10.2.

Unlike the mode and the median, the mean takes all the values in the distribution into account, which makes it especially sensitive to extreme scores or outliers. Extreme scores draw the mean toward their direction. For example, suppose Table 10.1 contained another response, from Respondent U, who reported 100 hours of radio and television use. The new mean would then be approximately 18.71, an increase of about 28% due to the addition of only one large number.

One way to look at the mean is that it could be assigned to each individual or element if the total were evenly distributed among all members of the sample. It is also the only measure of central tendency that can be defined algebraically. As we show later, this allows the mean to be used in a variety of situations. It also suggests that the data used to calculate the mean should be at the interval or ratio level (see Chapter 2).

Two factors must be considered in decisions about which of the three measures of central tendency to report for a given set of data. First, the level of measurement used may determine the choice: If the data are at the nominal level, only the mode is meaningful; with ordinal data, either the mode or the median may be used. All three measures are appropriate for interval and ratio data, however, and it may be desirable to report more than one.

Second, the purpose of the statistic is important. If the ultimate goal is to describe a set of data, the measure that is most typical of the distribution should be used. To illustrate, suppose the scores on a statistics exam are 100, 100, 100, 100, 0, and 0. To say that the mean grade is 67 does not accurately portray the distribution; the mode provides a more characteristic description.

Table 10.6 *Calculation of Mean from Frequency Distribution*

Hours	Frequency	*fx*
6	1	6
8	2	16
9	1	9
11	3	33
12	2	24
14	2	28
15	1	15
16	1	16
18	1	18
19	2	38
21	2	42
23	1	23
25	1	25
	$N = 20$	$\Sigma fX = 293$

$$\overline{X} = \frac{293}{20} = 14.65$$

Dispersion. A second type of descriptive statistics is used to measure **dispersion,** or variance. Measures of central tendency determine the typical score of a distribution; dispersion measures describe the way the scores are spread out about this central point. Dispersion measures can be particularly valuable in comparisons of different distributions. For example, suppose the average grades for two classes in research methods are the same; however, one class has several excellent students and many poor students, whereas the other class has students who are all about average. A measure of dispersion must be used to reflect this difference. In many cases, a data set can be described adequately by simply reporting a measure of central tendency (usually the mean) and an index of dispersion.

The three measures of dispersion, or variation, are range, variance, and standard deviation. (Some statisticians include a fourth measure—sum of squares.) The simplest measure, **range** (R), is the difference between the highest and lowest scores in a distribution of scores. The formula used to calculate the range is

$$R = X_{\text{hi}} - X_{\text{lo}}$$

where X_{hi} is the highest score and X_{lo} is the lowest score. The range is sometimes reported simply as "the range among scores is 40."

Since the range uses only two scores out of the entire distribution, it is not particularly descriptive of the data set. In addition, the range often increases with the sample size because larger samples tend to include more extreme values (more outliers). For these reasons, the range is seldom used in mass media research as the sole measure of dispersion.

A second measure, **variance**, is a mathematical index of the degree to which scores deviate from, or are at variance with, the mean. A small variance indicates that most of the scores in the distribution lie fairly close to the mean—the scores are very much the same; a large variance represents widely scattered scores. Therefore, variance is directly proportional to the degree of dispersion or difference among the group of scores.

To compute the variance of a distribution, the mean is first subtracted from each score; these *deviation scores* are then squared, and the squares are summed and divided by $N-1$. (Strictly speaking, this formula is used to find the variance of a sample of scores, where the sample variance is used to estimate the population variance. If a researcher is working with a population of scores, the denominator becomes N rather than $N-1$.) The formula for variance (usually symbolized as S^2, although many textbooks use a different notation) is:

$$S^2 = \frac{\Sigma(X - \overline{X})^2}{N - 1}$$

[In many texts, the expression $(X - \overline{X})^2$ is symbolized by x^2.] The numerator in this formula, $\Sigma(X - \overline{X})^2$, is called the *sum of squares*. Although this quantity is usually not reported as a descriptive statistic, the sum of squares is used to calculate several other statistics. An example using this variance formula is shown in Table 10.7.

This equation may not be the most convenient for calculating variance, especially if N is large. A simpler, equivalent formula is

$$S^2 = \frac{\Sigma X^2}{N} - \overline{X}^2$$

The expression ΣX^2 indicates to square each score and sum the squared scores. [Note that this is not the same as $\Sigma\ (X)^2$, which indicates to sum all the scores and then square the sum.]

Variance is a commonly used and highly valuable measure of dispersion. In fact, it is at the heart of one powerful technique, *analysis of variance* (see Chapter 12), which is widely used in inferential statistics. However, variance does have one minor inconvenience: It is expressed in terms of squared deviations from the mean rather than in terms of the original measurements. To ob-

Table 10.7 *Calculation of Variance: X = Score*

X	$\overline{X}$	$X - \overline{X}$	$(X - \overline{X})^2$
6	14.65	−8.65	74.8
8	14.65	−6.65	44.2
8	14.65	−6.65	44.2
9	14.65	−5.65	31.9
11	14.65	−3.65	13.3
11	14.65	−3.65	13.3
11	14.65	−3.65	13.3
12	14.65	−2.65	7.0
12	14.65	−2.65	7.0
14	14.65	−0.65	0.4
14	14.65	−0.65	0.4
15	14.65	0.35	0.1
16	14.65	1.35	1.8
18	14.65	3.35	10.2
19	14.65	4.35	18.9
19	14.65	4.35	18.9
21	14.65	6.35	40.3
21	14.65	6.35	40.3
23	14.65	8.35	69.7
25	14.65	10.35	107.1

$$S^2 = \frac{\Sigma(X - \overline{X})^2}{N - 1} = \frac{558}{19} = 29.4$$

tain a measure of dispersion that is calibrated in the same units as the original data, it is necessary to take the *square root of the variance.* This quantity, called the **standard deviation,** is the third type of dispersion measure. The standard deviation is more meaningful than the variance because it is expressed in the same units as the measurement used to compute it.

To illustrate, assume that a research project involves a question on household income that produces a variance of $90,000—interpreted as 90,000 "squared dollars." Because the concept of "squared dollars" makes no sense, a researcher would choose to report the standard deviation: 300 "regular dollars" ($\sqrt{90{,}000} = 300$). Usually symbolized as S (or SD), standard deviation is computed using either of these formulas:

$$S = \sqrt{\frac{\Sigma(X - \overline{X})^2}{N - 1}}$$

$$S = \sqrt{\frac{\Sigma X^2}{N - 1} - \overline{X}^2}$$

Note that these two equations correspond to the two variance formulas given earlier. Standard deviation represents a given distance of a score from the mean of a distribution. (Another way to consider standard deviation is to think of it as each element's "average difference" from the mean of the data set.)

The standard deviation is especially helpful in describing the results of standardized tests. For example, most modern intelligence tests have a mean of 100 and a standard deviation of 15. A person with a score of 115 is 1 standard deviation above the mean; a person with a score of 85 is 1 standard deviation below the mean.

The notions of variance and standard deviation are easier to understand if they are visualized. Figure 10.5 shows two sets of frequency curves. Which curve in each set has the larger S^2 and S?

By computing the mean and standard deviation of a set of scores or measurements, researchers can compute **standard scores** (**z-scores**) for any distribution of data. z-scores allow researchers to compare scores or measurements obtained from totally different

Figure 10.5 *Variance As Seen in Frequency Curves*

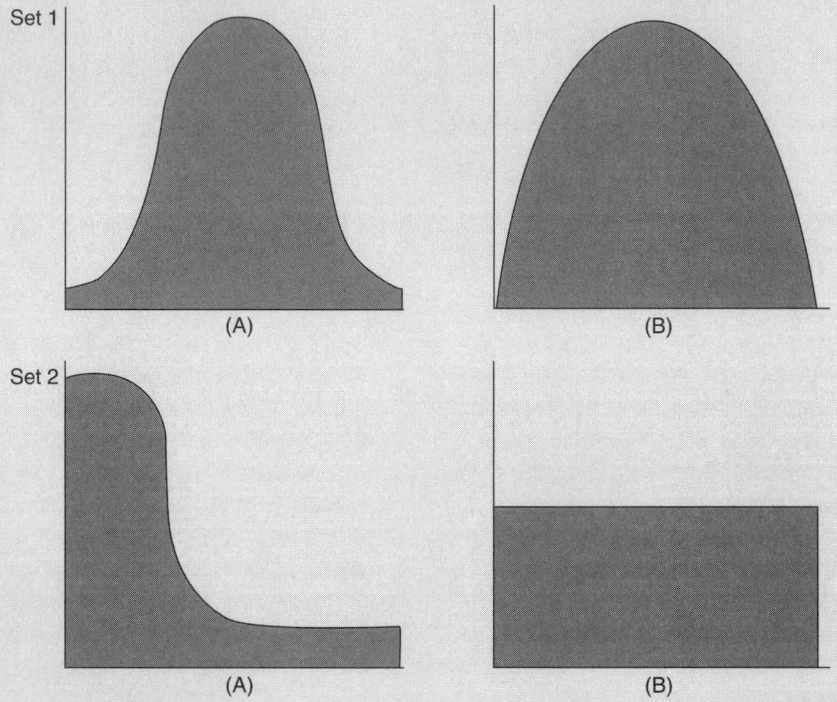

methods; they allow for comparisons of "apples and oranges." This is possible because all z-score computations are based on the same metric; they all have a mean of 0 and a standard deviation of 1.

z-scores are extremely useful and are easy to compute and interpret. They are probably one of the most widely used statistics in private-sector mass media research (see the "Readings" section on the authors' textbook website: *www.wimmerdominick.com*). The formula for computing z-scores is simply the score (X) minus the mean ($\overline{X}$), divided by the standard deviation (S):

$$z = \frac{X - \overline{X}}{S}$$

Interpretation is easy because each score represents how many standard deviation units a score, rating, or entity is above or below the mean of the data set.

The computation of z-scores and the ability to compare different measurements or methods can be demonstrated with a brief example. Suppose that two roommates are in different sections of a mass media research course. On a particular day, the two sections are given different exams, and both students score 73. However, the first roommate receives a letter grade of C, whereas the second roommate gets an A. How can this be? To understand how the professors arrived at the different grades, it is necessary to look at each section's z-scores.

Table 10.8 shows the hypothetical data for the two research sections. Each section contains 20 students. The scores in the first roommate's section range from a low of 68 to a high of 84 (range = 16), whereas the scores

Table 10.8 *z-Score Hypothetical Data*

	First Roommate's Section			Second Roommate's Section			
	Scores	(Computation)	*z* Score	Scores	(Computation)	*z* Score	
B grade	84	(84−74.6)/4.9=	1.9	73	(73− 43.9)/7.5=	3.9	A grade
B grade	81	(81−74.6)/4.9=	1.3	50	(50−43.9)/7.5=	.8	C grade
B grade	81	(81−74.6)/4.9=	1.3	50	(50−43.9)/7.5=	.8	C grade
C grade	79	(79−74.6)/4.9=	.9	47	(47−43.9)/7.5=	.4	C grade
C grade	79	(79−74.6)/4.9=	.9	46	(46−43.9)/7.5=	.3	C grade
C grade	79	(79−74.6)/4.9=	.9	45	(45−43.9)/7.5=	.2	C grade
C grade	78	(78−74.6)/4.9=	.7	43	(43−43.9)/7.5=	−.1	C grade
C grade	77	(77−74.6)/4.9=	.5	43	(43−43.9)/7.5=	−.1	C grade
C grade	77	(77−74.6)/4.9=	.5	42	(42−43.9)/7.5=	−.2	C grade
C grade	75	(75−74.6)/4.9=	.1	41	(41−43.9)/7.5=	−.4	C grade
C grade	73	(73−74.6)/4.9=	−.3	41	(41−43.9)/7.5=	−.4	C grade
C grade	71	(71−74.6)/4.9=	−.7	41	(41−43.9)/7.5=	−.4	C grade
C grade	71	(71−74.6)/4.9=	−.7	40	(40−43.9)/7.5=	−.5	C grade
C grade	71	(71−74.6)/4.9=	−.7	40	(40−43.9)/7.5=	−.5	C grade
C grade	70	(70−74.6)/4.9=	−.9	40	(40−43.9)/7.5=	−.5	C grade
C grade	70	(70−74.6)/4.9=	−.9	40	(40−43.9)/7.5=	−.5	C grade
C grade	70	(70−74.6)/4.9=	−.9	40	(40−43.9)/7.5=	−.5	C grade
D grade	69	(69−74.6)/4.9=	−1.1	39	(39−43.9)/7.5=	−.6	C grade
D grade	68	(68−74.6)/4.9=	−1.3	38	(38−43.9)/7.5=	−.8	C grade
D grade	68	(68−74.6)/4.9=	−1.3	38	(38−43.9)/7.5=	−.8	C grade
		Mean 74.6		Mean 43.9			
		S 4.9		*S* 7.5			

in the second roommate's section range from a low of 38 to a high of 73 (range = 35). The differences in scores can be due to a variety of things, including the difficulty of the tests, the ability of students in each section, and the teaching approach used by the professors.

The mean score in the first roommate's section is 74.6, with a standard deviation of 4.9 (43.9 and 7.5, respectively, in the other roommate's section). If we assume that the professors strictly followed the normal curve (discussed later in the chapter), it is easy to see why a score of 73 can result in different grades. The first roommate's performance is about average in comparison to the other students in the section; the second roommate is clearly above the performance of the other student.

The distribution of scores in Table 10.8 is not normal (discussed later). In reality, the professors might transform (change to a different metric) the scores to produce a more normal distribution, or they might set grade cutoffs at other scores to spread the grades out. When any collection of raw scores is transformed into *z*-scores, the resulting distribution possesses certain characteristics. Any score below the mean becomes a *negative* z-score, and any score above the mean is *positive*. The mean of a distribution of *z*-scores is always 0, which is also the *z*-score assigned to a person whose raw score equals the mean. As mentioned, the variance and the standard deviation of a *z*-score distribution are always both 1.00. *z*-scores are expressed in units of the standard deviation; thus a *z*-score of 3.00 means that the score is 3 standard deviation units above the mean.

z-scores are used frequently in all types of research because they allow researchers to directly compare the performances of different subjects on tests using different measurements (assuming the distributions have similar shapes). Assume for a moment that the apple harvest in a certain year was 24 bushels per acre, compared to an average annual yield of 22 bushels per acre, with a standard deviation of 10. During the same year, the orange crop yielded 18 bushels per acre, compared to an average of 16 bushels, with a standard deviation of 8. Was it a better year for apples or for oranges? The standard score formula reveals a *z*-score of .20 for apples [(24 − 22)/10] and .25 for oranges [(18 − 16)/ 8]. Relatively speaking, oranges had a better year.

	Apples	Oranges
Average bushel yield	22	16
Standard deviation	10	8
Current bushel yield	24	18
z-score	.20	.25

The Normal Curve

An important tool in statistical analysis is the normal curve, which was introduced briefly in Chapter 3. *z*-scores not only enable comparisons to be made between dissimilar measurements, but, when used in connection with the normal curve, also allow statements to be made regarding the frequency of occurrence of certain variables. Figure 10.6 shows an example of the familiar normal curve. The curve is symmetrical and achieves its maximum height at the mean, which is also its median and its mode. Also note that the curve in Figure 10.6 is calibrated in standard score units. When the curve is expressed in this way, it is called a **standard normal curve** and has all the properties of a *z*-score distribution.

Statisticians have studied the normal curve closely to describe its properties, most of which are discussed in articles available on the Internet. The most important of these properties is that a fixed proportion of the area below the curve lies between the mean and any unit of standard deviation. The area under a certain segment of the curve represents the frequency of the scores that fall therein. From Figure 10.7, which portrays the areas under the normal curve between several key standard deviation units, it can be

Figure 10.6 *The Normal Curve*

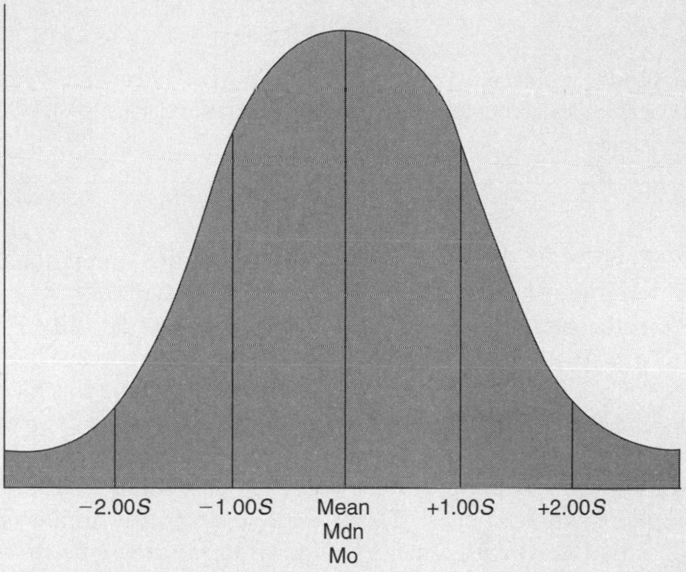

Figure 10.7 *Areas Under the Normal Curve*

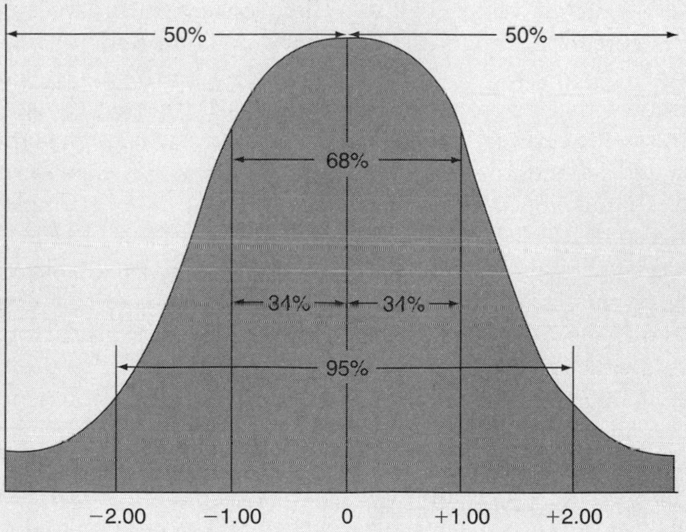

AN INSIDE LOOK

z-Scores

z-scores are often used to predict the probability of an event or occurrence. An online calculator for this computation is located at: *http://www.fourmilab.ch/rpkp/experiments/analysis/zCalc.html*

determined that roughly 68% of the total area (the scores) lies within −1 and +1 standard deviations from the mean; about 95% lies within −2 and +2 standard deviations; and so forth.

This knowledge, together with the presence of a normal distribution, allows researchers to make useful predictive statements. For example, suppose that TV viewing is normally distributed with a mean of 2 hours per day and a standard deviation of 0.5. What proportion of the population watches between 2 and 2.5 hours of TV? First, we convert the raw scores to *z*-scores:

$$\frac{2-2}{0.5} = 0 \quad \text{and} \quad \frac{2.5-2}{0.5} = 1.00$$

In other words, the *z*-score for 2 hours of TV watching is 0; the *z*-score for 2.5 hours of TV watching is 1.00.

Figure 10.7 shows that approximately 34% of the area below the curve is contained between the mean and 1 standard deviation. Thus, 34% of the population watches between 2 and 2.5 hours of television daily.

The same data can be used to find the proportion of the population that watches more than 3 hours of TV per day. Again, the first step is to translate the raw figures into *z*-scores. In this case, 3 hours corresponds to a *z*-score of 2.00. A glance at Figure 10.7 shows that approximately 98% of the area under the curve falls below a score of 2.00 (50% in the left half of the curve plus about 48% from the mean to the 2.00 mark). Thus only 2% of the population view more than 3 hours of TV daily.

Table 3 in Appendix 1 lists all the areas under the normal curve between the mean of the curve and some specified distance. To use this table, we match the row and the column represented by some standard score. For example, let's assume that the *z*-score of a normally distributed variable is 1.79. In Table 3, first find the row labeled 1.7, and then find the column labeled .09. At the intersection of the 1.7 row and the .09 column is the number .4633. The area between the mean of the curve (the midpoint) and a *z*-score of 1.79 is .4633, or roughly 46%. To take another example, what is the distance from the midpoint of the curve to the *z*-score of −1.32? According to Table 3, 40.66% of the curve lies between these two values. (In the left-hand column, find 1.3; then go over to the column labeled .02.) Note that the area is always positive even though the *z*-score was expressed as a negative value.

To make this exercise more meaningful, let's go back to our example of the two roommates (see Table 10.8). Assume that the scores were normally distributed in the class that had a mean of 74.6 and a standard deviation of 4.9. The instructor decided to assign the letter grade "C" to the middle 50% of the class. What numerical scores would receive this grade? To begin, remember that "the middle 50% of the grades" actually means "25% above the mean and 25% below the mean." Which standard deviation unit corresponds to this distance? To answer this question, it is necessary to reverse the process performed above.

Specifically, the first thing that we must do is examine the body of Table 3 in Appendix 1 for the corresponding z value of .2500. Unfortunately, it does not appear. There are, however, two percentages bracketing it—.2486 (z = .67) and .2517 (z = .68). Since .2486 is a little closer to .2500, let's use it as our area. Examining the row and column intersection at .2486, we find that it corresponds to 0.67 standard deviation units. We can now quickly calculate the test scores that receive Cs. First, we find the upper limit of the C range by taking the mean (74.6) and adding it to 0.67 × 4.9, or 3.28. This yields 77.88, which represents the quarter of the area above the mean. To find the lower limit of the range, we take the mean (74.6) and subtract from it 0.67 × 4.9, or 74.6 – 3.28. This gives us 71.32. After rounding, we find that all students who scored between 71 and 78 would receive the C grade.

The normal curve is important because many of the variables encountered by mass media researchers are distributed in a normal manner, or normally enough that minor departures can be overlooked. Furthermore, the normal curve is an example of a probability distribution that is important in inferential statistics. Finally, many of the more advanced statistics discussed in later chapters assume normal distribution of the variable(s) under consideration.

▪ Sample Distribution

A **sample distribution** is the distribution of some characteristic measured on the individuals or other units of analysis that were part of a sample. If a random sample of 1,500 college students is asked how many movies they attended in the last month, the resulting distribution of the variable "number of movies attended" is a sample distribution, with a mean ($\overline{X}$) and variance (S^2). It is theoretically possible (though not practical) to ask the same question of every college student in the United States. This would create a **population distribution** with a mean (μ) and a variance (σ^2). *A statistic is a measure based on a sample, whereas a parameter is a measure taken from a population.* Ordinarily, the precise shape of the population distribution and the values of μ and σ^2 are unknown and are estimated from the sample. This estimate is called a **sampling distribution.**

Characteristic	Sample statistic	Population parameter
Average	$\overline{X}$ (or M)	μ (mu)
Variance	S^2	σ^2 (sigma squared)
Standard deviation	S (or SD)	σ (sigma)

In any sample drawn from a specified population, the mean of the sample, $\overline{X}$, probably differs somewhat from the population mean, μ. For example, suppose that the average number of movies seen by each college student in the United States during the past month was exactly 3.8. It is unlikely that a random sample of 10 students from this population would produce a mean of exactly 3.8. The amount that the sample mean differs from μ is called the *sampling error.* If more random samples of 10 were selected from this population, the values calculated for $\overline{X}$ that are close to the population mean would become more numerous than the values of $\overline{X}$ that are greatly different from μ. If this process were repeated an infinite number of times and each mean was placed on a frequency curve, the curve would form a sampling distribution.

Once the sampling distribution has been identified, statements about the *probability* of occurrence of certain values are possible. There are many ways to define the concept of probability. Stated simply, the probability that an event will occur is equal to the relative frequency of occurrence of that event in the population under consideration (Roscoe, 1975). To illustrate, suppose a large urn contains 1,000 marbles, of which 700 are red and 300 white. The probability of drawing a red marble at random is 700/1,000, or 70%. It is also possible to calculate probability when the relative frequency of occurrence of an event is determined theoretically. For example, what is the probability of randomly guessing the answer to a true/false question? One out of two, or 50%. What is the probability of guessing the right answer on a four-item multiple-choice question? One out of four, or 25%. Probabilities can range from 0 (no chance) to 1 (a sure thing). The sum of all the probable events in a population must equal 1.00, which is also the sum of the probabilities that an event will and will not occur. For instance, when a coin is tossed, the probability of it landing face up ("heads") is .50, and the probability of it not landing face up ("tails") is .50 (.50 + .50 = 1.00).

There are two important rules of probability. The "addition rule" states that the probability that any one of a set of mutually exclusive events will occur is the sum of the probabilities of the separate events. (Two events are mutually exclusive if the occurrence of one precludes the other. In the marble example, the color of the marble is either red or white; it cannot be both.) To illustrate the addition rule, consider a population in which 20% of the people read no magazines per month, 40% read only one, 20% read two, 10% read three, and 10% read four. What is the probability of selecting at random a person who reads at least two magazines per month? The answer is .40 (.20 + .10 + .10), the sum of the probabilities of the separate events.

The "multiplication rule" states that the probability of a combination of independent events occurring is the product of the separate probabilities of the events. (Two events are independent when the occurrence of one has no effect on the other. For example, getting "tails" on the flip of a coin has no impact on the next flip.) To illustrate the multiplication rule, calculate the probability that an unprepared student will guess the correct answers to the first four questions on a true/false test. The answer is the product of the probabilities of each event: .5 (chance of guessing right on Question 1) × .5 (chance of guessing right on Question 2) × .5 (chance of guessing right on Question 3) × .5 (chance of guessing right on Question 4) = .0625.

Probability is important in inferential statistics because sampling distributions are a type of probability distribution. When the concept of probability is understood, a formal definition of "sampling distribution" is possible. A sampling distribution *is a probability distribution of all possible values of a statistic that would occur if all possible samples of a fixed size from a given population were taken.* For each outcome, the sampling distribution determines the probability of occurrence. For example, assume that a population consists of six college students. Their film viewing for the last month was as follows:

Student	Number of films seen
A	1
B	2
C	3
D	3
E	4
F	5

$$\mu = \frac{1 + 2 + 3 + 3 + 4 + 5}{6} = 3.00$$

Suppose a study is conducted using a sample of two ($N = 2$) from this population. As is evident, there is a limit to the number of combinations that can be generated, assuming that sampling is done without replacement (putting elements back into the population after they have already been selected).

Table 10.9 shows the possible outcomes. The mean of this sampling distribution is equal to μ, the mean of the population. The likelihood of drawing a sample whose mean is 2.0 or 1.5 or any other value is found simply by reading the figure in the far right-hand column.

Table 10.9 is an example of a sampling distribution determined by empirical means. Many sampling distributions, however, are not derived by mathematical calculations but are determined theoretically. For example, sampling distributions often take the form of a normal curve. When this is the case, the researcher can make use of everything that is known about the properties of the normal curve. Consider a hypothetical example using dichotomous data—data with only two possible values. (This type of data is chosen because it makes the mathematics less complicated. The same logic applies to continuous data, but the computations are elaborate.) A TV ratings firm is attempting to estimate from the results of a sample the total number of people in the population who saw a given program. One sample of 100 people might produce an estimate of 40%, a second an estimate of 42%, and a third an estimate of 39%. If, after a large number of samples have been taken, the results are expressed as a sampling distribution, probability theory predicts that it would have the shape of the normal curve with a mean equal to μ. This distribution is shown in Figure 10.8. It is interesting that if a person draws samples of size *N* repeatedly from a given population, the sampling distribution of the means of these samples, assuming *N* is large enough, will almost always be normal. This holds even if the population itself is not normally distributed. Furthermore, the mean of the sampling distribution will equal the population mean—the parameter.

In earlier discussions of the normal curve, the horizontal divisions along the base of the curve were expressed in terms of standard deviation units. With sampling distributions, this unit is called the **standard error of the mean** (*SE*) and serves as the criterion for determining the probable accuracy of an estimate. As is the case with the normal curve,

Table 10.9 *Generating a Sampling Distribution Population* = (1,2,3,3,4,5) *N* = 2

$\overline{X}$	Number of possible sample combinations producing this $\overline{X}$	Probability of occurrence
1.5	2 (1,2) (2,1)	2/30 or .07
2.0	4 (1,3) (1,3) (3,1) (3,1)	4/30 or .13
2.5	6 (1,4) (2,3) (2,3) (3,2) (3,2) (4,1)	6/30 or .20
3.0	6 (1,5) (2,4) (3,3) (3,3) (4,2) (5,1)	6/30 or .20
3.5	6 (2,5) (3,4) (3,4) (4,3) (4,3) (5,2)	6/30 or .20
4.0	4 (3,5) (3,5) (5,3) (5,3)	4/30 or .13
4.5	2 (4,5) (5,4)	2/30 or .07
		1.00

Total number of possible sample combinations = 30

Figure 10.8 *Hypothetical Sampling Distribution*

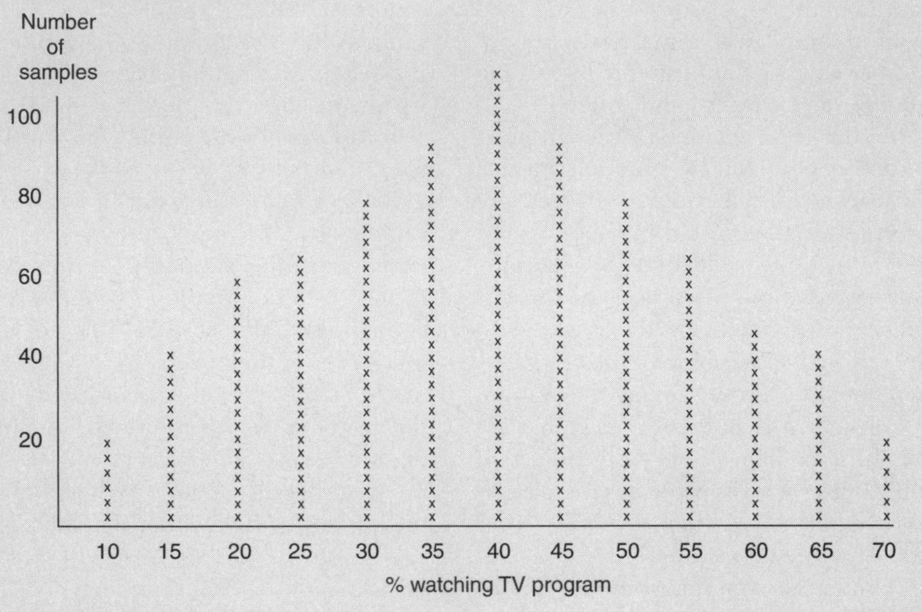

roughly 68% of the sample falls within ±1 standard error of the population mean, and about 95% falls within ±2 standard errors.

In most actual research studies, a sampling distribution is not generated by taking large numbers of samples and computing the probable outcome of each, and the standard error is not computed by taking the standard deviation of a sampling distribution of means. Instead, a researcher takes only one sample and uses it to estimate the population mean and the standard error. The process of inference from only one sample works in the following way: The sample mean is used as the best estimate of the population mean, and the standard error is calculated from the sample data. Suppose that in the foregoing TV viewing example, 40 of a sample of 100 people were watching a particular program. This number, in this case symbolized as p because the data are dichotomous, is 40% (dichotomous data require this unique formula). The formula for standard error in a dichotomous situation is

$$SE = \sqrt{\frac{pq}{N}} \times \text{Confidence level}$$

where p is the proportion viewing, $q = 1 - p$, and N is the number in the sample. In the example, the standard error at the 95% confidence level (corresponding z-score is 1.96) is

$$\sqrt{\frac{(.4)(.6)}{100}} \times 1.96 = \sqrt{\frac{.24}{100}} \times 1.96 =$$
$$.096 = \text{or } 9.6\%$$

Standard error is used in conjunction with the **confidence interval** (*CI*) set by the researcher. Recall from Chapter 4 that a confidence interval establishes an interval in which researchers state, with a certain degree of probability, that the statistical result found will fall. In the previous example, this means that at the 68% confidence interval, 68% of all possible samples taken will fall within the interval of plus and minus one standard error, or 35.2 (40 − 4.8) and 44.8 (40 + 4.8), and at the 95% confidence level, 95% of all samples will fall between plus and minus 1.96 (*SE*) or 30.4 (40 − 9.6) and 49.6 (40 + 9.6). The most commonly used confidence level is .95, which is expressed by this formula:

$$.95CI - p \pm 1.96SE$$

where *p* is the proportion obtained in the sample, *SE* is the standard error, and 1.96 is the specific value to use for enclosing exactly 95% of the scores in a normal distribution.

As an example, consider that a television ratings firm sampled 400 people and found that 20% of the sample was watching a certain program. What is the .95 confidence interval estimate for the population mean? The standard error is equal to the square root of [(.20)(.80)]/ 400, or .02. Inserting this value into the formula above yields a .95 confidence interval of .20 ±(1.96) (.02), or .16 – .24. In other words, there is a .95 chance that the population average lies between 16% and 24%. There is also a 5% chance of error—that is, that μ lies outside this interval. If this 5% chance is too great a risk, it is possible to compute a .99 confidence interval estimate by substituting 2.58 for 1.96 in the formula. (In the normal curve, 99% of all scores fall within ±2.58 standard errors of the mean.) For a discussion of confidence intervals using continuous data, consult Hays (1973) and the Internet.

The concept of sampling distribution is important to statistical inference. Confidence intervals represent only one way in which sampling distributions are used in inferential statistics. They are also important in hypothesis testing, where the probability of a specified sample result is determined under assumed population conditions.

▪ Data Transformation

Most statistical procedures are based on the assumption that the data are normally distributed. Although many statistical procedures are "robust," or conservative, in their requirement of normally distributed data, in some instances the results of studies using data that show a high degree of skewness may be invalid. The data used for any study should be checked for normality, a procedure accomplished very easily with most statistical software.

Most nonnormal distributions are created by outliers. When such anomalies arise, researchers can attempt to transform the data to achieve normality. Basically, transformation involves performing some type of mathematical adjustment to each score to try to bring the outliers closer to the group mean. This may take the form of multiplying or dividing each score by a certain number, or even taking the square root or log of the scores.

It makes no difference what procedure is used (although some methods are more powerful than others), as long as the same procedure is applied to all the data. This is known as a **monotonic transformation.**

Transformation is a simple process and can be computed either in statistical software packages or on spreadsheets. Here is an example of transformation that demonstrates how two transformations (square root and $\log_{10}$ of the original scores) "pull in" the outliers. The data remain the same as long as the same transformation is used for all scores. In other words, any statistical test conducted on the original scores will have the same result if the square root or $\log_{10}$ scores are used.

There are a variety of transformation methods available, depending on the type of distribution found in the data. Rummel (1970) describes these procedures in more detail, and there are many references on the Internet—search for "data transformation."

Table 10.10: *Example of Monotonic Transformation*

	Original score	Square root	Log_{10}
	98	9.9	1.99
	84	9.2	1.92
	82	9.1	1.91
	78	8.8	1.89
	75	8.7	1.88
	68	8.2	1.83
	61	7.8	1.79
	50	7.1	1.70
	48	6.9	1.68
	11	3.3	1.04
Mean	65.5	7.9	1.8
SD	24.6	1.9	0.3
High score	98	9.9	1.99
Low score	11	1.9	1.04

▪▪▪ Summary

This chapter introduced some of the more common descriptive and inferential statistics used by mass media researchers. Little attempt has been made to explain the mathematical derivations of the formulas and principles presented; rather, the emphasis here (as throughout the book) has been on understanding the reasoning behind these statistics and their applications. Unless researchers understand the logic underlying such concepts as mean, standard deviation, and standard error, the statistics themselves are of little value.

Key Terms

Abscissa
Bar chart
Central tendency
Confidence interval
Confidence level
Cumulative frequency
Data transformation
Descriptive statistics
Dispersion
Distribution
Frequency curve
Frequency distribution
Frequency polygon
Histogram
Mean
Median
Mode
Monotonic transformation
Normal curve
Ordinate
Outlier
Population distribution
Range
Sample distribution
Sampling distribution
Sigma
Skewness
Standard deviation
Standard error of the mean
Standard normal curve
Standard scores
Summary statistics
Variance
z-score

Using the Internet

1. The Internet is a wonderful source for information about statistics. Virtually any topic in statistics can be found on the Internet, and there are many very interesting bits of information. For example, although many references are in French, see the Internet for "Quetelet" and "Laplace."
2. There are many excellent statistical software packages available at reasonable prices. Search the Internet for "statistical methods" and "statistical tests." One good site is *http://www.superstats.com/index.html.*
3. Go to *http://nilesonline.com/stats* for an interesting perspective on statistics as used by journalists. Another site that includes several test problems for you to compute is located at *http://www.gcse.com/Maths/teach/esstat.htm.*
4. Go to *http://www.execpc.com/~helberg/statistics.html* for a listing of all types of statistical sites on the Internet.
5. *z*-scores are used in several areas such as the stock market and banking. Search the Internet

for "z-scores" to see some examples of how the statistic is used in non-media areas.

Questions and Problems for Further Investigation

1. Find the mean, variance, and standard deviation for these two sets of data (answers appear at the end of the exercises):

   Group 1: 5, 5, 5, 6, 7, 5, 4, 8, 4, 5, 8, 8, 7, 6, 3, 3, 2, 5, 4, 7
   Group 2: 19, 21, 22, 27, 16, 15, 18, 24, 26, 24, 22, 27, 16, 15, 18, 21, 20

2. From a regular deck of playing cards, what is the probability of randomly drawing an ace? An ace or a nine? A spade or a face card?
3. Assume that scores on the Mass Media History Test are normally distributed in the population with a μ of 50 and a population standard deviation of 5. What are the probabilities of these events?
   a. Someone picked at random has a score between 50 and 55.
   b. Someone picked at random scores 2 standard deviations above the mean.
   c. Someone picked at random has a score of 58 or higher.
4. Assume that a population of scores is 2, 4, 5, 5, 7, and 9. Generate the sampling distribution of the mean if $N = 2$ (sampling without replacement).
5. Search the Internet for more information on confidence intervals and probability. How are the two concepts related?
6. If you are using InfoTrac College Edition, you can read another explanation of descriptive statistics (with examples taken from sports) by retrieving: "A statistics primer: descriptive measures for continuous data" by Mary Lou V. H. Greenfield, John E. Kuhn, and Edward M. Wojtys in the October–November issue of the *Journal of Sports Medicine*.

Answers to Question 1:

Group 1: $\overline{X} = 5.35$, $S^2 = 3.08$, $S = 1.76$

Group 2: $\overline{X} = 20.6$, $S^2 = 16.2$, $S = 4.0$

For additional information on these and related topics, see

http://www.wimmerdominick.com

References and Suggested Readings

Blalock, H. M. (1972). *Social statistics.* New York: McGraw-Hill.

Champion, D. J. (1981). *Basic statistics for social research* (2nd ed.). New York: Macmillan.

Hays, W. L. (1973). *Statistics for the social sciences.* New York: Holt, Rinehart & Winston.

Hurlburt, R. T. (1998). *Comprehending behavioral statistics* (2nd ed.). Pacific Grove, CA: Brooks/Cole.

Jaccard, J., & Becker, M. A. (1996). *Statistics for the behavioral sciences* (3rd ed.). Belmont, CA: Wadsworth.

Lehmann, E. L. (1991). *Testing statistical hypotheses* (2nd ed.). Belmont, CA: Wadsworth.

Maleske, R. T. (1994). *Foundations for gathering and interpreting behavioral data: An introduction to statistics.* Pacific Grove, CA: Brooks/Cole.

Mason, R. D., Lind, D. A., & Marchal, W. G. (1998). *Statistics: An introduction.* Belmont, CA: Duxbury.

Moore, D. S. (1998). *Introduction to the practice of statistics.* New York: W. H. Freeman.

Nunnally, J. (1994). *Psychometric theory* (3rd ed.). New York: McGraw-Hill.

Rasmussen, S. (1992). *An introduction to statistics with data analysis.* Pacific Grove, CA: Brooks/Cole.

Roscoe, J. T. (1975). *Fundamental research statistics for the behavioral sciences.* New York: Holt, Rinehart & Winston.

Rummel, R. J. (1970). *Factor analysis.* Chicago: Northwestern University Press.

Siegel, S. (1988). *Nonparametric statistics for the behavioral sciences.* New York: McGraw-Hill.

Toothaker, L. E. (1996). *Introductory statistics for the behavioral sciences* (2nd ed.). Pacific Grove, CA: Brooks/Cole.

Williams, F. (1992). *Reasoning with statistics* (2nd ed.). New York: Holt, Rinehart & Winston.

Chapter 11

Hypothesis Testing

Scientists rarely begin a research study without a problem or a question to test. That would be similar to holding a cross-country race without telling the runners where to start. Both events need an initial step: The cross-country race needs a starting line, and the research study needs a question or statement to test. This chapter describes the procedures for developing research questions and the steps involved in testing them.

■ *Research Questions and Hypotheses*

Mass media researchers use a variety of approaches to answer questions. Some research is informal and seeks to solve relatively simple problems; some research is based on theory and requires formally worded questions. All researchers, however, must start with some tentative generalization regarding a relationship between two or more variables. These generalizations may take two forms: *research questions* and *statistical hypotheses.* The two are identical except for the aspect of prediction—hypotheses predict an outcome; research questions do not.

Research Questions

Research questions are used frequently in problem- or policy-oriented studies where the researcher is not interested in testing the statistical significance of the findings. For example, researchers analyzing television program preferences or newspaper circulation may be concerned only with discovering general *indications,* not with gathering data for statistical testing. However, research questions can be tested for statistical significance. They are not merely weak hypotheses; they are valuable tools for many types of research.

Research questions are frequently used in areas that have been studied only marginally or not at all. Studies of this type are classified as *exploratory research* because researchers have no idea what they may find. They have no prior information to base predictions on. Exploratory research is intended to search for data *indications* rather than to attempt to find causality (Tukey, 1962, 1986). The goal is to gather *preliminary* data, to be able to refine research questions, and possibly to develop hypotheses—an approach often used by graduate students for theses and dissertations.

Research questions may be stated as simple questions about the relationship between two or more variables or about the components of a phenomenon. As Tukey (1986) states, exploratory research responds to the question: What appears to be going on? For example, researchers might ask, "What are the characteristics of environmental reporters?" (Detjen, Fico, Li, & Kim, 2000) or "Do wire services differ in how they cover AIDS-HIV in different world regions?" (Bardhan, 2001). Walsh-Childers, Chance, and Swain (1999) posed several research questions about the way daily newspapers cover health care: (1) To what extent are health issues covered in daily newspapers relative to other topics? (2) How often does coverage include information about organization, delivery, and financing of health services? (3) Do major national and regional newspapers cover health issues differently than other newspapers?

Benefits of Hypotheses

Provide direction for a study
Eliminate trial-and-error research
Help rule out intervening and confounding variables
Allow for quantification of variables

Criteria for Good Hypotheses

Compatible with current knowledge
Logically consistent
Succinct
Testable

Research Hypotheses

In countless situations, researchers develop studies based on existing theory and are thus able to make predictions about the outcome of their work. Tukey (1986) says that hypotheses ask, Do we have firm evidence that such-and-such is happening (has happened)? King (2000), drawing upon various theories about the functions of humor, hypothesized that hero wisecracks accompanying violent actions in a fictional action film will decrease audience distress reactions to the film. Her experimental results supported her reasoning. Krcmar and Cooke (2001) drew upon theories of moral reasoning to hypothesize that younger children were more likely to perceive a violent act as correct and justified if the perpetrator went unpunished for the act than if punishment occurred. Their results were consistent with their prediction.

To facilitate the discussion of research testing, the remainder of this chapter uses only the word *hypothesis*. But recall that research questions and hypotheses are identical except for the absence of the element of prediction in the former.

Purposes of Hypotheses

Hypotheses offer researchers a variety of benefits. First, they *provide direction for a study*. As indicated at the opening of the chapter, research that begins without hypotheses offers no starting point; there is no blueprint of the sequence of steps to follow. Hypothesis development is usually the culmination of a rigorous literature review and emerges as a natural step in the research process. Without hypotheses, research lacks focus and clarity.

A second benefit of hypotheses is that they *eliminate trial-and-error research*—that is, the haphazard investigation of a topic in the hope of finding something significant. Hypothesis development requires researchers to isolate a specific area for study. Trial-and-error research is time-consuming and wasteful. The development of hypotheses eliminates this waste.

Hypotheses also help rule out intervening and confounding variables. Since hypotheses focus research to precise testable statements, other variables, whether relevant or not, are

AN INSIDE LOOK
Syllogisms

A syllogism is a sequence of three propositions such that the first two propositions imply the third proposition, the conclusion. There are three major types of syllogism. The most common is the "hypothetical syllogism," which is demonstrated by the Stevie Wonder example on page 268. The hypothetical syllogism uses the first premise as a conditional hypothesis: If p then q, then continues (p), and concludes with therefore (q).

excluded. For instance, researchers interested in determining how the media are used to provide consumer information must develop a specific hypothesis stating what media are included, what products are being tested, for what specific demographic groups, and so on. Through this process of narrowing, extraneous and intervening variables are eliminated or controlled. This does not mean that hypotheses eliminate all error in research, however; nothing can do that. Error in some form is present in every study.

Finally, hypotheses allow for quantification of variables. As stated in Chapter 2, any concept or phenomenon can be quantified if it is given an adequate operational definition. All terms used in hypotheses must have an operational definition. For example, to test the hypothesis "There is a significant difference between recall of television commercials for subjects exposed to low-frequency broadcasts and that for subjects exposed to high-frequency broadcasts," researchers need operational definitions of *recall, low-frequency,* and *high-frequency.* Words that cannot be quantified cannot be included in a hypothesis.

In addition, some concepts have a variety of definitions, such as *violence.* The complaint of many researchers is not that violence cannot be quantified, but rather that it can be operationally defined in more than one way. Therefore, before one can compare the results of studies of media violence, it is necessary to consider the definition of violence used in each study. Contradictory results may be due to the definitions used, not to the presence or absence of violence.

Criteria for Useful Hypotheses

A useful hypothesis should possess at least four essential characteristics: It should be compatible with current knowledge in the area, it should be logically consistent, it should be stated concisely, and it should be testable.

That hypotheses must be in harmony with current knowledge is obvious. If available literature strongly suggests one point of view, researchers who develop hypotheses that oppose this knowledge without basis only slow the development of the area. For example, it has been demonstrated beyond a doubt that most people obtain their news from television. It would be rather wasteful for a researcher to develop a hypothesis suggesting that this is not true. There is simply too much evidence to the contrary. (This is not to say that existing knowledge cannot be challenged; significant advances in science are made sometimes by doubting conventional wisdom, but researchers who do challenge existing knowledge should have a compelling reason to do so.)

The criterion of logical consistency means that if a hypothesis suggests that A = B and B = C, then A must also equal C. That is, if reading the *New York Times* implies a knowledge of current events, and a knowledge of current events means greater participation in social activities, then readers of the *New York Times* should exhibit greater participation in social activities. (Logical consistency relates to Aristotle's notion of syllogism, which produces such pop culture "logical consistencies" as: God is Love/Love is blind/ (therefore) Stevie Wonder is God.)

It should come as no surprise that hypotheses must be stated as succinctly as possible. A hypothesis such as "Intellectual and psychomotor creativity possessed by an individual positively coincides with the level of intelligence of the individual as indicated by standardized evaluative procedures measuring intelligence" is not exactly concise. Stated simply, the same hypothesis could read, "Psychomotor ability and IQ are positively related."

Most researchers agree that developing an untestable hypothesis is unproductive, but there is a fine line between what is and what is not testable. We agree that untestable hypotheses will probably create a great deal of frustration, and the information collected and tested will probably add nothing to the development of knowledge. However, the situation here is similar to some teachers who say (and really mean) on the first day of class, "Don't ever be afraid to ask me a question because you think it's stupid. The only stupid question is the one that is not asked." We consider hypothesis development a similar situation. It is much better to form an untestable hypothesis than to form none at all. The developmental process itself is a valuable experience, and researchers will no doubt soon find their error. The untestable ("stupid") hypothesis may eventually become a respectable research project. Our suggestion is to try not to develop untestable hypotheses but to accept the fact when it happens, correct it, and move on. Beginning researchers should not try to solve the problems of the world. Take small steps.

What are some unrealistic and untestable hypotheses? Read the following list of hypotheses (some relate to areas other than mass media) and determine what is wrong with each one. Feldman (1987) was used in preparing some of these statements.

1. Watching too many soap operas on television creates antisocial behavior.
2. Clocks run clockwise because most people are right-handed.
3. High school students with no exposure to television earn higher grades than those who watch television.
4. Students who give teachers gifts tend to earn higher grades.
5. People who read newspapers wash their hands more frequently than those who do not read newspapers.
6. Movies rated XXX are 10 times worse than movies rated XX and 20 times worse than movies rated X.
7. College students who cut classes have more deceased relatives than students who attend classes.
8. Einstein's theory of relativity would not have been developed if he had had access to television.
9. Sales of Fords in America would be higher if Lexus did not exist.
10. World opinion of the United States would be different if Richard Nixon had never been the president.

The Null Hypothesis

The **null hypothesis** (also called the "hypothesis of no difference") asserts that the statistical differences or relationships being analyzed are due to *chance* or *random error.* The null hypothesis (H_0) is the logical alternative to the research hypothesis (H_1). For example, the hypothesis "The level of attention paid to radio commercials is positively related to the amount of recall of the commercial" has its logical alternative (null hypothesis): "The level of attention paid to radio commercials is *not* related to the amount of recall of the commercial."

In practice, researchers rarely state the null hypothesis. Since every research hypothesis does have its logical alternative, stating the null form is redundant (Williams, 1979). However, the null hypothesis is always present and plays an important role in the rationale underlying hypothesis testing.

Testing Hypotheses for Statistical Significance

In hypothesis testing, or significance testing, the researcher either rejects or accepts the null hypothesis. That is, if H_0 is accepted (supported), it is assumed that H_1 is rejected; and if H_0 is rejected, H_1 must be accepted.

To determine the statistical significance of a research study, the researcher must set a **probability level,** or *significance level,* against which the null hypothesis is tested. If the results of the study indicate a probability lower than this level, the researcher can reject the null hypothesis. If the research outcome has a high probability, the researcher must support (or, more precisely, fail to reject) the null hypothesis. In reality, since the null hypothesis is not generally stated, acceptance and rejection apply to the research hypothesis, not to the null hypothesis. The probability level is expressed by a lowercase letter p (indicating probability), followed by a "less than" or "less than or equal to" sign, and then a value. For example, "$p \leq .01$" means that the null hypothesis is being tested at the .01 level of significance and that the results will be considered statistically significant if the probability is equal to or lower than this level. A .05 level of significance indicates that the researcher has a 5% chance of making a wrong decision about rejecting the null hypothesis (or accepting the research hypothesis). Establishing a level of significance depends on the amount of error researchers are willing to accept (in addition to other factors peculiar to the particular research study). The question of error is discussed in greater detail later in the chapter.

It is common practice in mass media research studies to set the probability level at .01 or .05, which means that either one or five times out of 100, significant results of the study occur because of random error or chance. There is no logical reason for using these figures; the practice has been followed for many years because Sir Ronald A. Fisher, who developed the concept of significance testing, formulated tables based on the areas under the normal curve defined by .01 and .05. In many research areas, however, researchers set the significance level according to the purpose of the study rather than by general convention. Some studies use .10 or .20, depending on the goals of the research. In exploratory research especially, levels that are more liberal are generally used; these are made more restrictive as further information is gathered.

In a theoretical sampling distribution (a graphed display of sampling results), the proportion of the area in which the null hypothesis is rejected is called the **region of rejection.** This area is defined by the level of significance chosen by the researcher. If the .05 level of significance is used, then 5% of the sampling distribution becomes the critical region. Conversely, the null hypothesis is retained in the region between the two rejection values (or levels).

As Figure 11.1 shows, the regions of rejection are located in the tails, or outer edges, of the sampling distribution. The terms *one-tail testing* and *two-tail testing* refer to the type of prediction made in a research study. A one-tail test predicts that the results will fall in only one direction—either positive or negative. This approach is more stringent than the two-tail test, which does not predict a direction. Two-tail tests are generally used when little information is available about the

Figure 11.1 *Regions of Rejection for $p \leq .05$ (Two-Tail)*

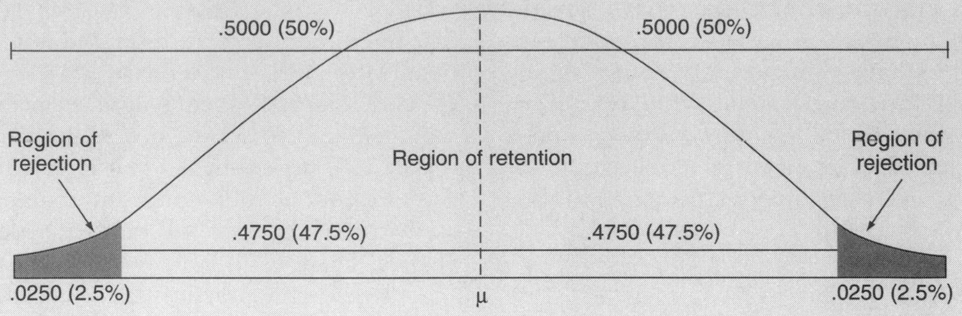

research area. One-tail tests are used when researchers have more knowledge of the area and are able to more accurately predict the outcome of the study.

Consider, for example, a study of the math competency of a group of subjects who receive a special learning treatment, possibly a series of television programs on mathematics. The hypothesis is that the group, after viewing the programs, will have scores on a standardized math test significantly different from those of the remainder of the population, which has not seen the programs. The level of significance is set at .05, indicating that for the null hypothesis to be rejected, the mean test score of the sample must fall outside the boundaries in the normal distribution that are specified by the statement "$p \leq .05$." These boundaries, or values, are determined by a simple computation. First, the critical values of the boundaries are found by consulting the normal distribution table (see Appendix 1, Table 3).

In Figure 11.1 the area from the middle of the distribution, or μ (mu), the hypothesized mean (denoted by the vertical broken line), to the end of the tails is 50%. At the .05 level, with a two-tail test, there is a 2.5% (.0250) area of rejection tucked into each tail. Consequently, the area from the middle of the distribution to the region of rejection is equal to 47.5% (50% − 2 .5% = 47.5%).

It follows that the corresponding z values that define the region of rejection are those that cut off 47.5% (.4750) of the area from μ to each end of the tail. To find this z value, use Table 3 of Appendix 1 (Areas Under the Normal Curve). This table provides a list of the proportions of various areas under the curve as measured from the midpoint of the curve out toward the tails. The far left column displays the first two digits of the z value. The row across the top of the table contains the third digit. For example, find the 1.0 row in the left-hand column. Next, find the entry under the .08 column in this row. The table entry is .3599. This means that 35.99% of the curve is found between the midpoint and a z value of 1.08. Of course, another 35.99% lies in the other direction, from the midpoint to a z value of −1.08. In our current example, it is necessary to work backward. We know the areas under the curve that we want to define (.4750 to the left and right of μ), and we need to find the z values. An examination of the body of Table 3 shows that .4750 corresponds to a z value of ±1.96.

These values are then used to determine the region of rejection:

Figure 11.2 *Regions of Rejection for Math Test*

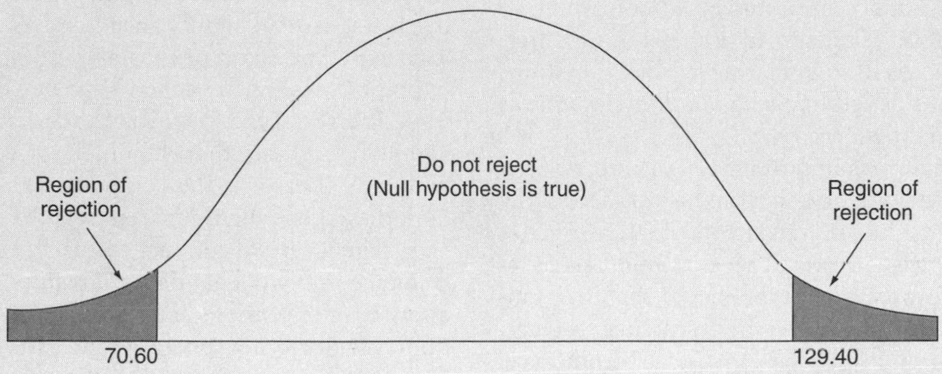

$$-1.96\ \alpha_m + \mu = \text{lower boundary}$$
$$+1.96\ \alpha_m + \mu = \text{upper boundary}$$

where α_m is the standard deviation of the distribution and μ is the population mean. Assume that the population mean for math competency is 100 and the standard deviation is 15. Thus, the sample must achieve a mean math competency score either lower than 70.60 or higher than 129.40 for the research study to be considered significant:

$$-1.96(15) + 100 = 70.60$$
$$+1.96(15) + 100 = 129.40$$

If a research study produces a result between 70.60 and 129.40, then the null hypothesis cannot be rejected; the instructional television programs had no significant effect on math levels. When we use the normal distribution to demonstrate these boundaries, the area of rejection is illustrated in Figure 11.2.

The Importance of Significance

The concept of significance testing causes problems for many people, primarily because too many researchers overemphasize the importance of statistical significance. When researchers find that the results of a study are nonsignificant, it is common to "talk around" the results—to deemphasize the finding that the results were not statistically significant. But there is really no need to use this approach.

There is no difference in value between a study that finds statistically significant results and a study that does not. Both studies provide valuable information. Discovering that some variables are not significant is just as important as determining which variables are significant. The nonsignificant study can save time for other researchers working in the same area by ruling out worthless variables. Nonsignificant research is important in collecting information about a theory or concept.

Also, there is nothing wrong with the idea of proposing a null hypothesis as the research hypothesis. For example, a researcher could formulate this hypothesis: "There is no significant difference in comprehension of program content between a group of adults (ages 18–49) with normal hearing that views a television program with closed-captioned phrases and a similar group that views the same program without captions." A scientific research study does not always have to test for significant relationships; it can also test for nonsignificance.

However, sloppy research techniques and faulty measurement procedures can add to error variance in a study and contribute to the failure to reject a hypothesis of no difference as well as jeopardize the entire study. This is a danger in using a null hypothesis as a substantive hypothesis.

Finally, it's important to remember that a statistically significant result is not necessarily a meaningful result. A significant statistical test simply tells the researcher that an observed result is probably not the result of chance or random error. It's up to the researcher to determine if that result has any social significance. For example, suppose a company is interested in buying a new software program that claims to improve keyboard skills. A researcher conducts an experiment where one group uses the software program and the other does not. The keyboard skills of the two groups are then measured. Suppose the group using the software typed an average of 65 words per minute while the other group averaged 63. Given a large sample and a small variance in scores, it's entirely possible that this two-point difference might be significant at the .05 level. However, is this two-point gain a meaningful difference? Is it enough of a difference to justify spending a considerable amount of money to buy the software and require all keyboard personnel to use the program? The statistical significance is only one factor that needs to be considered in making the decision.

Salkind (2000) offers the following considerations when evaluating the importance of statistical significance:

- Significance is not very meaningful unless the study has a sound conceptual base that lends meaning to the results.
- Significance cannot be interpreted independently of the context in which it occurs.
- Significance should not be the end-all of all research. If a study is designed correctly, failing to reject the null hypothesis might be an important finding.

Error

As with all steps in the research process, testing for statistical significance involves error. Two types of error particularly relevant to hypothesis testing are called **Type I error** and **Type II error.** Type I error is the rejection of a null hypothesis that should be accepted, and Type II error is the acceptance of a null hypothesis that should be rejected. To elaborate, whenever we conduct research, there is a chance that we'll get data that support our alternative hypothesis simply by luck or random accident, not because our alternative hypothesis is actually true. When this happens we incorrectly reject a null hypothesis that actually should be retained. This is Type I error. By the same token, random error could work the other way and we could end up with data that do not support our alternative hypothesis even though our alternative hypothesis is actually true. When this happens, we fail to reject a null hypothesis that should be rejected. This is Type II error.

Maybe an analogy will help. Assume that you think you have a problem with your car's steering and you take your car to a mechanic. Further, assume that you are omniscient and all-knowing and know that there is actually nothing wrong with your car's steering. Ultimately, the mechanic can tell you one of two things: (1) There is a problem with the steering, or (2) There is no problem with the steering. If the mechanic says "No problem," that's great. That's the correct decision. However, the mechanic might misread some test results and say "There is a problem." This is an error. In this situation, we have falsely rejected a true null hypothesis ("There's nothing wrong with the steering.") and have committed a Type I error.

Now suppose there *really* is something wrong with the steering. If the mechanic says, "You have a problem," that's great. That's a correct decision. But the mechanic may be having a bad day, overlook some test results, and say, "There's no problem." This is an error. We

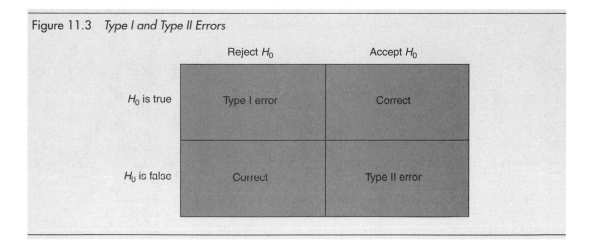

Figure 11.3 *Type I and Type II Errors*

	Reject H_0	Accept H_0
H_0 is true	Type I error	Correct
H_0 is false	Correct	Type II error

Figure 11.4 *Inverse Relationship Between Type I and Type II Errors*

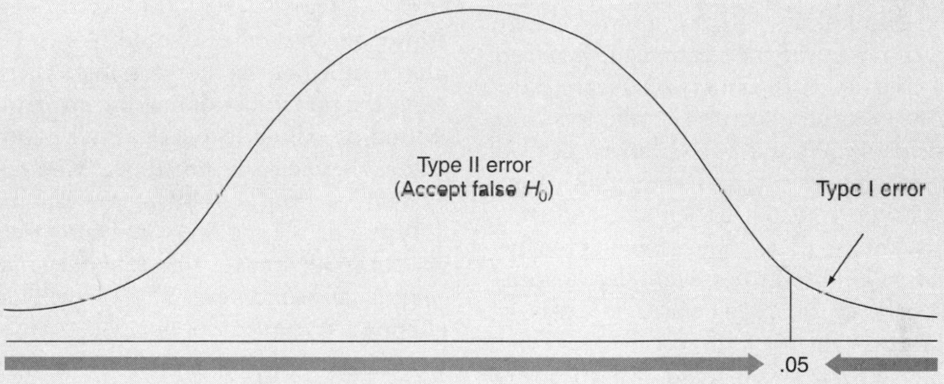

have failed to reject a false null hypothesis. We have committed a Type II error. These error types are represented in Figure 11.3.

The probability of making a Type I error (sometimes called *alpha error*) is equal to the established level of significance and is therefore under the direct control of the researcher. That is, to reduce the probability of Type I error, the researcher can simply set the level of significance closer to zero.

Type II error, often called *beta error*, is a bit more difficult to conceptualize. The researcher does not have direct control over Type II error; instead, Type II error is controlled, though indirectly, by the design of the research. In addition, the level of Type II error is inversely proportional to the level of Type I error: As Type I error decreases, Type II error increases, and vice versa. The potential magnitude of Type II error depends in part on the probability level and in part on which of the possible alternative hypotheses actually is true. Figure 11.4 shows the inverse relationship between the two types of error.

As mentioned earlier, most research studies do not state the null hypothesis because it

Figure 11.5 *Use of the Research Hypothesis to Distinguish Between Type I and Type II Errors*

	Where one exists	Where none exists
Significant difference found	Correct	Type I error
No significant difference found	Type II error	Correct

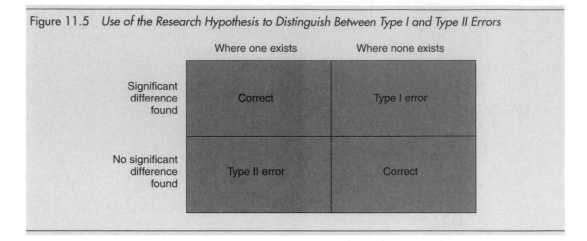

is assumed. However, there is a way to depict Type I and Type II errors without considering the null hypothesis, and this approach may help to demonstrate the relationship between Type I and Type II errors. As Figure 11.5 demonstrates, the research hypothesis is used to describe Type I and Type II errors instead of the null hypothesis. To use the table, start at the desired row on the left side and then read the column entry that completes the hypothesis to be tested. For example, "Significant difference found where none exists = Type I error."

Let's illustrate Type I and Type II errors one more time with a hypothetical example. Consider a research study to determine the effects of a short-term public relations campaign promoting the use of seat belts in automobiles. Suppose that the effort was highly successful and indeed changed the behavior of a majority of subjects exposed to the campaign. (This information is, of course, unknown to the researcher.) If the researcher finds that a significant effect was created by the campaign, the conclusion is a correct one; if the researcher does not find a significant effect, a Type II error is committed. On the other hand, if the campaign actually had no effect but the researcher concludes that the campaign was successful, a Type I error is committed.

Balancing Type I and Type II Error

Although researchers would like to be right all the time, it's just not possible. There is always the possibility of making an error in rejecting or failing to reject a null hypothesis. Under these circumstances, researchers must evaluate the various consequences of making a Type I or a Type II error. There are different consequences for different decisions. Setting a significance level at .0001 will virtually eliminate Type I error but will dramatically increase the odds of Type II error. Suppose a researcher is testing the efficacy of several new drugs. Which result is more harmful? Making a Type I error and claiming that a drug works when it does not, or making a Type II error and overlooking some drugs that might actually work?

There is no easy answer to the problem of balancing these two error types, but one procedure to help researchers deal with this issue is called power analysis.

Power

The concept of power is intimately related to Type I and Type II errors. **Power** refers to the probability of rejecting the null hypothesis

> *AN INSIDE LOOK*
> **Power Analysis**
>
> Another example might help here. This time go back to the software program that was touted as improving keyboard skills. In the example, using the program resulted in an average gain of two words per minute (what we might call a small effects size). However, it's possible that the program might have had a more pronounced effect, maybe improving scores by five words (we might call this a medium effects size) or ten words (we might call this a large effects size.) A powerful statistical test would be able to detect all of these differences; a less powerful test might only detect the large effects size.

when it is true. In other words, power indicates the probability that a statistical test of a null hypothesis will result in the conclusion that the phenomenon under study actually exists (Cohen, 1988). This is the situation that researchers want to achieve; if there is a difference, researchers want a statistical test that can detect it.

Let's go back to the steering problem and the mechanic example mentioned earlier. First, what are the consequences of a Type I and a Type II error in this situation? If your car's steering is *really* broken but your mechanic, for whatever reason, fails to notice it (a Type II error), you might drive off a cliff. On the other hand, if your steering is *really* working properly and the mechanic mistakenly says it's broken (a Type I error), the consequences are bad (you'll pay for unnecessary repair) but not as bad as driving off a cliff. Obviously, if you really have a problem with your steering, you want a mechanic who will be able to discover it. Similarly, if there is a difference between two variables in a research project, you want a statistic that is powerful enough to detect it.

Statistical power is a function of three parameters: probability level, sample size, and effects size. As we know, the probability level is under the direct control of the researcher and predetermines the probability of committing a Type I error. Sample size refers to the number of subjects used in an experiment. The most difficult concept is effects size. Basically, the effects size is the degree to which the null hypothesis is rejected; this can be stated either in general terms (such as any nonzero value) or in exact terms (such as .40). That is, when a null hypothesis is false, it is false to some degree; researchers can say the null hypothesis is false and leave it at that, or they can specify exactly how false it is. The larger the effects size, the greater the degree to which the phenomenon under study is present (Cohen, 1988).

Researchers seldom know the exact value of the effects size, and in these cases, they can use one of three alternatives:

1. Estimate the effects size based on knowledge in the area of investigation or indications from previous studies in the area, or simply state the size as "small," "medium," or "large." (Cohen describes these values in greater detail.)
2. Assume an effects size of "medium."
3. Select a series of effects sizes and experiment.

The technical definition of the power of a statistical test is 1—the probability of Type II error. When the probability level, sample size, and effects size are known, researchers can consult power tables (see "Using the Internet" at the end of this chapter) to determine the level of power in their study. Power tables consist of sets of curves that represent different sample sizes, levels of significance (.05 and so on), and types of tests (one- or two-tail). For example, in a two-tail test with a probability of .05 and a sample size of 10, the probability of rejecting the null hypothesis (that is, assuming that it is false) is .37 and the probability of accepting or retaining the hypothesis is .63. The power tables show that by increasing the sample size to 20, the probability of rejecting the null hypothesis jumps to .62 and the probability of retaining the hypothesis drops to .38. Many researchers suggest a desirable power value is .80 when working at the .05 level of significance. Researchers can find out what sample size will yield a power of .80 by consulting online power calculators or power curves.

A determination of power is important for two reasons. First and most important, if a low power level prevents researchers from arriving at statistical significance, a Type II error may result. If the power of the statistical test is increased, however, the results may become significant. Second, the high power level may help interpret the research results. If an experiment just barely reaches the significance level but has high power, researchers can place more faith in the results. Without power figures, researchers have to be more hesitant in their interpretations.

Statistical power should be considered in all research studies. Although power is only an approximation, computation of the value helps control Type II error. In addition, as power increases, there is no direct effect on Type I error; power acts independently of Type I error. Chase and Tucker (1975) conducted power analyses on articles published in nine communications journals. They found that 82% of the 46 articles analyzed had an average power for medium effects of less than .80 (the recommended minimum power value). In addition, more than half the articles had an average power of less than .50, which suggests a significant increase in the probability of Type II error.

▪ ▪ ▪ Summary

Hypothesis development in scientific research is important because the process refines and focuses the research by excluding extraneous variables and permitting variables to be quantified. Rarely will researchers conduct a project without developing some type of research question or hypothesis. Research without this focus usually proves to be a waste of time (although some people may argue that many inventions, theories, and new information have been found without the focus provided by a research question or hypothesis).

An applicable hypothesis must be compatible with current related knowledge, and it must be logically consistent. It should also be stated as simply as possible and, generally speaking, it should be testable. Hypotheses must be tested for statistical significance. This testing involves error, particularly Type I and Type II error. Error must be considered in all research. An understanding of error such as Type I and Type II does not make research foolproof, but it makes the process somewhat easier because researchers must pay closer attention to the elements involved in the project.

Too much emphasis is often placed on significance testing. It is possible that a nonsignificant test may add information to an available body of knowledge simply by finding what "does not work" or "should not be investigated." However, some nonsignificant research projects may be more valuable if the statistical power is analyzed.

Key Terms

Effects size
Exploratory research
Hypothesis
Null hypothesis
One-tail and two-tail tests

Power
Probability level
Region of rejection
Research question
Statistical significance
Type I and Type II error

Using the Internet

There are several sites that are relevant to the topics discussed in this chapter.

1. *http://psychology.wadsworth.com/workshops/hypothesis1.html* This site contains a discussion of hypothesis testing written in plain English that contains easy-to-understand examples. Related sites discuss Type I and Type II errors and power analysis.
2. *http://ebook.stat.ucla.edu/calculators/powercalc/normal/n-1/n-1-samp.html* This site includes an online calculator that will compute the needed sample size for a given statistical power. A related site will calculate the power of a statistical test given a sample size.
3. *http://www.dssresearch.com/SampleSize/use_avg2.asp* Another power calculator that helps determine *sample* size when dealing with mean differences between two groups. Very easy to use. Requires only an estimation of effect size and sample standard deviation. Another part of site calculates power given a sample size.
4. *http://cc.uoregon.edu/cnews/summer2000/statpower.html* A *Computing News* article that presents a good discussion of power analysis. The section on effect size is particularly helpful.

Questions and Problems for Further Investigation

1. Develop three research questions and three hypotheses in any mass media area that could be investigated or tested.
2. What is your opinion about using levels of significance .10 or greater in exploratory research?
3. Conduct a brief review of published research in mass media. What percentage of the studies report the results of a power analysis calculation?
4. Explain the relationship between Type I errors and Type II errors.
5. Under what circumstances might a researcher use a probability level of .001?
6. If a researcher's significance level is set at $p = \leq .02$ and the results of the experiment indicate that the null hypothesis cannot be rejected, what is the probability of a Type I error?

For additional information on these and related topics, see

http://www.wimmerdominick.com

References and Suggested Readings

Bardhan, N. (2001). Transnational AIDS-HIV news narratives. *Mass Communication & Society,* 4(3), 283–309.

Chase, L. J., & Tucker, R. K. (1975). A power-analytic examination of contemporary communication research. *Speech Monographs,* 42, 29–41.

Cohen, J. (1988). *Statistical power analysis for the behavioral sciences.* New York: Academic Press.

Detjen, J., Fico, F., Li, X., & Kim, Y. (2000). Changing work environment of environmental reporters. *Newspaper Research Journal,* 21(1), 2–12.

Feldman, D. (1987). *Why do clocks run clockwise?* New York: Harper & Row.

King, C. M. (2000). Effects of humorous heroes and villains in violent action films. *Journal of Communication,* 50(1), 5–24.

Krcmar, M., & Cooke, M. C. (2001). Children's moral reasoning and their perceptions of television violence. *Journal of Communication,* 51(2), 300–316.

Roscoe, J. T. (1975). *Fundamental research statistics for the behavioral sciences.* New York: Holt, Rinehart & Winston.

Salkind, N. (2000). *Statistics for people who think they hate statistics.* Thousand Oaks, CA: Sage.

Tukey, J. W. (1962). The future of data analysis. *Annals of Mathematical Statistics,* 33, 1–67.

Tukey, J. W. (1986). *The collected works of John W. Tukey, Vols III and IV.* Belmont, CA: Wadsworth and Brooks/Cole.

Walsh-Childers, K., Chance, J., & Swain, K. (1999). Daily newspaper coverage of the organization, delivery and financing of health care. *Newspaper Research Journal,* 20(2), 2–22.

Williams, F. (1979). *Reasoning with statistics* (2nd ed.). New York: Holt, Rinehart & Winston.

Chapter 12

Basic Statistical Procedures

Before we begin the discussion of statistics, we would like to address one question we hear repeatedly, "Why do I need to learn about statistics? It's boring." Well, boring as they may be, statistics are necessary when you follow the scientific method of knowing. In order to have valid and reliable results, any question—regardless of what it relates to—must be analyzed using some type of statistical method. If not, the "results" of the analysis will be based on the methods of intuition, tenacity, or authority. And we already know that results from these methods cannot be verified. We apologize if you're bored with statistics, but learning about them is a necessary evil. Statistics is how we advance our knowledge of everything, including our understanding of the mass media. So let's get to it.

Researchers often wish to do more than merely describe a sample. In many cases researchers want to use their results to make inferences about the population from which the sample has been taken. Tukey (1986), in his typically nonpresumptuous manner, identifies four purposes of statistics:

1. To aid in summarization
2. To aid in "getting at what is going on"
3. To aid in extracting "information" from the data
4. To aid in communication

With these four purposes as a foundation, this chapter describes some of the basic inferential statistical methods used in mass media research and suggests ways in which these methods may help answer questions.

History of Small-Sample Statistics

Using a sample to investigate a problem or question has been done for many centuries. Documented use of sampling in scientific research is found as long ago as 1627, when Sir Francis Bacon published an account of tests he had conducted to measure wheat seed growth in various forms of fertilizer. In 1763, Arthur Young began a series of experiments to discover the most profitable method of farming, and in 1849, James Johnston published a book called *Experimental Agriculture,* in which he provided advice on scientific research (Cochran, 1976).

One of the best-known investigators of the early 20th century was William S. Gossett, who in 1908 attempted to quantify experimental results in a paper entitled *The Probable Error of the Mean.* Under the pen name "Student," Gossett published the results of small-sample investigations he had conducted while working in a Dublin brewery. The *t*-distribution statistics Gossett developed were not widely accepted at the time; in fact, it took more than 15 years before other researchers began to have an interest in his work. The *t*-test, however, as will be seen, is now one of the most widely used statistical procedures in all areas of research.

Sir Ronald Fisher (1890–1962) provided a stepping-stone from early work in statistics and sampling procedures to modern statistical inference techniques. Fisher introduced the idea of "likelihood," that is, what the likelihood is that an event will occur. This

> **AN INSIDE LOOK**
>
> **Statistical Calculations**
>
> There are at least four basic ways that you can calculate the statistics mentioned in this chapter:
>
> 1. Do them by hand.
> 2. Use statistical calculators found on web sites.
> 3. Use a spreadsheet program such as *Excel* or *Quattro Pro*.
> 4. Use a statistical program such as *SPSS*.

idea provided the basis for developing statistical approaches to answer such questions. Fisher also developed the concept of probability and established the use of the .01 and .05 levels of probability testing (see Chapter 10). Until Fisher, statistical methods were not perceived as practical in areas other than agriculture, for which they were originally developed.

Although we recognize that most students will not calculate statistics by hand, we think it is useful for students to see the basic logic behind the statistic. Thus we have provided formulas and simple examples for readers to follow. Understanding how the numbers are used by the statistic will make it easier for students to make sense of the results of web statistical calculators, spreadsheets, and *SPSS*.

▪ Nonparametric Statistics

Statistical methods are commonly divided into two broad categories: **parametric** and **nonparametric.** Historically, researchers have recognized three primary differences between parametric and nonparametric statistics:

1. Nonparametric statistics are appropriate with only nominal and ordinal data. Parametric statistics are appropriate for interval and ratio data.
2. Nonparametric results cannot be generalized to the population. Generalization is possible only with parametric statistics.
3. Nonparametric statistics make no assumption about normally distributed data, whereas parametric statistics assume normality. Nonparametric statistics are said to be "distribution-free."

For the most part, the distinctions in items 1 and 2 have vanished. We agree with most researchers who argue that both parametric statistics and nonparametric statistics can be used successfully with all types of data and that both are appropriate for generalizing results to the population.

The following sections introduce some of the basic statistical procedures encountered by and used by mass media research. As we have stated before, this text is not a statistics text. For more information about any of these basic procedures, consult a statistics book or search for the specific methodology on the Internet.

Chi-Square Goodness of Fit

Mass media researchers often compare the observed frequencies of a phenomenon with the frequencies that might be expected or hypothesized. For example, assume a researcher wants to determine if the sales of television sets by four manufacturers in the current year are the same as the sales during the previous year. A logical hypothesis might be: "Television set sales of four major manufacturers are significantly different this year from those of the previous year."

Suppose the previous year's television set sales were distributed as follows:

Manufacturer	Percent of sales
RCA	22
Sony	36
JVC	19
Mitsubishi	23

From these previous year's sales, the researcher can calculate the expected frequencies (using a sample of 1,000) for each manufacturer's sales by multiplying the percentage of each company's sales by 1,000. These are the expected frequencies:

Manufacturer	Expected frequency
RCA	220
Sony	360
JVC	190
Mitsubishi	230

Next, the researcher surveys a random sample of 1,000 households known to have purchased one of the four manufacturers' television sets during the current year. The data from this survey provide the following information:

Manufacturer	Expected frequency	Observed frequency
RCA	220	180
Sony	360	330
JVC	190	220
Mitsubishi	230	270

The researcher now must interpret these data to determine whether the change in frequency is actually significant. This can be done by reducing the data to a chi-square statistic and performing a test known as the chi-square "goodness of fit" test.

A **chi-square** (X^2) is simply a value that shows the relationship between expected frequencies and observed frequencies. It is computed by this formula:

$$X^2 = \Sigma \frac{(O_i - E_i)^2}{E_i}$$

where O_i is the observed frequencies and E_i is the expected frequencies. This means that the difference between each expected and observed frequency must be squared and then divided by the expected frequency. The sum of the quotients is the *chi-square* for those frequencies. For the frequency distribution above, chi-square is calculated as follows:

$$\begin{aligned}
X^2 &= \frac{(O_1 - E_1)^2}{E_1} + \frac{(O_2 - E_2)^2}{E_2} \\
&+ \frac{(O_3 - E_3)^2}{E_3} + \frac{(O_4 - E_4)^2}{E_4} \\
&= \frac{(180 - 220)^2}{220} + \frac{(330 - 360)^2}{360} \\
&+ \frac{(220 - 190)^2}{190} + \frac{(270 - 230)^2}{230} \\
&= \frac{(-40)^2}{220} + \frac{(-30)^2}{360} + \frac{(30)^2}{190} + \frac{(40)^2}{230} \\
&= \frac{1{,}600}{220} + \frac{900}{360} + \frac{900}{190} + \frac{1{,}600}{230} \\
&= 7.27 + 2.50 + 4.73 + 6.95 \\
&= 21.45
\end{aligned}$$

(See *www.georgetown.edu/cball/webtools/web_chi.html* for an Internet calculator for the chi-square statistic.)

Once the chi-square value is known, the goodness-of-fit test determines whether this value represents a significant difference in frequencies. To do this, two values are necessary. The first is the probability level, which is predetermined by the researcher; the second, called **degrees of freedom** (*df*), is the number of scores in any particular test that are free to vary in value. For example, if one has three unknown values (x, y, and z) such that $x + y + z = 10$, there are two degrees of freedom: Any two of the three variables may be assigned any value without affecting the total, but the value of the third will then be predetermined. Thus, if $x = 2$ and $y = 5$, then z must be 3.

In the goodness-of-fit test, degrees of freedom are expressed in terms of $K = 1$, where K is the number of categories. In the television sales study, $K = 4$ and $df = 4 - 1 = 3$. Next, a chi-square significance table is consulted (see Appendix 1, Table 4). These tables are arranged by probability level and degrees of freedom. A portion of the chi-square table relevant to the hypothetical study is reproduced here to show how the table is used:

	Probability			
df	.10	.05	.01	.001
1	2.706	3.841	6.635	10.827
2	4.605	5.991	9.210	13.815
3	6.251	7.815	11.345	16.266
4	7.779	9.488	13.277	18.467

If the calculated chi-square value equals or exceeds the value found in the table, the differences in the observed frequencies are considered to be statistically significant at the predetermined alpha level; if the calculated value is smaller, the results are nonsignificant.

In the television sales example, suppose the researcher finds a chi-square value of 21.45, with degrees of freedom of 3, and has established a probability level of .05. The chi-square table shows a value of 7.815 at this level when $df = 3$. Since 21.45 is greater than 7.815, the difference is significant, and the hypothesis is accepted (supported): Television set sales of the four manufacturers are significantly different in the current year from sales in the previous year.

The chi-square goodness-of-fit test can be used in a variety of ways to measure changes—for example, in studying audience perceptions of advertising messages over time, in planning changes in television programming, and in analyzing the results of public relations campaigns. Idsvoog and Hoyt (1977) used a chi-square test to analyze the professionalism and performance of television journalists. The authors attempted to determine whether "professionalism" was related to several other characteristics, including the desire to look for employment, educational level, and job satisfaction. The results indicated that journalists classified "high" because of questionnaire responses differed significantly from those classified as "medium" or "low" professionals.

There are limitations to the use of the goodness-of-fit test. Since this is a nonparametric statistical procedure, the variables must be measured at the nominal or ordinal level. The categories must be mutually exclusive, and each observation in each category must be independent from all others. Additionally, because the chi-square distribution is sharply skewed (see Chapter 10) for small samples, Type II (see Chapter 11) errors may occur: Small samples may not produce significant results in cases that could have yielded significant results if a larger sample had been used. To avoid this problem, most researchers suggest that each category contain at least five observations. Other researchers suggest that 20% of the cells should have an expected frequency of at least 5, and none should have expected frequencies of 0.

As an alternative to the chi-square goodness-of-fit test, some researchers prefer the Kolomogorov-Smirnov test, which is considered to be more powerful than the chi-square approach. In addition, a minimum number of expected frequencies in each cell is not required, as in the chi-square test.

Figure 12.1 *Description of Random Sample of Media Users in Study of Sources of New Product Information*

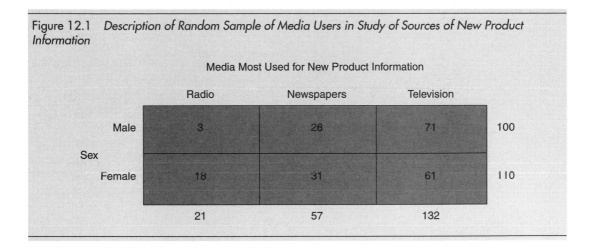

		Media Most Used for New Product Information			
		Radio	Newspapers	Television	
Sex	Male	3	26	71	100
	Female	18	31	61	110
		21	57	132	

Contingency Table Analysis

Another nonparametric procedure used in mass media research is the contingency table analysis, frequently called **cross-tabulation,** or simply **crosstabs.** Crosstab analysis is an extension of the goodness-of-fit test. The primary difference is that two or more variables can be tested simultaneously. Consider a study to determine the relationship between gender and use of the media to obtain information on new products. Suppose a researcher selects a random sample of 210 adults and obtains the information displayed in Figure 12.1.

The next step is to calculate the expected frequencies for each cell. This procedure is similar to that used in the goodness-of-fit test, but it involves a slightly more detailed formula:

$$E_{ij} = \frac{R_i C_j}{N}$$

where E_{ij} is the expected frequency for the cell in row i, column j; R_i is the sum of frequencies in row i; C_j is the sum of frequencies in column j; and N is the sum of frequencies for all cells. Using this formula, the researcher in the hypothetical example can calculate the expected frequencies:

$$\text{Male/radio} = \frac{100 \times 21}{210} = \frac{2{,}100}{210} = 10$$

$$\text{Female/radio} = \frac{110 \times 21}{210} = \frac{2{,}300}{210} = 11$$

and so forth. Each expected frequency is placed in a small square in the upper right-hand corner of the appropriate cell, as illustrated in Figure 12.2.

After the expected frequencies have been calculated, the investigator must compute the chi-square using this formula:

$$X_2 = \Sigma \frac{(O_{ij} - E_{\iota j})^2}{E_{ij}}$$

With the same example:

$$X^2 = \frac{(3 - 10)^2}{10} + \frac{(26 - 27)^2}{27} + \frac{(71 - 63)^2}{63} + \frac{(18 - 11)^2}{11}$$

Figure 12.2 *Random Sample of Media Users Showing Expected Frequencies*

Media Most Used for New Product Information

Sex		Radio	Newspapers	Television	
	Male	3 [10]	26 [27]	71 [63]	100
	Female	18 [11]	31 [30]	61 [69]	110
		21	57	132	

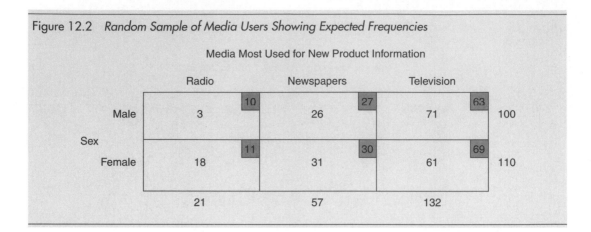

$$+ \frac{(31 - 30)^2}{30} + \frac{(61 - 69)^2}{69}$$

$$= \frac{49}{10} + \frac{1}{27} + \frac{64}{63} + \frac{49}{11} + \frac{1}{30} + \frac{64}{69}$$

$$= 4.90 + 0.04 + 1.01 + 4.45 + 0.03 + 0.92$$

$$= 11.35$$

To determine statistical significance, it is necessary to consult the chi-square table. In a crosstab analysis, the degrees of freedom are expressed as $(R - 1)(C - 1)$, where R is the number of rows, and C is the number of columns. If $p = \leq .05$, the chi-square value is listed in Table 4 of Appendix 1 as 5.991, which is lower than the calculated value of 11.35. Therefore, there is a significant relationship between gender and the media used to acquire new product information. The test indicates that the two variables are somehow related, but it does not tell exactly how. To find this out, we need to go back and examine the original crosstab data in Figure 12.1. According to the distribution, it is easy to see that females use radio more and television less than males do.

For a 2×2 crosstab (where $df = 1$), computational effort is saved when the corresponding cells are represented by the letters A, B, C, and D, such as

A	B
C	D

The following formula can then be used to compute chi-square:

$$X^2 = \frac{N(AD - BC)^2}{(A + B)(C + D)(A + C)(B + D)}$$

Crosstab analysis is used frequently in mass media research and can be conducted on almost any computer statistics package.

▪ Parametric Statistics

The sections that follow discuss the parametric statistical methods usually used with interval and ratio data. Recall that these methods assume that data are normally distributed. The most basic parametric statistic is the *t*-test, a procedure widely used in all areas of mass media research. (Keep in mind that there are several *t*-test calculators on the Internet.)

The t-test

Many research studies test two groups of subjects: One group receives some type of treatment, and the other serves as the control. After the treatment has been administered, both groups are tested, and the results are compared to determine whether a statistically significant difference exists between the groups. In other words, did the treatment have an effect on the results of the test? In cases such as this, the mean score for each group is compared with a *t*-test. [*Note:* The Internet provides a variety of *t*-test programs; in addition, consult Bruning and Kintz (1997) for a step-by-step algorithm for *t*-tests.]

The ***t*-test** is the most elementary method for comparing two groups' mean scores. A variety of *t*-test alternatives is available depending on the problem under consideration and the situation of a particular research study. Variations of the *t*-test are available for testing independent groups, related groups, and cases in which the population mean is either known or unknown (Champion, 1981; Roscoe, 1975).

The *t*-test assumes that the variables in the populations from which the samples are drawn are normally distributed (see Chapter 10). The test also assumes that the data have homogeneity of variance—that is, that they deviate equally from the mean.

The basic formula for the *t*-test is relatively simple. The numerator of the formula is the difference between the sample mean and the hypothesized population mean, and the denominator is the estimate of the standard error of the mean (S_m):

$$t = \frac{\overline{X} - \mu}{S_m}$$

where

$$S_m = \sqrt{\frac{SS}{n-1}} \quad \text{and} \quad SS = \Sigma(X - \overline{X})^2$$

One of the more commonly used forms of the *t*-test is the test for independent groups or means. This procedure is used to study two independent groups for differences (the type of study described at the beginning of this section). The formula for the independent *t*-test is

$$t = \frac{\overline{X}_1 - \overline{X}_2}{S_{\overline{x}_1 - \overline{x}_2}}$$

where $\overline{X}_1$ is the mean for Group 1, $\overline{X}_2$ is the mean for Group 2, and $S_{\overline{x}_1 - \overline{x}_2}$ is the standard error for the groups. The standard error is an important part of the *t*-test formula and is computed as follows:

$$S_{\overline{x}_1 - \overline{x}_2} = \sqrt{\left(\frac{SS_1 + SS_2}{n_1 + n_2 - 2}\right)\left(\frac{1}{n_1} + \frac{1}{n_2}\right)}$$

where SS_1 is the sum of squares for Group 1, SS_2 is the sum of squares for Group 2, n_1 is the sample size for Group 1, and n_2 is the sample size for Group 2.

To illustrate a *t*-test, consider a research problem to determine the recall of two groups of subjects about a television commercial for a new household cleaner. One group consists of 10 males, and the other consists of 10 females. Each group views the commercial once and then completes a 15-item questionnaire. The hypothesis predicts a significant difference between the recall scores of males and females.

The data are listed in Table 12.1. Using the *t*-test formula, the researcher computes the standard error for the groups by using the previous formula:

$$S_{\overline{x}_1 - \overline{x}_2} = \sqrt{\left(\frac{110 + 106}{10 + 10 - 2}\right)\left(\frac{1}{10} + \frac{1}{10}\right)}$$
$$= 1.55$$

Table 12.1 *Data on Recall Scores for Men and Women*

Female recall scores			Male recall scores		
X	x	$x^2(SS)$	X	x	$x^2(SS)$
4	−4	16	2	−4	16
4	−4	16	3	−3	9
5	−3	9	4	−2	4
7	−1	1	4	−2	4
7	−1	1	4	−2	4
8	0	0	6	0	0
9	1	1	6	0	0
9	1	1	8	2	4
12	4	16	10	4	16
15	7	49	13	7	49
80		110	60		106
$\overline{X} = 8$			$\overline{X} = 6$		

The researcher then substitutes this standard error value into the t-test formula:

$$t = \frac{8 - 6}{1.55}$$
$$= 1.29$$

To determine whether the t value of 1.29 is statistically significant, a t-distribution table is consulted. The t-distribution is a family of curves closely resembling the normal curve. The portion of the t-distribution table relevant to the sample problem is reproduced in Table 12.2. Again, to interpret the table, two values are required: degrees of freedom and level of probability. (For a complete t-distribution table, see Appendix 1, Table 2.)

For purposes of the t-test, degrees of freedom are equal to $n_1 + n_2 - 2$, where n_1 and n_2 are the sizes of the respective groups. In the example of advertising recall, $df = 18$ $(10 + 10 - 2)$. If the problem is tested at the .05 level of significance, a t value of 2.101 is required for the results to be considered statistically significant. However, since the sample problem is a "two-tail test" (the hypothesis predicts only a difference between the two groups, not that one particular group will have the higher mean score), the required values are actually $t \leq -2.101$ or $t \geq +2.101$. The conclusion of the hypothetical problem is that there is no significant difference between the recall scores of the female group and the recall scores of the male group because the calculated t does not equal or exceed the table values.

There are many examples of the t-test in mass media research that demonstrate the

Table 12.2 *Portion of the t-Distribution Table for the Two-Tail Test*

	Probability			
n	.10	.05	.01	.001
1	6.314	12.706	63.657	636.619
2	2.920	4.303	9.925	31.598
*				
*				
*				
17	1.740	2.110	2.898	3.965
18	1.734	2.101	2.878	3.992
19	1.729	2.093	2.861	3.883
*				
*				
*				

versatility of the method. For example, Garramone (1985) investigated political advertising by exploring the roles of the commercial sponsor (the source of the message) and the rebuttal commercial (a message that charges as false the claims of another commercial). Among six separate hypotheses that were tested, Garramone predicted:

H_1: Viewers of a negative political commercial will perceive an independent sponsor as more trustworthy than a candidate sponsor.

H_2: Viewers of an independent commercial opposing a candidate will demonstrate

a. more negative perceptions of the target's image.
b. lesser likelihood of voting for the target than viewers of a candidate commercial.

H_3: Viewers of an independent commercial opposing a candidate will demonstrate

a. more positive perceptions of the target's opponent.
b. greater likelihood of voting for the target's opponent than viewers of a candidate commercial.

Among other findings, Garramone concluded that

> The first hypothesis . . . was not supported. [However] hypotheses 2 and 3 . . . were supported. Viewers of an independent commercial opposing a candidate demonstrated a more negative perception of the target's image, $t(110) = 2.41, p \leq .01$, and a lesser likelihood of voting for the target, $t(110) = 1.83, p \leq .05$, than did viewers of a candidate commercial. Also as predicted, viewers of an independent

commercial demonstrated a more positive perception of the target's opponent, $t(110) = 1.89$, $p \leq .05$, and a greater likelihood of voting for the target's opponent, $t(110) = 2.45$, $p \leq .01$, than did viewers of a candidate commercial.

Analysis of Variance

The *t*-test allows researchers to investigate the effects of one independent variable on two samples of people, such as the effect of room temperature on subjects' performance on a research exam. One group may take the test in a room at 70°F, while another group takes the same test in a room at 100°F. The mean test scores for each group are used to calculate *t*. In many situations, however, researchers want to investigate several levels of an independent variable (rooms set at 70°, 80°, 90°, and 100°F), or possibly several independent variables (heat and light), and possibly several different groups (freshmen, sophomores, and so on). A *t*-test is inappropriate in these cases because the procedure is valid for only one single comparison. What may be required is an **analysis of variance** (ANOVA).

ANOVA is essentially an extension of the *t*-test. The advantage of ANOVA is that it can be used to simultaneously investigate several independent variables, also called *factors*. An ANOVA is named according to the number of factors involved in the study: A one-way ANOVA investigates one independent variable, a two-way ANOVA investigates two independent variables, and so on. An additional naming convention is used to describe an ANOVA that involves different levels of an independent variable. A 2×2 ANOVA studies two independent variables, each with two levels. For example, using the room temperature study just described, an ANOVA research project may include two levels of room temperature (70° and 100°F) and two levels of room lighting (dim and bright). This provides four different effects possibilities on test scores: 70°, dim lighting; 70°, bright lighting; 100°, dim lighting; and 100°, bright lighting.

ANOVA allows the researcher in this example to look at four unique situations at the same time. ANOVA is a versatile statistic that is widely used in mass media research. However, the name of the statistic is somewhat misleading because the most common form of ANOVA tests for significant differences between two or more group means and says little about the analysis of variance differences. Additionally, ANOVA breaks down the total variability in a set of data into its different sources of variation; that is, it "explains" the sources of variance in a set of scores on one or more independent variables.

An ANOVA identifies or explains two types of variance: systematic and error. **Systematic variance** in data is attributable to a *known* factor that predictably increases or decreases all the scores it influences. One such factor commonly identified in mass media research is gender: Often an increase or decrease in a given score can be predicted simply by determining whether a subject is male or female. **Error variance** in data is created by an *unknown* factor that most likely has not been examined or controlled in the study. A primary goal of all research is to eliminate or control as much error variance as possible (a task that is generally easier to do in the laboratory—see Chapter 9).

The ANOVA model assumes (1) that each sample is normally distributed, (2) that the variances in each group are equal, (3) that the subjects are randomly selected from the population, and (4) that the scores are statistically independent—that they have no concomitant (related) relationship with any other variable or score. The ANOVA procedure begins with the selection of two or more random samples. The samples may be from the same or different populations. Each group is subjected to different experimental treatments, followed by some type of test or measurement. The scores from the measurements are then used to calculate a ratio of variance, known as the **F ratio** (F).

To understand this calculation, it is necessary to examine in detail the procedure known as sum of squares (discussed briefly in Chapter 10). In the sum of squares procedure, raw scores or deviation scores are squared and summed to eliminate dealing with negative numbers. The squaring process does not change the meaning of the data as long as the same procedure is used on all the data (monotonic transformation); it simply converts the data into a more easily interpreted set of scores.

In ANOVA, sums of squares are computed *between groups* (of subjects), *within groups* (of subjects), and in *total* (the sum of the between and within figures). The sums of squares between groups and within groups are divided by their respective degrees of freedom (as will be illustrated) to obtain a *mean square:* mean squares between (MS_b) and mean squares within (MS_w). The F ratio is then calculated using this formula:

$$F = \frac{MS_b}{MS_w}$$

where $MS_b df = K - 1$; $MS_w df = N - K$; K is the number of groups; and N is the total sample. The F ratio derived from the formula is then compared to the value in the F-distribution table (Tables 5 and 6 in Appendix 1) that corresponds to the appropriate degrees of freedom and the desired probability level. If the calculated value equals or exceeds the tabled value, the ANOVA is considered to be statistically significant. The F table is similar to the t table and the chi-square table except that two different degrees of freedom are used, one for the numerator of the F ratio and one for the denominator.

The ANOVA statistic can be illustrated with an example from advertising. Suppose that three groups of five subjects each are selected randomly to determine the credibility of a newspaper advertisement for a new laundry detergent. The groups are exposed to versions of the advertisement that reflect varying degrees of design complexity: easy, medium, and difficult. The subjects are then asked to rate the advertisement on a scale of 1 to 10, with 10 indicating believable and 1 indicating not believable. The null hypothesis is advanced: "There is no significant difference in credibility among the three versions of the ad."

To test this hypothesis, it is first necessary to calculate the three sums of squares: total, within, and between. The formulas for sums of squares (SS) are:

$$\text{Total}_{SS} = \Sigma X^2 - \frac{(\Sigma X)^2}{N}$$

where N represents total sample size,

$$\text{Within}_{SS} = \Sigma X^2 - \frac{\Sigma(\Sigma X)^2}{n_K}$$

where n_K represents the sample size of each group, and

$$\text{Between}_{SS} = T_{SS} - W_{SS}$$

The scores for the three groups furnish the data shown next:

Group A (easy)		Group B (medium)		Group C (difficult)	
X	X^2	X	X^2	X	X^2
1	1	4	16	6	36
2	4	5	25	7	49
4	16	6	36	7	49
4	16	6	36	8	64
5	25	8	64	10	100
16	62	29	177	38	298

$$\Sigma X = (16 + 29 + 38) = 83$$
$$\Sigma X^2 = (62 + 177 + 298) = 537$$

Figure 12.3 *Values for One-Way ANOVA Example*

Sources of variation	*df*	Sums of squares	Mean square	*F*
Between groups	2 ($K-1$)	49	24.50	10.19
Within groups	12 ($n-K$)	28.8	2.4	xxxx
Total	14 ($n-1$)	77.8	xxxx	

By inserting the data into the formulas, the researchers are able to calculate the sums of squares as follows:

$$T_{SS} = \Sigma X^2 - \frac{(\Sigma X)^2}{N} = 537 - \frac{(83)^2}{15}$$
$$= 537 - 459.2 = 77.8$$
$$W_{SS} = \Sigma X^2 - \frac{\Sigma(\Sigma X)^2}{n_K}$$
$$= 537 - \frac{16^2}{5} - \frac{29^2}{5} - \frac{38^2}{5}$$
$$= 537 - 51.2 - 168.2 - 288.8 = 28.8$$
$$B_{SS} = T_{SS} - W_{SS} = 77.8 - 28.8 = 49$$

With this information, we can calculate the mean squares between and within groups (SS/*df*), which can then be divided (MS_b/MS_w) to obtain the value of the *F* ratio. These results are displayed in Figure 12.3.

If we assume a significance level of .05, the *F*-distribution data (Table 5, Appendix 1) for degrees of freedom of 2 and 12 indicate that the *F* ratio must be 3.89 or greater to show statistical significance. Since the calculated value of 10.2 is greater than 3.89, there is a significant difference in credibility among the three types of advertisements, and the researchers must reject the null hypothesis.

Two-Way ANOVA

Researchers often examine more than one independent variable in a study. In the preceding example, we may have wanted to investigate simultaneously a second independent variable, product knowledge. If so, then we could have used a two-way ANOVA. In a two-way ANOVA, the data are gathered and organized in table form, as with the one-way ANOVA, but the two-way table has both rows and columns, where each row and column represents an independent variable. The dependent variable score, represented by the letter *X* for each subject, is entered into each cell of the table. This procedure is demonstrated in Figure 12.4.

The two-way ANOVA can save time and resources because studies for each independent variable are being conducted simultaneously. In addition, we are able to calculate two types of independent variable effects on the dependent variable: main effects and interactions. (A one-way ANOVA tests for only main effects.) A **main effect** is simply the influence of an independent variable on the dependent variable. **Interaction** refers to the concomitant influence of two or more independent variables on the single dependent

Figure 12.4 *Two-Way ANOVA Design*

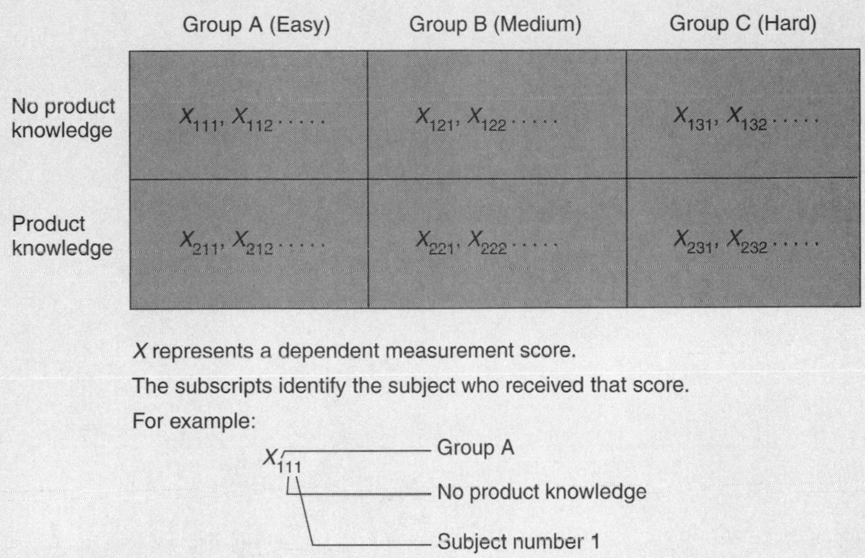
Group A (Easy)
Group B (Medium)
Group C (Hard)
No product knowledge
Product knowledge
$X_{111}, X_{112} \ldots$
$X_{121}, X_{122} \ldots$
$X_{131}, X_{132} \ldots$
$X_{211}, X_{212} \ldots$
$X_{221}, X_{222} \ldots$
$X_{231}, X_{232} \ldots$
X represents a dependent measurement score.
The subscripts identify the subject who received that score.
For example:
X_{111}
Group A
No product knowledge
Subject number 1

variable. For example, it may be found that a subject's educational background has no effect on media used for entertainment, but education and socioeconomic status may interact to create a significant effect.

The main effects plus interaction in a two-way ANOVA create a summary table slightly different from that shown for the one-way ANOVA, as illustrated by comparing Figures 12.3 and 12.4. Instead of computing only one F ratio as in one-way ANOVA, a two-way ANOVA involves four F ratios, and each is tested for statistical significance on the F distribution table (Between columns, Between rows, Interaction, Within cells). "Between columns" (a main effect) represents the test of the independent variable levels located in the columns of a two-way ANOVA. (From the preceding example, this would be a test for the differences between groups "easy," "medium," and "hard.") "Between rows" is another main effects test; it represents the significance between levels of the independent variable identified in the rows of the two-way ANOVA (product knowledge and no product knowledge). The "Interaction" section is the test for interaction between both independent variables in the study, and "Within cells" tests for significant differences between each cell in the study to determine how each individual group performed in the analysis. F ratios are not computed for the "Total," which accounts for the X's in the mean square and F columns.

Basic Correlational Statistics

Assume that a researcher hypothesizes an association between the number of pictures on the front page of a newspaper and the total number of copies sold at newsstands. If the observations reveal that more papers are sold when more pictures are used, there may be a

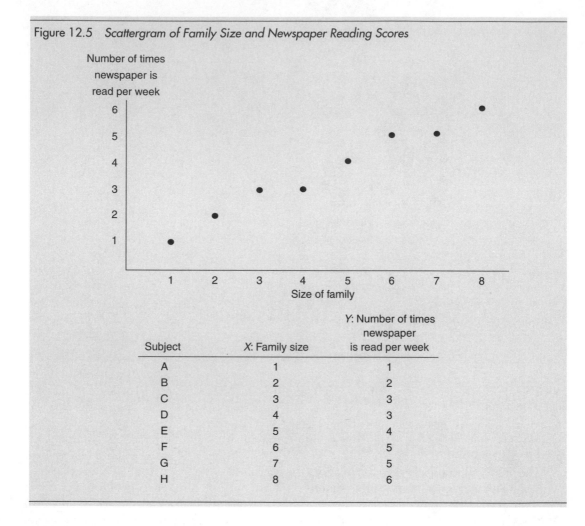

Figure 12.5 *Scattergram of Family Size and Newspaper Reading Scores*

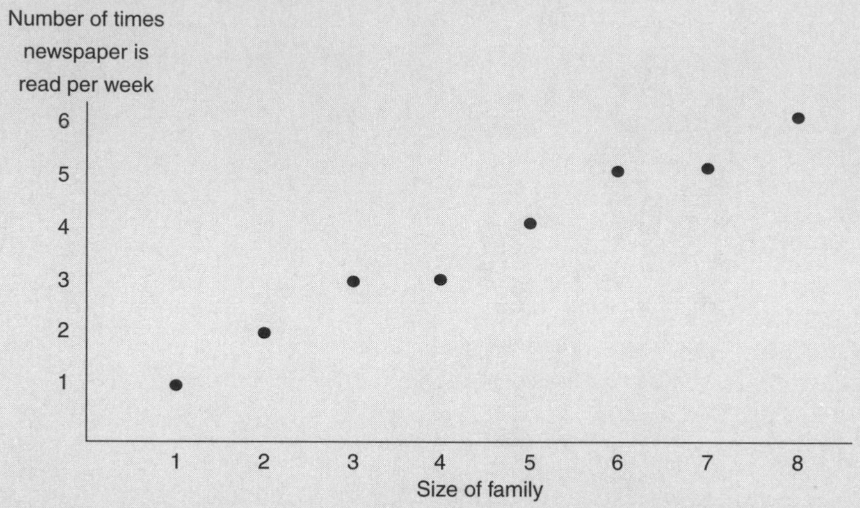

Subject	X: Family size	Y: Number of times newspaper is read per week
A	1	1
B	2	2
C	3	3
D	4	3
E	5	4
F	6	5
G	7	5
H	8	6

relationship between the two variables. Numerical expressions of the degree to which two variables change in relation to each other are called *measures of association,* or **correlation.** When making two different measurements of the same entity or person, researchers commonly designate one measure as the *X variable* and the other as the *Y variable.* For example, in a study of whether a relationship exists between the size of a subject's family and the frequency with which that person reads a newspaper, the measure of family size could be the *X* variable and the measure of newspaper reading the *Y* variable. Note that each subject in the group under study must be measured for both variables.

Figure 12.5 shows hypothetical data collected from a study of eight subjects. The *Y* variable is the number of times per week the newspaper is read; the *X* variable is the number of persons in the household. The two scores for each subject are plotted on a **scattergram,** a graphic technique for portraying a relationship between two or more variables.

Figure 12.6 *Scattergram of Possible Relationships*

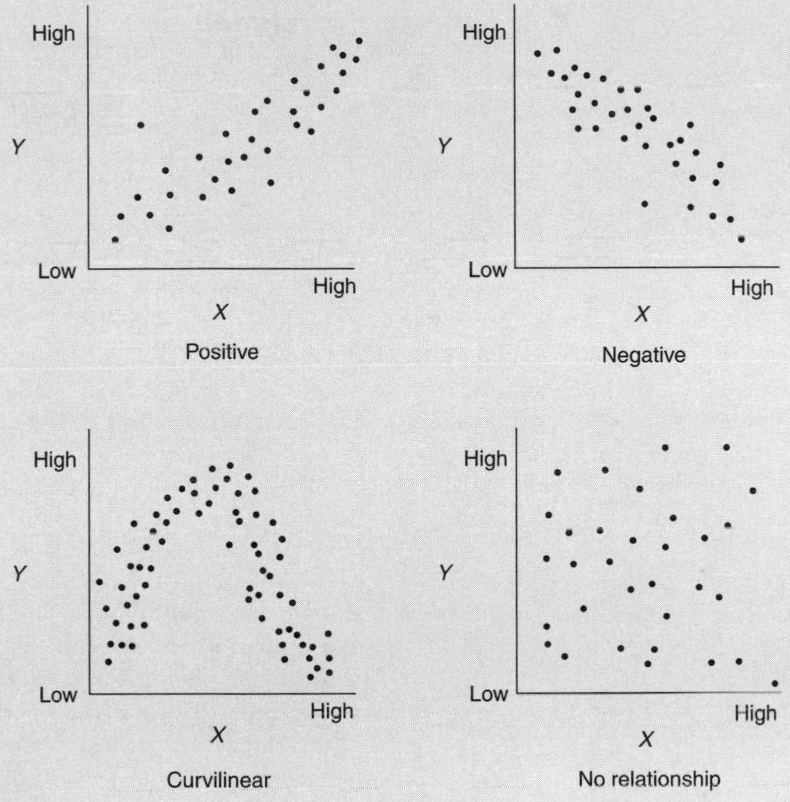

As indicated, family size and newspaper reading increase together. This is an example of a *positive relationship*.

An *inverse* (or *negative*) *relationship* exists when one variable increases while the other decreases. Sometimes the relationship between two variables is positive up to a point and then becomes inverse (or vice versa). When this happens, the relationship is said to be *curvilinear.* When there is no tendency for a high score on one variable to be associated with a high or low score on another variable, the two are said to be *uncorrelated.* Figure 12.6 illustrates these relationships.

Many statistics are available to measure the degree of relationship between two variables, but the most commonly used is the *Pearson product-moment correlation,* commonly symbolized as *r.* It varies between −1.00 and +1.00. A correlation coefficient of +1.00 indicates a perfect positive correlation: *X* and *Y* are completely covariant (they vary together). A Pearson *r* of −1.00 indicates a perfect relationship in the negative direction. The lowest value that the Pearson *r* can have is 0.00. This represents absolutely no relationship between two variables. Thus the Pearson *r* contains two pieces of information:

AN INSIDE LOOK

Computing a Correlation

Some researchers are concerned about all the calculations needed to compute a Pearson correlation, but don't worry about this since most computer spreadsheets include a macro that makes the calculation very simple. For example, the only command in *Excel* to compute a correlation is =*correl*

(1) an estimate of the strength of the relationship, as indicated by the number, and (2) a statement about the direction of the relationship, as shown by the sign. Keep in mind that the strength of the relationship depends solely on the number; strength of relationship must be interpreted in terms of absolute value. A correlation of $-.83$ is a stronger relationship than one of $+.23$.

The formula for calculating r looks sinister, but it actually includes only one new expression:

$$r = \frac{N\Sigma XY - \Sigma X \Sigma Y}{\sqrt{[N\Sigma X^2 - (\Sigma X)^2]\,[N\Sigma Y^2 - (\Sigma Y)^2]}}$$

where X and Y stand for the original scores, N is the number of pairs of scores, and again is the summation symbol. The only new term is ΣXY, which stands for the sum of the products of each X and Y. To find this quantity, simply multiply each X variable by its corresponding Y variable and then add the results. Table 12.3 demonstrates a computation of r.

A correlation coefficient is a pure number; it is not expressed in feet, inches, or pounds, nor is it a proportion or percent. The Pearson r is independent of the size and units of measurement of the original data. (In fact, the original scores do not have to be expressed in the same units.) Because of its abstract nature, r must be interpreted with care. In particular, it is not as easy as it sounds to determine whether a correlation is large or small. Some writers have suggested various adjectives to describe certain ranges of r. For example, an r between .40 and .70 might be called a "moderate" or "substantial" relationship, whereas an r of .71 to .90 might be termed "very high."

These labels are helpful, but they may lead to confusion. The best advice is to consider the nature of the study. For example, an r of .70 between frequency of viewing television violence and frequency of arrest for violent crimes would be more than substantial; it would be phenomenal. Conversely, a correlation of .70 between two coders' timings of the lengths of news stories on the evening news is low enough to call the reliability of the study into question. Additionally, correlation does not in itself imply causation. Newspaper reading and income might be strongly related, but this does not mean that earning a high salary causes people to read the newspaper. Correlation is just one factor in determining causality.

Furthermore, a large r does not necessarily mean that the two sets of correlated scores are equal. What it does mean is that there is a high likelihood of being correct when predicting the value of one variable by examining another variable that correlates with it. For example, there may be a correlation of .90 between the amount of time people spend reading newspapers and the amount of time they spend watching television news. That is, the amount of time reading newspapers correlates with the amount of time watching tel-

Table 12.3 *Calculation of r*

Subject	X	X^2	Y	Y^2	XY
A	1	1	1	1	1
B	2	4	2	4	4
C	3	9	3	9	9
D	4	16	3	9	12
E	4	16	4	16	16
F	5	25	5	25	25
G	6	36	5	25	30
H	8	64	6	36	48
$N = 8$	$\Sigma X = 33$	$\Sigma X^2 = 171$	$\Sigma Y = 29$	$\Sigma Y^2 = 125$	$\Sigma XY = 145$

$$(\Sigma X)^2 = 1{,}089$$
$$(\Sigma Y)^2 = 841$$

$$r = \frac{(8)(145) - (33)(29)}{\sqrt{[(8)(171) - 1{,}089][(8)(125) - 841]}}$$
$$= \frac{203}{\sqrt{(279)(159)}} = \frac{203}{(16.7)(12.6)}$$
$$= \frac{203}{210.62} = .964$$

r formula:

$$\frac{N\Sigma XY - \Sigma X \Sigma Y}{\sqrt{[N\Sigma X^2 - (\Sigma X)^2]\ [N\Sigma Y^2 - (\Sigma Y)^2}}$$

evision news. The correlation figure says nothing about the *amount* of time spent with each medium. It suggests only that there is a strong likelihood that people who spend time reading newspapers also spend time watching TV news.

Perhaps the best way to interpret r is in terms of the **coefficient of determination,** or the proportion of the total variation of one measure that can be determined by the other. This is calculated by squaring the Pearson r to arrive at a ratio of the two variances: The denominator of this ratio is the total variance of one of the variables, and the numerator is the part of the total variance that can be attributed to the other variable. For example, if $r = .40$, then $r^2 = .16$. One variable explains 16% of the variation in the other. Or to put it another way, 16% of the information necessary to make a perfect prediction from one variable to another is known. Obviously, if $r = 1.00$, then $r^2 = 100\%$; one variable allows perfect predictability of the other. The quantity $1 - r^2$ is usually called the **coefficient of nondetermination** because it represents that proportion of the variance left unaccounted for or unexplained.

Suppose that a correlation of .30 is found between a child's aggression and the amount of television violence the child views. This means that 9% of the total variance in aggression is accounted for by television violence. The other 91% of the variation is unexplained (it is not accounted for by the television variable). Note that the coefficient of determination is not measured on an equal interval scale: .80 is twice as large as .40, but this does not mean that an r of .80 represents twice as strong a relationship between two variables as an r of .40. In fact, the r of .40 explains 16% of the variance, while the r of .80 explains 64%—four times as much.

The Pearson r can be computed between any two sets of scores. For the statistic to be a valid description of the relationship, however, three assumptions must be made: (1) the data represent interval or ratio measurements; (2) the relationship between X and Y is linear, not curvilinear; and (3) the distributions of the X and Y variables are symmetrical and comparable. (Pearson's r can also be used as an inferential statistic. When this is the case, it is necessary to assume that X and Y come from normally distributed populations with similar variances.) If these assumptions cannot be made validly, then the researcher must use another kind of correlation coefficient, such as Spearman's rho or Kendall's *W*. For a thorough discussion of these and other correlation coefficients, consult Nunnally (1994).

Partial Correlation

Partial correlation is a method researchers use when they believe that a confounding or spurious variable may affect the relationship between the independent variables and the dependent variable: If such an influence is perceived, they can "partial out" or control the confounding variable. For example, consider a study of the relationship between being exposed to television commercials and purchasing the advertised products. The researchers select two commercials for a liquid laundry detergent (a "straight sell" version with no special video or audio effects, and a "hard sell" version that does use special effects). The commercials are shown to two groups of subjects: people who use only powdered detergent and people who use only liquid detergent. The study design is shown in Figure 12.7.

If the results show a very low correlation, indicating that any prediction made based on these two variables would be very tenuous, the researchers should suspect the presence of a confounding variable. An examination might reveal, for example, that the technicians had problems adjusting the color definition of the recording equipment; instead of its natural blue color, the detergent appeared dingy brown on the television screen. The study could be repeated to control (statistically eliminate) this variable by filming new commercials with the color controls properly adjusted. The design for the new study is shown in Figure 12.8. The partial correlation statistical procedure would enable the researchers to determine the influence of the controlled variable. With the new statistical method, the correlation might increase from the original study.

Cutler and Danowski (1981) used partial correlation in their study of older persons' use of television. The authors found it necessary, based on suggestions from earlier analyses, to control for gender and education when determining the correlation between political interest and television use. When these variables were partialed out (controlled), they found that media use varied

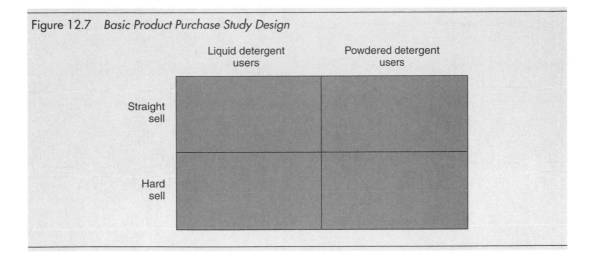

Figure 12.7 *Basic Product Purchase Study Design*

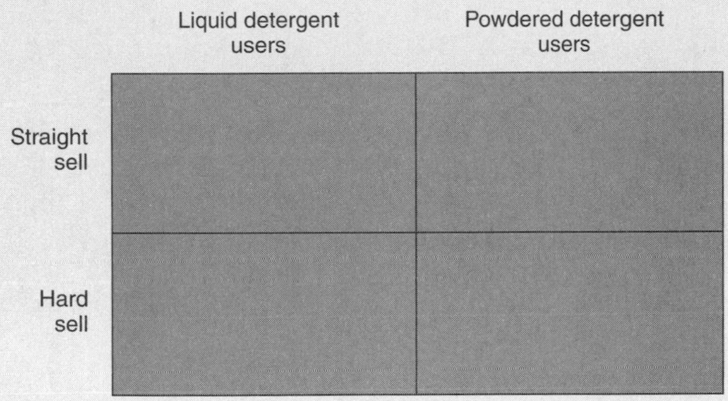

Figure 12.8 *Product Purchase Study Design Incorporating Partial Correlation Analysis*

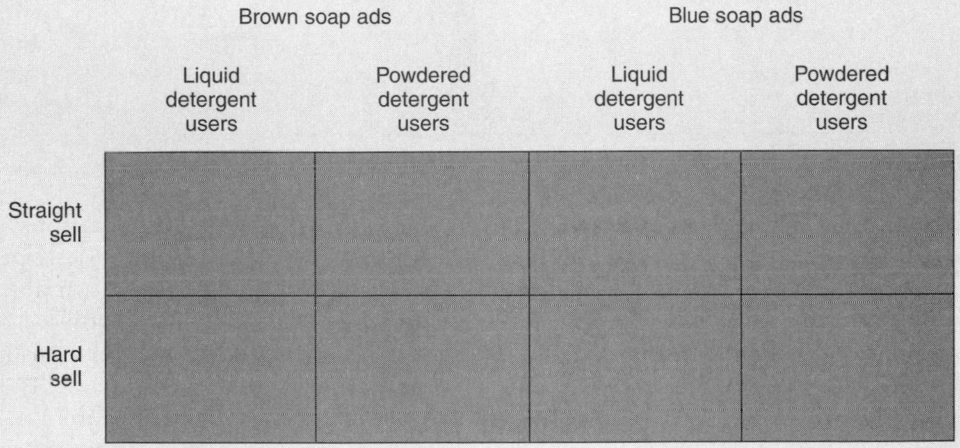

with the subject's age and when the media were used during the campaign.

Simple Linear Regression

Simple correlation involves measuring the relationship between two variables. The statistic is used to determine the degree to which one variable changes with a given change in another variable. Thus linear regression is a way of using the association between two variables as a method of prediction. Let's take the simplest case to illustrate the logic behind this technique.

Suppose two variables are perfectly related ($r = 1.00$). Knowledge of a person's score on one variable allows the researcher to

Figure 12.9 *Perfect Linear Correlation*

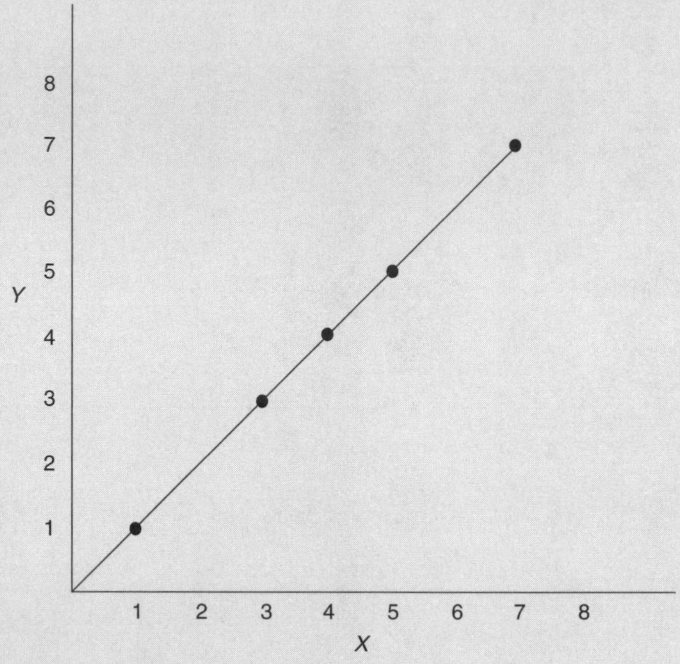

determine the score on the other. Figure 12.9 is a scattergram that portrays this situation. Note that all the points lie on a straight line, the *regression line.* Unfortunately, relationships are never this simple, and scattergrams more often resemble the one shown in Figure 12.10(a). Obviously, no single straight line can be drawn through all the points in the scattergram. It is possible, however, to mathematically construct a line that best fits all the observations in the figure. This line comes the closest to all the dots even though it might not pass through any of them. Mathematicians have worked out a technique to calculate such a line. German mathematician Karl Gauss, who used it successfully to relocate Ceres, the first recorded asteroid, after it was tracked for 41 days, developed this procedure, known as the "least squares" method, in 1794.

The least squares technique produces a line that is the best summary description of the relationship between two variables. For example, Figure 12.10(a) shows the data points that represent the relationship between eight x and y variables. The least squares technique determines the line equation for the data points such that the line passes through, or near, the greatest number of points. The computed line is then compared to the true, or perfect, line to determine the accuracy of the computed (predicted) line. The closer the computed line is to the true line, the more accurate the prediction.

The solid line in Figure 12.10(b) represents the best fitting line that passes through, or closest to, the greatest number of data points. The broken line connects the actual data points. It is clear that the broken line does not fall on the true line. The data points

Figure 12.10 *(a) Scattergram of X and Y; (b) Scattergram with Regression Line*

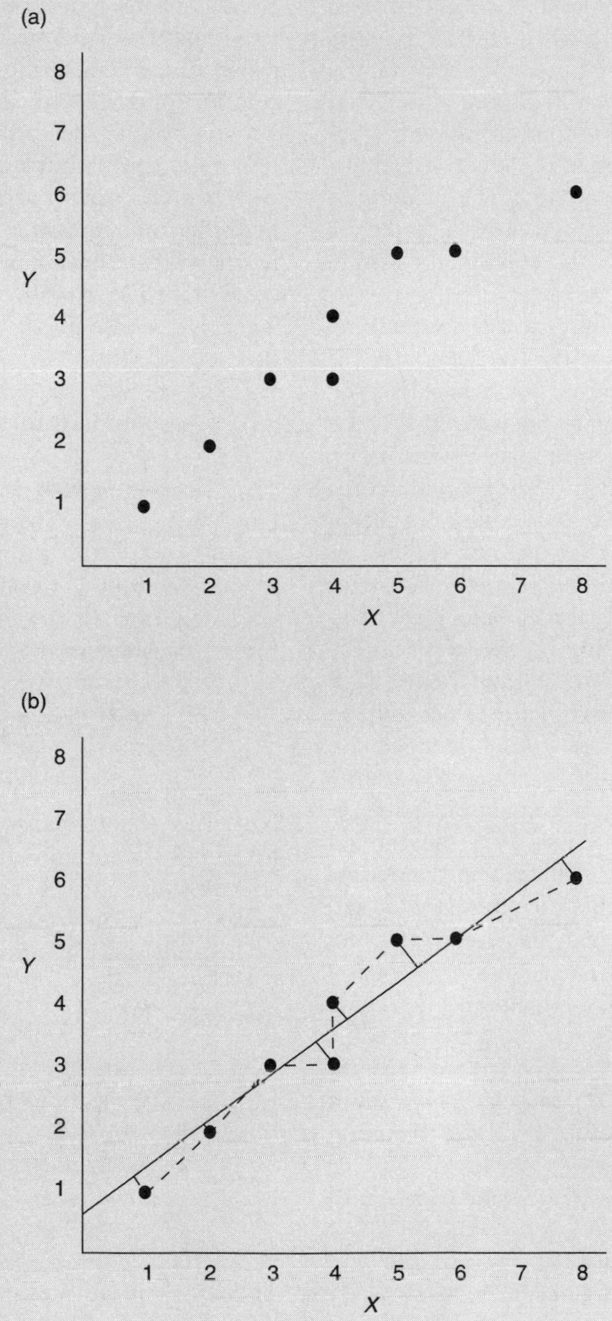

Note: The solid perpendicular lines connecting the data points to the computer line in (b) show the distances that must be determined and squared.

are some distance away from the true line (showing that the prediction is not perfect).

The method of least squares involves measuring the distances from the data points to the perfect line, then *squaring* the distances to eliminate negative values, and adding the squared distances. The computer does this repeatedly until the sum of the squared distance is the smallest (least squares). The smaller the sum of the squared distances, the greater the accuracy with which the computed formula predicts the dependent variable.

At this point it is necessary to review some basic analytical geometry. The general equation for a line is $Y = a + bX$, where Y is the variable we are trying to predict and X is the variable we are predicting from. Furthermore, a represents the point at which the line crosses the y-axis (the vertical axis), and b is a measure of the slope (or steepness) of the line. In other words, b indicates how much Y changes for each change in X. Depending on the relationship between X and Y, the slope can be positive or negative. To illustrate, Figure 12.9 shows that every time X increases one unit, so does Y. In addition, the a value is 0 because the line crosses the vertical axis at the origin.

Strictly speaking, the equation for a regression line is not the same as the general equation for a line, since the Y in the regression equation does not represent the actual variable Y but rather a predicted Y. Hence, the Y in the regression equation is usually symbolized $\hat{Y}$. Thus the regression equation is written $\hat{Y} = a + bX$.

Now let us put this general equation into more concrete terms. Assume that we have data on the relationship between years of education and number of minutes spent looking at the newspaper per day. The regression equation is

$$\text{Minutes reading newspaper} = 2 + 3\ (\text{education})$$

What can we assume from this? In the first place, the a value tells us that a person with no formal education spends 2 minutes per day looking at the newspaper. The b value indicates that time spent with the newspaper increases 3 minutes with each additional year of education. What is the prediction for someone with 10 years of education? Substituting, we have $\hat{Y} = 2 + 3(10) = 32$ minutes spent with the newspaper each day.

To take another example, consider the hypothetical regression equation predicting hours of TV viewed daily from a person's IQ score: $\hat{Y} = 5 - .01(\text{IQ})$. How many hours of TV are viewed daily by someone with an IQ of 100?

$$\hat{Y} = 5 - (.01)(100) = 5 - 1 = 4 \text{ hours}$$

Thus, according to this equation, TV viewing per day decreases 0.01 hour for every point of IQ.

The arithmetic calculation of the regression equation is straightforward. First, to find b, the slope of the line, use

$$b = \frac{N\Sigma XY - (\Sigma X)(\Sigma Y)}{N\Sigma X^2 - (\Sigma X)^2}$$

Note that the numerator is the same as that for the r coefficient, and the denominator corresponds to the first expression in the denominator of the r formula. Thus, b is easily calculated once the quantities necessary for r have been determined. To illustrate, using the data from Table 12.3, we have

$$\begin{aligned} b &= \frac{8(145) - (33)(29)}{[8(171) - 1{,}089]} \\ &= \frac{203}{279} \\ &= 0.73 \end{aligned}$$

The value of the $\hat{Y}$ intercept (a) is found by the following:

$$a = \overline{Y} - b\overline{X}$$

Again, using the data in Table 12.3 and the calculation of b, we get

$$\begin{aligned} a &= 3.63 - (0.73)(4.125) \\ &= 3.63 - 3.01 \\ &= 0.62 \end{aligned}$$

The completed regression equation is $\hat{Y} = 0.62 + 0.73X$.

Of course, as the name suggests, simple linear regression assumes that the relationship between X and Y is linear (the data increase or decrease in the same way). If an examination of the scattergram suggests a curvilinear relationship, other regression techniques are necessary. The notion of regression can be extended to the use of multiple predictor variables to predict the value of a single criterion variable.

Multiple Regression

Multiple regression, an extension of linear regression, is another parametric technique used to analyze the relationship between two or more independent variables and a single dependent (criterion) variable. Though similar in some ways to an analysis of variance, multiple regression serves basically to *predict* the dependent variable using information derived from an analysis of the independent variables.

In any research problem, the dependent variable is affected by a variety of independent variables. The primary goal of multiple regression is to develop a formula that accounts for, or explains, as much variance in the dependent variable as possible. It is widely used by researchers to predict success in college, sales levels, and so on. These dependent variables are predicted by *weighted linear combinations* of independent variables. A simple model of multiple regression is shown in Figure 12.11.

Linear combinations of variables play an important role in higher-level statistics. To understand the concept of a weighted linear combination, consider two methods of classroom grading. One instructor determines each student's final grade by his or her performance on five exams: The scores on these exams are summed and averaged to obtain each final grade. A student receives the following scores

Figure 12.11 *Multiple Regression Model*

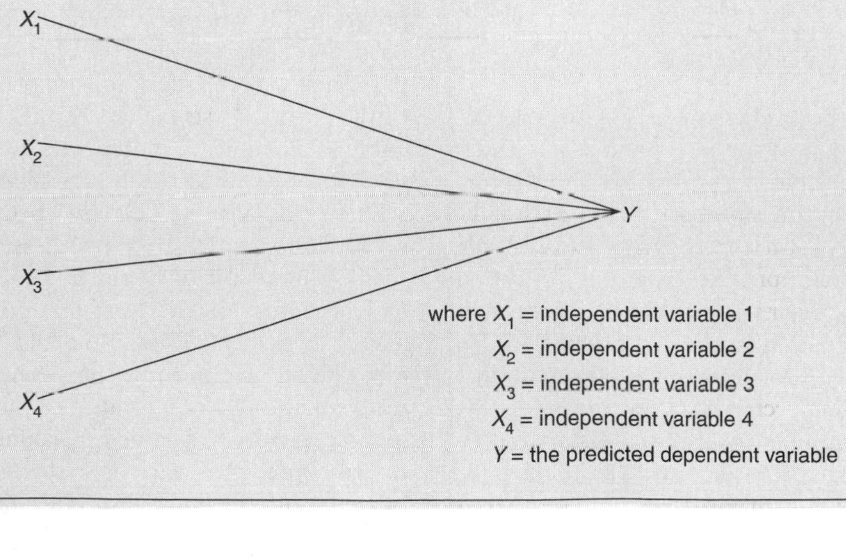

for the five exams: B (3.0), D+ (1.5), B (3.0), B+ (3.5), and A (4.0); thus the final grade is a B (15/5 = 3.0). This grade is the dependent variable determined by the linear combination of five exam scores (the independent variables). No test is considered more important than another; hence the linear combination is not said to be weighted (except in the sense that all the scores are "weighted" equally).

The second instructor also determines the final grades by students' performances on five exams; however, the first exam counts 30%, the last exam 40%, and the remaining three exams 10% each in the determination. A student with the same five scores as above thus receives a final grade of 3.3. Again, the scores represent a linear combination, but it is a weighted linear combination: The first and last exam contribute more to the final grade than do the other tests. The second grading system is used in multiple regression. The independent variables are weighted and summed to predict a dependent variable. The weight of each variable in a linear combination is referred to as its *coefficient*.

A multiple regression formula may involve any number of independent variables, depending on the complexity of the dependent variable. A simple formula of this type might look like this (hypothetical values are used):

$$\hat{Y} = 0.89X_1 + 2.5X_2 - 3$$

where $\hat{Y}$ is the predicted score or variable, X_1 is Independent Variable 1, and X_2 is Independent Variable 2. The number 3 in the formula, a constant subtracted from each subject's scores, is derived as part of the multiple regression formula. All formulas produced by multiple regression analyses represent a line in space; that is, the dependent variable is interpreted as a linear combination, or line, of independent variables. The slope of this line is determined by the *regression coefficients* assigned to the variables (Cohen & Cohen, 1975; Thorndike, 1978). The goal of the researcher is to derive a formula for a line that coincides as closely as possible with the true line (a mathematically determined line that represents a perfect prediction) of the dependent variable: The closer the computed line comes to the true line, the more accurate is the prediction.

Another important value that must be calculated in a multiple regression analysis is the *coefficient of correlation* (R), which represents the product-moment correlation between the predicted $\hat{Y}$ score and the weighted linear combination of the X scores. The square of this coefficient (R^2) indicates the proportion of variance in the dependent variable that is accounted for by the predictor variables. The higher the R^2 (that is, the closer the figure is to 1.00), the more accurate the prediction is considered to be.

Drew and Reeves (1980) conducted a multiple regression analysis to determine what factors affect the way children learn from television news stories. They defined the dependent variable, "learning," in terms of performance on a 10-point questionnaire regarding a news program the children watched in an experimental setting. The selection of independent variables was based on the results of previous studies; they decided to measure: (1) whether the children liked the program, (2) whether the children liked the particular news story, (3) the credibility of the program, and (4) the informational content of the particular story. The results, shown in Table 12.4, indicate that all the independent variables were statistically significant in their relation to learning. As the **beta weights** show, "informational content" seems to be the best predictor of learning, and "credibility" accounts for the least amount of variance. The multiple R of .546 could be considered highly significant; however, since it means that only 30% (.546²) of the variance in the dependent variable is accounted for by the four predictor variables, this value may not substantially explain the variance.

Table 12.4 *Drew and Reeves' Multiple Regression Analysis*

Predictor variables	Beta weights
Like program	.15**
Credibility	.10*
Informational content	.39***
Like story	.25***
Multiple *R*	.546
R^2	.298

*$p < .05$
**$p < .01$
***$p < .001$

▪▪▪ Summary

Mass media research has made great strides in both the number of research studies completed and the types of statistical methods used. This chapter introduced some of the more widely used basic statistical procedures involving one dependent variable and one or more independent variables. The information is intended to help beginning researchers read and analyze published research.

The emphasis in this chapter was on using statistical methods rather than on the statistics themselves. The basic formula for each statistic was briefly outlined so that beginning researchers can understand how the data are derived; the goal, however, has been to convey a knowledge of how and when to use each procedure. It is important that researchers be able to determine not only what the problem or research question is, but also which statistical method most accurately fits the requirements of a particular research study.

Key Terms

Analysis of variance
ANOVA
Beta weight
Chi-square goodness of fit
Coefficient of determination
Coefficient of nondetermination
Contingency table
Correlation
Crosstab
Cross-tabulation
Degrees of freedom
Error variance
F ratio
Interaction
Linear regression
Main effect
Multiple regression
Nonparametric statistics
Parametric statistics
Partial correlation
Pearson *r*
Scattergram
Sources of variation
Sum of squares
Systematic variance
t-test
Two-way ANOVA
Weighted linear combination

Using the Internet

1. Go to *www.vassar.edu/~lowry/VassarStats.html* for online statistical programs to run ANOVA, correlation, and partial correlation.
2. A variety of statistical calculators are available on the Internet. One source is located at: *www.vassar.edu/,lowry/VassarStats.html.*
3. The Internet is a valuable source for a great deal of information about statistics. For example, search for "analysis of variance," "linear regression," "Sir Ronald Fisher," "multiple regression," "multicolinearity," and "multiple dependence."

Questions and Problems for Further Investigation

1. Design a mass media study for which a chi-square analysis is appropriate. Consult the Internet for help, using "mass media questions" as a starting point.
2. In the chi-square example of television set sales, assume that the observed sales frequencies are 210 (RCA), 350 (Sony), 200 (JVC), and 240 (Mitsubishi). What is the chi-square value? Is it significant?

3. What are the advantages of using an ANOVA rather than conducting several separate *t*-tests of the same phenomena?
4. How could multiple regression be used to predict a subject's television viewing, radio listening, and newspaper reading behavior?
5. On page 296 we state that a Pearson *r* can be computed between any two sets of scores. Does that mean that all Pearson correlations will be logical? See the Internet for numerous interesting discussions by conducting a search on "pseudoscience" or "paranormal."
6. Calculate *r* for the following sets of scores:

   X: 1 1 3 2 2 4 5 7
   Y: 8 6 5 4 3 5 2 3

7. If you are using InfoTrac College Edition, you can read a short research article that shows how chi-square can be used in a cross-tabulation. See "Gender stereotypes: A bias against men" by Martin S. Fiebert and Mark W. Meyer in *The Journal of Psychology,* July 1997.

For additional information on these and related topics, see

http://www.wimmerdominick.com

References and Suggested Readings

Atwood, L. E., & Sanders, K. R. (1976). Information sources and voting in a primary and general election. *Journal of Broadcasting,* 20, 291–301.

Bruning, J. L., & Kintz, B. L. (1997). *Computational handbook of statistics.* New York: Longman.

Champion, D. J. (1981). *Basic statistics for social research.* New York: Macmillan.

Cochran, W. G. (1976). Early development of techniques in comparative experimentation. In D. B. Owen (Ed.), *On the history of statistics and probability.* New York: Marcel Dekker.

Cohen, J., & Cohen, P. (1975). *Applied multiple regression/correlation analysis for the behavioral sciences.* Hillsdale, NJ: Lawrence Erlbaum.

Cutler, N. E., & Danowski, J. A. (1981). Process gratification in aging cohorts. *Journalism Quarterly,* 57, 269–276.

Drew, D., & Reeves, B. (1980). Learning from a television news story. *Communication Research,* 7, 121–135.

Garramone, G. (1985). Effects of negative political advertising: The roles of sponsor and rebuttal. *Journal of Broadcasting and Electronic Media,* 29, 147–159.

Genova, B. K. L., & Greenberg, B. S. (1979). Interests in news and the knowledge gap. *Public Opinion Quarterly,* 43, 79–91.

Idsvoog, K. A., & Hoyt, J. L. (1977). Professionalism and performance of television journalists. *Journal of Broadcasting,* 21, 97–109.

Jeffres, L. (1978). Cable TV and viewer selectivity. *Journal of Broadcasting,* 22, 167–178.

Kerlinger, F. N., & Pedhazur, E. J. (1997). *Multiple regression in behavioral research* (3rd ed.). New York: Holt, Rinehart & Winston.

Krull, R., & Husson, W. (1980). Children's anticipatory attention to the TV screen. *Journal of Broadcasting,* 24, 35–48.

Metallinos, N., & Tiemens, R. (1977). Asymmetry of the screen: The effect of left versus right placement of television images. *Journal of Broadcasting,* 21, 21–34.

Nie, N. H., Hull, C. H., Jenkins, J. G., Steinbrenner, K., & Bent, D. H. (1975). *Statistical package for the social sciences.* New York: McGraw-Hill.

Nunnally, J. C. (1994). *Psychometric theory* (4th ed.). New York: McGraw-Hill.

Presser, S., & Schuman, H. (1980). The measurement of a middle position in attitude surveys. *Public Opinion Quarterly,* 44, 70–85.

Reeves, B., & Miller, M. (1977). A multidimensional measure of children's identification with television characters. *Journal of Broadcasting,* 22, 71–86.

Roscoe, J. T. (1975). *Fundamental research statistics for the behavioral sciences.* New York: Holt, Rinehart & Winston.

Siegel, S. (1988). *Nonparametric statistics for the behavioral sciences.* New York: McGraw-Hill.

Thorndike, R. M. (1978). *Correlational procedures for research.* New York: Gardner Press.

Tukey, J. W. (1986). *The collected works of John W. Tukey, Vols. III and IV.* Belmont, CA: Wadsworth.

Wakshlag, J. J., & Greenberg, B. S. (1979). Programming strategies and the popularity of television programs for children. *Journal of Communication,* 6, 58–68.

Winer, B. J. (1971). *Statistical principles in experimental design.* New York: McGraw-Hill.

Winkler, R., & Hays, W. (1975). *Statistics: Probability, inference, and decision.* New York: Holt, Rinehart & Winston.

Chapter 13

Research in the Print Media

Methodologies used to study the print media are similar to those used in most areas of research; academic and commercial research organizations often use content analysis, experiments, focus groups, and surveys, among other procedures, to study newspapers and magazines. Print media research, however, tends to be more narrowly focused and more oriented toward practical application. This chapter provides a brief overview of the most common types of studies in newspaper and magazine research, with a special emphasis on the research most likely to be conducted by advertiser-supported publications.

This chapter does not address basic market studies and advertising exposure studies. A basic market study provides a demographic or psychographic portrait of the potential readers of a newspaper or magazine; this market research technique is more fully described by Green, Tull, and Albaum (1988). Advertising exposure studies (also called reader traffic studies) are conducted to determine which ads are noticed or read by a publication's audience; for more information on these studies, see Chapter 16.

■ *Background*

Magazines and newspapers were one of the first subjects of mass media research. The initial interest in such research came from colleges and universities. In 1924 the Association of American Schools and Departments of Journalism first published the *Journalism Bulletin.* The first issue contained an article by William Bleyer entitled "Research Problems and Newspaper Analysis," which presented a list of possible research topics in journalism. Among them were the effects of form and typography on the ease and rapidity of newspaper reading, the effects of newspaper content on circulation, and the analysis of newspaper content. Bleyer's article was remarkably accurate in predicting the types of studies that would characterize newspaper and magazine research in the coming years.

Much of early print media research was qualitative. The first volume of *Journalism Quarterly,* founded in 1928 to succeed the *Journalism Bulletin,* contained articles on press law, history, international comparisons, and ethics. Soon, however, quantitative research began to make its appearance in this academic journal: An article published in March 1930 surveyed the research interests of those currently working in the newspaper and magazine field and found the most prevalent type of study to be the survey of reader interest in newspaper content. The June 1930 issue contained an article by Ralph Nafziger, "A Reader Interest Survey of Madison, Wisconsin," which served as the prototype for hundreds of future research studies. The 1930s also saw the publication of many studies designed to assess the results of print media advertising. This led to studies in applied research, and several publications began to sponsor their own readership surveys. Mostly, however, the results of these studies were considered proprietary.

As the techniques of quantitative research became more widely known and adopted, newspaper and magazine research became more empirical. Wilbur Schramm (1957) first recognized this trend in an article in *Public Opinion Quarterly* that reviewed 20 years of research as reported in *Journalism Quarterly.* Schramm found that only 10% of the 101 articles published between 1937 and 1941 concerned quantitative analyses; by 1952–1956, however, nearly half the 143 articles published were quantitative, a fivefold increase in only 15 years. The reasons for this trend, according to Schramm, were the growing availability of basic data, the development of more sophisticated research tools, and the increase in institutional support for research.

By 1960, newspapers and magazines were competing with television as well as radio for audience attention and advertiser investment. This situation greatly spurred the growth of private-sector research. The Bureau of Advertising of the American Newspaper Publishers Association (subsequently called the Newspaper Advertising Bureau) began conducting studies on all aspects of the press and its audience. In the 1970s, it founded the News Research Center, which reports the results of research to editors. The Magazine Publishers Association also began to sponsor survey research at this time. The continuing interest of academics in print media research led to the creation of the *Newspaper Research Journal* in 1979, a publication devoted entirely to research that has practical implications for newspaper management.

In 1976 the Newspaper Readership Project was instituted to study the problems of declining circulation and sagging readership. As a major part of the 6-year, $5-million study, a news research center was set up at Syracuse University to abstract and synthesize the results of more than 300 private and published studies of newspaper reading habits. The Newspaper Advertising Bureau produced dozens of research reports and conducted extensive focus group studies. In addition, regional workshops were held across the country to explain to editors the uses and limitations of research. By the time the Readership Project ended, most editors had accepted research as a necessary tool of the trade. Bogart (1991) presents a thorough history of the Readership Project.

In 1977 the Newspaper Research Council (NRC), a subgroup of the Newspaper Advertising Bureau, was incorporated with 75 members. This group was involved with the American Society of Newspaper Editors in a circulation retention study and with the International Newspaper Marketing Association on how to convert Sunday-only readers to daily readers. In 1992 the Newspaper Advertising Bureau merged with the American Newspaper Publishers Association to create the Newspaper Association of America (NAA). The NAA continued the efforts of the NRC in the research area by sponsoring a number of studies that looked at such topics as attracting younger readers and how to use advertising to encourage newspaper reading. The most recent effort of the NAA, launched in 1999, was a 5-year readership initiative study that examines the relationship of newspaper content to its readers.

Most newspapers with a circulation of at least 100,000 now have an in-house research department. The Vancouver, Washington, *Columbian* (circulation 48,000) recently hired a research manager, as did the Rochester, Minnesota, *Post-Bulletin* (circulation 39,000). The growth of group-owned newspapers—about 75% of U.S. dailies in 2001—has also increased the trend toward research because many small papers can call upon their corporate research staffs for aid. Cox Ohio Publishing, consisting of the Dayton *Daily News* and the Springfield *News-Sun,* started its in-house research operation in 2000. In addition, newspapers that don't have an in-house department often hire outside researchers to do their research. However it is conducted, research is a common activity at newspapers. Beam (1998) reported that about three-fourths of the newspapers in his sample said that they did some kind of research. Lallande (2000) provides an overview of the various kinds of research done by newspapers at the beginning of the new century.

Research touches nearly every corner of the publishing industry: advertising, marketing, circulation, readership, and news-editorial. Print media research is conducted by commercial research firms, in-house research organizations, professional associations, and colleges. Moreover, print media research is likely to continue its growth. The advent of online newspapers and magazines has prompted a busy new research area as traditional newspapers and magazines try to assess the competition from the Internet and examine how online versions relate to the traditional paper counterparts.

Types of Print Media Research

Newspaper and magazine researchers conduct six basic types of studies: readership, circulation, management, typography/makeup, readability, and online media use. Most of their research focuses on readership; studies of circulation and management rank next. Studies about online media examine two main topics (1) the potential competition between Internet news sites and traditional newspapers and (2) the relationship between a newspaper's web version and its print version. Only a few studies have been conducted of typography/makeup and readability.

Readership Research

Many readership studies were done in the United States in the years immediately preceding and following World War II. The George Gallup organization was a pioneer in developing the methodology of these studies—namely, a personal interview in which respondents were shown a copy of a newspaper and asked to identify the articles they had read. A comprehensive study of newspaper readership was undertaken by the American Newspaper Publishers Association (ANPA), whose *Continuing Studies of Newspapers* involved more than 50,000 interviews with readers of 130 daily newspapers between 1939 and 1950 (Swanson, 1955).

Readership research became important to management during the 1960s and 1970s, as circulation rates in metropolitan areas began to level off or decline. Concerned with holding the interests of their readers, editors and publishers began to depend on surveys for the detailed audience information they needed to shape the content of a publication. The uncertain economy at the beginning of the new century and increasing competition from traditional and online media have made readership research even more important today. This is most evident in the Readership Institute's continuing Impact Study that examines the readership habits of 37,000 consumers in one hundred daily newspaper markets across the United States (Fitzgerald, 2000).

Research into newspaper readership is composed primarily of five types of studies: reader profiles, item-selection studies, reader-nonreader studies, uses and gratifications studies, and editor-reader comparisons.

Reader Profiles. A **reader profile** provides a demographic summary of the readers of a particular publication. For example, in 2002 *PC Magazine* reported that the median income of its readers was $68,170; they had a median age of 40; 54% were college graduates; and 48% owned cell phones. These data can be used to focus the content of the publication, prepare advertising promotions, and increase subscriptions.

Because there may be significant differences in the nature and extent of newspaper reading among individuals who have the same demographic characteristics, researchers recently have turned to psychographic and lifestyle segmentation studies to construct reader profiles. Both procedures go beyond the traditional demographic portrait and describe readers in terms of what they think or how they live. **Psychographic studies** usually ask readers to indicate their level of agree-

AN INSIDE LOOK

Readership Research: What Isn't Investigated

While many national advertisers use insert advertising (the various forms of advertising inserted into a newspaper, usually in the Sunday edition), the companies do not conduct research on the effectiveness of these inserts. The advertisers do not know what types of messages these inserts communicate. They merely insert them and hope for the best.

ment or disagreement with a large number of attitudinal statements. Subsequently, patterns of response are analyzed to see how they correlate or cluster together. People who show high levels of agreement with questions that cluster together can be described with labels that summarize the substance of the questions. On the one hand, people who tend to agree with statements such as "I like to think I'm a swinger," "I'm a night person," and "Sex outside marriage can be a healthy thing" might be called "progressives." On the other hand, people who agree with items such as "Women's lib has gone too far," "Young people have too much freedom," and "The good old days were better" might be labeled "traditionalists." For example, the Canadian magazine *Saturday Night* did a psychographic study of its subscribers and found that they had a high need for achievement, possessed a high degree of self-confidence, and considered themselves more sophisticated than the average Canadian.

Lifestyle segmentation research takes a similar approach. Respondents are asked a battery of questions concerning their activities, hobbies, interests, and attitudes. Again, the results are analyzed to see which items cluster together. Groups of individuals who share the same attitudes and activities are identified and labeled. To illustrate, Davis (2001) describes newspaper industry research that segmented readers on the basis of how people manipulated time. The research identified three groups of readers: routinized, relaxed, and harried. The strategy for improving readership could then be tailored to each specific segment.

Both psychographic and lifestyle segmentation studies are designed to provide management with additional insights about editorial aims, target audiences, and circulation goals. In addition, they give advertisers a multidimensional portrait of the publications' readers. Two of the most popular scales designed to measure these variables are the List of Values (LOV) and the recently revised Values and Life Styles test (VALS II). Descriptions and comparisons of these scales are found in Novak and MacEvoy (1990). Other social factors might also be important. Loges and Ball-Rokeach (1993) note that newspaper readership is related to several sociological variables—including social understanding, self-understanding, and action orientation—that explain more of the variation in readership than do traditional demographic variables.

Item-Selection Studies. A second type of newspaper readership study, the **item selection study**, is used to determine who reads specific parts of the paper. The readership of a particular item is usually measured by means of **aided recall**, whereby the interviewer shows a copy of the paper to the respondent to find out which stories the respondent remembers. In one variation on this technique, the interviewer preselects items for which readership data are to be gathered and asks subjects about those items only. Because of the expense involved in conducting personal interviews, some researchers now use phone interviews to collect readership data. Calls are made on the same day the issue of the paper is published. The interviewer asks the respondent to bring a copy of the paper to the phone, and together they go over each page, with the respondent identifying the items he or she has read. Although this method saves money, it excludes from study those readers who do not happen to have a copy of the paper handy.

Stamm, Jackson, and Jacoubovitch (1980) suggested a more detailed method of item-selection analysis, which they called a **tracking study.** They supplied their respondents with a selection of colored pencils and asked them to identify which parts of an article (headline, text, photo, cutline) they had read, using a different colored pencil each time they began a new *reading episode* (defined as a stream of uninterrupted reading). The results showed a wide degree of variability in the readership of the elements that made up an item: For one story, 27% of the subjects had read the headline, 32% the text, and 36% the cutline. There was also variation in the length and type of articles read per reading episode.

The unit of analysis in an item-selection study is a specific news article (such as a front-page story dealing with a fire) or a specific content category (such as crime news, sports, obituaries). The readership of items or categories is then related to certain audience demographic or psychographic characteristics. For example, Griswold and Moore (1989) found that readers of a small daily newspaper most often read local news, obituaries, police news, state news, and weather forecasts. Gersh (1990) reported that teenage readers have reading habits different from adults. The most popular sections of the newspaper among teens were comics, sports, and entertainment; finance, food, and home sections were the least popular. Stone and Boudreau (1995) compared data from a 1985 survey of newspaper reader preferences with data gathered in 1994. They found that content preferences changed remarkably little during the time period. More recently, an industry study of item readership (Astor, 2000) found that local news was the number one category of news preferred by readers. Fashion news ranked last. The Newspaper Association of American (2001) reported that readers rank news items first, followed by general entertainment content.

Reader-Nonreader Studies. The third type of newspaper readership research is called the **reader-nonreader study.** This type of study can be conducted via personal, telephone, or mail interviews with minor modifications. It is difficult, however, to establish an operational definition for the term *nonreader.* In some studies, a nonreader is determined by a "no" answer to the question "Do you generally read a newspaper?" Others have used the more specific question "Have you read a newspaper yesterday or today?" (The rationale is that respondents are more likely to admit they have not read a paper today or yesterday than that they never read one.) A third form of this question uses multiple-response categories. Respondents are asked, "How often do you read a daily paper?" and they are given five choices of response: "very often," "often," "sometimes," "seldom," and "never." Nonreaders are defined as those who check the "never" response, or in some studies "seldom" or "never." Obviously, the form of the question has an impact on how many people are classified as nonreaders. The largest percentage of nonreaders generally occurs when researchers ask, "Have you read a newspaper today or yesterday?" (Penrose, Weaver, Cole, & Shaw, 1974); the smallest number is obtained by requiring a "never" response to the multiple-response question (Sobal & Jackson-Beeck, 1981).

Once the nonreaders have been identified, researchers typically attempt to describe them by means of traditional demographic variables. For example, Sobal and Jackson-Beeck (1981) reported that nonreaders tend to be older, to have less education and lower incomes, and to have more often been widowed or divorced than readers. A study by Stone (1994) found that education was a better predictor of newspaper readership than race among a sample of 18- to 34-year-olds. Davis (2001) reported that as today's young people get older, they are more likely to become nonreaders. Finally, a significant part of the Readership Institute's project mentioned above focuses on why people are not reading newspapers.

Several studies of nonreaders have attempted to identify the reasons people do not read the newspaper. One way to collect these data is to ask nonreaders to tell in their own words why they do not read. Responses are analyzed and the most frequent reasons reported. Bogart (1991), for example, identified four reasons: depressing news, cost, lack of interest, and inability to spend sufficient time at home. More recently, Wanta, Hu, and Wu (1995) differentiated newspaper readers and nonreaders using the uses and gratifications approach (discussed later). They found that nonreaders displayed low motivations to use the newspaper to help them understand what's going on and to keep up with current events. Qualitative research has also been useful. Mason (2000) did field observation and interviews in a donut shop. She found that some people didn't read because they didn't have the exact change necessary to buy a paper from a vending machine. Lyon (1998) reported the results of focus groups where nonreaders mentioned such things as having to recycle the paper, perceived bias, and a reliance on TV for news as reasons for their not reading a paper.

Broader studies in this area have included variables that are beyond the control of the newspaper. In a longitudinal study, Chaffee and Choe (1981) found that changes in marital status, residence, and employment had an impact on newspaper readership. Cobb-Walgren (1990) focused on why teenagers do not read the newspaper. She found that both teenagers' home environment and their image of the newspaper were important in determining why teens do not read newspapers. Nonreader teens perceived that reading the paper took too much time and effort, and they were more likely to have parents who also did not read newspapers.

Uses and Gratifications Studies. A **uses and gratifications study** is used to study all media content. For newspapers it can determine the motives that lead to newspaper reading and the personal and psychological rewards that result from it. The methodology of the uses and gratifications study is straightforward: Respondents are given a list of possible uses and gratifications and are asked whether any of these are the motives behind their reading. For example, a reader might be presented with this question:

> Here is a list of some things people have said about why they read the newspaper.
>
> How much do you agree or disagree with each statement?
>
> 1. I read the newspaper because it is entertaining.
> 2. I read the newspaper because I want to kill time.
> 3. I read the newspaper to keep up to date with what's going on around me.
> 4. I read the newspaper to relax and to relieve tension.
> 5. I read the newspaper so I can find out what other people are saying about things that are important to me.

The responses are then summed and an average score for each motivation item is calculated.

Several studies have taken this approach to explain readership. For example, Weaver, Wilhoit, and Reide (1979) found that the three motivations most common in explaining general media use are the need to keep tabs on what is going on around one, the need to be entertained, and the need to kill time. The authors also noted differences among demographic groups regarding which of these needs was best met by the newspaper. For example, young males, young females, and middle-aged males were most likely to say they read a newspaper to satisfy their need to keep tabs on things, but they preferred other forms of media for entertainment and killing time. A study done in Hawaii (Blood, Keir, & Kang, 1983) reinforced these conclusions. The two factors that were the best predictors of readership were "use in daily living" and "fun to read." In addition, gratifications from reading the newspaper seemed to differ across ethnic groups. The most recent uses and gratifications study in this area compare the gratifications of a print newspaper with those of an online version. See below for more details about this type of study.

Payne, Severn, and Dozier (1988) studied uses and gratifications as indicators of magazine readership. They found three main classes of gratifications: surveillance, diversion, and interaction. In addition, readers' scores on these three categories were consistent with the magazines they chose to read. Bramlett-Solomon and Merrill (1991), in their study of newspaper use in a retirement community, found that readers used the newspaper to keep involved with the community. Perse and Courtright (1993) found that print media were seen as most useful in fulfilling learning needs but were not rated high for social, arousal, or companionship needs.

Editor-Reader Comparisons. In the final area of newspaper readership research, **editor-reader comparisons**, a group of editors is questioned about a certain topic, and their answers are compared to those of their readers to see whether there is any correspondence between the two groups. Bogart (1989) presented two examples of such research. In one study, a group of several hundred editors was asked to rate 23 attributes of a high-quality newspaper. The editors ranked "high ratio of staff-written copy to wire service copy" first, "high amount of nonadvertising content" second, and "high ratio of news interpretations . . . to spot news reports" third. When a sample of readers ranked the same list, the editors' three top attributes were ranked 7th, 11th, and 12th, respectively. The readers rated "presence of an action line column" first, "high ratio of sports and feature news to total news" second, and "presence of a news summary" and "high number of letters to the editor per issue" in a tie for third. In short, there was little congruence between the two groups in their perceptions of the attributes of a high-quality newspaper.

In a related study, Bogart gave readers an opportunity to design their own newspaper. Interviewers presented a sample of readers with 34 subjects and asked how much space they would give to each in a paper tailor-made to their own interests. Major categories of news were omitted from the listings because they were topics over which editors have little control. When the results were tabulated, the contents of a sample of newspapers were analyzed to see whether the space allocations made by editors matched the public's preferences. The resulting data indicated that readers wanted more of certain content than they were getting (consumer news; health, nutritional, and medical advice; home maintenance; travel) and that they were getting more of some topics than they desired (sports news; human interest stories; school news; crossword puzzles; astrology). Gladney (1996) explored whether editors and readers agreed on what makes a good newspaper. A survey revealed that both

AN INSIDE LOOK

Readership: Measuring Daily or Weekly

Since it began, newspaper readership research has been geared to measuring the amount of readership garnered by daily newspapers. One of the most common questions used to measure readership has been, "Did you read a newspaper today or yesterday?" This question, however, is not adequate to measure weekly newspaper reading. Surveys done on Mondays, Tuesdays, Wednesdays, Saturdays, and Sundays would probably not accurately assess the reading of a weekly that appears on Thursday.

Thurlow and Milo (1993) suggest that more research should be devoted to the readership of weeklies. Their study of college students revealed that about half of them reported reading every issue of their campus weekly and a local weekly. In contrast, 56% of the students reported that they never read the local daily and only about 3% were classified as every-day readers. The authors note that it is important to track these students to see if they continue to favor the weekly over the daily or if they join the ranks of nonreaders.

groups agreed on the importance of many journalistic standards, but readers didn't value professional staffing goals and enterprise reporting as highly as the editors did. More recently, Bernt, Fee, Gifford, and Stempel (2000) compared editor's estimates of readers' interest in certain news topics with actual estimates taken from a survey. The results demonstrated that editors overestimated readers' interest in crime, religion, stock market, and local business news.

Magazine Readership Research. Magazine **readership surveys** are fundamentally similar to those conducted for newspapers but tend to differ in the particulars. Some magazine research is done by personal interview; respondents are shown a copy of the magazine under study and asked to rate each article on a four-point scale ("read all," "read most," "read some," or "didn't read"). The mail survey technique, also frequently used, involves sending a second copy of the magazine to a subscriber shortly after the regular copy has been mailed, with instructions on how to mark the survey copy. For example, the respondents might be instructed to mark with a check the articles they scanned, to draw an X through articles read in their entirety, and to underline titles of articles that were only partly read. Laitin (1997) presents a basic outline of the methods used to survey magazine subscribers.

Most consumer magazines use audience data compiled by the Simmons Market Research Bureau (SMRB) and Mediamark Research Inc. (MRI). Both companies select a large random sample of households and interview readers. Before 1994, SMRB and MRI used different techniques to measure readership. Simmons screened its respondents by first showing them cards with magazine logos printed on them and then stripped-down issues of actual magazines. Those people who reported reading one or more magazines were then interviewed again. Mediamark presented logo cards to respondents to identify readers and then gathered more detailed data in a single interview. Since the two research companies used different techniques, their readership data did not always agree, and the discrepancy was a source of some concern in the magazine industry. In 1994, however, partly as a money-saving strategy, SMRB announced that it was adopting a technique similar to that used by MRI.

Both MRI and SMRB face a troublesome problem caused by the proliferation of magazines targeted for a narrow readership. It is difficult to draw a sample that includes enough readers of specialized publications to generate statistically reliable results. In that connection, MRI announced in 1997 that it was planning to expand its sample size from 20,000 to 30,000 households (Wilson, 1997). As of 2001, MRI was interviewing about 26,000 people.

Many magazines maintain *reader panels* of 25 to 30 people who are selected to participate for a predetermined period. All feature articles that appear in each issue of the magazine are sent to these panel members, who rate each article on a number of scales, including interest, ease of reading, and usefulness. Over time, a set of guidelines for evaluating the success of an article is drawn up, and future articles can be measured against that standard. The primary advantage of this form of panel survey is that it can provide information about audience reactions at a modest cost. Other publications might use surveys that are included with the magazine itself.

The most recent trend is to use online reader panels. The sample size of the online panel is much larger than that of a traditional panel, and much more information can be gathered. The downside of the online panel is that it is probably not a representative sample of all readers. *Smithsonian* and *Elle* are just two of the many publications that use Internet panels. As of 2001, the *Elle* survey was a lengthy instrument that asked questions about web site and print version readership, other magazine subscriptions, and general consumer attitudes.

Other magazine research involves item-selection and editor-reader comparisons. For example, *Glamour* generally surveys reader response to every issue (Smith, 1992). Questionnaires are mailed to readers asking them about the articles, the cover, and their general reading habits. *Travel & Leisure* has a similar system. The McGraw-Hill magazine group spends approximately $250,000 a year on readership research. *Good Housekeeping* takes a random survey of its subscribers each month to determine what stories were enjoyed and what recipes were tried. Harcourt Brace Jovanovich does both pretesting and posttesting in its health care journals. The company sends the titles of 15 articles printed on a single sheet of paper to 400 or 500 physicians. The respondents are asked to rate each article as having high, moderate, or low interest value.

In addition to traditional readership studies, many magazines conduct focus groups. Harcourt Brace Jovanovich depends particularly on focus groups to help fine-tune the content of new publications. Ziff Communications does the same. *Farmer* uses focus group sessions for reader reaction to headlines, graphics, and general editorial feedback. Other magazines use focus groups as supplements to their monthly questionnaires.

Circulation Research

The term **circulation research** is applied to two different forms of newspaper and magazine study. The first type of circulation research uses a particular group of readers as its unit of analysis. It attempts to measure circulation in terms of the overall characteristics of a particular market—for example, to determine the proportion of households in a given market that are reached by a particular newspaper or the circulation pattern of a magazine among certain demographic groups or in specific geographic areas. For example, in a study of 69 Canadian daily newspaper markets, Alperstein (1980) discovered that newspaper circulation was positively related to the proportion of reading households within the newspaper's home city. In addition, daily newspaper circulation was inversely related to weekly newspaper circulation. More recently, Albers (2000) reported that loyal subscribers to the newspaper were more likely to be long-term residents who identify with the community. Individuals who cancelled subscriptions after a short time were younger and more likely to have young children at home.

Four studies in the 1990s examined the impact of content variables on circulation. Lacy and Fico (1991) demonstrated that measures of the content quality of a newspaper were positively related to circulation figures. Somewhat similarly, Lacy and Sohn (1990) found limited support for the hypothesis that the amount of space given to specific content sections in metropolitan newspapers correlates with circulation in suburban areas. McCleneghan (1997) examined the relationship between analytical content and newspaper circulation. Lastly, Ha and Litman (1997) conducted a longitudinal analysis of the impact of magazine advertising clutter on the circulation of 10 magazines. They found that increased clutter had a negative impact on the circulation of entertainment magazines but not of news magazines.

Another trend in circulation research is the identification of other market level or market structure variables that have an impact on circulation. Stone and Trotter (1981) found that the number of households in the local community and measures of broadcast media availability were the two best predictors of circulation. Blankenburg (1981) analyzed market structure variables and determined that county population and distance from the point of publication were strong predictors of circulation. Hale (1983) concluded from a regression analysis of Sunday newspaper sales in all 50 states that degree of urbanization, population density, and affluence were key predictors of circulation. Moore, Howard, and Johnson (1988) discovered that there was no relationship between viewing television news programs and afternoon newspaper circulation. Market size and location showed a stronger relationship with circulation. In sum, it appears from these studies that many factors outside the control of the newspaper publisher have an impact on circulation.

Economic influences have also been examined. Blankenburg and Friend (1994) discovered that circulation figures were not related to the percentage of a newspaper's budget that was spent on news-editorial expenses, nor was there a relationship between money spent on promotion and circulation. There was, however, an influence of newspaper price; papers that cost more tended to lose circulation. Similarly, Lewis (1995) found that increases in price were related to declines in circulation. Marchetti (1996) detailed several economic factors, including increased advertising cost, cutbacks in newsstand distribution, and a concentration on core market areas, that were related to declining circulation.

The second type of circulation research uses the individual reader as the unit of analysis to measure the effects of certain aspects of delivery and pricing systems on reader behavior. For example, McCombs, Mullins, and Weaver (1974) studied why people cancel their subscriptions to newspapers. They found that the primary reasons had less to do with content than with circulation problems, such as irregular delivery and delivery in unreadable condition. These reasons were substantiated in a 1992 Paragon Research study of circulation of the two newspapers in Denver, Colorado. Seamon (2000) looked at several newspaper delivery variables and concluded that the age of the carrier was not a factor in missed or late delivery.

Magazine publishers often conduct this type of circulation research by drawing samples of subscribers in different states and checking on the delivery dates of their publication and its physical condition when received. Other publications contact subscribers who do not renew to determine what can be done to prevent cancellation (Sullivan, 1993). Studies have even been conducted to find out why some people do not pay their subscription bills promptly.

The Gannett Company's Newspaper Division conducted research that discovered that customer billing was a prime cause of their newspapers losing circulation. Subsequently, Gannett interviewed 1,000 subscribers and conducted several focus groups to devise a billing system that was more responsive to consumer needs. Some circulation research uncovers facts that management would probably never be aware of. For example, at the *Wichita Eagle,* management was puzzled about circulation losses. A survey found that many subscribers were canceling because the plastic delivery bags used by the paper on rainy days were not heavy enough, and many readers were fed up with soggy papers. In short, this type of circulation research investigates the effect on readership or subscription rates of variables that are unrelated to a publication's content.

Newspaper Management Research

A growing research area in the last two decades has been newspaper management practices. This growth was due to three factors. First, newspaper companies expanded their holdings, which created a more complicated management structure. Second, media competition became more intense. Newspapers with efficient management techniques had a greater advantage in the new competitive environment. Third, the newspaper industry became more labor-intensive. Skilled and experienced personnel form the backbone of a successful newspaper. More and more managers turned to research to determine how to keep employees satisfied and productive.

The techniques used to study newspaper management are the same as those used to study any business activity: surveys, case studies, descriptive content analysis, and mathematical models. The main topics that have attracted the most research attention in the last 5 years are goal setting by management, organizational structure, employee job satisfaction, and effects of competition and ownership on newspaper content and quality.

One representative example of management research into goal setting is Demers and Wackman's (1988) study of the effect of chain (group) ownership on management's objectives. Secondary analysis of data collected from a sample of 101 newspaper managers revealed that editors at chain-owned daily newspapers were more likely to say that profit was a goal driving their organization. Analogous results were found in a follow-up study (Demers, 1991). In a similar study, Busterna (1989) administered a survey to 42 newspaper executives, most of them from weekly papers, asking them to rate several managerial goals in terms of their relative importance to their newspapers. Managers who also owned their papers placed less emphasis on maximizing profits as a goal, whereas non-owner managers ranked it first.

The effects of various management structures at newspapers and magazines is a fairly new research area. Neuzil, Hansen, and Ward (1999) analyzed the impact of participatory management and topic teams on employee's feelings of empowerment. They found little evidence that such an approach was beneficial. A study conducted by the Readership Institute (2001) looked at the management culture of 90 newspapers across the United States. Their results suggested that the culture at more than 70 of the papers could be classified as "defensive," whereas only 17 evidenced what was called a "constructive" atmosphere.

Job satisfaction among newspaper employees has been the topic of several studies.

Stamm and Underwood's (1993) survey of 429 newsrooms revealed that job satisfaction was negatively related to a newspaper's emphasis on business over journalism but positively related to an emphasis on journalistic quality. Bramlett-Solomon (1993) discovered that the job satisfaction motivations of black journalists were not very different from those of white journalists. Technological innovations, such as computer pagination, did not relate to measures of job satisfaction (Stamm, Underwood, & Giffard, 1995). Finally, McQuarrie (1999) studied the link between the "professional mystique" of journalism and job dissatisfaction.

A related issue that has garnered recent attention is job burnout among journalists. Data collected from employees at five newspapers (Cook & Banks, 1993) revealed that the person most likely to suffer from burnout is a young, entry-level journalist working as a copyeditor at a small daily newspaper. It is not surprising that journalists with a high level of job satisfaction are unlikely to experience burnout. In a related study, Cook, Banks, and Turner (1993) reported that several work environment variables, including supervisor support and peer cohesion, are also related to burnout.

Research on the impact of concentration of ownership includes Akhavan-Majid, Rife, and Gopinah's (1991) study of editorial positions taken by Gannett-owned papers. They found that the Gannett papers were more likely than other newspapers to endorse similar editorial positions. Lacy (1990) found that local market monopoly newspapers used a smaller number of wire services than did papers in competitive markets, which supports earlier findings that competition encourages more spending on the news-editorial department. Coulson (1994) sampled 773 journalists at independent and group-owned papers about the quality of their publication. Reporters at independently owned papers were more likely to rate their paper's commitment to quality local coverage as excellent. Coulson and Hansen (1995) examined the news content of the *Louisville Courier-Journal* after its purchase by the Gannett organization. Results indicated that the total amount of news space increased but that the average length of stories and the amount of hard news coverage decreased. Finally, Hollifield (1999) found that newspapers owned by Thomson, a Canadian-based company, ran more editorials against the independence movement in Quebec than did non-Canadian papers.

Typography and Makeup Research

Another type of print media research measures the effects of news design elements—specifically typeface and page makeup—on readership, reader preferences, and comprehension. By means of this approach, researchers have tested the effects of different typography and makeup elements, including amount of white space, presence of paragraph headlines, size and style of type, variations in column width, and use of vertical or horizontal page makeup.

The experimental method (see Chapter 10) is used most often in typography and makeup studies. Subjects are typically assigned to one or more treatment groups, exposed to an experimental stimulus (typically in the form of a mock newspaper or magazine page), and asked to rate what they have seen according to a series of dependent variable measures.

Among the dependent variables that have been rated by subjects are the informative value of a publication, interest in reading a publication, image of a page, recall of textual material, readability, and general preference for a particular page. A common practice is to measure these variables by means of a semantic differential rating scale. For example, Siskind (1979) used a nine-point,

20-item differential scale with such adjective pairs as "messy/neat," "informative/uninformative," "unpleasant/pleasant," "easy/difficult," "clear/unclear," "bold/timid," and "passive/active." She obtained a general reader preference score by having subjects rate a newspaper page and summing their responses to all 20 items. Other studies have measured reader interest by using the rating scale technique or the 0–100 "feeling thermometer" (see Figure 7.1). Comprehension and recall are typically measured by a series of true/false or multiple-choice questions on the content that is being evaluated.

Haskins and Flynne (1974) conducted a typical design study to test the effects of different typefaces on the perceived attractiveness of and reader interest in the women's section of a newspaper. They hypothesized that some typefaces would be perceived as more feminine than others and that headlines in such typefaces would create more reader interest in the page. The authors showed an experimental copy of a newspaper prepared specially for the study to a sample of 150 female heads of households: One subsample saw a paper with headlines in the women's section printed in Garamond Italic (a typeface experts had rated as feminine), while a second group saw the same page with Spartan Black headlines (considered to be a masculine typeface). A third group served as a control and saw only the headline copy typed on individual white cards. The subjects were asked to evaluate each article for reading interest. Additionally, each woman was shown a sample of 10 typefaces and asked to rate them on a semantic differential scale with 16 adjective pairs.

The researchers discovered that typeface had no impact on reader interest scores. In fact, the scores were about the same for the printed headlines as they were for those typed on white cards. Analysis of the typeface ratings revealed that readers were able to differentiate between typefaces; Garamond Italic was rated the second most feminine typeface, whereas Spartan Black was rated most masculine, thus confirming the judgment of the expert raters.

Studies of page layout have been used to help magazine editors make decisions about the mechanics of editing and makeup. Click and Baird (1993) provided a summary of the more pertinent research in this area. Some of their conclusions are listed here to illustrate the types of independent variables that have been studied:

- Large illustrations attract more readers than small ones.
- Unusually shaped pictures irritate readers.
- A small amount of text and a large picture on the opening pages of an article increase readership.
- Readers do not like to read type set in italics.
- For titles, readers prefer simple, familiar typefaces.
- Readers and graphic designers seldom agree about what constitutes superior type design.
- Roman type can be read more quickly than other typefaces.

Wanta and Gao (1994) performed a similar study of newspaper design elements that young readers found desirable. They found that their sample of high school students preferred newspapers that used pullout quotes, large graphics, and many small photographs. In a similar study, Wanta and Remy (1995) investigated the effects of design elements on recall with a sample of high school students. Information in pullout quotes was remembered best, whereas facts embedded in graphics were remembered the least.

The popularity of *USA Today,* with its ground-breaking illustrations and use of color, has prompted several studies. Two studies by Geraci (1984a, 1984b) compared the photographs, drawings, and other illustrations used by *USA Today* with those in traditional papers. Click and Stempel (1982) used seven front-page formats ranging from a modular page with a four-color halftone (the format favored by *USA Today*) to a traditional format with no color. Respondents were shown a slide of each page for 15 seconds and were asked to rate the page using 20 semantic differential scales. The results indicated that readers preferred modular pages and color.

The impact of graphics on reader understanding and comprehension has also been examined, and the studies have had fairly consistent results. Kelly (1989) found that embellished graphic presentations of data (as commonly used by *USA Today*) were no better than unembellished graphics in helping readers retain information. Ward (1992) investigated whether using a sidebar graphic illustration along with a news story aided comprehension. He found that bar charts, tables, and an adorned bar chart were less effective in aiding comprehension than a straight sidebar story that accompanied the main story. On the other hand, Griffin and Stevenson (1992) reported that background material presented in both text and graphic forms increased readers' understanding of a complex story. These same researchers also found that including geographic information, either in the text or with a map, raised comprehension scores on a news article (Griffin & Stevenson, 1994).

Page layout and design have become important topics for Internet websites in recent years. This body of research is discussed below.

Readability Research

Simply defined, **readability** is the sum total of all the elements and their interactions that affect the success of a piece of printed material. Success is measured by the extent to which readers understand the piece, are able to read it at an optimal speed, and find it interesting (Dale & Chall, 1948).

Several formulas have been developed to determine objectively the readability of text. One of the best known is the **Flesch** (1948) **reading ease formula,** which requires the researcher to select systematically 100 words from the text, determine the total number of syllables in those words (wl), determine the average number of words per sentence (sl), and perform the following calculation:

$$\text{Reading ease} = 206.835 - 0.846wl - 1.015sl$$

The score is compared to a chart that provides a description of style (such as "very easy") or a school grade level for the potential audience. (*Microsoft Word* automatically computes the Flesch reading ease value as well as the Flesch-Kincaid grade level. The chapter you are currently reading, for example, has a Flesch-Kincaid score of 12.0).

Another measure of readability is the **Fog Index,** which was developed by Gunning (1952). To compute the Fog Index, researchers must systematically select samples of 100 words each, determine the mean sentence length by dividing the number of words by the number of sentences, count the number of words with three or more syllables, add the mean sentence length to the number of words with three or more syllables, and multiply this sum by 0.4. Like the Flesch index, the Gunning formula suggests the educational level required for understanding a text. The chief advantages of the Fog Index are that the syllable count and the overall calculations are simpler to perform. (See the Internet for online calculation programs to compute the Fog Index.)

McLaughlin (1969) proposed a third readability index called **SMOG Grading** (for Simple Measure Of Gobbledygook). The SMOG Grading is quick and easy to calculate: The researcher merely selects 10 consecutive sentences near the beginning of the text, 10 from the middle, and 10 from the end, and then counts every word of three or more syllables and takes the square root of the total. The number thus obtained represents the reading grade that a person must have reached to understand the text. McLaughlin's index can be calculated quickly using a small, easily measured sample. Although the procedure is related to that for the Fog Index, it appears that the SMOG grade is generally lower.

Taylor (1953) developed yet another method for measuring readability called the **Cloze procedure.** This technique departs from the formulas described above in that it does not require an actual count of words or syllables. Instead, the researcher chooses a passage of about 250–300 words, deletes every fifth word from a random starting point and replaces it with a blank. The researcher then gives the passage to subjects and asks them to fill the blanks with what they think are the correct words; he or she then counts the number of times the blanks are replaced with the correct words. The number of correct words or the percentage of correct replacement constitutes the readability score for that passage. The following paragraph is a sample of what a passage might look like after it has been prepared for the Cloze procedure:

> The main stronghold of the far left _______ to be large _______ centers of north Italy. _______ is significant, however, that _______ largest relative increase in _______ leftist vote occurred in _______ areas where most of _______ landless peasants live—in _______ and south Italy and Sicily and Sardinia. The _______ had concentrated much of its efforts on winning the _______ of those peasants.

Nestvold (1972) found that Cloze procedure scores were highly correlated with readers' own evaluations of content difficulty. The Cloze procedure was also found to be a better predictor of evaluations than several other common readability tests.

Finally, Mosenthal and Kirsch (1998) have developed the PMOSE/IKIRSCH readability formula expressly designed for assessing the complexity of documents. The formula takes into account such elements as lists, schedules, tables, and graphs in its estimation of readability.

Although they are not used extensively in print media research, readability studies can provide valuable information. Smith (1984) found differences in readability among categories of newspaper content, with features and entertainment more readable than national-international or state and local news. Smith also noted that three popular readability formulas did not assign the same level of reading difficulty to his sample of stories. Porter and Stephens (1989) found that a sample of Utah managing editors consistently underestimated the Flesch readability scores of five different stories from five different papers. They also found that the common claim that reporters write front-page stories at an 8th-grade level was a myth. The hard news stories they analyzed were written at an average 12th-grade level. McAdams (1992/1993) computed a Fog Index for 14 news stories that were then given to a sample of readers. Results suggest that a high Fog Index did not adversely affect readers who found a story to have high overall quality. Last, Bodle (1996) compared the readability levels of a sample of student newspapers with a sample of private-sector papers and found that the private-sector dailies had a higher score than the student papers.

▪ *Print Media Research and the Internet*

As of 2001 more than a thousand newspapers were publishing both traditional print and online versions. The total number of magazines online is harder to pin down. A recent issue of the *Net.Journal Directory* listed more than 10,000 magazines, newsletters, and journals available online. Since the online newspaper and magazine is a relatively recent phenomenon, most of the research is still at a rather basic level.

One group of studies is concerned with describing what types of newspapers have websites, how they are trying to make a profit, and how their online version relates to the print version. For example, Peng, Tham, and Hao (1999) conducted a survey of more than 60 editors of online papers and performed a content analysis of the sites of 80 papers. They found that almost all types of papers had online versions and that the two main reasons for starting the digital version were to gain more readers and to increase revenues. The researchers found no clear pattern in how the online papers generated their revenues. Chyi and Lasorsa (1999) looked at the relationship between online readers and print newspaper readers. They found that readers on the online editions of local papers also read the print version. On the other hand, the readers of online editions of national papers were unlikely to read the print counterpart. Last, Tewksbury and Althaus (2000) conducted an experiment that compared the effects of exposure to the print and online versions of the *New York Times*. The results revealed that people who read the online version read fewer national and international news stories and had less recall of information.

A second research focus looks at the time readers spend with print newspapers and Internet news sites. The concern among newspaper publishers is that consumers will turn to the web for news rather than to the traditional newspaper. Research results in this area have been mixed. Bartlett (2001) reports data that seem to suggest that publishers have a valid concern. Survey results indicated that those with greater experience and access, typically younger individuals, rely more on the Internet and less on the newspaper for their news. Kayani and Yelsma (2000) reported similar findings. Their survey revealed that newspaper reading went down as Internet usage went up. On the other hand, Stempel, Hargrove, and Bernt (2000) found that Internet users were more likely to be newspaper readers. Similarly, a study by the Scarborough Research Company (Newspaper Association of America, 2000) reported that 82% of people who got news from online sources read the newspaper with the same or increased frequency.

Not surprisingly, researchers are also interested in the uses and gratifications of receiving news online instead of with a traditional paper. Papacharissi and Rubin (2000) found five main motivations for using the Internet: interpersonal utility, passing time, convenience, information seeking, and entertainment. Lee (2001) surveyed college students and compared their motives for reading an online paper with their motives for reading a print paper. He found that motives were generally similar but that convenience and entertainment were more important factors for online newspaper readers.

The design and make-up of online newspapers has been a popular topic. Li (1998) analyzed the web page design of *USA Today*, the *New York Times*, and the *Washington Post*. He concluded that the papers gave more priority to text than graphics and that all provided a number of related links for readers to visit. Online newspaper readers seem to prefer a portrait or vertical screen layout as opposed to a landscape layout (Wearden, Fidler, Schierhorn, & Schierhorn, 1999). Lowrey (1999) interviewed web creative directors and found general agreement that traditional print design features can be translated to the web. Last, Sundar (2000) conducted an experiment that examined the impact of multimedia presentations in online news sites. The results indicated that multimedia hindered memory for story content and led to more negative evaluations of the site.

AN INSIDE LOOK

Journalism Research: The Journalist As Researcher

Print media reporters and social scientists now have more in common with each other, thanks to several recent trends. One of these is **precision journalism,** a technique of inquiry in which social science research methods are used to gather the news. Popularized by reporter and researcher Philip Meyer in his book, *Precision Journalism* (1973), the method relies primarily on the procedures of content analysis and survey research to generate quantitative data that are reported as news stories. For example, the *Detroit News* content analyzed almost 36,000 drunk-driving conviction records and discovered that big-city judges gave more lenient penalties than rural judges. Similarly, the *Charlotte Observer* analyzed campaign finance reports and noted a link between voting patterns and contributions.

A second trend is known as **database journalism.** Pioneered by reporter Elliot Jaspin, this form of reporting relies on computer-assisted analysis of existing information files, an approach that has been accepted at many newspapers. Jaspin, for example, researching a story on school bus safety, studied computerized records of traffic citations over a 3-year period and found that many bus drivers had frightful driving records.

The popularity of precision and database journalism suggests that competent journalists need a basic knowledge of social science techniques. To be specific, precision journalism requires knowledge of measurement, research techniques, questionnaire design, sampling, statistics and data presentation—the same skills needed by many mass communication researchers.

▪▪▪ Summary

Magazine and newspaper research began in the 1920s and for much of its early existence was qualitative in nature. Typical research studies dealt with law, history, and international press comparisons. During the 1930s and 1940s, readership surveys and studies of the effectiveness of print media advertising were frequently done by private firms. By the 1950s, quantitative research techniques became common in print media research. The continuing competition between television and radio for advertisers and audiences during the past three decades has spurred the growth of private sector research. Professional associations have started their own research operations.

Research in the print media encompasses readership studies, circulation studies, management studies, typography and makeup studies, and readability studies. Readership research is the most extensive area; it serves to determine who reads a publication, what items are read, and what gratifications the readers get from their choices. Circulation studies examine the penetration levels of newspapers and magazines in various markets as well as various aspects of the delivery and pricing systems. Management studies look at goal setting and at job satisfaction. Typography and makeup are studied to determine the impact of different newspaper and magazine design elements on readership and item preferences. Readability studies investigate the textual elements that affect comprehension of a message. A more recent research area examines the online versions of print media.

Key Terms

Aided recall
Circulation research
Cloze procedure
Database journalism
Editor-reader comparison
Flesch formula
Fog Index
Item-selection study
Lifestyle segmentation
Magazine readership surveys
Precision journalism
Psychographic studies
Readability
Reader-nonreader study
Reader profile
SMOG Grading
Tracking study
Uses and gratifications study

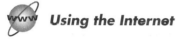

Using the Internet

There are many sites that contain useful information for anyone interested in print media research. The sites mentioned below represent only a small sampling.

1. *http://www.smithsonianmagresearch.com* You can join the Smithsonian magazine's online reader panel at this site. Note the kind of information the magazine wants to know about its readers.
2. *http://readership.org* Site of the Readership Institute of the Media Management Center at Northwestern University. Contains links to reports of surveys, content analyses, and management studies pertaining to newspapers.
3. *http://www.magazine.org/resources/research.html* The Magazine Publishing Association maintains this site that contains links to magazine readership and advertising data.
4. *http://www.bsu.edu/web/aejmcmagazine/journal/default.html* Online home of the *Journal of Magazine and News Media Research*, a publication sponsored by the magazine division of the Association for Education in Journalism and Mass Communication. Each issue contains an assortment of media research.
5. *http://www.naa.org* The Newspaper Association of America's home page. Contains links to several research studies concerning both print and online newspapers.

Questions and Problems for Further Investigation

1. Assume that you are the editor of an afternoon newspaper faced with a declining circulation. What types of research projects could you conduct to help increase your readership?
2. Now suppose you have decided to publish a new magazine about women's sports. What types of research could you conduct before starting publication? Why?
3. Conduct a pilot uses and gratifications study of 15–20 people to determine why they read the local daily newspaper.
4. Using any five pages from this chapter as a sample, calculate the Flesch reading ease formula, the Gunning Fog Index, and McLaughlin's SMOG Grading.
5. Make a catalog of existing websites that are relevant to a local newspaper reporter. Now make a list of sites that are of interest to a social scientist. Are there any similarities?

For additional information on these and related topics, see

http://www.wimmerdominick.com

References and Suggested Readings

Akhavan-Majid, A. M., Rife, A., & Gopinah, S. (1991). Chain ownership and editorial independence. *Journalism Quarterly*, 68(1/2), 59–66.

Albers, R. R. (2000). Masterminding circulation. *Presstime*, 22(4), 46–53.

Alperstein, G. (1980). *The influence of local information on daily newspaper household penetration in Canada* (ANPA News Research Report No. 26). Reston, VA: ANPA News Research Center.

Astor, D. (2000). Relative readership of syndicated stuff. *Editor & Publisher*, 133(33), 21.

Bartlett, M. (22 June, 2001). Study predicts black skies ahead for newspapers. Available online at *www.newsbytes.com*.

Beam, R. (1998). What it means to be a market-oriented newspaper. *Newspaper Research Journal,* 19(3), 2–20.

Bernt, J. P., Fee, F. E., Gifford, J., & Stempel, G. (2000). How well can editors predict reader interest in news? *Newspaper Research Journal,* 21(2), 2–11.

Blankenburg, W. R. (1987). Predicting newspaper circulation after consolidation. *Journalism Quarterly,* 64(3), 585–587.

Blankenburg, W. R., & Friend, R. (1994). Effects of cost and revenue strategies on newspaper circulation. *Journal of Media Economics,* 7(2), 1–14.

Bleyer, W. (1924). Research problems and newspaper analysis. *Journalism Bulletin,* 1(1), 17–22.

Blood, R., Keir, G., & Kang, N. (1983). Newspaper use and gratification in Hawaii. *Newspaper Research Journal,* 4(4), 43–52.

Bodle, J. V. (1996). Assessing news quality: A comparison between community and student daily newspapers. *Journalism and Mass Communication Quarterly,* 73(3), 672–686.

Bogart, L. (1989). *Press and public.* Hillsdale, NJ: Lawrence Erlbaum.

Bogart, L. (1991). *Preserving the press.* New York: Columbia University Press.

Bramlett-Solomon, S. (1993). Job satisfaction factors important to black journalists. *Newspaper Research Journal,* 14(3/4), 60–68.

Bramlett-Solomon, S., & Merrill, B. (1991). Newspaper use and community ties in a model retirement community. *Newspaper Research Journal,* 12(2), 60–68.

Busterna, J. C. (1989). How managerial ownership affects profit maximization in newspaper firms. *Journalism Quarterly,* 66(2), 302–307.

Chaffee, S., & Choe, S. (1981). Newspaper reading in longitudinal perspective. *Journalism Quarterly,* 58(2), 201–211.

Chyi, H. I., & Lasorsa, D. (1999). Access, use and preferences for online newspapers. *Newspaper Research Journal,* 20(4), 2–13.

Ciotta, R. (1996). Baby, you should drive this CAR. *American Journalism Review,* 18(2), 34–39.

Click, J. W., & Baird, R. (1993). *Magazine editing and production* (6th ed.). Dubuque, IA: Brown & Benchmark.

Click, J. W., & Stempel, G. (1982). *Reader response to front pages with modular format and color* (ANPA News Research Report No. 35). Reston, VA: ANPA News Research Center.

Cobb-Walgren, C. J. (1990). Why teenagers do not read all about it. *Journalism Quarterly,* 67(2), 340–347.

Cook, B., & Banks, S. (1993). Predictors of job burnout in reporters and copy editors. *Journalism Quarterly,* 70(1), 108–117.

Cook, B., Banks, S., & Turner, R. (1993). The effects of work environment on burnout in the newsroom. *Newspaper Research Journal,* 14(3/4), 123–136.

Coulson, D. (1994). Impact of ownership on newspaper quality. *Journalism Quarterly,* 71(2), 403–410.

Coulson, D., & Hansen, A. (1995). The *Louisville Courier-Journal's* news content after purchase by Gannett. *Journalism and Mass Communication Quarterly,* 72(1), 205–215.

Dale, E., & Chall, J. S. (1948). A formula for predicting readability. *Education Research Journal,* 27(1), 11–20.

Davis, N. (2001). Measures for measures. *Presstime,* 23(4), 38–44.

Demers, D. P. (1991). Corporate structure and emphasis on profits and product quality at U.S. daily newspapers. *Journalism Quarterly,* 68(1/2), 15–26.

Demers, D. P., & Wackman, D. B. (1988). Effect of chain ownership on newspaper management goals. *Newspaper Research Journal,* 9(2), 59–68.

Fisher, C. (1993, July 26). Newspaper readers get choosier. *Advertising Age,* p. 22.

Fitzgerald, M. (2000). Reading edge report. *Editor & Publisher,* 133(41), 22–27.

Flesch, R. (1948). A new readability yardstick. *Journal of Applied Psychology,* 32(2), 221–233.

Geraci, P. (1984a). Comparison of graphic design and illustration use in three Washington, DC, newspapers. *Newspaper Research Journal,* 5(2), 29–40.

Geraci, P. (1984b). Newspaper illustration and readership: Is *USA Today* on target? *Journalism Quarterly,* 61(2), 409–413.

Gersh, D. (1990, April 7). Reaching the teenage reader. *Editor & Publisher,* p. 18.

Gladney, G. A. (1996). How editors and readers rank and rate the importance of eighteen traditional standards of newspaper excellence. *Journalism and Mass Communication Quarterly,* 73(2), 319–331.

Green, P. E., Tull, D. S., & Albaum, G. (1988). *Research for marketing decisions.* Englewood Cliffs, NJ: Prentice-Hall.

Griffin, J., & Stevenson, R. (1992). Influence of text and graphics in increasing understanding of foreign news content. *Newspaper Research Journal,* 13(1/2), 84–98.

Griffin J., & Stevenson, R. (1994). The effectiveness of locator maps in increasing reader understanding of the geography of foreign news. *Journalism Quarterly,* 71(4), 937–946.

Griswold, W. F., & Moore, R. L. (1989). Factors affecting readership of news and advertising in a small daily newspaper. *Newspaper Research Journal,* 10(2), 55–66.

Gunning, R. (1952). *The technique of clear writing.* New York: McGraw-Hill.

Ha, L., & Litman, B. R. (1997). Does advertising clutter have diminishing and negative returns? *Journal of Advertising,* 26(1), 31–42.

Hale, D. (1983). Sunday newspaper circulation related to characteristics of the 50 states. *Newspaper Research Journal,* 5(1), 53–62.

Harper, C. (1996). Online newspapers: Going somewhere or going nowhere? *Newspaper Research Journal,* 17(3/4), 2–13.

Haskins, J. B., & Flynne, L. (1974). Effects of headline typeface variation on reader interest. *Journalism Quarterly,* 51(4), 677–682.

Hollifield, A. (1999). Effects of foreign ownership on media content. *Newspaper Research Journal,* 20(1), 65–82.

Janofsky, M. (1993, July 22). A survey shows Tina Brown's *New Yorker* is attracting more and wealthier readers. *New York Times,* p. D21.

Kayani, J. M., & Yelsma, P. (2000). Displacement effects on online media in the socio-technical contexts of households. *Journal of Broadcasting and Electronic Media,* 44(2), 215–229.

Kelly, J. D. (1989). The data-ink ratio and accuracy of newspaper graphics. *Journalism Quarterly,* 66(3), 623–639.

Lacy, S. (1990). Newspaper competition and number of press services carried. *Journalism Quarterly,* 67(1), 79–82.

Lacy, S., & Fico, F. (1991). The link between content quality and circulation. *Newspaper Research Journal,* 12(2), 46–56.

Lacy, S., & Sohn, A. (1990). Correlations of newspaper content with circulation in the suburbs. *Journalism Quarterly,* 67(4), 785–793.

Laitin, J. A. (1997, June 1). Subscriber surveys that sing. *Folio,* 26(8), 88–89.

Lallande, A. (2000). More for the money. *Presstime,* 22(6), 59–66.

Lee, D. W. (2001). A comparative study: Use of online vs. print media newspapers and gratifications. Unpublished master's thesis. Department of Telecommunication, University of Georgia, Athens, Georgia.

Lewis, R. (1995). Relation between newspaper subscription price and circulation. *Journal of Media Economics,* 8(1), 25–41.

Li, X. (1998). Web page design and the graphics of three U.S. newspapers. *Journalism and Mass Communication Quarterly,* 75(2), 353–365.

Loges, W., & Ball-Rokeach, S. (1993). Dependency relationships and newspaper readership. *Journalism Quarterly,* 70(3), 602–614.

Lowrey, W. (1999). From map to machine. *Newspaper Research Journal,* 20(4), 14–28.

Lyon, C. (1998). Women grade the newspaper. *Presstime,* 20(12), 65.

Mason, K. (2000). Price vs. sales. *Presstime,* 22(11), 37–40.

Marchetti, M. (1996). The scoop on circulation. *Sales & Marketing Management,* 148(3), 61–62.

McAdams, K. (1992/1993). Readability reconsidered. *Newspaper Research Journal,* 13/14(4/1), 50–59.

McCleneghan, S. J. (1997). Searching for analysis in the Southwest. *Social Science Journal,* 34(1), 21–33.

McCombs, M., Mullins, L. E., & Weaver, D. (1974). *Why people subscribe and cancel: A stop-start survey of three daily newspapers* (ANPA News Research Bulletin No. 3). Reston, VA: ANPA News Research Center.

McLaughlin, H. (1969). SMOG grading: A new readability formula. *Journal of Reading,* 22(4), 639–646.

McQuarrie, F. (1999). Professional mystique and journalists' dissatisfaction. *Newspaper Research Journal,* 20(3), 20–28.

Meyer, P. (1973). *Precision journalism.* Bloomington: Indiana University Press.

Moore, B. A., Howard, H. H., & Johnson, G. C. (1988). TV news viewing and the decline of the afternoon newspaper. *Newspaper Research Journal,* 10(1), 15–24.

Mosenthal, P. B., & Kirsch, I. S. (1998). A new measure for assessing document complexity. *Journal of Adolescent and Adult Literacy,* 41(8), 638–657.

Nafziger, R. (1930). A reader interest survey of Madison, Wisconsin. *Journalism Quarterly,* 7(2), 128–141.

Nestvold, K. (1972). Cloze procedure correlation with perceived readability. *Journalism Quarterly,* 49(3), 592–594.

Neuzil, M., Hansen, K. & Ward, J. (1999). Twin Cities journalists' assessment of topic teams. *Newspaper Research Journal,* 20(1), 2–16.

Newspaper Association of America. (2000). Newspaper voice and online services. Available online at *www.naa.org/irc/facts99/18.html.*

Newspaper Association of America, (2001). Facts about newspapers, 2001. Vienna, VA: NAA.

Novak, T. P., & MacEvoy, B. (1990, June). On comparing alternative schemes: LOV and VALS. *Journal of Consumer Research,* 17(1), 105–109.

Papacharissi, Z., & Rubin, A. R. (2000). Predictors of Internet use. *Journal of Broadcasting and Electronic Media,* 44(2), 175–196.

Payne, G. A., Severn, J. J., & Dozier, D. M. (1988). Uses and gratifications motives as indicators of magazine readership. *Journalism Quarterly,* 65(4), 909–913.

Peng, F. Y., Tham, N. I., & Hao, X. (1999). Trends in online newspapers. *Newspaper Research Journal,* 20(2), 52–63.

Penrose, J., Weaver, D., Cole, R., & Shaw, D. (1974). The newspaper non-reader ten years later. *Journalism Quarterly,* 51(4), 631–639.

Perse, E., & Courtright, A. (1993). Normative images of communication media. *Human Communication Research,* 19(4), 485–503.

Porter, W. C., & Stephens, F. (1989). Estimating readability: A study of Utah editors' abilities. *Newspaper Research Journal,* 10(2), 87–96.

Readership Institute. (2001). *Impact study.* Evanston, IL: Northwestern University Media Management Center.

Schramm, W. (1957). Twenty years of journalism research. *Public Opinion Quarterly,* 21(1), 91–108.

Seamon, M. (2000). How demographic variables affect newspaper delivery. *Newspaper Research Journal,* 21(1), 91–101.

Siskind, T. (1979). The effect of newspaper design on reader preference. *Journalism Quarterly,* 56(1), 54–62.

Smith, A. M. (1992, April). The measure of editorial success. *Folio,* pp. 95–98.

Smith, R. (1984). How consistently do readability tests measure the difficulty of newswriting? *Newspaper Research Journal,* 5(4), 1–8.

Sobal, J., & Jackson-Beeck, M. (1981). Newspaper nonreaders: A national profile. *Journalism Quarterly,* 58(1), 9–13.

Stamm, K., Jackson, K., & Jacoubovitch, D. (1980). Exploring new options in newspaper readership methods. *Newspaper Research Journal,* 1(2), 63–74.

Stamm, K., & Underwood, D. (1993). The relationship of job satisfaction to newsroom policy changes. *Journalism Quarterly,* 70(3), 528–541.

Stamm, K., Underwood, D., & Giffard, A. (1995). How pagination affects job satisfaction of editors. *Journalism and Mass Communication Quarterly,* 72(4), 851–862.

Stempel, G. H., Hargrove, T., & Bernt, J. P. (2000). Relation of growth of use of Internet to changes in media use, 1995–1999. *Journalism and Mass Communication Quarterly,* 77(1), 71–79.

Stone, G. (1994). Race yields to education as predictor of newspaper use. *Newspaper Research Journal,* 15(1), 115–126.

Stone, G., & Boudreau, T. (1995). 1985, 1994: Comparison of reader content preferences. *Newspaper Research Journal,* 16(4), 13–28.

Stone, G., & Trotter, E. (1981). Community traits and predictions of circulation. *Journalism Quarterly,* 58(3), 460–463.

Sullivan, C. (1993, November 1). Expire research is no dead end. *Folio,* pp. 39–40.

Sundar, S. S. (2000). Multimedia effects on processing and perception of online news. *Journalism and Mass Communication Quarterly,* 77(3), 480–499.

Swanson, C. (1955). What they read in 130 daily newspapers. *Journalism Quarterly,* 32(3), 411–421.

Sylvie, G. (1996). Departmental influences on interdepartmental cooperation in daily newspapers. *Journalism and Mass Communication Quarterly,* 73(1), 230–241.

Taylor, W. (1953). Cloze procedure: A new tool for measuring readability. *Journalism Quarterly,* 30(4), 415–433.

Tewksbury, D., & Althaus, S. (2000). Differences in knowledge acquisition among readers of the paper and online versions of a national newspaper. *Journalism and Mass Communication Quarterly,* 77(3), 457–479.

Thurlow, G., & Milo, K. (1993). Newspaper readership. *Newspaper Research Journal,* 14(3/4), 34–43.

Wanta, W., & Gao, D. (1994). Young readers and the newspaper. *Journalism Quarterly,* 71(4), 926–936.

Wanta, W., & Remy, J. (1995). Information recall of four elements among young newspaper readers. *Newspaper Research Journal,* 16(2), 112–123.

Wanta, W., Hu, Y. W., & Wu, Y. C. (1995). Getting more people to read more newspapers. *Newspaper Research Journal,* 16(1), 103–115.

Ward, D. B. (1992). The effect of sidebar graphics. *Journalism Quarterly,* 69(7), 318–328.

Wearden, S. T., Fidler, R., Schierhorn, A. B., & Schierhorn, C. (1999). Portrait vs. landscape: Potential users' preferences for screen orientation. *Newspaper Research Journal,* 20(4), 50–62.

Weaver, D., Wilhoit, C., & Reide, P. (1979). *Personal needs and media use* (ANPA News Research Report No. 21). Reston, VA: ANPA News Research Center.

Wilson, S. (1997, October 1). Changes in syndicated research coming soon. *Folio,* 26(13), 17–19.

Chapter 14

Research in the Electronic Media

Research in the electronic media has become commonplace because managers need to know what their target audiences want. As Phil LoCascio (1998), program director of WARW-FM in Washington, D.C. says:

> Research is the only way to find out about a target audience and what they want from a station. Research helps us determine when we must adjust our business to meet new demands. This is important because changes in broadcasting can happen in a matter of minutes. We have no factories to re-tool and no raw materials to order and we must have accurate information very quickly.
>
> The ratings winners in broadcasting use quality research and accurately analyze the data. There are stations that conduct research yet lose in the ratings because they either have used inferior research information or have come to the wrong conclusions. In broadcasting, there is no replacement for quality research information.

There are many types of researchers in the electronic media who provide the quality information that is needed. For example, there are professional research companies, in-house research departments in most radio, television, cable, TV networks, and satellite operations, and many research departments or divisions in colleges and universities. Electronic media research is a multimillion-dollar business that continually changes as a result of advancements in technology and improved research methodologies. This chapter introduces some of the more widely used research procedures in this area.

■ Background

Broadcast research developed rapidly in sophistication and volume since its beginnings in the 1920s. In the early years of broadcasting, the broadcasters were experimenters and hobbyists who were interested mainly in making sure that their signal was being sent and received. The popularity of radio was unknown, and there was no reason to be concerned with audience size at that time.

The situation changed rapidly during the 1930s as radio became a popular mass medium. When radio began to attract large audiences, concern emerged over how radio would be financed. After much discussion, advertising emerged as the choice over government financing or taxes on sales of equipment. The acceptance by radio listeners of advertising on radio was the first step in the development of electronic media research.

Advertisers, not broadcasters, were the initiators of broadcast research. When commercials began airing on radio stations, advertisers naturally wondered how many listeners were exposed to their messages and how effective the messages were. It became the responsibility of broadcasters to provide empirical evidence of the size and characteristics of their audience. This situation still exists—advertisers continually want information about the people who hear and see their commercial announcements.

In addition to information about audience size, advertisers became interested in *why* people behave the way they do. This led to the development of the research area known as psychographics (why people behave they way they do). But because psychographics data are rather vague, they were not adequate predictors of audience behavior; advertisers wanted more information. Research procedures were then designed to study lifestyle patterns and how they affect media use and buying behavior. Such information is valuable in designing advertising campaigns: If advertisers understand the lifestyle patterns of the people who purchase their products, they can design commercials to match those lifestyles.

Electronic media research studies today fall into two main categories: ratings and nonratings research. The remainder of this chapter is devoted to a discussion of these two areas.

▪ *Ratings Research*

When radio first became popular and advertisers began to grasp its potential for attracting customers, they were faced with the problem of documenting audience size. The print media were able to provide circulation figures, but broadcasters had no equivalent "hard" information—merely estimates. The early attempts at audience measurement failed to provide adequate data. Volunteer mail from listeners was the first source of data, but it is a well-known axiom of research that volunteers do not necessarily represent the general audience. Advertisers and broadcasters quickly realized that more information was urgently needed.

Since 1930, when a group called the Cooperative Analysis of Broadcasting conducted one of the first audience surveys for radio, several individuals and companies have attempted to provide syndicated audience information. The bulk of syndicated information for radio and television stations and cable is provided by two companies: Nielsen Media Research for local market and network TV and cable TV, and Arbitron Inc. for local market radio. The country is divided into more than 200 markets, and no city is included in more than one market. In most markets, the Arbitron and Nielsen companies provide ratings data throughout the year (called *continuous measurement*), not just during certain times of the year.

Located in Northbrook, Illinois, Nielsen Media Research is a subsidiary of ACNielsen (see *www.acnielsen.com* and *www.nielsemedia.com*). The original company (A. C. Nielsen) was founded in 1945 and was purchased by VNU (a Netherlands company;*www.vnu.com*) in February 2001. ACNielsen is one of the world's largest market research companies, and its television and cable ratings (via Nielsen Media Research) are well known throughout the world. Arbitron (*www.arbitron.com*) was founded in 1949 as The American Research Bureau (ARB). The company name was changed to The Arbitron Company in 1972, then to The Arbitron Ratings Company in 1982, back to The Arbitron Company in 1989, and now Arbitron, Inc. Arbitron's headquarters are in Laurel, Maryland. For more information about the history of broadcast ratings, see Beville (1988).

Nielsen Media Research is involved in television ratings in both the United States and Canada, and includes ratings for "national broadcast and cable networks, regional networks, syndicators, television stations, local cable TV systems, satellite distributors, advertising agencies and advertisers, program producers, station representatives and buying services." (*www.nielsenmedia.com*).

Nielsen Media Research ratings are divided into two broad categories: *national* and *local*. In the national ratings, Nielsen uses an electronic measurement device called the Nielsen People Meter. According to Nielsen's website,

> These meters are placed in a sample of 5,000 households (13,000 persons) in the U.S., randomly selected and recruited by Nielsen Media. The People Meter is placed on each TV in the sample household. The meter measures two things—what program or channel is being tuned and who is watching. The People Meter is used to collect audience estimates for broadcast and cable networks, nationally distributed syndicated programs and satellite distributors.
>
> Which TV source (broadcast, cable, etc.) is being watched in the sample homes is continually recorded by one part of the meter which has been calibrated to identify which station, network or satellite is carried on each channel in the home. Channel changes are electronically monitored by the meter. Nielsen Media Research gathers and maintains a database of information about source and time of telecast for TV programs, and when this information is combined with source tuning data from the sample homes, we can credit audience to specific TV programs.
>
> Who is watching is measured by another portion of the Nielsen People Meter which uses an electronic "box" at each TV set in the home and accompanying remote control units. Each family member in the sample household is assigned a personal viewing button (identified by name or symbol) on the People Meter. The Nielsen Media Research representative who recruits the household links the assigned button to the age and gender of each person in the household. Whenever the television set is turned on a red light flashes from time to time on the meter, reminding viewers to press their assigned button to indicate if they are watching television. Additional buttons on the meter enable guests in a sample home to report when they watch TV by entering their age and gender and pushing a visitor button.

Nielsen conducts local audience measurement in 53 of the largest markets in the United States. The local measurement uses a different type of meter that provides TV ratings information on a daily basis. According to Nielsen,

> This information is used by local television stations, local cable systems, advertisers and their agencies to make programming decisions as well as to buy and sell commercial advertising. In each of these markets, approximately 400–500 households are recruited (not the same homes as the national People Meter sample), and electronic meters are attached to each TV set in the sample home.
>
> Homes recruited for local samples are not equipped with People Meters, so the information is limited to "set tuning" information from which Nielsen Media Research can determine which channel the TV set is tuned. This information is augmented at least four months a year with demographic viewing data which are collected from separate samples of households which each maintain a paper viewing diary for one week. Household members are asked to write down what programs they and their guests watch in their home over the course of that week. Standard reports which combine the meter and diary data are issued regularly.

Nielsen's diary methodology is used in each of the 210 television markets in the United States in November, February, May, and July of each year (some larger markets also have ratings conducted during January, March, and October). These measurement periods are known in the industry as the **sweeps.**

Nielsen Media Research produces a variety of audience measurement reports, such as the *National Television Index* (NTI) for national measurements, and the *National Station Index* (NSI) for local measurements. These publications, as well as other informa-

> ### AN INSIDE LOOK
> ### *Audience Ratings—What to Expect*
>
> Mass media researchers will certainly be involved in audience ratings and will be faced constantly with questions about the "correctness" of the ratings. If a radio or TV station receives low ratings for a given ratings period, researchers will hear something like, "There must be something wrong with the ratings. Find out what it is." While there may be instances where the ratings companies do provide incorrect information, the researcher must find out why the station's ratings are down. The answer usually relates to some type of programming decision, something management doesn't want to hear.

tion from Nielsen are discussed on the company's website.

The metered data are used for NTI and NSI reports and for **overnights**, which are preliminary ratings data gathered to give network and station executives, program producers, advertising agencies, and others an indication of the performance of the previous night's programs. Because the sample sizes involved in overnights are small, the actual ratings for the programs do not appear until several days later, when an additional sample is added to increase statistical reliability.

Arbitron is best known in the United States for its radio audience measurement, although the company states that it is "an international media and marketing research firm serving radio and TV broadcasters, cable companies, advertisers and advertising agencies, magazines, newspapers and the online industry in the United States and Europe."

For several years, Arbitron provided ratings for local television, but it stopped producing television ratings in 1995. Currently, Arbitron produces only radio ratings by collecting information via diaries. Although most of the larger markets in the United States are continually measured, the most important ratings "books" are produced in the winter, spring, summer, and fall. The only network radio ratings are gathered by Statistical Research, Inc., which is hired by networks to produce a RADAR report (Radio's All-Dimension Audience Research).

Controversy. Broadcast ratings create controversy in many areas. TV viewers complain that "good" shows are canceled; radio listeners complain that their favorite station's format is changed; producers, actors, and other artists complain that numbers are no judge of artistic quality (they are not intended to be); radio and television station owners and operators complain that the results are not reliable; and advertisers balk at the lack of reliable information. Although there may be merit to these complaints, one basic fact remains: Until further refinements are made, ratings as they currently exist will remain the primary decision-making tool in programming and advertising.

Since ratings will continue to be used for some time, it is important to understand some basic points about them. First, ratings are *only approximations or estimates of audience size.* They do not measure either the quality of programs or opinions about the programs. Second, not all ratings are equally dependable: Different companies produce different ratings figures for the same market during the same time period. (See *www.nielsenmedia.com/wtrrm.html* for an article entitled "What the ratings really mean.")

The important point to remember when discussing or using ratings is that the figures are riddled with error. The data must be interpreted in light of several limitations (which are always printed in the last few pages of every ratings book). Individuals who depend on ratings as though they were facts are misusing the data.

Ratings Methodology

The research methodologies used by Arbitron and Nielsen are complex, and each company publishes several texts describing its methods and procedures that should be consulted for specific information. The data for ratings surveys are currently gathered by two methods: diaries and electronic meters. Each method has its own advantages and disadvantages. (As of mid-2002, Arbitron is testing a meter device (Portable People Meter) for gathering radio listening data.)

Broadcast ratings provide a classic example of the need to sample the population. With about 105.5 million households in the United States, it would be impossible for any ratings company to conduct a census of media use. The companies naturally resort to sampling to produce data that can be generalized to the population. For example, Nielsen's national samples are selected using national census data and involve multistage area probability sampling that ensures that the sample reflects actual population distributions. That is, if Los Angeles accounts for 10% of the television households in the United States, Los Angeles households should comprise 10% of the sample as well. Nielsen uses four stages in sampling: selection of counties in the country, selection of block groups within the counties, selection of certain blocks within the groups, and selection of individual households within the blocks. Nielsen claims that about 20% of the households in the NTI-metered sample of approximately 5,000 households are replaced each year.

To obtain samples for producing broadcast listening and viewing estimates, Arbitron and Nielsen use recruitment by telephone, which includes calls to both listed and unlisted telephone numbers. Although all the ratings companies begin sample selection from telephone directories, each firm uses a statistical procedure to ensure that unlisted telephone numbers are included. This eliminates the bias that would be created if only people or households listed in telephone directories were asked to participate in broadcast audience estimates. Nielsen calls its procedure a Total Telephone Frame; Arbitron uses Expanded Sample Frame.

Target sample sizes for local audience measurements vary from market to market. Each ratings service uses a formula to establish a minimum sample size required for a specific level of statistical efficiency, but there is no guarantee that this number of subjects will actually be produced. Although many people may agree to participate in an audience survey, there is no way to force them all to complete the diaries they are given or to use electronic meters accurately. Additionally, completed diaries are often rejected because they are illegible or obviously inaccurate. The companies are often lucky to get a 50% response rate in their local market measurements.

In addition, since participation by minority groups in audience surveys is generally lower than for the remainder of the population, the companies make an extra effort to collect data from these groups by contacting households by telephone or in person to assist them in completing the diary. [These methods are generally used in high-density Hispanic (HDHA) and high-density African-American areas (HDBA); otherwise, return rates could be too low to provide any type of audience estimates.] When the return (or in-tab) rate is low, statistical weighting or sample balancing is used to compensate for the shortfall. This topic is discussed later.

Perhaps the best-known method of gathering ratings data from a sample is by means of electronic ratings-gathering instruments, in particular the Nielsen People Meter, which was introduced as the *audimeter* in 1936 to record radio use on a moving roll of paper. (A. C. Nielsen purchased the audimeter from Robert Elder and Louis Woodruff, professors at the Massachusetts Institute of Technology.) Today's audimeter, the storage instantaneous audimeter (SIA), is a sophisticated device that automatically records the time each set in a household is turned on or off, the broadcasting station, the amount of time each set stays on a channel, and the channel changes. The central computer in Dunedin, Florida, calls each NTI household each day to retrieve the stored data. These data are used to compute the National Television Index. The data collection is automatic and does not require participation by anyone in the NTI households.

For the second major form of data collection, subjects are asked to record in diaries the channels they watch or the stations they listen to, the time periods, and the number of people viewing or listening to each program or daypart, a segment of the broadcast day such as "prime time" (8:00 P.M.–11:00 P.M. EST). Arbitron uses diaries for radio; Nielsen uses diaries for the households in its NAC sample to supplement the information gathered from the SIA households because the audimeter cannot record the number of people who are watching each television set. The instruction pages from Arbitron and Nielsen diaries are shown in Figures 14.1 and 14.2.

The third major technique used to collect data—the telephone—is not being used in the broadcast industry as of early 2002. The only company that used telephone data collection until late 2001 was Strategic Media Research, located in Chicago, which produced ratings known as *AccuTrack*.

Arbitron and Nielsen do use the telephone to conduct a variety of special studies, however, allowing clients to request almost any type of survey research project. One of the most frequent types of custom work is the **telephone coincidental.** This procedure measures the size of the medium's audience at a given time; the survey coincides with actual viewing or listening. The method involves selecting a sample of households at random and calling these homes during the viewing or listening period of interest. Respondents are simply asked what they are watching or listening to at that moment. This method avoids having respondents try to recall information from the previous day. Coincidentals are inexpensive (generally a few thousand dollars) and are frequently used by station management to receive immediate feedback about the success of special programming. In most cases, coincidentals are used for advertising sales purposes.

The fourth method of ratings data collection, People Meters, was started in the mid-1980s by A. C. Nielsen to attempt to improve the accuracy of ratings information and to obtain "single-source data," whereby research companies collect television ratings data, demographic data, and even household member purchasing behavior at the same time. (See *www.nielsenmedia.com/wtrrm.html* for a discussion of the People Meter.)

Traditional television meters indicate only whether the television set is on or off and the channel to which the set is tuned; there are no data about who is watching. Such information must be obtained by pooling TV meter data with information from households in the diary samples. People Meters attempt to simplify this data collection task by requiring each person in the household, as well as all

Figure 14.1 *Arbitron Radio Diary Instruction Page*

You count in the radio ratings!

No matter how much or how little you listen, you're important!
You're one of the few people picked in your area to have the chance to tell radio stations what you listen to.

This is *your* ratings diary. Please make sure you fill it out yourself.

Here's what we mean by "listening":
"Listening" is any time you can hear a radio – whether you choose the station or not.

When you hear a radio between Thursday, August 23, and Wednesday, August 29, write it down – whether you're at home, in a car, at work or someplace else.

When you hear a radio, write down:

TIME

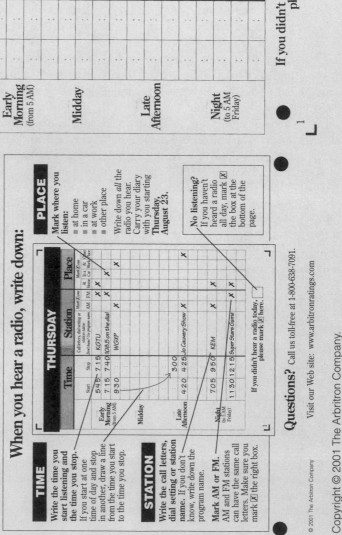

Write the time you start listening and the time you stop. If you start at one time of day and stop in another, draw a line from the time you start to the time you stop.

STATION

Write the call letters, dial setting or station name. If you don't know, write down the program name.

Mark AM or FM. AM and FM stations can have the same call letters. Make sure you mark ☒ the right box.

THURSDAY

	Time: Start	Time: Stop	Station: Call letters, dial setting or station name (Don't know? Use program name.)	Mark ☒ one: AM	FM	Place: Mark ☒ one: At Home	In a Car	At Work	Other Place
Early Morning (from 5 AM)	545	7 15	KGTU		✗	✗			
	7 15	7 40	108.5 on the dial		✗		✗		
	930	:	WGXP	✗				✗	
Midday									
	:	300							
Late Afternoon	420	425	Jo Cauvery Show	✗					✗
Night (to 5 AM Friday)	705	950	KEM	✗		✗			
	1130	1215	Super Stars Game		✗	✗			

If you didn't hear a radio today, please mark ☒ here. ☐

1

PLACE

Mark where you listen:
- at home
- in a car
- at work
- other place

Write down *all* the radio you hear. Carry your diary with you starting **Thursday, August 23.**

No listening? If you haven't heard a radio all day, mark ☒ the box at the bottom of the page.

Questions? Call us toll-free at 1-800-638-7091.

Visit our Web site: www.arbitronratings.com

THURSDAY

	Time: Start	Time: Stop	Station: Call letters, dial setting or station name (Don't know? Use program name.)	Mark ☒ one: AM	FM	Place: Mark ☒ one: At Home	In a Car	At Work	Other Place
Early Morning (from 5 AM)	:	:							
Midday	:	:							
Late Afternoon	:	:							
Night (to 5 AM Friday)	:	:							

If you didn't hear a radio today, please mark ☒ here. ☐

1

Figure 14.2 *Nielsen TV Ratings Diary Instruction Page*

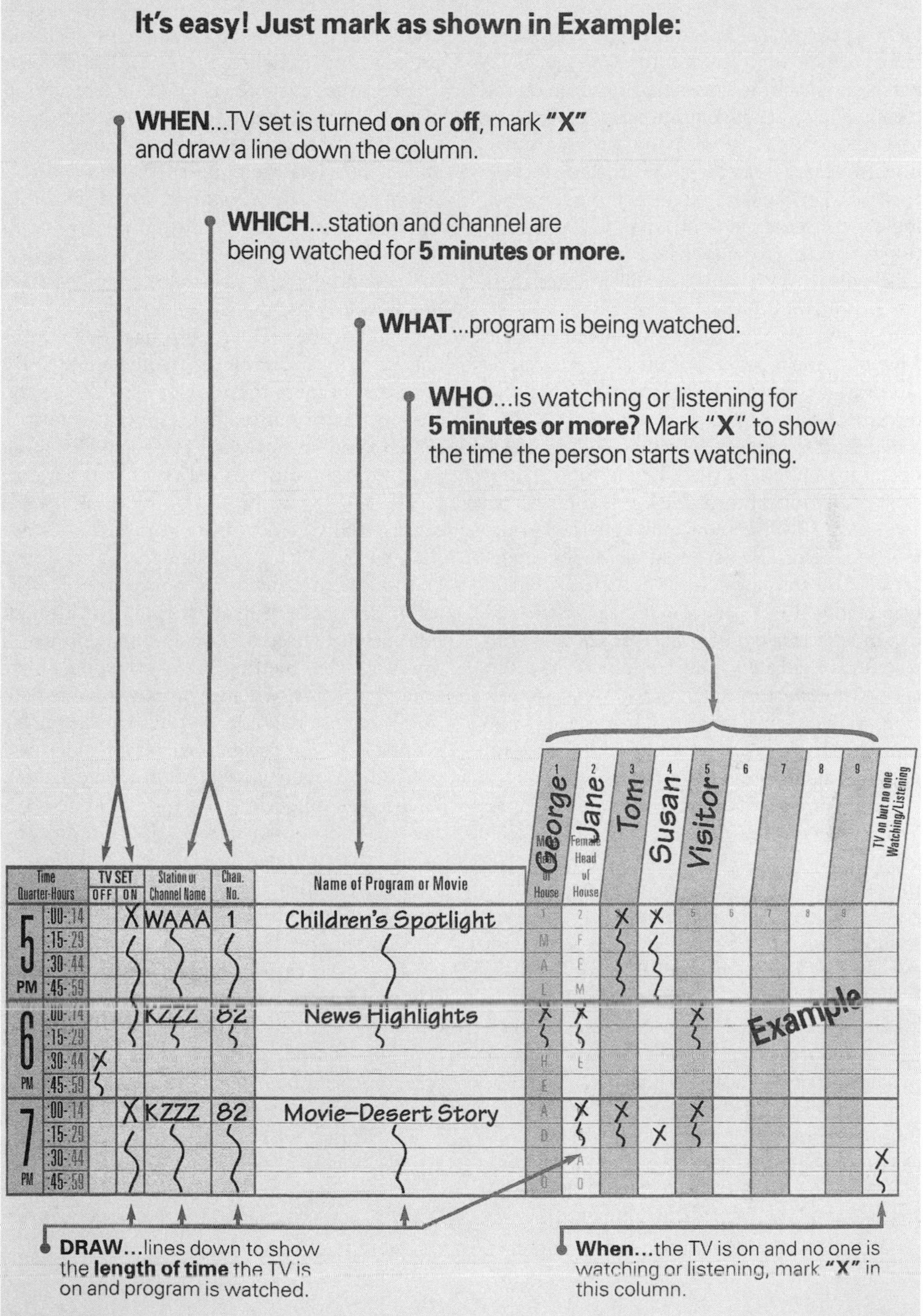
It's easy! Just mark as shown in Example:
WHEN...TV set is turned on or off, mark "X" and draw a line down the column.
WHICH...station and channel are being watched for 5 minutes or more.
WHAT...program is being watched.
WHO...is watching or listening for 5 minutes or more? Mark "X" to show the time the person starts watching.
Time Quarter-Hours
TV SET OFF ON
Station or Channel Name
Chan. No.
Name of Program or Movie
George Male Head of House
Jane Female Head of House
Tom
Susan
Visitor
TV on but no one Watching/Listening
5 PM :00-:14 :15-:29 :30-:44 :45-:59
6 PM
7 PM
WAAA 1 Children's Spotlight
KZZZ 82 News Highlights
KZZZ 82 Movie—Desert Story
Example
DRAW...lines down to show the length of time the TV is on and program is watched.
When...the TV is on and no one is watching or listening, mark "X" in this column.

visitors, to push a specific button on a mechanical unit that records the viewing. Each person in the home is assigned a button on the meter. The meter instantaneously records information about how many people in the household are watching and the identity of each viewer. The data from each night's viewing are collected via computer. This information is valuable for advertisers and their agencies, who can more accurately target their advertising messages.

Nielsen is convinced that using People Meters is the way to obtain accurate television ratings information. The company's interest in People Meters was spawned in 1987, when Audits of Great Britain (AGB) introduced the meters to the United States. However, AGB pulled out of the U.S. People Meter service in 1988, leaving only Nielsen to develop a universally accepted system of single-source data collection. In 1991, when Arbitron was involved in television ratings, it tried to expand the concept of single-source data with a system called *ScanAmerica*. The plan was to collect purchasing data and network television viewing information from the same household. *ScanAmerica* was unsuccessful and was discontinued in late 1992.

In theory, People Meters are quite simple: When a person begins or stops watching television, he or she pushes a button to document the behavior. The button may be located on a hand-held device or enclosed in a small box mounted on top of the television set. However, theory and reality are often misaligned. In late 1989, a survey funded by ABC, CBS, and NBC found that People Meters "turned off" participants, especially with children's programming on Saturday mornings. Additional criticisms about low television viewing numbers produced by the People Meters continued in the mid-1990s.

The major problem with People Meters is that participants tire of pushing buttons to record when they watch television, and children cannot be depended upon to push the proper buttons when they turn on the set. The reality is that television ratings produced by People Meters are lower than those produced by meters and diaries. Broadcasters and advertisers are concerned. Broadcasters claim the data underestimate actual viewing; advertisers who pay ad costs that are based on audience size, claim the data are probably correct and that they are therefore paying too much money for their commercials.

Each of the audience-estimate procedures has its critics: Simple electronic meters are criticized because they do not provide specific audience information; diaries, because participants may fail to record viewing or listening as it happens and may rely on recall to complete the diary at the end of the week. In addition, many critics contend that diaries are used to "vote" for or against specific shows and that actual viewing is not recorded. Critics of data collection by telephone (although not currently used by any national company) say that the method favors responses by younger people, who are more willing to talk on the telephone; older respondents generally do not have the patience to answer the questions about their viewing or listening habits. Finally, People Meters are condemned because of participant fatigue and a failure by many participants (especially children) to remember to push the required buttons when they watch television.

One thing is certain: Debate about the accuracy of the various audience ratings methods will continue. Research companies, including Arbitron and Nielsen, will be forced to try to develop more valid and reliable research procedures. The next phase of ratings development will take the form of an electronic storage system for radio ratings. This system is considered necessary by some researchers to eliminate the problems inherent in the hand-entry paper diaries used by Arbitron and Nielsen.

Interpreting the Ratings

Interpreting broadcast ratings and understanding the terminology used can best be explained with an example. While this example uses television networks, the procedures are the same for radio ratings. In addition, the example has been simplified by using only three commercial television networks; local market ratings books include many more stations.

Let's assume that Nielsen has collected the following data for a certain daypart on "traditional" network television:

Network	Households viewing
ABC	1,100
CBS	1,000
NBC	895
Not watching	2,005
Total	5,000

Recall that Nielsen's NTI sample includes about 5,000 households in the United States, and the data collected from them are generalized to the total population of about 105.5 million television households. The first number to compute is the rating for each network.

Rating. An audience **rating** is the percentage of people or households in a population with a television or radio tuned to a specific station, channel, or network. Thus the rating is expressed as the station or network's audience divided by the total number of television households or people in the target population:

$$\text{Rating} = \frac{\text{People or Households}}{\text{Population}}$$

For example, ABC's rating using the hypothetical data is computed as

$$\frac{1{,}100}{5{,}000} = 0.22, \text{ or } 22\%$$

This indicates that approximately 22% of the sample of 5,000 households was tuned to ABC at the time of the survey. (Note that even though ratings and related statistical values are percentages, when the data are reported, the decimal points are eliminated to ease reading.)

The combined ratings of all the networks or stations during a specific time period provide an estimate of the total number of *homes using television* (HUT). Since radio ratings deal with persons rather than households, the term *persons using radio* (PUR) is used. The HUT or PUR can be found either by adding together the households or persons using radio or television or by computing the total rating and multiplying that times the sample (or population when generalized). The total rating in the sample data is 59.9, which is computed as follows:

$$\text{ABC} \quad \frac{1{,}100}{5{,}000} = 0.22, \text{ or } 22\%$$

$$\text{CBS} \quad \frac{1{,}000}{5{,}000} = 0.20, \text{ or } 20\%$$

$$\text{NBC} \quad \frac{895}{5{,}000} = 0.179, \text{ or } 17.9\%$$

$$\text{HUT} = 2{,}995 \qquad \text{Total rating} = 59.9\%$$

In other words, about 59.9% of all households (HH) with television were watching one of the three networks at the time of the survey. As mentioned, the HUT can also be computed by multiplying the total rating times the sample size: $0.599 \times 5{,}000 = 2{,}995$. The same formula is used to project to the population. The population HUT is computed as $0.599 \times$ 105.5 million = 63,194,500.

Stations, networks, and advertisers naturally wish to know the estimated number of households in the HUT tuned to specific channels. The data from the sample of 5,000 households are again generalized to find a rough estimate of the households viewing each network (or station).

Network	Rating		Population		Rough Population HH estimate
ABC	0.220	×	105,500,000	=	23,210,000
CBS	0.200	×	105,500,000	=	21,100,000
NBC	0.179	×	105,500,000	=	18,884,500
Total	*0.599*				*63,194,500*

Network	Share		HUT		Exact Population HH Estimate
ABC	36.7	×	63,194,500	=	23,192,382
CBS	33.4	×	63,194,500	=	21,106,963
NBC	29.9	×	63,194,500	=	18,895,156
Total	*100*				*63,194,500*

Share. A **share** of the audience is the percentage of the HUT or PUR that is tuned to a specific station, channel, or network. It is determined by dividing the number of households or persons tuned to a station or network by the number of households or persons using their sets:

$$\frac{\text{People or Households}}{\text{HUT or PUR}}$$

In the example, the sample HUT is 2,995 (1,100 + 1,000 + 895), or 59.9% of 5,000. The audience share for ABC would thus be

$$\frac{1{,}100}{2{,}995} = 0.367, \text{ or } 36.7\%$$

That is, of the households in the sample whose television sets were on at the time of the survey, 36.7% were tuned to ABC. (People may not have been watching the set but recorded that they did.) The shares for CBS and NBC are computed in the same manner: CBS share = 1,000/2,995, or 33.4%; NBC share = 895/2,995, or 29.9%.

Shares are also used to estimate the number of households in the target population. The preceding example demonstrating how to compute households is considered a *rough estimate.* There is often need for a more exact method. This is achieved by multiplying the share times the HUT or PUR. The exact household estimates for each network are shown in the accompanying box (rough estimates are for comparison).

Cost Per Thousand. Stations, networks, and advertisers need to be able to assess the efficiency of advertising on radio and television so that they can determine which advertising buy is the most cost effective. One common way to express advertising efficiency is in **cost per thousand (CPM),** or what it costs an advertiser to reach 1,000 households or persons. The CPM provides no information about the effectiveness of a commercial message, only a dollar estimate of its reach. It is computed according to the following formula:

$$\text{CPM} = \frac{\text{Cost of advertisement}}{\text{Audience size (in thousands)}}$$

AN INSIDE LOOK

The Stability of Radio Ratings

Anyone involved in radio ratings has encountered situations where their radio station's ratings and shares "bounce around" from one ratings book to another. This is a common complaint about Arbitron and one that all broadcasters must understand. Although a radio station's ratings and shares may change as a result of changes in actual listening, a primary reason for the change is that different samples are used for each rating's period. By virtue of using different samples of listeners, there are different sampling error percentages. Even if no programming changes were made, radio broadcasters must expect changes in their radio station's ratings. This problem is not faced by ACNielsen since the company uses respondent panels for ratings information, which are more stable and reliable.

With the hypothetical television survey presented earlier, assume that a single 30-second commercial on ABC costs $275,000. The CPM for a commercial on ABC is computed as

$$\text{CPM} = \frac{\$275{,}000}{23{,}192(000)} = \$11.85$$

In other words, it costs an advertiser $11.85 to reach each 1,000 households when the commercial is aired. If we assume that the advertising costs were the same for CBS and NBC, the corresponding CPMs are: CBS = $13.02 and NBC = $14.55.

The CPM is used regularly when advertisers buy commercial time. Advertisers and stations or networks often negotiate an advertising contract using CPM figures; the advertiser might agree to pay $11.50 per thousand households. In some cases, no negotiation is involved; a station or network simply offers a program to advertisers at a specified CPM.

The CPM is seldom the only criterion used in purchasing commercial time. Other information, such as audience demographics and the type of program on which the advertisement will be aired, is considered before a contract is signed. An advertiser may be willing to pay a higher CPM to a network or station that is reaching an audience that is more desirable for its product. Cost per thousand should be used as the sole purchasing criterion *only* when all else is equal: demographics, programming, advertising strategy, and so on.

Related Ratings Concepts

Ratings, shares, and other figures are computed for a variety of survey areas and are split into several demographic categories. For an additional fee, ratings companies also provide custom information such as ratings in specific zip codes. Although ratings and shares are important in audience research, a number of other computations can be performed with the data.

A **metro survey area (MSA)** corresponds to the Consolidated Metropolitan Statistical Areas (CMSA) for the country, as defined by the U.S. Office of Management and Budget. The MSA generally includes the town, the county, or some other designated area closest to the station's transmitter. The **designated market area (DMA)**, another area for which ratings data are gathered, defines each television or radio market in exclusive terms. (At one time Arbitron used the term *area of* *dominant influence,* or ADI, to describe the DMA, but has since changed to Nielsen's designation.) Each county in the United States belongs to one and only one DMA, and rankings are determined by the number of television households in the DMA. Radio ratings use the DMAs established from television households; they are not computed separately.

The **total survey area (TSA)** includes the DMA and MSA as well as some other areas the market's stations reach (known as adjacent DMAs). Broadcasters are most interested in TSA data because they represent the largest number of households or persons. In reality, however, advertising agencies look at DMA figures when purchasing commercial time for television stations, and MSA figures when purchasing radio time. The TSA is used infrequently in the sale or purchase of advertising time; it serves primarily to determine the reach of the station, or the total number of people or households that listened to or watched a station or a channel. Nielsen uses the term NSI area as equivalent to Arbitron's TSA.

Ratings books contain information about the TSA/NSI, DMA, and MSA. Each area is important to stations and advertisers for various reasons, depending on the type of product or service being advertised and the goals of the advertising campaign. For instance, a new business that places a large number of spots on several local stations may be interested in reaching as many people in the area as possible. In this case, the advertising agency or individual client may ask for TSA/NSI numbers only, disregarding the DMA and metro data.

The **average quarter-hour (AQH)** is an estimate of the number of persons or households tuned to a specific station for at least 5 minutes during a 15-minute time segment. These estimates are provided for the TSA/NSI, DMA, and MSA in all ratings books. Stations are obviously interested in obtaining high AQH figures in all demographic areas because these figures indicate how long an audience is tuned in, and thus how loyal the audience is to the station. The AQH data are used to determine the average radio listener's **time spent listening (TSL)** during a given day or daypart. All stations try to increase their audience TSL because it means that the audience is not continually switching to other stations.

The **cume** (cumulative audience) or **reach** is an estimate of the number of persons who listened to or viewed at least 5 minutes within a given daypart. The cume is also referred to as the "unduplicated audience." For example, a person who watches a soap opera at least 5 minutes a day Monday through Friday would be counted only once in a cume rating, whereas the person's viewing would be "duplicated" five times in determining average quarter-hours.

The **gross rating points (GRPs)** are a total of a station's ratings during two or more dayparts and estimate the size of the gross audience. Advertising purchases are often made via GRPs. For example, a radio advertiser who purchases 10 commercials on a station may wish to know the gross audience that will be reached. Using hypothetical data, the GRP calculation is shown in Table 14.1. The gross rating point indicates that about 32.4% of the listening audience will be exposed to the 10 commercials.

A useful figure for radio stations is the **audience turnover,** or the number of times the audience changes during a given daypart. A high turnover is not always a negative factor in advertising sales; some stations have naturally high turnover (such as Top 40 stations, whose audiences comprise mostly younger people who tend to change stations frequently). A high turnover simply means that an advertiser needs to run more spots to reach the station's audience. Usually such stations compensate by charging less for commercial spots than stations with low turnovers.

Turnover is computed by dividing a station's cume audience by its average persons total. (Both these figures are reported in rat-

Table 14.1 *Calculation of GRP for Five Dayparts*

Daypart	Number of spots		Station rating		GRP (%)
M–F, 6 A.M.–9 A.M.	2	×	3.1	=	6.2
M–F, 12 P.M.–3 P.M.	2	×	2.9	=	5.8
M–F, 1 P.M.–6 P.M.	2	×	3.6	=	7.2
Sat, 6 A.M.–9 A.M.	2	×	2.5	=	5.0
Sun, 3 P.M.–6 P.M.	2	×	4.1	=	8.2
	10				32.4

ings books.) Consider three stations in the Monday–Friday, 3:00–6:00 P.M. daypart, as shown in Table 14.2. In this market, an advertiser on Station C would need to run more commercials to reach all listeners than one who advertises on Station A. However, Station C, in addition to having a smaller audience, may have the demographic audience most suitable for the advertiser's product.

Reading a Ratings Book

When many people see their first radio or TV ratings book, the thousands of numbers included on the pages usually amaze them. However, although radio and TV ratings are organized differently, they are easy to read once you learn the layout. Remember that even though most numbers in ratings books are percentages, all decimal points are deleted and all numbers are rounded.

A sample page from Nielsen's May 2001 Denver NSI ratings book is shown in Figure 14.3. The page is taken from the "Program Averages" section of the book. Only a portion of this page is shown because the numbers in the actual book are very small, and only some of the TV stations are shown on this sample page. The page shows the 6:00 P.M. time period. On page 1 of the report, Nielsen states that the DMA audience estimates were based on an average in-tab meter sample of 379 DMA TV households, combined with 2,167 diaries used to gather demographic information.

We will use KMGH to describe how to read the data. First, notice that each column is numbered, beginning with columns 1 and 2 at the left under "Metro HH," to column 43 for Children. During the 4-week rating

Table 14.2 *Computation of Turnover for Three Stations*

Station	Cume audience		Average persons		Turnover
A	2,900	÷	850	=	3.4
B	1,750	÷	850	=	3.4
C	960	÷	190	=	5.1

Figure 14.3 *Sample Page from Denver Nielsen NSI Ratings Book*

DENVER, CO

WK1 4/26-5/02 WK2 5/03-5/09 WK3 5/10-5/16 WK4 5/17-5/23

PROGRAM AVERAGES

METRO HH RTG	METRO HH SHR	STATION DAY PROGRAM	DMA HOUSEHOLD RATINGS WEEKS 1	2	3	4	MULTI-WEEK AVG RTG	MULTI-WEEK AVG SHR	HUT	DMA RATINGS PERSONS 2+	18+	12-24	12-34	18-34	18-49	21-49	25-54	35+	35-64	50+	WOMEN 18+	12-24	18-34	18-49	21-49	25-49	25-54	50+	WKG	MEN 18+	18-34	18-49	21-49	25-49	25-54	TNS 12-17	CHILD 2-11	CHILD 6-11
1	2		3	4	5	6	7	8	14	15	16	17	18	19	20	21	22	23	24	25	26	27	28	29	30	31	32	33	34	35	36	37	38	39	40	41	42	43
2		*R.S.E. THRESHOLDS 25+%*	*3*	*3*	*3*	*3*	*2*			*1*	*1*	*6*	*3*	*3*	*2*	*2*	*2*	*2*	*2*	*2*	*2*	*9*	*6*	*3*	*3*	*3*	*2*	*4*	*3*	*2*	*7*	*3*	*3*	*3*	*3*	*11*	*7*	*10*
1		*(1 S.E.) 4 WK AVG 50+%*	*1*	*1*	*1*	*1*	*LT*			*LT*	*LT*	*1*	*1*	*1*	*1*	*1*	*LT*	*LT*	*1*	*LT*	*LT*	*2*	*2*	*1*	*1*	*1*	*1*	*1*	*1*	*LT*	*2*	*1*	*1*	*1*	*1*	*3*	*2*	*3*
		6:00PM																																				
4	7	KMGH MON 7 NEWS-6PM	4	5	3	4	4	8	53	2	3		1	1	2	2	2	4	3	6	3	1	2	2	2	2	3	6	2	2	1	1	1	1	2	1		
4	8	TUE 7 NEWS-6PM	5	5	3	4	5	9	50	3	4			1	2	2	2	5	4	8	4		1	2	2	2	2	7	2	3		1	1	2	2			
5	9	WED 7 NEWS-6PM	7	4	3	5	5	9	53	2	3		1	1	1	1	2	4	3	7	4		1	1	2	2	2	8	2	3	1	1	1	1	1			
4	8	THU 7 NEWS-6PM	4	6	4	4	4	9	51	2	3		1	1	1	1	2	4	3	6	4		1	2	2	2	2	7	2	2		1	1	1	1			
4	8	FRI 7 NEWS-6PM	4	5	3	3	4	8	49	2	3		1	1	1	1	1	4	3	7	3	1	1	1	1	2	1	6	1	3		1	1	1	1	1		
4	*8*	*AV5 7 NEWS-6PM*	*5*	*5*	*3*	*4*	*4*	*8*	*51*	*2*	*3*		*1*	*1*	*1*	*1*	*2*	*4*	*3*	*7*	*3*		*1*	*2*	*2*	*2*	*2*	*7*	*2*	*3*	*1*	*1*	*1*	*1*	*1*			
4	10	SAT JEOPARDY-WKND	6	4	5	3	4	10	44	3	3	1	1	1	1	1	2	4	3	7	4	1	1	2	2	2	2	9	2	2	1	1	1	1	1	1	1	2
6	11	SUN ABC SU-SHW-5/6		5			5	9	59	5	4	3	5	4	4	5	5	4	5	3	4	4	6	4	4	5	5	3	5	5	3	5	5	6	5	6	6	
9	15	SUN CLSC-BLPRS-ABC				7	7	13	56	4	5	2	3	3	5	5	5	6	6	5	6		2	5	6	6	5	6	6	4	3	5	5	5	5	3		
7	14	SUN WONDRF-DSN-ABC	7		7		7	14	53	6	6	3	3	2	4	5	5	7	6	8	7	3	4	6	6	6	6	10	7	4	1	3	3	3	3	5	12	14
1	1	KPXC MON SPRMK SWP2-PAX	1	<<	1	1	1	1	53																													
1	2	TUE SPRMK SWP2-PAX	1	1	1	1	1	2	50																													
1	2	WED SPRMK SWP2-PAX	1	1	1	1	1	2	53														1	1	1	1	1		1									1
1	2	THU SPRMK SWP2-PAX	1	1	1	1	1	1	51														1															
1	2	FRI SPRMK SWP2-PAX	1	2	1	1	1	2	49									1		1	1							2										
1	*2*	*AV5 SPRMK SWP2-PAX*	*1*	*1*	*1*	*1*	*1*	*1*	*51*																													
1	3	SAT BONANZA-7P 5/5		1			1	3	50		1						1	1	1	1	1						1	2	1								1	
1	2	SAT MASTR-ILSN-PAX	1			1	1	2	45			1	1									2			1	1	1		1							2		
1	2	SAT MOMS-ENC-PAX			1		1	2	41				1	1									1	1	1	1	1		1									
1	3	SUN CANDID CM1-PAX	1	2	2	1	1	3	51	1	1				1	1	1	2	2	2	1			1	1	1	1	2	1	1		1	1	1	1			1
2	3	KRMA MON NEWSHOUR-LEHR	1	1	2	1	1	2	55	1	1						1	1	1	2	1	1	1	1			1	2		1					1			
1	3	TUE NEWSHOUR-LEHR	1	1	1	1	1	2	51	1	1							1	1	2	1							1	1	1								
1	3	WED NEWSHOUR-LEHR	2	1	1	1	1	2	53	1	1						1	1	1	2	1						1	2	1	1								
1	2	THU NEWSHOUR-LEHR		1	1	1	1	2	53	1	1							1	1	2	1	1						1		1								
2	4	FRI NEWSHOUR-LEHR		2	1	2	2	3	49	1	1							2	1	3	1	1						2		2								
2	*3*	*AV5 NEWSHOUR-LEHR*	*1*	*1*	*1*	*1*	*1*	*2*	*52*	*1*	*1*							*1*	*1*	*2*	*1*							*2*		*1*								
2	5	SAT LAWRENCE WELK		2	1	2	2	4	45	1	1							2	1	4	1							4		1								
2	3	SUN OCEAN WILDS		1	<<	2	1	2	52	1	1	1	1	1		1	1	1	1	2	1	2	1	1	1	1	1	2		1	1					2		
5	8	KTVD MON JUDGE JUDY	4	5	4	4	4	8	53	2	3	1	1	2	2	2	2	4	2	6	4	1	2	2	2	2	3	8	4	2	1	1	1	1	1			
4	7	TUE JUDGE JUDY	3	4	3	3	3	7	50	2	2		1	1	1	1	2	2	2	4	3		3	2	2	2	3	6	3	1						1		
5	9	WED JUDGE JUDY	5	5	4	3	4	8	53	2	3		1	1	1	1	2	3	2	6	4		2	2	2	2	3	7	3	2	1	1	1	1	1			
5	10	THU JUDGE JUDY	3	6	5	5	5	9	51	2	3	2	1	1	2	2	2	4	3	6	4	1	2	2	2	2	2	7	2	3	1	2	2	2	2	1		
5	10	FRI JUDGE JUDY	5	5	3	4	4	8	49	2	3	2	3	3	3	3	3	3	3	5	4	3	3	3	2	2	3	6	3	3	4	3	3	3	3			
5	*9*	*AV5 JUDGE JUDY*	*4*	*5*	*4*	*4*	*4*	*8*	*51*	*2*	*3*	*1*	*1*	*2*	*2*	*2*	*2*	*3*	*2*	*5*	*4*	*1*	*2*	*2*	*2*	*2*	*3*	*7*	*3*	*2*	*1*	*1*	*1*	*1*	*2*			
4	9	SAT NASH BRIDGES	2	5	2	3	3	7	45	2	2		1	1	1	1	2	2	2	3	3		1	2	2	2	4	5	5						1		2	2
3	6	SUN NASH BRDGES R	1		3	2	2	4	52	1	1		1	1	1	1	2	1	2	2	2		2	2	2	2	3	2	4	1					1			
7	13	KUSA MON 9NWS-600PM	7	7	6	6	7	12	53	3	4		1	1	3	3	4	5	5	7	5		2	3	4	4	5	8	5	3	1	2	2	2	3			
8	15	TUE 9NWS-600PM	7	7	6	7	7	14	50	3	4		1	2	3	3	4	5	5	7	4	1	2	3	3	3	4	7	5	4	2	2	3	3	4			
7	13	WED 9NWS-600PM	7	8	5	8	7	13	53	4	5		1	2	3	3	4	6	6	8	6		3	4	4	5	6	9	6	4	1	2	2	2	3			
8	15	THU 9NWS-600PM	7	6	8	7	7	14	51	3	5		1	1	3	4	4	6	5	7	5		2	4	4	5	5	8	5	4	1	3	3	3	4			
5	11	FRI 9NWS-600PM	4	6	5	4	5	10	49	3	4		1	1	2	2	3	5	4	6	4		1	2	2	3	3	8	4	3	2	2	3	3	3			
7	*13*	*AV5 9NWS-600PM*	*7*	*7*	*6*	*7*	*7*	*13*	*51*	*3*	*4*		*1*	*2*	*3*	*3*	*4*	*5*	*5*	*7*	*5*		*2*	*3*	*4*	*4*	*4*	*8*	*5*	*4*	*1*	*2*	*3*	*3*	*3*			
2	5	SAT CHEERS			2		2	5	40	1	1							2	2	3	2							5										
3	6	SAT NBA PLSAT-.NBC				3	3	7	44	1	1	1	3	4	2	2	2		1	1	2		4	2	2	2	2	1	2	1	4	2	2	2	2	1		
5	10	KWGN MON FRIENDS	6	4	5	5	5	9	53	3	3	6	5	6	4	4	3	2	2	1	5	11	9	6	6	4	4	2	5	2	3	2	2	2	2	4	3	2
7	13	TUE FRIENDS	7	5	6	6	6	12	50	4	4	8	8	9	6	6	4	2	2	1	5	11	11	7	7	6	5	1	5	3	7	5	5	4	3	5	2	2
7	14	WED FRIENDS	6	5	7	6	6	12	53	4	4	11	7	8	5	5	3	3	3	2	6	16	11	7	7	4	4	3	5	3	5	3	3	2	2	6	2	1
7	14	THU FRIENDS	5	7	5	7	6	12	51	4	4	10	8	9	6	6	4	2	3	1	6	13	11	8	8	5	5	2	4	3	6	4	4	3	2	6		1
5	11	FRI FRIENDS	5		5		5	11	44	4	3	8	6	6	4	4	3	2	2	1	4	11	8	5	5	3	3	2	3	3	4	4	4	3	3	7	4	3
6	*12*	*AV5 FRIENDS*	*6*	*5*	*6*	*6*	*6*	*11*	*51*	*4*	*4*	*9*	*7*	*8*	*5*	*5*	*4*	*2*	*2*	*1*	*5*	*12*	*10*	*7*	*7*	*5*	*5*	*2*	*5*	*3*	*5*	*4*	*3*	*3*	*3*	*5*	*2*	*2*
2	4	SAT ADRENALINE TV	1				1	3	46	1	1	1	1	1		1		1		1	1	2	2	1	1		1	1	1									
2	3	SUN JAMIE FOXX-WB		2	1	1	1	3	50	1		2	1					1		1								1								4		
2	5	SUN POPSTRS4/29-WB	2				2	4	52																													
		6:15PM																																				
3	5	KUSA SAT NBA PL-SA.-NBC		3			3	6	52	2	2		2	3	2	2	2	2	2	2	1		2	1	1	1	1	2		3	4	3	3	3	3			
		6:30PM																																				
<<		KBDI MON WORLD NEWS-TV	<<	1	1	<<	1	1	56													1	1															
<<		TUE WORLD NEWS-TV	<<	<<	<<	<<	<<		51																													
1	1	WED WORLD NEWS-TV	1	<<	<<	1	1	1	54		1	1			1			1		1		1	1	1						1								
1	1	THU WORLD NEWS-TV	1	<<	<<	<<	1	1	54																													
<<		FRI WORLD NEWS-TV	1	1	<<	<<	<<		50																			1										
<<		*AV5 WORLD NEWS-TV*	*1*	*<<*	*<<*	*<<*	*<<*		*53*																													
5	9	KCNC MON HOLLYWD SQUARS	4	5	4	4	4	8	56	2	3		1	1	1	2	2	3	3	5	3		1	2	2	2	2	6	2	2	1	1	1	1	1		1	1
5	10	TUE HOLLYWD SQUARS	4	4	5	5	4	9	51	2	2	1	1	1	1	1	2	3	3	5	3	1	1	1	1	2	2	6	2	2	1	1	1	1	1	2		
4	8	WED HOLLYWD SQUARS	5	3	4	5	4	8	54	2	2			1	1	1	2	3	3	5	3			2	2	2	2	6	2	2	1	1	1	1	2			
5	10	THU HOLLYWD SQUARS	5	6	4	4	5	9	54	3	3	1	1	1	2	2	3	4	4	6	3	1	1	2	2	2	3	6	4	3	2	2	2	2	2	1	1	1
4	9	FRI HOLLYWD SQUARS	5	3	4	4	4	8	50	2	3	2	1	1	2	1	2	4	3	6	4	1		2	2	2	2	8	3	2	2	1	1	1	1	1		
5	*9*	*AV5 HOLLYWD SQUARS*	*4*	*4*	*4*	*4*	*4*	*8*	*53*	*2*	*3*	*1*	*1*	*1*	*1*	*1*	*2*	*4*	*3*	*5*	*3*	*1*	*1*	*2*	*2*	*2*	*2*	*6*	*3*	*2*	*1*	*1*	*1*	*1*	*1*	*1*		
4	8	SAT GREG MOODY SHW	3	4	4	4	4	8	46	2	3				1	1	1	4	4	8	3			1	1	1	1	8	2	3				1	1			
1	2		3	4	5	6	7	8	14	15	16	17	18	19	20	21	22	23	24	25	26	27	28	29	30	31	32	33	34	35	36	37	38	39	40	41	42	43

See Program Index for complete details of program start time, duration and weeks of telecast.

period, KMGH aired "7 News" Monday through Friday. The "AV5" line shows the average rating and share information for "7 News" during the 4 weeks. Columns 1 and 2 show the average metro rating and share as 4 and 8, the same rating and share KMGH received for the multi-week DMA averages shown in columns 7 and 8.

Columns 3–6 show the DMA ratings for each of the 4 weeks, columns 7 and 8 are the averages for the DMA for the survey, and column 14 shows the DMA HUT. The remaining columns (15–43) show the DMA ratings for specific age and gender cells. Recall that this is only one page from the May 2001 Denver NSI book, which includes 281 pages.

Now compare the results for KUSA, one of KMGH's competitors. It's easy to see that more people watch KUSA than KMGH.

Although information on ratings and shares is computed the same way for radio and television audience measurements, the information is presented very differently. Radio books usually contain more than 10 individual sections (such as Target Audience Estimates, Audience Composition, and various trend and rank data) and then concentrate on presenting audience estimates in terms of dayparts, not individual programs. Also, because there are so many radio stations in any given market, the emphasis in radio books is on shares, not ratings. Radio broadcasters rarely, if ever, use ratings to sell advertising; audience share is the key to radio advertising sales. In addition, metro shares, not DMA or TSA shares, are the most important numbers in radio.

A sample page from an Arbitron radio book (for the Denver–Boulder area in Spring 2001) is shown in Figure 14.4. The page is taken from the Target Listener Trends—Persons 12+ (not all of the stations in the Denver market are shown on this sample page). Reading a radio ratings book is somewhat different from reading a television ratings book. We will use KOA, an AM news/talk station, to describe how to read this page.

First, notice that the stations are listed from top to bottom in alphabetical order. Next, the data are listed in five major columns for five different radio dayparts. The first column shows the total week data (Monday–Sunday, 6 A.M.-MID), while the remaining four columns shows other specific dayparts during the week.

Notice that listed for each column are four pieces of information: Average Quarter-Hour people, shown as AQH (00), Average Quarter-Hour Cume, shown as Cume (00), followed by AQH rating and AQH share. Note that AQH (average quarter-hour) is listed in 100s; that is, "00" is eliminated from the reported data. For example, KOA's AQH for Spring '01 is listed as 173. This means that about 17,300 people age 12 and over were listening for at least 5 minutes during any given quarter-hour between 6 A.M. and midnight (this is down slightly from 17,900 in the Spring '00 book).

The AQH RTG (or rating) for KOA's Spring '01 book is .9, which means that the station attracts about .9% of all quarter-hour listening by people 12+ Monday–Sunday, 6 A.M. to midnight (this is also down from the 1.0 in the Spring '00 book). KOA's audience share for Spring '01—6.1—is the same as its share in Spring '00.

The Spring '01 Arbitron book shows that KOA is a consistent radio station. KOA does show a high share of 7.6 in the Fall '00 book, but this is probably due to sports broadcasts and is not a typical KOA audience share number.

Adjusting for Unrepresentative Samples

Since ratings are computed using samples from the population, a certain amount of error is always associated with the data. This error, designated by the notation $SE(p)$, is known as standard error. Standard error must always be considered before ratings are interpreted, to

Figure 14.4 *Sample Page from Denver–Boulder Spring 2001 Arbitron Ratings Book*

Target Listener Trends

Persons 12+

	Monday-Sunday 6AM-MID				Monday-Friday 6AM-10AM				Monday-Friday 10AM-3PM				Monday-Friday 3PM-7PM				Monday-Friday 7PM-MID			
	AQH (00)	Cume (00)	AQH Rtg	AQH Shr	AQH (00)	Cume (00)	AQH Rtg	AQH Shr	AQH (00)	Cume (00)	AQH Rtg	AQH Shr	AQH (00)	Cume (00)	AQH Rtg	AQH Shr	AQH (00)	Cume (00)	AQH Rtg	AQH Shr
KKHK-FM																				
SP '01	70	1541	.4	2.5	83	692	.4	2.0	124	764	.6	2.9	93	796	.5	2.6	28	320	.1	2.4
WI '01	79	1588	.4	2.8	125	848	.6	2.9	138	715	.7	3.3	102	829	.5	3.0	13	289	.1	1.2
FA '00	96	1973	.5	3.4	127	986	.7	3.0	167	1005	.9	3.9	119	1168	.6	3.3	29	454	.2	2.6
SU '00	98	1850	.5	3.4	133	932	.7	3.2	154	982	.8	3.5	122	1074	.7	3.6	39	512	.2	3.6
4-Book	***86***	***1738***	***.5***	***3.0***	***117***	***865***	***.6***	***2.8***	***146***	***867***	***.8***	***3.4***	***109***	***967***	***.6***	***3.1***	***27***	***394***	***.2***	***2.5***
SP '00	95	2040	.5	3.2	141	995	.8	3.2	157	885	.8	3.6	133	1171	.7	3.7	27	485	.1	2.2
KLVZ-AM																				
SP '01	12	232	.1	.4	13	110	.1	.3	17	94	.1	.4	17	115	.1	.5	2	54		.2
WI '01	14	211	.1	.5	23	106	.1	.5	21	108	.1	.5	20	137	.1	.6	1	37		.1
FA '00	**	**	**	**	**	**	**	**	**	**	**	**	**	**	**	**	**	**	**	**
SU '00	**	**	**	**	**	**	**	**	**	**	**	**	**	**	**	**	**	**	**	**
4-Book	**	**	**	**	**	**	**	**	**	**	**	**	**	**	**	**	**	**	**	**
SP '00	**	**	**	**	**	**	**	**	**	**	**	**	**	**	**	**	**	**	**	**
KLZ -AM																				
SP '01	21	541	.1	.7	33	225	.2	.8	36	279	.2	.8	26	217	.1	.7	6	134		.5
WI '01	41	677	.2	1.5	49	315	.3	1.1	66	347	.3	1.6	56	389	.3	1.6	19	203	.1	1.8
FA '00	34	593	.2	1.2	47	312	.2	1.1	47	309	.2	1.1	40	344	.2	1.1	17	136	.1	1.5
SU '00	26	490	.1	.9	28	201	.1	.7	41	258	.2	.9	30	219	.2	.9	9	105		.8
4-Book	***31***	***575***	***.2***	***1.1***	***39***	***263***	***.2***	***.9***	***48***	***298***	***.2***	***1.1***	***38***	***292***	***.2***	***1.1***	***13***	***145***	***.1***	***1.2***
SP '00	28	605	.1	1.0	25	276	.1	.6	51	344	.3	1.2	32	296	.2	.9	11	163	.1	.9
KMXA-AM																				
SP '01	38	398	.2	1.3	78	280	.4	1.9	64	208	.3	1.5	40	187	.2	1.1	5	86		.4
WI '01	21	387	.1	.7	26	201	.1	.6	31	170	.2	.7	22	125	.1	.6	7	61		.7
FA '00	20	274	.1	.7	39	173	.2	.9	38	159	.2	.9	17	153	.1	.5	3	21		.3
SU '00	17	296	.1	.6	40	194	.2	1.0	26	197	.1	.6	10	108	.1	.3	4	63		.4
4-Book	***24***	***339***	***.1***	***.8***	***46***	***212***	***.2***	***1.1***	***40***	***184***	***.2***	***.9***	***22***	***143***	***.1***	***.6***	***5***	***58***		***.5***
SP '00	32	335	.2	1.1	54	244	.3	1.2	40	212	.2	.9	24	134	.1	.7	19	79	.1	1.6
KNUS-AM																				
SP '01	27	547	.1	1.0	53	323	.3	1.3	27	187	.1	.6	39	258	.2	1.1	21	128	.1	1.8
WI '01	27	462	.1	1.0	62	261	.3	1.4	34	165	.2	.8	41	231	.2	1.2	8	95		.8
FA '00	23	551	.1	.8	56	257	.3	1.3	20	208	.1	.5	42	279	.2	1.2	12	137	.1	1.1
SU '00	15	351	.1	.5	25	168	.1	.6	17	148	.1	.4	22	134	.1	.6	15	106	.1	1.4
4-Book	***23***	***478***	***.1***	***.8***	***49***	***252***	***.3***	***1.2***	***25***	***177***	***.1***	***.6***	***36***	***226***	***.2***	***1.0***	***14***	***117***	***.1***	***1.3***
SP '00	16	377	.1	.5	16	121	.1	.4	19	120	.1	.4	32	195	.2	.9	11	128	.1	.9
KOA -AM																				
SP '01	173	3658	.9	6.1	270	1745	1.4	6.4	277	1751	1.4	6.5	175	1792	.9	4.9	117	1081	.6	10.0
WI '01	175	3433	.9	6.2	360	2032	1.9	8.4	309	1642	1.6	7.3	167	1562	.9	4.9	44	561	.2	4.2
FA '00	217	4254	1.1	7.6	342	1977	1.8	8.0	382	1807	2.0	9.0	176	1536	.9	5.0	56	706	.3	5.0
SU '00	174	3340	.9	6.1	206	1308	1.1	4.9	290	1513	1.5	6.6	184	1594	1.0	5.4	96	862	.5	9.0
4-Book	***185***	***3671***	***1.0***	***6.5***	***295***	***1766***	***1.6***	***6.9***	***315***	***1678***	***1.6***	***7.4***	***176***	***1621***	***.9***	***5.1***	***78***	***803***	***.4***	***7.1***
SP '00	179	3279	1.0	6.1	264	1622	1.4	6.1	281	1530	1.5	6.5	196	1587	1.0	5.4	112	1085	.6	9.2
KOSI-FM																				
SP '01	151	2370	.8	5.3	226	1248	1.2	5.4	259	1183	1.3	6.1	183	1293	.9	5.2	47	526	.2	4.0
WI '01	146	2457	.8	5.2	207	1212	1.1	4.8	271	1238	1.4	6.4	168	1328	.9	4.9	64	627	.3	6.0
FA '00	180	2903	.9	6.3	277	1551	1.4	6.5	332	1437	1.7	7.8	219	1639	1.1	6.2	49	689	.3	4.4
SU '00	182	2679	1.0	6.4	285	1470	1.5	6.8	328	1511	1.7	7.5	202	1279	1.1	5.9	50	637	.3	4.7
4-Book	***165***	***2602***	***.9***	***5.8***	***249***	***1370***	***1.3***	***5.9***	***298***	***1342***	***1.5***	***7.0***	***193***	***1385***	***1.0***	***5.6***	***53***	***620***	***.3***	***4.8***
SP '00	175	2814	.9	6.0	250	1462	1.3	5.7	307	1396	1.6	7.1	212	1513	1.1	5.8	64	696	.3	5.2
KQKS-FM																				
SP '01	123	2318	.6	4.3	171	1269	.9	4.1	145	1118	.8	3.4	149	1325	.8	4.2	84	876	.4	7.2
WI '01	140	2653	.7	5.0	177	1379	.9	4.1	192	1324	1.0	4.5	188	1635	1.0	5.5	91	1003	.5	8.6
FA '00	125	2535	.6	4.4	145	1345	.8	3.4	147	1266	.8	3.5	157	1462	.8	4.4	96	1036	.5	8.6
SU '00	154	2462	.8	5.4	188	1287	1.0	4.5	207	1357	1.1	4.7	179	1465	1.0	5.3	97	974	.5	9.1
4-Book	***136***	***2492***	***.7***	***4.8***	***170***	***1320***	***.9***	***4.0***	***173***	***1266***	***.9***	***4.0***	***168***	***1472***	***.9***	***4.9***	***92***	***972***	***.5***	***8.4***
SP '00	187	2639	1.0	6.4	249	1540	1.3	5.7	195	1374	1.0	4.5	248	1760	1.3	6.8	147	1203	.8	12.0

** Station(s) not reported this survey.
* Listener estimates adjusted for reported broadcast schedule.
+ Station(s) changed call letters – see Page 13.
4-Book: Avg. of current and previous 3 surveys.
2-Book: Avg. of most recent 2 surveys.

ARBITRON

AN INSIDE LOOK
Comparing Ratings Data

Because of seasonal differences in listening to radio and watching TV, comparisons of a radio station, TV station, or network's performance should be made to "like" books; that is, compare Spring to Spring, or November to November. For example, in radio, it isn't correct to compare Spring to Summer or Fall to Winter; in television, it isn't correct to compare May to November, and so on.

determine whether a certain gender/age group has been undersampled or oversampled.

There are several approaches to calculating standard error. One standard formula is

$$SE(p) = \sqrt{\frac{p(100 - p)}{n}} \times 1.96$$

where p is the sample percentage or rating, n is sample size, SE is the standard error, and 1.96 is the corresponding z-score for the 95% confidence interval. For example, suppose a random sample of 1,200 households produces a rating of 20. The standard error can be expressed as follows:

$$\begin{aligned} SE(p) &= \sqrt{\frac{20(100 - 20)}{1{,}200}} \times 1.96 \\ &= \sqrt{\frac{20(80)}{1{,}200}} \times 1.96 \\ &= \sqrt{1.33} \times 1.96 \\ &= \pm 2.26 \end{aligned}$$

The rating of 20 has a standard error of ±2.26 points, which means that at the 95% confidence level, the rating ranges from 17.74 to 22.26. Standard error formulas are included in all ratings books; Arbitron has simplified the procedure by publishing tables in the back of each book.

Weighting is another procedure used by ratings companies to adjust for samples that are not representative of the population. In some situations, a particular gender/age group cannot be adequately sampled, and a correction must be made.

Assume that population estimates for a DMA indicate that it includes 41,500 men ages 18–34 and that this group accounts for 8.3% of the population over the age of 12. The researchers distribute diaries to a sample of the DMA population, of which 950 are returned and usable (known as in-tab diaries). They would expect about 79 of these to be from men ages 18–34 (8.3% of 950). However, they find that only 63 of the diaries are from this demographic group—16 short of the anticipated number. The data must be weighted to adjust for this deficiency. The weighting formula is:

$$\begin{aligned} \text{Weight}_{\text{MSA men, 18}-34} &= \frac{0.083}{0.066} \\ &= 1.25 \end{aligned}$$

This figure must be multiplied by the number of persons in the group that each diary would normally represent. That is, instead of representing 525 men (41,500 ÷ 79), each diary would represent 656 men (525 × 1.25). The ideal weighting value is 1.00, indicating that the group was adequately represented in the sample. On occasion, a group may be oversampled, in which case the weighting value is a number less than 1.00.

Both Arbitron and Nielsen provide detailed explanations of error rates, weighting, and other methodological considerations. Each company includes pages of information in ratings books on how to interpret the data considering different sample sizes and weighting. In reality, however, the vast majority of people who interpret and use broadcast and cable ratings consider the printed numbers as gospel. If they are considered at all, error rates, sample sizes, and other problems are important only when an owner or manager's station performs poorly in the ratings.

▪ Nonratings Research

Although audience ratings are the most visible research data used in broadcasting, broadcasters, production companies, advertisers, and broadcast consultants use numerous other methodologies. Ratings provide estimates of audience size and composition. Nonratings research provides information about what the audience likes and dislikes, analyses of different types of programming, demographic and lifestyle information about the audience, and much more. These data provide decision makers with information they can use to eliminate some of the guesswork involved in giving the audience what it wants. Nonratings research is important to broadcasters in all markets, and one characteristic of all successful broadcast or cable operations is that the management uses research in all types of decision making.

What is the importance of nonratings research to a newcomer to the broadcast field? Frank Bell, VP/Programming for Keymarket Communications, Inc. (1999) says:

> Imagine yourself as a pilot, attempting to safely guide your plane through a bank of thunderstorms and all of your navigation instruments are out of commission. As heavy turbulence bounces your craft up and down, passengers, each with a different perspective, shout suggestions: "Pull up, watch out for the mountains ahead!" "Don't fly into those clouds; they're full of lightning!" "Hey, there's another plane off to the right!" That's what it is like to program a radio or TV station today without the benefit of ongoing local market research.
>
> If you don't know the strengths and weaknesses of your own station and your primary competitors, if you don't have a handle on your market's tastes, if you're unsure what would happen if a new competitor signed on tomorrow, then you are truly "flying blind." Better keep your parachute packed!
>
> Local market research provides something unattainable from inside a radio or TV station: the unvarnished perspective of those wonderful people who actually tune in every week and keep us in business. As a wise man said many years ago, "The only reality that counts is that of the audience."

The following section describes some of the nonratings research conducted in the electronic media.

Program Testing

Research is an accepted step in the development and production of programs and commercials. It is now common to test these products in each state of development: initial idea or plan, rough cut, and postproduction. A variety of research approaches can be used in each stage, depending on the purpose of the study, the amount of time allowed for testing, and the types of decisions that will be made with the results. The researcher must determine what information the decision makers will need to know and must design an analysis to provide that information.

Since major programs and commercials are very expensive to produce, producers and directors are interested in gathering preliminary reactions to a planned project. It would be ludicrous to spend thousands or millions of dollars on a project that has no audience appeal.

Although the major TV networks, large advertising agencies, and production companies conduct most program testing, many local TV stations are involved in programming research. Stations test promotional campaigns, prime-time access scheduling, the acceptability of commercials, and various programming strategies.

One basic way to collect preliminary data is to have respondents read a short statement that summarizes a program or commercial and ask them for their opinions about the idea, their willingness to watch the program, or their intent to buy the product based on the description. The results may provide an indication of the potential success of a program or commercial.

However, program or commercial descriptions usually cannot adequately describe the characters and their relationships to other characters in the program or commercial. This can be done only through the program dialogue and the characters' on-screen performance. For example, the NBC-TV program "ER" might have been described as follows:

> *ER:* A drama about a hospital emergency room showing the "real" events faced by doctors and nurses. Each week the program concentrates on a number of medical emergencies and the relationships among the personnel in the hospital.

To many people this statement might describe the type of show generally referred to as a "bomb." However, the indescribable on-screen relationships between the doctors and nurses and the other cast members, as well as the story lines, has made "ER" one of the most popular television shows since the mid-1990s. If producers relied only on program descriptions in testing situations, many successful shows would never reach the air.

If an idea tests well in the preliminary stages (or if the producer or advertiser wishes to go ahead with the project regardless of what the research indicates), a model or simulation is produced. These media "hardware" items are referred to as *rough cuts, storyboards, photomatics, animatics,* or *executions.* The **rough cut** is a simplistic production that usually uses amateur actors, little or no editing, and makeshift sets. The other models are photographs, pictures, or drawings of major scenes designed to give the basic idea of a program or commercial to anyone who looks at them.

Testing rough cuts is not expensive, which is important if the tests show a lack of acceptance or understanding of the product. The tests provide information about the script, characterizations, character relationships, settings, cinematic approach, and overall appeal. Rough cut tests seldom identify the reasons why a program or commercial tests poorly, but they provide an overall indication that something is wrong and provide information for more specific tests.

When the final product is available, postproduction research can be conducted. Finished products are tested in experimental theaters, in shopping centers (where mobile vans are used to show commercials or programs), at respondents' homes in cities where cable systems provide test channels, or via telephone, in the case of radio commercials. Results from postproduction research often indicate that, for example, the ending of a program is unacceptable and must be reedited or reshot. Many problems that were not foreseen during production may be encountered in postproduction research, and the data usually provide producers with an initial audience reaction to the finished, or partially finished, product.

The major TV networks use their own approaches to testing new programs. One approach is to test pilot programs on cable TV outlets throughout the country, where respondents are prerecruited to watch the program. Another approach is to test pilot programs in large focus group settings. Regardless of the

AN INSIDE LOOK

Hook Testing

Numerous proprietary research studies show that a hook of between 5 and 15 seconds is all that is needed to test a familiar song, although the majority of hooks are between 5 and 7 seconds because respondents in all radio formats tend to rate a familiar song in 3 seconds or less.

type of pretesting, the networks continually test the programs using a variety of qualitative and quantitative approaches such as focus groups and telephone interviews.

Several research companies use a variety of methods to test commercials or programs. Some companies test commercials and consumer products by showing different versions of commercials on cable systems. Test commercials can be "cut into" a program (that is, they can replace a regularly scheduled commercial with a test spot) in target households. The other households on the cable system view the regular spot. Some time after the airing of the test commercial to the target households, follow-up research is conducted to determine the success of the commercial or the response to a new consumer product.

Commercials can also be tested in focus groups, shopping center intercepts, and auditorium-type situations. Commercials are not usually shown on television until they are tested in a variety of situations. The sponsors (even radio and television managers who wish to advertise their own station) do not want to communicate the wrong message to the audience.

Music Research

Music is the product of a music radio station, and failing to analyze the product is courting disaster. To provide the radio station's listeners with music they like to hear and to avoid the songs that they do not like or are tired of hearing (*burned out*), radio programmers use two primary research procedures—auditorium music testing and callout research.

Auditorium tests are designed to evaluate *recurrents* (songs that were recently popular) and oldies (songs that have been around for years). **Callout research** is used to test music on the air (currents). New music releases cannot be tested adequately in the auditorium or with call-out procedures. New music is often tested on the air during programs titled "Smash or Trash," where listeners call in and voice their opinion about new releases. Sometimes new music is tested in focus group situations where the respondents listen to the entire song.

Auditorium tests and callout research serve the same purpose: to provide a program director or music director with information about the songs that are liked, disliked, burned, or unfamiliar. This information allows the program director to make decisions based on audience reaction rather than gut feelings or guessing.

Both music testing methods involve playing **hooks** (short segments) of several songs for a sample of listeners. A hook is a 5- to 15-second representative sample of the song—enough for respondents to identify the song if it is already familiar to them and to rate the song on some type of evaluation scale.

Research companies and program directors have a variety of scales for listeners to use in evaluating the music they hear. For example, respondents can be asked to rate a hook on a 5- or 7-point scale, where 1 represents "hate" and 5 or 7 represents "like a lot" or "favorite." There are also options for "unfamiliar" and "tired of hearing." (A respondent who is unfamiliar with a song is asked not to rate it.) Which scale is best? Research conducted over several years by the senior author indicates that the 7-point scale provides the most reliable results.

Sometimes researchers ask respondents to rate whether each song "fits" the music they hear on their favorite radio station. This additional question helps program directors determine which of the tested songs might not be appropriate for their station.

In addition, some research companies ask listeners whether they would like radio stations in the area to play a particular song more, less, or the same amount as they currently do. This is a highly inefficient and inaccurate way to determine the frequency with which a song should be played. The reason is that there is no common definition of more, less, or same, and listeners are extremely poor judges of how often a station currently plays the songs.

The bottom line in all music testing is that program directors should use the data as a guide for selecting their radio station's music. The data should not be used as a music "bible."

Auditorium Testing. In this method, between 75 and 200 people are invited to a large room or hall, often a hotel ballroom. Subjects always match specific screening requirements determined by the radio station or the research company, such as listeners between the ages of 25 and 40 who listen to soft rock stations in the client's market. Respondents are usually recruited by a field service that specializes in recruiting people for focus groups or other similar research projects. Respondents are generally paid between $25 and $150 for their cooperation. The auditorium setting—usually a comfortable location away from distractions at home—allows researchers to test several hundred hooks in one 90–120-minute session. Usually between 200 and 600 hooks are tested, although some companies routinely test up to 800 hooks in a single session. However, after 600 songs subject fatigue becomes evident by explicit physical behavior (looking around the room, fidgeting, talking to neighbors), and statistical reliability decreases. It is easy to demonstrate that scores for songs after 600 are not reliable (Wimmer, 2001), specifically in reference to unstable standard deviations for the songs.

Auditorium music testing is designed to test only recurrents and oldies. It cannot be used for new releases because people cannot be expected to rate an unfamiliar recording based on a 5- to 15-second hook.

Although auditorium music testing looks like an easy research process, there are many things to consider. Among numerous procedures and steps, some basic procedures to follow when conducting an auditorium music test include:

1. The key to a successful test is a good introduction that explains the purpose of the test and how important the respondents' answers are to hearing good music on the radio. It is important to stress that there are no right or wrong answers in the test and that the goal is to collect a variety of opinions.
2. The moderator must be in total control over the situation to ensure that respondents do not talk amongst themselves or try to influence other respondents' answers.
3. Adequate breaks must be taken during the session. Respondents shouldn't listen to more than 200 songs without a break.
4. The moderator must make sure that all respondents understand the scoring system. After the test begins, the moderator

AN INSIDE LOOK

Callout Research Costs

A correctly conducted callout research project testing 20 hooks with 100 respondents takes about 100 hours for professional interviewers to complete. The typical field service or research company fee for interviewing time is about $22.00 per hour, which means that the company's direct costs are about $2,200 for the project. However, some callout companies charge less than $1,000 per project. How can this be accomplished? Only by cutting corners. As mentioned elsewhere in this book, when it comes to buying research, follow the axiom "*caveat emptor.*"

should check to see that each person is rating the songs correctly.

5. The moderator should not allow the respondents to sing along with the songs. This tends to disrupt the entire room.
6. After conducting music tests for more than 20 years, we know that it is important to mention that a moderator should expect the unexpected. This includes electricity going out, sick respondents, equipment failures, or problems with the hotel arrangement.

In the late 1990s, a few radio research companies developed alternative approaches to the firmly established (reliable and valid) auditorium music testing methodology. One method is to test music hooks over the telephone; the other tests hooks via the Internet. Both methods face the same problem of relinquishing control over the testing situation, and there is no way to know who is actually rating the songs. While our experience shows that telephone and Internet music testing should not be used because there is no publicly available research evidence to show that they are reliable and valid, we know that many program directors and general managers will use them anyway. The only advice we have is "*caveat emptor.*"

Callout Research. The purpose of callout research is the same as that of auditorium testing; only the procedure for collecting the data is changed. Instead of people being invited to a large hall or ballroom, randomly selected or prerecruited subjects are called on the telephone. Subjects are given the same rating instructions as in the auditorium test; they listen to the hook and provide a verbal response to the researcher making the telephone call. Callout research is used to test only newer music releases. (The reliability and validity of using the telephone for callout research is better than using the telephone for auditorium testing because only a small number of songs are tested in callout).

While callout methodology is adequate because only a few songs are tested, the limitation on the songs tested is also the methodology's major fault. Well-designed callout research involves testing a maximum number of 20 songs because subject fatigue sets in very quickly over the telephone. Other problems include the distractions that are often present in the home, the poor quality of sound transmission created by the telephone equipment, and the fact that there is no way to determine exactly who is answering the questions.

Even with such limitations, many radio stations throughout the country use callout research. Since callout research is inexpensive compared with the auditorium method, the research can be conducted on a continual basis to track the performance of songs in a particular market. Auditorium research, which can cost between $20,000 and $40,000 to test approximately 800 songs, is generally conducted only once or twice per year.

Programming Research and Consulting

Dozens of companies conduct mass media research. They can be found on the Internet by searching "television research," "radio research," or "program research." Although each company specializes in specific areas of broadcasting and uses different procedures, they all have a common goal: to provide management with data to be used in decision making. These companies offer custom research in almost any area of broadcasting—from testing call letters and slogans to air talent, commercials, music, importance of news programs, and the overall sound or look of a station.

Broadcast consultants can be equally versatile. The leading consultants have experience in broadcasting and offer their services to radio and television stations. Although some of their recommendations are based on research, many are based on past experience. A good consultant can literally "make or break" a broadcast station, and the task of a consultant is probably best described by E. Karl (1992, p. 1), a former leading international radio consultant, who was asked to describe what a consultant does for a radio station. He states:

> A consultant works with research data to help plan a strategy for a station. A consultant puts research information into a package that will position the station correctly in listeners' minds, and helps market the station to bring listeners in to try out the station. The consultant does anything from designing music rotations, creating "clock hours" on the station, and selecting air talent . . . to developing television commercials to advertise the station, executing direct marketing campaigns to ask listeners to listen, and working with the station staff to make sure the "promise" of the station's position stays on track.

Performer Q

Producers and directors in broadcasting naturally want to have an indication of the popularity of various performers and entertainers. A basic question in the planning stage of any program is: What performer or group of performers should be used to give the show the greatest appeal? Not unreasonably, producers prefer to use the most popular and likable performers in the industry rather than taking a chance on an unknown entertainer.

Marketing Evaluations, Inc., of Manasset, New York, meets the demand for information about performers, entertainers, and personalities (*www.qscores.com*). The company conducts nationwide telephone surveys using panels of about 1,250 households and interviewing about 5,400 people 6 years of age and older. The surveys are divided into seven types of "Q" scores, such as the Performer Q, TVQ, and Cartoon Q. The Performer Q portion of the analysis provides Familiarity and Appeal scores for more than 1,000 different personalities. The Target Audience Rankings provide a rank-order list of all personalities for several different target audiences, such as women aged 18–49. The target rank tells producers and directors which personalities appeal to specific demographic groups.

Focus Groups

The focus group, discussed in Chapter 5 and on *www.wimmerdominick.com* is a common research procedure in electronic media research, probably because of its versatility. Focus groups are used to develop questionnaires for further research and to provide preliminary information on a variety of topics, such as format and programming changes, personalities, station images, and lifestyle characteristics of the audience. Data in the last category are particularly useful when the focus group consists of a specific demographic segment.

The popularity and use of focus groups were demonstrated in the December 13, 1998, edition of CBS's "60 Minutes," which showed how Bill Clinton used focus group information to formulate his responses to his problems with Monica Lewinsky.

Miscellaneous Research

The electronic media are unique, and each requires a different type of research. Here are examples of research conducted by and for stations:

1. *Market studies.* A market study investigates the opinions and perceptions of the entire market, usually within a specific age range, such as 25- to 54-year-olds. There are no requirements for respondents to meet in terms of station listening or viewing, and the sample matches the population distribution and makeup of the market.

2. *Format studies.* A format study for a radio station involves a sample of respondents who listen to or prefer a certain type of music. These respondents are asked a series of questions to determine which stations provide the best service in a variety of areas, such as music, news, traffic reports, and community activities.

3. *Format search studies.* The title of the study explains its purpose—to find an available radio format in a given market.

4. *Program element importance.* A program element importance study identifies the specific elements on radio or television that are most important to a specific audience. Station managers use this information to ensure that they are providing what the audience wants.

5. *Station image.* It is important for a station's management to know how the public perceives the station and its services. Public misperception of management's purpose can decrease an audience's size and, consequently, advertising revenue. For example, suppose a radio station has been CHR (contemporary hits radio) for 10 years and switches to a country format. It is important that the audience and advertisers be aware of this change and have a chance to voice their opinions. This can be accomplished through a station image study, in which respondents to telephone calls are asked questions such as "What type of music does radio station WAAA play?" "What types of people do you think listen to WAAA radio?" and "Did you know that WAAA now plays country music?" If research reveals that few people are aware of the change in format, management can develop a new promotional strategy. Or the station might find that the current promotional efforts have been successful and should not be changed. Station image studies are conducted periodically by most larger stations to acquire current information on how the audience perceives each station in the market. If station managers are to provide the services that listeners and viewers want, they must keep up to date with audience trends and social changes.

6. *Personality (talent) studies.* Radio and television managers of successful stations constantly test the on-air personalities. Announcers (DJs), news anchors, and all other personalities are tested for their overall appeal and fit with other station personalities. Personality studies are often conducted for stations to find new talent from other markets, or even to test personalities who are on other stations in the market with the intent of hiring them in the future.

7. *Advertiser (account) analysis.* To increase the value of their service to advertisers, many stations administer questionnaires to local business executives. Some typical ques-

tions are, "When did your business open?" "How many people own this business?" "How much do you invest in advertising per year?" "When are advertising purchase decisions made?" and "What do you expect from your advertising?" Information obtained from client questionnaires is used to help write more effective advertising copy, to develop better advertising proposals, and to allow the sales staff to know more about each client. Generally, the questionnaires are administered before a business becomes an advertiser on the station, but they can also be used for advertisers who have done business with the station for several years.

8. *Account executive research.* Radio and television station managers throughout the country conduct surveys of advertising agency personnel, usually buyers, to determine how their sales executives are perceived. It is vitally important to know how the buyers perceive the salespeople. The results of the survey indicate which salespeople are performing very well and which ones may need additional help. Many times a survey discloses that a problem between a sales executive and a buyer is purely a personality difference, and the station can easily correct the problem by assigning another salesperson to the advertising agency.

9. *Sales research.* In an effort to increase sales, many stations themselves conduct research for local clients. For example, a station may conduct a "bank image" study of all banks in the area to determine how residents perceive each bank and the service it provides. The results from such a study are then used in an advertising proposal for the banks in the area. For example, if it is discovered that First National Bank's 24-hour automatic teller service is not well understood by local residents, the station might develop an advertising proposal to concentrate on this point.

10. *Diversification analyses.* The goals of any business are to expand and to achieve higher profits. In an effort to reach these goals, most larger stations, partnerships, and companies engage in a variety of studies to determine where investments should be made. Should other stations be purchased? What other types of activity should the business invest in? Such studies are used for forecasting and represent a major portion of the research undertaken by larger stations and companies. The changes in broadcast ownership rules made by the FCC have significantly increased the amount of acquisition research conducted by individuals, group owners, and other large companies in the broadcasting industry.

11. *Qualitative research.* Managers of successful broadcasting and cable operations leave nothing to chance; they test every aspect of their station. Research is conducted to test billboard advertising, logo designs, bumper stickers, bus advertising, direct mail campaigns, and programming interests.

12. *TV programming research.* This is a broad category that includes testing local news programs, promotional materials used by the station (known as *topicals*), entertainment programming, and everything else that might appear on the station.

▪▪▪ Summary

This chapter has introduced some of the more common methodologies used in broadcast research. Ratings are the most visible form of research used in broadcasting as well as the most influential in the decision-making process. However, nonratings approaches such as focus groups, music research, image studies, and program testing are all used frequently to collect data. The importance of research is fueled by an ever-increasing desire by management to learn more about broadcast audiences and their uses of the media.

Audience fragmentation is now an accepted phenomenon of the electronic media, and the competition for viewers and listeners has created a need for research data. Broadcast owners and managers realize that they can no longer rely on gut feelings when making programming, sales, and marketing decisions. The discussions in this chapter have been designed to emphasize the importance of research in all areas of broadcasting.

Key Terms

ACNielsen
Arbitron, Inc.
Audience turnover
Auditorium music test
Average quarter-hour
Callout research
Cost per thousand (CPM)
Cume
Daypart
Designated market area
Gross rating points
Hook
HUT
Metro survey area
Nonratings research
Overnights
People Meter
PUR
Psychographics
Rating
Reach
Rough cut
Share
Standard error
Sweeps
Telephone coincidental
Time spent listening
Total survey area

Using the Internet

1. For extensive information about research in the electronic media, search the Internet for these sources:
   - Broadcast research
   - Radio history
   - Television history
   - Cable television history
   - Psychographics
   - People Meter
   - Gross rating point
   - Cost per thousand

   In addition, visit Arbitron, ACNielsen, *Variety,* and *Advertising Age* at *www.arbitron.com, www.nielsenmedia.com, www.variety.com,* and *www.adage.com* for more information about broadcast ratings.

Questions and Problems for Further Investigation

1. Assume that a local television market has three stations: Channel 2, Channel 7, and Channel 9. There are 200,000 television households in the market. A ratings company samples 1,200 households at random and finds that 25% of the sample is watching Channel 2; 15%, Channel 7; and 10%, Channel 9.
   a. Calculate each station's share of the audience.
   b. Project the total number of households in the population that watch each channel.
   c. Calculate the CPM for a $1,000, 30-second spot on Channel 2.
   d. Calculate the standard error involved in Channel 2's rating.
2. What are the major data-gathering problems associated with each instrument?
   a. Electronic meters
   b. Diaries
   c. Telephone interviews
   d. People Meters
3. Find out what is happening in the development of electronic diaries. This information is available in several of the weekly broadcasting trade publications. If you can develop a replacement for the paper diary on your own, please be sure to send an email letter to us!
4. Search the Internet for websites for radio and TV stations in your market. Can you detect any type of research the station may have used in designing its site?
5. Perform your own music call-out research. Edit several 15-second selections of recordings on a cassette or CD and ask people to rate them on a 7-point scale. Compute means and standard deviations for the results. What can you conclude?
6. If you are using InfoTrac College Edition, you can keep up to date on the latest Nielsen TV ratings by simply doing a key word search on "Nielsen ratings."

For additional information on these and related topics, see

http://www.wimmerdominick.com

References and Suggested Readings

Arbitron Inc. (2001). *Description of methodology.* New York: Arbitron Inc.

The Arbitron Company. (1996). *A guide to understanding and using radio audience estimates.* New York: Arbitron.

The Arbitron Company. (1998). *Radio today: How America listens to radio.* New York: Arbitron.

Bell, F. (1999). Personal correspondence to Roger Wimmer.

Beville, H. M. (1988). *Audience ratings: Radio, television, cable* (Rev. ed.). Hillsdale, NJ: Lawrence Erlbaum.

Birch, T. (1989). Anatomy of the Birch radio telephone interview. *Radio & Records,* 818, 30.

Birch Radio. (1989a). *The Birch method of measurement and processing environment.* Birch Research Corporation.

Birch Radio. (1989b). *How Birch measures radio: The complete Birch radio sourcebook.* Birch Research Corporation.

Hudson, M. (1998). Personal correspondence to Roger Wimmer.

Hawkins, W. J. (1990, February). TV views viewers. *Popular Science,* pp. 74–75.

Karl, E. (1992). Personal correspondence to Roger Wimmer.

LoCascio, P. (1998). Personal correspondence to Roger Wimmer.

Nielsen, A. C. (1997–98). *Reference supplement: Nielsen station index.* Nielsen Media Research.

Nielsen, A. C. (1992a). *Media news.* New York: A. C. Nielsen.

Nielsen, A. C. (1992b). *Nielsen Media Research . . . The quality behind the numbers.* Northbrook, IL: Nielsen Media Research.

Webster, J., and Lichty, L. (1991). *Ratings analysis.* Hillsdale, NJ: Lawrence Erlbaum.

Wimmer, R. D. (2000). Research in advertising. In Chakrapani, C. (Ed.) *Marketing research: State-of-the-art perspectives.* New York: American Marketing Association.

Wimmer, R. D. (2001). An analysis of the reliability of auditorium music tests. Denver: Wimmer Research. (Proprietary data.)

Chapter 15

Research in Advertising

For many years, research was not widely used in advertising and decisions were made on an intuitive basis. However, with increased competition, mass markets, and mounting costs, more and more advertisers have come to rely on research as a basic management tool (Haskins & Kendrick, 1993).

Much of the research in advertising is **applied research,** which attempts to solve a specific problem and is not concerned with theorizing or generalizing to other situations. Advertising researchers want to answer questions such as should a certain product be packaged in blue or red? Is *Cosmopolitan* a better advertising buy than *Vogue?* Advertising research does not involve any special techniques; the methods discussed earlier—laboratory, survey, field research, focus groups, and content analysis—are in common use. They have been adapted, however, to provide specific types of information that meet the needs of this industry.

This chapter discusses the more common areas of advertising research and the types of studies they entail. In describing these research studies, we aim to convey the facts the reader must know to understand the methods and to use them intelligently.

A significant portion of the research in these areas involves market studies conducted by commercial research firms; these studies form the basis for much of the more specific research that follows in either the academic sector or the private sector. The importance of market research notwithstanding, this chapter does not have sufficient space to address this topic. Readers who want additional information about market research techniques should consult Boyd, Westfall, and Stasch (1989) and McQuarrie (1996).

The three functional research areas in advertising are copy research, media research, and campaign assessment research. Each is discussed in turn, and the syndicated research available in each case is described when appropriate.

▪ *Copy Testing*

Everyone who does advertising research agrees that the term *copy testing* is misleading. The word *copy* implies that only the words in the ad are tested. This, of course, is not the case: Every element in an ad (layout, narration, music, illustration, size, length, and so on) is a possible variable in copy testing. Leckenby (1984) suggested that the term *advertising stimulus measurement and research* (ASMAR) be substituted for *copy testing,* but the term has not gained wide use. Likewise, the term *message research* is a less frequently used synonym. Thus, we continue to use the traditional term despite its shortcomings.

Copy testing refers to research that helps develop effective advertisements and then determines which of several advertisements is the most effective. Copy testing takes place at every stage of the advertising process. Before a campaign starts, copy pretesting indicates what to stress and what to avoid. Once the content of the ad has been established, tests must be performed to ascertain the most effective way to structure these ideas. For example, in studying the illustration copy of a proposed magazine spread, a researcher might show to two or more groups of subjects an illustration of the product photographed from different angles. The headline might be evaluated by having potential users rate the typefaces used in several versions of the ad. The copy might be tested for readability and recall. In all cases, the aim is to determine whether the variable tested significantly affects the liking or the recall of the ad.

In TV, a rough cut of an entire commercial might be produced. The rough cut is a filmed or taped version of the ad in which amateur actors are used, locations are simplified, and the editing and narration lack the smoothness characteristic of broadcast (final cut) commercials. In this way, variations in the ad can be tested without incurring great expense.

The final phase of copy testing, which occurs after the finished commercials have appeared, serves to determine whether the campaign is having the desired effects. Any negative or unintended effects can be corrected before serious damage is done to a company's sales or reputation. This type of copy testing requires precisely defined goals. Some campaigns, for example, are designed to draw customers away from competitors; others are conducted to retain a company's present customers. Still others are intended to enhance the image of a firm and may not be concerned with consumers' purchase preferences. As we discuss later, this type of copy testing blends in with campaign assessment research.

There are several different ways to categorize copy testing methods. Perhaps the most useful, summarized by Leckenby and Wedding (1982), suggests that there are appropriate copy testing methods for each of the three dimensions of impact in the persuasion process. Although the model suggests a linear process starting with the cognitive dimension (knowing) and continuing through the affective dimension (feeling) to the conative dimension (doing), it is not necessary for the steps to occur in this order—see Table 15.1. In any event, the model does serve as a convenient guide for discussing copy research testing methods.

Table 15.1 *Typology of Copy Testing Effects*

Dimension of impact	Typical dependent variables
Cognitive	Attention
	Exposure
	Awareness
	Recognition
	Comprehension
	Recall
Affective	Attitude change
	Liking/disliking
	Involvement
Conative	Intention to buy
	Purchase behavior

The Cognitive Dimension

In the cognitive dimension, the key dependent variables are attention, awareness, exposure, recognition, comprehension, and recall. Studies that measure attention to advertising can use various methods. One strategy involves a consumer jury, where a group of 50–100 consumers are shown test ads and asked which ad was best at catching their attention. A physiological measurement technique, known as an *eye-tracking study,* is also used to determine which parts of an ad are noticed. A camera records the movement of the eye as it scans printed and graphic material. Analyzing the path the eye follows allows researchers to determine which parts of the ad attracted initial attention.

A tachistoscope (or T-scope) is one way to measure recognition of an ad. The T-scope is actually a slide projector with adjustable levels of illumination and with projection speeds that can be adjusted down to a tiny fraction of a second. Ads are tested to determine how long it takes a consumer to recognize the product, the headline, or the brand name.

Ad comprehension is an important factor in advertising research. One study found that all 60 commercials used in a test were misunderstood by viewers (Jacoby & Hofer, 1982). To guard against results such as these, advertising researchers typically test new ads with focus groups (see Chapter 5) to make sure their message is getting across as intended. The T-scope is also used to see how long it takes subjects to comprehend the theme of an ad—an important consideration for outdoor advertising, where drivers may have only a second or two of exposure.

Awareness, exposure, and recall are determined by several related methods. Primarily the print media use one measurement technique that taps these variables: Subjects are shown a copy of a newspaper or magazine and are asked which advertisements they remember seeing or reading. The results are used to tabulate a "reader traffic score" for each ad.

This method is open to criticism because some respondents confuse the advertisements or the publications in which they saw the ads, and some try to please the interviewer by reporting that they saw more than they actually did. To control this problem, researchers often make use of aided recall techniques. For instance, they might also show the respondent a list of advertisers, some of whose advertisements actually appeared in the publication and some of whose did not. For obvious reasons, this type of **recall study** is not entirely suitable for testing radio and television commercials; a more commonly used method in such cases is the telephone survey. Two variations of this approach are sometimes used. In aided recall, the interviewer mentions a general class of products and asks whether the respondent remembers an ad for a specific brand. A typical question might be "Have you seen or heard any ads for soft drinks lately?" In the **unaided recall** technique, researchers ask a general question such as "Have you seen any ads that interested you lately?" Obviously, it is harder for the consumer to respond to the second type of question. Only truly memorable ads score high on this form of measurement. Some researchers suggest that the most sensitive way to measure recall is to ask consumers whether they remember any recent advertising for each particular brand whose advertising is of interest (Haskins & Kendrick, 1993).

In that same connection, Sutherland and Friedman (2000) propose a difference between measuring "ad awareness" and "advertising awareness." Advertising awareness is measured by asking a question such as "Have you seen any advertising for Sears lately?" In contrast, ad awareness is measured by asking, "Can you describe the ad you recently saw for Sears?" Sutherland and Friedman argue that both concepts are important in determining the cognitive impact of advertising.

Perhaps a better understanding can be gained by looking at the several research companies that offer syndicated services in this area. For example, Perception Research Services (PRS) uses an eye-tracking camera to measure which parts of an ad were most noticed and the sequence in which consumers viewed the various elements of the ad. This is followed by an interview in which respondents report their feelings and attitudes toward the ad. Davis (1997) describes a PRS study for Bombay Gin that disclosed that respondents were not reading the ad copy and not looking at the Bombay bottle pictured in the ad. The interviews revealed that respondents found the ad confusing and did not understand the connection between the message and the artwork. The ad agency subsequently redesigned the ad to clear up these problems.

A method of posttesting television commercials is the InTeleTest service provided by

AN INSIDE LOOK

Ethics in Advertising Research

All of the general ethical concerns mentioned in Chapter 3 apply to advertising research. In addition, there are some ethical concerns that are unique to this area. Two of the most controversial are research about advertising to children and "push-polling."

A tremendous amount of advertising is directed toward children. Not surprisingly, much advertising research is conducted with children. Is it ethical to conduct research that uncovers new ways of making advertising effective with this group? Many social critics argue that children are a vulnerable audience and should be shielded from all forms of advertising. These same people would argue that research that helps advertisers further manipulate this group is not ethical. In 1999, a group of psychologists called on the American Psychological Association to restrict the use of psychological research designed to help sell toys, snack foods, video games, and other products to kids.

The second area, "push-polling," often crops up in political campaigns. At its worst, push-polling involves a bogus public opinion poll put into the field by candidate A in an attempt to spread dirt about candidate B. The push-poll would contain negative and often incorrect information about Candidate B designed to push the voters away from supporting him or her. Most researchers would condemn this form of polling as unethical. The line becomes less clear, however, in other situations. When constructing an ad campaign for a candidate, it is often helpful to know what negatives about the opponent should be stressed. Some legitimate polling might include information that might have negative connotations, (e.g., "Are you aware that Candidate B has been twice divorced?"). The appropriate amount of negative items to include can be a difficult ethical problem.

Gallup & Robinson. Gallup & Robinson measures the percentage of respondents who remember seeing the commercial and the percentage of those who can remember specific points. Additionally, they provide a score indicating the degree of favorable attitude toward the product, based on positive statements made by the subjects during the interview. Gallup & Robinson also conducts pretests and posttests of magazine advertisements. Their Magazine Impact Research Service (MIRS) measures the recall of advertisements that appear in general-interest magazines. Copies of a particular issue containing the advertisement under study are mailed to approximately 150 readers. (In the case of a pretest, the MIRS binds the proposed advertisement into each magazine.) The day after delivery of the magazines, respondents are telephoned and asked which advertisements they noticed in the magazine and what details they can remember about them. These results are reported to the advertiser.

One of the best-known professional research firms is Starch Advertising Research (now part of Roper ASW), which conducts posttest recall research. The company's Message Report Service routinely measures advertising readership in more than 100 magazines and newspapers. Using a sample of approximately 300 people, Starch interviewers take a copy of the periodical under study to respondents' homes. If a subject has already looked through that particular publication, he or she is questioned at length. The interviewer shows the respondent an advertisement and asks whether he or she has seen or read any part of it. If the answer is no, the interviewer moves on to another advertisement; if the answer is yes, more questions are asked to determine how much was read. This procedure continues until the respondent has been questioned about every advertisement in that issue up to 90 (at which point the interview is terminated to avoid subject fatigue). Starch places each respondent into one of four categories for each advertisement:

1. Nonreader (did not recall seeing the advertisement).
2. Noted reader (remembered seeing the advertisement).
3. Associated reader (not only saw the advertisement but also read some part of it that clearly indicated the brand name).
4. Read most reader (read more than half the written material in the advertisement).

The Starch organization reports the findings of its recall studies in a novel manner. Advertisers are given a copy of the magazine in which readership scores printed on yellow stickers have been attached to each advertisement. Figure 15.1 is an example of a "Starched" advertisement.

Starch also offers its AD+IMPACT service. This system measures all aspects of communication and their effect on the image and health of a brand. The system uses both qualitative and diagnostic measures allied with quantitative ratings. The service can tell what element of the ad is getting viewers' attention and the proportion of people who will pay attention to it. In addition, it will examine if the ad is moving viewers closer to the brand and the effect this has on the brand image and health.

The Affective Dimension

The affective dimension usually involves research into whether a consumer's attitudes toward a particular product have changed because of exposure to an ad or a campaign. The techniques used to study the affective dimension include projective tests, theater testing, physiological measures, semantic differential scales, and rating scales. Projective tests provide an alternative to the straightforward "Do you like this ad?" approach. Instead, respondents are asked to draw a picture or complete a story that involves the ad or the product mentioned in the ad. Analysis of these responses provides additional insight and depth into the consumer's feelings. Davis (1997) describes other projective procedures, including the personification technique in which the respondent is asked to relate a product to a well-known person. For example, "Think about vacuum cleaners. If the Oreck vacuum could turn into a celebrity or famous person, who would it be?" The answers might reveal something about brand image that could not be tapped through other measures.

Theater tests involve bringing an audience to a special facility where they are shown television commercials that are embedded in a TV show. Respondents are given electronic response indicators (ERIs—similar to hand-held calculators) that allow them to instantaneously rate each commercial they see. The ERI is a device with five buttons ranging from one labeled "feel very positive" to one labeled "feel very negative." The respondents press these buttons while watching a commercial. The miniaturization of these hand-held rating devices allows tests to be conducted in focus room facilities or in specially equipped vans parked outside shopping malls. These tests have been criticized because they require respondents to make too many responses, analyze content that

Figure 15.1 *A "Starched" Ad*

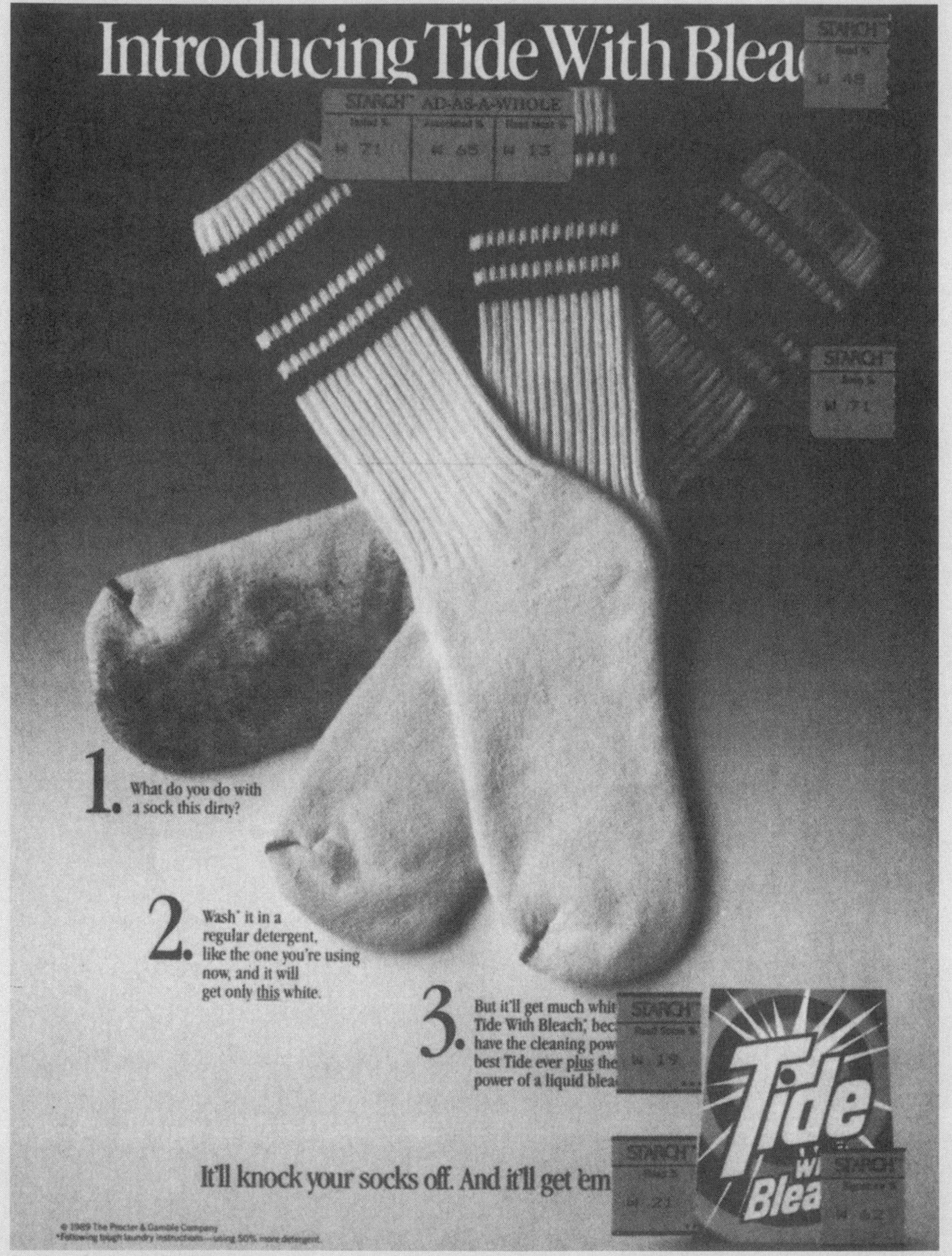

Source: Starch INRA Hooper, Inc. Readership Report for *Southern Living*, October 1989, page 129. Reprinted by permission.

may be too minute to be put into practical use, and do not allow respondents to change their answers since the answers are recorded instantaneously in a computer. Sometimes a researcher's desire to use technology to impress clients overshadows the validity and reliability of a research approach.

Four physiological tests are used in this area. In the pupilometer test, a tiny camera focused on the subject's eye measures the amount of pupil dilation that occurs while the person is looking at an ad. Changes in pupil diameter are recorded because findings from psychophysiology suggest that people tend to respond to appealing stimuli with dilation (enlargement) of their pupils. Conversely, when unappealing, disagreeable stimuli are shown, the pupil narrows. The second test measures galvanic skin response, or GSR (that is, changes in the electrical conductance of the surface of the skin). A change in GSR rating while the subject is looking at an ad is taken to signify emotional involvement or arousal. The third technique, brain wave analysis, monitors brain activity during exposure to a television commercial in order to measure the level of interest and involvement by a viewer (Percy & Rossiter, 1997).

Hazlett (1999) described a method whereby a facial electromyography (EMG—a technique that measures the electrical activity of facial muscles) was used to tap consumers' responses to TV commercials. The results suggested that EMG was a better measure of emotion than relying on viewers' self-reports.

Semantic differential scales and rating scales (see Chapter 2) are used most often to measure attitude change. For these measurements to be most useful, it is necessary to (1) obtain a picture of the consumer's attitudes before exposure to the ad, (2) expose the consumer to the ad or ads under examination, and (3) remeasure the attitude after exposure. To diminish the difficulties associated with achieving all three of these goals in testing television ads, many researchers prefer a **forced-exposure** method. In this technique, respondents are invited to a theater for a special screening of a TV program. Before viewing the program, they are asked to fill out questionnaires concerning their attitudes toward several different products, one of which is of interest to the researchers. Next, everyone watches the TV show, which contains one or more commercials for the product under investigation as well as ads for other products. When the show is over, all respondents again fill out the questionnaire concerning product attitudes. Change in evaluation is the essential variable of interest. The same basic method can be used in testing attitudes toward print ads except that the testing is done individually, in each respondent's home. Typically, a consumer is interviewed about product attitudes, a copy of a magazine that includes the test ad (or ads) is left at the house, and the respondent is asked to read or look through the publication before the next interview. A short time later, the interviewer calls the respondent and asks whether the magazine has been read. If it has, product attitudes are once again measured.

The importance of the affective dimension was emphasized by Walker and Dubitsky (1994), who noted that the degree of liking expressed by consumers toward a commercial was significantly related to awareness, recall, and greater persuasive impact. Indeed, several advertising researchers have suggested that liking an ad is one of the most important factors in determining its impact (Haley, 1994).

Several research companies offer services designed to measure attitudes. As part of their In-View service, Gallup & Robinson tests attitude change by calling eligible respondents and inviting them to participate in viewing a test program. During this call, the interviewer records attitudes about six products, three of which will be advertised on the test show. Comparison data are collected from nonviewers of the program. After they view the program, respondents are called back and asked the same attitude questions. Changes in attitude are presumed to be the result of viewing the commercial. In magazine measurement, Gallup & Robinson constructs a special issue of a magazine containing the ads under consideration. Respondents are selected randomly from the phone book, visited at home, and given a copy of the magazine. The next day, to establish readership, respondents are asked questions about the magazine's contents. The interviewer next reads a list of products and asks whether the magazine contained ads for each product. Each time a respondent remembers seeing a product ad, the interviewer asks for a description of the ad as well as the respondent's attitudes toward the product after reading the ad.

The Conative Dimension

The conative dimension deals with actual consumer behavior, and, in many instances, it is the most pertinent of all dependent variables. The two main categories of behavior usually measured are buying predisposition and actual purchasing behavior. In the first category, the usual design is to gather precampaign predisposition data and reinterview the subjects after the advertising has been in place. Subjects are typically asked a question along these lines: "If you were going shopping tomorrow to buy breakfast cereal, which brand would you buy?" This might be followed by "Would you consider buying any other brands?" and "Are there any cereals you would definitely not buy?" (The last question is included to determine whether the advertising campaign has had any negative effects.) Additionally, some researchers (Haskins, 1976) suggest using a buying intention scale and instructing respondents to check the one position on the scale that best fits their intention. Such a scale might look like this:

_____ I'll definitely buy this cereal as soon as I can.

_____ I'll probably buy this cereal sometime.

_____ I might buy this cereal, but I don't know when.

_____ I'll probably never buy this cereal.

_____ I wouldn't eat this cereal even if somebody gave it to me.

The scale allows advertisers to see how consumers' buying preferences change during and after the campaign.

Perhaps the most reliable methods of posttesting are those that measure actual sales, direct response, and other easily quantifiable behavior. In the print media, direct response might be measured by inserting a coupon that readers can mail in for a free sample. Different forms of an ad might be run in different publications to determine which elicits the most inquiries. Another alternative suitable for use in both print media advertising and electronic media advertising is to include a toll-free 800 number that consumers can call for more information or to order the product.

Two recent studies illustrate how researchers can examine behavioral response. Bates and Buckley (2000) examined the influence of exposure to TV commercials that urged people to return their 2000 census forms on the actual rate of returned forms. They found that exposure to advertising was related to knowing more about the census but that there was no relationship between exposure to the ads and actually returning a form. Burton, Lictenstein, and Netemeyer (1999) discovered that exposure to an advertising sales flyer for retail supermarkets resulted in more than a 100% increase in the number of advertised products that were purchased.

Some research companies measure direct response by means of a laboratory store. Usually used in conjunction with theater testing, this technique involves giving people chits with which they can buy products in a special store. (Most of the time this is a special trailer or field service conference room furnished to look like a store.) Subjects are then shown a program containing some test commercials, given more chits, and allowed to shop again. Changes in pre- and post-exposure choices are recorded.

Actual sales data can be obtained in many ways. Consumers may be asked directly: "What brand of breakfast cereal did you most recently purchase?" The findings from this survey would be subject to error, however, as a result of faulty recall, courtesy bias, and so forth; for this reason, more direct methods are generally preferred. If enough time and money are available, direct observation of people's selections in the cereal aisles at a sample of supermarkets can be a useful source of data. Store audits that list the total number of boxes sold at predetermined times are another possibility. Last, and possibly most expensive, is the household audit technique, in which an interviewer visits the homes of a sample of consumers and actually inspects their kitchen cupboards to see what brands of cereals are there. In addition to the audit, a traditional questionnaire is used to gather further information about the respondents' feelings toward the commercials.

Many professional research firms conduct surveys that deal with purchasing behavior. Information Resources Inc., for example, provides a service called BehaviorScan. The BehaviorScan system delivers different TV ads to selected homes within the same market and measures the impact of the advertising on consumers' actual purchasing behavior. The AdTel Company offers a similar service.

In the print area, Ipsos-ASI uses a technique that measures pseudopurchase behavior. A test magazine containing the client's ad is left at the house. The respondent is asked to read the magazine, told there will be a prize for participation, and asked which brands would be preferred if he or she is a grand prize winner. After the test ads have been looked at, the respondent is again asked about prize preferences. Changes in pre- and post-exposure scores are carefully noted.

Copy Research and Validity

All the methods of copy research discussed in the preceding sections are based on the assumption that this research identifies ads that will work well in the marketplace. To test this assumption, the Advertising Research Foundation (ARF) sponsored a research validity project to determine which copy testing measures were effective (Haley & Baldinger, 1991). To begin, ARF selected five pairs of TV commercials. Since one of the ads in each of these pairs had already been shown to produce major sales differences in test markets, ARF researchers used the ads in a field experiment that included many common copy-testing measures.

The experiment revealed a strong correlation between ads that copy tested well and ads that performed well in the marketplace. For example, measuring reaction to commercials on an affective scale (like/dislike) predicted the more effective ad of the pair 87% of the time. Top-of-mind awareness (unaided recall) measures correctly classified the more effective ad 73% of the time. Less effective were measures that asked respondents to recall the main point of the ad. In a reanalysis of the ARF data, Rossiter and Eagleson (1994) suggested that another measure—a pretest–posttest difference in replies to the item "I will definitely buy this product"—is also useful. In sum, it appears that copy testing research can help predict what ad will be most effective in generating sales.

The current trend in copy testing is multiple measures of copy research effectiveness. A technique called Advertising Response Modeling (ARM) provides a conceptual model that integrates several measurements to evaluate ad effectiveness (Mehta & Purvis, 1997). ARM differentiates between high and low involvement situations and includes measures such as recall, liking, buying interest, and brand rating. The technique highlights the observation that different ads can be successful for a variety of reasons.

▪ Media Research

The two important terms in media research are *reach* and *frequency*. **Reach** is the total number of households or persons that will be exposed to a message in a particular medium at least once over a certain period (usually 4 weeks). Reach can be thought of as the cumulative audience, and it is usually expressed as a percentage of the total universe of households that have been exposed to a message. For example, if 25 of a possible 100 households are exposed to a message, then the reach is 25%. **Frequency** refers to the number of exposures to the same message that each household receives. Of course, not every household in the sample will receive exactly the same number of messages. Consequently, advertisers prefer to use the average frequency of exposure, expressed by this formula:

$$\frac{\text{Total exposures for all households}}{\text{Reach}} = \text{Average frequency}$$

Thus, if the total number of exposures for a sample of households is 400 and the reach is 25, the average frequency is 16. In other words, the average household was exposed 16 times. Notice that if the reach were 80%, the frequency would be 5. As reach increases, average frequency drops. (Maximizing both reach and frequency would require an unlimited budget, something most advertisers lack.)

A concept closely related to reach and frequency is gross rating points (GRPs), introduced in Chapter 14. GRPs are useful when it comes to deciding between two media alternatives. For example, suppose Program A has a reach of 30% and an average frequency of 2.5, whereas Program B has a reach of 45% and a frequency of 1.25. Which program offers a better reach–frequency relationship? First, determine the GRPs of each program using the following formula:

$$\text{GRPs} = \text{Reach} \times \text{Average frequency}$$

For A:

$$\text{GRPs} = 30 \times 2.5 = 75.00$$

For B:

$$\text{GRPs} = 45 \times 1.25 = 56.25$$

In this example, Program A scores better in the reach–frequency combination, and this would probably be a factor in deciding which was the better buy.

Media research falls into three general categories: studies of the size and composition of an audience of a particular medium or media (reach studies), studies of the relative efficiency of advertising exposures provided by various combinations of media (reach and frequency studies), and studies of the advertising activities of competitors.

Audience Size and Composition

Analyses of audiences are probably the most commonly used advertising studies in print and electronic media research. Since advertisers spend large amounts of money in the print and electronic media, they have an understandable interest in the audiences for those messages. In most cases, audience information is gathered using techniques that are compromises between the practical and the ideal.

Table 15.2 *Determining Advertising Efficiency from Ad Cost and Circulation Data*

	Newspaper X	Newspaper Y
Ad cost	\$1,800	\$2,700
Circulation	180,000	300,000
Cost per thousand circulated copies	$\frac{\$1,800}{180} = \$10.00$	$\frac{\$2,700}{300} = \$9.00$

The audience size of a newspaper or magazine is commonly measured in terms of the number of copies distributed per issue. This number, which is called the publication's **circulation,** includes all copies delivered to subscribers as well as those bought at newsstands or from other sellers. Because a publication's advertising rate is determined directly by its circulation, the print media have developed a standardized method of measuring circulation and have instituted an organization, the Audit Bureau of Circulations (ABC), to verify that a publication actually distributes the number of copies per issue that it claims. (The specific procedures used by the ABC are discussed later in this chapter.)

Circulation figures are used to compute the CPMs of various publications. For example, suppose Newspaper X charges \$1,800 for an advertisement and has an ABC-verified circulation of 180,000, whereas Newspaper Y, with a circulation of 300,000, charges \$2,700 for the same-size space. Table 15.2 shows that Newspaper Y is the more efficient advertising vehicle.

Note that this method considers only the number of circulated copies of a newspaper or magazine. This information is useful, but it does not necessarily indicate the total number of readers of the publication. To estimate the total audience, the circulation figure must be multiplied by the average number of readers of each copy of an issue. This information is obtained by performing audience surveys.

A preliminary step in conducting such surveys is to define operationally the concept *magazine reader* or *newspaper reader.* There are many possible definitions, but the one most commonly used is fairly liberal: A *reader* is a person who has read or at least looked through an issue.

Three techniques are used to measure readership. The most rigorous is the unaided recall method, in which respondents are asked whether they have read any newspapers or magazines in the past month (or other time period). If the answer is yes, subjects are asked to specify the magazines or newspapers they read. When a publication is named, the interviewer attempts to verify reading by asking questions about the contents of that publication. The reliability of the unaided recall method is open to question (as has been discussed) because of the difficulty respondents often have in recalling specific content.

A second technique is aided recall. In this method, the interviewer names several publications and asks whether the respondent has read any of them lately. Each time the respondent claims to have read a publication, the interviewer asks whether he or she remembers seeing the most recent copy. The interviewer may jog a respondent's memory by describing the front page or the cover. Finally, the respondent is asked to recall anything that

Table 15.3 *Determining Ad Efficiency from an Extended Database*

	Newspaper X	Newspaper Y
Ad cost	$1,800	$2,700
Circulation	180,000	300,000
CPM	$10.00	$9.00
Number of people who read the issue	630,000 (3.5 readers per copy)	540,000 (1.8 readers per copy)
Revised CPM	$2.86	$5.00

was seen or read in that particular issue. (In a variation on this process, **masked recall,** respondents are shown the front page or the cover of a publication with the name blacked out and are asked whether they remember reading that particular issue. Those who respond in the affirmative are asked to recall any items they have seen or read.)

The third technique, called the **recognition** method, entails showing respondents the logo or cover of a publication. For each publication the respondent has seen or read, the interviewer produces a copy and the respondent leafs through it to identify the articles or stories he or she recognizes. All respondents who definitely remember reading the publication are counted in its audience. To check the accuracy of the respondent's memory, dummy articles may be inserted into the interviewer's copy of the publication; respondents who claim to have read the dummy items thus may be eliminated from the sample or given less weight in the analysis. Many advertising researchers consider the recognition technique to be the most accurate predictor of readership scores.

Once the total audience for each magazine or newspaper has been tabulated, the advertiser can determine which publication is the most efficient buy. For example, returning to the example of Table 15.2, let us suppose that Newspaper X and Newspaper Y have the audience figures listed in Table 15.3. Based on these figures, Newspaper X is seen to be the more efficient choice.

Another variable to be considered in determining the advertising efficiency (or **media efficiency**) of a newspaper or magazine is the number of times a person reads each issue. For example, imagine two newspapers or magazines that have exactly the same number of readers per issue. Publication A consists primarily of pictures and contains little text; people tend to read it once and not look at it again. Publication B, on the other hand, contains several lengthy and interesting articles; people pick it up several times. Publication B would seem to be a more efficient advertising vehicle because it provides several possible exposures to an advertisement for the same cost as Publication A. Unfortunately, a practical and reliable method for measuring the number of exposures per issue has yet to be developed.

Perhaps the most important gauge of advertising efficiency is the composition of the audience. It matters little if 100,000 people see an advertisement for farm equipment if only a few of them are in the market for such products. To evaluate the number of potential customers in the audience, an advertiser must first conduct a survey to determine cer-

Table 15.4 *Calculation of Ad Efficiency Incorporating Demographic Survey Results*

	Newspaper X	Newspaper Y
Ad cost	$1,800	$2,700
Circulation	180,000	300,000
CPM	$10.00	$9.00
Number of people who read average issue	630,000	540,000
Number of potential beer drinkers	150,000	220,000
Number of potential fast-food customers	300,000	200,000
CPM (beer drinkers)	$12.00	$12.27
CPM (fast-food customers)	$6.00	$13.50

tain demographic characteristics of the people who tend to purchase a particular product. For example, potential customers for beer might be described typically as males between the ages of 18 and 49; those for fast-food restaurants might be households in which the primary wage earner is between ages 18 and 35 and there are at least two children under 12. These demographic characteristics of the typical consumer are then compared with the characteristics of a publication's audience for the product. The cost of reaching this audience is also expressed in CPM units, as shown in Table 15.4. An examination of these figures indicates that Newspaper X is slightly more efficient as a vehicle for reaching potential beer customers and much more efficient in reaching fast-food restaurant patrons.

Because of the ephemeral nature of radio and television broadcasts, determining audience size and composition in the electronic media poses special problems for advertising researchers. One problem in particular involves the use of the CPM measure for media planning. The various measures of program audience discussed in Chapter 14 may or may not reflect the number of people who actually view a TV program. Lloyd and Clancy (1991) suggest a new measure, the CMPI, or cost per thousand involved persons, as a solution. Constructing this measure consists of asking viewers to respond to statements about their viewing, such as:

- There were parts in this show that really touched my feelings.
- I was really involved in the program. I wished it had lasted longer.

Answers to these items reveal audience differences in program involvement, and the authors suggest that a program whose audience is small but involved might be a better advertising buy than a program with a large but marginally involved audience.

Frequency of Exposure in Media Schedules

An advertiser working within a strict budget to promote a product or service may be limited to the use of a single vehicle or medium. Often, however, an advertising campaign is conducted via several advertising vehicles simultaneously. But which combination of vehicles and media will provide the greatest reach and frequency for the advertiser's product? A substantial amount of recent media research has been devoted to this question, much of it concentrated on the development of mathematical models of advertising media and their audiences. The mathematical derivations of these models are beyond the scope of this book. However, the following material describes in simplified form the concepts underlying two models: stepwise analysis and decision calculus. Readers who wish to pursue these topics in more rigorous detail should consult Rust (1986).

Stepwise analysis is called an iterative model because the same series of instructions to the computer is repeated over and over with slight modifications until a predetermined best or optimal solution is reached. The Young & Rubicam agency pioneered development in this area with its stepwise "high-assay" model. Stepwise analysis constructs a media schedule in increments, initially choosing a particular vehicle based on the lowest cost per potential customer reached. After this selection has been made, all the remaining media vehicles are reevaluated to determine whether the optimal advertising exposure rate has been achieved. If not, the second most efficient vehicle is chosen and the process is repeated until the optimal exposure rate is reached. This method is called the "high-assay" model because it is analogous to gold mining. The easiest-to-get gold is mined first, followed by less accessible ore. In like manner, the consumers who are the easiest to reach are targeted first, followed by those consumers who are harder to find and more costly to reach.

Decision calculus models make use of an **objective function,** a mathematical statement that provides a quantitative value for a given media combination (also known as a schedule). This value represents the schedule's effectiveness in providing advertising exposure. The advertising researcher determines which schedule offers the maximum exposure for a given product by calculating the objective functions of various media schedules.

Calculations of objective functions are based on values generated by studies of audience size and composition for each vehicle or medium. In addition, a schedule's objective function value takes into account such variables as the probability that the advertisement will be forgotten, the total cost of the media schedule compared with the advertiser's budget, and the "media option source effect"—that is, the relative impact of exposure in a particular advertising vehicle. (For example, an advertisement for men's clothes is likely to have more impact in *Gentlemen's Quarterly* than in *True Detective.*) Many software programs are available for media planners that help them determine the most effective media combinations. More recently, Zufryden (2000) described the ZAPEM methodology that takes into account cumulative penetration and repeat purchase patterns and their impact on various media schedules.

Media Research by Private Firms

As mentioned earlier, the Audit Bureau of Circulations (ABC) supplies advertisers with data on the circulation figures of newspapers and magazines. As of 2001, ABC measured the circulation of about 75% of all print media vehicles in the United States and Canada. ABC requires publishers to submit a detailed report of their circulation every 6 months; it verifies these reports by sending field workers to conduct an audit at each publication. The auditors typically examine records of the publications' press runs, newsprint bills, or other invoices for paper, as well as transcripts of circulation records and related files.

The ABC audit results, as well as overall circulation data, coverage maps, press times, and market data, are published in an annual report and distributed to ABC members and advertisers. ABC now provides a Reader Profile that contains demographic data about readers as well as circulation figures.

Mediamark Research Inc. (MRI) provides comprehensive feedback about magazine readership. MRI uses the measurement technique called the *recent reading method*. The company selects a large random sample of readers and shows them the logos of about 70 magazines to determine which ones they have recently read or looked through. At the same time, data are gathered about the ownership, purchase, and use of a variety of products and services. This information is tabulated by MRI and released in a series of detailed reports on the demographic makeup and purchasing behavior of each magazine's audience. Using these data, advertisers can determine the cost of reaching potential buyers of their products or services. A portion of an MRI Magazine Total Audience Report is reproduced in Table 15.5. The Simmons Market Research Bureau offers a similar service.

Two companies—Arbitron and AC-Nielsen—supply broadcast audience data for advertisers. Arbitron measures radio listening in about 270 markets across the United States, and ACNielsen provides audience estimates for network TV and local television markets. (Chapter 14 has more information on the methods used by these two companies and others.)

Measuring the Internet Audience

The Internet poses special problems for audience measurement. Reliable data on who is looking at web pages and banner advertising are important because without such data advertisers are reluctant to spend money on Internet advertising. As in other media, advertisers want to know who is visiting a website, how often they visit, and whether the CPM is reasonable. Obtaining such data, however, is difficult.

The first attempts to monitor web page traffic consisted of software programs that measured the number of "hits," or the number of times someone logs onto the page. These numbers were unreliable because the programs measured hits in different ways, depending on the server. Moreover, there were programs available that called websites over and over and could be used to inflate the number of hits. Advertisers preferred to have an independent organization count the numbers (Green, 1998), and it wasn't long before Internet rating companies came into existence.

As of 2002, the two most visible organizations that measure the Internet audience are Media Metrix and Nielsen//NetRatings. Both of these companies use a media panel of consumers to collect their data. Media Metrix provides its panel members with software that monitors online and offline activity and also collects demographic and behavioral data. Media Metrix measures both home and work Internet activity. Nielsen//NetRatings collects realtime data from more than 70,000 panel members in the United States. The U.S. panel sample consists of 62,000 at-home users and 8,000 at-work users. Like Media Metrix, Nielsen provides its panel members with software that tracks their online activity.

Both of these firms face a difficult problem in gathering accurate web data. Much web surfing is done at work, and many businesses have been reluctant to allow ratings companies to install tracking software on office computers because they fear the software might also be used to access confidential memos or sales data. As a result, all research firms probably underreport office use. Both of these companies are working to improve their methods and to solve these problems because they know that the rewards will be

Table 15.5 *Example of Mediamark Report*

	AUDIENCE (000)			MEDIAN AGE			MEDIAN H/D INCOME			CIRCULATION	READERS PER COPY		
	TOTAL ADULTS	TOTAL MEN	TOTAL WOMEN	ADULTS	MEN	WOMEN	ADULTS	MEN	WOMEN	(000)	ADULTS	MEN	WOMEN
TOTAL ADULT POPULATION	180.974	86.307	94.667	40.8	39.9	41.7	31.717	33.829	29.538	-	-	-	-
AIR GROUP ONE (GR)	1.882	1.075	807	39.0	37.9	40.0	57.245	61.194	55.116	659	2.86	1.63	1.22
AMERICAN BABY	3.557	558	2.999	29.5	31.3	29.2	33.146	39.515	31.852	1.143	3.11	.19	2.62
AMERICAN HEALTH	3.851	1.175	2.676	40.8	42.7	40.2	37.115	35.287	37.483	1.102	3.49	1.07	2.43
AMERICAN LEGION	3.313	2.031	1.282	59.1	61.3	56.3	28.078	27.734	28.641	2.825*	1.17	.72	.45
AMERICAN WAY	1.062	528	534	45.2	44.3	47.7	59.750	61.967	52.500	245*	4.33	2.16	2.18
ARCHITECTURAL DIGEST	3.147	1.607	1.540	38.2	37.7	38.7	56.446	57.246	55.685	624	5.04	2.58	2.47
AUDUBON	1.580	616	964	42.7	41.7	44.5	38.528	33.737	43.117	453*	3.49	1.36	2.13
BABY TALK	2.258	403	1.855	27.9	31.6	27.2	23.636	33.096	21.667	964*	2.34	.42	1.92
BASSMASTER	3.202	2.742	460	34.9	35.6	31.7	34.747	34.986	32.031	539	5.94	5.09	.85
BETTER HOMES & GARDENS	31.367	7.527	23.840	42.5	41.8	42.9	34.643	37.057	33.855	8.078	3.88	.93	2.95
BHG/LHJ COMBO (GR)	49.749	9.264	40.485	42.8	42.1	42.9	33.924	36.290	33.430	13.161	3.78	.70	3.08
BLACK ENTERPRISE	1.904	983	921	37.6	36.2	38.9	26.061	33.476	17.443	239	7.97	4.11	3.85
BON APPETIT	4.631	1.111	3.520	40.0	38.2	40.6	41.081	41.389	41.027	1.389	3.33	.80	2.53
BRIDE'S MAGAZINE	3.957	592	3.365	25.7	25.8	25.7	33.170	34.097	33.076	390	10.15	1.52	8.63
BUSINESS WEEK	6.136	4.341	1.795	37.4	38.1	36.3	45.881	48.094	42.012	929	6.60	4.67	1.93
THE CABLE GUIDE	14.852	7.401	7.451	36.5	35.5	37.3	39.966	40.799	39.102	7.684*	1.93	.96	.97
CAR & DRIVER	5.327	4.641	686	29.5	29.3	30.7	38.282	38.237	38.632	870*	6.12	5.33	.79
CAR CRAFT	2.506	2.257	249	29.1	28.4	33.7	31.271	31.576	28.092	435	5.76	5.19	.57
CHANGING TIMES	3.426	1.886	1.540	49.1	46.9	51.0	40.650	40.014	41.530	1.250	2.74	1.51	1.23
CHICAGO TRIBUNE MAGAZINE	2.336	1.143	1.193	42.7	42.4	43.0	44.888	46.855	43.154	1.130	2.07	1.01	1.06
COLONIAL HOMES	2.294	772	1.522	38.8	36.2	40.6	36.067	38.259	34.372	581*	3.95	1.33	2.62
CONDE NAST LIMITED (GR)	21.230	6.201	15.029	34.1	31.1	35.8	39.487	40.174	39.224	3.835	5.54	1.62	3.92
CONDE NAST WOMEN (GR)	28.258	3.178	25.080	30.0	30.5	29.9	36.392	42.740	36.035	5.936	4.76	.54	4.23
CONSUMERS DIGEST	4.676	2.682	1.994	40.7	40.9	40.4	39.012	38.900	39.132	935	5.00	2.87	2.13
COSMOPOLITAN	12.118	1.916	10.202	30.9	31.9	30.7	34.449	34.659	34.410	2.512	4.82	.76	4.06
COUNTRY HOME	5.762	1.563	4.199	38.3	37.5	38.6	38.741	42.211	37.851	976*	5.90	1.60	4.30
COUNTRY LIVING	10.372	2.700	7.672	39.5	38.0	40.1	37.262	40.876	36.359	1.748	5.93	1.54	4.39
CREATIVE IDEAS FOR LIVING	2.310	339	1.971	38.4	36.1	38.9	31.024	34.432	30.120	725	3.19	.47	2.72
DELTA SKY	1.255	691	564	40.2	38.2	41.6	57.540	56.905	57.861	397*	3.16	1.74	1.42
DIAMANDIS MAGAZINE NTWK (GR)	22.748	18.733	4.015	31.4	30.8	33.3	38.800	38.970	37.951	4.273	5.32	4.38	.94
DISCOVER	5.132	3.207	1.925	35.8	34.3	39.1	37.500	38.527	36.250	948	5.41	3.38	2.03
DISNEY CHANNEL MAGAZINE	5.710	2.389	3.321	36.2	36.5	36.0	40.547	43.816	37.874	4.664*	1.22	.51	.71
EAST/WEST NETWORK (GR)	3.849	2.244	1.605	39.1	38.7	39.6	52.133	58.272	43.262	1.329	2.90	1.69	1.21
EBONY	9.519	4.120	5.399	36.2	35.4	36.7	22.466	28.044	18.754	1.774	5.37	2.32	3.04
ELLE	2.298	299	1.999	29.7	36.1	29.1	45.038	47.961	43.562	751	3.06	.40	2.66
ESQUIRE	3.672	2.230	1.442	34.3	33.9	35.4	36.020	37.716	30.097	724	5.07	3.08	1.99
ESSENCE	3.484	987	2.497	34.3	32.0	35.0	25.205	31.369	22.592	921*	3.78	1.07	2.71
FAMILY CIRCLE	24.570	3.240	21.330	43.5	42.4	43.6	33.527	37.948	32.797	5.195	4.73	.62	4.11
FAMILY CIRCLE/MCCALLS (GR)	41.859	5.100	36.759	43.5	42.1	43.7	32.821	35.579	32.439	10.384	4.03	.49	3.54
FAMILY HANDYMAN	4.022	2.546	1.476	44.6	43.7	46.8	35.380	36.231	33.490	1.494	2.69	1.70	.99
FIELD & STREAM	13.794	10.385	3.409	37.0	37.0	37.0	32.582	33.383	29.889	2.104	6.56	4.94	1.62
FLOWER & GARDEN	3.620	1.007	2.613	43.1	42.9	43.1	28.540	29.911	27.370	606	5.97	1.66	4.31
FLOWER & GRDN/WORKBENCH (GR)	6.366	2.854	3.512	42.9	43.2	42.5	31.312	33.116	29.494	1.498	4.25	1.91	2.34
FOOD & WINE	2.722	1.184	1.538	38.7	38.3	38.9	40.618	43.936	39.581	884	3.08	1.34	1.74
FORBES	3.284	2.229	1.055	42.1	40.3	46.3	52.252	54.021	48.828	777	4.23	2.87	1.36
FORTUNE	3.307	2.254	1.053	38.5	36.6	42.5	51.495	50.956	52.516	704	4.70	3.20	1.50
4 WHEEL & OFF ROAD	2.816	2.423	393	25.7	26.0	24.4	32.862	33.353	28.786	331	8.51	7.32	1.19
FOUR WHEELER	2.046	1.799	247	25.9	25.3	31.8	34.565	35.342	23.565	311	6.58	5.78	.79
GAMES	1.648	816	832	36.1	32.6	39.1	34.495	34.035	35.000	682	2.42	1.20	1.22
GLAMOUR	8.984	768	8.216	30.6	31.4	30.5	35.591	47.444	34.890	2.141	4.20	.36	3.84
GOLF DIGEST	4.449	3.599	850	42.1	41.3	46.6	45.188	44.478	51.768	1.284	3.46	2.80	.66
GOLF DIGEST/TENNIS (GR)	6.076	4.618	1.458	40.1	39.2	42.6	44.297	43.726	47.703	1.826	3.33	2.53	.80
GOLF MAGAZINE	3.804	2.937	867	40.0	39.7	41.7	44.017	42.925	48.889	987	3.85	2.98	.88
GOOD HOUSEKEEPING	24.811	3.699	21.112	43.1	43.6	42.9	32.695	34.647	32.298	4.880	5.08	.76	4.33
GOURMET	2.850	741	2.109	43.0	41.2	43.9	47.023	50.198	45.833	767	3.72	.97	2.75
GQ (GENTLEMEN'S QUARTERLY)	4.369	3.185	1.184	26.1	26.3	25.7	37.190	38.196	33.278	633	6.90	5.03	1.87

great for the company that becomes the industry standard.

In addition to Media Metrix and Nielsen, other organizations offer audits and verifications of traffic at a particular website. The Audit Bureau of Circulations, for example, provides an ABC Interactive audit that assures that the data reported by the website's log is accurate and supports any claim of viewership made by the website owner.

Measuring the Effectiveness of Internet Advertising

As the Internet emerged as a new medium for advertising, many companies were interested in discovering how effective their ads were in generating interest and new business. The Internet offered a unique advantage over traditional media: the potential for directly measuring results. Advertisers have always had problems linking exposure to a given advertisement and a sale. With the Internet, however, things were different. In addition to simply viewing a banner ad on a website, consumers could also click on that ad and be given more specific information about a product and even buy it online. Not surprisingly, in addition to wanting to know how many times websites were visited, advertisers also wanted information about what viewers did when they were there.

The first type of measurement that was used was a behavioral one, the "click-through," that measured the number of times a visitor clicked on a banner ad at the site. In addition, advertisers could also track how many actual sales resulted from these click-throughs. For many years, this was the industry standard and everybody seemed pleased. In the mid-1990s click-through rates for some banner ads were around 30%. In the past few years, however, as the novelty of banner ads has worn off and as more and more banners clutter website pages, there has been a dramatic fall-off in click-through rates. A 2001 study revealed that the click-through rate had plummeted to only 0.3 percent (Green & Elgin, 2001).

In response, web advertising has shifted from the traditional banner ad to new forms. These included the *skyscraper ad* (tall and skinny ads at the right and left side of a website), *pop-up ads* (ads that appear when a webpage is opened and have to be closed in order to view the content underneath), and larger square and rectangular ads that appear at various places in the website. It is too early to determine if these innovations are more effective than the traditional banner ads.

Moreover, new methods of tracking have become available. DynamicLogic has designed a system whereby a "cookie" is placed on a viewer's computer that tracks where people visit in the days or weeks after seeing an ad. Another method involves randomly selecting visitors to a website who are then given the opportunity to take a brief online survey about what ads they saw.

Advertisers are also moving away from the behavioral measure, the click-through, to more cognitive and conative measures. Some companies aren't interested in selling their products online. Instead, they are using online advertising to build brand recognition. Many in the industry also realize that a person doesn't have to click on an ad for that ad to have an impact. Research firms are now reporting data about brand awareness, message recall, and brand attitude as well as purchasing interest.

Competitors' Activities

Advertisers like to know the media choices of their competitors. This information can help advertisers avoid making the mistakes of less successful competitors and to imitate the strategies of more successful competitors. In addition, advertisers seeking to promote a new product who know that the three leading competitors are using the same media mix might feel that their approach is valid (but this is not always true).

An advertiser can collect data on competitors' activity either by setting up a special research team or by subscribing to the services of a syndicated research company. Since the job of monitoring the media activity of a large number of firms advertising in several media is so difficult, most advertisers rely on a syndicated service. The companies gather data by direct observation—that is, by tabulating the advertisements that appear in a given medium. In addition to information about the frequency of advertisements, cost figures are helpful; these estimates are obtained from the published rate cards of the various media vehicles.

Advertisers also find it helpful to know what competitors are saying. To acquire this information, many advertising agencies conduct systematic content analyses of the messages in a sample of the competitors' advertisements. The results often provide insight into the persuasive themes, strategies, and goals of competitors' advertising. It is because of such studies that many commercials look and sound alike: Successful commercial approaches are often mimicked.

The most comprehensive information about advertisers' activities and expenditures is provided by Competitive Media Reporting (CMR). CMR tracks ad spending in 15 national consumer and business media. Its MultiMedia Service reports advertising expenditures in ten major media, including newspapers, magazines, television, and radio. CMR's Ad Spender reports on advertising expenditures for 100,000 major brands across all media for the past five years. CMR recently began reporting on advertising activity on the Internet through its CMRi division that measures online ad expenditures on the top 350 ad-supported websites.

▪ Campaign Assessment Research

Campaign assessment research builds on copy and media research, but its research strategies are generally different from those used in the other areas. In general, there are two kinds of assessment research. The *pretest/posttest method* takes measurements both before and after the campaign, and *tracking studies* assess the impact of the campaign by measuring effects at several times during the progress of the campaign.

The major advantage of a tracking study is that it provides important feedback to the advertiser while the campaign is still in progress. This feedback might lead to changes in the creative strategy or the media strategy. No matter what type of assessment research is chosen, one of the problems is deciding upon the dependent variable. The objective of the campaign should be spelled out before the campaign is executed so that assessment research is most useful. For example, if the objective of the campaign is to increase brand awareness, this measure should be the dependent variable rather than recall of ad content or actual sales increases. Schultz and Barnes (1994) list several campaign objectives that might be examined, including liking for the brand, ad recall, brand preference, and purchasing behavior.

Pretest/posttest studies typically use personal interviews to collect data. At times, the same people are interviewed before the campaign starts and again after its close (a panel study), or two groups are chosen and asked the same questions (a trend study; see Chapter 8). In any case, measures before and after the campaign are examined to gauge the effects of advertising. Winters (1983) reports several pretest/posttest studies done for a major oil company. In one study a pretest showed that about 80% of the sample agreed that a particular oil company made too much profit. Five months later a posttest revealed that the percentage had dropped slightly among those who had seen an oil company newspaper ad but had remained the same among those who had not seen the ad. Additionally, the study disclosed that people who saw both print ads and TV ads showed less attitude change than those who saw only the TV ads, suggesting that the print ad might have had a dampening effect.

Tracking studies also rely on personal or telephone interviews as their main data collection devices. Thomas (1997) notes that tracking studies can be continuous (a certain number of interviews are conducted every day or every week for a certain time period) or pulsed (the interviews are conducted in waves, perhaps every 3 or 6 months). Continuous tracking is more expensive but it smoothes out the effect of short-term factors, such as bad weather or bad publicity. Pulsed tracking can be timed to coincide with specific schedules of ads, thus offering a more precise before–after comparison.

For example, Block and Brezen (1990) analyzed a tracking study of 223 households over 88 weeks concerning their spaghetti sauce purchases. They discovered that brand loyalty was the most important variable in predicting buying behavior. More recently, Jones (1995) reported the results of an elaborate tracking study of the advertising and purchasing behavior of 2,000 homes and 142 brands over an entire year. The study found evidence of pronounced short-term effects of advertising, but long-term effects were more difficult to isolate. Browne (1997) described the tracking study done by Boston Market. The company began a new advertising push in 1996 and found that sandwich sales increased by 20%, but that did not help the company—it declared bankruptcy in mid-1998. A search of the Internet will reveal a large number of private research firms that offer advertising tracking studies.

Tracking studies are tremendously useful, but they are not without drawbacks. Perhaps the biggest problem is cost. Tracking studies typically require large samples; in fact, a sample of less than 1,500 cases per year is unusual. If a detailed analysis of subgroups is needed, the sample must be much larger. Furthermore, if the product is a national one, test markets across the country might be necessary to present a complete picture of the results. Finally, the use of sophisticated research methods, such as single-source data, makes the research even more expensive. For those who can afford it, however, the tracking study provides continuous measurement of the effects of a campaign and an opportunity to fine-tune the copy and the media schedule.

▪ A Final Note on Advertising Research

The perception of many people who are *outside* the advertising community is that all businesses and their advertising agencies use the latest and most effective forms of advertising; that print and electronic advertising is on the "cutting edge." With all due respect to advertising agencies and others involved in the development of advertising, this is not true. An example will help with this misperception.

When it comes to television viewing, it is common knowledge that about 75% of all TV viewers do not watch the TV screen all the time. (This has been documented in proprietary research by the senior author for more than 10 years.) Instead of constantly watching the TV screen, these people *listen* to TV while they participate in such other activities as reading, eating, playing with children, and so on. The people who simultaneously participate in two or more activities, such as TV viewing and reading, belong to a category known as **polychronic behavior.** In computer terms, they "multitask." The people who do not participate simultaneously in two or more activities belong to a category known as **monochromic behavior.** Monochronic people watch TV and do nothing else.

Now, since the majority of TV viewers are polychronic, it is scientifically logical that commercials should include both visual *and* audio information. Audio information does not mean music. It means spoken words. TV commercials that include visual information only (this includes commercials that have words that must be read) are a complete and total waste for as much as 75% of the audience. In other words, a polychronic viewer obtains no information from a visual-only commercial. This is demonstrated easily in tests of TV commercials where respondents are asked to rate commercials by looking away from the TV screen. When visual-only commercials are tested and the respondents are asked to rate the commercial or explain what information they obtained from it, the answer to both questions is always, "I don't know."

Therefore, it is clear from the countless number of visual-only commercials on

American television that advertising experts do not incorporate "cutting edge" research into the development of commercials. Instead, advertising agencies create commercials for other reasons—to win awards, to be considered "artistic," or to mimic other advertising agencies. There is no concern about the success of the ad in relation to its ability to communicate a message to the audience. Many advertisers waste a lot of money.

For more information about this topic, see Wimmer (2000).

▪ ▪ ▪ Summary

The three main areas of advertising research are copy testing, media research, and campaign assessment research. Copy testing consists of studies that examine the advertisement or the commercial itself. The three main dimensions of impact examined by copy testing are cognitive (knowing), affective (feeling), and conative (doing). Media research helps determine which advertising vehicles are the most efficient and what type of media schedule will have the greatest impact. Campaign assessment studies examine the overall response of consumers to a complete campaign. The two main types of campaign assessment research are the pretest/posttest and the tracking study. Many private firms specialize in supplying copy, media, and assessment data to advertisers. A new area in advertising research involves measuring the impact of Internet advertising.

Key Terms

Aided recall
Applied research
Circulation
Copy testing
Forced exposure
Frequency
Gross rating points
Masked recall
Media efficiency
Monochronic behavior
Objective function
Polychronic behavior
Reach
Recall study
Recognition
Tracking study
Unaided recall

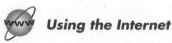

Using the Internet

Some of the more useful sites for information about advertising research are:

1. *www.arfsite.org* This is the site of the Advertising Research Foundation, an organization founded in 1936 whose members consist of advertisers, advertising agencies, research firms, media companies, and colleges. The site contains links to various advertising reports, the organization's newsletter, and award-winning ad campaigns.
2. *www.esomar.nl* ESOMAR is the World Association of Opinion and Marketing Research Professionals. The site contains a directory of companies across the globe that provide advertising research, links to codes of good conduct in advertising and marketing research, and recent news about advertising research.
3. *www.warc.com* The World Advertising Research Center maintains this site, which contains a huge amount of advertising data. This is a paid access site but you can sign up for a free trial.
4. *www.asiresearch.com* Ipsos-ASI bills itself as "The Advertising Research Company." Their site contains a description of the types of reports and other products that are available from a big research company. One link describes their ad tracking service.
5. *www.aef.com* The home of the Advertising Educational Foundation. Once registered on the site, visitors can read the online version of *Advertising & Society Review* that often contains articles about research.

Questions and Problems for Further Investigation

1. Suppose you have developed a new diet soft drink and are ready to market it. Develop a research study for identifying the elements and topics that should be stressed in your advertising.
2. A full-page advertisement costs $16,000 in Magazine A and $26,000 in Magazine B. Magazine A has a circulation of 100,000 and 2.5

readers per copy, whereas Magazine B has a circulation of 150,000 and 1.8 readers per copy. In terms of CPM readers, which magazine is the most efficient advertising vehicle?

3. Select a sample of newspaper and magazine advertisements for two airlines. Conduct a content analysis of the themes or major selling points in each advertisement. What similarities and differences are there?
4. If you are using InfoTrac College Edition, several articles are available that examine the copy testing issue. Do a title search using "copy testing" and read the most recent conclusions.

For additional information on these and related topics, see

http://www.wimmerdominick.com

References and Suggested Readings

Bates, N., & Buckley, S. K. (2000). Exposure to paid advertising and returning a census form. *Journal of Advertising Research,* 40(1/2), 65–73.

Beatty, S., & Hawkins, D. I. (1989). Subliminal stimulation: Some new data and interpretation. *Journal of Advertising,* 18(3), 4–8.

Block, M. P., & Brezen, T. S. (1990). Using database analysis to segment general media audiences. *Journal of Media Planning,* 5(4), 1–12.

Boyd, H. W., Westfall, R., & Stasch, S. F. (1989). *Marketing research: Text and cases* (7th ed.). Homewood, IL: Irwin.

Browne, A. (1997). Does your advertising work? *Colorado Business Magazine,* 24(5), 72–75.

Burton, S., Lictenstein, D. R. & Netemeyer, R. G. (1999). Exposure to sales flyers and increased purchases in retail supermarkets. *Journal of Advertising Research,* 39(5), 7–14.

Davis, J. J. (1997). *Advertising research.* Upper Saddle River, NJ: Prentice Hall.

Dunn, S. W., Barban, A. M., Krugman, D. K., & Reid, L. N. (1990). *Advertising: Its role in modern marketing.* Chicago: Dryden.

Fletcher, A., & Bowers, T. (1991). *Fundamentals of advertising research* (4th ed.). Belmont, CA: Wadsworth.

Green, H. (1998, April 27). The new web ratings game. *Business Week,* pp. 73–78.

Green, H., & Elgin, B. (2001, Jan. 22). Do e-adds have a future? *Business Week,* pp. EB46–51.

Green, P. E., Tull, D. S., & Albaum, G. (1988). *Research for marketing decisions.* Englewood Cliffs, NJ: Prentice-Hall.

Haley, R. (1994). A rejoinder to conclusions from the ARF's copy research validity project. *Journal of Advertising Research,* 34(3), 33–34.

Haley, R. I., & Baldinger, A. L. (1991, April/March). The ARF copy research validity project. *Journal of Advertising Research,* 31(2), 11–32.

Haskins, J. (1976). *An introduction to advertising research.* Knoxville, TN: Communication Research Center.

Haskins, J., & Kendrick, A. (1993). *Successful advertising research methods.* Lincolnwood, IL: NTC Business Books.

Hawkins, D. (1970). The effects of subliminal stimulation on drive level and brand preference. *Journal of Marketing Research,* 7(3), 322–326.

Hazlett, R. L. (1999). Emotional response to television commercials. *Journal of Advertising Research,* 39(2), 7–23.

Jacoby, J., & Hofer, W. D. (1982). Viewers' miscomprehension of televised communication. *Journal of Marketing,* 46(4), 12–27.

Jones, J. (1995). Single-source research begins to fulfill its promise. *Journal of Advertising Research,* 35(3), 9–11.

Katz, H. (1988). The role and function of media research at major U.S. advertising agencies. *Journal of Media Planning,* 3(2), 47–53.

Krugman, D., Fox, R., Fletcher, J., Fischer, P., & Rojas, T. (1994). Do adolescents attend to warnings in cigarette advertising? *Journal of Advertising Research,* 34(6), 39–52.

Lauzen, M. (1995). A comparison of issues managers' and PR educators' worldviews. *Journalism Educator,* 49(4), 36–46.

Leckenby, J. (1984). Current issues in the measurement of advertising effectiveness. Paper presented to the International Advertising Association, Tokyo, Japan.

Leckenby, J., & Wedding, N. (1982). *Advertising management.* Columbus, OH: Grid Publishing.

Lloyd, D. W., & Clancy, K. J. (1991, August/September). CPMs vs. CPMIs: Implications for media planning. *Journal of Advertising Research,* 34(4), 34–43.

McQuarrie, E. F. (1996). *The market research toolbox.* Thousand Oaks, CA: Sage Publications.

Mehta, A., & Purvis, S. C. (1997). Evaluating advertising effectiveness through advertising response modeling. In W. D. Wells (Ed.), *Measuring advertising effectiveness* (pp. 325–334). Mahwah, NJ: Lawrence Erlbaum.

Morton, L., & Warren, J. (1992/1993). Newspapers' art preferences from public relations sources. *Newspaper Research Journal,* 13/14(4/1), 121–129.

Percy, L., & Rossiter, J. R. (1997). A theory-based approach to pretesting advertising. In W. D. Wells (Ed.), *Measuring advertising effectiveness* (pp. 267–282). Mahwah, NJ: Lawrence Erlbaum.

Rossi, P., & Freeman, H. (1982). *Evaluation: A systematic approach.* Beverly Hills, CA: Sage Publications.

Rossiter, J., & Eagleson, G. (1994). Conclusions from the ARF's copy research validity project. *Journal of Advertising Research,* 34(3), 19–32.

Rust, R. T. (1986). *Advertising media models.* Lexington, MA: D. C. Heath.

Ryan, M., & Martinson, D. C. (1990). Social science research, professionalism and PR practitioners. *Journalism Quarterly,* 67(2), 377–390.

Schultz, D., & Barnes, B. (1994). *Strategic advertising campaigns.* Lincolnwood, IL: Business Books.

Sutherland, M., & Friedman, L. (2000). Do you model ad awareness or advertising awareness? *Journal of Advertising Research,* 40(5), 32–36.

Thomas, J. W. (1997). Tracking can determine if your advertising works. *Business First—Louisville,* 13(42), 38–41.

Walker, D., & Dubitsky, T. (1994). Why liking matters. *Journal of Advertising Research,* 34(3), 9–18.

Wimmer, R. D. (2000). Research in advertising. In Chakrapani, C. (Ed.) *Marketing research: State-of-the-art perspectives.* New York: American Marketing Association.

Winski, J. M. (1992, January 20). Who we are, how we live, what we think. *Advertising Age,* pp. 16–20.

Winters, L. (1983). Comparing pretesting and posttesting of corporate advertising. *Journal of Advertising Research,* 23(1), 33–38.

Zufryden, F. S. (2000). Predicting trial, repeat and sales response from alternative media plans. *Journal of Advertising Research,* 40(6), 65–73.

Chapter 16

Research in Public Relations

(The authors would like to acknowledge the assistance of Dr. Lynne Sallot in preparing this chapter.)

Much like advertising, public relations has become more research-oriented in recent years. As a leading text points out (Baskin, Aronoff, & Lattimore, 1997, p. 107):

> Research is a vital function in the process of public relations. It provides the initial information necessary to plan public relations action and to evaluate its effectiveness. Management demands hard facts, not intuition or guesswork.

The trend toward research is evident from many sources. A study by Lindenmann (1990) found that 75% of public relations practitioners agreed that research was an integral part of the public relations process. Wiesendanger (1994) reported that of the 80 projects completed in 1993 by Ketchum Public Relations, 57% pertained specifically to public relations evaluation research, up from 24% in 1988. Hon (1998) reported that most of the public relations practitioners she interviewed favored more systematic public relations research. Finally, the downturn in the U.S. economy at the beginning of the new century prompted a new era of accountability in public relations that will make research much more important.

Traditional research techniques are widely used in the field. An analysis of the empirical studies reported in the 1998, 1999, and 2000 issues of the *Journal of Public Relations Research,* an academic journal, disclosed that qualitative methods were used in 44% of the studies, with intensive interviewing and case studies the most popular approaches. Of the 56% that used quantitative methods, survey research was by far the most popular method. As for private-sector research, a survey done by the industry newsletter *pr reporter* found that focus groups, surveys, and personal interviews were the three most frequently used techniques in 1993 (Wiesendanger, 1994). A recent survey of small and medium-size public relations firms found that content analysis, focus groups, in-depth interviews, and surveys were used the most (McCleneghan, 2000). However, public relations researchers use these methods for a highly specific reason: to improve communication with various publics.

Types of Public Relations Research

Pavlik (1987) defined three major types of public relations research: applied, basic, and introspective. **Applied research** examines specific practical issues; in many instances, it is conducted to solve a specific problem. A branch of applied research, **strategic research,** is used to develop public relations campaigns and programs. According to Broom and Dozier (1990), strategic research is "deciding where you want to be in the future . . . and how to get there." A second branch, **evaluation research,** is conducted to assess the effectiveness of a public relations program and is discussed in more detail later.

Basic research in public relations creates knowledge that cuts across public relations situations. It is most interested in examining the underlying processes and in constructing theories that explain the public relations

AN INSIDE LOOK

Public Relations Research Methods: A Brief Overview

Public relations researchers use a wide variety of research techniques. An examination of the 1998–2000 issues of the *Journal of Public Relations Research* found 31 articles that used 41 different empirical research methods. Quantitative studies were used 56% of the time, while qualitative methods were used 44% of the time. Five studies used both techniques. The survey was by far the most popular quantitative technique, used in 70% of the studies. The mail survey was the most used data collection method. Experiments ranked second, followed by content analysis. The two most popular qualitative techniques were intensive interviewing and case studies.

The introspective nature of the field is highlighted by the fact that about 42% of the studies focused on the attitudes, perceptions, and behaviors of public relations practitioners. They may not be at the top of the list but public relations professionals must rank among the most studied group of people in existence.

process. For example, Moffitt (1994) examined the utility of collapsing the concepts of "public" and "image" into a new theory. Woodward (2000) offered a theoretical model based on transactional philosophy that could be used in public relations operations. Finally, Bruning and Ledingham (1999) developed a scale to measure the underlying relationships between organizations and their publics.

The third major type of public relations research is **introspective research,** which examines the field of public relations. Of all the media professions discussed in this book, public relations tends to be the most self-analytical. To illustrate, Neupauer (1998) examined the percentages of women in the sports information field. Moss, Warnaby, and Newman (2000) surveyed public relations professionals across a number of specialty areas to determine how practitioners were involved in strategic management. Berkowitz and Hristodoulakis (1999) surveyed members of the Public Relations Student Society of America and professionals in the Public Relations Society of America concerning their opinions of the proper roles of public relations practitioners.

▪ Research in the Public Relations Process

Perhaps a more helpful way to organize public relations research is to examine the various ways research is used in the public relations process. A leading public relations textbook (Cutlip, Center, & Broom, 1994) presents a four-step model of the public relations process:

1. Defining public relations problems.
2. Planning public relations programs.
3. Implementing public relations programs through actions and communications.
4. Evaluating the program.

The rest of this chapter uses this model to organize the various forms of public relations research.

Defining public relations problems

The first phase in the process consists of gathering information that helps define and anticipate possible public relations problems. Several techniques are useful at this stage: environmental monitoring (also called boundary scanning), public relations audits, communications audits, and social audits.

Environmental Monitoring Programs. Researchers use **environmental monitoring programs** to observe trends in public opinion and social events that may have a significant impact on an organization. Generally, two phases are involved. The "early warning" phase, an attempt to identify emerging issues, often takes the form of a systematic content analysis of publications likely to signal new developments. For example, one corporation may conduct a content analysis of scholarly journals in the fields of economics, politics, and science; another company may sponsor a continuing analysis of trade and general newspapers. Gregory (2001) presents a typology of monitoring that divides the environment into four sectors: political, economic, social, and lifestyles. Gronstedt (1999) describes the "SWOT" technique of analyzing a company's *strengths* and *weaknesses* in meeting the *opportunities* and *threats* in the external environment. An alternative method is to perform panel studies of community leaders or other influential and knowledgeable citizens. These people are surveyed regularly about the ideas they perceive to be important, and the interviews are analyzed to identify new topics of interest.

Brody and Stone (1989) list other forms of monitoring. One technique is to have the monitors look for a **trigger event,** which is an event or activity that might focus public concern on a topic or issue. For example, the Exxon oil spill in Alaska brought heavy visibility to environmental concerns, and the Columbine High School tragedy sparked interest in school safety and teenage alienation. However, there is no scientific way to determine what is or what may become a trigger event. Monitors are left to trust their instincts and judgment. Dyer (1996) presented a conceptual model of environmental monitoring that takes into account the salience of the issue, the type of media coverage, and the amount of coverage. Models such as this are useful to practitioners in structuring their monitoring.

The technique of precursor analysis is similar to trigger events analysis. **Precursor analysis** assumes that leaders establish trends that ultimately trickle down to the rest of society. For example, Japanese businesses tend to lead in innovative management techniques, many of which have caught on in the United States. At home, California tends to be a leader in insurance concerns and Florida in health issues. Monitors are instructed to pay particular attention to developments in these states.

The second phase of environmental monitoring consists of tracking public opinion on major issues. Typically, this involves either a longitudinal panel study, in which the same respondents are interviewed several times during a specified interval, or a cross-sectional opinion poll, in which a random sample is surveyed only once. To illustrate, since 1959 the Roper organization has surveyed public attitudes about media credibility. AT&T, General Electric, General Motors, and the Dow Chemical Company have also conducted elaborate tracking studies. DDB Needham reported the latest installment of its 16-year trend study of American lifestyles (Winski, 1992). Their data failed to support the popular idea that Americans were returning to traditional family values. The American Council on Life Insurance conducts a program called Monitoring the Attitudes of the Public. This continuing nationwide study examines enduring consumer attitudes that affect the life insurance industry and looks at such things as the image of life insurers and how the public perceives the value of the life insurance product.

An **omnibus survey** is a regularly scheduled personal interview, with questions provided by various clients. Survey questions might ask about a variety of topics, ranging from political opinions to basic market research information. For example, the Opinion Research Corporation sponsors CARAVAN, a twice-weekly national telephone omnibus consumer survey of public opinion.

Public relations professionals who specialize in political campaigns make extensive use of public opinion surveys. Some of the polling techniques used include:

- Baseline polling. An analysis of the current trends in public opinion in a given state or community that could be helpful for a candidate.
- Threshold polling. Surveys that attempt to assess public approval of changes in services, taxation, fees, etc. Such a poll can be used to establish positions on various issues.
- Tracking polls. Polls that take place after a baseline poll and that are used to look at trends over time.

Online databases have made monitoring studies more efficient. Hauss (1995) describes how the new online technologies can be used to track news events. Moreover, several commercial firms provide Internet monitoring services. *i-clip,* for example, tracks publicity about a company or product on thousands of news and information sites, discussion groups, and on other areas of the Web. The company's report is a web page itself, with links to all the relevant sites mentioned. Additionally, public relations firms are using online surveys and online focus groups to gather data (Johnson, 1997). *Pollingreport.com* contains a large database of public opinion polls on topics ranging from politics to the economy.

Public Relations Audits. The **public relations audit,** as the name suggests, is a comprehensive study of the public relations position of an organization. Such studies are used to measure a company's standing both internally (employee perceptions) and externally (opinions of customers, stockholders, community leaders, and so on). In short, as summarized by Simon (1986, p. 150), the public relations audit is a "research tool used specifically to describe, measure, and assess an organization's public relations activities and to provide guidelines for future public relations programming."

The first step in a public relations audit is to list the segments of both internal and external groups that are most important to the organization. This phase has also been called *identifying the key stakeholders in the organization.* These might include customers, employees, investors, regulators, and the public. This stakeholder analysis is usually conducted via personal interviews with key management in each department and by a content analysis of the company's external communications. The second step is to determine how the organization is viewed by each of these audiences. This involves conducting a corporate image study—that is, a survey of audience samples. The questions are designed to measure familiarity with the organization (Can the respondents recognize the company logo? Identify a product it manufactures? Remember the president's name?) as well as attitudes and perceptions toward it.

Ratings scales are often used. For example, respondents might be asked to rank their perceptions of the ideal electric company on a seven-point scale for a series of adjective pairs, as shown in Figure 16.1. Later the respondents would rate a specific electric company on the same scale. The average score for each item would be tabulated and the means connected by a zigzag line to form a composite profile. Thus, in Figure 16.2, the ideal electric company's profile is represented by a broken line and the actual electric company's standing by a solid line. By comparing the two lines, public relations researchers can

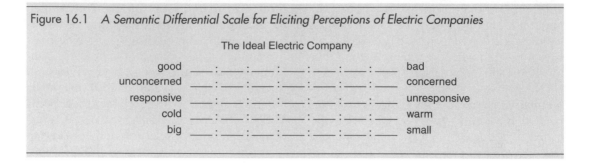

Figure 16.1 *A Semantic Differential Scale for Eliciting Perceptions of Electric Companies*

The Ideal Electric Company

good	___	___	___	___	___	___	___	bad
unconcerned	___	___	___	___	___	___	___	concerned
responsive	___	___	___	___	___	___	___	unresponsive
cold	___	___	___	___	___	___	___	warm
big	___	___	___	___	___	___	___	small

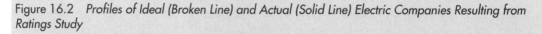

Figure 16.2 *Profiles of Ideal (Broken Line) and Actual (Solid Line) Electric Companies Resulting from Ratings Study*

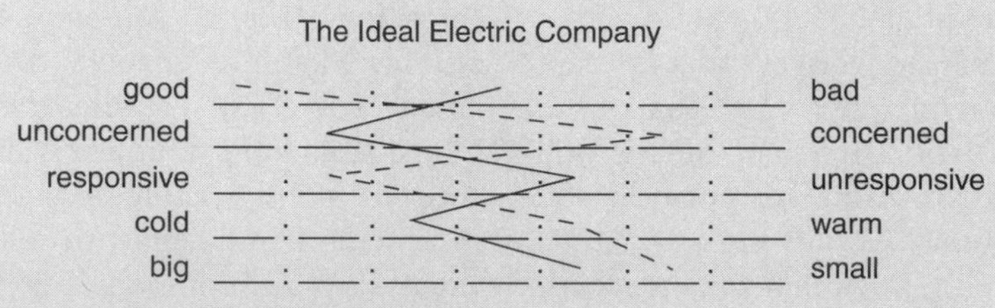

readily identify the areas in which a company falls short of the ideal. Corporate image studies can be conducted before the beginning of a public relations campaign and again at the conclusion of the campaign to evaluate its effectiveness. An example of a public relations audit is described in Croft (1996).

Communication Audits. The **communication audit** resembles a public relations audit but has narrower goals; it concerns the internal and external means of communication used by an organization rather than the company's entire public relations program. The two research techniques generally used in conducting such an audit are readership surveys and readability studies. Readership studies are designed to measure how many people read certain publications (such as employee newsletters or annual reports) and remember the messages they contain. The results are used to improve the content, appearance, and method of distribution of the publications. Sparks (1997), for example, measured the attitudes of employees and retirees of a large public utility toward its newsletter. She found several areas where readers thought the publication might improve. Readability studies help a company gauge the ease with which its employee publications and press releases can be read. An internal audit would also include an analysis of channels of communication within the organization.

Social Audits. A **social audit** is a small-scale environmental monitoring program designed to measure an organization's social performance—that is, how well it is living up to its public responsibilities. The audit provides feedback on company-sponsored social action programs such as minority hiring, environmental cleanup, and employee safety.

AN INSIDE LOOK

Analyzing Annual Reports

The top management of most publicly owned companies is very interested in how their company's annual report is received. It is not unusual for a company to spend $50,000 or more to analyze its annual report.

Social audits are the newest form of public relations research and the most challenging.

Researchers are currently studying such questions as which activities to audit, how to collect data, and how to measure the effects of the programs. Nevertheless, several large companies, including General Motors and Celanese, have already conducted lengthy social audits. When the Unilever company acquired Ben & Jerry's ice cream in 2000, Unilever agreed to conduct a social audit so that the company would continue to carry out the original social missions of Ben & Jerry's.

Planning Public Relations Programs

After gathering the information from the various methods of environmental scanning, the next step in the process is to interpret the information to identify specific problems and opportunities that can be addressed by a systematic public relations program. For example, the results of the public relations audit can be used to identify the needs of each of the key stakeholder groups and construct behavioral objectives that can be achieved with each group. A behavioral objective concerning customers might be to take occasional users of the product and turn them in to loyal users. Among investors, the goal might be to increase stock purchases by small investors.

To cite a specific instance, Moss (1990) reports the case of the United Kingdom's Prudential Corporation. Research uncovered that the company was perceived as "convenient" but also as "big," "lumbering," and "old-fashioned." As a result, a new corporate identity program was launched to attempt to change these perceptions.

To take a more recent example, environmental monitoring by the U.S. Army turned up the fact that recruitment numbers were down and young people were voicing negative attitudes about the military. The army asked a public relations agency to plan a program to increase recruitment. As a first step, the agency needed to find out what sorts of specific public relations problems the Army faced. Surveys and focus group research uncovered the fact that young people valued such qualities as independence and individualism, things they thought lacking in a military career. In fact, the Army was viewed as authoritarian and repressive. The image of the Army among 17- to 20-year-olds was one of screaming generals, pushups, and no respect.

Using this knowledge, the agency designed a new marketing and public relations program. The new program dropped the old "Be All You Can Be" slogan and replaced it with a new tag line—"An Army of One"—that emphasized individuality. The agency pilot tested a number of variations and executions of this theme. Approaches that did not reflect their target group were scrapped. Eventually, an acceptable program was launched. Measurable goals included increasing recruitment, increasing the number of hits on *goarmy.com*, and an increased number of calls to the Army's 800 number. Although too early for a definitive conclusion, the new program did increase hits to the Army's website by 30% (How research helps, 2001).

Additionally, the qualitative techniques discussed in Chapter 5 can also be used in the planning phase. For example, State Farm Insurance conducts a campaign in which the company tries to identify the ten most hazardous intersections in the United States. In an attempt to find a name for the campaign that would resonate with consumers, the company conducted a number of focus groups to try to identify which word would embody the essence of the campaign. Several adjectives were discussed, including "deadly," "crash-prone," and "hazardous," but most focus group participants thought that "dangerous" was the most appropriate. As a result, State Farm labeled its campaign "The Ten Most Dangerous Intersections." In addition, researchers also conducted intensive interviews with local officials in those communities with the dangerous intersections to see how they would react to being named in the "Ten Most Dangerous" list. The results of the interviews suggested that most public officials would welcome the publicity because they felt it might help them fix the problem and that State Farm would experience no significant public relations problems as a result of the campaign (Russell, 2000).

The planning phase also involves research that attempts to determine the most effective media for delivering the program. At its most basic level, this research entails finding the reach, frequency, and demographic characteristics of the audiences for the various mass and specialized communication media.

A second type of media research is the **media audit.** A media audit is a survey of reporters, editors, and other media personnel that asks about their preferences for stories and how they perceive the public relations agency's clients. Most media audit surveys contact about 50 to 75 media professionals. (Media audits, 2000). For example, the public relations division at a leading telecommunications market research company conducted a media audit with reporters at 16 trade publications. The survey revealed that the reporters had little knowledge about the firm or understanding about what it did. Other questions asked what kinds of information the reporters would most like to receive from companies. Responses revealed that case studies were the preferred format. As a result, the company changed its public relations approach and was able to place stories in trade and national publications such as *USA Today.* (Score big hits, 2001). Media audits can also target certain influential journalists. Theaker (2001) reports a case study concerning a British financial organization, the Bristol & West Building Society. Public relations researchers prepared a profile of a prominent journalist who frequently wrote about mortgages and financial markets. Using content analysis, the researchers compiled a list of topics that the journalist most often covered. On the basis of this analysis, the company was able to focus its press release approach on this reporter. Tailoring press releases about their products to match the journalist's favorite topics allowed the company to have more success in getting its message out.

Implementing Public Relations Programs

The most common type of research during the implementation phase consists of monitoring the efforts of the public relations program. Two of the most frequently used monitoring techniques are **gatekeeping research** and **output analysis.**

Gatekeeping Research. A gatekeeping study analyzes the characteristics of press releases and video news releases that allow them to "pass through the gate" and appear in a mass medium. Both content and style variables are typically examined. For example, Morton and Ramsey (1994) studied 129 national news releases carried over a public relations wire service and found that 22 were carried by newspapers and that releases dealing with financial matters were more likely to be used than those dealing with other topics. News releases with localized facts—that is, rewritten to be of interest to the paper where it is being sent—were more apt to be published than general releases (Morton & Warren, 1992). The same authors also examined which type of artwork newspaper gatekeepers preferred. They found that smaller-circulation newspapers favored hometown photos. Walters, Walters, and Starr (1994) examined the differences between the grammar and syntax of original news releases and published versions. They found that editors typically shorten the releases and make them easier to read before publication. In sum, it appears that a news release most likely to pass through the gate is one that is short, simply written, deals with localized financial matters, and is accompanied by a hometown photo. Gaschen (2001) surveyed TV stations about their use of VNRs (video news release) and found that those stations that used VNRs generally used some of the visuals that accompanied the story but seldom ran the entire package. Cameron, Sallot, and Curtin (1997) provide a summary of the research on source-reporter relations.

Output Analysis. Lindenmann (1997) defines outputs as the *short-term or immediate results of a particular public relations program or activity.* Output analysis measures how well the organization presents itself to others and the amount of exposure or attention that the organization receives. Several techniques can be used in output analysis. One way is to measure the total number of stories or articles that appear in selected mass media. In addition, it is also possible to gauge the tone of the article. A public relations campaign that results in a large number of stories that are negative about the organization is less useful than a campaign that results in positive coverage. It is also possible to measure non-media outputs such as speaking engagements, white papers, and the number of people attending special public relations events.

Lindenmann (1997) lists several types of specific output analysis. For example, traditional content analysis is used to determine the type of story that appeared in the media (news, feature, editorial, etc.); the source of the story that was used (press release, press conference, special event); degree of exposure (column inches in print media or number of minutes of air time in the electronic media); and topic variables such as what company officials were quoted, what issues were covered, how much coverage was given to competitors, etc. Additionally, content analysis is used to look at more subtle qualities. Public relations researchers can judge the tone of the article, whether it is positive, neutral, or negative; balanced or unbalanced; favorable or unfavorable. As Lindenmann points out, this type of analysis must be based on clearly defined criteria for assessing positives and negatives.

Not surprisingly, output analysis can also be extended to cyberspace. Analysis of how a company is described on various websites and in chat rooms, forums, and newsgroups can also offer clues about the effectiveness of a public relations campaign. The number of hits on a company website and the number of site visitors who requested additional information or filled out feedback forms can also be measured.

Non-media activities can also be studied with output analysis, such as the attendance at special events and trade shows. In addition, attendees can be analyzed according to the types of people who show up and their level of influence within the field. Researchers can also tabulate the number of promotional materials distributed and the number of interviews or speaking engagements generated by the event.

Another facet of output analysis is measuring the total number of impressions attributed to a public relations campaign. This measurement is determined by calculating the reach and frequency of the various media in which campaign-related stories appeared to determine the number of people who might have been exposed to the message. The reach of a print publication is usually based on its total audited circulation. For example, if an article related to a public relations campaign appeared in the *San Francisco Chronicle,* which has an audited circulation of about 500,000, that article generated 500,000 impressions or opportunities to see the story. If two stories appeared, that would create one million impressions. In addition, researchers can also determine how many of those impressions actually reached an organization's target group by examining detailed media audience data as compiled by firms such as Mediamark and Nielsen (see Chapter 14).

The problem with using impressions is that the researcher has to make several assumptions. For instance, it is assumed that all readers included in the circulation reports actually read the articles associated with the campaign and that everyone who visits the company web site has also read the item. In sum, the impressions method does not measure *actual exposure* to the message, but it does estimate the potential audience that might be reached.

Evaluation Research. Evaluation research refers to the process of judging the effectiveness of program planning, implementation, and impact. Baskin, Aronoff, and Lattimore (1997) suggest that evaluation should be involved in virtually every phase of a program. Specifically, they propose the following specific phases:

1. *Implementation checking:* This phase investigates whether the intended target audience is actually being reached by the message.
2. *In-progress monitoring:* Shortly after the campaign starts, researchers check to see if the program is having its intended effects. If there are unanticipated results or if results seem to be falling short of objectives, the program might still be modified.
3. *Outcome evaluation:* When the campaign is finished, the program's results are assessed. These findings are used to suggest changes for the future.

Broom and Dozier (1990) compare evaluation research to a field experiment (discussed in Chapter 5). The public relations campaign is similar to an experimental treatment and the target publics are similar to the subjects in the experiment. If possible, public relations researchers should try to construct control groups to isolate campaign effects from other spurious factors. The public relations researcher takes before-and-after measures and determines if any significant differences exist that can be attributed to the campaign. However, Broom and Dozier call attention to the fact that public relations campaigns occur in dynamic settings, and like most field experiments, it is difficult to control extraneous variables. As a result, it may not be scientifically possible to *prove* the program caused the results. But from a management standpoint, systematic evaluation research may still represent the best available evidence of program effectiveness.

Evaluation researchers are interested in the same three levels of effect that were mentioned in Chapter 15's discussion of copy research: cognitive, affective, and conative. At the cognitive level, researchers attempt to find out how much people learned from the public relations campaign. At the affective level, measures of changes in attitudes, opinions, or perceptions are used frequently. Finally, behavioral change, at the conative level, is an important way to gauge public relations impact. Obviously, the techniques used in advertising campaign effectiveness studies—pretest/posttest and tracking studies—can be applied in measuring the impact dimension of public relations campaigns.

AN INSIDE LOOK
Positive Perceptions

Although public relations studies may show that consumers perceive a company in a positive way, it does not mean that those same consumers will buy products or services from the company. For example, while Sears may be perceived positively, many people may not shop at Sears because they have a difficult time finding a salesperson in the store to help them.

Public relations researchers should be aware of some common mistakes that can affect evaluation research. Baskin, Aronoff, and Lattimore (1997) caution against the following:

1. Confusing volume with results. This is a case of confusing output research with outcome research. A huge pile of press clippings may document effort, but the pile does not document that the clippings had an effect.
2. Substituting estimation for measurement. Public relations practitioners should not substitute intuition or approximations for objective measurement—guesswork has no place in evaluation research (or any research).
3. Using unrepresentative samples. Analyzing only volunteer or convenience samples may lead to errors.
4. Confounding knowledge and attitudes. It is possible that a public might have gained more knowledge as the result of a public relations campaign, but this increased knowledge does not necessarily mean that attitudes have been positively influenced.
5. Confusing attitudes with behavior. Similar to item 4, it is incorrect to assume that favorable attitudes will result in favorable behavior.

Benchmarking is a method to assess an impact that is gaining popularity. A benchmark is a standard of comparison used by a company to track its public relations progress; research is conducted before the campaign to establish the standards of comparison. Other ways to establish a benchmark might include examining existing data to find industry averages and looking at past performance numbers.

For example, Lindenmann (1988) discusses several examples of evaluation research used by corporations. The Aetna Life and Casualty Company has used before-and-after polling during the last few years as part of a campaign to introduce a long-term health care plan for elderly Americans. The company's precampaign polling revealed that a large majority of Americans incorrectly believed that Medicare coverage routinely extended to nursing home stays. After a communication campaign, the company's polls found that more people were aware of Medicare's limitations than had been before. Similarly, Sears, Roebuck and Co. recently scored a public relations victory by placing a positive story about the company on "The Oprah Winfrey Show." The story described Sears' donation of $20,000 worth of Christmas gifts to several needy families. With help from a public relations research firm, Sears collected benchmark data before the program aired. They collected similar data from *Oprah* viewers after the show aired. Their results showed that agreement with the statement "Sears is a quality company" increased from 58% to 65% and that those who expressed their intent to shop at Sears increased from 59% to 70%.

Gronstedt (1999) describes a continuing benchmarking study done by a top European design firm. The company annually surveys its employees with questions such as "My job makes good use of my abilities," and "There are sufficient opportunities for me to improve my skills in my current job." Employee responses are then compared to a benchmark average calculated from a large-scale survey given other employees in more than 40 countries.

▪ ▪ ▪ Summary

Research in public relations takes place at all phases of the public relations process. Research such as environmental monitoring, public relations audits, communication audits, and social audits are used to define problems. During the planning stage, quantitative and qualitative techniques are used to test various public relations strategies, and media audits are done to identify the most effective media for a campaign. Gatekeeping research and output analysis are done during the program implementation phase. Finally, evaluation research is done both during and after a campaign to assess whether the stated goals were achieved. Benchmarking is a method of evaluation research that is gaining popularity.

Key Terms

Applied research	Media audit
Basic research	Omnibus survey
Benchmarking	Output analysis
Communication audit	Precursor analysis
Environmental monitoring	Public relations audit
Evaluation research	Social audit
Gatekeeping research	Strategic research
Introspective research	Trigger event

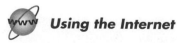

Using the Internet

There are several websites that contain useful information about public relations research.

1. *www.pollingreport.com.* Calling itself "an independent, non-partisan resource on trends in American public opinion," this site contains mountains of data about public opinion.
2. *www.silveranvil.org.* The Silver Anvil is to public relations campaigns what the Emmy is to TV programs. The site has an archive of past winning campaigns. Visitors can learn how research played a role in the way the campaign was planned, executed, and evaluated.
3. *www.prsa.org.* This is the home of the Public Relations Society of America. The site contains a Professional Resource Center that is helpful for researchers.
4. *www.instituteforpr.com.* The Institute for Public Relations is an independent foundation whose main concerns are research and education. Several articles directly related to public relations research are available on this site.

Questions and Problems for Further Investigation

1. Assume you are the public relations director for a large auto company. How would you go about conducting an environmental monitoring study?
2. How would you assess the effectiveness of a public relations campaign designed to encourage people to conserve water?
3. What is the difference between an output measure and an outcome measure?
4. What factors might account for the relatively large numbers of introspective studies done in the public relations field?

For additional information on these and related topics, see

http://www.wimmerdominick.com

References and Suggested Readings

Baskin, O., Aronoff, C., & Lattimore, D. (1997). *Public relations: The profession and the practice.* New York: Irwin/McGraw-Hill.

Berkowitz, D., & Hristodoulakis, I. (1999). Practitioner roles, public relations education and professional socialization. *Journal of Public Relations Research,* 11(1), 91–103.

Brody, E. W., & Stone, G. C. (1989). *Public relations research.* New York: Praeger.

Broom, G. M., & Dozier, D. M. (1990). *Using research in public relations.* Englewood Cliffs, NJ: Prentice-Hall.

Bruning, S. D., & Ledingham, J. A. (1999). Relationships between organizations and publics. *Public Relations Review,* 25(2), 157–170.

Cameron, G. J., Sallot, L., & Curtin, P. (1997). Public relations and the production of news. In B. Burleson (Ed.), *Communication Yearbook 20,* (pp. 111–155). Thousand Oaks, CA: Sage Publications.

Croft, A. C. (1996). Look in the mirror with a public relations agency performance audit. *Public Relations Quarterly,* 42(2), 6–10.

Cutlip, S., Center, A., & Broom, G. (1994). *Effective public relations* (7th ed.). Englewood Cliffs, NJ: Prentice-Hall.

Dyer, D. S. (1996). Descriptive model for public relations scanning. *Journal of Public Relations Research,* 8(3), 137–150.

Gaschen, D. (June, 2001). What TV stations really think about VNRs. *Public Relations Tactics,* p. 10.

Gregory, A. (2001). Public relations and management. In A. Theaker (Ed.), *The public relations handbook* (pp. 35–51), London: Routledge.

Gronstedt, A. (1999). The role of research in public relations strategy and planning. Internet document found at *http://courses.smsu.edu/scd950f/powerpoint/med-510/caywood-3.pdf.*

Hauss, D. (1995, May). Technology gives early warning on news breaks. *Public Relations Journal,* pp. 18–22.

Hon, L. C. (1998). Demonstrating effectiveness in public relations. *Journal of Public Relations Research,* 10(2), 103–136.

How research helps the Army be all it can be. (2001) *Ragan's PR Intelligence,* p. 1.

Johnson, M. A. (1997). Public relations and technology. *Journal of Public Relations Research,* 9(3), 213–236.

Lindenmann, W. K. (1988). Beyond the clipbook. *Public Relations Journal,* 44(12), 22–26.

Lindenmann, W. K. (1990). Research, evaluation and measurement: A national perspective. *Public Relations Review,* 16(2), 8–16.

Lindenmann, W. (1997). *Guidelines and standards for measuring and evaluating PR effectiveness.* Gainesville, FL: The Institute for Public Relations.

McCleneghan, S. (2000). CEOs and research at small-to-medium PR firms in selected Western States. *Public Relations Quarterly,* 45(2), 31–34.

Media audits are a growing trend. (5 June, 2000). *Media Relations Report,* p. 1.

Moffitt, M. (1994). Collapsing and integrating concepts of public and image into a new theory. *Public Relations Review,* 20(2), 155–170.

Morton, L., & Ramsey, S. (1994). A benchmark study of the PR news wire. *Public Relations Review,* 20(2), 171–182.

Morton, L., & Warren, J. (1992). Proximity: Localization vs. distance in PR news releases. *Journalism Quarterly,* 69(4), 1023–1028.

Moss, D. (1990). *Public relations in practice.* London: Routledge.

Moss, D., Warnaby, G., & Newman, A. (2000). Public practitioners role enactment at the senior management level within U.K. companies. *Journal of Public Relations Research,* 12(4), 277–308.

Neupauer, N. C. (1998). Women in the male dominated world of sports information directing. *Public Relations Quarterly,* 43(1), 27–30.

Pavlik, J. V. (1987). *Public relations: What the research tells us.* Beverly Hills, CA: Sage Publications.

Pincus, J. D., Rayfield, R. E., & Cozzens, M. D. (1991). The chief executive officer: Internal communications role. In L. A. Grunig and J. E. Grunig (Eds.), *Public Relations Research Annual* (Vol. 3). Hillsdale, NJ: Lawrence Erlbaum.

Russell, F. (28 February, 2000). Dangerous intersections. *Marketing News,* 34(5), 18–19.

Score big hits with audits. (2001). *Ragan's PR Intelligence,* p. 2.

Simon, R. (1986). *Public relations: Concepts and practices.* Columbus, OH: Grid Publishing.

Sparks, S. D. (1997). Employee newsletter readability for a large public utility. *Public Relations Quarterly,* 42(3), 37–40.

Theaker, A. (2001). *The public relations handbook.* London: Routledge.

Walters, T., Walters, L., & Starr, D. (1994). After the highwayman: Syntax and successful placement of press releases in newspapers. *Public Relations Review,* 20(4), 345–356.

Wiesendanger, B. (1994, May). A research roundup. *Public Relations Journal,* pp. 22–24.

Winski, J. M. (1992, January 20). Who we are, how we live, what we think. *Advertising Age,* pp. 16–20.

Woodward, W. (2000). Transactional philosophy as a basis for dialog in public relations. *Journal of Public Relations Research,* 12(3), 255–275.

Chapter 17

Research in Media Effects

Chapters 14–16 focused on research conducted in a professional or industry setting; however, a great deal of mass media research is done at colleges and universities. As we mentioned in Chapter 1, there are several differences between research in the academic and the private sectors. To summarize briefly:

- Academic research tends to be more theoretical in nature; private sector research is generally more applied.
- The data used in academic research are public, whereas much industry research is based on proprietary data.
- Top management often determines private-sector research topics; academic researchers have more freedom in their choice of topics.
- Projects in private sector research usually cost more to conduct than do academic investigations.

The two research settings also have some common features:

- Many research techniques and approaches used in the private sector emerged from academic research.
- Industry and academic researchers use the same basic research methodologies and approaches.
- The goal of research is often the same in both settings—to explain and predict audience and consumer behavior.

This chapter describes some of the more popular types of research carried out by academic investigators and shows how this work relates to private-sector research.

Obviously, not every type of scholarly research used in colleges and universities can be covered in one chapter. What follows is not an exhaustive survey but rather an illustrative overview of the history, methods, and theoretical development of five research areas: antisocial and prosocial effects of specific media content, uses and gratifications, agenda setting by the media, cultivation of perceptions of social reality, and the social impact of the Internet. Readers who want a more comprehensive treatment of media effects research should consult Sparks (2002).

■ *Antisocial and Prosocial Effects of Media Content*

The antisocial effect of viewing television and motion pictures is one of the most heavily researched areas in all mass media studies. Comstock, Chaffee, and Katzman (1978) reported that empirical studies focusing on this topic outnumbered work in all other problem areas by four to one, and this emphasis is still apparent more than a decade later. Paik and Comstock (1994) reviewed the results of 217 such studies conducted between 1959 and 1990.

The impact of **prosocial** content is a newer area and grew out of the recognition that the same principles underlying the learning of antisocial activities ought to apply to more positive behavior. Applied and academic researchers share an interest in this area: All the major networks have sponsored such research, and the effects of antisocial and prosocial content have been popular topics on college and university campuses for the past 30 years. It is not surprising that there has been a certain amount of friction between academic researchers and industry executives.

History

Concern over the social impact of the mass media was evident as far back as the 1920s, when many critics charged that motion pictures had a negative influence on children. In 1928 the Motion Picture Research Council, with support from the Payne Fund, a private philanthropic organization, sponsored a series of 13 studies on the movies' influence on children. After examination of film content, information gain, attitude change, and influence on behavior, it was concluded that the movies were potent sources of information, attitudes, and behavior for children. Furthermore, many of the things that children learned had antisocial overtones. In the early 1950s, another medium, the comic book, was chastised for its alleged harmful effects (Wertham, 1954).

In 1960 Joseph Klapper (1960) summarized what was then known about the social impact of mass communication. In contrast to many researchers, Klapper downplayed the potential harmful effects of the media. He concluded that the media most often reinforced an individual's existing attitudes and predispositions. Klapper's viewpoint, which became known as the *minimal effects position,* was influential in the development of a theory of media effects.

In the late 1950s and early 1960s, concern over the antisocial impact of the media shifted to television. Experiments on college campuses by Bandura and Berkowitz (summarized in Comstock & Paik, 1991) showed that aggressive behavior could be learned by viewing violent media content and that a stimulation effect was more probable than a cathartic (or cleansing) effect. Senate subcommittees examined possible links between viewing violence on television and juvenile delinquency, and in 1965, one subcommittee concluded that televised crime and violence were related to antisocial behaviors among juvenile viewers.

The civil unrest and assassinations in the middle and late 1960s prompted the formation of the National Commission on the Causes and Prevention of Violencc, chaired by Milton Eisenhower. The staff report of the Eisenhower Commission, which concluded that television violence taught the viewer how to engage in violence, included a series of recommendations about reducing the impact of television violence.

The early 1970s saw extensive research on the social effects of the mass media. Just 3 years after the publication of the Eisenhower Commission report came the release of a multi-volume report sponsored by the Surgeon General's Scientific Advisory Committee on Television and Social Behavior (1972, p. 10). In *Television and Growing Up,* the committee cautiously summarized its research evidence:

> There is a convergence of fairly substantial evidence on short-run causation of aggression among children by viewing violence . . . and the much less certain evidence from field studies that . . . violence viewing precedes some long-run manifestation of aggressive behavior. This convergence . . . constitutes some preliminary evidence of a causal relationship.

The committee tempered this conclusion by noting that in accordance with the reinforcement notion, "any sequence by which viewing television violence causes aggressive behavior is most likely applicable only to some children who are predisposed in that direction" (p. 10).

At about the same time, the three television networks were sponsoring research in this area. CBS commissioned two studies: a field experiment that found no link between television viewing and subsequent imitation of antisocial behavior (Milgram & Shotland,

1973) and a longitudinal study in Great Britain that found an association between viewing violence on television and committing antisocial acts such as damaging property and hurting others (Belson, 1978). ABC sponsored a series of studies by two mental health consultants who concluded that television stimulated aggression to only a tiny extent in children (Heller & Polsky, 1976). NBC began a large-scale panel study, but results were not released until 1983. In addition to television violence, the potential antisocial impact of pornography was under scrutiny. The Commission on Obscenity and Pornography (1970), however, reported that such material was not a factor in determining antisocial behavior. The commission's conclusions were somewhat controversial in political circles, but in general they supported the findings of other researchers in human sexuality (Tan, 1986). Subsequent efforts in this area were directed primarily toward examining links between pornography and aggression.

Along with violence and pornography, the contrasting prosocial effect of television was investigated as well. One stimulus for this research was the success of the television series "Sesame Street." A substantial research effort went into the preparation and evaluation of these children's programs. It was found that the series was helpful in preparing young children for school but not very successful in narrowing the information gap between advantaged and disadvantaged children (Minton, 1975). Other studies by both academic researchers and industry researchers demonstrated the prosocial impact of other programs. For example, the series "Fat Albert and the Cosby Kids" was found to be helpful in teaching prosocial lessons to children (CBS Broadcast Group, 1974).

Studies of these topics continued between 1975 and 1985, although there were far fewer than in the early 1970s. An update to the 1972 Surgeon General's Report, issued in 1982, reflected a broader research focus than the original document; it incorporated investigations of socialization, mental health, and perceptions of social reality. Nonetheless, its conclusions were even stronger than those of its predecessor: "The consensus among most of the research community is that violence on television does lead to aggressive behavior" (National Institute of Mental Health, 1982, p. 8). Other researchers, notably Wurtzel and Lometti (1984) and Bear (1984), argued that the report did not support the conclusion of a causal relationship, whereas Chaffee (1984) and Murray (1984), among others, contended that the conclusions are valid.

Not long after the Surgeon General's report was updated, the results of the NBC panel study begun in the early 1970s were published (Milavsky, Kessler, Stipp, & Rubens, 1983). This panel study, which used state-of-the-art statistical analyses, found a nonsignificant relationship between viewing television violence during the early phases of the study and subsequent aggression. The NBC data have been reexamined by others, and at least one article suggests that the data from this survey do show a slight relationship between violence viewing and aggression among at least one demographic subgroup—middle-class girls (Cook, Kendzierski, & Thomas, 1983).

From 1985 to 2001, the controversy subsided, but this topic remained popular among academic researchers. Williams (1986) conducted an elaborate field experiment in three Canadian communities. One town was about to receive television for the first time, another received Canadian TV, and the third received both Canadian and U.S. programs. Two years later, Williams and her colleagues found that when compared to children in the other two communities, children in the town that had just received TV scored higher on measures of physical and verbal aggression.

Additional evidence on the topic of television and violence comes from a series of panel studies conducted by an international team of researchers (Huesmann & Eron, 1986). Data were gathered from young people in the United States, Finland, Australia, Israel, and Poland. Findings from the U.S. and Polish studies reached a similar conclusion: Early TV viewing was related to later aggression. The Finnish study found this relationship for boys but not for girls. The Israeli study found that TV viewing seemed to be related to aggression for children living in urban areas but not for those in rural areas. The Australian study failed to find a relationship. In all countries where a relationship between TV viewing and violence was found, the relationship was relatively weak. Rosenthal (1986), who concluded that even a weak relationship could have substantial social consequences, examined the practical implications of this weak relationship.

More recently, Congress passed the Telecommunications Act of 1996. Part of the act specified that newly manufactured TV sets had to contain a V-chip, a computer chip that allows parents to block out violent and other objectionable programming from their TV sets. The chip would work in concert with a ratings system developed by the industry. (Recent research suggests that the V-chip has been largely ignored by consumers. One study found that 53% of consumers who had recently purchased a new TV set were not even aware they had a V-chip. A Kaiser Family Foundation study discovered that only 17% of families were using the V-chip to screen programs.)

Another recent research area examined mediating effects on the viewing of TV violence. Nathanson (1999), for example, confirmed that parental mediation of TV viewing helped curtail the antisocial inclinations of their children. The same researcher (Nathanson, 2001) also examined the influence of peer mediation on antisocial TV viewing. She found that peer influence was more frequent and more potent than parental mediation and that it tended to promote a positive attitude toward antisocial TV.

The violence at Columbine High School in Littleton, CO, and in other high schools at the end of the century sparked renewed interest in media violence among parents and policy makers. Media leaders were called before a congressional committee investigating this topic. In 2001, the Surgeon General issued a report entitled *Youth Violence,* a document that included a study of the factors that contributed most to antisocial behavior among young people. The report concluded that media violence was less of a risk factor than family influences, peer group attitudes, socioeconomic status, and substance abuse (U.S. Department of Health and Human Services, 2001).

Despite this renewed interest, the number of research studies examining media violence has decreased in the last few years. *Communications Abstracts* lists a total of only 3 audience studies in 1999 and 2000 that addressed this topic.

The increasing popularity of video games during the early years of this decade opened up another avenue of inquiry for researchers. Since more than 90% of young people report that they sometimes play these games, and since some of the more popular games feature graphic and explicit violence, social concern over their impact was widespread. Results of some of the early studies in this area (for example, Silvern & Williamson, 1987) suggest that playing video games can lead to increased aggression levels in young children and is related to their self-concepts (Funk & Buchman, 1996). Research that is more recent has reinforced this conclusion. Anderson and Dill (2000) measured aggressive personality traits, recent delinquent behaviors, and video-game playing habits of 227 college students. Those who reported playing more violent video games in the past engaged in more aggressive behavior and had lower academic grades in college. Sherry (2001) conducted a meta-analysis on 20 studies that examined a possible link between video game playing and antisocial attitudes and behaviors. He concluded that, like the research results on exposure to TV violence and antisocial behavior, there was a weak but statistically significant link between playing violent video games and aggression.

Research interest in the antisocial effects of pornography increased in the late 1980s—averaging approximately 8 studies per year as listed in *Communication Abstracts*—but declined by the end of the century. Only one audience study about pornography was listed in the 1999 and 2000 editions of *Communication Abstracts*. The most controversial research in this area examined whether prolonged exposure to nonviolent pornography had any antisocial effects (Donnerstein, Linz, & Penrod, 1987; Zillmann & Bryant, 1989; Allen, D'Alessio, & Brezgel, 1995).

Research interest in the prosocial effects of media exposure decreased in the 1980s and mid-1990s. Sprafkin and Rubinstein (1979) reported on a correlational study in which the viewing of prosocial television programs accounted for only 1% of the variance in an index of prosocial behavior exhibited in school. The apparent lack of a strong relationship between these two variables, coupled with the absence of general agreement on a definition of *prosocial content*, might have discouraged researchers from selecting this area. In any case, an average of less than one study per year appears in the 1986–2000 editions of *Communication Abstracts*, and many of these are content analyses (for example, Potter & Ware, 1989).

Methods

Researchers who study the effects of mass media have used most of the techniques discussed in this book: content analysis, laboratory experiments, surveys, field experiments, observations, and panels. In addition, they have used some advanced techniques, such as meta-analysis, that have not been discussed. Given the variety of methods used, it is not possible to describe a typical approach. Instead, this section focuses on five different methods as illustrations of some research strategies.

The Experimental Method. A common design used to study the antisocial impact of the media is to show one group of subjects violent media content, while a control group sees nonviolent content. This was the approach used by Berkowitz and Bandura in their early work. The dependent variable, aggression, is measured immediately after exposure—either by a pencil-and-paper test or by a mechanical device like the one described below. For example, Liebert and Baron (1972) divided children into two groups. The first group saw a 3.5-minute segment from a television show depicting a chase, two fistfights, two shootings, and a knifing. Children in the control group saw a segment of similar length in which athletes competed in track and field events. After viewing, the children were taken one at a time into another room that contained an apparatus with two buttons, one labeled "Help" and the other labeled "Hurt." An experimenter explained to the children that wires from the device were connected to a game in an adjacent room. The subjects were told that in the adjacent room, another child was starting to play a game. (There was, in fact, no other child.) At various times, by pressing the appropriate buttons, each child was given a chance either to help the unseen child win the game or to hurt the child. The results showed that children who had seen the violent segment were significantly more likely than the control group to press the "Hurt" button. Of course, there are many variations on this basic design. For example, the type of violent content shown to the subjects can be manipulated (cartoon versus live violence, entertainment versus newscast violence, justified versus unjustified violence). Also, some subjects may be frustrated before exposure. The degree of association between the media violence and the subsequent testing situation may be high or low. Subjects can watch alone or with others who praise or condemn the media violence. Media exposure can be a one-time event, or it can be manipulated over time. For a thorough summary of this research, see Comstock and Paik (1991) and Liebert and Sprafkin (1992).

Experimental studies to examine the impact of media exposure on prosocial behavior have used essentially the same approach. Subjects see a televised segment that is either prosocial or neutral, and the dependent variable is then assessed. For example, Forge and Phemister (1987) randomly assigned preschoolers to one of four conditions: prosocial animated program ("The Get-along Gang"), neutral animated ("Alvin and the Chipmunks"), prosocial nonanimated ("Mr. Rogers' Neighborhood"), and neutral nonanimated ("Animal Express"). The children watched the program and were then placed in a free-play situation where their prosocial behaviors were observed and recorded. The results demonstrated an effect for the program variable (prosocial programs prompted more prosocial behaviors than did neutral programs) but no effect for the animated versus nonanimated variable.

The operational definitions of *prosocial behavior* have varied widely: Studies have examined cooperative behaviors, sharing, kindness, altruism, friendliness, creativity, and absence of stereotyping. Almost any behavior with a positive social value seems to be a candidate for study, as exemplified by the experiment by Baran, Chase, and Courtright (1979): Third-graders were assigned to one of three treatment conditions. One group saw a condensed version of a segment of "The Waltons" demonstrating cooperative behavior; the second group saw a program portraying noncooperative behavior; and the third group saw no program. After answering a few written questions dealing with the program, each subject left the viewing room only to encounter a confederate of the experimenter who passed the doorway and dropped an armload of books. There were two dependent measures: whether the subject attempted to retrieve the books, and how much time elapsed until the subject began to help. The group that saw the cooperative content was more likely to help, and their responses were quicker than those of the control group. It is interesting that there was no difference in helping behavior or in time elapsed between the group that saw "The Waltons" and the group that saw the noncooperative content.

The Survey Approach. Most survey studies have used questionnaires that incorporate measures of media exposure (such as viewing television violence or exposure to pornography) and a pencil-and-paper measure of antisocial behavior or attitudes. In addition, many recent studies have included measures of demographic and sociographic variables that mediate the exposure–antisocial behavior relationship. Results are usually expressed as a series of correlations.

A survey by McLeod, Atkin, and Chaffee (1972) illustrates this approach. Their questionnaire contained measures of violence viewing, aggression, and family environment. They tabulated viewing by giving respondents a list of 65 prime-time television programs with a scale measuring how often each was viewed. An index of overall violence viewing was obtained by using an independent rating of the violence level of each show and multiplying it by the frequency of viewing. Aggression was measured by seven scales. One measured respondents' approval of manifest physical aggression (sample item: "Whoever insults me or my family is looking for a fight"). Another examined approval of aggression ("It's all right to hurt an enemy if you are mad at him"). Respondents indicated their degree of agreement with each of the items on the separate scales. Family environment was measured by asking about parental control over television, parental emphasis on nonaggressive punishment (such as withdrawal of privileges), and other variables. The researchers found a moderate positive relationship between the respondents' level of violence viewing and their self-reports of aggression. Family environment showed no consistent association with either of the two variables.

Sprafkin and Rubinstein (1979) used the survey method to examine the relationship between television viewing and prosocial behavior. They used basically the same approach as McLeod, Atkin, and Chaffee (1972), except their viewing measure was designed to assess exposure to television programs established as prosocial by prior content analysis. Their measure of prosocial behaviors was based on peer nominations of persons who reflected 12 prosocial behaviors, including helping, sharing, following rules, staying out of fights, and being nice. The researchers found that when the influence of the child's gender, the parents' educational level, and the child's academic level were statistically controlled, exposure to prosocial television explained only 1% of the variance in prosocial behaviors.

Field Experiments. The imaginative and elaborate field work used to study the antisocial effects of the media by Milgram and Shotland (1973) was discussed in Chapter 9. Parke, Berkowitz, and Leyens (1977) conducted a field experiment in a minimum-security penal institution for juveniles. The researchers exposed groups to unedited feature-length films that were either aggressive or nonaggressive. On the day after the last film was shown, in the context of a bogus learning experiment, the boys were told they had a chance to hurt a confederate of the experimenters who had insulted one group of boys and had been neutral to the other. The results on an electric shock measure similar to the one used in the Liebert and Baroa (1972) study, described previously, revealed that the most aggressive of all the experimental groups were the boys who had seen the aggressive films and had been insulted. In addition to this laboratory measure, the investigators collected observational data on the boys' aggressive interpersonal behavior in their everyday environment. These data showed that boys who saw the violent movies were more interpersonally aggressive. However, there was no apparent cumulative effect of movies on aggression. The boys who watched the diet of aggressive films were just as aggressive after the first film as after the last.

Figure 9.11 (page 236) illustrates the design of the Canadian field experiment (Williams, 1986) discussed earlier. The dependent variable of aggression was measured in three ways: observations of behavior on school playgrounds, peer ratings, and teacher ratings. On the observational measure, the aggressive acts of children in the town labeled A (the town that just received TV) increased from an average of 0.43 per minute in Phase 1 to 1.1 per minute in Phase 2. Children in the other towns showed only a slight and statistically insignificant increase in the same period. Peer and teacher ratings tended to support the behavioral data. As yet, there have been no large-scale field experiments examining prosocial behavior.

Panel Studies. Primarily because of the time and expense involved in panel studies, this method is seldom used to examine the antisocial effects of the media. Three studies relevant to this topic are briefly reviewed here. Lefkowitz, Eron, Waldner, and Huesmann (1972), using a catch-up panel design, reinterviewed 427 of 875 youthful subjects 10 years after they had participated in a study of mental health. Measures of television viewing and aggression had been administered to these subjects when they were in the third grade, and data on the two variables were gathered again a decade later. Slightly different methods were used to measure television viewing on the two occasions. Viewing in the third grade was established on the basis of mothers' reports of their children's three favorite television shows. Ten years later, respondents rated their own frequency of viewing. The data were subjected to cross-lagged correlations and path analysis. The results supported the hypothesis that aggression in later life was caused in part by television viewing during early years. However, the panel study by Milavsky and colleagues (1983), sponsored by NBC, found no evidence of a relationship.

The difference between the results of these studies might be due to several factors. The Milavsky study did not vary its measure of "violent television viewing" throughout its duration. In addition, the NBC researchers used LISREL (linear structural equations), a more powerful statistical technique, which was not available at the time of the Lefkowitz study. Finally, the Lefkowitz measures were taken 10 years apart; the maximum time lag in the NBC study was 3 years.

Another panel study of the media and possible antisocial effects was conducted by Huesmann and Eron (1986). The investigators followed 758 children who were in the first and third grades in 1977 and reinterviewed them in 1978 and 1979. Aggression was measured by both peer nominations and self-ratings. Multiple regression analyses disclosed that, for both boys and girls, watching TV violence was a significant predictor of the aggression they would later demonstrate. Other significant variables were the degree to which children identified with violent TV characters, the perceived reality of the violence, and the amount of a child's aggressive fantasizing. More recently, Valkenburg and Van der Voort (1995) conducted a 1-year panel study that examined the influence of viewing TV violence on children's daydreaming. They found that exposure to violent programs stimulated an aggressive-heroic daydreaming style.

Meta-analysis. A complete description of the techniques of meta-analysis is beyond the scope of this book. For our purposes, **meta-analysis** is defined as the quantitative aggregation of many research findings and their interpretations. It allows researchers to draw general conclusions from an analysis of many studies that have been conducted concerning a definable research topic. Its goal is to provide a synthesis of an existing body of research. Given the large number of research studies that have been conducted concerning antisocial and prosocial behavior, it is not surprising that the mid- to late 1990s saw the growth in popularity of meta-analytic research in this area. Five examples of meta-analysis are mentioned next.

Paik and Comstock (1994) performed a meta-analysis on 217 studies from 1959 to 1990 that tested 1,142 hypotheses. They concluded that the magnitude of the impact of exposure to media violence varied with the method used to study it. Experiments produced the strongest effects, and time-series studies the weakest. Nonetheless, there was overall a highly significant positive association between exposures to portrayals of violence and antisocial behavior. In addition, they found that males were affected by exposure to media violence only slightly more than females and that violent cartoons and fantasy programs produced the greatest magnitude of effects. The latter finding is at odds with the conventional argument that cartoon violence does not affect viewers because it is unrealistic.

A second meta-analysis on the impact of exposure to pornography and subsequent aggressive behavior was done by Allen, D'Alessio, and Brezgel (1995). They analyzed the results of 30 studies and found that there was indeed a connection between exposure to pornography and subsequent antisocial behavior. More specifically, they noted that exposure to nudity actually decreased aggressive behavior. In contrast, consumption of material depicting nonviolent sexual activity increased aggressive behavior, while exposure to violent sexual activity generated the highest levels of aggression. These findings are in accord with those discussed by Paik and Comstock (1994). A meta-analysis of studies examining exposure to pornography and acceptance of rape myths (Allen, Emmers, Gebhardt, & Geiry, 1995) revealed that experimental studies showed a positive relationship between pornography and rape myth acceptance but nonexperimental studies displayed no such effects.

Friedlander (1993) reported the results of a meta-analysis that compared the magnitude of effects reported by studies that looked at antisocial behavior with those that examined prosocial behavior. He found that, with few exceptions, the effects found for prosocial media messages were larger than the effect found for antisocial messages. Finally, Hogben (1998) looked at the results of 56 analyses from 30 studies and concluded that viewing televised violence was associated with a small increase in viewer aggression. In addition, there was a correlation between the year a study was done and the effect size; the later the study, the greater the effect size, suggesting that prolonged exposure has a greater effect on viewers. Last, justified violence and violence that did not accurately portray the consequence of violence generated greater effect sizes.

Summary. Experiments and surveys have been the most popular research strategies used to study the impact of media on antisocial and prosocial behavior. The more elaborate techniques of field experiments and panel studies have been used infrequently. Laboratory experiments have shown a stronger positive relationship between viewing media violence and aggression than have the other techniques. Meta-analyses have offered general conclusions about the scope and magnitude of these effects.

Theoretical Developments

One of the earliest theoretical considerations in the debate on the impact of media violence was the controversy of catharsis versus stimulation. The **catharsis** approach suggests that viewing fantasy expressions of hostility reduces aggression because a person who watches filmed or televised violence is purged of his or her aggressive urges. This theory has some obvious attraction for industry executives because it implies that presenting violent television shows is a prosocial action. The **stimulation theory** argues the opposite: Viewing violence prompts more aggression on the part of the viewer. Research findings in this area have indicated little support for the catharsis position. A few studies did find a lessening of aggressive behavior after viewing violent content, but these results apparently were an artifact of the research design. The overwhelming majority of studies found evidence of a stimulation effect.

Since these early studies, many experiments and surveys have used social learning as their conceptual basis. As spelled out by Bandura (1977), the theory explains how people learn from direct experience or from observation (or modeling). Some key elements in this theory are attention, retention, motor reproduction, and motivations. According to Bandura, *attention* to an event is influenced by characteristics of the event and by characteristics of the observer. For example, repeated observation of an event by a person who has been paying close attention should increase learning. *Retention* refers to how well an individual remembers behaviors that have been observed. *Motor reproduction* is the actual behavioral enactment of the observed event. For example, some people can accurately imitate a behavior after merely observing it, but others need to experiment. The *motivational* component of the theory depends on the reinforcement or punishment that accompanies performance of the observed behavior.

Applied to the effects area, social learning theory predicts that people can learn antisocial or prosocial acts by watching films or television. The model further suggests that viewing repeated antisocial acts makes people more likely to perform these acts in real life. Another suggestion is that *desensitization* accounts for people who are heavily exposed to violence and antisocial acts becoming less anxious about the consequences.

Bandura (1977) summarized much of the research on social learning theory. In brief, some key findings in laboratory and field experiments suggest that children can easily perform new acts of aggression after a single exposure to them on television or in films. The similarity between the circumstances of the observed antisocial acts and the post-observation circumstances is important in determining whether the act is performed. If a model is positively reinforced for performing antisocial acts, the observed acts are performed more frequently in real life. Likewise, when children are promised rewards for performing antisocial acts, they exhibit more antisocial behavior. Other factors that facilitate the performance of antisocial acts include the degree to which the media behavior is perceived to be real, the emotional arousal of the subjects, and the presence of cues in the post-observation environment that elicit antisocial behavior. Finally, as predicted by the theory, desensitization to violence can occur through repeated exposure to violent acts.

Other research has continued to refine and reformulate some of the elements in social learning theory. For example, the *arousal hypothesis* (Tannenbaum & Zillmann, 1975) suggests that, for a portrayal to have a demonstrable effect, increased arousal may be necessary. According to this model, if an angered person is exposed to an arousing stimulus, such as a pornographic film, and is placed in a situation to which aggression is a possible response, the person will become more aggressive. (*Excitation transfer* is the term used by the researchers.)

Zillmann, Hoyt, and Day (1979) offer some support for this model. It appears that subjects in a high state of arousal after seeing a violent film will perform more prosocial acts than nonaroused subjects. Like aggressive behavior, prosocial behavior seems to be facilitated by media-induced arousal (Mueller, Donnerstein, & Hallam, 1983).

Other research has shown that social learning theory can be applied to the study of the effects of viewing pornography. Zillmann and Bryant (1982) showed that heavy exposure to pornographic films apparently desensitized subjects to the seriousness of rape and led to decreased compassion for women as rape victims. A similar finding was obtained by Linz, Donnerstein, and Penrod (1984). Men who viewed five movies depicting erotic situations involving violence toward women perceived the films as less violent and less degrading to women than did a control group not exposed to the films. In sum, social learning theory is a promising framework for integrating many findings in this area.

Another promising theory, outlined by Berkowitz and Rogers (1986), is based on priming effects analysis. Drawing upon the concepts of cognitive neo-associationism, *priming effects analysis* posits that elements of thought or feeling or memories are parts of a network connected by associative pathways. When a thought element is activated, the activation spreads along the pathways to other parts of the network. Thus, for some time after a concept is activated, there is an increased probability that it and other associated parts of the network will come to mind again, thus creating the priming effect. As a result, aggressive ideas prompted by viewing media violence trigger other semantically related thoughts, thereby increasing the probability that associated aggressive thoughts will come to mind. Berkowitz and Rogers note that priming analysis can explain why much exposure to media violence results in short-term, transient effects. They point out that the priming effect attenuates over time to lower the probability of subsequent violent effects.

Van Evra (1990) suggests that "script theory" might also be useful in explaining the impact of viewing TV violence. Since most viewers, particularly younger ones, have little real-life experience with violence but see a lot of it on TV, their behavior patterns or scripts might be influenced by the TV exposure. Those who watch a large amount of violent TV might store these scripts in their memory and display violence when an appropriate stimulus triggers the acting out of their scripts. Moreover, Huesmann and Eron (1986) argue that if a young child learns early in his or her developmental cycle that aggression is a potent problem-solving technique, that behavior will be hard to change because the script has been well rehearsed by the child.

Drawing upon the above information, Comstock and Paik (1991) proposed a three-factor explanation of the influence of media violence on antisocial and aggressive behavior:

1. Violent portrayals that are unique, compelling, and unusual are likely to prompt viewer aggression because of their high attention and arousal.
2. Social cognition theory suggests that repetitive and redundant portrayals of violence prompt viewers to develop expectations and perceptions of violence.
3. Violent media content encourages the early acquisition of stable and enduring traits. Some violent scripts may be learned by children who are only 3 or 4 years old.

More recently, Sander (1997) proposed a new theoretical approach, the dynamic transaction model, to explain how viewers perceive violence. The model posits that a person's reaction to media violence is a function of the precise form of the media stimulus and the interpretive ability of the receiver. A quasi-experimental study of viewers revealed that audience members and researchers perceive violence differently and that specific content variables (physical vs. psychological violence, serious vs. comic violence, real vs. fantasy violence, etc.) have the greatest influence on perceptions, followed by the emotional state of the receiver while watching violence. Krcmar's (1998) study suggested that family communication patterns are also important in determining how children perceive violence. These last two studies support the idea that perceptions of violence may be a key concept in formulating theories about the impact of this kind of material.

▪ Uses and Gratifications

The **uses and gratifications** perspective takes the view of the media consumer. It examines how people use the media and the gratifications they seek and receive from their media behaviors. Uses and gratifications researchers assume that audience members are aware of and can articulate their reasons for consuming various media content.

History

The uses and gratifications approach has its roots in the 1940s, when researchers became interested in why people engaged in various forms of media behavior, such as radio listening or newspaper reading. These early studies were primarily descriptive, seeking to classify the responses of audience members into meaningful categories. For example,

Herzog (1944) identified three types of gratification associated with listening to radio soap operas: emotional release, wishful thinking, and obtaining advice. Berelson (1949) took advantage of a New York newspaper strike to ask people why they read the paper. The responses fell into five major categories: reading for information, reading for social prestige, reading for escape, reading as a tool for daily living, and reading for a social context. These early studies had little theoretical coherence; in fact, many were inspired by the practical needs of newspaper publishers and radio broadcasters to know the motivations of their audience in order to serve them more efficiently. (Chapter 13 notes that the uses and gratifications approach is still one of the major types of research performed by those interested in understanding newspaper readership.)

The next step in the development of this research began during the late 1950s and continued into the 1960s. In this phase the emphasis was on identifying and operationalizing the many social and psychological variables that were presumed to be the antecedents of different patterns of consumption and gratification. For example, Schramm, Lyle, and Parker (1961), in their extensive study, found that children's use of television was influenced by individual mental ability and relationships with parents and peers, among other things. Gerson (1966) concluded that race was important in predicting how adolescents used the media. These studies and many more conducted during this period reflected a shift from the traditional effects model of mass media research to the functional perspective.

According to Windahl (1981), a primary difference between the traditional effects approach and the uses and gratifications approach is that a media effects researcher usually examines mass communication from the perspective of the communicator, whereas the uses and gratifications researcher uses the audience member as a point of departure. Windahl argues for a synthesis of the two approaches, believing that it is more beneficial to emphasize their similarities than to stress their differences. He has coined the term *conseffects* of media content and use to categorize observations that are partly results of content use in itself (a viewpoint commonly adopted by effects researchers) and partly results of content mediated by use (a viewpoint adopted by many uses and gratifications researchers).

Windahl's perspective links the earlier uses and gratifications approach to the third phase in its development. Recently, uses and gratifications research has become more conceptual and theoretical as investigators have offered data to explain the connections between audience motives, media gratifications, and outcomes. As Rubin (1985, p. 210) notes: "Several typologies of mass media motives and functions have been formulated to conceptualize the seeking of gratifications as variables that intervene before media effects." For example, Rubin (1979) found a significant positive correlation between the viewing of television to learn something and the perceived reality of television content: Those who used television as a learning device thought television content was more true to life. DeBock (1980) notes that people who experienced the most frustration at being deprived of a newspaper during a strike were those who used the newspaper for information and those who viewed newspaper reading as a ritual. These and many other recent studies have revealed that a variety of audience gratifications are related to a wide range of media effects. These "uses and effects" studies (Rubin, 1985) have bridged the gap between the traditional effects approach and the uses and gratifications perspective.

In the last few years the uses and gratifications approach has been used to explore the impact of new technologies on the audience.

For example, Lin (1993) posited that audience activity (planning viewing, discussing content, remembering the program) would be an important intervening variable in the gratification-seeking process because of the viewing options opened up by cable, VCRs, and remote controls. Her results supported her hypothesis. Viewers who were most active had a greater expectation of gratification and also reported obtaining greater satisfaction.

Albarran and Dimmick (1993) combined the uses and gratifications approach with niche theory in their study of the utility of the video entertainment industries. They found that broadcast TV was the most diverse in serving the cognitive gratifications of the audience, whereas cable TV and the VCR were the most effective in meeting needs related to feeling and emotional states.

The advent of the Internet has spurred a renaissance in uses and gratifications research as investigators describe Internet motivations and compare and contrast their results with the uses and gratifications from traditional media. To illustrate, Valkenburg and Soeters (2001) found that Internet use among their sample of 8- to 13-year-olds was most related to an enjoyment of using computers and finding information. Ferguson and Perse (2000) examined the World Wide Web as a functional alternative to TV and discovered that many of the motivations for using the web were similar to those for viewing television. Finally, Papacharissi and Rubin (2000) came up with a set of five motivations for using the Internet: utility, passing time, seeking information, convenience, and entertainment.

Methods

Uses and gratifications researchers have relied heavily on the survey method to collect their data. As a first step, researchers have conducted focus groups or have asked respondents to write essays about their reasons for media consumption. Closed-ended Likert-type scales are then constructed based on what was said in the focus group or written in the essays. The closed-ended measures are typically subjected to multivariate statistical techniques such as factor analysis, which identifies various dimensions of gratifications

For example, in their study of the uses and gratifications of VCRs, Rubin and Bantz (1989) first asked selected groups of respondents to list 10 ways in which they used their VCRs and to provide reasons for those uses. This procedure resulted in a list of categories and statements describing VCR usage. A questionnaire was then developed from this master list and administered to respondents, who were asked to indicate how frequently they used their VCRs for these purposes and to rate how much importance they placed on the statements detailing the reasons for usage. After revisions, a final questionnaire was developed; it contained 95 motivational statements. This questionnaire was administered to a sample of 424 VCR owners.

Through factor analysis, the 95 statements were then reduced to eight main motivational categories. These are some examples of the factors and statements that went with them: "I want to keep a permanent copy of the program" (library storage); "I use music video for parties" (music videos); "I don't have to join an exercise class" (exercise tapes). Rubin and Bantz then correlated these factors with demographic and media exposure variables.

Note that this technique assumes that the audience is aware of its reasons and can report them when asked. The method also assumes that the pencil-and-paper test is a valid and reliable measurement scale. Other assumptions include an active audience with goal-directed media behavior; expectations for media use that are produced from individual predispositions, social interaction, and environmental factors; and media selection initiated by the individual.

AN INSIDE LOOK

Media Effects Research: Whether the Weather Makes a Difference

Uses and gratifications research has shed a good deal of light on viewer motivations for watching TV, but the approach has not been particularly successful in predicting the actual amount of television use. Roe and Vandebosch (1996) suggest that one reason for the inability to predict is that researchers sometimes overlook the obvious—such as the weather.

Seasonal variations in TV viewing are well documented: People watch more in the winter and less in the summer. Roe and Vandebosch, however, suggest that specific weather effects occur with each season. The researchers gathered detailed meteorological data in Belgium for a year, including temperature, precipitation amount, wind speed, cloud cover, barometric pressure, and hours of sunlight. They also collected television viewing statistics encompassing the percentage viewing and the daily average amount of time spent watching.

Their results showed strong correlations between all their weather-related measures, except for barometric pressure, and viewing with some correlations reaching as high as .75. Furthermore, there was consistency within each individual season. People watched more TV when there were fewer hours of daylight, when the temperature was low, when wind speed was high, and when there was some precipitation.

The implication in this finding for broadcasters was clear. The single most important determiner of TV audience size was wholly beyond their control.

The experimental method has not been used widely in uses and gratifications research. When it has been chosen, investigators typically manipulated the subjects' motivations and measured differences in their media consumption. To illustrate, Bryant and Zillmann (1984) placed their subjects in either a state of boredom or a state of stress and then gave them a choice of watching a relaxing or a stimulating television program. Stressed subjects watched more tranquil programs, and bored subjects opted for the exciting fare. McLeod and Becker (1981) had their subjects sit in a lounge that contained public affairs magazines. One group of subjects was told that they would soon be tested about the current situation in Pakistan; a second group was told they would be required to write an essay on U.S. military aid to Pakistan; while a control group was given no specific instructions. As expected, subjects in the test and essay conditions made greater use of the magazines than did the control group. The two test groups also differed in the type of information they remembered from the periodicals. Experiments such as these two indicate that different cognitive or affective states facilitate the use of media for various reasons, as predicted by the uses and gratifications rationale.

Theoretical Developments

As mentioned earlier, researchers in the academic sector are interested in developing theory concerning the topics they investigate. This tendency is well illustrated in the history of uses and gratifications research. Whereas early studies tended to be descriptive, later scholars have attempted to integrate research findings into a more theoretical context.

In an early explanation of the uses and gratifications process, Rosengren (1974) suggested that certain basic needs interact with personal characteristics and the social environment of the individual to produce perceived problems and perceived solutions. The problems and solutions constitute different motives for gratification behavior that can come from using the media or from other activities. Together the media use or other behaviors produce gratification (or nongratification) that has an impact on the individual or society, thereby starting the process anew. After reviewing the results of approximately 100 uses and gratifications studies, Palmgreen (1984) stated that "a rather complex theoretical structure . . . has begun to emerge." He proposed an integrative gratifications model that suggested a multivariate approach.

The gratifications sought by the audience form the central concept in the model. There are, however, many antecedent variables such as media structure, media technology, social circumstances, psychological variables, needs, values, and beliefs that all relate to the particular gratification pattern used by the audience. Additionally, the consequences of the gratifications relate directly to media and nonmedia consumption behaviors and the perceived gratifications that are obtained. As Palmgreen admits, this model suffers from lack of parsimony and needs strengthening in several areas, but it does represent an increase in our understanding of the mass media process. Further refinements in the model will come from surveys and experiments designed to test specific hypotheses derived from well-articulated theoretical rationales and from carefully designed descriptive studies. For example, Levy and Windahl (1984) examined the assumption of an active audience in the uses and gratifications approach. They derived a typology of audience activity and prepared a model that linked activity to various uses and gratifications, thus further clarifying one important postulate in the uses and gratifications process.

Swanson (1987) called for more research to encourage the theoretical grounding of the uses and gratifications approach. Specifically, Swanson urged that research focus on (1) the role of gratification seeking in exposure to mass media, (2) the relationship between gratification and the interpretive frames through which audiences understand media content, and (3) the link between gratifications and media content. Van Evra (1990) presents an integrated theoretical model of television's impact in which the use of the medium is considered along with the amount of viewing, presence of information alternatives, and perceived reality of the medium. Her description highlights the complex interactions that need to be examined in order to understand the viewing process. Additionally, uses and gratifications researchers have incorporated a theory from social psychology, expectancy-value theory, into their formulations (Babrow, 1989). This theory suggests that audience attitude toward media behavior is an important factor in media use.

Rubin (1994) summarized the growth of theory in the area and concludes that single-variable explanations of media effects are inadequate. He suggests that more attention be given to antecedent, mediating, and consequent exposure conditions. Finn (1997) investigated a five-factor personality model as a correlate of mass media use. He found that persons who scored high on the extroversion and agreeableness dimensions of a personality measure were more likely to choose nonmedia activities (such as conversation) to meet their communication needs. In a comprehensive review of the theoretical developments relevant to uses and gratifications theory, Ruggiero (2000) argues that researchers must expand the uses and gratifications model to accommodate the unique features of the Internet such as interactivity and demassification. He also contends that the growing popularity of the Internet will make the uses and gratifications approach even more valuable in the future.

The uses and gratifications approach also illustrates the difference in emphasis between academic and applied research objectives. Newspaper publishers and broadcasting executives, who want guidance in attracting readers, viewers, and listeners, seem to be particularly interested in determining what specific content is best suited to meeting the needs of the audience. College and university researchers are interested not only in understanding content characteristics but also in developing theories that explain and predict the public's media consumption based on sociological, psychological, and structural variables.

▪ Agenda Setting by the Media

Agenda setting theory proposes that "the public agenda—or what kinds of things people discuss, think, and worry about (and sometimes ultimately press for legislation about)—is powerfully shaped and directed by what the news media choose to publicize" (Larson, 1994). This means that if the news media decide to give the most time and space to covering the budget deficit, this issue will become the most important item on the audience's agenda. If the news media devote the second most coverage to unemployment, audiences will also rate unemployment as the second most important issue to them, and so on. Agenda setting research examines the relationship between media priorities and audience priorities in the relative importance of news topics.

History

The notion of agenda setting by the media can be traced back to Walter Lippmann (1922), who suggested that the media were responsible for the "pictures in our heads." Forty years later, Cohen (1963) further articulated the idea when he argued that the media may not always be successful in telling people what to think, but they are usually successful in telling them what to think about. Lang and Lang (1966, p. 468) reinforced this notion by observing, "The mass media force attention to certain issues. . . . They are constantly presenting objects, suggesting what individuals in the mass should think about, know about, have feelings about."

The first empirical test of agenda setting came in 1972, when McCombs and Shaw (1972) reported the results of a study done during the 1968 presidential election. They found strong support for the agenda-setting hypothesis. There were strong relationships between the emphasis placed on different campaign issues by the media and the judgments of voters regarding the importance of various campaign topics. This study inspired a host of others, many of them concerned with agenda setting as it occurred during political campaigns. For example, Tipton, Haney, and Baseheart (1975) used cross-lagged correlation (see Chapter 8) to analyze the impact of the media on agenda setting during statewide elections. Patterson and McClure (1976) studied the impact of television news and television commercials on agenda setting in the 1972 election. They concluded that television news had minimal impact on public awareness of issues but that television campaign advertising accounted for increased audience awareness of candidates' positions on issues.

Agenda setting continued to be a popular research topic through the 1980s and 1990s. Its focus has expanded from looking at political campaigns to examining other topics. The agenda-setting technique is now being used in a variety of areas: history, advertising, foreign news, and medical news. McCombs (1994) and Wanta (1997) present useful summaries of this topic.

In recent years the most popular subjects in agenda-setting research are (1) how the media agenda is set (this research is also called *agenda building*), and (2) how the media choose to portray the issues they cover (called **framing analysis**). With regard to agenda building, Wanta, Stephenson, Turk, and McCombs (1989) noted some correlation between issues raised in the president's State of the Union address and the media coverage of those issues. Similarly, Wanta (1991) discovered that the president can have an impact on the media agenda, particularly when presidential approval ratings are high. Boyle (2001) found that major party candidate political ads can have an influence on media coverage of a campaign. Reese (1990) presents a review of the agenda-building research.

Framing analysis recognizes that the media can impart a certain perspective, or "spin," to the events that they cover and that this, in turn, might influence public attitudes on an issue. Framing analysis has been called the second level of agenda setting. As Ghanem (1997, p. 3) put it:

> Agenda setting is now detailing a second level of effects that examines how media coverage affects both what the public thinks about and how the public thinks about it. This second level of agenda setting deals with the specific attributes of a topic and how this agenda of attributes also influences public opinion.

For example, Iyengar and Simon (1993) found a framing effect in their study of news coverage of the Gulf War. Respondents who relied the most on television news, where military developments were emphasized, expressed greater support for a military rather than a diplomatic solution to the crisis. In their study of the way media framed breast cancer coverage in the 1990s, Andsager and Powers (1999) discovered that women's magazines offered more personal stories and more comprehensive information, while news magazines focused more on the economic angle, stressing research funding and insurance. Finally, Andsager (2000) analyzed the attempts by interest groups to frame the abortion debate of the late 1990s and the impact their efforts had with news media. She found that the pro-life group was more successful in getting their interpretation into press coverage.

Methods

The typical agenda-setting study involves several of the approaches discussed in earlier chapters. Content analysis (Chapter 6) is used to define the media agenda, and surveys (Chapter 7) are used to collect data on the audience agenda. In addition, since determining the media agenda and surveying the audience are not done simultaneously, a longitudinal dimension (Chapter 8) is present. More recently, some studies have used the experimental approach (Chapter 9).

Measuring the Media Agenda. Several techniques have been used to establish the media agenda. The most common method involves grouping coverage topics into broad categories and measuring the amount of time or space devoted to each category. The operational definitions of these categories are important because the more broadly a topic area is defined, the easier it is to demonstrate an agenda-setting effect. Ideally, the content analysis should include all media: television, radio, newspaper, and magazines. Unfortunately, this is too large a task for most researchers to handle comfortably, and most studies have been confined to one or two media, usually television and the daily newspaper. For example, Williams and Semlak (1978) tabulated the total air time for each topic mentioned in the three television network newscasts over a 19-day period. The topics were rank-ordered according to their total time. At the same time, the newspaper agenda was constructed by measuring the total column inches devoted to each topic on the front and editorial pages of the local newspaper. McLeod, Becker, and Byrnes (1974) content-analyzed local newspapers for a 6-week period, totaling the number of inches devoted to each topic, including headlines and pertinent pictures on the front and editorial pages. Among other things, they found that the front and editorial pages adequately represented the entire newspaper in their topical areas.

The development of new technologies has created problems for researchers when it comes to measuring the media agenda. Cable TV, fax machines, email, online computer services, and the Internet have greatly expanded the information outlets available to the public. The role of these new channels of communication in agenda setting is still unclear.

Measuring Public Agendas. The public agenda has been measured in at least four ways. First, respondents are asked an open-ended question such as "What do you feel is the most important political issue to you personally?" or "What is the most important political issue in your community?" The phrasing of this question can elicit either the respondent's intrapersonal agenda (as in the first example) or interpersonal agenda (the second example). A second method asks respondents to rate in importance the issues in a list compiled by the researcher. The third technique is a variation of this approach. Respondents are given a list of topics selected by the researcher and asked to rank-order them according to perceived importance. The fourth technique uses the paired-comparisons method. Each issue on a preselected list is paired with every other issue, and the respondent is asked to consider each pair and to identify the more important issue. When all the responses have been tabulated, the issues are ordered from the most important to the least important.

As with all measurement, each technique has its own advantages and disadvantages. The open-ended method gives respondents great freedom in nominating issues, but it favors those people who are better able to verbalize their thoughts. The closed-ended ranking and rating techniques make sure that all respondents have a common vocabulary, but they assume that each respondent is aware of all the public issues listed and restrict the respondent from expressing a personal point of view. The paired-comparisons method provides interval data, which allows for more sophisticated statistical techniques, but it takes longer to complete than the other methods, and this might be a problem in some forms of survey research.

Three important time frames used in collecting the data for agenda-setting research are (1) the duration of the media agenda measurement period, (2) the time lag between measuring the media agenda and measuring the personal agenda, and (3) the duration of the audience agenda measurement. Unfortunately, there is little in the way of research or theory to guide the investigator in this area. To illustrate, Mullins (1977) studied media content for a week to determine the media agenda, but Gormley (1975) gathered media data for 4.5 months. Similarly, the time lag between media agenda measurement and audience agenda measurement has varied from no time at all (McLeod et al., 1974) to a lag of 5 months (Gormley, 1975). Wanta and Hu (1994a) discovered that different media have different optimum time lags. Television, for example, has a more immediate impact, whereas newspapers are more effective in the long term.

It is not surprising that the duration of the measurement period for audience agendas has also varied widely. Hilker (1976) collected a public agenda measure in a single day, whereas McLeod and colleagues (1974) took 4 weeks. Eyal, Winter, and DeGeorge (1981) suggested that methodological studies should be carried out to determine the optimal effect span or peak association period between the media emphasis and public emphasis. Winter and Eyal (1981), in an example of one of these methodological studies, found an optimal effect span of 6 weeks for agenda setting on the civil rights issue. Similarly, Salwen (1988) found that it took from 5 to 7 weeks of news media coverage of environmental issues before they became salient on the public's agenda.

In a large-scale agenda-setting study of German television, Brosius and Kepplinger (1990) found that the nature of the issue had an impact on the time lag necessary to demonstrate an effect. For general issues such as environmental protection, a lag of a year or two might be appropriate. For issues raised in political campaigns, 4 to 6 weeks might be the appropriate lag. For a breaking event within an issue, such as the Chernobyl disaster, a lag of a week might be sufficient.

Agenda-setting researchers are now incorporating more complicated longitudinal analysis measures into their designs. Gonzenbach and McGavin (1997), for example, present descriptions of time series analysis and time series modeling and a discussion of nonlinear analysis techniques.

Several researchers have used the experimental technique to study the causal direction in agenda setting. For example, Heeter, Brown, Soffin, Stanley, & Salwen (1989) examined the agenda-setting effect of teletext. One group of subjects was instructed to abstain from all traditional news media for 5 consecutive days and instead spend 30 minutes each day with a teletext news service. The results indicated that a week's worth of exposure did little to alter subjects' agendas. The experimental method has also been employed to measure the impact of different message frames. Valentino, Buhr, and Beckmann (2001) manipulated the frame of a news story about a politician by creating one version in which an elected official's policy decision was represented as a sincere choice to benefit constituents and another version in which the same decision was represented as a selfish effort to win votes in the next election. The frame that emphasized the vote-getting effort produced more negative reactions than did the sincere choice interpretation.

Theoretical Developments

The theory of agenda setting is still at a formative level. In spite of the problems in method and time span mentioned earlier, the findings in agenda setting are consistent enough to permit some first steps toward theory building. To begin, longitudinal studies of agenda setting have permitted some tentative causal statements. Most of this research has supported the interpretation that the media's agenda causes the public agenda; the rival causal hypothesis—that the public agenda establishes the media agenda—has not received much support (Behr & Iyengar, 1985; Roberts & Bachen, 1981). Thus, much of the recent research has attempted to specify the audience-related and media-related events that condition the agenda-setting effect.

It is apparent that constructing an agenda-setting theory will be a complicated task. Williams (1986), for example, posited eight antecedent variables that should have an impact on audience agendas during a political campaign. Four of these variables (voter interest, voter activity, political involvement, and civic activity) have been linked to agenda setting (Williams & Semlak, 1978). In addition, several studies have suggested that a person's "need for orientation" should be a predictor of agenda holding. (Note that such an approach incorporates uses and gratifications thinking.) For example, Weaver (1977) found a positive correlation between the need for orientation and a greater acceptance of media agendas.

These antecedent variables define the media-scanning behavior of the individual

(McCombs, 1981). Important variables at this stage of the process are the use of media and the use of interpersonal communication (Winter, 1981). Other influences on the individual's agenda setting behavior are the duration and obtrusiveness of the issues themselves and the specifics of media coverage (Winter, 1981). Three other audience attributes that are influential are the credibility given to the news media, the degree to which the audience member relies on the media for information, and the level of exposure to the media (Wanta & Hu, 1994b).

Despite the tentative nature of the theory, many researchers continue to develop models of the agenda-setting process. Manheim (1987), for example, developed a model of agenda setting that distinguished between content and salience of issues. Brosius and Kepplinger (1990) used time series analysis in their study of German news programs to test both a linear model and a nonlinear model of agenda setting. The linear model assumes a direct correlation between coverage and issue importance; an increase or decrease in coverage results in a corresponding change in issue salience. Four nonlinear models were also examined: (1) the threshold model—some minimum level of coverage is required before the agenda-setting effect is seen; (2) the acceleration model—issue salience increases or decreases to a greater degree than coverage; (3) the inertia model—issue importance increases or decreases to a lesser degree than coverage; and (4) the echo model—extremely heavy media coverage prompts the agenda-setting effect long after coverage recedes. Their data showed that the nature of the issue under study was related to the model that best described the results. The acceleration model worked better for issues that were considered subjectively important by the audience (taxes) and for new issues. The linear model seemed to work better with enduring issues (the environment). Some support was also found for the threshold model. There was, however, little support for the inertia model, and not enough data were available for a convincing test of the echo model. In sum, these data suggest an agenda-setting process more complicated than that envisioned by the simple linear model.

▪ Cultivation of Perceptions of Social Reality

How do the media affect audience perceptions of the real world? The basic assumption underlying the cultivation, or enculturation, approach is that repeated exposures to consistent media portrayals and themes influence our perceptions of these items in the direction of the media portrayals. In effect, learning from the media environment is generalized, sometimes incorrectly, to the social environment.

As was the case with agenda-setting research, most of the enculturation research has been conducted by investigators in the academic sector. Industry researchers are aware of this work and sometimes question its accuracy or meaning (Wurtzel & Lometti, 1984), but they seldom conduct it or sponsor it themselves.

History

Some early research studies indicated that media portrayals of certain topics could have an impact on audience perceptions, particularly if the media were the main information sources. Siegel (1958) found that children's role expectations about a taxi driver could be influenced by hearing a radio program about the character. DeFleur and DeFleur (1967) found that television had a homogenizing effect on children's perceptions of occupations commonly shown on television.

The more recent research on viewer perceptions of social reality stems from the Cultural Indicators project of George Gerbner and his associates. Since 1968, they have collected data on the content of television and have analyzed the impact of heavy exposure on the audience. Some of the many variables that have been content analyzed are the demographic portraits of perpetrators and victims of television violence, the prevalence of violent acts, the types of violence portrayed, and the contexts of violence. The basic hypothesis of cultivation analysis is that the more time one spends living in the world of television, the more likely one is to report conceptions of social reality that can be traced to television portrayals (Gross & Morgan, 1985).

To test this hypothesis, Gerbner and his associates have analyzed data from adults, adolescents, and children in cities across the United States. The first cultivation data were reported more than two decades ago (Gerbner & Gross, 1976). Using data collected by the National Opinion Research Center (NORC), Gerbner found that heavy television viewers scored higher on a "mean world" index than did light viewers. [Sample items from this index are "Do you think people try to take advantage of you?" and "You can't be too careful in dealing with people (agree/disagree)."] Data from both adult and child NORC samples showed that heavy viewers were more suspicious and distrustful. Subsequent studies reinforced these findings and found that heavy television viewers were more likely to overestimate the prevalence of violence in society and their own chances of being involved in violence (Gerbner, Gross, Jackson-Beeck, Jeffries-Fox, & Signorielli, 1978). In sum, their perceptions of reality were cultivated by television.

Not all researchers have accepted the cultivation hypothesis. In particular, Hughes (1980) and Hirsch (1980) reanalyzed the NORC data using simultaneous rather than individual controls for demographic variables, and they were unable to replicate Gerbner's findings. Gerbner responded by introducing **resonance** and **mainstreaming**, two new concepts to help explain inconsistencies in the results (Gerbner, Gross, Morgan, & Signorielli, 1986). When the media reinforce what is seen in real life, thus giving an audience member a "double dose," the resulting increase in the cultivation effect is attributed to resonance. Mainstreaming is a leveling effect. Heavy viewing, resulting in a common viewpoint, washes out differences in perceptions of reality usually caused by demographic and social factors. These concepts refine and further elaborate the cultivation hypothesis, but they have not satisfied all the critics of this approach. Condry (1989) presents a comprehensive review of the cultivation analysis literature and of cultivation analysis and an insightful evaluation of the criticisms directed against it. Shanahan and Morgan (1999) also present a comprehensive review of cultivation research.

Additional research on the cultivation hypothesis indicates that the topic may be more complicated than first thought. There is evidence that cultivation may be less dependent on the total amount of TV viewing than on the specific types of programs viewed (O'Keefe & Reid-Nash, 1987). Weaver and Wakshlag (1986) found that the cultivation effect was more pronounced among active TV viewers than among low-involvement viewers, and that personal experience with crime was an important mediating variable that affected the impact of TV programs on cultivating an attitude of vulnerability toward crime. Additionally, Potter (1986) found that the perceived reality of the TV content had an impact on cultivation. Other research (Rubin, Perse, & Taylor, 1988) demonstrated that the wording of the attitude and the perceptual questions used to measure cultivation influenced the results. Potter (1988) found that variables such as identification with TV characters, anomie, IQ, and informational needs of the viewer

AN INSIDE LOOK

Cultivating the Paranormal

Many television programs focus on the paranormal—"The X-Files," "Unsolved Mysteries," "Sightings," and more. Could heavy viewing of these programs have a cultivation effect? This general question was examined by Sparks, Nelson, and Campbell (1997) in a survey of 120 residents of a midwestern city. Respondents were asked to estimate the total amount of time they spent watching TV and how often they had seen specific programs that featured paranormal content. The researchers next developed a 20-item scale to assess respondents' belief in paranormal activities, including UFOs, ESP, ghosts, palm reading, telekinesis, and astrology. This scale was factor-analyzed to yield two distinct elements: belief in supernatural beings and belief in psychic energy. The researchers also asked respondents to report whether they had had any paranormal experiences. TV viewing was then correlated with the measures of belief in the paranormal.

The total number of hours of TV viewing was not related to either of the paranormal belief factors. Exposure to paranormal TV shows showed no correlation with belief in psychic energy. There was a significant relationship, however, between paranormal TV show viewing and belief in supernatural beings among those who had some prior experience with paranormal events. This relationship persisted even after controlling for several demographic variables. The authors suggest that this finding should have implications for journalists and program producers of content related to paranormal themes.

had differential effects on cultivation. In other words, different people react in different ways to TV content, and these different reactions determine the strength of the cultivation effect.

More recently, there have been three key trends in cultivation research. The first is expanding the focus of cultivation into other countries and cultures. *Cultivation Analysis: New Directions in Media Effects Research* (Signorielli & Morgan, 1990) contains chapters on research done in Britain, Sweden, Asia, and Latin America. The results regarding the cultivation effect were mixed. The second trend, discussed in more detail in the next section, is a closer examination of the measurements used in cultivation. Results suggest that the way TV viewing is quantified and the way the cultivation questions are framed all have an impact on the results. The final trend concerns the conceptual mechanisms that result in the occurrence of the cultivation effect and are discussed in the Theoretical Developments section, immediately following the Methods section.

Method

There are two discrete steps in performing a cultivation analysis. First, descriptions of the media world are obtained from periodic content analyses of large blocks of media content. The result of this content analysis is the identification of the messages of the television world. These messages represent consistent patterns in the portrayal of specific issues, policies, and topics that are often at odds with their occurrence in real life. The identification of the consistent portrayals is followed by the construction of a set of questions designed to detect a cultivation effect. Each question poses two or more alternatives. One alternative is more consistent with the world as seen on television, while another is more in line with the real world. For example, according to the content analyses performed by Gerbner and colleagues (1977), strangers commit about 60% of television homicides. In real life, according to government statistics, only 16% of homicides occur between strangers. The question based on this discrepancy was, "Does fatal violence occur between strangers or between relatives and acquaintances?" The response "strangers" was considered to be the television answer. Another question was, "What percentage of all males who have jobs work in law enforcement and crime detection? Is it 1% or 5%?" According to census data, 1% of men in real life have such jobs, compared with 12% in television programs. Thus 5% is the television answer.

Condry (1989) points out that the cultivation impact seems to depend upon whether respondents are making judgments about society or about themselves. Societal level judgments, such as the examples given above, seem to be more influenced by the cultivation effect, but personal judgments (such as "What is the likelihood that you will be involved in a violent crime?") seem to be harder to influence. In a related study, Sparks and Ogles (1990) demonstrated a cultivation effect when respondents were asked about their fear of crime but not when they were asked to give their personal rating of their chances of being victimized. Measures of these two concepts were not related. Related findings were reported by Shanahan, Morgan, and Stenbjerre (1997), who found that TV viewing was associated with a general state of fear about the state of the environment but not related to viewers' perceptions of specific sources of environmental threats.

The second step involves surveying audiences about their television exposure, dividing the sample into heavy and light viewers (4 hours of viewing a day is usually the dividing line), and comparing their answers to the questions that differentiate the television world from the real world. In addition, data are often collected on possible control variables such as gender, age, and socioeconomic status. The basic statistical procedure consists of correlational analysis between the amount of television viewing and the scores on an index reflecting the number of television answers to the comparison questions. Also, partial correlation is used to remove the effects of the control variables. Alternatively, sometimes the *cultivation differential* (CD) is reported. The CD is the percentage of heavy viewers minus the percentage of light viewers who gave the television answers. For example, if 73% of the heavy viewers gave the television answer to the question about violence being committed between strangers or acquaintances compared to 62% of the light viewers, the CD would be 11%. Laboratory experiments use the same general approach, but they usually manipulate the subjects' experience with the television world by showing an experimental group one or more preselected programs.

Measurement decisions can have a significant impact on cultivation findings. Potter and Chang (1990) gauged TV viewing using five different techniques: (1) total exposure (the traditional way used in cultivation analysis); (2) exposure to different types of television programs; (3) exposure to program types while controlling for total exposure; (4) measure of the proportion of each program type viewed, obtained by dividing the time spent per type of program by the total time spent viewing; and (5) a weighted proportion calculated by multiplying hours viewed per week by the proportional measure mentioned in the fourth technique.

The results showed that total viewing time was not a strong predictor of cultivation scores. The proportional measure proved to be the best indicator of cultivation. This suggests that a person who watches 20 hours of

TV per week, with all of the hours being crime shows, will score higher on cultivation measures of fear of crime than a person who watches 80 hours of TV a week with 20 of them consisting of crime shows. The data also showed that all of the alternative measures were better than a simple measure of total TV viewing.

Potter (1991a) demonstrated that deciding where to put the dividing point between heavy viewers and light viewers is a critical choice that can influence the results of a cultivation analysis. He showed that the cultivation effect may not be linear, as typically assumed. This finding may explain why cultivation effects in general are small in magnitude; simply dividing viewers into heavy and light categories cancels many differences among subgroups. Diefenbach and West (2001) offer another insight into possible ways of measuring the cultivation effect. In their study of the cultivation effect, they found no relationship between TV viewing and estimates of murder and burglary rates in society when using the traditional regression model. However, when they used a different form of regression analysis, one based on non-normally distributed dependent variables, they detected a cultivation effect.

Theoretical Developments

What does the research tell us about cultivation? After an extensive literature review in which they examined 48 studies, Hawkins and Pingree (1981) concluded that there was evidence for a link between viewing and beliefs regardless of the kind of social reality in question. Was this link real or spurious? The authors concluded that the answer did, in fact, depend on the type of belief under study. Relationships between viewing and demographic aspects of social reality held up under rigorous controls. As far as causality was concerned, the authors concluded that most of the evidence went in one direction—namely, that television causes social reality to be interpreted in certain ways. Twelve years later, Shrum and O'Guinn (1993) echoed the earlier conclusion by saying that cultivation research has demonstrated a modest but persistent effect of television viewing on what people believe the social world is like. More recently, Morgan and Shanahan (1997) performed a meta-analysis of 82 published cultivation studies and concluded that there is a small but reliable and pervasive cultivation effect that accounts for about 1% of the variance in people's perceptions of the world. The authors argue that although the effect is small, it is not socially insignificant.

How does this process take place? The most recent publications in this area have focused on conceptual models that explain the cognitive processes that cause cultivation. Potter (1993) presents an extensive critique of the original cultivation formulation and offers several suggestions for future research, including developing a typology of effects and providing a long-term analysis. Van Evra (1990) posits a multivariate model of cultivation, taking into account the use to which the viewing is put (information or diversion), the perceived reality of the content, the number of information alternatives available, and the amount of viewing. She suggests that maximum cultivation occurs among heavy viewers who watch for information, believe the content to be real, and have few alternative sources of information. Potter (1991b) proposes a psychological model of cultivation incorporating the concepts of learning, construction, and generalization. He suggests that cultivation theory needs to be extended and revamped in order to explain how the effect operates.

Tapper (1995) presents a possible conceptual model of the cultivation process that is divided into two phases. Phase one deals with content acquisition and takes into account such variables as motives for viewing, selective viewing, the type of genre viewed, and perceptions of the reality of the content. Phase two is the storage phase and elaborates those constructs that might affect long-term memory. Tapper's model allows for various cultivation effects to be examined according to a person's viewing and storage strategies.

Shrum and O'Guinn (1993) present a psychological model of the cultivation process based on the notion of accessibility of information in a person's memory. They posit that human memory works much like a storage bin. When new information is acquired, a copy of that new information is placed on top of the appropriate bin. Later, when information is being retrieved for decision making, the contents of the bin are searched from the top down. Thus, information deposited most recently and most frequently stands a better chance of being recalled. A person who watches a lot of TV crime shows, for example, might file away many exaggerated portrayals of crime and violence in the appropriate bin. When asked to make a judgment about the frequency of real-life crime, the TV images are the most accessible and the person might base his or her judgment of social reality on them.

Shrum and O'Guinn reported the results of an empirical test of this notion. They reasoned that the faster a person is able to make a response, the more accessible is the information retrieved. Consequently, when confronted with a social reality judgment, heavy TV viewers should be able to make judgments faster than light viewers and their judgments should also demonstrate a cultivation effect. The results of Shrum and O'Guinn's experiment supported this reasoning. Shrum (1996) reported a study that replicated these findings. In this experiment, subjects who were heavier viewers of soap operas were more likely to show a cultivation effect and also responded faster to the various cultivation questions that were asked of them. The same author (Shrum, 2001) presents evidence that the cognitive information-processing strategy employed by the viewer has an impact on cultivation. Specifically, when subjects were asked to respond to questions about estimates of crime and occupations spontaneously, a cultivation effect was found. On the other hand, when subjects were asked to think systematically about their answers, the cultivation effect was not found. Shrum argues that those who thought systematically were more likely to discount TV as a source of their information and rely on other sources, thus negating a cultivation effect.

In sum, cultivation has proven to be an evocative and heuristic notion. It is likely that future research will concentrate on identifying key variables important to the process and on specifying the psychological processes that underlie the process.

▪ Social Impact of the Internet

Recall from Chapter 1 that mass media research follows a typical pattern when a new medium develops. Phase 1 concerns an interest in the medium itself: the technology used, functions, access, cost. Phase 2 deals with the users of the medium: who they are, why they use it, what other media it displaces. Phase 3 pertains to the social, psychological, and physical effects of the medium, particularly any harmful effects. Finally, Phase 4 involves research about how the medium can be improved.

Research examining the Internet has generally followed this pattern. Much of the research done during the mid-1990s described the technology involved in the Internet and some of the possible functions that it might serve (see, for example, Porter, 1997). Most of the studies reviewed in this section fall into Phase 2.

The Internet is such a recent development that this section departs from the organizational structure we used earlier. It is too early to write the history of Internet research or to talk about theoretical developments. The methods used to study the net are those discussed earlier in this book: surveys, content analysis, and the occasional experiment. Moreover, new research methods that use the unique resources of the Internet will probably continue to emerge. Consequently, this section divides the research into relevant topic categories.

Audience Characteristics

According to the 2000 Census, about 44 million U.S. households (about 42% of all households) had at least one member online. About 95 million people used the Internet in 2000, up from 57 million in 1998.

By the beginning of 2002, the demographic profile of the average Internet user was similar to that of the average American. According to Nielsen//NetRatings data, 52% of online users were women, a percentage that almost exactly mirrors that of the general population. In addition, the average household income of the online population was only slightly higher than that of the U.S. population. The Internet population was still generally younger, with 76% of the online users between 18 and 49, compared to 63% in the general population. Older Americans, however, were among the fastest-growing age category of Internet users. Education is related to Internet use. A Mediamark survey found that 80% of users had attended college, a proportion greater than the U.S. average. Research by the Pew Center (2001) found this same general pattern.

Longitudinal usage data suggest that the Internet deviates from the pattern followed by other new media. Lindstrom (1997) points out that initial use of a medium is abnormally high during the novelty phase and then declines over time as the medium becomes familiar. During the 1950s, for example, individuals who bought TV sets watched more TV during their first few months of ownership than they did during the rest of the year. Lindstrom cites data from a Nielsen survey, however, showing that Internet use actually increased in the 12-month period following initial use. He hypothesizes that it requires both learning and practice to get the most utility out of the Internet, thus increasing use over time. A 2000 survey by the Stanford Institute for the Quantitative Study of Society lends support to this hypothesis (Nie & Erbring, 2000). Amount of Internet use was positively correlated with the number of years respondents had had Internet access.

Recent research on Internet usage suggests that time spent on the net displaces time spent on other media, particularly television. Television viewing suffers because a great deal of Internet usage is in the evening hours, when people traditionally watch TV (Weaver, 1998). The Stanford study found that 65% of their respondents who were online more than 10 hours per week reported they spent less time watching TV. Time spent on the Internet was also negatively related to time spent reading newspapers, but the effect was not as great as with TV (Nie & Erbring, 2000). Radio listening occurs mainly in cars and as a result does not seem to be affected by Internet use. When it comes to news, however, using the Internet seems to have little impact. Stempel, Hargrove, and Bernt (2000) found that Internet users and nonusers were alike in their viewing of local and network newscasts, and, in a finding that is at odds with the Stanford results, they found that users actually were more regular readers of the daily newspaper.

The audience still relies on and trusts traditional news sources for most of their information about the world. A Gallup survey of more than 1,000 Americans conducted in 1998 revealed that only a few people (about 11%) frequently used the Internet as a source of news. In addition, about 45% of the

Gallup sample reported that they cannot trust the accuracy of what's on the net. Only infomercials and talk shows were viewed with more distrust than the Internet (Newport & Saad, 1998). Johnson and Kaye (1998) found similar results. About 14% of their survey respondents rated online newspapers and online magazines as moderately or very credible sources. When compared to their traditional counterparts, however, online information sources fare relatively well. Flanagin and Metzger (2000) found that their respondents rated the credibility of Internet information sites as highly as they rated the credibility of information obtained from television, radio, and magazines. Only the traditional newspaper was rated higher in credibility.

Functions and Uses

It appears that research concerning the Internet has reached Phase 2, with the advent of studies examining how people are using the Internet. Although a definitive list of uses and gratifications has yet to be drawn up, some preliminary results show some general trends. At the risk of oversimplifying, the main functions seem to be (1) information, (2) communication, (3) entertainment, and (4) affiliation.

The primary use seems to be information gathering. The Pew Center survey mentioned above found that more than 80% of their sample had used the net to find information on some specific topic. A Nielsen survey found that about 75% used the net for informational needs, with most looking for information about products or services

The communication function is best exemplified by the use of email. About 90% of the Pew Center survey respondents used the net to send email. The Stanford survey turned up a comparable result (Nie & Erbring, 2000).

Surfing the web and generally exploring websites illustrate the entertainment function of the Internet. The Stanford survey found a little more than a third of their respondents surf the web and play games for fun. The Pew Center found an even greater percentage: 68% said they surf the web to be entertained.

The last function, affiliation, may be the most interesting. A Georgia Tech study found that 45% of respondents reported that after going on the net they felt more "connected" to people like themselves (GVU survey, 1998). About 35% of the Pew Center respondents reported participating in an online support group. Finally, the frequency of Internet uses seems to be related to age. Younger people use the net more for entertainment and socializing, whereas older people use it more for information (Cortese, 1997).

Social Effects

Since the Internet is so new, Phase 3 research about the effects of the medium has yet to emerge. Nonetheless, there are some indications about what is to come. Stevens (1998) raises questions about the impact of pornographic web sites, particularly on young people. DeKeseredy, Schwartz, and Bergen (1998) suggest a connection among viewing pornography on the Internet, male peer support, and abuse of women in dating. This area will probably be examined closely in subsequent years.

Another potential harmful effect has been labeled "Internet addiction" (Young, K., 1998). This condition is typified by a psychological dependence on the Internet that causes persons to turn into "onlineaholics" who ignore family, work, and friends as they devote most of their time to surfing the net. Young estimated that perhaps 5 million people may be addicted. Surveys have shown that middle-aged women, the unemployed, and newcomers to the net are most at risk (Hurley, 1997). Students are also susceptible. One study reported that one in three students knew someone whose grades had suffered because of heavy net use. Another found a positive correlation between high Internet use and dropout rate (Young, J., 1998). In New York an Internet addiction support group has started regular meetings to help addicts kick the habit. (*http://netaddiction.com/resources/test* has a test you can take online to see whether you suffer from Internet addiction.)

A 1998 study done at Carnegie Mellon University raised some interesting questions about the relationship between Internet use and feelings of depression and loneliness (Harmon, 1998). Somewhat unexpectedly, a 2-year panel study of 169 individuals found that Internet use appeared to cause a decline in psychological well-being. Even though most panel members were frequent visitors to chat rooms and used email heavily, their feelings of loneliness increased as they reported a decline in their amount of interaction with family members and friends. The researchers hypothesized that online communication does not provide the kind of support obtained from conventional face-to-face communication. These findings were reinforced by the results of the Stanford survey. Nie and Erbring report that heavy Internet users spent less time talking to family and friends over the phone and spent less time with family and friends in person. On the other hand, the Pew survey found the opposite. Their results suggested that Internet use actually sustained and strengthened social and family ties. Perhaps subsequent research studies will clear up the inconsistency.

■ ■ ■ Summary

Academic research and private sector research are both similar and different. They share common techniques and try to predict and explain behavior, but academic research is public, is more theoretical in nature, is generally determined more by the individual researcher than by management, and usually costs less than private-sector research. Five main areas of mass media effects research conducted by the academic sector are (1) prosocial and antisocial effects of specific media content, (2) uses and gratifications, (3) agenda setting, (4) perceptions of social reality, and (5) the Internet. Each of these areas is typified by its own research history, method, and theoretical formulation.

Key Terms

Agenda setting
Catharsis
Cultivation
Desensitization
Framing analysis
Mainstreaming
Meta-analysis
Prosocial content
Resonance
Stimulation
Uses and gratifications
V-chip

Using the Internet

Some helpful web sites for more information about media effects research include:

1. *http://www.pewinternet.org.* The Pew Internet & American Life Project creates and funds original, academic-quality research that explores the impact of the Internet on children, families, communities, the workplace, schools, health care and civic/political life. This is a good source for current data on Internet usage.
2. *http://www.mbcnet.org/ETV/A/htmlA/audienceresec/audienceresec.htm.* This link is part of the Museum of Broadcast Communications web site. It contains a short but useful summary of cultivation analysis. Contains a helpful bibliography.
3. *http://www.surgeongeneral.gov/library/youthviolence/chapter4/appendix4b.html.* This rather ungainly link will take you to Appendix 4B of the Surgeon General's Report on Youth Violence. This appendix is entitled "Violence in the Media and Its Effect on Youth Violence" and it contains a readable and succinct summarization of the TV violence literature.
4. *http://www.colostate.edu/Depts/Speech/rccs/theory15.htm.* A brief but helpful introduction to uses and gratifications research.

Questions and Problems for Further Investigation

1. List some topics in addition to those mentioned in this chapter that might interest both private sector researchers and academic researchers.
2. What problems arise when the experimental technique is used to study agenda setting?
3. Assume that, as a consultant for a large metropolitan newspaper, you are designing a uses and gratifications study of newspaper reading. What variables would you include in the analysis? If you were instead an academic researcher interested in the same question, how might your investigation differ from the private sector study?
4. List some perceptions of social reality, in addition to those discussed in the chapter, that might be cultivated by heavy media exposure.
5. What other social effects might arise from increased use of the Internet?
6. The debate about the impact of media violence is too complicated to be covered fully in a short section. If you are using InfoTrac College Edition, do a search on "television violence" to see the many different viewpoints on this topic.

For additional information on these and related topics, see

http://www.wimmerdominick.com

References and Suggested Readings

Albarran, A., & Dimmick, J. (1993). An assessment of utility and competition superiority in the video entertainment industries. *Journal of Media Economics,* 6(2), 45–51.

Allen, M., D'Alessio, D., & Brezgel, K. (1995). A meta-analysis summarizing the effects of pornography II. *Human Communication Research,* 22(2), 258–283.

Allen, M., Emmers, T., Gebhardt, L., & Geiry, M. (1995). Pornography and acceptance of rape myths. *Journal of Communication,* 45(2), 5–27.

Anderson, C., & Dill, K. E. (2000). Video games and aggressive thoughts, feelings, and behavior in the laboratory and in life. *Journal of Personality & Social Psychology,* 78(4), 772–791.

Andsager, J. L. (2000). How interest groups attempt to shape public opinion with competing news frames. *Journalism and Mass Communication Quarterly,* 77(3), 577–592.

Andsager, J. L. & Powers, A. (1999). Social or economic concerns: How news and women's magazines framed breast cancer in the 1990s. *Journalism and Mass Communication Quarterly,* 76(3), 531–550.

Babrow, A. J. (1989). An expectancy-value analysis of the student soap opera audience. *Communication Research,* 16, 155–178.

Bandura, A. (1977). *Social learning theory.* Englewood Cliffs, NJ: Prentice Hall.

Baran, S. B., Chase, L., & Courtright, J. (1979). Television drama as a facilitator of prosocial behavior. *Journal of Broadcasting,* 23(3), 277–284.

Bear, A. (1984). The myth of television violence. *Media Information Australia,* 33, 5–10.

Behr, R., & Iyengar, S. (1985). TV news, real-world clues and changes in the public agenda. *Public Opinion Quarterly,* 49(1), 38–57.

Belson, W. (1978). *Television violence and the adolescent boy.* Hampshire, England: Saxon House.

Berelson, B. (1949). What missing the newspaper means. In P. Lazarsfeld & F. Stanton (Eds.), *Communication research, 1948–49.* New York: Harper & Row.

Berkowitz, L., & Rogers, K. H. (1986). A priming effect analysis of media influences. In J. Bryant & D. Zillmann (Eds.), *Perspectives on media effects* (pp. 57–82). Hillsdale, NJ: Lawrence Erlbaum.

Boyle, T. P. (2001). Intermedia agenda setting in the 1996 presidential election. *Journalism and Mass Communication Quarterly,* 78(1), 26–44.

Brand, J., & Greenberg, B. (1994). Commercials in the classroom. *Journal of Advertising Research,* 34(1), 18–27.

Brosius, H. B., & Kepplinger, H. M. (1990). The agenda-setting function of TV news. *Communication Research,* 17(2), 183–211.

Brosius, H. B., & Kepplinger, H. M. (1992). Linear and non-linear models of agenda setting in television. *Journal of Broadcasting and Electronic Media,* 36(1), 5–24.

Bryant, J., & Zillmann, D. (1984). Using television to alleviate boredom and stress. *Journal of Broadcasting,* 28(1), 1–20.

Bryant, J., & Zillmann, D. (Eds.). (1994). *Media effects.* Hillsdale, NJ: Lawrence Erlbaum.

CBS Broadcast Group. (1974). *Fat Albert and the Cosby kids.* New York: CBS Office of Social Research.

Chaffee, S. (1984). Defending the indefensible. *Society,* 21(6), 30–35.

Cohen, B. (1963). *The press, the public and foreign policy.* Princeton, NJ: Princeton University Press.

Commission on Obscenity and Pornography. (1970). *The report of the commission on obscenity and pornography.* Washington, DC: U.S. Government Printing Office.

Comstock, G., Chaffee, S., & Katzman, N. (1978). *Television and human behavior.* New York: Columbia University Press.

Comstock, G., & Paik, H. (1991). *Television and the American child.* New York: Academic Press.

Condry, J. (1989). *The psychology of television.* Hillsdale, NJ: Lawrence Erlbaum.

Cook, T., Kendzierski, D., & Thomas, S. (1983). The implicit assumptions of television research. *Public Opinion Quarterly,* 47(2), 161–201.

Cortese, A. (1997, May 5). A census in cyberspace. *Business Week,* 3525, 84–85.

CyberStats, Spring '98. (1998). Available at *http://www.mediamark.com/pages/cs.*

DeBock, H. (1980). Gratification frustration during a newspaper strike and a TV blackout. *Journalism Quarterly,* 57(1), 61–66.

DeFleur, M., & DeFleur, L. (1967). The relative contribution of television as a learning source for children's occupational knowledge. *American Sociological Review,* 32, 777–789.

DeKeseredy, W. S., Schwartz, M. D., & Bergen, R. K. (1998). *Issues in intimate violence.* Thousand Oaks, CA: Sage Publications.

Diefenbach, D. L., & West, M. D. (2001). Violent crime and Poisson regression: A measure and a method for cultivation analysis. *Journal of Broadcasting and Electronic Media,* 45(3), 432–445.

Donnerstein, E., Linz, D., & Penrod, S. (1987). *The question of pornography: Research findings and policy implications.* New York: Free Press.

Dyrli, O. E. (1998). Internet stats making news. *Technology & Learning,* 18(9), 60.

Eyal, C., Winter, J., & DeGeorge, W. (1981). The concept of time frame in agenda setting. In G. Wilhoit & H. deBock (Eds.), *Mass communication review yearbook* (Vol. II). Beverly Hills, CA: Sage Publications.

Ferguson, D., & Perse, E. (2000). The world wide web as a functional alternative to television. *Journal of Broadcasting and Electronic Media,* 44(2), 155–176.

Finn, S. (1997). Origins of media exposure. *Communication Research,* 24(5), 507–529.

Flanagin, A. J., & Metzger, M. J. (2000). Perceptions of Internet information credibility. *Journalism and Mass Communication Quarterly,* 77(3), 515–540.

Forge, K. L., & Phemister, S. (1987). The effect of prosocial cartoons on preschool children. *Child Study Journal,* 17(2), 83–86.

Friedlander, B. (1993). Community violence, children's development and mass media. *Psychiatry,* 56(1), 66–81.

Funk, J. B., & Buchman, D. D. (1996). Playing violent video and computer games and adolescent self concept. *Journal of Communication,* 46(2), 19–32.

Gerbner, G., & Gross, L. (1976). Living with television: The violence profile. *Journal of Communication,* 26(2), 173–179.

Gerbner, G., Gross, L., Eleey, M. F., Jackson-Beeck, M., Jeffries-Fox, S., & Signorielli, N. (1977). TV violence profile no. 8. *Journal of Communication,* 27(2), 171–180.

Gerbner, G., Gross, L., Jackson-Beeck, M., Jeffries-Fox, S., & Signorielli, N. (1978). Cultural indicators: Violence profile no. 9. *Journal of Communication,* 28(3), 176–207.

Gerbner, G., Gross, L., Morgan, M., & Signorielli, N. (1986). Living with television: The dynamics of the cultivation process. In J. Bryant & D. Zillmann (Eds.), *Perspectives on media effects* (pp. 17–40). Hillsdale, NJ: Lawrence Erlbaum.

Gerson, W. (1966). Mass media socialization behavior: Negro-white differences. *Social Forces,* 45, 40–50.

Ghanem, S. (1997). Filling in the tapestry. The second level of agenda setting. In M. McCombs, D. Shaw, & D. Weaver (Eds.), *Communication and democracy* (pp. 3–15). Mahwah, NJ: Lawrence Erlbaum.

Gonzenbach, W. J., & McGavin, L. (1997). A brief history of time: A methodological analysis of agenda setting. In M. McCombs, D. Shaw, & D. Weaver (Eds.), *Communication and democracy* (pp. 97–114). Mahwah, NJ: Lawrence Erlbaum.

Gormley, W. (1975). Newspaper agendas and political elites. *Journalism Quarterly,* 52(2), 304–308.

Gross, L., & Morgan, M. (1985). Television and enculturation. In J. Dominick & J. Fletcher (Eds.), *Broadcasting research methods.* Boston: Allyn & Bacon.

GVU's Ninth Internet Survey. (1998). Available at *http://www.cc.gatech.edu/gvu.*

Harmon, A. (1998, August 30). Internet increases loneliness, researchers find. *Atlanta Journal-Constitution,* Section A, p. 18.

Hawkins, R., & Pingree, S. (1981). Using television to construct social reality. *Journal of Broadcasting,* 25(4), 347–364.

Heeter, C., Brown, N., Soffin, S., Stanley, C., & Salwen, M. (1989). Agenda-setting by electronic text news. *Journalism Quarterly,* 66(1), 101–106.

Heller, M., & Polsky, S. (1976). *Studies in violence and television.* New York: American Broadcasting Company.

Herzog, H. (1944). What do we really know about daytime serial listeners? In P. Lazarsfeld & F. Stanton (Eds.), *Radio research, 1942–43.* New York: Duell, Sloan & Pearce.

Hilker, A. (1976, November 10). Agenda-setting influence in an off-year election. *ANPA Research Bulletin,* pp. 7–10.

Hirsch, P. (1980). The "scary world" of the non-viewer and other anomalies. *Communication Research, 7,* 403–456.

Hogben, H. (1998). Factors moderating the effect of televised aggression on viewer behavior. *Communication Research,* 25(2), 220–247.

Huesmann, L. R., & Eron, L. D. (1986). *Television and the aggressive child: A cross-national comparison.* Hillsdale, NJ: Lawrence Erlbaum.

Hughes, M. (1980). The fruits of cultivation analysis: A re-examination of some effects of television viewing. *Public Opinion Quarterly,* 44(3), 287–302.

Hunter, C. D. (1997). The uses and gratifications of Project Agora. Available at *http://www.asc.upenn.edu/usr/hunter/agora_uses.*

Hurley, M. (1997, September 1): But can it lead to the harder stuff? *U.S. News and World Report,* 123(8), 12.

Internet drawing more women for research, purchases. (1998). *Media Report to Women,* 26(1), 4.

Isler, L., Popper, E. T., & Ward, S. (1987). Children's purchase requests and parental response. *Journal of Advertising Research,* 27(5), 28–39.

Iyengar, S., & Simon, A. (1993). News coverage of the Gulf crisis and public opinion. *Communication Research,* 20(3), 265–283.

Johnson, J., Jackson, J., & Gatto, L. (1995). Violent attitudes and deferred academic aspirations. *Basic and Applied Social Psychology,* 16(1/2), 27–41.

Johnson, T. J., & Kaye, B. K. (1998). Cruising is believing?: Comparing Internet and traditional sources on media credibility measures. *Journalism and Mass Communication Quarterly,* 75(2), 325–340.

Klapper, J. (1960). *The effects of mass communication.* Glencoe, IL: Free Press.

Krcmar, M. (1998). The contribution of family communication patterns to children's interpretations of television violence. *Journal of Broadcasting and Electronic Media,* 42(2), 250–264.

Lang, K., & Lang, G. (1966). The mass media and voting. In B. Berelson & M. Janowitz (Eds.), *Reader in public opinion and communication.* New York: Free Press.

Larson, C. U. (1994). *Persuasion* (7th ed.). Belmont, CA: Wadsworth.

Lefkowitz, M., Eron, L., Waldner, L., & Huesmann, L. (1972). Television violence and child aggression. In G. Comstock & E. Rubinstein (Eds.), *Television and social behavior: Vol. III. Television and adolescent aggressiveness.* Washington, DC: U.S. Government Printing Office.

Levy, M., & Windahl, S. (1984). Audience activity and gratifications. *Communication Research,* 11, 51–78.

Liebert, R., & Baron, R. (1972). Short-term effects of televised aggression on children's aggressive behavior. In J. Murray, E. Rubinstein, & G. Comstock (Eds.), *Television and social behavior: Vol. II. Television and social learning.* Washington, DC: U.S. Government Printing Office.

Liebert, R. M., & Sprafkin, J. (1992). *The early window* (3rd ed.). New York: Pergamon Press.

Lin, C. (1993). Modeling the gratification-seeking process of television viewing. *Human Communication Research,* 20(2), 224–244.

Lindstrom, P. (1997). The Internet: Nielsen's longitudinal research on behavioral changes in use of this counter intuitive medium. *Journal of Media Economics,* 10(2), 35–40.

Linz, D., Donnerstein, D., & Penrod, S. (1984). The effects of multiple exposure to film violence against women. *Journal of Communication,* 34(3), 130–147.

Lippmann, W. (1922). *Public opinion.* New York: Macmillan. (reprint, 1965). New York: Free Press.

Manheim, J. B. (1987). A model of agenda dynamics. In M. L. McLaughlin (Ed.), *Communication yearbook* (Vol. 10, pp. 499–516). Beverly Hills, CA: Sage Publications.

McCombs, M. (1981). The agenda setting approach. In D. Nimmo & K. Sanders (Eds.), *Handbook of political communication.* Beverly Hills, CA: Sage Publications.

McCombs, M. (1994). News influence on our pictures of the world. In J. Bryant and D. Zillmann (Eds.), *Media Effects.* Hillsdale, NJ: Lawrence Erlbaum.

McCombs, M., & Shaw, D. (1972). The agenda-setting function of mass media. *Public Opinion Quarterly,* 36(2), 176–187.

McLeod, J., Atkin, C., & Chaffee, S. (1972). Adolescents, parents and television use. In G. Comstock & E. Rubinstein (Eds.), *Television and social behavior: Vol. III. Television and adolescent aggressiveness.* Washington, DC: U.S. Government Printing Office.

McLeod, J., & Becker, L. (1981). The uses and gratifications approach. In D. Nimmo & K. Sanders (Eds.), *Handbook of political communication.* Beverly Hills, CA: Sage Publications.

McLeod, J., Becker, L., & Byrnes, J. (1974). Another look at the agenda setting function of the press. *Communication Research,* 1(2), 131–166.

Milavsky, J., Kessler, R., Stipp, H., & Rubens, W. (1983). *Television and aggression.* New York: Academic Press.

Milgram, S., & Shotland, R. (1973). *Television and antisocial behavior.* New York: Academic Press.

Minton, J. (1975). The impact of "Sesame Street" on readiness. *Sociology of Education,* 48(2), 141–155.

Montgomery, K. (1995). *Prosocial behavior in films.* Unpublished master's thesis, University of Georgia.

Morgan, M., & Shanahan, J. (1997). Two decades of cultivation research. In B. R. Burleson (Ed.),

Communication yearbook 20 (pp. 1–47). Thousand Oaks, CA: Sage Publications.

Mueller, C., Donnerstein, E., & Hallam, J. (1983). Violent films and prosocial behavior. *Personality and Social Psychology Bulletin,* 9, 183–189.

Mullins, E. (1977). Agenda setting and the younger voter. In D. Shaw & M. McCombs (Eds.), *The emergence of American political issues.* St. Paul, MN: West.

Murray, J. (1984). A soft response to hard attacks on research. *Media Information Australia,* (33), 11–16.

Nathanson, A. I. (1999). Identifying and explaining the relationship between parental mediation and children's aggression. *Communication Research,* 26(2), 124–143.

Nathanson, A. I. (2001). Parents vs. peer. *Communication Research,* 28(3), 251–274.

National Institute of Mental Health. (1982). *Television and behavior: Ten years of scientific progress and implications for the 1980s.* Washington, DC: U.S. Government Printing Office.

Newhagen, J., & Lewenstein, M. (1992). Cultivation and exposure to television following the 1989 Loma Prieta earthquake. *Mass Communication Review,* 19(1/2), 49–56.

Newport, F., & Saad, L. (1998, July/August). A matter of trust. *American Journalism Review,* 20(6), 30–33.

Nie, N. H., & Erbring, L. (2000). *Internet and society: A preliminary report.* Palo Alto, CA: Stanford Institute for the Quantitative Study of Society.

O'Keefe, G. J., & Reid-Nash, K. (1987). Crime news and real world blues. *Communication Research,* 14(2), 147–163.

Paik, H., & Comstock, G. (1994). The effects of television violence on antisocial behavior: A meta-analysis. *Communication Research,* 21(4), 516–546.

Palmgreen, P. (1984). Uses and gratifications: A theoretical perspective. In R. Bostrom (Ed.), *Communication yearbook 8.* Beverly Hills, CA: Sage Publications.

Palmgreen, P., & Lawrence, P. A. (1991). Avoidances, gratifications and consumption of theatrical films. In B. A. Austin (Ed.), *Current research in film, Vol. 5* (pp. 39–55). Norwood, NJ: Ablex.

Papacharissi, Z., & Rubin, A. (2000). Predictors of Internet use. *Journal of Broadcasting and Electronic Media,* 44(2), 175–196.

Parke, R., Berkowitz, L., & Leyens, J. (1977). Some effects of violent and nonviolent movies on the behavior of juvenile delinquents. *Advances in Experimental Social Psychology,* 16, 135–172.

Patterson, T., & McClure, R. (1976). *The unseeing eye.* New York: G. P. Putnam's.

Pew Research Center (18 February 2001). Internet and American life: More online doing more. *www.pewinternet.org/reports.*

Porter, D. (1997). *Internet culture.* New York: Routledge.

Porter, W. C., & Stephens, F. (1989). Estimating readability: A study of Utah editors' abilities. *Newspaper Research Journal,* 10(2), 87–96.

Potter, W. J. (1986). Perceived reality and the cultivation hypothesis. *Journal of Broadcasting and Electronic Media,* 30(2), 159–174.

Potter, W. J. (1988). Three strategies for elaborating the cultivation hypothesis. *Journalism Quarterly,* 65(4), 930–939.

Potter, W. J. (1991a). The linearity assumption in cultivation research. *Human Communication Research,* 17(4), 562–583.

Potter, W. J. (1991b). Examining cultivation from a psychological perspective. *Communication Research,* 18(1), 77–102.

Potter, W. J. (1993). Cultivation theory and research. *Human Communication Research,* 19(4), 564–601.

Potter, W. J., & Chang, I. C. (1990). Television exposure and the cultivation hypothesis. *Journal of Broadcasting and Electronic Media,* 34(3), 313–333.

Potter, W. J., & Ware, W. (1989). The frequency and context of prosocial acts on prime time TV. *Journalism Quarterly,* 66(2), 359–366.

Reese, S. D. (1990). Setting the media's agenda. In J. Anderson (Ed.), *Communication yearbook, No. 14.* Newbury Park, CA: Sage Publications.

Roberts, D., & Bachen, C. (1981). Mass communication effects. In M. Rosenzweig & L. Porter (Eds.), *The uses of mass communication.* Beverly Hills, CA: Sage Publications.

Robertson, T. S., Ward, S., Gatignon, H., & Klees, D. M. (1989). Advertising and children: A cross-cultural study. *Communication Research,* 16(4), 459–485.

Roe, K., & Vandebosch, H. (1996). Weather to view or not. *European Journal of Communication,* 11(2), 201–216.

Rosengren, K. E. (1974). Uses and gratifications: A paradigm outlined. In J. G. Blumler & E. Katz (Eds.), *The uses of mass communication.* Beverly Hills, CA: Sage Publications.

Rosenthal, R. (1986). Media violence, antisocial behavior, and the social consequences of small effects. *Journal of Social Issues,* 42(3), 141–154.

Rubin, A. (1979). Television use by children and adolescents. *Human Communication Research,* 5(2), 109–120.

Rubin, A. (1985). Uses and gratifications. In J. Dominick and J. Fletcher (Eds.), *Broadcasting Research Methods.* Boston: Allyn and Bacon.

Rubin, A. M. (1994). Media uses and effects. In J. Bryant & D. Zillmann (Eds.), *Media effects.* Hillsdale, NJ: Lawrence Erlbaum.

Rubin, A. M., Perse, E. M., & Taylor, D. S. (1988). A methodological examination of cultivation. *Communication Research,* 15(2), 107–136.

Rubin, A. R., & Bantz, C. R. (1989). Uses and gratifications of videocassette recorders. In J. L. Salvaggio & J. Bryant (Eds.), *Media use in the information age.* Hillsdale, NJ: Lawrence Erlbaum.

Ruggiero, T. (2000). Uses and gratifications theory in the 21st century. *Mass Communication and Society,* 3(1), 3–38.

Salwen, M. B. (1988). Effect of accumulation of coverage on issue salience in agenda setting. *Journalism Quarterly,* 65(1), 100–106.

Sander, I. (1997). How violent is TV violence? *European Journal of Communication,* 12(1), 43–98.

Schramm, W., Lyle, J., & Parker, E. (1961). *Television in the lives of our children.* Stanford, CA: Stanford University Press.

Shanahan, J., & Morgan, M. (1999). *Television and its viewers.* Cambridge, NY: Cambridge University Press.

Shanahan, J., Morgan, M., & Stenbjerre, M. (1997). Green or brown? Television and the cultivation of environmental concern. *Journal of Broadcasting and Electronic Media,* 41(3), 305–323.

Sherry, J. L. (2001). The effects of violent video games on aggression. *Human Communication Research,* 27(3), 409–431.

Shrum, L. (1996). Psychological processes underlying cultivation effects. *Human Communication Research,* 22(4), 482–509.

Shrum, L. (2001). Processing strategy moderates the cultivation effect. *Human Communication Research,* 27(1), 94–120.

Shrum, L., & O'Guinn, T. (1993). Process and effects in the construction of social reality. *Communication Research,* 20(3), 436–471.

Siegel, A. (1958). The influence of violence in the mass media upon children's role expectations. *Child Development,* 29, 35–56.

Signorielli, N., & Morgan, M. (1990). *Cultivation analysis: New directions in media effects research.* Newbury Park, CA: Sage Publications.

Silvern, S., & Williamson, P. A. (1987). The effects of video game play on young children's aggressive, fantasy and prosocial behavior. *Journal of Applied Developmental Psychology,* 8, 453–462.

Sparks, G. (2002). *Media effects research.* Belmont, CA: Wadsworth.

Sparks, G., Nelson, C. L., & Campbell, R. G. (1997). The relationship between exposure to televised messages about paranormal phenomena and paranormal beliefs. *Journal of Broadcasting and Electronic Media,* 41(3), 345–359.

Sparks, G., & Ogles, R. M. (1990). The difference between fear of victimization and the probability of being victimized. *Journal of Broadcasting and Electronic Media,* 34(3), 351–358.

Sprafkin, J., & Rubinstein, E. (1979). Children's television viewing habits and prosocial behavior. *Journal of Broadcasting,* 23(7), 265–276.

Stempel, G. H., Hargrove, T., & Bernt, J. (2000). Relation of growth of use of Internet to changes in media use from 1995 to 1999. *Journalism and Mass Communication Quarterly,* 77(1), 71–79.

Stevens, B. (1998, May). Click here. *Off Our Backs,* 28(5), 8–9.

Surgeon General's Scientific Advisory Committee on Television and Social Behavior. (1972). *Television and social behavior. Television and growing up* (summary report). Washington, DC: U.S. Government Printing Office.

Swanson, D. L. (1987). Gratification seeking, media exposure, and audience interpretations. *Journal of Broadcasting and Electronic Media,* 31(3), 237–254.

Tan, A. S. (1986). *Mass communication theories and research* (2nd ed.). Columbus, OH: Grid Publications.

Tannenbaum, P., & Zillmann, D. (1975). Emotional arousal in the facilitation of aggression through communication. In L. Berkowitz (Ed.), *Advances in experimental social psychology.* New York: Academic Press.

Tapper, J. (1995). The ecology of cultivation. *Communication Theory,* 5(1), 36–57.

Tipton, L., Haney, R., & Baseheart, J. (1975). Media agenda setting in city and state election campaigns. *Journalism Quarterly,* 52(1), 15–22.

Turk, J. V., & Franklin, B. (1987). Information subsidies: Agenda setting traditions. *Public Relations Review,* 13(4), 29–41.

U.S. Department of Health and Human Services. (2001). *Youth Violence: A Report of the Surgeon General.* Rockville, MD: U.S. Department of Health and Human Services.

Valentino, N. A., Buhr, T. A., & Beckmann, M. N. (2001). When the frame is the game. *Journalism and Mass Communication Quarterly,* 78(1), 93–112.

Valkenburg, P., & Van der Voort, T. (1995). The influence of television on children's daydreaming styles. *Communication Research,* 22(3), 267–287.

Valkenburg, P., & Soeters, K. E. (2001). Children's positive and negative experiences with the Internet. *Communication Research,* 28(5): 652–675.

Van Evra, J. (1990). *Television and child development.* Hillsdale, NJ: Lawrence Erlbaum.

Wanta, W. (1991). Presidential approval ratings as a variable in the agenda-building process. *Journalism Quarterly,* 68(4), 672–679.

Wanta, W. (1997). *The public and the national agenda.* Mahwah, NJ: Lawrence Erlbaum.

Wanta, W., & Hu, Y. (1994a). Time-lag differences in the agenda-setting process. *International Journal of Public Opinion Research,* 6(3), 225–240.

Wanta, W., & Hu, Y. (1994b). The effects of credibility reliance and exposure on media agenda setting. *Journalism Quarterly,* 71(1), 90–98.

Wanta, W., Stephenson, M. A., Turk, J. V., & McCombs, M. E. (1989). How president's State of Union talk influenced news media agendas. *Journalism Quarterly,* 66(3), 537–541.

Weaver, A. (1998). Net worth. *Working Woman,* 23(1), 20.

Weaver, D. (1977). Political issues and voter need for orientation. In M. McCombs & D. Shaw (Eds.), *The emergence of American political issues.* St. Paul, MN: West.

Weaver, J., & Wakshlag, J. (1986). Perceived vulnerability in crime, criminal victimization experience, and television viewing. *Journal of Broadcasting and Electronic Media,* 30(2), 141–158.

Wertham, F. (1954). *The seduction of the innocent.* New York: Holt, Rinehart & Winston.

Williams, T. B. (1986). *The impact of television.* New York: Academic Press.

Williams, W., & Semlak, W. (1978). Campaign 76: Agenda setting during the New Hampshire primary. *Journal of Broadcasting,* 22(4), 531–540.

Windahl, S. (1981). Uses and gratifications at the crossroads. In G. Wilhoit & H. deBock (Eds.), *Mass communication review yearbook.* Beverly Hills, CA: Sage Publications.

Winter, J. (1981). Contingent conditions in the agenda setting process. In G. Wilhoit & H. deBock (Eds.), *Mass communication review yearbook.* Beverly Hills, CA: Sage Publications.

Winter, J., & Eyal, C. (1981). Agenda setting for the civil rights issue. *Public Opinion Quarterly,* 45(3), 376–383.

Wurtzel, A., & Lometti, G. (1984). Researching TV violence. *Society,* 21(6), 22–30.

Young, J. R. (1998, February 6). Students are vulnerable to Internet addiction, article says. *Chronicle of Higher Education,* 44(22), A25.

Young, K. S. (1998). *Caught in the net.* New York: John Wiley.

Zillmann, D., & Bryant, J. (1982). Pornography, sexual callousness, and the trivialization of rape. *Journal of Communication,* 32(4), 10–21.

Zillmann, D., & Bryant, J. (1989). *Pornography: Research advances and policy considerations.* Hillsdale, NJ: Lawrence Erlbaum.

Zillmann, D., Hoyt, J., & Day, K. (1979). Strength and duration of the effect of violent and erotic communication on subsequent aggressive behavior. *Communication Research,* 1, 286–306.

Chapter 18

Mass Media Research and the Internet

- *Brief History of the Internet*
- *Research and the Internet—Background*
- *Internet Data Collection Approaches*
- *Frequently Asked Questions*
- *Sample Internet Survey*
- *Advantages of Internet Research*
- *Disadvantages of Internet Research*
- *Practical and Ethical Considerations of Internet Research*
- *The Future of Internet Research*
- *Internet Research Companies*

Summary

Key Terms

Using the Internet

Questions and Problems for Further Investigation

References and Suggested Readings

"Internet research" can mean two distinctly different things. First, the Internet can be used as an electronic library for information on almost any topic. Second, the Internet can be used to collect research information—a primary data-gathering tool. This chapter focuses on the second approach. A wealth of information about using the Internet as a library resource can be found by conducting a search for "Internet research."

As any online user knows, the Internet has grown at a blazing speed. It was only in the mid-1990s that the Internet became a reality for average computer users, but since that time, the Internet has grown rapidly and it affects almost every area of our lives. Estimates show that there will be about 165 million online users in United States in 2002. The rapid growth of the Internet has also affected research in all types of businesses, including mass media research.

The Internet has had a dramatic affect on the way people communicate, conduct business, and process information, and it has affected mass media research. For example, the Internet has:

- Created new methods for gathering mass media data.
- Changed the way researchers search for and disseminate information.
- Simplified collaboration and interaction among researchers.
- Provided new material for analysis.

Although the Internet offers exciting possibilities for mass media researchers, using the Internet is not universally accepted as reliable and valid. But before discussing how to use the Internet for research, we need to present a brief history of the development of the Internet.

Brief History of the Internet

The idea behind the Internet is usually traced to a 1962 memo written by an MIT scientist who discussed a "galactic network" of interconnected computers through which everybody could connect to everybody else. This concept was particularly interesting to the RAND Corporation, a think tank then wrestling with the problem of how the U.S. military might communicate after an atomic attack. (Keep in mind that the early 1960s was the height of the Cold War with the Soviet Union. It was also the time of the Cuban missile crisis when nuclear war was a distinct possibility.) In 1964, RAND presented a revolutionary proposal for a computer network that would have no central authority and would continue to function even if a large part of it were destroyed. The basic principle behind this system was simple. Each computer in the network would be equal to all the other computers, and each would decide on its own the best way to send, route, and receive messages. Thus, if a number of computers were destroyed, the remaining computers would figure out the best way to route messages through the system, bypassing the disabled computers.

In order for this system to work, computer-generated messages would be disassembled into "packets" of information, similar to breaking down a written letter into its component paragraphs and putting each paragraph in a separate envelope. These individual packets would be transferred from computer to computer until they were all reassembled at their destination. The route each individual packet would take did not matter as long as they all got to where they were sent.

In 1969, the Pentagon's Advanced Research Projects Agency (ARPA) put together the first packet-switching network that linked four supercomputers. The network was named ARPANET after its sponsor. By 1972, more than 35 computers had been linked via ARPANET. Although long-distance computer programming and calculating were supposed to be the main functions of ARPANET, it was quickly discovered that scientists were using the system primarily to send news and personal messages to one another via electronic mail, or email.

By the mid-1970s, more advanced programs were developed for handling information packets. A standard format, called TCP/IP for Transmission Control Protocol/Internet Protocol, made it easier for many different kinds of computers to be linked to ARPANET. As a result, more than 580 host computers were linked to the Internet by 1983. On January 1, 1983, the U.S. military broke away from ARPANET to form its own network, MILNET; this date is considered the official start date of the Internet.

In 1984, the National Science Foundation (NSF) entered the picture when it announced plans to link several supercomputers at various U.S. universities. For technical reasons, ARPANET was not the best way to link these machines, so the NSF started its own faster and upgraded computer network (NSFNET) that also used the Internet Protocol. Other computer networks were soon linked to the new NSF network, and the name "Internet" began to stick for this new collection of computer links. In 1989, ARPANET itself was formally transferred to the Internet.

Soon many companies and social organizations owned powerful computers, and linking them to the Internet was easy. Since the initial philosophy behind the Internet was decentralization, there was no central authority that would prevent anyone from linking up. In fact, the opposite was true. The Internet community welcomed organizations and corporations. Connecting to the Internet did not cost the taxpayer anything because each network handled its own financing and technical needs. The more networks that joined, the more valuable the system became as a communication channel. As a result, the Internet grew quickly.

Two other inventions also encouraged growth. In 1990 scientists in Europe created *hypertext,* a language system that links electronic documents, including text and graphics. The result was an interconnected web of pages that became known as the *World Wide Web* (WWW). Any person or company could create a web page, as long as it used the standard protocol developed in Europe. Many commercial organizations took advantage of the web's graphical possibilities and established websites. The WWW got another boost in 1993 with the invention of web *browsers,* or programs that searched the web for requested information, described it, and configured it for display.

▪ Research and the Internet—Background

Several chapters in this book discuss a variety of methods researchers use to collect data. One underlying similarity with all of these methods is that they are expensive. For example, although costs vary depending on the type of study, the *direct cost* for a typical 20-minute telephone study with 400 respondents is about $15,000. This cost is out of range for many researchers in both the private and the academic sectors.

Although researchers often have lofty ideas about the type of project to conduct, the reality of research is that most projects are designed to fit the constraints of the research budget. In most cases, researchers trim sample sizes and questionnaire length to meet these constraints. While the research may be conducted, the validity and/or reliability of the data are often compromised because of the high costs of conducting research. This is not a new problem. It has existed since the first days of mass media research.

Many things changed when the Internet became available to the public. One change was how researchers in public and private sectors use the Internet. Almost immediately upon the Internet's debut to the public, researchers saw the opportunity to use the new vehicle as a research tool, specifically an inexpensive data collection tool. The Internet was viewed immediately (and embraced) as a replacement for telephone interviews, mail questionnaires, diaries, and other types of data collection methods. That is why research on the Internet has taken off like wildfire—data collection costs can be reduced substantially, and in some cases, the data can be collected without any cost.

However, while cutting research costs is a benefit, it is the foundation for a significant problem in private-sector research. In most private-sector research situations, the cost of data collection takes precedence over the quality of data. Many researchers and managers who want research data have placed reduced costs ahead of the validity and reliability of research in terms of what is important. Are the Internet-collected data correct? It doesn't matter because they are cheap. Are the data gathered from the correct respondents? It doesn't matter because the data are cheap. Are the results comparable to other types of data collection procedures? Once again, it doesn't matter because they're cheap.

The word "cheap" has become the guideline for conducting mass media research. Many researchers and managers do not consider whether the data are good because the data are cheap. And that's wrong.

This doesn't mean that this problem will hinder using the Internet as a data collection tool. That won't happen. In fact, the opposite will happen. Internet data collection will continue to grow rapidly. In addition, Internet data collection has opened the door to all types of researchers. Collecting data no longer requires expertise of any kind or a huge budget. Virtually anyone can now conduct a research study via the Internet. The reduced costs open the research door to people in both the private and public sectors. Academicians, students, and private sector researchers who were once unable to conduct research can now pursue almost any type of project.

This chapter focuses on the various methods of Internet data collection and the advantages and disadvantages of the methodology.

▪ Internet Data Collection Approaches

There are several methods currently used to attempt to gather data from Internet users. Any person with a limited knowledge of computers and the Internet can use these approaches, or one of several dozen Internet research companies can be hired to complete the project. However, keep in mind that costs escalate if an outside company is used in any phase of a study.

The current Internet data collection procedures include:

Email. Respondents receive an email that includes a questionnaire in the body of the letter; has a questionnaire attached; or directs the respondent to a website. The respondent completes the questionnaire and sends the data back to the source by clicking on a "submit" button or via fax after printing the completed questionnaire. Email addresses can be collected from a variety of areas such as the Internet, or they can be purchased from companies that sell such information.

Database email: Respondents who voluntarily agree to have their name included on a company's database receive an email inviting them to the company's website (or other location) to participate in a research project. This methodology is widely used by radio and television stations.

Pop-up: An invitation to participate in a research study pops-up in a small box on the user's monitor when he/she visits a website. To participate, the user simply clicks on a button contained in the pop-up and is directed to the questionnaire.

Randomly selected pop-up: The procedure is the same as in the pop-up, but respondents are selected randomly, usually every *n*th visitor to a website. For example, the offer to participate in a research project can be presented to every 15th visitor to the website.

Prerecruit: Respondents are contacted by telephone, the Internet, regular mail, or email and are invited to participate in a research study. If the respondent agrees to participate, the person is given an Internet address to visit to take part in the project.

Instant messaging: Respondents participate in focus groups and other discussions by simultaneously logging onto the same instant message service or proprietary site.

Stationary display: A company website includes a permanent display, usually a small box at the side of the screen, that invites users to participate in a research project. Respondents click on a button and are directed to the questionnaire.

The basic email approach is the easiest to use, but it requires more work in the data entry phase of the study since the data must be coded and entered. But don't be afraid to pursue any of the procedures. One advantage of using the Internet to collect data is that there are many software packages (some are free) to aid researchers.

In addition, the knowledge of the Internet, websites, and computer programming vary depending on the type of procedure used. A study can be as complicated as the researcher desires. The email approach requires the least amount of computer and Internet expertise, whereas the fully automated approach used in pop-up questionnaires and other "turnkey" approaches requires the most expertise.

All material on the Internet uses a language known as **HTML (hypertext markup language)**, but it is not necessary to learn HTML; this factor will be addressed shortly. The next step is to understand the process of using the Internet for data collection.

▪ Frequently Asked Questions

Most first-time users of the Internet for data collection usually perceive the process as an insurmountable task that requires expertise beyond their abilities. In reality, however, the process is extremely simple and requires learning only a few things about questionnaire design, file uploading and downloading, and data analysis.

Our experience with Internet research during the past several years has shown that novice researchers tend to worry about the same things when it comes to Internet research. In fact, nearly all researchers new to

AN INSIDE LOOK
The Sample Survey

If you are interested in viewing this sample survey on the Internet, go to the readings page on *http://wimmerdominick.com*. As mentioned, this survey is only a simple example of an Internet questionnaire. By the way, if you do view the survey on the Internet and decide to answer the questions, do not hit the "SUBMIT" button because that portion of the questionnaire is not designed to work.

the Internet ask the same four questions. To make things easy, we will first address the four most frequently asked questions about using the Internet to collect research data. They are:

- How do I design my questionnaire?
- How much knowledge of HTML do I need?
- How do I upload my questionnaire to the Internet?
- How do I download my data from the Internet?

The best way to answer these four questions is to use an example. We'll design a basic email survey and address the four most frequently asked questions.

How Do I Design My Questionnaire?

Questionnaire design for Internet research is virtually the same as questionnaire design for any other type of respondent-directed research. The most important rule is to ensure that the questionnaire and directions are clear and unambiguous since the respondent has no opportunity to ask questions immediately. The complexity of the questionnaire depends on the knowledge of the person or company designing the questionnaire and the purposes of the study. There are virtually no limits to the types of questions that can be asked.

How Much Knowledge of HTML Do I Need?

As mentioned, all website pages are written in a language called HyperText Markup Language, or HTML. However, using the Internet for research requires no knowledge of HTML, regardless of whether the project is email based or website based. Email uses either HTML or simple text language, but the writer does not need to understand HTML because email programs automatically convert an email to HTML (if HTML is selected by the writer). This is also true in website-based research because software packages such as Microsoft's *Front Page* and Macromedia's *DreamWeaver* automatically convert questionnaires and other website material to HTML. The process is very simple.

For example, shown on page 433 is a very simple email survey that includes three open-ended questions. The questionnaire was written using *FrontPage 2002* by Microsoft. The text portion of the questionnaire was typed just as it would be using any word processor. The table for the respondents' answers was imported from a macro template website.

The sample below shows what was developed using *FrontPage 2002*. It shows how the questionnaire will look on the Internet. Keep in mind that the survey can be colored or highlighted in almost any way. The sample here is just a simple design.

Sample Internet Survey—Typed Version

Hi! Thanks for agreeing to participate in our radio research project. Please understand that there are no right or wrong answers to the questions. We are interested only in your opinions, so please feel free to "speak your mind." Your name and answers will be kept confidential.

Please answer the following questions and then press the SUBMIT button. Although the answer spaces look small, your answer can be as long as you want. Just keep typing. Hit the TAB key or use your cursor to go from one answer space to another. DO NOT hit the "Enter" key to go to the next answer space or you'll screw it up. When you're done, click on the SUBMIT button and your answers will be sent automatically to our research company.

You can read and edit your answer. When you complete your answer, you can use your arrow keys to go backwards or forwards. You can also go back to an answer by clicking your mouse in the answer space you want to read or edit.

If you have any questions, please go to survey at *samplesurvey.com*

Name

What is your favorite radio station?

What do you like most about your favorite radio station?

Submit | Clear

That is all there is to it. The sample survey was written in the same way it would be written on a word processor, and the response section was imported from an outside source. The imported section also included the "Submit" and "Clear" buttons shown at the bottom of the questionnaire.

As the material, in this case the sample questionnaire, is typed into the *FrontPage 2002* software, the program simultaneously converts the material into HTML. This automatic conversion process has opened the door for Internet research to anyone who can type who has access to an Internet website.

The HTML code for the sample survey that was converted by *FrontPage 2002* is shown on page 434. You'll notice the unique codes used by HTML to convert English language into computer language. For example, the fifth line states <BODY bgcolor="#FFFFFF">. This means that the background color of the questionnaire is white, as identified by "bgcolor="#FFFFFF." " If the background of the questionnaire were brilliant blue, the HTML code would read, <BODY bgcolor="#0000FF">

A few other HTML codes in the sample survey are:

Code	Action
.	Space
<HTML>	Begin HTML
</HTML>	End HTML
<b>	Begin bold font
</b>	End bold font
<I>	Begin italics
</I>	End italics

Following is the complete HTML code for the sample survey:

Sample Internet Survey—HTML Version

```
<HTML>

<HEAD>

<TITLE>MMR Sample Survey</TITLE>

</HEAD>

<BODY bgcolor="#FFFFFF">

<H2><font size="4">Sample Internet Survey</font></H2>

<P>

Hi!  Thanks for agreeing to participate in our radio research project.  Please understand
that there are no right or wrong answers to the questions.  We are interested only in your
opinions, so please feel free to &quot;speak your mind.&quot;  Your name and answers will
be kept confidential.

<P>

Please answer the following questions and then press the SUBMIT button. Although the
answer spaces look small, your answer can be as long as you want. Just keep typing. 
Hit the TAB key or use your cursor to go from one answer space to another.  DO NOT hit the
&quot;Enter&quot; key to go to the next answer space or you'll mess it up.  When you're
done, click on the SUBMIT button and your answers will be sent automatically to our research
company.<P>You can read and edit your answer.  When you complete your answer, you can
use your arrow keys to go backwards or forwards.  You can also go back to an answer by
clicking your mouse in the answer space you want to read or edit.<P>If you have any questions,
please go to samplesurvey.com

<P>

<FORM METHOD="POST">

<TABLE BORDER=0 CELLPADDING=0 CELLSPACING=5 height="200">

<TR>

<TD height="44"><B>Name</B></TD>

<TD height="44"><INPUT NAME="required-Name" TYPE="text"
SIZE="35"><BR></TD>

</TR>

<TR>

<TD height="44">

<p style="margin-top: 0; margin-bottom: 0"><B>What is your favorite radio station?
 </B></p>
```

```
</TD>
<TD height="44">INPUT NAME="Favorite radio station" TYPE="text" SIZE="35">
<BR></TD>
</TR>
<TR>
<TD height="44"><b>What do you like most about your favorite radio station?</b>
</TD>
<TD height="44"><INPUT NAME="Like most" TYPE="text" SIZE="35"><BR></TD>
</TR>
</TABLE>
<BR>
<BR>
<INPUT TYPE="submit" VALUE="Submit"><INPUT TYPE="reset"
VALUE="Clear"></FORM>
</BODY>
</HTML>
```

When a respondent completes the questions and hits the "SUBMIT" button, the person's answers are automatically sent to a designated email address or other file.

Using an HTML editor is virtually the same as using any major word processing package. Almost all formatting and editing can be accomplished with a click of a button, and all editors include spell-checking options. In addition, there are many macros available to use for complicated questionnaire items, and there are a countless number of useful tips available on the Internet. In addition, any person with knowledge of HTML can "tweak" the HTML language.

How Do I Upload My Questionnaire to a Website?

Researchers who use an Internet research company to conduct a project do not have to worry about uploading and downloading information. The company does this.

However, uploading and downloading files by researchers who conduct the study alone is not complicated. Most Internet users have free web space available from their **Internet service provider** (ISP) to use for personal web pages. This free space can be used to conduct research, although it is important to read the agreement since some do not allow the free web space to be used for certain purposes.

In addition to the free web space, users are usually provided with a free upload package that allows the users to transfer their files to the ISP's server (computer). The generic term for transferring files is known as **file transfer protocol**, or **FTP**. One commonly used FTP software package is *CuteFTP* by GlobalSCAPE. Uploading files such as questionnaires is simply a "point and click" process—users click on the files they want to

> ### AN INSIDE LOOK
> ## Web Page Names
>
> Researchers who use their free web space provided by their ISP will not have a unique address such as *www.researchproject.com* for their project. Instead, the address will be something like: *http://members.home.com/rogerwimmer/researchproject.htm*. Researchers who wish to use a unique address must purchase the name (about $75.00 for 3 years) and then contract with an Internet web-hosting company such as NTTVerio to manage the account (about $40.00 per month).

upload and hit the "upload" button. (The software sends only the HTML for the file, not the standard typed information.) When the file transfer is done—after only a few seconds—the material is available to view on the Internet for anyone in the world who knows the address for the material.

To upload the sample survey, we use a commercial FTP package or the package provided by the ISP. After we click on the FTP package to start it, the program logs onto the Internet. The next step is to go to the file named "*mmrsamplesurvey.html*" (the name of the file for the sample survey) on our computer. A right click on the mouse on the file name opens a menu of options, one of which is "Upload." If we click this option, the survey is uploaded to the ISP's computer. The questionnaire is now available to view by anyone in the world who knows the address for the survey.

How Do I Download My Data from the Internet?

The data download process is the most difficult step of Internet research, but commercially available software and Internet research companies make even this step simple.

Email data collection requires no additional software, programming, or expense, which explains why most novice researchers use email for their projects. The process is simple: The researcher sends an email questionnaire and receives the completed questionnaires as a reply. The data are then entered into a statistical software package or input into a spreadsheet for analysis.

While many software packages make the downloading procedure very simple for individual users, several Internet research companies have developed extremely sophisticated procedures to collect, sort, and analyze the data. In fact, some of the companies allow researchers and clients to view their data real time—the researcher or client logs onto a protected site and can literally view the respondents' answers as they are submitted.

▪ Advantages of Internet Research

The list of advantages of using the Internet to conduct research shows why the methodology has become popular so quickly. Some of the advantages of using the Internet include:

1. Internet surveys are easy to conduct. Once a researcher understands the process, a project can be designed and available in only a few hours for respondents on the Internet anywhere in the world.
2. Questionnaires can be changed almost immediately if a change is re-

AN INSIDE LOOK
Uploading Questionnaires

Information on the Internet is open for anyone to see unless the website or specific file is protected by a username and password. Protecting user access to Internet information is easy and is accomplished by selecting a "protection" option on the ISP used for the study. For example, in our sample survey, we could go to the ISP and protect "mmrsamplesurvey.html" with a username and password that make it virtually impossible for anyone to randomly get to the site and answer the questions.

This process works well, and it is easy to see who answers the survey and whether someone is trying to hack into the questionnaire by viewing the website's Log Files on the ISP. All website operators can see who has logged onto their site. The information may not be specific enough to identify a specific person, but the operators will at least know that someone is attempting break into the site.

quired, especially if a researcher works without an Internet research company. The ability to change questionnaires saves time and money as compared to the process necessary if changes are required in telephone surveys or mail surveys. In many cases, changes cannot be made in the other approaches once the study is under way.

3. Costs for data collection and data analysis are substantially reduced or almost eliminated if an Internet research company is not used.
4. Each respondent can proceed at his or her own speed and can read questions several times if necessary. In addition, many software packages and Internet research companies include options to allow the respondent to complete the questionnaire in several sessions. Respondents answer as many questions as time allows, and when they sign back in, they are taken directly to the point when they stopped in a previous session.
5. Unlike laws in some areas of the United States regulating telephone solicitation, there are currently no laws related to conducting Internet research.
6. The turnaround of results is very quick. As mentioned earlier, some Internet research companies offer users an option to view results in real time as respondents submit them.
7. There is almost no limit to the type of questions that can be asked, including questions that have audio or visual information for the respondents to hear or see. Respondents can listen to several minutes of audio, such as a new song, or they can watch a video, such as a proposed TV commercial.
8. Questionnaires can be interactive, meaning that researchers can include complicated skips to ensure that the questionnaire meets each respondent's answers. For example, in a survey about television, respondents who watch reality programming can be directed to a specific section of the questionnaire that relates to this type of program.
9. The Internet allows access to all types of people, including high-income users and professionals. Access doesn't

AN INSIDE LOOK

Internet Questionnaire Design

Just as with any type of research, it is necessary to conduct a pilot study or run-through of the procedures. If you do get involved in Internet research, always remember to upload your materials and go through them yourself several times to ensure that everything is clear. In addition, it is wise to ask a few friends or colleagues to go to the site and complete your questionnaire. After these people are done, be sure to ask them about the experience to find out if what you planned is what actually happened.

necessarily mean acceptance or completion, but the Internet provides an opportunity to reach people who cannot be reached by telephone or mail. In addition, high-income people and professionals often volunteer to have their names included on databases.

10. Research projects can be replicated frequently if necessary, or the project can be on-going and last as long as the researcher desires. This flexibility allows researchers to track respondents' answers over time.
11. There are few restrictions on geography; respondents in many areas of the world can be recruited easily.
12. Large samples are easy to achieve if the project is interesting and relevant to many respondents. However, keep in mind that a large sample does not mean that the sample is good. It's entirely possible to have a large sample of the wrong type of respondents.
13. Internet use is no longer restricted only to certain types of respondents. Internet users are quickly becoming representative of the total population. Unlike some other consumer products and services that continually escalate in price, costs for computers and Internet access continually fall. This has opened the door to a wide variety of respondents.

▪ Disadvantages of Internet Research

Although Internet research has become popular very quickly, the popularity of the methodology does not mean that the methodology is inherently valid and reliable. Researchers must address several problems if they plan to conduct Internet research because the method is not universally accepted as a valid methodology. There is a lack of reputable research comparing Internet research to other universally accepted data collection procedures.

With that in mind, let's consider some of the problems with Internet research.

1. The most significant problem related to Internet research relates to control over the research situation—researchers do not know who answers an Internet questionnaire. This problem also exists with mail surveys, but mail surveys are conducted very infrequently in mass media research.

   However, to be honest, most people in the "real world" of private-sector research do not care about the problem of not knowing who answers Internet surveys. In a countless number of situations, the senior author has told clients about the problem, and the usual response is something like, "But at least it's cheap and we get a lot of responses."

The importance of this problem cannot be overlooked. If you are a mass media researcher, or a person who plans to enter the field, you must have a clear and unambiguous answer for someone who asks, "Who answered this survey?" And the only clear and unambiguous answer is, "There is no way to know who answers the survey."

The only way to deal with the problem now is to look at the data to search for outliers. In other words, if respondents are asked how many hours they watch TV each day and the average shows 3.5 hours (that's hypothetical), and a few respondents say "More than 15 hours," or something significantly different than the other respondents, the outliers can be dropped from the data. This does not mean that these people are not telling the truth because there is no way to know that, but at least eliminating outliers will eliminate wide swings in the data. Another indication of an outlier is a respondent who answers the same way to several questions, such as rating everything a "5" if ratings questions are used. These are called **response sets** and provide an indication that the respondent probably does not belong in the sample.

2. Although a variety of people use the Internet and the representativeness of Internet users appears to be approaching the general characteristics of most populations, there is currently no way to determine if the Internet sample is representative of the population from which the sample was selected or volunteered. This relates to the first problem—there is no way to determine who completed the survey.
3. Many Internet users are concerned with security and refuse to participate in any type of Internet research project. These people think their answers will be available to anyone in the world; their identity will be used for sales of products or services; or they will receive unsolicited email from the researcher or other companies that may purchase their email address from the researcher.
4. While responses from the same computer can be controlled so that one computer cannot answer the survey more than once (accomplished by identifying the computer's IP address), there is still no way to identify the respondent of a computer that is used to complete a survey.
5. There are no research data about the appropriate length of Internet surveys. For example, we know that a telephone survey should have a maximum length of about 20 minutes, but this information is not available for Internet research.
6. People who have absolutely no knowledge of research have become Internet researchers. In the radio industry, for example, several former program directors who have no research background have developed websites to conduct radio research. This is a detriment not only to the respondents who participate in the project but also to the radio managers who hire these people.

Practical and Ethical Considerations of Internet Research

Media researchers who plan to gather data over the Internet face some special difficulties. First, if a website is going to be used, the researcher must have access to space on a server and design the research materials using HTML. Second,

AN INSIDE LOOK
Paying Respondents

Although paying respondents an incentive fee for an Internet research study will obviously increase costs for a project, this is not viewed as a problem by researchers in either the public or private sectors. If we assume that respondents are paid as much as $25.00 for their participation, the cost is less than the costs to conduct the survey on the telephone.

just because a website exists does not mean that people will visit it. Publicizing the site and informing the relevant population are important steps in web data collection. Furthermore, a researcher who decides to post a questionnaire on the web should keep in mind that there is a potential audience of many millions of people who might respond. Extra care must be taken to ensure that the questionnaire is not offensive, that it contains nonsexist language, and that it reflects well on the researcher and the sponsoring organization.

In addition, certain ethical considerations are unique to the net. In academic research, there must be a mechanism for subjects to provide informed consent before participating in a web experiment or filling out a web questionnaire. In addition, in traditional experiments and surveys, a "debriefing" session is often needed to explain the goals of the research and give feedback to the participants. Special provisions to do this must be made for online research, although sending a standard email explanation might be sufficient for most projects.

Researchers who analyze the content of bulletin boards, newsgroups, list servers, chat rooms, and email need to consider the ethical implications of examining the communication of others without their consent or knowledge. The traditional ethical guidelines state that researchers who study people in public places usually do not require informed consent, whereas those who study people in places where some degree of privacy is expected need to obtain consent. The distinction between public and private may be blurry in cyberspace. Is a chat room public or private? Are messages posted to a newsgroup or a list server private? What if a person must subscribe or pay a fee to belong? Can deception be used to gather data? For example, misrepresenting oneself as a single parent in order to gain access to a chat room for single parents and win their confidence raises ethical questions about deception in data gathering. Is it ethical to gather data from a bulletin board or a list server operator about subscribers? Duncan (1996) provides some general ethical guidelines for online research. An interesting discussion of the ethics involved in data collection through the Internet can be found in Rimm (1995). In sum, the Internet brings new opportunities for mass communication research even as it raises new concerns.

▪ The Future of Internet Research

Despite some definite problems, Internet research has many more advantages than disadvantages. When the problems of not knowing who is answering a questionnaire and sample representativeness are addressed in the next few years, Internet research will probably become the primary data collection method used by researchers in all fields. Until that time, Internet research can be used as an adjunct approach to attempt to support or refute data collected with other methods.

Another thing that will help Internet research grow is when researchers or Internet research companies figure out a way to pay respondents via some type of electronic cash. Although there are a few ways to pay respondents online, such as PayPal (see *www.paypal.com*), a universally accepted method has not been developed. At present, research projects that involve co-op payments to the respondents use regular mail to send the money to respondents. In addition, a few researchers and Internet research companies are testing online coupons as respondent co-op payments.

Internet Research Companies

Even at this early stage of Internet research, there are dozens of companies operating now that are available for hire to conduct the study. (Keep in mind that costs escalate as the involvement by the Internet research company increases.) Just as with typical field services and research companies, there are several types of Internet research companies. Some are boutiques that offer only questionnaire design, while others are "turn-key" operations that participate in all phases of the research.

However, while there are many types of Internet research companies, the majority follow the same approach: provide a data collection vehicle for a client in two ways:

1. Provide a full-service approach where the company designs, collects, and analyzes data.
2. Sell a software package that allows the user to perform the tasks.

Although the costs involved in hiring an Internet research company to collect data via the Internet are less than conducting the study via well-established data collection procedures, there is still a cost involved. We mentioned earlier that the Internet has opened research to almost anyone, but these companies do not solve the problem of research expense.

The list of Internet research companies shown below is not an endorsement of the companies, but rather examples of the types of companies now conducting Internet research. Each site has a detailed explanation of the services the company offers.

Some of the companies involved in Internet research as of mid-2002 are:

- Business Research Lab at *http://www.busreslab.com/onlinesurvey.htm*
- Free Surveys Online.com at *http://freeonlinesurveys.com*
- Hosted Surveys.com at *http://www.hostedsurvey.com*
- InfoSurv at *http://www.infosurv.com*
- Inquisite at *http://www.inquisite.com*
- MarketTools at *http://www.markettools.com*
- Questionbuilder.com at *http://www.questionbuilder.com*
- Super Survey at *http://www.supersurvey.com*
- SurveyPro at *http://www.surveypro.com*
- SurveySite at *http://www.surveysite.com*
- WebSurveyor at *http://www.websurveyor.com*

For other companies involved in online surveys, search the Internet for "online surveys."

In addition, several sites on the Internet provide a great deal of information about Internet research. Two of them are:

- Internet Research: Electronic Networking, Applications and Policy at: *http://www.emeraldinsight.com/intr.htm*
- ResearchBuzz at *http://www.researchbuzz.com*

Just as with using any non-Internet research company, it is important to investigate an Internet research company before contracting with the company to conduct a study. It is easy to develop a fancy-looking website, but it is not easy to conduct the research correctly. In most cases, the Internet research companies will allow new users to try the research software or proprietary method for free to see how everything works.

▪ ▪ ▪ Summary

Researchers in all fields and businesses have quickly embraced the Internet as a data collection tool, but that does not mean that the methodology is reliable and valid. While there are several advantages in using the Internet to collect research data, there are several disadvantages that researchers need to consider before they take the Internet "plunge."

As mentioned in the chapter, even though using the Internet as a data collection tool has several problems, these problems will eventually be solved, and the Internet will become a valuable research tool for mass media researchers.

One goal of this chapter is to dispel the fear that many novice researchers may have in using the Internet for data collection. Although this chapter is only an introduction to the process of using the Internet, we hope that all researchers will understand that using the Internet is a very simple process.

Key Terms

File Transfer Protocol (FTP)
HyperText Markup Language (HTML)
Internet Service Provider (ISP)
Response set

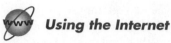

Using the Internet

Literally any topic discussed in this chapter can be found on the Internet. For more information, search the Internet for any of the terms or concepts discussed in the chapter. For example, to learn more about HTML, conduct a search for "HTML." It's that simple.

Questions and Problems for Further Investigation

1. Although you may not be an expert in Internet research, what is your opinion of using the Internet as a data collection tool? Don't only rely on the information in this chapter. Consider other things such as internal and external validity.
2. As mentioned in the chapter, most Internet research companies allow new users to try the software for free. Go to a few of the sites mentioned in the chapter, or search for others on the Internet, and experiment with the software.
3. The primary problem with Internet research mentioned in the chapter is that of not knowing who answers a questionnaire. Even if you are not an expert in the Internet or in research procedures, what types of things do you think researchers could do to help solve this problem?
4. Would you participate in an Internet research project if your incentive was a coupon to your favorite music store? Some people immediately say "yes," while others immediately say "no." Why do you think some respondents would refuse to participate even though they would receive a coupon to one of their favorite stores?

For additional information on these and related topics, see

http://www.wimmerdominick.com

References and Suggested Readings

December, John. (1996). Units of analysis for Internet communication. *Journal of Communication,* 46(1), 21–99.

Dreze, X., & Zufryden, F. (1997). Testing Web site design and promotional content. *Journal of Advertising Research,* 37(2) 77–91.

Duncan, G. T. (1996). Is my research ethical? *Communications of the ACM,* 39(12), 67–68.

Eighmey, J. (1997). Profiling user responses to commercial Web sites. *Journal of Advertising Research,* 37(3), 59–66.

Fleitas, J. (1998). Spinning tales from the World Wide Web. *Qualitative Health Research,* 8(2), 283–292.

Herzog, A., Dinoff, B., & Page, J. (1997). Animal rights talk. *Qualitative Sociology,* 20(3), 399–418.

Hill, K. A., & Hughes, J. E. (1997). Computer-mediated political communication: The USENET and political communities. *Political Communication,* 14 (1), 3–27.

Johnson, T. J., & Kaye, B. K. (1998). Cruising is believing? Comparing Internet and traditional sources on media credibility measures. *Journalism and Mass Communication Quarterly,* 75(2), 325–340.

Jones, S. (1997, March). Using the news: An examination of the value and use of news sources in CMC. *Journal of Computer Mediated Communication,* 2(4).

McLaughlin, M. L. (1996). The art site on the World Wide Web. *Journal of Communication,* 46(1), 51–79.

Miller, H. (1995). The presentation of self in electronic life: Goffman on the Internet. Paper presented at the Embodied Knowledge and Virtual Space Conference, London. (Available at *http://ntu.ac.uk/soc/psych/miller/goffman.html*)

Newhagen, J. E., Cordes, J. W., & Levy, M. (1995). Nightly©nbc.com: Audience scope and the perception of interactivity in viewer mail on the Internet. *Journal of Communication,* 45(3), 164–175.

Newhagen, J. E., & Rafaeli, S. (1996). Why communication researchers should study the Internet. *Journal of Communication,* 46(1), 4–13.

Palmer, J. W., & Griffith, D. A. (1998). An emerging model of Web site design for advertising. *Communications of the ACM,* 41(3), 44–51.

Parks, M. R., & Floyd, K. (1996). Making friends in cyberspace. *Journal of Communication,* 46(1), 80–96.

Pratt, L. (1996). Impression management in organizational e-mail communication. Paper presented at the Speech Communication Association Conference. (Available at *http://www.public.asu.edu/~corman/scaorgcomm/pratt.html*)

Rice, R. P. (1997). An analysis of stylistic variables in e-mail. *Journal of Business and Technical Communication,* 11(11), 5–23.

Rimm, M. (1995). Marketing pornography on the Internet. *Georgetown Law Review,* 83(2), 1849–2008.

Salam, A. F., Rao, H. R., & Pegels, C. C. (1998). Content of corporate Web pages as advertising media. *Communications of the ACM,* 41(3), 76–77.

Walters, A. (1996). An analysis of purposes and forms of personal homepages on the World Wide Web. Unpublished thesis, Sloan School of Management, Massachusetts Institute of Technology. (Available at *http://tranquility.mit.edu/alison/thesis.html*)

Williams, D. A. (1997). Wanted: Info on you and your interests. *Advertising Age,* May 19, pp. 60–62.

Wylie, K. (1997). NFO exec sees most research going to the Internet. *Advertising Age,* May 19, p. 50.

Appendix

Tables

- *Table 1 Random Numbers*
- *Table 2 Distribution of t*
- *Table 3 Areas Under the Normal Curve*
- *Table 4 Distribution of Chi-Square*
- *Table 5 Distribution of F: .05 Level*
- *Table 6 Distribution of F: .01 Level*

Table 1 *Random Numbers*

0	8	9	5	6	4	4	8	9	4	0	7	5	9	7	0	4	5	3	1	2	7	8	6	6
8	2	4	4	8	8	0	2	6	5	5	0	3	5	9	1	3	8	6	8	8	3	1	8	5
3	1	2	3	7	6	4	1	1	4	3	5	2	7	4	9	3	2	7	5	5	4	7	6	2
2	3	8	1	8	6	6	1	0	8	4	1	0	5	0	4	8	5	3	7	8	7	6	5	7
0	0	4	3	6	5	5	2	3	5	2	4	3	3	9	3	2	5	2	0	8	4	6	2	1
1	2	8	9	7	5	8	9	7	8	6	7	4	0	4	0	4	9	7	8	5	0	2	9	8
9	8	4	6	9	9	0	8	0	2	3	2	8	0	5	4	5	0	6	7	6	2	3	9	8
0	7	3	6	9	5	1	6	3	8	0	5	9	0	0	2	0	9	3	6	8	8	2	4	3
2	2	3	9	5	7	9	4	0	6	7	3	6	9	6	4	1	7	3	6	5	1	8	2	6
4	9	5	6	9	3	1	4	7	8	1	5	6	7	2	2	4	0	3	0	5	4	2	1	2
4	0	6	6	8	5	4	3	7	8	3	2	6	8	1	2	2	7	0	6	5	3	5	8	4
6	3	3	2	0	3	9	7	0	2	3	6	9	5	3	4	1	6	1	8	3	9	4	3	3
0	6	1	8	4	2	1	8	6	7	5	4	1	9	0	3	2	4	1	5	7	7	4	0	8
2	2	4	2	9	6	8	5	8	2	6	1	0	7	6	1	7	9	2	0	9	2	8	7	8
8	3	2	3	0	7	4	3	5	8	9	0	8	0	5	8	8	7	1	3	6	0	1	3	9
2	3	1	8	2	3	1	0	9	0	0	8	9	1	2	0	3	7	0	2	0	1	8	1	7
0	8	7	3	4	4	5	1	8	7	4	5	1	9	9	0	3	2	2	3	1	2	6	4	6
5	8	5	6	7	6	1	0	1	6	7	0	2	1	9	1	6	3	2	0	1	1	5	5	9
6	1	1	0	5	1	3	6	7	7	7	8	2	4	5	9	3	0	7	6	7	9	1	1	6
5	3	6	1	2	7	2	6	2	7	3	3	6	8	2	6	5	5	8	4	2	4	2	1	8
8	7	3	9	5	1	1	8	4	1	8	5	6	6	0	6	9	2	2	6	8	2	5	8	5
2	9	1	9	9	5	6	1	8	6	6	4	0	5	0	0	8	8	2	5	9	2	0	1	2
8	1	0	2	1	7	2	0	2	7	6	8	4	8	0	2	6	2	8	0	8	3	6	0	7
9	7	1	5	5	7	4	6	1	5	6	5	9	9	2	2	7	1	2	7	0	0	5	0	9
6	3	7	9	8	8	7	4	9	5	0	3	3	0	3	7	0	7	5	8	1	2	8	3	1
9	4	2	2	1	3	2	0	5	6	0	6	0	9	0	9	3	1	7	8	1	2	3	1	1
5	2	8	5	1	0	2	4	6	0	8	3	4	2	9	0	2	4	0	5	2	7	8	8	8
7	9	7	1	3	7	2	4	6	3	8	4	0	2	5	5	4	0	1	0	5	4	0	3	0
0	1	5	0	6	5	1	1	8	0	9	4	1	1	2	6	1	4	2	0	8	6	3	1	0
5	8	1	7	4	7	5	6	2	1	9	3	7	4	0	4	6	4	6	9	6	7	5	0	6
2	5	0	7	5	1	6	0	4	0	4	1	9	4	9	8	3	6	3	8	0	0	1	7	9
8	8	3	7	8	1	4	6	3	8	0	5	6	4	4	3	5	0	6	9	5	5	0	6	0
4	3	1	8	7	3	4	1	7	1	6	1	5	2	7	9	4	0	2	9	9	6	8	7	6
9	1	4	7	7	4	3	7	4	2	5	5	0	2	1	1	1	4	0	6	4	7	5	9	6
8	6	0	8	2	9	3	4	3	4	7	6	9	6	1	8	2	3	3	8	3	4	6	8	3
3	3	0	6	2	3	8	7	4	3	8	3	1	1	5	9	7	4	4	4	9	7	6	0	9
1	8	2	0	2	9	8	8	0	1	6	8	0	7	5	6	0	8	3	9	2	1	1	2	0
4	7	4	1	1	8	5	9	6	9	7	7	8	0	8	0	8	5	7	2	6	9	4	6	7
7	2	8	1	1	0	4	0	5	0	0	8	2	5	7	4	9	4	0	6	9	7	1	8	0
8	4	0	0	8	1	8	7	1	5	0	1	3	7	3	1	1	4	1	9	7	1	7	8	5
1	5	0	5	3	1	9	7	5	0	3	7	6	3	4	7	2	2	0	5	0	0	7	5	1
6	8	5	1	2	4	1	0	4	6	2	5	9	9	3	2	5	6	0	1	2	0	6	7	7
7	6	5	5	4	6	1	9	1	1	7	9	9	9	6	6	7	1	3	7	7	4	8	8	2
7	8	2	4	2	1	6	4	3	9	7	2	6	6	5	7	0	1	2	8	9	7	1	4	5
9	0	3	3	8	1	3	5	1	4	2	8	7	7	0	3	5	8	0	8	4	2	6	6	4
5	5	4	8	6	5	6	8	0	3	2	0	4	8	4	5	6	6	5	4	7	1	3	1	2
0	6	4	9	7	7	9	8	0	6	4	0	9	2	4	7	8	2	5	1	7	2	3	5	2
6	0	6	7	8	0	8	7	6	8	5	0	1	3	4	3	0	4	7	0	5	2	4	1	3
1	6	3	6	4	9	6	5	3	5	5	3	0	3	3	8	3	7	9	1	1	5	8	2	2
2	1	5	9	7	1	2	6	4	4	5	0	2	1	4	5	1	1	7	0	4	0	1	3	0

Table 1 *Random Numbers (continued)*

5	0	3	9	1	8	3	8	9	5	5	6	7	3	0	6	7	9	7	1	4	9	2	3	3
3	5	8	1	8	1	6	3	4	7	0	6	7	7	8	9	6	2	0	8	5	0	4	3	7
7	0	6	4	0	6	9	0	5	9	3	3	7	7	1	1	4	4	3	8	0	6	2	1	8
1	0	4	9	2	7	8	1	6	4	4	9	3	2	9	6	7	3	2	4	2	6	4	9	6
7	7	7	0	3	2	5	7	9	3	0	5	6	6	5	8	7	6	2	8	5	2	5	3	8
3	1	4	2	0	1	2	3	5	8	0	4	9	9	9	5	6	4	8	6	4	3	5	0	8
8	7	9	8	4	6	4	1	7	0	8	6	0	0	6	1	7	0	9	0	2	9	8	4	2
5	0	6	9	7	6	4	6	4	9	6	6	0	5	3	2	7	9	2	4	4	4	0	6	5
0	9	7	6	2	3	7	3	6	5	7	7	4	8	5	9	4	9	6	6	0	9	5	6	3
1	1	2	9	9	4	6	0	0	6	3	7	1	3	1	9	1	2	6	6	0	8	7	5	2
9	5	5	5	1	9	7	5	9	0	3	2	1	5	6	1	1	1	2	8	3	5	9	5	5
5	6	2	2	6	5	2	0	4	0	5	8	1	8	6	1	2	3	9	0	3	4	3	0	3
3	0	8	5	5	8	7	5	1	7	1	0	7	0	2	7	4	9	9	5	4	9	3	4	6
1	9	4	1	2	5	8	1	2	4	4	9	7	5	9	7	5	8	8	6	2	2	2	4	0
1	6	0	1	7	5	6	9	4	1	7	3	2	2	6	5	1	4	5	9	8	9	9	2	4
9	4	3	4	6	5	3	2	3	0	8	5	6	6	1	1	0	6	6	6	9	6	0	1	1
3	8	5	2	2	5	3	1	3	4	8	8	2	8	7	5	4	6	4	6	4	0	3	3	4
6	5	9	8	7	5	1	5	0	1	3	1	3	5	7	1	1	7	6	6	6	6	8	4	5
9	9	7	6	9	8	8	7	0	6	1	5	7	9	7	1	5	9	7	9	2	6	7	1	1
3	2	8	0	3	7	7	6	8	3	1	2	6	3	0	8	1	4	8	6	1	2	6	6	8
8	9	9	2	9	7	7	4	2	3	3	5	9	2	3	5	8	6	7	3	0	6	4	9	9
5	2	2	0	3	2	8	7	3	4	1	2	6	8	9	6	8	9	4	1	7	6	8	2	9
9	3	7	1	9	8	3	6	0	2	8	6	3	5	3	0	1	6	1	3	3	8	3	4	8
0	6	7	9	9	0	3	7	7	2	6	0	7	7	1	1	8	1	2	9	9	7	8	0	6
6	5	3	1	0	4	2	4	5	1	4	9	5	3	9	0	2	2	4	5	9	9	9	0	0
4	1	8	9	1	7	4	3	6	4	4	6	6	6	0	7	6	3	2	5	8	2	0	6	8
4	5	4	7	1	1	4	5	0	4	7	9	4	0	6	1	2	1	9	4	9	9	0	2	3
2	5	4	3	3	6	3	1	4	0	9	3	7	9	1	1	8	8	1	8	0	3	1	9	5
4	3	6	4	0	1	7	8	2	0	4	9	5	9	7	9	0	3	3	7	2	9	9	4	0
2	3	8	5	4	4	3	3	0	6	1	0	7	3	5	3	1	3	2	0	6	0	9	1	7
1	6	4	8	7	9	9	9	1	3	1	0	8	6	7	5	6	9	0	3	1	6	8	2	0
4	8	1	6	3	4	5	0	2	7	5	7	0	8	3	2	4	8	5	3	2	9	6	8	1
4	2	1	9	4	6	2	3	0	1	1	6	1	0	7	2	2	3	4	8	7	9	1	4	6
4	0	7	6	5	4	2	9	5	3	3	9	0	6	3	0	2	5	4	9	5	3	6	0	8
8	4	9	3	0	8	2	8	4	0	4	5	6	9	0	6	8	1	1	4	6	7	4	8	1
1	7	6	3	8	1	4	6	2	2	9	4	5	0	3	5	7	0	0	2	4	1	7	1	2
5	6	4	6	9	0	1	5	1	5	5	0	3	1	4	5	1	2	7	0	2	4	9	9	6
0	3	6	0	7	1	4	8	0	3	5	4	8	8	0	4	0	6	7	3	3	1	1	7	4
6	7	2	9	0	4	2	9	2	6	4	6	4	6	4	6	9	4	6	2	3	9	4	8	8
0	3	1	4	5	9	5	0	8	2	6	5	0	8	5	8	0	7	5	0	9	5	3	1	5
7	3	0	9	3	6	1	9	3	1	3	9	8	3	9	7	7	6	6	5	3	0	2	6	8
8	6	7	9	6	6	8	3	4	0	5	9	5	1	7	8	0	1	0	8	9	7	1	4	6
4	9	5	8	6	8	0	4	4	4	5	6	7	4	8	1	7	1	4	9	2	9	5	1	9
6	0	3	9	9	5	8	4	4	1	5	4	0	6	8	6	0	2	0	0	1	8	8	8	0
4	1	0	5	3	6	3	5	0	6	4	0	0	1	2	1	8	2	9	5	4	8	7	2	5
5	2	7	9	6	5	7	4	5	1	3	3	8	8	4	4	0	4	1	8	9	1	1	6	5
3	4	6	1	2	1	8	7	4	7	6	3	3	5	0	0	7	9	1	6	4	0	7	4	6
8	2	2	0	8	8	8	7	3	8	3	1	5	8	4	9	5	1	9	1	7	9	7	9	9
4	8	7	0	7	8	9	4	3	0	9	2	3	5	4	7	2	1	4	6	6	8	6	3	2
9	0	4	3	8	0	1	5	7	6	7	1	6	3	0	5	7	3	7	1	0	9	5	6	6

Table 1 *Random Numbers (continued)*

8	2	8	9	7	9	6	9	7	9	0	8	2	9	8	1	5	6	9	3	2	9	2	3	3
9	4	6	9	2	6	8	4	4	7	8	3	5	1	0	1	3	9	9	2	9	0	4	0	8
5	6	7	4	2	7	4	1	2	7	3	1	5	8	3	1	0	7	3	8	7	5	2	5	1
8	0	9	9	8	3	2	9	7	5	5	8	0	5	2	1	3	4	2	3	8	6	8	3	6
6	7	0	3	7	9	8	8	2	0	9	1	0	6	0	7	2	4	5	1	3	3	5	1	0
8	1	3	0	0	8	3	4	8	8	3	4	8	9	9	2	0	4	3	9	6	7	6	5	7
1	7	6	2	5	8	6	2	6	6	8	0	8	3	9	8	8	7	4	2	1	3	3	3	2
9	9	7	1	7	5	9	1	3	2	4	6	0	5	9	0	7	3	8	2	3	5	4	7	1
0	4	6	4	0	1	7	9	9	3	6	8	1	5	3	7	1	1	9	5	1	0	1	4	8
9	7	8	2	1	2	9	7	2	0	6	4	2	5	2	7	0	8	1	1	9	7	7	7	0
2	4	6	4	6	3	6	7	5	2	0	0	5	4	7	3	3	4	1	0	7	4	4	0	9
8	5	4	5	4	7	7	4	0	0	5	0	6	4	2	8	8	0	8	0	9	9	0	5	8
5	8	6	7	6	6	4	7	0	1	4	9	9	5	7	2	1	4	1	1	9	7	7	3	5
1	3	8	1	4	7	0	7	4	8	8	4	4	0	1	2	5	1	4	8	1	7	7	3	2
4	1	5	9	7	9	5	6	6	7	4	5	6	1	8	8	8	2	8	9	0	0	9	2	5
9	5	4	7	0	6	8	1	2	1	4	0	4	5	8	3	1	6	0	1	9	7	5	6	0
3	7	2	7	4	1	4	8	3	6	4	1	6	1	9	0	4	1	3	2	6	8	9	2	5
9	7	1	8	1	0	8	3	6	0	1	7	5	0	6	3	2	7	9	2	5	6	2	9	9
9	9	9	9	1	9	4	2	6	9	5	8	5	6	8	3	9	8	6	9	9	6	8	2	5
9	3	0	1	8	1	5	8	8	1	1	4	4	6	6	4	1	0	9	6	6	7	5	5	8
7	9	4	6	8	9	0	6	6	9	5	4	3	1	9	5	1	9	5	6	2	8	2	7	4
3	5	5	4	5	2	5	2	2	1	4	8	2	0	9	1	8	4	3	5	0	3	2	6	5
6	7	2	1	9	0	5	4	3	3	9	8	9	0	1	2	6	6	1	3	0	4	5	4	1
4	0	5	3	9	2	6	3	2	2	0	4	2	0	9	1	0	0	8	8	8	0	2	8	1
2	1	5	7	3	7	3	6	2	8	9	3	2	8	7	9	6	7	9	5	1	9	5	5	4
8	2	9	1	7	6	5	0	5	7	4	2	4	7	5	1	4	2	8	4	0	2	0	4	5
0	4	9	2	5	9	9	8	7	4	7	3	2	2	1	7	7	1	9	5	1	4	4	9	4
3	8	6	7	5	6	1	5	3	0	9	0	8	4	0	4	6	7	2	2	6	8	4	3	5
7	1	8	8	3	6	3	7	4	3	6	3	3	0	1	3	4	9	7	3	8	9	2	3	6
2	3	0	4	7	4	6	9	9	9	8	7	4	4	2	8	1	4	4	4	0	0	6	0	8
8	6	4	4	0	7	1	2	9	6	3	1	3	4	9	1	6	2	9	3	7	6	1	1	0
0	5	5	4	6	7	7	9	6	9	0	2	5	5	3	5	8	5	1	2	9	6	9	3	9
5	7	4	3	2	8	8	4	4	2	0	8	9	6	3	0	5	1	1	2	7	3	7	8	0
8	3	2	7	1	2	7	0	2	9	1	1	7	1	5	4	8	1	9	1	2	5	0	5	3
3	1	2	1	0	7	7	3	0	4	7	1	3	8	9	3	8	7	2	7	5	1	4	8	9
0	7	9	7	0	6	4	5	3	0	5	8	2	7	3	7	3	0	6	2	4	3	3	9	1
9	0	3	4	4	3	1	8	2	1	0	4	5	9	7	2	9	0	5	5	4	7	1	5	9
1	5	7	9	2	9	5	2	8	9	1	8	6	4	2	3	4	0	6	1	4	1	7	9	9
7	3	8	2	7	8	4	7	5	9	3	4	2	9	9	4	8	3	1	1	6	5	1	5	6
2	4	0	4	4	0	4	5	0	7	6	4	9	2	0	5	3	9	2	8	1	1	8	0	2
2	9	9	9	6	6	8	0	6	9	4	0	8	4	2	4	0	4	6	0	2	1	2	2	4
5	8	2	2	2	1	7	7	2	5	9	4	2	1	7	2	1	7	7	9	3	3	5	9	8
7	3	7	4	3	6	3	0	9	9	1	6	3	9	2	3	0	2	6	8	9	8	9	0	7
8	8	9	7	6	2	9	9	0	1	2	0	0	1	0	2	4	7	8	9	6	6	9	7	8
1	4	0	9	6	1	0	9	8	7	0	5	8	0	6	5	8	0	5	0	1	9	3	0	1
1	6	4	2	4	7	6	7	7	3	5	9	3	2	2	9	2	7	8	6	3	7	7	8	1
1	2	9	8	1	2	5	7	7	9	6	8	4	4	0	6	3	3	1	1	6	7	2	5	8
5	7	7	5	3	5	5	5	6	7	9	4	3	1	5	7	2	7	6	9	7	6	1	0	3
2	4	7	9	1	7	2	8	3	4	4	1	1	1	3	0	6	9	1	4	8	8	7	5	6
0	2	5	9	4	0	8	2	5	6	0	4	7	1	6	3	6	5	5	6	1	1	6	7	6

Table 1 *Random Numbers (continued)*

8	9	0	8	8	8	7	4	1	9	9	9	5	5	1	8	2	1	3	7	5	7	8	7	1
1	1	0	4	2	7	2	3	9	9	5	7	5	0	9	5	3	9	6	8	6	7	4	9	0
0	0	6	6	6	3	1	5	6	3	8	9	7	2	9	0	9	8	4	9	4	2	5	0	0
2	8	5	9	9	3	5	2	5	2	1	1	7	4	0	7	9	0	1	4	9	1	9	8	9
7	5	8	0	7	9	4	5	7	9	3	2	0	7	6	3	2	6	3	6	0	9	7	8	5
2	8	1	2	4	9	9	2	0	1	9	7	9	7	2	0	8	1	4	9	2	8	6	5	9
1	6	5	9	5	2	6	8	5	8	1	8	0	6	1	2	2	7	1	0	8	6	1	9	9
3	8	0	2	2	2	0	4	5	5	5	4	5	6	9	9	1	4	2	6	7	3	9	3	5
7	0	7	8	2	1	9	6	3	1	1	8	1	1	7	8	1	6	0	3	9	6	7	1	0
9	5	9	2	6	6	6	7	4	1	9	5	1	9	8	4	2	7	9	3	8	5	5	0	8
9	9	3	7	7	0	5	3	1	2	2	4	7	0	2	2	4	0	2	1	4	5	2	6	9
2	8	6	7	5	0	2	8	7	0	4	2	5	4	1	5	3	3	7	0	7	8	8	0	8
5	8	4	6	5	0	3	6	4	5	2	4	7	9	6	7	7	3	1	5	9	7	7	4	2
2	7	9	4	0	0	1	7	0	7	2	0	0	5	1	8	6	4	9	7	9	7	0	4	8
3	2	0	4	1	5	9	2	4	0	8	3	9	0	6	9	8	3	7	7	2	6	0	6	8
9	4	4	2	4	3	1	3	1	3	0	2	2	8	2	7	5	6	8	5	3	2	9	9	9
1	4	7	7	0	3	1	3	3	5	9	6	5	1	6	4	0	6	9	7	3	9	2	1	6
2	7	4	6	7	2	6	2	7	2	5	1	3	8	7	7	8	2	1	9	2	5	0	9	0
5	3	2	1	6	4	9	4	4	6	2	5	3	3	3	5	2	5	4	9	5	7	4	4	6
6	0	9	6	4	0	0	9	3	2	7	7	6	6	7	9	7	8	1	8	0	4	1	8	1
6	8	6	5	0	5	3	4	2	3	3	7	5	7	7	9	7	4	7	0	5	6	5	1	3
7	2	1	3	4	1	7	8	1	8	4	4	1	6	6	6	2	5	6	6	2	0	4	1	9
7	5	9	1	3	2	7	1	2	6	3	1	3	3	1	2	9	0	9	8	9	8	6	9	8
8	7	7	6	8	8	8	1	6	8	6	1	8	8	6	1	7	5	6	8	6	4	3	6	9
0	4	6	4	6	1	9	6	1	4	5	9	1	1	3	6	1	4	5	7	0	8	2	5	4
9	6	8	6	1	6	3	0	3	7	0	4	9	8	8	7	7	6	8	1	7	1	5	0	8
7	6	9	7	0	9	8	7	1	2	0	9	0	3	8	5	3	9	3	7	4	1	1	5	7
3	2	7	0	9	2	7	5	8	0	4	7	8	1	4	2	4	0	0	9	6	5	9	2	5
4	2	6	8	9	1	9	0	4	2	1	3	4	3	2	0	6	7	4	7	1	3	9	7	9
6	8	6	5	1	4	1	3	0	6	7	0	9	5	2	8	7	0	9	3	8	5	1	3	5
6	3	5	7	2	0	2	8	6	3	3	8	5	3	1	0	4	6	6	3	1	7	9	9	7
7	3	7	7	3	4	5	2	3	6	2	3	6	5	5	3	9	2	1	7	0	6	4	2	0
6	0	1	2	5	0	2	9	4	9	8	3	5	9	5	7	4	5	2	8	4	7	6	6	4
2	6	6	8	6	5	0	7	7	5	5	4	9	1	2	0	3	4	8	9	6	4	9	8	9
3	6	8	7	2	9	9	2	7	5	6	0	9	0	6	5	8	8	2	8	3	4	7	4	0
4	2	5	5	7	2	6	5	9	4	3	8	7	5	6	5	3	6	3	4	3	8	5	4	7
3	2	3	1	1	5	6	5	8	3	9	6	2	2	0	2	9	0	9	3	1	1	3	1	4
0	2	3	6	6	9	4	4	6	6	0	9	9	7	4	0	1	3	2	5	6	9	4	5	1
6	5	6	9	4	1	6	8	8	6	7	0	0	6	0	8	8	3	9	7	8	4	1	7	6
7	3	1	3	9	1	2	0	7	1	5	2	1	2	0	7	0	1	7	8	6	4	6	6	3
3	5	2	5	5	9	9	0	1	5	3	2	1	7	0	1	9	3	6	3	3	4	5	0	9
2	7	6	2	3	9	6	7	5	3	6	1	5	0	2	0	3	2	9	1	6	2	1	4	6
7	8	9	1	3	0	3	0	0	2	8	5	5	4	3	8	9	6	8	2	2	1	8	8	1
1	1	0	8	2	7	9	9	8	5	5	1	9	0	7	1	2	5	7	6	8	5	8	2	8
9	6	3	9	6	2	1	1	1	0	3	2	1	7	5	0	6	9	0	6	2	0	9	5	1
1	0	3	2	4	6	1	9	9	8	8	6	5	7	6	9	8	9	1	2	4	9	1	3	5
2	3	7	1	5	7	2	5	8	1	1	7	6	6	4	9	1	3	0	3	5	2	6	3	3
2	3	6	4	7	5	3	4	7	7	7	6	4	3	5	9	6	3	8	7	8	0	1	3	2
9	3	6	1	5	4	4	5	3	3	5	4	1	5	2	3	4	6	4	5	3	7	6	9	2
0	4	0	4	6	7	0	2	9	4	3	5	9	9	7	4	9	0	6	8	7	5	9	3	6

Table 1 *Random Numbers (concluded)*

9	3	6	4	8	6	5	9	2	6	4	5	1	6	9	9	0	8	6	7	4	5	7	2	8
1	1	5	8	8	6	9	0	3	3	6	8	4	1	8	1	3	9	0	8	3	4	5	6	5
7	2	8	1	8	8	3	7	4	4	3	5	0	2	1	3	1	9	9	1	1	1	7	0	0
1	8	4	9	4	8	6	2	6	5	1	7	6	9	5	8	8	2	8	4	0	6	2	7	8
2	7	3	0	6	1	3	6	4	1	9	2	4	5	4	4	9	5	4	7	1	4	2	0	0
2	1	0	3	9	9	3	2	8	0	0	3	4	6	2	9	2	5	5	9	6	5	0	7	8
5	1	2	1	7	3	1	5	7	1	5	8	7	7	5	7	9	8	0	8	5	3	2	5	8
2	5	3	5	4	8	4	5	2	5	7	7	2	8	7	1	8	2	3	9	3	1	5	9	9
0	6	1	5	3	1	9	8	0	4	3	2	0	1	4	5	4	2	9	8	2	9	1	5	5
4	7	0	9	2	7	5	8	6	1	5	4	0	9	9	7	3	9	6	5	5	4	0	1	4
4	6	1	4	8	5	7	1	9	7	0	9	4	2	8	0	1	3	6	4	0	4	9	7	2
8	5	2	7	5	0	5	6	6	3	3	3	1	8	1	6	7	3	2	4	9	6	6	8	9
1	9	5	1	2	4	1	4	7	2	9	8	7	7	4	9	5	1	2	8	6	7	0	0	7
1	1	7	5	2	6	4	7	5	9	2	9	2	7	0	9	3	3	1	6	2	1	0	8	2
6	0	4	0	7	7	9	9	5	0	3	8	6	9	8	9	1	2	5	2	6	3	3	6	5
4	2	8	8	4	2	2	6	5	9	7	6	4	5	2	4	4	4	7	2	3	3	8	0	1
6	3	1	3	5	0	4	8	3	4	1	7	2	9	0	6	3	3	5	0	4	0	4	5	1
4	9	9	6	2	8	3	1	8	4	8	1	1	0	9	4	6	4	2	1	5	9	4	8	6
5	5	8	5	7	3	5	3	1	0	8	9	8	0	1	0	6	2	1	6	9	7	3	5	1
0	8	3	6	4	9	7	5	6	2	8	7	3	8	9	0	2	2	0	0	4	9	9	0	9
5	6	2	1	3	3	7	4	0	7	1	9	3	8	7	6	5	8	9	0	8	3	7	1	4
6	7	6	6	5	2	7	1	5	0	1	5	8	3	1	5	3	5	5	2	2	4	2	5	4
1	0	2	9	2	0	9	5	4	1	6	9	6	8	4	0	2	6	5	3	2	2	1	3	9
9	7	3	0	4	1	8	8	6	5	9	3	9	1	2	2	0	7	2	3	8	9	9	7	8
3	6	6	7	1	6	5	6	6	9	6	7	8	6	2	1	4	1	1	0	8	8	5	4	0
2	4	3	9	7	6	0	0	6	2	8	4	3	4	4	1	1	5	9	3	7	9	4	8	3
0	4	7	0	4	1	0	7	2	9	6	4	5	2	7	2	9	8	3	4	5	6	8	8	2
6	0	5	9	1	1	1	4	4	6	9	7	8	8	6	3	6	7	6	0	5	1	0	5	5
1	1	5	1	6	6	0	5	1	5	6	0	7	5	2	7	3	7	2	4	8	6	2	5	4
3	4	2	3	2	5	9	4	7	1	7	8	4	1	3	8	8	5	3	7	6	8	8	6	4
8	3	3	6	5	8	0	5	9	6	6	1	3	4	5	4	2	8	3	9	5	0	8	9	1
9	2	1	2	4	7	6	5	9	3	6	0	5	0	7	5	3	7	9	3	8	5	1	7	6
2	6	6	8	4	7	5	4	7	0	8	4	2	6	8	3	1	4	5	9	8	7	5	0	6
6	6	4	6	5	8	8	5	9	8	5	9	4	6	5	2	4	0	7	1	4	1	8	7	0
1	1	6	5	4	5	4	0	4	1	7	2	1	5	7	5	8	5	7	4	4	8	2	6	2
3	0	8	3	7	1	3	1	9	0	7	7	5	2	2	7	6	3	9	9	9	0	3	8	6
8	0	2	6	1	8	5	9	3	1	7	9	4	7	5	5	4	9	6	4	6	1	6	0	1
4	5	2	7	5	1	0	6	4	2	1	6	2	4	9	1	8	3	1	8	8	2	7	4	1
0	5	6	1	3	8	3	9	8	3	6	9	4	9	1	5	2	5	6	5	8	4	5	1	9
7	4	1	5	0	4	4	3	4	8	7	4	8	7	4	5	1	3	9	2	4	1	2	2	5
7	4	5	7	0	9	8	3	4	9	7	8	1	3	2	2	8	3	7	3	8	5	2	6	1
5	8	8	2	4	5	4	9	5	6	5	5	0	1	7	6	3	6	1	6	6	5	6	8	9
1	4	9	9	2	0	5	4	1	2	6	4	3	8	4	3	4	3	2	4	4	2	9	5	6
2	3	5	4	3	3	6	9	2	8	2	1	1	5	5	0	7	1	4	5	0	5	6	3	0
9	6	1	5	9	9	1	2	9	2	5	3	9	9	4	1	6	2	3	4	0	8	8	6	9
0	7	2	9	3	7	5	5	5	0	5	7	3	3	6	8	6	2	7	2	1	5	0	0	3
6	2	8	1	5	1	1	4	8	2	9	5	5	6	5	2	0	6	7	3	3	9	2	2	2
2	7	8	8	9	0	4	1	4	6	9	7	5	4	9	2	4	4	0	6	9	5	4	4	4
4	3	3	9	1	2	1	3	6	3	4	3	4	8	8	6	9	3	2	3	3	4	7	1	2
8	8	0	5	2	2	8	0	8	5	3	0	3	7	4	9	6	0	1	8	5	3	8	6	4

Table 2 *Distribution of t*

df	*Level of significance for one-tailed test*					
	.10	.05	.025	.01	.005	.0005
	Level of significance for two-tailed test					
	.20	.10	.05	.02	.01	.001
1	3.078	6.314	12.706	31.821	63.657	636.619
2	1.886	2.920	4.303	6.965	9.925	31.598
3	1.638	2.353	3.182	4.541	5.841	12.941
4	1.533	2.132	2.776	3.747	4.604	8.610
5	1.476	2.015	2.571	3.365	4.032	6.859
6	1.440	1.943	2.447	3.143	3.707	5.959
7	1.415	1.895	2.365	2.998	3.499	5.405
8	1.397	1.860	2.306	2.896	3.355	5.041
9	1.383	1.833	2.262	2.821	3.250	4.781
10	1.372	1.812	2.228	2.764	3.169	4.587
11	1.363	1.796	2.201	2.718	3.106	4.437
12	1.356	1.782	2.179	2.681	3.055	4.318
13	1.350	1.771	2.160	2.650	3.012	4.221
14	1.345	1.761	2.145	2.624	2.977	4.140
15	1.341	1.753	2.131	2.602	2.947	4.073
16	1.337	1.746	2.120	2.583	2.921	4.015
17	1.333	1.740	2.110	2.567	2.898	3.965
18	1.330	1.734	2.101	2.552	2.878	3.992
19	1.328	1.729	2.093	2.539	2.861	3.883
20	1.325	1.725	2.086	2.528	2.845	3.850
21	1.323	1.721	2.080	2.518	2.831	3.819
22	1.321	1.717	2.074	2.508	2.819	3.792
23	1.319	1.714	2.069	2.500	2.807	3.767
24	1.318	1.711	2.064	2.492	2.797	3.745
25	1.316	1.708	2.060	2.485	2.787	3.725
26	1.315	1.706	2.056	2.479	2.779	3.707
27	1.314	1.703	2.052	2.473	2.771	3.690
28	1.313	1.701	2.048	2.467	2.763	3.674
29	1.311	1.699	2.045	2.462	2.756	3.659
30	1.310	1.697	2.042	2.457	2.750	3.646
40	1.303	1.684	2.021	2.423	2.704	3.551
60	1.296	1.671	2.000	2.390	2.660	3.460
120	1.289	1.658	1.980	2.358	2.617	3.373
∞	1.282	1.645	1.960	2.326	2.576	3.291

Table abridged from Table III of Fisher and Yates, *Statistical Tables for Biological, Agricultural, and Medical Research,* published by Longman Group Ltd., London (previously published by Oliver and Boyd Ltd., Edinburgh), by permission of the authors and publishers.

Table 3 *Areas Under the Normal Curve. Proportion of Area Under the Normal Curve Between the Mean and a z Distance from the Mean*

$\frac{x}{\sigma}$ or z	.00	.01	.02	.03	.04	.05	.06	.07	.08	.09
.0	.0000	.0040	.0080	.0120	.0160	.0199	.0239	.0279	.0319	.0359
.1	.0398	.0438	.0478	.0517	.0557	.0596	.0636	.0675	.0714	.0753
.2	.0793	.0832	.0871	.0910	.0948	.0987	.1026	.1064	.1103	.1141
.3	.1179	.1217	.1255	.1293	.1331	.1368	.1406	.1443	.1480	.1517
.4	.1554	.1591	.1628	.1664	.1700	.1736	.1772	.1808	.1844	.1879
.5	.1915	.1950	.1985	.2019	.2054	.2088	.2123	.2157	.2190	.2224
.6	.2257	.2291	.2324	.2357	.2389	.2422	.2454	.2486	.2517	.2549
.7	.2580	.2611	.2642	.2673	.2704	.2734	.2764	.2794	.2823	.2852
.8	.2881	.2910	.2939	.2967	.2995	.3023	.3051	.3078	.3106	.3133
.9	.3159	.3186	.3212	.3238	.3264	.3289	.3315	.3340	.3365	.3389
1.0	.3413	.3438	.3461	.3485	.3508	.3531	.3554	.3577	.3599	.3621
1.1	.3643	.3665	.3686	.3708	.3729	.3749	.3770	.3790	.3810	.3830
1.2	.3849	.3869	.3888	.3907	.3925	.3944	.3962	.3980	.3997	.4015
1.3	.4032	.4049	.4066	.4082	.4099	.4115	.4131	.4147	.4162	.4177
1.4	.4192	.4207	.4222	.4236	.4251	.4265	.4279	.4292	.4306	.4319
1.5	.4332	.4345	.4357	.4370	.4382	.4394	.4406	.4418	.4429	.4441
1.6	.4452	.4463	.4474	.4484	.4495	.4505	.4515	.4525	.4535	.4545
1.7	.4554	.4564	.4573	.4582	.4591	.4599	.4608	.4616	.4625	.4633
1.8	.4641	.4649	.4656	.4664	.4671	.4678	.4686	.4693	.4699	.4706
1.9	.4713	.4719	.4726	.4732	.4738	.4744	.4750	.4756	.4761	.4767
2.0	.4772	.4778	.4783	.4788	.4793	.4798	.4803	.4808	.4812	.4817
2.1	.4821	.4826	.4830	.4834	.4838	.4842	.4846	.4850	.4854	.4857
2.2	.4861	.4864	.4868	.4871	.4875	.4878	.4881	.4884	.4887	.4890
2.3	.4893	.4896	.4898	.4901	.4904	.4906	.4909	.4911	.4913	.4916
2.4	.4918	.4920	.4922	.4925	.4927	.4929	.4931	.4932	.4934	.4936
2.5	.4938	.4940	.4941	.4943	.4945	.4946	.4948	.4949	.4951	.4952
2.6	.4953	.4955	.4956	.4957	.4959	.4960	.4961	.4962	.4963	.4964
2.7	.4965	.4966	.4967	.4968	.4969	.4970	.4971	.4972	.4973	.4974
2.8	.4974	.4975	.4976	.4977	.4977	.4978	.4979	.4979	.4980	.4981
2.9	.4981	.4982	.4982	.4983	.4984	.4984	.4985	.4985	.4986	.4986
3.0	.4987	.4987	.4987	.4988	.4988	.4989	.4989	.4989	.4990	.4990
3.1	.4990	.4991	.4991	.4991	.4992	.4992	.4992	.4992	.4993	.4993
3.2	.4993	.4993	.4994	.4994	.4994	.4994	.4994	.4995	.4995	.4995
3.3	.4995	.4995	.4995	.4996	.4996	.4996	.4996	.4996	.4996	.4997
3.4	.4997	.4997	.4997	.4997	.4997	.4997	.4997	.4997	.4997	.4998
3.5	.4998									
4.0	.49997									
4.5	.499997									
5.0	.4999997									

Table 4 *Distribution of Chi-Square*

	Probability					
df	.20	.10	.05	.02	.01	.001
1	1.642	2.706	3.841	5.412	6.635	10.827
2	3.219	4.605	5.991	7.824	9.210	13.815
3	4.642	6.251	7.815	9.837	11.345	16.266
4	5.989	7.779	9.488	11.668	13.277	18.467
5	7.289	9.236	11.070	13.388	15.086	20.515
6	8.558	10.645	12.592	15.033	16.812	22.457
7	9.803	12.017	14.067	16.622	18.475	24.322
8	11.030	13.362	15.507	18.168	20.090	26.125
9	12.242	14.684	16.919	19.679	21.666	27.877
10	13.442	15.987	18.307	21.161	23.209	29.588
11	14.631	17.275	19.675	22.618	24.725	31.264
12	15.812	18.549	21.026	24.054	26.217	32.909
13	16.985	19.812	22.362	25.472	27.688	34.528
14	18.151	21.064	23.685	26.873	29.141	36.123
15	19.311	22.307	24.996	28.259	30.578	37.697
16	20.465	23.542	26.296	29.633	32.000	39.252
17	21.615	24.769	27.587	30.995	33.409	40.790
18	22.760	25.989	28.869	32.346	34.805	42.312
19	23.900	27.204	30.144	33.687	36.191	43.820
20	25.038	28.412	31.410	35.020	37.566	45.315
21	26.171	29.615	32.671	36.343	38.932	46.797
22	27.301	30.813	33.924	37.659	40.289	48.268
23	28.429	32.007	35.172	38.968	41.638	49.728
24	29.553	33.196	36.415	40.270	42.980	51.179
25	30.675	34.382	37.652	41.566	44.314	52.620

Table 4 *Distribution of Chi-Square (continued)*

	Probability					
df	.20	.10	.05	.02	.01	.001
26	31.795	35.563	38.885	42.856	45.642	54.052
27	32.912	36.741	40.113	44.140	46.963	55.476
28	34.027	37.916	41.337	45.419	48.278	56.893
29	35.139	39.087	42.557	46.693	49.588	58.302
30	36.250	40.256	43.773	47.962	50.892	59.703
32	38.466	42.585	46.194	50.487	53.486	62.487
34	40.676	44.903	48.602	52.995	56.061	65.247
36	42.879	47.212	50.999	55.489	58.619	67.985
38	45.076	49.513	53.384	57.969	61.162	70.703
40	47.269	51.805	55.759	60.436	63.691	73.402
42	49.456	54.090	58.124	62.892	66.206	76.084
44	51.639	56.369	60.481	65.337	68.710	78.750
46	53.818	58.641	62.830	67.771	71.201	81.400
48	55.993	60.907	65.171	70.197	73.683	84.037
50	58.164	63.167	67.505	72.613	76.154	86.661
52	60.332	65.422	69.832	75.021	78.616	89.272
54	62.496	67.673	72.153	77.422	81.069	91.872
56	64.658	69.919	74.468	79.815	83.513	94.461
58	66.816	72.160	76.778	82.201	85.950	97.039
60	68.972	74.397	79.082	84.580	88.379	99.607
62	71.125	76.630	81.381	86.953	90.802	102.166
64	73.276	78.860	83.675	89.320	93.217	104.716
66	75.424	81.085	85.965	91.681	95.626	107.258
68	77.571	83.308	88.250	94.037	98.028	109.791
70	79.715	85.527	90.531	96.388	100.425	112.317

Table 5 *Distribution of F: .05 Level*

df_2 / df_1	1	2	3	4	5	6	7	8	9	10	12	15	20	24	30	40	60	120	∞
1	161.4	199.5	215.7	224.6	230.2	234.0	236.8	238.9	240.5	241.9	243.9	245.9	248.0	249.1	250.1	251.1	252.2	253.3	254.3
2	18.51	19.00	19.16	19.25	19.30	19.33	19.35	19.37	19.38	19.40	19.41	19.43	19.45	19.45	19.46	19.47	19.48	19.49	19.50
3	10.13	9.55	9.28	9.12	9.01	8.94	8.89	8.85	8.81	8.79	8.74	8.70	8.66	8.64	8.62	8.59	8.57	8.55	8.53
4	7.71	6.94	6.59	6.39	6.26	6.16	6.09	6.04	6.00	5.96	5.91	5.86	5.80	5.77	5.75	5.72	5.69	5.66	5.63
5	6.61	5.79	5.41	5.19	5.05	4.95	4.88	4.82	4.77	4.74	4.68	4.62	4.56	4.53	4.50	4.46	4.43	4.40	4.36
6	5.99	5.14	4.76	4.53	4.39	4.28	4.21	4.15	4.10	4.06	4.00	3.94	3.87	3.84	3.81	3.77	3.74	3.70	3.67
7	5.59	4.74	4.35	4.12	3.97	3.87	3.79	3.73	3.68	3.64	3.57	3.51	3.44	3.41	3.38	3.34	3.30	3.27	3.23
8	5.32	4.46	4.07	3.84	3.69	3.58	3.50	3.44	3.39	3.35	3.28	3.22	3.15	3.12	3.08	3.04	3.01	2.97	2.93
9	5.12	4.26	3.86	3.63	3.48	3.37	3.29	3.23	3.18	3.14	3.07	3.01	2.94	2.90	2.86	2.83	2.79	2.75	2.71
10	4.96	4.10	3.71	3.48	3.33	3.22	3.14	3.07	3.02	2.98	2.91	2.85	2.77	2.74	2.70	2.66	2.62	2.58	2.54
11	4.84	3.98	3.59	3.36	3.20	3.09	3.01	2.95	2.90	2.85	2.79	2.72	2.65	2.61	2.57	2.53	2.49	2.45	2.40
12	4.75	3.89	3.49	3.26	3.11	3.00	2.91	2.85	2.80	2.75	2.69	2.62	2.54	2.51	2.47	2.43	2.38	2.34	2.30
13	4.67	3.81	3.41	3.18	3.03	2.92	2.83	2.77	2.71	2.67	2.60	2.53	2.46	2.42	2.38	2.34	2.30	2.25	2.21
14	4.60	3.74	3.34	3.11	2.96	2.85	2.76	2.70	2.65	2.60	2.53	2.46	2.39	2.35	2.31	2.27	2.22	2.18	2.13

15	4.54	3.68	3.29	3.06	2.90	2.79	2.71	2.64	2.59	2.54	2.48	2.40	2.33	2.29	2.25	2.20	2.16	2.11	2.07
16	4.49	3.63	3.24	3.01	2.85	2.74	2.66	2.59	2.54	2.49	2.42	2.35	2.28	2.24	2.19	2.15	2.11	2.06	2.01
17	4.45	3.59	3.20	2.96	2.81	2.70	2.61	2.55	2.49	2.45	2.38	2.31	2.23	2.19	2.15	2.10	2.06	2.01	1.96
18	4.41	3.55	3.16	2.93	2.77	2.66	2.58	2.51	2.46	2.41	2.34	2.27	2.19	2.15	2.11	2.06	2.02	1.97	1.92
19	4.38	3.52	3.13	2.90	2.74	2.63	2.54	2.48	2.42	2.38	2.31	2.23	2.16	2.11	2.07	2.03	1.98	1.93	1.88
20	4.35	3.49	3.10	2.87	2.71	2.60	2.51	2.45	2.39	2.35	2.28	2.20	2.12	2.08	2.04	1.99	1.95	1.90	1.84
21	4.32	3.47	3.07	2.84	2.68	2.57	2.49	2.42	2.37	2.32	2.25	2.18	2.10	2.05	2.01	1.96	1.92	1.87	1.81
22	4.30	3.44	3.05	2.82	2.66	2.55	2.46	2.40	2.34	2.30	2.23	2.15	2.07	2.03	1.98	1.94	1.89	1.84	1.78
23	4.28	3.42	3.03	2.80	2.64	2.53	2.44	2.37	2.32	2.27	2.20	2.13	2.05	2.01	1.96	1.91	1.86	1.81	1.76
24	4.26	3.40	3.01	2.78	2.62	2.51	2.42	2.36	2.30	2.25	2.18	2.11	2.03	1.98	1.94	1.89	1.84	1.79	1.73
25	4.24	3.39	2.99	2.75	2.60	2.49	2.40	2.34	2.28	2.24	2.16	2.09	2.01	1.96	1.92	1.87	1.82	1.77	1.71
26	4.23	3.37	2.98	2.74	2.59	2.47	2.39	2.32	2.27	2.22	2.15	2.07	1.99	1.95	1.90	1.85	1.80	1.75	1.69
27	4.21	3.35	2.96	2.73	2.57	2.46	2.37	2.31	2.25	2.20	2.13	2.06	1.97	1.93	1.88	1.84	1.79	1.73	1.67
28	4.20	3.34	2.95	2.71	2.56	2.45	2.36	2.29	2.24	2.19	2.12	2.04	1.96	1.91	1.87	1.82	1.77	1.71	1.65
29	4.18	3.33	2.93	2.70	2.55	2.43	2.35	2.28	2.22	2.18	2.10	2.03	1.94	1.90	1.85	1.81	1.75	1.70	1.64
30	4.17	3.32	2.92	2.69	2.53	2.42	2.33	2.27	2.21	2.16	2.09	2.01	1.93	1.89	1.84	1.79	1.74	1.68	1.62
40	4.08	3.23	2.84	2.61	2.45	2.34	2.25	2.18	2.12	2.08	2.00	1.92	1.84	1.79	1.74	1.69	1.64	1.58	1.51
60	4.00	3.15	2.76	2.53	2.37	2.25	2.17	2.10	2.04	1.99	1.92	1.84	1.75	1.70	1.65	1.59	1.53	1.47	1.39
120	3.92	3.07	2.68	2.45	2.29	2.17	2.09	2.02	1.96	1.91	1.83	1.75	1.66	1.61	1.55	1.50	1.43	1.35	1.25
∞	3.84	3.00	2.60	2.37	2.21	2.10	2.01	1.94	1.88	1.83	1.75	1.67	1.57	1.52	1.46	1.39	1.32	1.22	1.00

This table is abridged from Table 18 of the *Biometrika Tables for Statisticians*, Vol. 1 (ed. 1), edited by E. S. Pearson and H. O. Hartley. Reproduced by the kind permission of E. S. Pearson and the trustees of *Biometrika*.

Table 6 *Distribution of F: .01 Level*

df_1 \ df_2	1	2	3	4	5	6	7	8	9	10	12	15	20	24	30	40	60	120	∞
1	4052	4999.5	5403	5625	5764	5859	5928	5982	6022	6056	6106	6157	6209	6235	6261	6287	6313	6339	6366
2	98.5	99.00	99.17	99.25	99.30	99.33	99.36	99.37	99.39	99.40	99.42	99.43	99.45	99.46	99.47	99.47	99.48	99.49	99.50
3	34.12	30.82	29.46	28.71	28.24	27.91	27.67	27.49	27.35	27.23	27.05	26.87	26.69	26.60	26.50	26.41	26.32	26.22	26.13
4	21.20	18.00	16.69	15.98	15.52	15.21	14.98	14.80	14.66	14.55	14.37	14.20	14.02	13.93	13.84	13.75	13.65	13.56	13.46
5	16.26	13.27	12.06	11.39	10.97	10.67	10.46	10.29	10.16	10.05	9.89	9.72	9.55	9.47	9.38	9.29	9.20	9.11	9.02
6	13.75	10.92	9.78	9.15	8.75	8.47	8.26	8.10	7.98	7.87	7.72	7.56	7.40	7.31	7.23	7.14	7.06	6.97	6.88
7	12.25	9.55	8.45	7.85	7.46	7.19	6.99	6.81	6.72	6.62	6.47	6.31	6.16	6.07	5.99	5.91	5.82	5.74	5.65
8	11.26	8.65	7.59	7.01	6.63	6.37	6.18	6.03	5.91	5.81	5.67	5.52	5.36	5.28	5.20	5.12	5.03	4.95	4.86
9	10.56	8.02	6.99	6.42	6.06	5.80	5.61	5.47	5.35	5.26	5.11	4.96	4.81	4.73	4.65	4.57	4.48	4.40	4.31
10	10.04	7.56	6.55	5.99	5.64	5.39	5.20	5.06	4.94	4.85	4.71	4.56	4.41	4.33	4.25	4.17	4.08	4.00	3.91
11	9.65	7.21	6.22	5.67	5.32	5.07	4.89	4.74	4.63	4.54	4.40	4.25	4.10	4.02	3.94	3.86	3.78	3.69	3.60
12	9.33	6.93	5.95	5.41	5.06	4.82	4.64	4.50	4.39	4.30	4.16	4.01	3.86	3.78	3.70	3.62	3.54	3.45	3.36
13	9.07	6.70	5.74	5.21	4.86	4.62	4.44	4.30	4.19	4.10	3.96	3.82	3.66	3.59	3.51	3.43	3.34	3.25	3.17
14	8.86	6.51	5.56	5.04	4.69	4.46	4.28	4.14	4.03	3.94	3.80	3.66	3.51	3.43	3.35	3.27	3.18	3.09	3.00
15	8.68	6.36	5.42	4.89	4.56	4.32	4.14	4.00	3.89	3.80	3.67	3.52	3.37	3.29	3.21	3.13	3.05	2.96	2.87
16	8.53	6.23	5.29	4.77	4.44	4.20	4.03	3.89	3.78	3.69	3.55	3.41	3.26	3.18	3.10	3.02	2.93	2.84	2.75
17	8.40	6.11	5.18	4.67	4.34	4.10	3.93	3.79	3.68	3.59	3.46	3.31	3.16	3.08	3.00	2.92	2.83	2.75	2.65
18	8.29	6.01	5.09	4.58	4.25	4.01	3.84	3.71	3.60	3.51	3.37	3.23	3.08	3.00	2.92	2.84	2.75	2.66	2.57
19	8.18	5.93	5.01	4.50	4.17	3.94	3.77	3.63	3.52	3.43	3.30	3.15	3.00	2.92	2.84	2.76	2.67	2.58	2.49

20	8.10	5.85	4.94	4.43	4.10	3.87	3.70	3.56	3.46	3.37	3.23	3.09	2.94	2.86	2.78	2.69	2.61	2.52	2.42
21	8.02	5.78	4.87	4.37	4.04	3.81	3.64	3.51	3.40	3.31	3.17	3.03	2.88	2.80	2.72	2.64	2.55	2.46	2.36
22	7.95	5.72	4.82	4.31	3.99	3.76	3.59	3.45	3.35	3.26	3.12	2.98	2.83	2.75	2.67	2.58	2.50	2.40	2.31
23	7.88	5.66	4.76	4.26	3.94	3.71	3.54	3.41	3.30	3.21	3.07	2.93	2.78	2.70	2.62	2.54	2.45	2.35	2.26
24	7.82	5.61	4.72	4.22	3.90	3.67	3.50	3.36	3.26	3.17	3.03	2.89	2.74	2.66	2.58	2.49	2.40	2.31	2.21
25	7.77	5.57	4.68	4.18	3.85	3.63	3.46	3.32	3.22	3.13	2.99	2.85	2.70	2.62	2.54	2.45	2.36	2.27	2.17
26	7.72	5.53	4.64	4.14	3.82	3.59	3.42	3.29	3.18	3.09	2.96	2.81	2.66	2.58	2.50	2.42	2.33	2.23	2.13
27	7.68	5.49	4.60	4.11	3.78	3.56	3.39	3.26	3.15	3.06	2.93	2.78	2.63	2.55	2.47	2.38	2.29	2.20	2.10
28	7.64	5.45	4.57	4.07	3.75	3.53	3.36	3.23	3.12	3.03	2.90	2.75	2.60	2.52	2.44	2.35	2.26	2.17	2.06
29	7.60	5.42	4.54	4.04	3.73	3.50	3.33	3.20	3.09	3.00	2.87	2.73	2.57	2.49	2.41	2.33	2.23	2.14	2.03
30	7.56	5.39	4.51	4.02	3.70	3.47	3.30	3.17	3.07	2.98	2.84	2.70	2.55	2.47	2.39	2.30	2.21	2.11	2.01
40	7.31	5.18	4.31	3.83	3.51	3.29	3.12	2.99	2.89	2.80	2.66	2.52	2.37	2.29	2.20	2.11	2.02	1.92	1.80
60	7.08	4.98	4.13	3.65	3.34	3.12	2.95	2.82	2.72	2.63	2.50	2.35	2.20	2.12	2.03	1.94	1.84	1.73	1.60
120	6.85	4.79	3.95	3.48	3.17	2.96	2.79	2.66	2.56	2.47	2.34	2.19	2.03	1.95	1.86	1.76	1.66	1.53	1.38
∞	6.63	4.61	3.78	3.32	3.02	2.80	2.64	2.51	2.41	2.32	2.18	2.04	1.88	1.79	1.70	1.59	1.47	1.32	1.00

Note: df_1 = rows of table (for degrees of freedom in denominator)—within
df_2 = columns of table (for degrees of freedom in numerator)—between

Glossary

acceptance rate: the percentage of the target sample that agrees to participate in a research project.

agenda setting: the theory that the media provide topics of discussion and importance for consumers.

aided recall: a survey technique in which the interviewer shows the respondent a copy of a newspaper, magazine, television schedule, or other item that might help him or her to remember a certain article, program, advertisement, and so on.

algorithm: a statistical procedure or formula.

analysis of variance (ANOVA): a statistical procedure used to decompose sources of variation into two or more independent variables.

analytical survey: a survey that attempts to describe and explain why certain conditions exist (usually by testing certain hypotheses).

anonymity: researcher cannot connect the names of research participants with the information they provide.

antecedent variable: (1) in survey research, the variable used to predict another variable; (2) in experimental research, the independent variable.

applied research: research that attempts to solve a specific problem rather than to construct a theory.

artifact: a variable that creates an alternative explanation of results (a confounding variable).

audience turnover: in radio research, an estimate of the number of times the audience changes stations during a given daypart.

auditorium music testing: a testing procedure in which a group of respondents simultaneously rate music hooks.

autonomy: ethical principle holding that each individual is responsible for his or her decisions and should not be exploited.

available sample: a sample selected on the basis of accessibility.

average quarter-hour (AQH): the average number of persons or households tuned in to a specific channel or station for at least 5 minutes during a 15-minute time segment.

bar chart: see histogram.

beneficence: ethical principle stating that a researcher should share the positive benefits of a research project with all involved.

beta weight: a mathematically derived value that represents a variable's contribution to a prediction or weighted linear combination (also called weight coefficient).

callout research: a procedure used in radio research to determine the popularity of recordings; see also *hook*.

case study: an empirical inquiry that uses multiple sources of data to investigate a problem.

catch-up panel: members of a previous cross-sectional sample who are relocated for subsequent observation.

CATI: computer-assisted telephone interviewing; video display terminals are used by interviewers to present questions and enter responses.

census: an analysis in which the sample comprises every element of a population.

central limit theorem: the sum of a large number of independent and identically distributed random variables that has an approximate normal distribution.

central location testing (CLT): research conducted with respondents who are invited to a field service facility or other research location.

central tendency: a single value that is chosen to represent a typical score in a distribution, such as the mean, the mode, or the median.

checklist question: a type of question in which the respondent is given a list of items and is asked to mark those that apply.

chi-square statistic: a measurement of observed versus expected frequencies; often referred to as *crosstabs.*

circulation: in the print media, the total number of copies of a newspaper or magazine that are delivered to subscribers plus all copies bought at newsstands or from other sellers.

circulation research: (1) a market-level study of newspaper and magazine penetration; (2) a study of the delivery and pricing systems used by newspapers and magazines.

closed-ended question: a question the respondent must answer by making a selection from a prepared set of options.

Cloze procedure: a method for measuring readability or recall in which every *n*th word is deleted from the message and readers are asked to fill in the blanks.

cluster sample: a sample placed into groups or categories.

codebook: a menu or list of responses used in coding open-ended questions.

coding: the placing of a unit of analysis into a particular category.

coefficient of determination: in correlational statistics, the amount of variation in the criterion variable that is accounted for by the antecedent variable.

coefficient of nondetermination: in correlational statistics, the amount of variation in the criterion variable that is left unexplained.

cohort analysis: a study of a specific population as it changes over time.

communication audit: in public relations, an examination of the internal and external means of communication used by an organization.

computer-assisted telephone interviewing (CATI): questionnaires are designed for the computer; interviewers enter respondents' answers directly into the computer for tabulation; question skips and response options are controlled by the computer.

concealment: withholding some information about a research project from a participant.

concept: an abstract idea formed by generalization.

confidence interval: an area within which there is a stated probability that the parameter will fall.

confidence level: the probability (for example, .05 or .01) of rejecting a null hypothesis that is, in fact, true; also called the alpha level.

confidentiality: researcher can connect the names of research participants with the information they provide but promises to keep connection secret.

constitutive definition: a type of definition in which other words or concepts are substituted for the word being defined.

construct: a combination of concepts that is created to describe a specific situation (for example, "authoritarianism").

constructive replication: an analysis of a hypothesis taken from a previous study that deliberately avoids duplicating the methods used in the previous study.

continuous variable: a variable that can take on any value over a range of values and can be meaningfully broken into subparts (for example, "height").

control group: subjects who do not receive experimental treatment and thus serve as a basis of comparison in an experiment.

control variable: a variable whose influence a researcher wishes to eliminate.

convenience sample: a nonprobability sample consisting of respondents or subjects who are available, such as college students in a classroom.

co-op (incentive): a payment given to respondents for participating in a research project.

copy testing: research used to determine the most effective way of structuring a message to achieve the desired results; also known as message research.

cost per interview (CPI): the dollar amount required to recruit or interview one respondent.

cost per thousand (CPM): the dollar cost of reaching 1,000 people or households by means of a particular medium or advertising vehicle.

criterion variable: (1) in survey research, the variable presumed to be the effects variable; (2) in experimental research, the dependent variable.

cross-lagged correlation: a type of longitudinal study in which information about two variables is gathered from the same sample at two different times; the correlations between variables at the same point in time are compared with the correlations at different points in time.

cross-sectional research: the collection of data from a representative sample at only one point in time.

cross-tabulation analysis (crosstabs): see *chi-square statistic.*

cross-validation: a procedure in which measurement instruments or subjects' responses are compared to verify their validity or truthfulness.

cultivation analysis: a research approach suggesting that heavy television viewing leads to perceptions of social reality that are consistent with the view of the world as presented on television.

cume: an estimate of the number of different persons who listened to or viewed a particular broadcast for at least 5 minutes during a given daypart; see also *reach.*

data archives: data storage facilities where researchers can deposit data for other researchers to use.

database journalism: a form of journalism that relies on computer-assisted analysis of existing information.

database marketing: research conducted with respondents whose names are included in databases, such as people who recently purchased a television set or members of a club or organization.

daypart: a given part of the broadcast day (for example, prime time: 8:00 P.M.–11:00 P.M.).

deception: deliberately misleading participants in a research project.

demand characteristic: the premise that subjects' awareness of the experimental condition may affect their performance in the experiment; also known as the Hawthorne effect.

deontological: ethical system based on rules.

dependent variable: the variable that is observed and whose value is presumed to depend on the independent variable(s).

descriptive statistics: statistical methods and techniques designed to reduce data sets to allow for easier interpretation.

descriptive survey: a survey that attempts to picture or document current conditions or attitudes.

design-specific results: research results that are based on, or specific to, the research design used.

designated market area (DMA): a term to define a TV market area; each county in the United States belongs to only one DMA.

discrete variable: a variable that can be conceptually subdivided into a finite number of indivisible parts (for example, the number of children in a family).

disk-by-mail (DBM) survey: a survey questionnaire on computer disk sent to respondents to answer at their leisure.

dispersion: the amount of variability in a set of scores.

disproportionate stratified sampling: overrepresentation of a specific stratum or characteristic.

distribution: a collection of scores or measurements.

double-barreled question: a single question that requires two separate responses (for example, "Do you like the price and style of this item?").

double-blind experiment: a research study in which experimenters and others do not know whether a given subject belongs to the experimental group or to the control group.

dummy variable: the variable created when a variable at the nominal level is transformed into a form more appropriate for higher order statistics.

editor-reader comparison: a readership study in which the perceptions of editors and readers are solicited.

environmental monitoring program: in public relations research, a study of trends in public opinion and events in the social environment that may have a significant impact on an organization.

equivalency: the internal consistency of a measure.

error variance: the error created by an unknown factor.

evaluation apprehension: a fear of being measured or tested, which may result in providing invalid data.

evaluation research: a small-scale environmental monitoring program designed to measure an organization's social performance.

exhaustivity: a state of a category system such that every unit of analysis can be placed into an existing slot.

experimental design: a blueprint or set of plans for conducting laboratory research.

external validity: the degree to which the results of a research study are generalizable to other situations.

factor analysis: a multivariate statistical procedure used primarily for data reduction, construct development, and the investigation of variable relationships.

factor score: a composite or summary score produced by factor analysis.

factorial design: a simultaneous analysis of two or more independent variables or factors.

feeling thermometer: a rating scale patterned after a weather thermometer on which respondents can rate their attitudes on a scale of 0 to 100.

field observation: a study of a phenomenon in a natural setting.

field service: a research company that conducts interviews, recruits respondents for research projects, or both.

filter question: a question designed to screen out certain individuals from participation in a study; also called a screener question.

File Transfer Protocol (FTP): Computer language/software to upload files to a server.

Flesch reading ease formula: an early readability formula based on the number of words per sentence and the number of syllables per word.

focus group: an interview conducted with 6–12 subjects simultaneously and a moderator who leads a discussion about a specific topic.

Fog Index: a readability scale based on sentence length and the number of syllables per word.

follow-back panel: a research technique in which a current cross-sectional sample is selected and matched with archival data.

forced-choice question: a question that requires a subject to choose between two specified responses.

forced exposure: a test situation in which respondents are required to be exposed to a specific independent or dependent variable.

framing: how the media choose to portray what they cover.

frequency: in advertising, the total number of exposures to a message that a person or household receives.

frequency curve: a graphical display of frequency data in a smooth, unbroken curve.

frequency distribution: a collection of scores, ordered according to magnitude, and their respective frequencies.

frequency polygon: a series of lines connecting points that represent the frequencies of scores.

gross incidence: the percent of qualified respondents reached of all contacts made.

gross rating points: the total of audience ratings during two or more time periods, representing the size of the gross audience of a radio or television broadcast.

group administration: conducting measurements with several subjects simultaneously.

histogram: a bar chart that illustrates frequencies and scores.

homogeneity: equality of control and experimental groups prior to an experiment; also called point of prior equivalency.

hook: a short representative sample of a recording used in call-out research.

hypertext: system that links electronic documents.

HyperText Markup Language (HTML): computer language used to develop web pages.

hypothesis: a tentative generalization about the relationship between two or more variables that predicts an outcome.

incidence: the percentage of a population that possesses the desired characteristics for a particular research study.

independent variable: the variable that is systematically varied by the researcher.

informed consent: ethical guideline stating that participants in a research project should have the basic facts of the project revealed to them before they make a decision to participate in the research.

instrument decay: the deterioration of a measurement instrument during the course of a study, which reduces the instrument's effectiveness and accuracy.

instrumental replication: the duplication in a research study of the dependent variable of a previous study.

intensive interview: a hybrid of the one-on-one personal interview.

interaction: a treatment-related effect dependent on the concomitant influence of two independent variables on a dependent variable.

intercoder reliability: in content analysis, the degree of agreement between or among independent coders.

internal consistency: the level of consistency of performance among items within a scale.

internal validity: a property of a research study such that results are based on expected conditions rather than on extraneous variables.

Internet Service Provider (ISP): company that provides user connection to the Internet.

interval level: a measurement system in which the intervals between adjacent points on a scale are equal (for example, a thermometer).

isomorphism: similarity of form or structure.

item pretest: a method of testing subjects' interest in reading magazine or newspaper articles.

item-selection study: a readership study used to determine who reads specific parts of a newspaper.

justice: ethical principle holding that all people should be treated equally.

leading question: a question that suggests a certain response or makes an implicit assumption (for example, "How long have you been an alcoholic?").

lifestyle segmentation research: a research project that investigates and categorizes respondents' activities, interests, attitudes, and behaviors.

Likert scale: a measurement scale in which respondents strongly agree, agree, are neutral, disagree, or strongly disagree with the statements.

literal replication: a study that is an exact duplication of a previous study.

longitudinal study: the collection of data at different points in time.

magazine readership survey: a survey of readers to determine which sections of the magazine were viewed, read, or both.

mail survey: the mailing of self-administered questionnaires to a sample of people; the researcher must rely on the recipients to mail back their responses.

mailing list: a compilation of names and addresses, sometimes prepared by a commercial firm, that is used as a sampling frame for mail surveys.

main effect: the effect of the independent variable(s) on the dependent variable (no interaction is present).

manipulation check: a test to determine whether the manipulation of the independent variable actually had the intended effect.

marker variable: a variable that highlights or defines the construct under study.

masked recall: a survey technique in which the interviewer shows respondents the front cover of a newspaper or magazine with the name of the publication blacked out to test unaided recall of the publication.

mean: the arithmetic average of a set of scores.

measurement: a procedure in which a researcher assigns numerals to objects, events, or properties according to certain rules.

measurement error: an inconsistency produced by the instruments used in a research study.

media efficiency: reaching the maximum possible audience at the least possible cost.

median: the midpoint of a distribution of scores.

medium variables: in a content analysis, the aspects of content that are unique to the medium under consideration (for example, typography to a newspaper or magazine).

meta-analysis: a quantitative aggregation of many research findings.

method of authority: a method of knowing in which something is believed because a source perceived as an authority says it is true.

method of intuition: a method of knowing in which something is believed because it is "self-evident" or "stands to reason"; also called a priori reasoning.

method of tenacity: a method of knowing in which something is believed because a person has always believed it to be true.

method-specific results: research results based on, or specific to, the research method used.

metro survey area (MSA): a region representing one of the Consolidated Metropolitan Statistical Areas (CMSA), as defined by the U.S. Office of Management and Budget.

mode: the score that occurs most often in a frequency distribution.

mortality: in panel studies and other forms of longitudinal research, the percent of original sample members who drop out of the research project for one reason or another.

multiple regression: an analysis of two or more independent variables and their relationship to a single dependent variable; used to predict the dependent variable.

multistage sampling: a form of cluster sampling in which individual households or persons, not groups, are selected.

mutually exclusive: a category system in which a unit of analysis can be placed in one and only one category.

net incidence: the number of respondents or subjects who actually participate in a research project.

nominal level: the level of measurement at which arbitrary numerals or other symbols are used to classify persons, objects, or characteristics.

nonmaleficence: ethical principle stating that a researcher should do no harm.

nonparametric statistics: statistical procedures used with variables measured at the nominal or ordinal level.

nonprobability sample: a sample selected without regard to the laws of mathematical probability.

normal curve: a symmetrical, bell-shaped curve that possesses specific mathematical characteristics.

normal distribution: a mathematical model of how measurements are distributed; a graph of a normal distribution is a continuous, symmetrical, bell-shaped curve.

null hypothesis: the denial or negation of a research hypothesis.

objective function: a mathematical formula that provides various quantitative values for a given media schedule of advertisements; used in computer simulations of advertising media schedules.

one-on-one interviews: sessions in which respondents are interviewed one at a time.

open-ended question: a question to which respondents are asked to generate an answer or answers with no prompting from the item itself (for example, "What is your favorite type of television program?").

operational definition: a definition that specifies patterns of behavior and procedures in order to experience or measure a concept.

operational replication: a study that duplicates only the sampling methodology and the experimental procedures of a previous study.

ordinal level: the level of measurement at which items are ranked along a continuum.

overnights: ratings surveys of a night's television viewing computed in five major U.S. cities by the ACNielsen Company.

panel study: a research technique in which the same sample of respondents is measured at different points in time.

parameter: a characteristic or property of a population.

parametric statistics: statistical procedures appropriate for variables measured at the interval or ratio level.

parsimony principle: the premise that the simplest method is the most preferable; also known as Occam's razor.

partial correlation: a method used to control a confounding or spurious variable that may affect the relationship between independent variables and dependent variables.

people meter: an electronic television audience data-gathering device capable of recording individual viewing behavior.

periodicity: any form of bias resulting from the use of a nonrandom list of subjects or items in selecting a sample.

personal interview: a survey technique in which a trained interviewer visits a respondent and administers a questionnaire in a face-to-face setting.

pilot study: a trial run of a study conducted on a small scale to determine whether the research design and methodology are relevant and effective.

population: a group or class of objects, subjects, or units.

population distribution: the frequency distribution of all the variables of interest as determined by a census of the population.

power: the probability of rejecting the null hypothesis when an alternative is true.

precision journalism: a technique of inquiry in which social science research methods are used to gather the news.

precursor analysis: a study assuming that leaders establish trends and that these trends ultimately trickle down to the rest of society.

predictor variable: see *antecedent variable.*

prerecruits: respondents who are recruited ahead of time to participate in a research project.

prestige bias: the tendency of a respondent to give answers that will make him or her seem more educated, successful, financially stable, or otherwise prestigious.

probability level: a predetermined value at which researchers test their data for statistical significance.

probability sample: a sample selected according to the laws of mathematical probability.

proportionate stratified sampling: representing population proportions of a specific stratum or characteristic.

proposition: a statement of the form "if *A*, then *B*" that links two or more concepts.

proprietary data: research data gathered by a private organization that are available to the general public only if released by that organization.

prosocial: having positive results for society.

protocol: a document that contains the procedures to be used in a field study.

psychographics: an area of research that examines why people behave and think as they do.

public relations audit: a comprehensive study of the public relations position of an organization.

purposive sample: a sample deliberately chosen to be representative of a population.

qualitative research method: a research method that uses flexible questioning.

quantitative research method: a research method that uses standardized questioning.

quasi-experiment: a research design that does not involve random assignment of subjects to experimental groups.

quota sample: a sample selected to represent certain characteristics of interest.

random digit dialing: a method of selecting telephone numbers that ensures that all telephone households have an equal chance of being selected.

random error: error in a research study that cannot be controlled by the researcher.

random sample: a subgroup or subset of a population selected in such a way that each unit in a population has an equal chance of being selected.

range: a measure of dispersion based on the difference between the highest and lowest scores in a distribution.

rating: an estimate of the percentage of people or households in a population that are tuned to a specific station or network.

ratio level: a level of measurement that has all the properties of an interval level scale and also has a true zero point.

reach in advertising: the total number of people or households exposed to a message at least once during a specific period of time; see also *cume.*

reactivity: a subject's awareness of being measured or observed and its possible impact on that subject's behavior.

readability: the total of all elements in a piece of printed material that affect the degree to which people understand the piece and find it interesting.

reader-nonreader study: a study that contrasts nonreaders of newspapers or magazines with regular readers.

reader profile: a demographic summary of the readers of a particular publication.

recall study: a study in which respondents are asked to remember which advertisements they remember seeing in the medium being investigated.

recognition: a measurement of readership in which respondents are shown the logo of a magazine or newspaper.

region of rejection: the proportion of an area in a sampling distribution that equals the level of significance; the region of rejection represents all the values of a test statistic that are highly unlikely, provided the null hypothesis is true.

relativistic: ethical system that takes into account the situation in which a decision is made.

reliability: the property of a measure that consistently gives the same answer at different times.

repeated-measures design: a research design in which numerous measurements are made on the same subjects.

replication: an independent verification of a research study.

research question: a tentative generalization about the relationship between two or more variables.

research supplier: a company that provides various forms of research to clients, from data collection only to a final written analysis and summary of the data.

response set: a pattern of answers given by a respondent, such as all "5" ratings on a 1–10 rating scale. These data are usually deleted from the data set.

retrospective panel: a study in which each respondent is asked questions about events and attitudes in his or her lifetime.

rough cut: a model or simulation of a final product.

sample: a subgroup or subset of a population or universe.

sample distribution: the frequency distribution of all the variables of interest as determined from a sample.

sample-specific results: research results that are based on, or specific to, the research sample used.

sampling distribution: a probability distribution of all possible values of a statistic that would occur if all possible samples of a fixed size were taken from a given population.

sampling error: the degree to which measurements obtained from a sample differ from the measurements that would be obtained from the population.

sampling frame: a list of the members of a particular population.

sampling interval: a random interval used for selecting subjects or units in the systematic sampling method.

sampling rate: the ratio of the number of people chosen in the sample to the total number in the population (for example, if 100 fraternity members were systematically chosen from a sampling frame of 1,000 fraternity members, the sampling rate would be 10%, or 1/10).

scale: a form of measurement such as 10-point scales, Likert, Guttman, or semantic differential.

scattergram: a graphic technique for portraying the relationship between two variables.

scientific method: a systematic, controlled, empirical, and critical investigation of hypothetical propositions about the presumed relationships among natural phenomena.

screener: a short survey or a portion of a survey designed to select only appropriate respondents for a research project.

secondary analysis: the use of data collected by a previous researcher or another research organization; also called data reanalysis.

semantic differential: a rating scale consisting of seven spaces between two bipolar adjectives (for example, "good _____ bad").

share: an estimate of the percentage of persons or households tuned to a specific station, channel, or network.

shopping center interview (intercept): a nonprobability study in which respondents are recruited and interviewed in a shopping mall.

sigma (Σ): the Greek capital letter symbolizing summation.

skewness: the degree of departure of a curve from the normal distribution (curves can be positively or negatively skewed).

SMOG Grading: a measure of readability based on the number of syllables per word.

social audit: in public relations research, an analysis of the social performance of an organization.

stability: the degree of consistency of the results of a measure at different times.

staged manipulation: a situation in which researchers construct events and circumstances so they can manipulate the independent variable.

standard deviation: the square root of the variance (a mathematical index of dispersion).

standard error: an estimate of the amount of error present in a measurement.

standard score: a measure that has been standardized in relation to a distribution's mean and standard deviation.

statistics: a science that uses mathematical methods to collect, organize, summarize, and analyze data.

straightforward manipulation: a situation in which materials and instructions are simply presented to respondents or subjects.

stratified sample: a sample selected after the population has been divided into categories.

structured interview: an interview in which standardized questions are asked in a predetermined order.

summary statistics: statistics that summarize a great deal of numerical information about a distribution, such as the mean and the standard deviation.

sweeps: a nationwide survey conducted by the ACNielsen Company of every television market; conducted in February, May, July, and November.

systematic random sampling: a procedure to select every *n*th subject for a study, such as every 10th person in a telephone directory.

systematic variance: a regular increase or decrease in all scores or data in a research study by a known factor.

teleological: ethical system based on the balancing of the likely effects of a decision.

telephone coincidental: a broadcasting research procedure in which random subjects or households are called and asked what they are viewing or listening to at that moment.

telephone survey: a research method in which survey data are collected over the telephone by trained interviewers who ask questions and record responses.

theory: a set of related propositions that presents a systematic view of phenomena by specifying relationships among concepts.

time spent listening (TSL): a quantitative statement about the average time a listener spends listening to a radio station (or several stations); stated in hours and minutes.

total observation: in field observation, a situation in which the observer assumes no role in the phenomenon being observed other than that of observer.

total participation: field observation in which the observer becomes a full-fledged participant in the situation under observation.

total survey area (TSA): a region in which an audience survey is conducted.

tracking study: a special readership measurement technique in which respondents designate material they have read (using a different color of pencil for each reading episode).

trend study: a longitudinal study in which a topic is restudied using different groups of respondents (for example, the Roper studies of the credibility of the media).

triangulation: using a combined quantitative and qualitative approach to solve a problem.

trigger event: an event or activity that might focus public concern on a topic or issue.

***t*-test:** a statistic used to determine the significance between group means.

Type I error: rejection of the null hypothesis when it should be accepted.

Type II error: acceptance of the null hypothesis when it should be rejected.

unaided recall: question format in which respondents are asked to recall certain information without help from the researcher.

unit of analysis: the smallest element of a content analysis; the thing that is counted whenever it is encountered.

unstructured interview: an interview in which the interviewer asks broad and general questions but retains control over the discussion.

uses and gratifications study: a study of the motives for media usage and the rewards that are sought.

utilitarianism: ethical system that weighs the potential benefits of a decision against potential harm.

validity: the degree to which a test actually measures what it purports to measure.

variable: a phenomenon or event that can be measured or manipulated.

variance: a mathematical index of the degree to which scores deviate from the mean.

voluntary participation: ethical guideline stating that subjects involved in a research project have a right to decline to participate or to leave the project at any time.

volunteer sample: a group of people who go out of their way to participate in a survey or experiment (for example, by responding to a newspaper advertisement).

web browser: a program that searches the World Wide Web.

weighting: a mathematical procedure used to adjust a sample to meet the characteristics of a given population; also called sample balancing.

World Wide Web: system of interconnected computers and electronic information sites.

Name Index

Subject Index